PSYCHOLOGY

THE PEARSON CUSTOM LIBRARY

Psychology for Life

PEARSON

Printed in the United States of America.

7 17

Copyright © 2014 by Pearson Learning Solutions

Please visit our website at *www.pearsonlearningsolutions.com*.

Attention bookstores: For permission to return any unsold stock, contact us at *pe-uscustomreturns@pearson.com*.

Pearson Learning Solutions, 501 Boylston Street, Suite 900, Boston, MA 02116
A Pearson Education Company
www.pearsoned.com

ISBN 10: 1-269-29281-1
ISBN 13: 978-1-269-29281-8

Table of Contents

Statistical Supplement

From Chapter 2 Supplement of *Psychology and Life*, 20th Edition. Richard J. Gerrig. Copyright © 2013 by Pearson Education, Inc.
All rights reserved.

Statistical Supplement

Understanding Statistics:
Analyzing Data and Forming Conclusions

As noted in the chapter text, psychologists use statistics to make sense of the data they collect. They also use statistics to provide a quantitative basis for the conclusions they draw. Knowing something about statistics, therefore, can help you appreciate the process by which psychological knowledge is developed. To demonstrate this point, I will follow a single project from its real-world inspiration to the statistical arguments the researchers used to draw conclusions.

The project began in response to the types of stories that appear on newspaper front pages, about shy individuals who became *sudden murderers*. Here's an example:

> *Fred Cowan was described by relatives, co-workers, and acquaintances as a "nice, quiet man," a "gentle man who loved children," and a "real pussycat." The principal of the parochial school Cowan had attended as a child reported that his former student had received A grades in courtesy, cooperation, and religion. According to a co-worker, Cowan "never talked to anybody and was someone you could push around." Cowan, however, surprised everyone who knew him when, one Valentine's Day, he strolled into work toting a semiautomatic rifle and shot and killed four co-workers, a police officer, and, finally, himself.*

This story has a common plot: A shy, quiet person suddenly becomes violent, shocking everyone who knows him. What did Fred Cowan have in common with other people who are suddenly transformed from gentle and caring into violent and ruthless? What personal attributes might distinguish them from us?

A team of researchers had a hunch that there might be a link between shyness and other personal characteristics and violent behavior (Lee et al., 1977). They began to collect some data that might reveal such a connection. The researchers reasoned that seemingly nonviolent people who suddenly commit murders are probably typically shy, nonaggressive individuals who keep their passions in check and their impulses under tight control. For most of their lives, they suffer many silent injuries. Seldom, if ever, do they express anger, regardless of how angry they really feel. On the outside, they appear unbothered, but on the inside they may be fighting to control furious rages. Because they are shy, they probably do not let others get close to them, so no one knows how they really feel. Then, suddenly, something explodes. At the slightest provocation—one more small insult, one more little rejection, one more bit of social pressure—the fuse is lit, and they release the suppressed violence that has been building up for so long. Because they did not learn to deal with interpersonal conflicts through discussion and verbal negotiation, these sudden murderers act out their anger physically.

The researchers' reasoning led them to the hypothesis that shyness would be more characteristic of *sudden murderers*—people who had engaged in homicide without any prior history of violence or antisocial behavior—than it would of *habitual criminal murderers*—those who had committed homicide but had had a previous record of violent criminal behavior. In addition, sudden murderers should have higher levels of control over their impulses than habitually violent people. Finally, their passivity and dependence would be manifested in more feminine and androgynous (both male and female) characteristics, as measured on a standard sex-role inventory, than those of habitual criminals.

To test their ideas about sudden murderers, the researchers obtained permission to administer psychological questionnaires to a group of inmates serving time for murder in California prisons. Nineteen inmates (all male) agreed to participate in the study. Prior to committing murder, some had committed a series of crimes, whereas the other part of the sample had had no previous criminal record. The researchers collected three kinds of data from these two types of participants: shyness scores, sex-role identification scores, and impulse control scores.

Shyness scores were collected using the Stanford Shyness Survey. The most important item on this questionnaire asked if the individual was shy; the answer could be either yes or no. The second questionnaire was the Bem Sex-Role Inventory (BSRI), which presented a list of adjectives, such as *aggressive* and *affectionate,* and asked how well each adjective described the individual (Bem, 1974, 1981). Some adjectives were typically associated with being "feminine," and the total score of these adjectives was an individual's femininity score. Other adjectives were considered "masculine," and the total score of those adjectives was an individual's masculinity score. The final sex-role score, which reflected the difference between an individual's femininity and masculinity, was calculated by subtracting the masculinity score from the femininity score. The third questionnaire was the Minnesota Multiphasic Personality Inventory (MMPI), which was designed to measure many different aspects of personality. The study used only the "ego-overcontrol" scale, which measures the degree to which a person acts out or controls impulses. The higher the individual's score on this scale, the more ego overcontrol the individual exhibits.

The researchers predicted that, compared with murderers with a prior criminal record, sudden murderers would (1) more often describe themselves as shy on the shyness survey, (2) select more feminine traits than masculine ones on the sex-role scale, and (3) score higher in ego overcontrol. What did they discover?

Before you find out, you need to understand some of the basic procedures that were used to analyze these data. The actual sets of data collected by the researchers are used here as the source material to teach you about some of the different types of statistical analyses and also about the kinds of conclusions they make possible.

Table 1 • Raw Data from the Sudden Murderers Study

Inmate	Shyness	BSRI Femininity–Masculinity	MMPI Ego Overcontrol
Group 1: **Sudden Murderers**			
1	Yes	+5	17
2	No	−1	17
3	Yes	+4	13
4	Yes	+61	17
5	Yes	+19	13
6	Yes	+41	19
7	No	−29	14
8	Yes	+23	9
9	Yes	−13	11
10	Yes	+5	14
Group 2: **Habitual Criminal Murderers**			
11	No	−12	15
12	No	−14	11
13	Yes	−33	14
14	No	−8	10
15	No	−7	16
16	No	+3	11
17	No	−17	6
18	No	+6	9
19	No	−10	12

ANALYZING THE DATA

For most researchers in psychology, analyzing the data is an exciting step. Statistical analysis allows researchers to discover if their predictions were correct. In this section, we will work step by step through an analysis of some of the data from the Sudden Murderers Study.

The *raw data*—the actual scores or other measures obtained—from the 19 inmates in the Sudden Murderers Study are listed in **Table 1.** As you can see, there were 10 inmates in the sudden murderers group and 9 in the habitual criminal murderers group. When first glancing at these data, any researcher would feel what you probably feel: confusion. What do all these scores mean? Do the two groups of murderers differ from one another on these various personality measures? It is difficult to know just by examining this disorganized array of numbers.

Psychologists rely on two types of statistics to help draw meaningful conclusions from the data they collect: descriptive and inferential. **Descriptive statistics** use mathematical procedures in an objective, uniform way to describe different aspects of numerical data. If you have ever computed your GPA, you already have used descriptive statistics. **Inferential statistics** use probability theory to make sound decisions about which results might have occurred simply through chance variation.

....

descriptive statistics Statistical procedures that are used to summarize sets of scores with respect to central tendencies, variability, and correlations.

inferential statistics Statistical procedures that allow researchers to determine whether the results they obtain support their hypotheses or can be attributed just to chance variation.

Descriptive Statistics

Descriptive statistics provide a summary picture of patterns in the data. They are used to describe sets of scores collected from one experimental participant or, more often, from different groups of participants. They are also used to describe relationships among variables. Thus, instead of trying to keep in mind all the scores obtained by each of the participants, researchers get indexes of the scores that are most *typical* for each group. They also get measures of how *variable* the scores are with respect to the typical score—whether the scores are spread out or clustered closely together. Let's see how researchers derive these measures.

Frequency Distributions How would you summarize the data in Table 1? To present a clear picture of how the various scores are distributed, we can draw up a **frequency distribution**—a summary of how frequently each of the various scores occurs. The shyness data are easy to summarize. Of the 19 scores, there are 9 *yes* and 10 *no* responses; almost all the *yes* responses are in Group 1, and almost all the *no* responses are in Group 2. However, the ego-overcontrol and sex-role scores do not fall into easy *yes* and *no* categories. To see how frequency distributions of numerical responses can allow informative comparisons between groups, we will focus on the sex-role scores.

Consider the sex-role data in Table 1. The highest score is +61 (most feminine) and the lowest is −33 (most masculine). Of the 19 scores, 9 are positive and 10 negative. This means that 9 of the murderers described themselves as relatively feminine and 10 as relatively masculine. But how are these scores distributed between the groups? The first step in preparing a frequency distribution for a set of numerical data is to *rank-order* the scores from highest to lowest. The rank ordering for the sex-role scores is shown in **Table 2**. The second step is to group these rank-ordered scores into a smaller number of categories called *intervals*. In this study, 10 categories were used, with each category covering 10 possible scores. The third step is to construct a frequency distribution table, listing the intervals from highest to lowest and noting the *frequencies*, the

Table 3 • Frequency Distribution of Sex-Role Difference Scores

Category	Frequency
+60 to +69	1
+50 to +59	0
+40 to +49	1
+30 to +39	0
+20 to +29	1
+10 to +19	1
0 to +9	5
−10 to −1	4
−20 to −11	4
−30 to −21	1
−40 to −31	1

number of scores within each interval. Our frequency distribution shows us that the sex-role scores are largely between −20 and +9 (see **Table 3**). The majority of the inmates' scores did not deviate much from zero. That is, they were neither strongly positive nor strongly negative.

The data are now arranged in useful categories. The researchers' next step was to display the distributions in graphic form.

Graphs Distributions are often easier to understand when they are displayed in graphs. The simplest type of graph is a *bar graph*. Bar graphs allow you to see patterns in the data. We can use a bar graph to illustrate how many more sudden murderers than habitual criminal murderers described themselves as shy (see **Figure 1**).

Table 2 • Rank Ordering of Sex-Role Difference Scores

Highest			
Highest	+61	−1	
	+41	−7	
	+23	−8	
	+19	−10	
	+6	−12	
	+5	−13	
	+5	−14	
	+4	−17	
	+3	−29	
		−33	**Lowest**

Note: + scores are more feminine; − scores are more masculine.

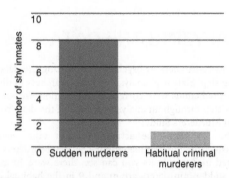

FIGURE 1 Shyness for Two Groups of Murderers (a Bar Graph)

....

frequency distribution A summary of how frequently each score appears in a set of observations.

For more complex data, such as the sex-role scores, we can use a *histogram,* which is similar to a bar graph except that the categories are intervals—number categories instead of the name categories used in the bar graph. A histogram gives a visual picture of the number of scores in a distribution that are in each interval. It is easy to see from the sex-role scores shown in the histograms (in **Figure 2**) that the distributions of scores are different for the two groups of murderers.

You can see from Figures 1 and 2 that the overall distributions of responses conform to two of the researchers' hypotheses. Sudden murderers were more likely to describe themselves as shy and were more likely to use feminine traits to describe themselves than were habitual criminal murderers.

Measures of Central Tendency   So far, we have formed a general picture of how the scores are *distributed.* Tables and graphs increase our general understanding of research results, but we want to know more—for example, the one score that is most typical of the group as a whole. This score becomes particularly useful when we compare two or more groups; it is much easier to compare the typical scores of two groups than their entire distributions. A single *representative* score that can be used as an index of the most typical score obtained by a group of participants is called a **measure of central tendency.** (It is located in the center of the distribution, and other scores tend to cluster around it.) Typically, psychologists use three different measures of central tendency: the *mode,* the *median,* and the *mean.*

The **mode** is the score that occurs more often than any other. For the measure of shyness, the modal response of the sudden murderers was *yes*—8 out of 10 said they were shy. Among habitual criminal murderers, the modal response was *no.* The sex-role scores for the sudden murderers had a mode of +5. Can you figure out what the mode of their ego-overcontrol scores is? The mode is the easiest index of central tendency to determine, but it is often the least useful. You will see one reason for this relative lack of usefulness if you notice that only one overcontrol score lies above the mode of 17, and six lie below it. Although 17 is the score obtained most often, it may not fit your idea of "typical" or "central."

The **median** is more clearly a central score; it separates the upper half of the scores in a distribution from the lower half. The number of scores larger than the median is the same as the number that is smaller. When there is an odd number of scores, the median is the middle score; when there is an even number of scores, researchers most often average the two scores at the middle. For example, if you rank-order the sex-role scores of only the habitual criminal murderers on a separate piece of paper, you will see that the median score is −10, with four scores higher and four scores lower. For the sudden murderers, the median is +5—the average of the fifth and sixth scores, each of which happens to be +5. The median is not affected by extreme scores. For example, even if the sudden murderers' highest sex-role score had been +129 instead of +61, the median value would still have been +5. That score would still separate the upper half of the data from the lower half. The median is quite simply the score in the middle of the distribution.

The **mean** is what most people think of when they hear the word *average.* It is also the statistic most often used to describe a set of data. To calculate the mean, you add up all the scores in a distribution and divide by the total number of scores. The operation is summarized by the following formula:

$$M = \frac{(\Sigma X)}{N}$$

In this formula, M is the mean, X is each individual score, Σ (the Greek letter sigma) is the summation of what

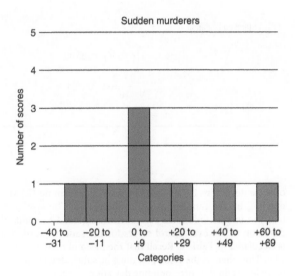

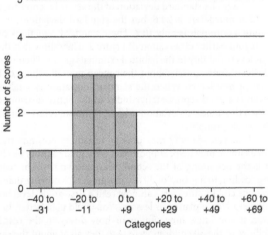

FIGURE 2 Sex-Role Scores (Histograms)

measure of central tendency A statistic, such as a mean, median, or mode, that provides one score as representative of a set of observations.

mode The score appearing most frequently in a set of observations; a measure of central tendency.

median The score in a distribution above and below which lie 50 percent of the other scores; a measure of central tendency.

mean The arithmetic average of a group of scores; the most commonly used measure of central tendency.

immediately follows it, and N is the total number of scores. Because the summation of all the sex-role scores (ΣX) is 115, and the total number of scores (N) is 10, the mean (M) of the sex-role scores for the sudden murderers would be calculated as follows:

$$M = \frac{(115)}{10} = 11.5$$

Try to calculate their mean overcontrol scores yourself. You should come up with a mean of 14.4.

Unlike the median, the mean *is* affected by the specific values of all scores in the distribution. Changing the value of an extreme score does change the value of the mean. For example, if the sex-role score of inmate 4 were +101 instead of +61, the mean for the whole group would increase from 11.5 to 15.5.

Variability   In addition to knowing which score is most representative of the distribution as a whole, it is useful to know how representative that measure of central tendency really is. Are most of the other scores fairly close to it or widely spread out? **Measures of variability** are statistics that describe the distribution of scores around some measure of central tendency. Take a look back at Figure 2. You can see that the sex-role scores for the habitual criminals seem to cluster more tightly together than do the scores for sudden murderers. That difference gives you a sense of what's meant by variability.

The simplest measure of variability is the **range**, the difference between the highest and the lowest values in a frequency distribution. For the sudden murderers' sex-role scores, the range is 90: (+61) – (−29). The range of their overcontrol scores is 10: (+19) – (+9). To compute the range, you need to know only two of the scores: the highest and the lowest.

The range is simple to compute, but psychologists often prefer measures of variability that are more sensitive and that take into account *all* the scores in a distribution, not just the extremes. One widely used measure is the **standard deviation (SD)**, a measure of variability that indicates the *average* difference between the scores and their mean. To figure out the standard deviation of a distribution, you need to know the mean of the distribution and the individual scores. The general procedure involves subtracting the value of each individual score from the mean and then determining the average of those mean deviations. Here is the formula:

$$SD = \sqrt{\frac{\Sigma(X - M)^2}{N}}$$

You should recognize most of the symbols from the formula for the mean. The expression $(X - M)$ means "individual score minus the mean" and is commonly called the *deviation score*. The mean is subtracted from each score, and each resulting score is squared (to eliminate negative values). Then the mean

....

measure of variability A statistic, such as a range or standard deviation, that indicates how tightly the scores in a set of observations cluster together.

range The difference between the highest and the lowest scores in a set of observations; the simplest measure of variability.

standard deviation (SD) The average difference of a set of scores from their mean; a measure of variability.

Table 4 • Calculating the Standard Deviation of Sudden Murderers' Ego-Overcontrol Scores

Squared Score (X)	Deviation (score minus mean) (X − M)	Deviations Squared (score minus mean)² (X − M)2
17	2.6	6.76
17	2.6	6.76
13	−1.4	1.96
17	2.6	6.76
13	−1.4	1.96
19	4.6	21.16
14	−0.4	0.16
9	−5.4	29.16
11	−3.4	11.56
14	−0.4	0.16

Standard deviation $= SD = \sqrt{\dfrac{\Sigma(X - M)^2}{N}}$

$\Sigma(X - M)^2 = 86.40$

$\sqrt{\dfrac{86.40}{10}} = \sqrt{8.64} = 2.94$

$SD = 2.94$

of these deviations is calculated by summing them up (Σ) and dividing by the number of observations (N). The symbol $\sqrt{}$ tells you to take the square root of the enclosed. The standard deviation of the overcontrol scores for the sudden murderers is calculated in **Table 4**. Recall that the mean of these scores is 14.4. This, then, is the value that must be subtracted from each score to obtain the corresponding deviation scores.

The standard deviation tells us how variable a set of scores is. The larger the standard deviation, the more spread out the scores are. The standard deviation of the sex-role scores for the sudden murderers is 24.6, but the standard deviation for the habitual criminals is only 10.7. These standard deviations confirm your earlier observation of Figure 2. They show that there was less variability in the habitual criminals group. Their scores clustered more closely about their mean than did those of the sudden murderers. When the standard deviation is small, the mean is a good representative index of the entire distribution. When the standard deviation is large, the mean is less typical of the whole group.

Can you see why measures of variability are important? An example may help. Suppose you are a grade-school teacher. It is the beginning of the school year, and you will be teaching reading to a group of 30 second graders. Knowing that the average child in the class can now read a first-grade-level book will help you to plan your lessons. You could plan better, however, if you knew how *similar* or how *divergent* the reading abilities of the 30 children were. Are they all at about the same level (low variability)? If so, then you can plan a fairly standard second-grade lesson. What if several can read advanced material and others can barely read at all (high variability)? Now the mean level is not so representative of the entire class, and you will have to plan a variety of lessons to meet the children's varied needs.

Correlation   Another useful tool in interpreting psychological data is the **correlation coefficient (r),** a measure of the nature and strength of the relationship between two variables (such as height and weight or sex-role score and ego-overcontrol score). It tells us the extent to which scores on one measure are associated with scores on the other. If people with high scores on one variable tend to have *high* scores on the other variable, then the correlation coefficient will be positive (greater than 0). If, however, most people with high scores on one variable tend to have *low* scores on the other variable, then the correlation coefficient will be negative (less than 0). If there is *no* consistent relationship between the scores, the correlation will be close to 0 (see also chapter discussion).

Correlation coefficients range from +1 (perfect positive correlation) through 0 to −1 (perfect negative correlation). The further a coefficient is from 0 in *either* direction, the more closely related the two variables are, positively or negatively. Higher coefficients permit better predictions of one variable, given knowledge of the other.

In the Sudden Murderers Study, the correlation coefficient (symbolized as *r*) between the sex-role scores and the overcontrol scores turns out to be +0.35. Thus the sex-role scores and the overcontrol scores are positively correlated. In general, individuals seeing themselves as more feminine also tend to be higher in overcontrol. However, the correlation is modest, compared with the highest possible value, +1.00, so we know that there are exceptions to this relationship.

Inferential Statistics

We have used a number of descriptive statistics to characterize the data from the Sudden Murderers Study, and now we have an idea of the pattern of results. However, some basic questions remain unanswered. Recall that the research team hypothesized that sudden murderers would be shyer, more overcontrolled, and more feminine than habitual criminal murderers. After we have used descriptive statistics to compare average responses and variability in the two groups, it appears that there are some differences between the groups. But how do we know if the differences are large enough to be meaningful? If we repeated this study, with other sudden murderers and other habitual criminal murderers, would we expect to find the same pattern of results, or could these results have been an outcome of chance? If we could somehow measure the entire population of sudden murderers and habitual criminal murderers, would the means and standard deviations be the same as those we found for these small samples?

Inferential statistics are used to answer these kinds of questions. They tell us which inferences we *can* make from our samples and which conclusions we can legitimately draw from our data. Inferential statistics use probability theory to determine the likelihood that a set of data occurred simply by chance variation.

The Normal Curve   To understand how inferential statistics work, we must look first at the special properties of a distribution called the *normal curve.* When data on a variable (for example, height, IQ, or overcontrol) are collected from a large number of individuals, the numbers obtained often fit a curve roughly similar to that shown in **Figure 3**. Notice that the curve is symmetrical (the left half is a mirror image of the right) and bell shaped—high in the middle, where most scores are, and lower the farther you get from the mean. This type of curve is called a **normal curve,** or *normal distribution.* (A *skewed* distribution is one in which scores cluster toward one end instead of around the middle.)

In a normal curve, the median, mode, and mean values are the same. A specific percentage of the scores can be predicted to fall under different sections of the curve. Figure 3 shows IQ scores on the Stanford-Binet Intelligence Test. These scores have a mean of 100 and a standard deviation of 15. If you indicate standard deviations as distances from the mean along the baseline, you find that a little over 68 percent of all the scores are between the mean of 100 and 1 standard deviation above and below—between IQs of 85 and 115. Roughly another 27 percent of the scores are found between the first and second standard deviations below the mean (IQ scores between 70 and 85) and above the mean (IQ scores between 115 and 130). Less than 5 percent of the scores fall in the third standard deviation above and below the mean, and very few scores fall beyond—only about one quarter of 1 percent. This normal distribution tells you how common or rare different outcomes would be (such as an individual having an IQ of 115 versus 170).

A normal curve is also obtained by collecting a series of measurements whose differences are due only to chance. Suppose you flip a coin 10 times in a row and record the number of heads and tails. If you repeat the exercise for a 100 sets of 10 tosses, you probably will get a few sets with all heads or no heads, more sets where the number is between these extremes, and, most typically, more sets where you get 5 heads and 5 tails. If you plotted your sets of tosses, you should get a graph that closely fits a normal curve with the mean at 5 heads and 5 tails.

Statistical Significance   But suppose you flipped the coin all those times, and you didn't get a mean of 5 heads and 5 tails. Suppose you plotted your data and, after all those sets of 10 tosses, the mean was 8 heads and 2 tails. You would almost certainly wonder if there were something dishonest about the coin. Here's the question you'd want to ask: Suppose the coin were in fact, a fair coin—what is the probability that you'd obtain an outcome as extreme as the one you got? That question is the core type of question addressed by inferential statistics. If the probability of getting 80% heads (just by random chance) was sufficiently low, then you could conclude that you hadn't been flipping a fair coin.

When researchers look at the outcomes of experiments, they ask how likely it is that whatever differences they obtained

....

correlational coefficient (*r*) A statistic that indicates the degree of relationship between two variables.

normal curve The symmetrical curve that represents the distribution of scores on many psychological attributes; allows researchers to make judgments of how unusual an observation or result is.

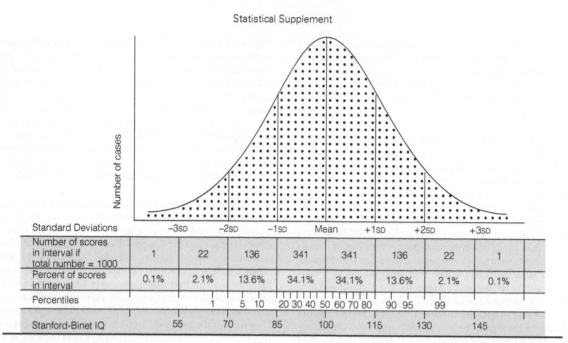

FIGURE 3 A Normal Curve

occurred simply by chance. Because chance differences have a normal distribution, a researcher can use the normal curve to answer this question. By common agreement, psychologists accept a difference as "real" when the probability that it might be due to chance is less than 5 in 100 (indicated by the notation $p < .05$). A **significant difference** is one that meets this criterion. However, in some cases, even stricter probability levels are used, such as $p < .01$ (less than 1 in 100) and $p < .001$ (less than 1 in 1,000). With a statistically significant difference, a researcher can draw a conclusion about the behavior that was under investigation.

There are many different types of tests for estimating the statistical significance of sets of data. The type of test chosen for a particular case depends on the design of the study, the form of the data, and the size of the groups. I will mention only one of the most common tests, the *t-test*, which may be used when an investigator wants to know if the difference between the means of two groups is statistically significant.

Let's return to the sex-role scores of the two groups of murderers. For the sudden murders, the scores had a mean of 11.5 and a standard deviation of 24.6; the habitual criminals had a mean of −10.2 and a standard deviation of 10.7. The *t*-test combines the information about the means and standard deviations to determine whether the scores of the sudden murderers are significantly different from those of the habitual criminal murderers. The *t*-test uses a mathematical procedure to confirm the conclusion you may have drawn from Figure 2: The distributions of sex-role scores for the two groups is sufficiently different to be "real." If we carry out the appropriate

calculations—which evaluate the difference between the two means as a function of the variability around those two means—we find that there is a very slim chance, less than 5 in 100 ($p < .05$), of obtaining such a large t value if no true difference exists. The difference is, therefore, statistically significant, and we can feel more confident that there is a real difference between the two groups. The sudden murderers *did* rate themselves as more feminine than did the habitual criminal murderers.

On the other hand, the difference between the two groups of murderers in overcontrol scores turns out not to be statistically significant ($p < .10$), so we must be more cautious in making claims about this difference. There is a trend in the predicted direction—the difference is one that would occur by chance only 10 times in 100. However, the difference is not within the standard 5-in-100 range. (The difference in shyness, analyzed using another statistical test for frequency of scores, is in fact significant.)

So, by using inferential statistics, we are able to answer some of the basic questions with which we began, and we are closer to understanding the psychology of people who suddenly change from mild-mannered, shy individuals into murderers. Any conclusion, however, is only a statement of the *probable* relationship between the events that were investigated; it is never one of certainty. Truth in science is provisional, always open to revision by later data from better studies, developed from better hypotheses.

You might take a moment to consider what else you'd like to know, to put these data in a richer context. For example, you might want to know how both types of murderers differ from individuals who have never committed murders on measures such as their sex-role scores. If we collected new data we could use descriptive and inferential statistics to answer such questions as whether all murderers are, on such dimensions, different from those who don't commit murders. What might you expect?

....

significant difference A difference between experimental groups or conditions that would have occurred by chance less than an accepted criterion; in psychology, the criterion most often used is a probability of less than 5 times out of 100, or $p < .05$.

BECOMING A WISE CONSUMER OF STATISTICS

Now that we have considered what statistics are, how they are used, and what they mean, let's talk briefly about how they can be misused. Many people accept unsupported so-called facts that are bolstered by the air of authority of a statistic. Others choose to believe or disbelieve what the statistics say without having any idea of how to question the numbers that are presented in support of a product, politician, or proposal. At the end of the chapter, you saw some suggestions about how you can become a wiser research consumer. Based on this brief survey of statistics, we can extend that advice to situations in which people make specific statistical claims.

There are many ways to give a misleading impression using statistics. The decisions made at all stages of research—from who the participants are to how the study is designed, what statistics are selected, and how they are used—can have a profound effect on the conclusions that can be drawn from the data.

The group of participants can make a large difference that can easily remain undetected when the results are reported. For example, a survey of views on abortion rights will yield very different results if conducted in a small conservative community in the South rather than at a university in New York City. Likewise, a pro-life group surveying the opinions of its membership will very likely arrive at conclusions that differ from those obtained by the same survey conducted by a pro-choice group.

Even if the participants are randomly selected and not biased by the methodology, the statistics can produce misleading results if the assumptions of the statistics are violated. For example, suppose 20 people take an IQ test; 19 of them receive scores between 90 and 110, and 1 receives a score of 220. The mean of the group will be strongly elevated by that one outlying high score. With this sort of a data set, it would be much more accurate to present the median, which would accurately report the group's generally average intelligence, rather than the mean, which would make it look as if the average member of this group had a high IQ. This sort of bias is especially powerful in a small sample. If, however, the number of people in this group were 2,000 instead of 20, the one extreme outlier would make virtually no difference, and the mean would be a legitimate summary of the group's intelligence.

One good way to avoid falling for this sort of deception is to check on the size of the sample. Large samples are less likely to be misleading than small ones. Another check is to look at the median or the mode as well as the mean. The results can be interpreted with more confidence if they are similar than if they are different. Always closely examine the methodology and results of the research reported. Check to see if the experimenters report their sample size, measures of variability, and significance levels.

Statistics are the backbone of psychological research. They are used to understand observations and to determine whether the findings are, in fact, correct. Through the methods you've seen, psychologists can prepare a frequency distribution of data and find the central tendencies and variability of the scores. They can use the correlation coefficient to determine the strength and direction of the association between sets of scores. Finally, psychological investigators can find out how representative the observations are and whether they are significantly different from what would be observed among the general population. Statistics can also be used poorly or deceptively, misleading those who do not understand them. But when statistics are applied correctly and ethically, they allow researchers to expand the body of psychological knowledge.

KEY TERMS

correlation coefficient (*r*)
descriptive statistics
frequency distribution
inferential statistics
mean

measure of central tendency
measure of variability
median
mode
normal curve

range
significant difference
standard deviation (SD)

10

Research Methods in Psychology

Research Methods
in Psychology

Research Methods
in Psychology

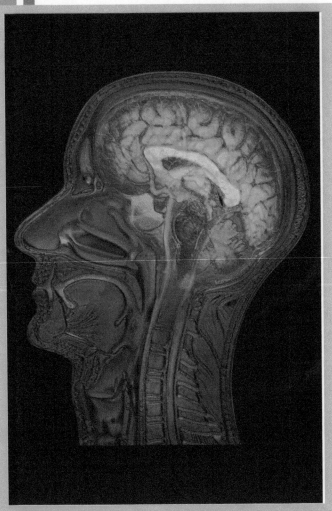

© Exactostock/SuperStock

Thinking like a psychologist involves questioning and finding answers to those questions. Past students of mine have expressed a range of interesting concerns that might be answered through the study of psychology. Here are some of their questions:

- Should I use my cell phone while I drive?
- Can memory research help me study for exams?
- How can I become more creative?
- Is it okay to put kids in day care?

In this chapter, we consider how psychologists generate answers to questions that matter most to students. The focus will be on the special way in which psychology applies the scientific method to its domain of inquiry. By the end of the chapter, you should understand how psychologists design their research: How can solid conclusions ever be drawn from the complex and often fuzzy phenomena that psychologists study—how people think, feel, and behave? Even if you never do any scientific research in your life, mastering the information in this section will be useful. The underlying purpose here is to help improve your *critical thinking skills* by teaching you how to ask the right questions and evaluate the answers about the causes, consequences, and correlates of psychological phenomena. The mass media constantly release stories that begin with, "Research shows that. . . ." By sharpening your intelligent skepticism, this chapter will help you become a more sophisticated consumer of the research-based conclusions that confront you in everyday life.

THE PROCESS OF RESEARCH

The research process in psychology can be divided into several steps that usually occur in sequence (see **Figure 1**). The process typically begins with *Step 1,* in which observations, beliefs, information, and general knowledge lead someone to come up with a new idea or a different way of thinking about a phenomenon. Where do researchers' questions originate? Some come from direct observations of events, humans, and nonhumans in the environment. Other research addresses traditional parts of the field: Some issues are considered to be "great unanswered questions" that have been passed down from earlier scholars. Researchers often combine old ideas in unique ways that offer an original perspective. The hallmark of the truly creative thinker is the discovery of a new truth that moves science and society in a better direction.

As psychologists accumulate information about phenomena, they create theories that become an important context to formulate research questions. A **theory** is an organized set of concepts that *explains* a phenomenon or set of phenomena. At the common core of most psychological theories is the assumption of **determinism,** the idea that all events—physical, mental,

....

 Watch the Video *The Big Picture: How to Answer Psychological Questions?* on MyPsychLab

theory An organized set of concepts that explains a phenomenon or set of phenomena.

determinism The doctrine that all events—physical, behavioral, and mental—are determined by specific causal factors that are potentially knowable.

Step 1 Initial observation or question

Similarity plays a large role in relationships, as does conversation. Perhaps conversation provides a context for couples to gauge similarity.

Step 2 Form a hypothesis

Couples whose style of language use is more similar will show more stability in their relationships.

Step 3 Design the study

Couples' instant messages for a 10-day period were assessed on a variety of linguistic features yielding an index of *language style* matching.

Three months later, couples indicated whether they were still dating.

Step 4 Analyze the data and draw conclusions

The data revealed that couples with more language style matching were more likely to still be dating.

Step 5 Report the findings

The article appeared in the prestigious journal *Psychological Science.*

Step 6 Consider open questions

The discussion in the article acknowledges that the direction of the effect remains open: More language style matching might lead to better relationships or might lead to more language style matching.

Step 7 Act on open questions

These or other researchers can undertake new research to answer the open questions.

FIGURE 1 Steps in the Process of Conducting and Reporting Research

To illustrate the steps in the scientific process, consider a study that examined the relationship between couples' language styles and the stability of their relationships (Ireland et al., 2011).

and behavioral—are the result of, or determined by, specific causal factors. These causal factors are limited to those in the individual's environment or within the person. Researchers also assume that behavior and mental processes follow *lawful patterns* of relationships, patterns that can be discovered and revealed through research. Psychological theories are typically claims about the causal forces that underlie such lawful patterns.

When a theory is proposed in psychology, it is generally expected both to account for known facts and, as *Step 2* in the research process, generate new hypotheses. A **hypothesis** is a tentative and testable statement about the relationship between causes and consequences. Hypotheses are often stated as if–then predictions, specifying certain outcomes from specific conditions. We might predict, for example, that *if* children view a lot of violence on television, *then* they will engage in more aggressive acts toward their peers. Research is required to verify the if–then link. For *Step 3*, researchers rely on the *scientific method* to put their hypotheses to the test. The scientific method is a general set of procedures for gathering and interpreting evidence in ways that limit sources of errors and yield dependable conclusions. Psychology is considered a science to the extent that it follows the rules established by the scientific method. Much of this chapter is devoted to describing the scientific method. Once researchers have collected their data, they proceed to *Step 4*, in which they analyze those data and generate conclusions.

If researchers believe that their data will have an impact on the field, they will move on to *Step 5* and submit the paper for publication in a journal. For publication to be possible, researchers must keep complete records of observations and data analyses in a form that other researchers can understand and evaluate. Secrecy is banned from the research procedure because all data and methods must eventually be open for *public verifiability*; that is, other researchers must have the opportunity to inspect, criticize, replicate, or disprove the data and methods.

Much psychological research appears in journals that are published by organizations such as the American Psychological Association or the Association for Psychological Science. When research manuscripts are submitted to most journals, they undergo a process of *peer review*. Each manuscript is typically sent to two to five experts in the field. Those experts provide detailed analyses of the manuscript's rationale, methodology, and results. Only when those experts have been sufficiently satisfied do manuscripts become journal articles. This is a rigorous process. For example, in 2010, journals published by the American Psychological Association (2011) rejected, on average, 71 percent of the manuscripts submitted to them. The process of peer review isn't perfect—no doubt some worthy research projects are overlooked and some uneven ones slip through—but, in general, this process ensures that the research you read in the vast majority of journals has met high standards.

At Step 5, psychologists also often try to disseminate their results to a wider public. In a presidential address to the American Psychological Association, George Miller (1969) reached the celebrated conclusion that the responsibility of professional psychologists "is less to assume the role of experts and try to apply psychology ourselves than to give it away to the people who really need it—and that includes everyone" (p. 1071). Individual psychologists often write books and give lectures that are directed toward broad audiences. Major professional organizations, such as the American Psychological Association and Association for Psychological Science, also issue press releases and create public forums in which researchers can give psychology away.

At *Step 6* of the research process, the scientific community reflects on the research and identifies questions the work leaves unresolved. Most research articles start this process in a *discussion* section in which the researchers lay out the implications and limitations of their work. They might explicitly describe the type of future research they consider desirable. When the data do not fully support a hypothesis, researchers must rethink aspects of their theories. Thus there is continual interaction between theory and research. At *Step 7*, the original researchers or their peers might act on open questions and begin the research cycle again.

This research process is centered around appropriate uses of the scientific method. The goal of the scientific method is to allow researchers to draw conclusions with maximum objectivity. Conclusions are *objective* when they are uninfluenced by researchers' emotions or personal biases. Each of the next two sections begins with a *challenge to objectivity* and then describes the *remedy* prescribed by the scientific method. ◉

Observer Biases and Operational Definitions

When different people observe the same events, they don't always "see" the same thing. This section describes the problem of *observer bias* and the steps researchers take as remedies.

The Challenge to Objectivity An **observer bias** is an error due to the personal motives and expectations of the viewer. At times, people see and hear what they expect rather than what is. Consider a rather dramatic example of observer bias. Around

....

◉ **Watch** the Video *What Do You Think About Psychological Research?* on MyPsychLab

hypothesis A tentative and testable explanation of the relationship between two (or more) events or variables; often stated as a prediction that a certain outcome will result from specific conditions.

observer bias The distortion of evidence because of the personal motives and expectations of the viewer.

Participants, as well as spectators and broadcast viewers, are subject to observer bias. How can you determine what really happened?

the beginning of the 20th century, a leading psychologist, Hugo Munsterberg, gave a speech on peace to a large audience that included many reporters. He summarized the news accounts of what they heard and saw in this way:

> The reporters sat immediately in front of the platform. One man wrote that the audience was so surprised by my speech that it received it in complete silence; another wrote that I was constantly interrupted by loud applause and that at the end of my address the applause continued for minutes. The one wrote that during my opponent's speech I was constantly smiling; the other noticed that my face remained grave and without a smile. The one said that I grew purple-red from excitement; and the other found that I grew chalk-white. (1908, pp. 35–36)

It would be interesting to go back to the original newspapers, to see how the reporters' accounts were related to their political views—then we might be able to understand why the reporters supposedly saw what they did.

You can look for examples of observer biases in your day-to-day life. Suppose, for example, you are in a close relationship. How might the motives and expectations you bring to that relationship affect the way you view your partner's behavior? Let's consider a study of 125 married couples.

Featured Study

The couples were videotaped while they had two different 10-minute conversations (Knobloch et al., 2007). For one conversation, the couples discussed a positive aspect of their relationship; for the other, they discussed a recent unexpected event that had changed how sure they were (for better or for worse) about the future of their relationship. After each conversation, the two spouses gave individual ratings about the quality of the interactions along dimensions such as how warm or cold they thought their partner had been and how much their partner attempted to dominate the conversation. The researchers also asked neutral raters—people who had no connections to the couples—to watch and evaluate the conversations. Against the baseline provided by those neutral ratings, the couples' ratings displayed consistent observer bias. The direction of the bias was determined by how certain each member reported him- or herself to be about the future of the relationship. The researchers noted, for example, that "participants who were sure about their marriage had strong positive reactions to conversations that seemed normal to the naked eye" (p. 173).

This study demonstrates how expectations can lead different observers to reach different conclusions. The biases of the observers act as *filters* through which some things are noticed as relevant and significant and others are ignored as irrelevant and not meaningful.

Let's apply this lesson to what happens in psychology experiments. Researchers are often in the business of making observations. Given that every observer brings a different set of prior experiences to making those observations—and often those experiences include a commitment to a particular theory—you can see why observer biases could pose a problem. Researchers must work hard to ensure that they are viewing behavior with a "naked eye," free of biases. What can researchers do to ensure that their observations are minimally affected by prior expectations?

The Remedy To minimize observer biases, researchers rely on standardization and operational definitions. **Standardization** means using uniform, consistent procedures in all phases of data collection. All features of the test or experimental situation should be sufficiently standardized so all research participants experience exactly the same experimental conditions. Standardization means asking questions in the same way and scoring responses according to preestablished rules. Having results printed or recorded helps ensure their comparability across different times and places and with different participants and researchers.

Observations themselves must also be standardized: Scientists must solve the problem of how to translate their theories into concepts with consistent meaning. The strategy for standardizing the meaning of concepts is called *operationalization*. An **operational definition** standardizes meaning within an experiment, by defining a concept in terms of specific operations or procedures used to measure it or to determine its presence. All the variables in an experiment must be given operational definitions. A **variable** is any factor that varies in amount or kind. Recall the experiment in Figure 1. The researchers assessed the variable *language style matching*, which could take on any value between 0 and 1.

In experimental settings, researchers most often wish to demonstrate a cause-and-effect relationship between two types of variables. Imagine, for example, that you wished to test the hypothesis we considered earlier: that children who view a lot of violence on television will engage in more aggressive acts toward their peers. To test that hypothesis, you might devise an experiment in which you manipulated the amount of violence each participant viewed. That factor you manipulate would be the **independent variable;** it functions as the causal part of the relationship. For each level of violence viewed, you could then assess how much aggression each participant displayed. Aggression is the effect part of the cause-effect relationship; it is the **dependent variable,** which is what the experimenter measures. If researchers' claims about cause and effect are correct, the value of the dependent variable will *depend* on the value of the independent variable. 👁

Let's take a moment to put these new concepts to use in the context of a real experiment. The research project we consider begins with a great philosophical question: Do people have free will, or is their behavior determined by forces of genetics and environment outside their control? The study didn't attempt to answer that question. Rather, the researchers argued that the

....

👁 **Watch** the Video *Distinguishing Independent and Dependent Variables* on MyPsychLab

standardization A set of uniform procedures for treating each participant in a test, interview, or experiment, or for recording data.

operational definition A definition of a variable or condition in terms of the specific operation or procedure used to determine its presence.

variable In an experimental setting, a factor that varies in amount and kind.

independent variable In an experimental setting, a variable that the researcher manipulates with the expectation of having an impact on values of the dependent variable.

dependent variable In an experimental setting, a variable that the researcher measures to assess the impact of a variation in an independent variable.

Is violent behavior caused by viewing violence on television? How could you find out?

way in which different individuals answer this question—their beliefs in *free will* versus *determinism*—has an impact on how they behave (Vohs & Schooler, 2008). The researchers reasoned that people who are guided by a worldview of determinism would feel less personal responsibility for bad behavior because they'd consider it out of their control. To test this hypothesis, the researchers gave students an opportunity to cheat!

Figure 2 presents important aspects of the experiment. The researchers recruited roughly 120 college undergraduates to serve as participants. The independent variable for the study was participants' beliefs in free will versus determinism. To manipulate this variable, the researchers presented students with a series of 15 statements and asked them to think about each statement for one minute. As you might expect, those statements were different for the free will and determinism conditions. Figure 2 provides examples.

To test their hypothesis, the researchers needed to provide the students with an opportunity to cheat. During the experiment, the students attempted to answer 15 problems from Graduate Record Examination (GRE) practice tests. They could earn $1 for each correct answer. Participants scored their own answers in the absence of the experimenter. That provided the context for cheating: The experimenter would never know if a participant paid him- or herself more money than was due. The dependent variable for the experiment was the amount of money participants paid themselves.

Figure 2 provides the results of the experiment. To determine how average students would actually score on the 15 GRE questions, the researchers had an extra condition in which they scored participants' performance themselves to see how much money the students would earn. The bar labeled "Baseline experimenter-scored" provides that information. As you can see from the other two bars in Figure 2, the independent variable had the effect on the dependent variable that the researchers expected. Those students who had been prompted to take the perspective of determinism paid themselves about $4 more than those students who focused on free will. Because of the experimenter-scored baseline—which shows free-will students at the same level as experimenter-scored students—we can infer that the determinism students were cheating. Take a moment to think about other ways in which you might operationalize the experimental variables, to test the same hypothesis by other means. You might, for example, want to measure cheating in some other fashion, to show that the results generalize to other

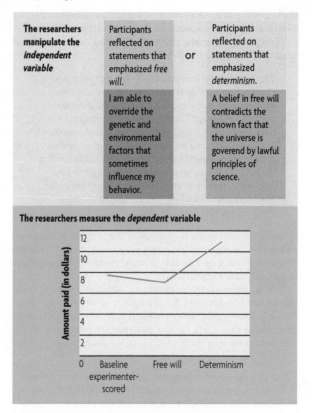

FIGURE 2 Elements of an Experiment

To test their hypotheses, researchers create operational definitions for the independent and dependent variables.

Data from Kathlee D. Vohs and Jonathan W. Schooler, The value of believing in free will: Encouraging a belief in determinism increases cheating, *Psychological Science*, January 1, 2008, pages 49–54. © 2008 by the Association for Psychological Science.

life circumstances. This type of concern provides a transition to an exploration of experimental methods.

Experimental Methods: Alternative Explanations and the Need for Controls

You know from day-to-day experience that people can suggest many causes for the same outcome. Psychologists face this same problem when they try to make exact claims about causality. To overcome causal ambiguity, researchers use **experimental methods:** They manipulate an independent variable to look for an effect on a dependent variable. The goal of this method is to make strong causal claims about the impact of one variable on the other. In this section, let's review the problem of *alternative explanations* and some steps researchers take to counter the problem.

The Challenge to Objectivity When psychologists test a hypothesis, they most often have in mind an explanation for

experimental method Research methodology that involves the manipulation of independent variables to determine their effects on the dependent variables.

why change in the independent variable should affect the dependent variable in a particular way. For example, you might predict, and demonstrate experimentally, that the viewing of television violence leads to high levels of aggression. But how can you know that it was precisely the viewing of *violence* that produced aggression? To make the strongest possible case for their hypotheses, psychologists must be very sensitive to the existence of possible *alternative explanations*. The more alternative explanations there might be for a given result, the less confidence there is that the initial hypothesis is accurate. When something other than what an experimenter purposely introduces into a research setting changes a participant's behavior and adds confusion to the interpretation of the data, it is called a **confounding variable.** When the real cause of some observed behavioral effect is *confounded*, the experimenter's interpretation of the data is put at risk. Suppose, for example, that violent television scenes are louder and involve more movement than do most nonviolent scenes. In that case, the superficial and violent aspects of the scenes are confounded. The researcher is unable to specify which factor uniquely produces aggressive behavior.

Although each different experimental method potentially gives rise to a unique set of alternative explanations, there are two types of confounds that apply to almost all experiments, which researchers call *expectancy effects* and *placebo effects*. Unintentional **expectancy effects** occur when a researcher or observer subtly communicates to the research participants the behaviors he or she expects to find, thereby producing the desired reaction. Under these circumstances, the experimenter's expectations, rather than the independent variable, actually help trigger the observed reactions.

In an experiment, 12 students were given groups of rats that were going to be trained to run a maze (Rosenthal & Fode, 1963). Half of the students were told their rats were from a special maze-bright breed. The other students were told their rats were bred to be maze-dull. As you might guess, their rats were actually all the same. Nonetheless, the students' results corresponded with their expectations for their rats. The rats labeled bright were found to be much better learners than those that had been labeled as dull.

How do you suppose the students communicated their expectations to their rats? Do you see why you should worry even more about expectancy effects when an experiment is carried out within species—with a human experimenter and human participants? Expectation effects distort the content of discovery.

A **placebo effect** occurs when experimental participants change their behavior in the *absence* of any kind of experimental manipulation. This concept originated in medicine to account for cases in which a patient's health improved after he or she had received medication that was chemically inert or a treatment that was nonspecific. The placebo effect refers to an improvement in health or well-being related to the individual's *belief* that the treatment will be effective. Some treatments with no genuine medical effects have been shown to produce good or excellent outcomes for patients on whom they were used (Colloca & Miller, 2011).

In a psychological research setting, a placebo effect has occurred whenever a behavioral response is influenced by a person's expectation of what to do or how to feel rather than by the specific intervention or procedures employed to produce that response. Recall the experiment relating television viewing to later aggression. Suppose we discovered that experimental participants who hadn't watched any television at all also showed high levels of aggression. We might conclude that these individuals, by virtue of being put in a situation that allowed them to display aggression, would expect they were *supposed* to behave aggressively and would go on to do so. Experimenters must always be aware that participants change the way they behave simply because they are aware of being observed or tested. For example, participants may feel special about being chosen to take part in a study and thus act differently than they would ordinarily. Such effects can compromise an experiment's results.

The Remedy: Control Procedures Because human and animal behaviors are complex and often have multiple causes, good research design involves anticipating possible confounds and devising strategies for eliminating them. Similar to defensive strategies in sports, good research designs anticipate what the other team might do and make plans to counteract it. Researchers' strategies are called **control procedures**—methods that attempt to hold constant all variables and conditions other than those related to the hypothesis being tested. In an experiment, instructions, room temperature, tasks, the way the researcher is dressed, time allotted, the way the responses are recorded, and many other details of the situation must be similar for all participants, to ensure that their experience is the same. The only differences in participants' experiences should be those introduced by the independent variable. Let's look at remedies for the specific confounding variables, expectancy and placebo effects.

Imagine, for example, that you enriched the aggression experiment to include a treatment group that watched comedy programs. You'd want to be careful not to treat your comedy and violence participants in different ways based on your expectations. Thus, in your experiment, we would want the research assistant who greeted the participants and later assessed their aggression to be unaware of whether they had watched a violent program or a comedy: We would keep the research assistant *blind* to the assignment of participants to conditions. In the best circumstances, bias can be eliminated by keeping *both* experimental assistants and participants blind to which

....

confounding variable A stimulus other than the variable an experimenter explicitly introduces into a research setting that affects a participant's behavior.

expectancy effect Result that occurs when a researcher or observer subtly communicates to participants the kind of behavior he or she expects to find, thereby creating that expected reaction.

placebo effect A change in behavior in the absence of an experimental manipulation.

control procedure Consistent procedure for giving instructions, scoring responses, and holding all other variables constant except those being systematically varied.

participants get which treatment. This technique is called a **double-blind control.** In our prospective aggression experiment, we couldn't keep participants from knowing whether they had watched comedy or violence. However, we would take great care to ensure that they couldn't guess that our later analyses would focus on their subsequent aggression.

To account for placebo effects, researchers generally include an experimental condition in which the treatment is not administered. This is a **placebo control.** Placebo controls fall into the general category of controls by which experimenters assure themselves they are making appropriate comparisons. Suppose you see a late-night TV commercial that celebrates the herbal supplement ginkgo biloba as an answer to all your memory problems. What might you expect if you buy a supply of ginkgo and take it weekly? One study demonstrated that university students who took ginkgo every morning for six weeks did, in fact, show improvements in their performance on cognitive tasks (Elsabagh et al., 2005). On one task, people were asked to view a series of 20 pictures on a computer screen, name them, and later recall those names. The participants were 14 percent better at this task after six weeks of ginkgo. However, participants who took a placebo—a pill with no active ingredients—also improved by 14 percent. The placebo control suggests that improvement on the task was the result of practice from the initial session. The data from control conditions provide an important baseline against which the experimental effect is evaluated.

The Remedy: Research Designs To implement control conditions, researchers make decisions about what type of research design best suits their goals. In some research designs, which are referred to as **between-subjects designs,** different groups of participants are *randomly assigned,* by chance procedures, to an experimental condition (exposed to one or more experimental treatments) or to a control condition (not exposed to an experimental treatment). **Random assignment** is one of the major steps researchers take to eliminate confounding variables that relate to individual differences among potential research participants. This is the procedure you'd want to use for the aggression experiment. The random assignment to experimental and control conditions makes it quite likely that the two groups will be similar in important ways at the start of an experiment because each participant has the same probability of being in a treatment condition as in a control condition. We shouldn't have to worry, for example, that everyone in the **experimental group** loves violent television and everyone in the **control group** hates it. Random assignment should mix both types of people together in each group. If outcome differences are found between conditions, we can be more confident that the differences were caused by a treatment or intervention rather than by preexisting differences.

Researchers also try to approximate randomness in the way they bring participants into the laboratory. Suppose you would like to test the hypothesis that 6-year-old children are more likely to lie than 4-year-old children. At the end of your experiment, you'd like your conclusions to apply to the whole **population** of 4-year-olds and 6-year-olds. However, you can bring only a very small subset—a **sample**—of the world's 4- and 6-year-olds into your laboratory. Typically, psychology experiments use from 20 to 100 participants. How should you choose your group of children? Researchers attempt to construct a **representative sample,** which is a sample that closely

matches the overall characteristics of the population with respect, for example, to the distribution of males and females, racial and ethnic groups, and so on. For example, if your study of children's lying included only boys, we wouldn't consider that a representative sample of the full population of 4- and 6-year-olds. To achieve a representative sample, researchers often use the procedure of **random sampling,** which means that every member of a population has an equal likelihood of participating in the experiment. (In the Statstical Supplement that goes along this chapter, we describe the procedures researchers use to determine whether experimental results can be generalized beyond a particular sample. Please read the Supplement in conjunction with this chapter.)

Another type of experimental design—a **within-subjects design**—uses each participant as his or her own control. For example, each participant might experience more than one level of the independent variable. Or, the behavior of an experimental participant before getting the treatment might be compared with behavior after. Consider an experiment that examined the accuracy of people's judgments about future exercise.

Suppose you are contemplating a visit to the gym. You're probably more likely to go if you think that you're going to enjoy the workout. But how accurate are your predictions about your future enjoyment? A team of researchers tested the hypothesis that people habitually underestimate the extent to which they'll enjoy their exercise (Ruby et al., 2011). To test their hypothesis, the researchers approached people who attended fitness classes regularly. Before a class began, they asked the participants to predict how much they

Featured Study

....

double-blind control An experimental technique in which biased expectations of experimenters are eliminated by keeping both participants and experimental assistants unaware of which participants have received which treatment.

placebo control An experimental condition in which treatment is not administered; it is used in cases where a placebo effect might occur.

between-subjects design A research design in which different groups of participants are randomly assigned to experimental conditions or to control conditions.

random assignment A procedure by which participants have an equal likelihood of being assigned to any condition within an experiment.

experimental group A group in an experiment that is exposed to a treatment or experiences a manipulation of the independent variable.

control group A group in an experiment that is not exposed to a treatment or does not experience a manipulation of the independent variable.

population The entire set of individuals to which generalizations will be made based on an experimental sample.

sample A subset of a population selected as participants in an experiment.

representative sample A subset of a population that closely matches the overall characteristics of the population with respect to the distribution of males and females, racial and ethnic groups, and so on.

random sampling A procedure that ensures that every member of a population has an equal likelihood of participating in an experiment.

within-subjects design A research design that uses each participant as his or her own control; for example, the behavior of an experimental participant before receiving treatment might be compared to his or her behavior after receiving treatment.

thought they would enjoy the class on a scale ranging from 1 (not at all) to 10 (very much). People, on average, gave a rating of 7.6. After the class, the people rated their actual enjoyment. They gave consistently higher ratings, with an average of 8.2 on the 10-point scale.

Because this study used a within-subjects design, the researchers could draw the strong conclusion that the participants were underestimating their future enjoyment. You might wonder why. The researchers suggested that people contemplating exercise are too focused on the beginning of the workout—which is often the worst part. In a later between-subjects experiment, they asked participants to imagine doing either the best part of their workout routine either first or last. Those people who imagined doing the best part first gave consistently higher average ratings (8.0 on the 10-point scale) than people who imagined doing the best part last (7.0). Do you see how you can harness this result the next time you contemplate getting some exercise?

The research methodologies we have considered so far all involve the manipulation of an independent variable to look for an effect on a dependent variable. Although this experimental method often allows researchers to make the strongest claims about causal relations among variables, several conditions can make this method less desirable. First, during an experiment, behavior is frequently studied in an artificial environment, one in which situational factors are controlled so heavily that the environment may itself distort the behavior from the way it would occur naturally. Critics claim that much of the richness and complexity of natural behavior patterns is lost in controlled experiments, sacrificed to the simplicity of dealing with only one or a few variables and responses. Second, research participants typically know they are in an experiment and are being tested and measured. They may react to this awareness by trying to please the researcher, attempting to "psych out" the research purpose, or changing their behavior from what it would be if they were unaware of being monitored. Third, some important research problems are not amenable to ethical experimental treatment. We could not, for example, try to discover whether the tendency toward child abuse is transmitted from generation to generation by creating an experimental group of children who would be abused and a control group of

children who would not be. The next section turns to a type of research method that often addresses these concerns.

Correlational Methods

Is intelligence associated with how long people live? Are optimistic people healthier than pessimists? Is there a relationship between experiencing child abuse and later mental illness? These questions involve variables that a psychologist could not easily or ethically manipulate. To answer these questions, researchers carry out studies using **correlational methods.** Psychologists use correlational methods when they want to determine to what extent two variables, traits, or attributes are related.

To determine the precise degree of correlation that exists between two variables, psychologists compute a statistical measure known as the **correlation coefficient (r).** This value can vary between $+1.0$ and -1.0, where $+1.0$ indicates a perfect positive correlation, -1.0 indicates a perfect negative correlation, and 0.0 indicates no correlation at all. A positive correlation coefficient means that as one set of scores increases, a second set also increases. The reverse is true with negative correlations; the second set of scores goes in the opposite direction to the values of the first scores (see **Figure 3**). Correlations that are closer to zero mean that there is a weak relationship or no relationship between scores on two measures. As the correlation coefficient gets stronger, closer to the ± 1.0 maximum, predictions about one variable based on information about the other variable become increasingly more accurate.

Correlational studies have led to important insights in the field of psychology. To whet your appetite, let's consider one example here.

A team of researchers wished to determine whether children's media habits (television, video games, and computer usage) had an impact on the likelihood that they would have sleep problems (Garrison et al., 2011). To address this question, the researchers asked the parents of 3- to 5-year-old children to keep "media diaries" (in which they recorded the children's media usage) for one week. The parents also completed a Sleep Habits Questionnaire that assessed how long it took children to fall asleep as well as the frequency of "repeated night wakings, nightmares, difficulty waking in the morning, and daytime tiredness" (p. 30). The data analyses indicated that each extra hour of nighttime media use resulted in more sleep problems. In addition, daytime consumption of violent media (but not other types of content) also predicted more sleep problems.

Can you see why a correlational design is appropriate to address this issue? You can't randomly assign children to watch lots of television or none at all. You must wait to see what patterns emerge from families' actual habits. Do these results suggest decisions you might make if you become a parent?

© Luca DiCecco/Alamy

Why do people underestimate how much they will enjoy an exercise session?

correlational method Research methodology that determines to what extent two variables, traits, or attributes are related.

correlation coefficient (r) A statistic that indicates the degree of relationship between two variables.

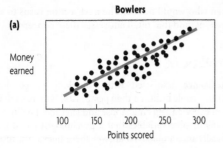

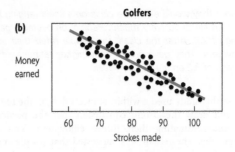

FIGURE 3 Positive and Negative Correlations

These imaginary data display the difference between positive and negative correlations. Each point represents a single bowler or golfer. (a) In general, the more points a professional bowler scores, the more money he or she will earn. Thus, there is a positive correlation between those two variables. (b) The correlation for golf is negative, because golfers earn more money when they make fewer strokes.

When we interpret correlational data, we always need to take care before we make causal claims. Let's stay with the topic of sleep. Research suggests that students who are at risk for sleep disorders are also more likely to have particularly low GPAs (Gaultney, 2010). Based on this result, you might want to take the next step and say that the way to improve students' GPAs would be to force them to sleep more. This intervention is misguided. A strong correlation indicates only that two sets of data are related in a systematic way; the correlation does not ensure that one causes the other. *Correlation does not imply causation.* The correlation could reflect any one of several cause-and-effect possibilities. Many of those possibilities involve a *third variable* that works in the background to bring about the correlation. Suppose, for example, that people both sleep better and get higher grades when they take easy courses. Under those circumstances, the difficulty of students' courses would be a third variable that would bring about a positive correlation between amount of sleep and GPA. It could also be that case people who study more efficiently get to bed sooner or that people who experience anxiety about schoolwork cannot fall asleep. You can see from these three possibilities that correlations most often require researchers to probe for deeper explanations. 👁

Let's consider a couple more examples of the difficulty of making causal claims from correlations. Recall the study we outlined in Figure 1. The main result was that couples with more language style matching were more likely to have relationships that endured over time (Ireland et al., 2011). The researchers acknowledged that the design was correlational: They couldn't be sure whether more language style matching leads to better relationships or better relationships lead to more language style matching. As a second example, consider a study that asked participants to examine photographs of the CEOs of Fortune 500 companies (Rule & Ambady, 2008). Based just on the photographs, participants indicated how good they thought each person would be at leading a company. On the whole, the CEOs who got the highest leadership ratings—again, based only on their photographs—led the most profitable companies. Why might this positive correlation emerge? The researchers were careful to acknowledge that more than one causal pathway

is possible: "Of course, we cannot draw any causal inferences as to whether more successful companies choose individuals with a particular appearance to be their CEOs or whether individuals with a particular appearance emerge as more successful in their work as CEOs" (p. 110). For each of these cases, you can see why correlation does not imply causation. You can also see how correlational research can call attention to intriguing patterns in the world.

We've already given you several examples of the outcomes of experiments. The next section fills in more about how psychologists measure important processes and dimensions of experience.

Stop *and* Review

① What is the relationship between theories and hypotheses?
② What steps can researchers take to overcome observer biases?
③ Why do researchers use double-blind controls?
④ What is meant by a within-subjects design?
⑤ Why does correlation not imply causation?

CRITICAL THINKING Consider the study in which participants predicted their future enjoyment for exercise. Why might the researchers have used people who exercise regularly as participants?

✔️ **Study** and **Review** on **MyPsychLab**

PSYCHOLOGICAL MEASUREMENT

Because psychological processes are so varied and complex, they pose major challenges to researchers who want to measure them. Although some actions and processes are easily seen, many, such as anxiety or dreaming, are not. Thus one task for a

....

👁 **Watch** the **Video** *Correlations Do Not Show Causation* on **MyPsychLab**

Psychology in Your Life

DOES WISHFUL THINKING AFFECT HOW YOU EVALUATE INFORMATION?

In the discussion of challenges to objectivity, observer biases loomed large: Scientists need to take careful measures to ensure that they don't see just what they want to see. However, the concern with observer bias is equally pressing in the real world. Think about all the information you have available through the wonders of the Internet. How do you evaluate all that information when you make important decisions? Researchers have demonstrated that people often engage in wishful thinking. Let's review one study that reached that conclusion.

To begin the study, the researchers defined two populations of participants by their attitudes toward day care (Bastardi et al., 2011). All the participants indicated that they planned to have children in the future. They also indicated that they thought home care was superior to day care. One group, which the researchers called the *unconflicted* group, said that they planned to use home care for their (future) children. The second group, which the researchers called the *conflicted* group, said that they planned to put their children in day care (even though they thought home care was better).

Next, the researchers described two studies to the participants about the relative effectiveness of the two types of child care. The studies differed in their conclusions: One favored day care and the other favored home care. They also differed in their methods: In one study the children were randomly assigned to the two types of care; in the other, the students were matched so that the children in each setting were highly similar.

The researchers asked the participants to indicate how valid and convincing they found each study. For example, the participants judged which study they thought would yield higher-quality conclusions on a scale that ranged from "random assignment much more valid" to "statistical matching much more valid." How would we see an impact of wishful thinking? Recall that the conflicted participants forecasted a future in which they would put their children in day care. As a consequence, they evaluated a study much more positively when it indicated the superiority of day care over home care. Note, of course, that the description of the study hadn't changed—the only thing that was different was the conclusion the participants wished the study to reach.

The researchers also asked the participants to rate the relative superiority of day care versus home care. Recall that both groups had initially rated home care as better. However, after learning about studies that provided balanced information, the conflicted group changed their attitudes dramatically in the direction of thinking that day care was better.

You can imagine yourself in the situation of the participants in the conflicted group. They are eager to find information that supports the difficult decision they foresee in their future. The study demonstrates how that eagerness—that wishful thinking—affects how they assess the information available to them. As you go through life making judgments about how to assess information, think what you might do to keep wishful thinking out of the process.

What procedures might you follow to determine the correlation between students' sleep habits and their success in college? How would you evaluate potential causal relationships underlying any correlation?

psychological researcher is to make the unseen visible, to make internal events and processes external, and to make private experiences public. You have already seen how important it is for researchers to provide operational definitions of the phenomena they wish to study. Those definitions generally provide some procedure for assigning numbers to, or *quantifying*, different levels, sizes, intensities, or amounts of a variable. Many measurement methods are available, each with its particular advantages and disadvantages. 👁

This review of psychological measurement begins with a discussion of the distinction between two ways of gauging the accuracy of a measure: reliability and validity. I then review different measurement techniques for data collection. By whatever means psychologists collect their data, they must use appropriate statistical methods to verify their hypotheses. A description of how psychologists analyze their data is given in the Statistical Supplement, which goes along with this chapter.

👁 **Watch** the **Video** *Research Methods* on **MyPsychLab**

Achieving Reliability and Validity

The goal of psychological measurement is to generate findings that are both reliable and valid. **Reliability** refers to the consistency or dependability of behavioral data resulting from psychological testing or experimental research. A reliable result is one that will be repeated under similar conditions of testing at different times. A reliable measuring instrument yields comparable scores when employed repeatedly (and when the thing being measured does not change). Consider the experiment that manipulated participants' beliefs about free will. That experiment used 122 participants. The experimenters' claim that the result was "reliable" means that they should be able to repeat the experiment with any new group of participants of comparable size and generate the same pattern of data.

Validity means that the information produced by research or testing accurately measures the psychological variable or quality it is intended to measure. A valid measure of *happiness,* for example, should allow us to predict how happy you are likely to be in particular situations. A valid experiment means that the researcher can generalize to broader circumstances, often from the laboratory to the real world. Suppose a professor instructs his class to meditate on free will just before an exam. That professor likely accepts as valid the idea that belief in free will lowers students' impulse to cheat. Tests and experiments can be reliable without being valid. We could, for example, use your shoe size as an index of your happiness. This would be reliable (we'd always get the same answer), but not valid (we'd learn very little about your day-to-day happiness level).

As you now read about different types of measures, try to evaluate them in terms of reliability and validity.

Self-Report Measures

Often researchers are interested in obtaining data about experiences they cannot directly observe. Sometimes these experiences are internal psychological states, such as beliefs, attitudes, and feelings. At other times, these experiences are external behaviors but—like sexual activities or criminal acts—not generally appropriate for psychologists to witness. In these cases, investigations rely on self-reports. **Self-report measures** are verbal answers, either written or spoken, to questions the researcher poses. Researchers devise reliable ways to quantify these self-reports so they can make meaningful comparisons between different individuals' responses.

Self-reports include responses made on questionnaires and during interviews. A *questionnaire* or *survey* is a written set of questions, ranging in content from questions of fact ("Are you a registered voter?"), to questions about past or present behavior ("How much do you smoke?"), to questions about

attitudes and feelings ("How satisfied are you with your present job?"). *Open-ended* questions allow respondents to answer freely in their own words. Questions may also have a number of *fixed alternatives* such as *yes, no,* and *undecided.*

An *interview* is a dialogue between a researcher and an individual for the purpose of obtaining detailed information. Instead of being completely standardized, like a questionnaire, an interview is *interactive.* An interviewer may vary the questioning to follow up on something the respondent said. Good interviewers are also sensitive to the process of the social interaction as well as to the information revealed. They are trained to establish *rapport,* a positive social relationship with the respondent that encourages trust and the sharing of personal information.

Although researchers rely on a wide variety of self-report measures, there are limits to their usefulness. Obviously, many forms of self-report cannot be used with preverbal children, illiterate adults, speakers of other languages, some mentally disturbed people, and nonhuman animals. Even when self-reports can be used, they may not be reliable or valid. Participants may misunderstand the questions or not remember clearly what they actually experienced. Furthermore, self-reports may be influenced by social desirability. People may give false or misleading answers to create a favorable (or, sometimes, unfavorable) impression of themselves. They may be embarrassed to report their true experiences or feelings.

Behavioral Measures and Observations

As a group, psychological researchers are interested in a wide range of behaviors. They may study a rat running a maze, a child drawing a picture, a student memorizing a poem, or a worker repeatedly performing a task. **Behavioral measures** are ways to study overt actions and observable and recordable reactions.

One of the primary ways to study what people do is *observation.* Researchers use observation in a planned, precise, and systematic manner. Observations focus on either the *process* or the

By watching from behind a one-way mirror, a researcher can make observations of a child without influencing or interfering with the child's behavior. Have you ever changed your behavior when you knew you were being watched?

....

reliability The degree to which a test produces similar scores each time it is used; stability or consistency of the scores produced by an instrument.

validity The extent to which a test measures what it was intended to measure.

self-report measure A self-behavior that is identified through a participant's own observations and reports.

behavioral measure Overt actions or reaction that is observed and recorded, exclusive of self-reported behavior.

products of behavior. In an experiment on learning, for instance, a researcher might observe how many times a research participant rehearsed a list of words (process) and then how many words the participant remembered on a final test (product). For *direct observations,* the behavior under investigation must be clearly visible and overt and easily recorded. For example, in a laboratory experiment on emotions, a researcher could observe a participant's facial expressions as the individual looked at emotionally arousing stimuli.

A researcher's direct observations are often augmented by technology. For example, contemporary psychologists often rely on computers to provide very precise measures of the time it takes for research participants to perform various tasks, such as reading a sentence or solving a problem. Although some forms of exact measurement were available before the computer age, computers now provide extraordinary flexibility in collecting and analyzing precise information. The newest technologies allow researchers to produce behavioral measures of a remarkable kind: pictures of the brain at work.

In **naturalistic observation,** some naturally occurring behavior is viewed by a researcher, who makes no attempt to change or interfere with it. In some cases, the observation takes place in a laboratory. For instance, a researcher behind a one-way mirror might observe how children use their verbal abilities to persuade their friends to help with tasks (McGrath & Zook, 2011). In other cases, researchers go out into the world to observe behavior.

When you enter a college classroom, do you notice people sitting together based on their physical similarity?

Featured Study

Consider this scenario: You enter a crowded classroom and you need to choose a seat. What factors influence your choice? A team of researchers suggested that "birds of a feather sit together": Specifically, they hypothesized that students choose to sit near people with whom they shared physical similarity (Mackinnon et al., 2011). To test this hypothesis, the researchers took digital photographs of 14 university classrooms with 2,228 students. You probably won't be surprised to learn that students were more likely to sit near other students of the same sex and race. However, the researchers' analyses also revealed that people were more likely to sit together based on whether they were wearing glasses as well as similarity in their hair length and hair color.

Do you see why naturalistic observation provides an excellent method to test the hypothesis? Meanwhile, it's very unlikely that students scan a classroom and think, "I'm going sit next to him because we both have long blond hair." This study allows you to reflect on ways in which physical similarity influences your behavior outside of your awareness.

Naturalistic observation is especially useful in the early stages of an investigation. It helps researchers discover the extent of a phenomenon or to get an idea of what the important variables and relationships might be. The data from naturalistic observation often provide clues for an investigator to use in formulating a specific hypothesis or research plan.

When they wish to test hypotheses with behavioral measures, researchers sometimes turn to *archival data.* Imagine all the types of information you might find in a library or on the Web: birth and death records, weather reports, movie attendance figures, legislators' voting patterns, and so on. Any of those types of information could become valuable to test the right hypothesis. Consider a study that examined whether men

and women differ in their level of *heroism* (Becker & Eagly, 2004). To address this question, the researchers couldn't create a laboratory test; they couldn't set a building on fire to see whether more men or women rushed in. Instead, they defined behaviors out in the world that were arguably heroic and then looked to archival records to assess the relative contributions of men and women. For example, the researchers examined participation in "Doctors of the World," an organization that sends medical personnel to all corners of the globe. Personnel in this program assume a "nonnegligible risk [by] delivering health and medical services in environments marked by local violence and unsanitary conditions" (Becker & Eagly, 2004, p. 173). What did the archival data show? More than half of the participants in Doctors of the World (65.8 percent) were women. You can see why archival data are essential to address certain types of questions.

Before we leave the topic of psychological measurement, you should be aware that many research projects combine both self-report measures and behavioral observations. Researchers may, for example, specifically look for a relationship between how people report they will behave and how they actually behave. In addition, rather than involving large numbers of participants, some research projects will focus all their measures on a single individual or small group in a **case study.** Intensive analyses of particular individuals can sometimes yield

naturalistic observation A research technique in which unobtrusive observations are made of behaviors that occur in natural environments.

case study Intensive observation of a particular individual or small group of individuals.

Table 1 • What's in a Name? Methods and Measures

	Research Goal	Dependent Measure		
			Self-Report	**Observation**
Correlational Methods	To assess the correlation between the frequency of people's names and their experience of happiness.		Each participant's assessment of his or her own happiness.	
	To assess the correlation between the frequency of children's names and their acceptance by peers.			Children's amount of social interaction on the playground.
Experimental Methods	To determine if people judge identical photos differently when different names are assigned to them.		Participants' ratings of baby pictures to which random names have been assigned.	
	To determine if people's actual social interactions change because of name-based expectations.			The number of positive facial expressions people produce in conversation with a stranger who has introduced himself as *Mark* or *Marcus*.

important insights into general features of human experience. For example, careful observations of single patients with brain damage provided the basis for important theories of the localization of language functions in the brain.

You have now seen several types of procedures and measures that researchers use. Before we move on, let's see how the same issue can be addressed in different research designs. Consider Shakespeare's question, "What's in a name?" In *Romeo and Juliet*, Juliet asserts, "That which we call a rose by any other name would smell as sweet." But is that correct? Do you think your name has an impact on the way other people treat you? Is it better to have a common, familiar name or a rare, distinctive one? Or does your name not matter at all? **Table 1** gives examples of combinations of measures and methods that researchers might use to answer those questions. As you read through Table 1, ask yourself how willing you would be to participate in each type of study. The next section discusses the ethical standards that govern psychological research.

Stop *and* Review

① Why can some measures be reliable but not valid?
② Why is it important for interviewers to establish rapport?

③ Suppose a researcher spends time observing children's behavior on a playground. What kind of measure would that be?

✓•─ **Study** and **Review** on **MyPsychLab**

ETHICAL ISSUES IN HUMAN AND ANIMAL RESEARCH

Respect for the basic rights of humans and animals is a fundamental obligation of all researchers (Bersoff, 2008). All research is conducted with respect to a critical question: How should the *potential gains* of a research project be weighed against the *costs* it incurs to those who are subjected to procedures that are risky, painful, stressful, or deceptive? For example, researchers have conducted classic experiments on *obedience to authority*. In those experiments, participants were deceived into believing that they were giving dangerous electric shocks to total strangers. Evidence from the experiments suggests that the participants were experiencing severe emotional distress. Although the research may be quite important to an understanding of human nature, it is difficult to assert that this gain in knowledge offsets the emotional costs to the participants. 👁

Beginning in 1953, the American Psychological Association published guidelines for ethical standards for researchers. Current research practice is governed by the 2002 revision of those guidelines (including a series of amendments made through 2010). To guarantee that these and other ethical principles are honored, special committees oversee every research proposal, imposing strict guidelines issued by the U.S. Department of Health and Human Services. Universities and colleges, hospitals, and research institutes each have *review boards* that approve and reject proposals for human and animal research. Let's review some of the factors those review boards consider.

Informed Consent

At the start of nearly all laboratory research with human subjects, participants undergo a process of **informed consent.** They are *informed* about the procedures they will experience as well as the potential risks and benefits of participation. Given that information, participants are asked to sign a statement indicating that they *consent* to continue. Participants are also assured that their privacy is protected: All records of their behavior are kept strictly confidential; they must approve any public sharing of them. In addition, participants are told in advance that they may leave an experiment any time they wish, without penalty, and they are given the names and phone numbers of officials to contact if they have any grievances. 👁

Risk/Gain Assessment

Most psychology experiments carry little risk to the participants, especially where participants are merely asked to perform routine tasks. However, some experiments that study more personal aspects of human nature—such as emotional reactions, self-images, conformity, stress, or aggression—can be upsetting or psychologically disturbing. Therefore, whenever a researcher conducts such a study, risks must be minimized, participants must be informed of the risks, and suitable precautions must be taken to deal with strong reactions. Where any risk is involved, it is carefully weighed by each institutional review board in terms of its necessity for achieving the benefits to the participants of the study, to science, and to society.

Intentional Deception

For some kinds of research, it is not possible to tell the participants the whole story in advance without biasing the results. If you were studying the effects of violence on television on aggression, for example, you would not want your participants to know your purpose in advance. But is your hypothesis enough to justify the deception?

The American Psychological Association's (2002) ethical principles give explicit instructions about the use of deception. The APA provides several restrictions: (1) The study must have sufficient scientific and educational importance to warrant deception; (2) researchers must not deceive participants about research that has a high likelihood of causing physical pain or severe emotional distress; (3) researchers must demonstrate that no equally effective procedures excluding deception

are available; (4) the deception must be explained to the participants by the conclusion of the research; and (5) participants must have the opportunity to withdraw their data once the deception is explained. In experiments involving deception, a review board may impose constraints, insist on monitoring initial demonstrations of the procedure, or deny approval.

Debriefing

Participation in psychological research should always be a mutual exchange of information between researcher and participant. The researcher may learn something new about a behavioral phenomenon from the participant's responses, and the participant should be informed of the purpose, hypothesis, anticipated results, and expected benefits of the study. At the end of an experiment, each participant must be given a careful **debriefing,** in which the researcher provides as much information about the study as possible and makes sure that no one leaves feeling confused, upset, or embarrassed. If it was necessary to mislead the participants during any stage of the research, the experimenter carefully explains the reasons for the deception. Finally, participants have the right to withdraw their data if they feel they have been misused or their rights abused in any way.

Issues in Animal Research

Should animals be used in psychological and medical research? This question has often produced very polarized responses. On one side are researchers who point to the very important breakthroughs research with animals has allowed in several areas of behavioral science (Carroll & Overmier, 2001: Mogil et al., 2010). The benefits of animal research have included discovery and testing of drugs that treat anxiety and mental illnesses as well as important knowledge about drug addiction. Animal research benefits animals as well. For example, veterinarians are able to provide improved treatments that emerged through animal research.

For defenders of animal rights, "ethical concerns about compromised animal welfare cannot be eased by human benefits alone" (Olsson et al., 2007, p. 1680). Ethicists encourage researchers to adhere to the three *Rs*: Researchers should devise tests of their hypothesis that enable them to *reduce* the number of animals they require or to *replace* the use of animals altogether; they should *refine* their procedures to minimize pain and distress (Ryder, 2006). Each animal researcher must judge his or her work with heightened scrutiny.

The American Psychological Association (APA) provides firm ethical guidelines for researchers who use nonhuman animals in their research (APA, 2002). The APA expects

....

👁 Watch the Video *Special Topics: Ethics* on MyPsychLab

👁 Watch the Video *Before Informed Consent: Robert Guthrie* on MyPsychLab

informed consent The process through which individuals are informed about experimental procedures, risks, and benefits before they provide formal consent to become research participants.

debriefing A procedure conducted at the end of an experiment in which the researcher provides the participant with as much information about the study as possible and makes sure that no participant leaves feeling confused, upset, or embarrassed.

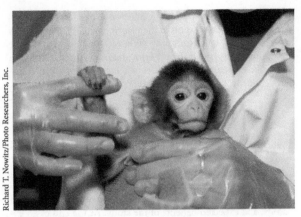

Researchers who use animal subjects are required to provide a humane environment. Do you think scientific gains justify the use of nonhuman animals in research?

researchers who work with animals to have received specific training to ensure the comfort and health of their subjects. Researchers must enforce humane treatment and take reasonable measures to minimize discomfort and pain. Psychologists may use procedures "subjecting animals to pain, stress, or privation only when an alternative procedure is unavailable and the goal is justified by its prospective scientific, educational, or applied value" (p. 1070). If you become a researcher, how might you make decisions about the costs and benefits of animal research?

Stop and Review

① What is the purpose of informed consent?
② What is the purpose of debriefing?
③ What are the three Rs of animal research?

✔—Study and Review on MyPsychLab

BECOMING A CRITICAL CONSUMER OF RESEARCH

The final section of this chapter focuses on the kinds of critical thinking skills you need to become a wiser consumer of psychological knowledge. Honing these thinking tools is essential for any responsible person in a dynamic society such as ours. Psychological claims are an ever-present aspect of the daily life of any thinking, feeling, and acting person in this psychologically sophisticated society. Unfortunately, much information on psychology does not come from the books, articles, and reports of accredited practitioners. Rather, this information comes from newspaper and magazine articles, TV and radio shows, pop psychology, and self-help books. To be a *critical thinker* is to go beyond the information as given and to delve

....

👁 Watch the Video *Thinking Like a Psychologist: Critical Thinking* on MyPsychLab

beneath slick appearances, with the goal of understanding the substance without being seduced by style and image. 👁

Studying psychology will help you make wiser decisions based on scientific evidence. Always try to apply the insights you derive from your formal study of psychology to the informal psychology that surrounds you: Ask questions about your own behavior or that of other people, seek answers to these questions with respect to rational psychological theories, and check out the answers against the evidence available to you.

Here are some general rules to keep in mind to be a more sophisticated shopper as you travel through the supermarket of knowledge:

- Avoid the inference that correlation is causation.
- Ask that critical terms and key concepts be defined operationally so that there can be consensus about their meanings.
- Consider first how to disprove a theory, hypothesis, or belief before seeking confirming evidence, which is easy to find when you're looking for a justification.
- Always search for alternative explanations to the obvious ones proposed, especially when the explanations benefit the proposer.
- Recognize how personal biases can distort perceptions of reality.
- Be suspicious of simple answers to complex questions or single causes and cures for complex effects and problems.
- Question any statement about the effectiveness of some treatment, intervention, or product by finding the comparative basis for the effect: compared to what?
- Be open-minded yet skeptical: Recognize that most conclusions are tentative and not certain; seek new evidence that decreases your uncertainty while keeping yourself open to change and revision.
- Challenge authority that uses personal opinion in place of evidence for conclusions and is not open to constructive criticism.

As you study psychology, try to apply open-minded skepticism. You shouldn't view your study of psychology as the acquisition of a list of facts. Instead, strive to participate in the joy of observing and discovering and putting ideas to the test.

A news interview with an expert may include misleading sound bites taken out of context or oversimplified "nutshell" descriptions of research conclusions. How could you become a wiser consumer of media reports?

Critical Thinking in Your Life

WHY IS SKILL WITH NUMBERS IMPORTANT?

Imagine that you've become a clinical psychologist. You are called upon to make an important judgment (Slovic et al., 2000):

Mr. James Jones has been evaluated for discharge from a mental health facility where he has been treated for the past several weeks. A prominent psychologist has reached this conclusion: Of every 100 patients similar to Mr. Jones, 10 percent are estimated to commit an act of violence to others during the first several months of discharge.

You must judge whether Mr. Jones is high, medium, or low risk for violent acts following discharge. What judgment would you make? Now consider a slightly different version of the scenario:

Of every 100 patients similar to Mr. Jones, 10 are estimated to commit an act of violence to others during the first several months of discharge.

Once again, what risk judgment would you make? Look closely: The two versions of the scenario describe exactly the same mathematical situation; 10 percent out of 100 equals 10 out of 100. Even so, people give quite different judgments. In one study, Mr. Jones was rated as "low risk" by 30.3 percent of participants who got "10 percent out of 100"; he was rated as "low risk" by just 19.4 percent of participants who got "10 out of 100" (Slovic et al., 2000). The researchers suggested that the difference arises from the "frightening images evoked by the frequency format" (p. 290). Specifically, it's relatively hard to form a firm mental image of 10 percent, whereas you can easily imagine surveying a room of 100 people and finding 10 who might be dangerous.

An important first lesson here is that a statistic's format can have a major impact on how people act on information.

But here's a second important lesson: People who have better numerical skills are less likely to be influenced by a statistic's presentation. In one study, researchers measured students' *numeracy* (a term that parallels *literacy*) by having them answer questions that captured knowledge of probability concepts (Peters et al., 2006). The researchers used the students' scores to divide them into *high numerate* and *low numerate* groups. In response to the scenario with Mr. Jones, the low-numerate students gave quite different risk ratings for the two versions. However, the high-numerate students gave virtually identical ratings. Numeracy also has an impact in real-world settings (Galesic & Garcia-Retamero, 2011). For example, as people make critical decisions about medical care, they must often evaluate data about factors such as hospital performance and costs. More-numerate people show better comprehension of such complex data and make higher-quality decisions (Reyna et al., 2009).

The good news is that college provides you with ample opportunities to become more numerate. Your coursework should lay the groundwork for you to make better data-based decisions well beyond your college years.

- In the scenario with Mr. Jones, people perceive more risk when they read "20 out of 100" versus "2 out of 10." Why might that be?

- How might you choose a statistic's format to influence public opinion?

Recapping Main Points

The Process of Research

- In the initial phase of research, observations, beliefs, information, and general knowledge lead to a new way of thinking about a phenomenon. The researcher formulates a theory and generates hypotheses to be tested.

- To test their ideas, researchers use the scientific method, a set of procedures for gathering and interpreting evidence in ways that limit errors.

- Researchers combat observer biases by standardizing procedures and using operational definitions.

- Experimental research methods determine whether causal relationships exist between variables specified by the hypothesis being tested.

- Researchers rule out alternative explanations by using appropriate control procedures.

- Correlational research methods determine if and how much two variables are related. Correlations do not imply causation.

Psychological Measurement

- Researchers strive to produce measures that are both reliable and valid.

- Psychological measurements include self-reports and behavioral measures.

Ethical Issues in Human and Animal Research

- Respect for the basic rights of human and animal research participants is the obligation of all researchers. Various safeguards have been enacted to guarantee ethical and humane treatment.

Becoming a Critical Consumer of Research

- Becoming a wise research consumer involves learning how to think critically and knowing how to evaluate claims about what research shows.

KEY TERMS

behavioral measure
between-subjects design
case study
confounding variable
control group
control procedure
correlation coefficient (r)
correlational method
debriefing
dependent variable
determinism
double-blind control

expectancy effect
experimental group
experimental method
hypothesis
independent variable
informed consent
naturalistic observation
observer bias
operational definition
placebo control
placebo effect
population

random assignment
random sampling
reliability
representative sample
sample
self-report measure
standardization
theory
validity
variable
within-subjects design

• Practice Test

1. A(n) _____ is an organized set of concepts that explains a phenomenon or set of phenomena.
a. theory
b. hypothesis
c. operational definition
d. correlation

2. When articles are submitted to most journals, they are sent out to experts for detailed analyses. This process is known as
a. debriefing.
b. informed consent.
c. peer review.
d. control procedures.

3. Professor Peterson is testing the hypothesis that people will cooperate less when a lot of people are in a group. In the experiment he plans, he will vary the number of people in each group. That will be his
a. placebo control.
b. independent variable.
c. double-blind control.
d. dependent variable.

4. Rahul is serving as a research assistant. In the first phase of the experiment, Rahul gives each participant a can of cola or a can of caffeine-free cola. In the second phase of the experiment, Rahul times the participants with a stopwatch while they play a video game. It sounds like this study is lacking a(n)
a. placebo control.
b. correlational design.
c. operational definition.
d. double-blind control.

5. Matt is participating in a two-day experiment. On Day 1, he takes a memory test after running on a treadmill for 2 minutes. On Day 2, he takes a similar test after running for 10 minutes. The experimenters plan to compare Matt's performance on the two tests. This sounds like a
a. within-subjects design.
b. double-blind control.
c. between-subjects design.
d. correlational design.

6. Shirley visits an antique store. The owner explains to her that the smaller an object is, the more he can charge for it. This is an example of a
a. correlation coefficient.
b. negative correlation.
c. positive correlation.
d. placebo effect.

7. Sally is about to travel from New York to Chicago. Although she prefers to drive, she has decided to get on an airplane. Sally reads a pair of articles about the relative safety of the two types of travel. She concludes that the one that favors air travel is considerably more valid. This sounds like an example of
a. determinism.
b. expectancy effects.
c. informed consent.
d. wishful thinking.

8. Dr. Paul is developing a new measure of hunger. He says, "I need a measure that will accurately predict how much food people will eat in their next meal." Dr. Paul's statement is about the _____ of the measure.
a. operational definition
b. standardization
c. validity
d. reliability

9. Giovanna is worried that the results of her experiment may be affected by her participants' desire to provide favorable impressions of themselves. It sounds as if she might be using _____ measures.
a. valid
b. self-report
c. reliable
d. operational

10. Ben believes that men are more likely to arrive late to classes than are women. To test this hypothesis most effectively, Ben should use
a. a within-subjects design.
b. a correlational design.
c. self-report measures.
d. naturalistic observation.

11. Andrew wishes to test the hypothesis that people give more freely to charities when the weather is pleasant. To test this hypothesis, Andrew is likely to make use of
a. double-blind controls.
b. expectancy effects.
c. laboratory observation.
d. archival data.

12. Before you participate in an experiment, the researcher should provide you with information about procedures, potential risks, and expected benefits. This process is called
a. a risk/gain assessment.
b. informed debriefing.
c. informed consent.
d. operational definitions.

13. Which one of these is *not* among the three Rs that ethicists suggest should guide research using nonhuman animals?
a. relate
b. refine
c. reduce
d. replace

14. Always search for _____ explanations to the obvious ones proposed.
a. optimistic
b. alternative
c. negative
d. opposite

15. You ask people to respond to scenarios that describe the risk associated with excess cell-phone usage. You expect people to give the highest risk estimates when they read that "_____ people suffer serious vocal chord damage."
a. 10 of every 100
b. 10 percent of
c. 20 of every 100
d. 20 percent of

ESSAY QUESTIONS

1. Why is it so important that research procedures be open for public verifiability?

2. Suppose you wanted to measure "happiness." What might you do to assess the validity of your measure?

3. With respect to ethical principles, how are risks and gains defined in the context of psychological research?

Stop and Review Answers

Stop and Review (The Process of Research)

1. Theories attempt to explain phenomena. Those explanations should generate new hypotheses—testable consequences of a theory.
2. Researchers can standardize their procedures and provide operational definitions for their variables.
3. Researchers use double-blind controls so that the expectations they bring to the research setting cannot have an impact on their studies' results.
4. When an experiment has a within-subjects design, each participant serves as his or her own control.
5. A correlation coefficient indicates the extent to which two variables are related—it does not give any indication of why that relationship exists.

Stop and Review (Psychological Measurement)

1. If a measure is reliable, it means that it yields a comparable value when researchers use it repeatedly. However, that value might still not accurately reflect the psychological variable that the researcher is after. That's why shoe size would be a reliable but not a valid measure of happiness.
2. Interviewers seek to create a context in which people are willing to provide information through self-reports that might be highly personal or sensitive.
3. The researcher is engaged in naturalistic observation of the children's behavior.

Stop and Review (Ethical Issues in Human and Animal Research)

1. Research participants must have the opportunity to understand their rights and responsibilities before they choose to engage in an experiment.
2. During debriefing, participants have an opportunity to learn something new about the psychological phenomena that were the topic of the study. In addition, through debriefing researchers can ensure that participants do not leave the study upset or confused.
3. The three Rs are reduce, replace, and refine.

Practice Test Answers

1. a	**5.** a	**9.** b	**13.** a
2. c	**6.** b	**10.** d	**14.** b
3. b	**7.** d	**11.** d	**15.** c
4. d	**8.** c	**12.** c	

References

American Psychological Association. (2002). Ethical principles of psychologists and code of conduct. *American Psychologist, 57,* 1060–1073.

American Psychological Association. (2011). Summary report of journal operations, 2010. *American Psychologist, 66,* 405–406.

Bastardi, A., Uhlmann, E. L., & Ross, L. (2011). Wishful thinking: Belief, desire, and the motivated evaluation of scientific evidence. *Psychological Science, 22,* 731–732.

Becker, S. W., & Eagly, A. H. (2004). The heroism of women and men. *American Psychologist, 59,* 163–178.

Bersoff, D. N. (Ed.) (2008). *Ethical conflicts in psychology* (4th ed.). Washington, DC: American Psychological Association.

Carroll, M. E., & Overmier, J. B. (Eds.). (2001). *Animal research and human health: Advancing human welfare through behavioral science.* Washington, DC: American Psychological Association.

Elsabagh, S., Hartley, D. E., Ali, O., Williamson, E. M., & File, S. E. (2005). Differential cognitive effects of *Ginkgo biloba* after acute and chronic treatment in healthy young volunteers. *Psychopharmacology, 179,* 437–446.

Galesic, M., & Garcia-Retamero, R. (2011). Do low-numeracy people avoid shared decision making? *Health Psychology, 30,* 336–341.

Garrison, M. M., Liekweg, K., & Christakis, D. A. (2011). Media use and child sleep: The impact of content, timing, and environment. *Pediatrics, 128,* 29–35.

Gaultney, J. F. (2010). The prevalence of sleep disorders in college students: Impact on academic performance. *Journal of American College Health, 59,* 91–97.

Ireland, M. E., Slatcher, R. B., Eastwick, P. W., Scissors, L. E., Finkel, E. J., & Pennebaker, J. W. (2011). Language style matching predicts relationship initiation and stability. *Psychological Science, 22,* 39–44.

Knobloch, L. K., Miller, L. E., Bond, B. J., & Mannone, S. E. (2007). Relational uncertainty and message processing in marriage. *Communication Monographs, 74,* 154–180.

Mackinnon, S. P., Jordan, C. H., & Wilson, A. E. (2011). Birds of a feather sit together: Physical similarity predicts seating choice. *Personality and Social Psychology Bulletin, 37,* 879–892.

McGrath, M. P., & Zook, J. M. (2011). Maternal control of girls versus boys: Relations to empathy and persuasive style with peers. *Journal of Child and Family Studies, 20,* 57–65.

Miller, G. A. (1969). Psychology as a means of promoting human welfare. *American Psychologist, 24,* 1063–1075.

Mogil, J. S., Davis, K. D., & Derbyshire, S. W. (2010). The necessity of animal models in pain research. *Pain, 151,* 12–17.

Olsson, I. A. S., Hansen, A. K., & Sandøe, P. (2007). Ethics and refinement in animal research. *Science, 317,* 1680.

Peters, E., Västfjäll, D., Slovic, P., Mertz, C. K., Mazzocco, K., & Dickert, S. (2006). Numeracy and decision making. *Psychological Science, 17,* 407–413.

Reyna, V. R., Nelson, W. L., Han, P. K., & Dieckmann, N. F. (2009). How numeracy influences risk comprehension and medical decision making. *Psychological Bulletin, 135,* 943–973.

Ruby, M. B., Dunn, E. W., Perrino, A., Gillis, R., & Viel, S. (2011). The invisible benefits of exercise. *Health Psychology, 30,* 67–74.

Rule, N. O., & Ambady, N. (2008). The face of success: Inferences from chief executive officers' appearance predict company profits. *Psychological Science, 19,* 109–111.

Ryder, R. D. (2006). Speciesism in the laboratory. In P. Singer (Ed.), *In defense of animals: The second wave.* Oxford, UK: Blackwell.

Slovic, P., Monahan, J., & MacGregor, D. G. (2000). Violence risk assessment and risk communication: The effects of using actual cases, providing instruction, and employing probability versus frequency formats. *Law and Human Behavior, 24,* 271–296.

Vohs, K. D., & Schooler, J. W. (2008). The value of believing in free will: Encouraging a belief in determinism increases cheating. *Psychological Science, 19,* 49–54.

Psychology and Life

© Form Advertising/Alamy

Why should you study psychology? The answer to that question is quite straightforward. Psychological research has immediate and crucial applications to important issues of everyday experience: your physical and mental health, your ability to form and sustain close relationships, and your capacity for learning and personal growth. One of the foremost goals of this text is to highlight the personal relevance and social significance of psychological expertise. ◉

Every semester when I begin to teach, I am faced with students who enter an introductory psychology class with some very specific questions in mind. Sometimes those questions emerge from their own experience ("What should I do if I think my mother is mentally ill?" "Will this course teach me how to improve my grades?"); sometimes those questions emerge from the type of psychological information that is communicated through the media ("Should I worry when people use cell phones while they're driving?" "Is it possible to tell when people are lying?") The challenge of introductory psychology is to bring the products of scientific research to bear on questions that matter to you.

Research in psychology provides a continuous stream of new information about the basic mechanisms that govern mental and behavioral processes. As new ideas replace or modify old ideas, psychologists are continually intrigued and challenged by the many fascinating pieces of the puzzle of human nature. I hope that, by the end of this journey through psychology, you too will cherish your store of psychological knowledge.

Foremost in the journey will be a scientific quest for understanding. We will inquire about the how, what, when, and why of human behavior and about the causes and consequences of behaviors you observe in yourself, in other people, and in animals. We will consider why you think, feel, and behave as you do. What makes you uniquely different from all other people? Yet why do you often behave so much like others? Are you molded by heredity, or are you shaped more by personal experiences? How can aggression and altruism, love and hate, and mental illness and creativity exist side by side in this complex creature—the human animal? In this chapter, we ponder how and why all these types of questions have become relevant to psychology's goals as a discipline. ◉

WHAT MAKES PSYCHOLOGY UNIQUE?

To appreciate the uniqueness and unity of psychology, you must consider the way psychologists define the field and the goals they bring to their research and applications. I hope you will begin to think like a psychologist. This first section will give you a strong idea of what that might mean.

Definitions

Many psychologists seek answers to this fundamental question: What is human nature? Psychology answers this question by looking at processes that occur within individuals as well as forces that arise within the physical and social environment. In this light, we'll define **psychology** as the scientific study of the behavior of individuals and their mental processes. Let's explore the critical parts of this definition: *scientific, behavior, individual,* and *mental.*

The scientific aspect of psychology requires that psychological conclusions be based on evidence collected according to the principles of the scientific method. The **scientific method** consists of a set of orderly steps used to analyze and solve problems. This method uses objectively collected information as the factual basis for drawing conclusions.

Behavior is the means by which organisms adjust to their environment. Behavior is action. The subject matter of psychology largely consists of the observable behavior of humans and other species of animals. Smiling, crying, running, hitting, talking, and touching are some obvious examples of behavior you can observe. Psychologists examine what the individual does and how the individual goes about doing it within a given behavioral setting and in the broader social or cultural context.

The subject of psychological analysis is most often an *individual*—a newborn infant, a college student adjusting to life in a dormitory, or a woman coping with the stress of her husband's deterioration from Alzheimer's disease. However, the subject might also be a chimpanzee learning to use symbols to communicate, a white rat navigating a maze, or a sea slug responding to a danger signal. An individual might be studied in its natural habitat or in the controlled conditions of a research laboratory.

Many researchers in psychology also recognize that they cannot understand human actions without also understanding *mental processes,* the workings of the human mind. Much human activity takes place as private, internal events—thinking, planning, reasoning, creating, and dreaming. Many psychologists believe that mental processes represent the most important aspect of psychological inquiry. As you shall soon see, psychological investigators have devised ingenious techniques to study mental events and processes—to make these private experiences public.

The combination of these concerns defines psychology as a unique field. Within the *social sciences,* psychologists focus largely on the behavior of individuals in various settings, whereas sociologists study social behavior of groups or institutions, and anthropologists focus on the broader context of behavior in different cultures. Even so, psychologists draw broadly from the insights of other scholars. Psychologists share many interests with researchers in *biological sciences,* especially with those who study brain processes and the biochemical bases of behavior. As part of *cognitive science,*

....

◉ Watch the Video *The Big Picture: Asking the Tough Questions* on MyPsychLab

◉ Watch the Video *How Much Do You Know About Psychology?* on MyPsychLab

psychology The scientific study of the behavior of individuals and their mental processes.

scientific method The set of procedures used for gathering and interpreting objective information in a way that minimizes error and yields dependable generalizations.

behavior The actions by which an organism adjusts to its environment.

Most psychological study focuses on individuals—usually human ones, but sometimes those of other species. Is there anything happening in your life that might make you want to conduct a research study?

psychologists' questions about how the human mind works are related to research and theory in computer science, philosophy, linguistics, and neuroscience. As a *health science*—with links to medicine, education, law, and environmental studies—psychology seeks to improve the quality of each individual's and the collective's well-being.

Although the remarkable breadth and depth of modern psychology are a source of delight to those who become psychologists, these same attributes make the field a challenge to the student exploring it for the first time. There is so much more to the study of psychology than you might expect initially—and, because of that, there will also be much of value that you can take away from this introduction to psychology. The best way to learn about the field is to learn to share psychologists' goals. Let's consider those goals. 👁

The Goals of Psychology

The goals of the psychologist conducting basic research are to describe, explain, predict, and control behavior. These goals form the basis of the psychological enterprise. What is involved in trying to achieve each of them?

Describing What Happens   The first task in psychology is to make accurate observations about behavior. Psychologists typically refer to such observations as their *data* (*data* is the plural, *datum* the singular). **Behavioral data** are reports of observations about the behavior of organisms and the conditions

under which the behavior occurs. When researchers undertake data collection, they must choose an appropriate *level of analysis* and devise measures of behavior that ensure *objectivity*.

To investigate an individual's behavior, researchers may use different *levels of analysis*—from the broadest, most global level down to the most minute, specific level. Suppose, for example, you were trying to describe a painting you saw at a museum (see **Figure 1**). At a global level, you might describe it by title, *Bathers*, and by artist, Georges Seurat. At a more specific level, you might recount features of the painting: Some people are sunning themselves on a riverbank while others are enjoying the water, and so on. At a very specific level, you might describe the technique Seurat used—tiny points of paint—to create the scene. The description at each level would answer different questions about the painting.

Different levels of psychological description also address different questions. At the broadest level of psychological analysis, researchers investigate the behavior of the whole person within complex social and cultural contexts. At this level, researchers might study cross-cultural differences in violence, the origins of prejudice, and the consequences of mental illness. At the next level, psychologists focus on

....

👁 **Watch** the **Video** *Thinking Like a Psychologist: Debunking Myths* on MyPsychLab

behavioral data Observational reports about the behavior of organisms and the conditions under which the behavior occurs or changes.

FIGURE 1 Levels of Analysis
Suppose you wanted a friend to meet you in front of this painting. How would you describe it? Suppose your friend wanted to make an exact copy of the painting. How would you describe it?

narrower, finer units of behavior, such as speed of reaction to a stop light, eye movements during reading, and children's grammatical errors while acquiring language. Researchers can study even smaller units of behavior. They might work to discover the biological bases of behavior by identifying the places in the brain where different types of memories are stored, the biochemical changes that occur during learning, and the sensory paths responsible for vision or hearing. Each level of analysis yields information essential to the final composite portrait of human nature that psychologists hope ultimately to develop.

However tight or broad the focus of the observation, psychologists strive to describe behavior *objectively*. Collecting the facts as they exist, and not as the researcher expects or hopes them to be, is of utmost importance. Because every observer brings to each observation his or her *subjective* point of view—biases, prejudices, and expectations—it is essential to prevent these personal factors from creeping in and distorting the data. Psychological researchers have developed a variety of techniques to maintain objectivity.

Explaining What Happens Whereas *descriptions* must stick to perceivable information, *explanations* deliberately go beyond what can be observed. In many areas of psychology, the central goal is to find regular patterns in behavioral and mental processes. Psychologists want to discover *how* behavior works. Why do you laugh at situations that differ from your expectations of what is coming next? What conditions could lead someone to attempt suicide or commit rape?

Explanations in psychology usually recognize that most behavior is influenced by a combination of factors. Some factors operate within the individual, such as genetic makeup, motivation, intelligence level, or self-esteem. These inner determinants tell something special about the organism. Other factors, however, operate externally. Suppose, for example, that a child tries to please a teacher to win a prize or that a motorist trapped in a traffic jam becomes frustrated and hostile. These behaviors are largely influenced by events outside the person. When psychologists seek to explain behavior, they almost always consider both types of explanations. Suppose, for example, psychologists want to explain why some people start smoking. Researchers might examine the possibility that some individuals are particularly prone to risk taking (an internal explanation) or that some individuals experience a lot of peer pressure (an external explanation)—or that both a disposition toward risk taking and situational peer pressure are necessary (a combined explanation).

Often a psychologist's goal is to explain a wide variety of behavior in terms of one underlying cause. Consider a situation in which your professor says that, to earn a good grade, each student must participate regularly in class discussions. Your roommate, who is always well prepared for class, never raises his hand to answer questions or volunteer information. Your professor chides him for being unmotivated and assumes he is not bright. That same roommate also goes to parties but speaks only to people he knows, doesn't openly defend his point of view when it is challenged by someone less informed, and rarely engages in small talk at the dinner table. What is your analysis? What underlying cause might account for this range of behavior? How about *shyness*? Like many other people who suffer from intense feelings of shyness, your roommate is unable to behave in desired ways (Zimbardo & Radl, 1999). We can use the concept of shyness to explain the full pattern of your roommate's behavior.

To forge such causal explanations, researchers must often engage in a creative process of examining a diverse collection of data. Master detective Sherlock Holmes drew shrewd conclusions from scraps of evidence. In a similar fashion, every researcher must use an informed imagination, which creatively *synthesizes* what is known and what is not yet known. A well-trained psychologist can explain observations by using her or his insight into the human experience along with the facts previous researchers have uncovered about the phenomenon in question. Much psychological research is an attempt to give accurate explanations for different behavioral patterns.

Predicting What Will Happen Predictions in psychology are statements about the likelihood that a certain behavior will occur or that a given relationship will be found. Often an accurate explanation of the causes underlying some form of behavior will allow a researcher to make accurate predictions about future behavior. Thus, if we believe your roommate to be shy, we could confidently predict that he would be uncomfortable when asked to give a speech in front of a large class. When different explanations are put forward to account for some behavior or relationship, they are usually judged by how well they can make accurate and comprehensive predictions. If your roommate was to speak happily to the class, we would be forced to rethink our diagnosis.

Just as observations must be made objectively, scientific predictions must be worded precisely enough to enable them to be tested and then rejected if the evidence does not support them. Suppose, for example, a researcher predicts that the presence of a stranger will reliably cause human and monkey babies, beyond a certain age, to respond with signs of anxiety. We might want to bring more precision to this prediction by examining the dimension of "stranger." Would fewer signs of anxiety appear in a human or a monkey baby if the stranger were also a baby rather than an adult, or if the stranger were of the same species rather than of a different one? To improve future predictions, a researcher would create systematic variations in environmental conditions and observe their influence on the baby's response.

A psychological prediction.

Controlling What Happens For many psychologists, control is the central, most powerful goal. Control means making behavior happen or not happen—starting it, maintaining it, stopping it, and influencing its form, strength, or rate of occurrence. A causal explanation of behavior is convincing if it can create conditions under which the behavior can be controlled.

The ability to control behavior is important because it gives psychologists ways of helping people improve the quality of their lives. Psychologists have devised many *interventions* to help people gain control over problematic aspects of their lives, such as treatments for mental illness. Such interventions enable people to harness psychological forces to eliminate unhealthy behaviors like smoking and initiate healthy behaviors like regular exercise.

What causes people to smoke? Can psychologists create conditions under which people will be less likely to engage in this behavior?

Psychologists have also studied what types of parenting practices can help parents maintain solid bonds with their children, as well as what forces make strangers reluctant to offer assistance in emergency situations and how those forces can be overcome. These are just a few examples of the broad range of circumstances in which psychologists use their knowledge to control and improve people's lives. In this respect, psychologists are a rather optimistic group; many believe that virtually any undesired behavior pattern can be modified by the proper intervention. Perhaps you will come to share that optimism.

Stop *and* Review

① What are the four components of the definition of psychology?
② What four goals apply to psychologists who conduct research?
③ Why is there often a close relationship between the goals of explanation and prediction?

✓ Study and Review on **MyPsychLab**

THE EVOLUTION OF MODERN PSYCHOLOGY

Today, it is relatively easy to define psychology and to state the goals of psychological research. As you begin to study psychology, however, it is important to understand the many forces that led to the emergence of modern psychology. At the core of this historical review is one simple principle: *Ideas matter*. Much of the history of psychology has been characterized by heated debates about what constitutes the appropriate subject matter and methodologies for a science of mind and behavior.

This historical review will be carried out at two levels of analysis. The first section will consider the period of history in which some of the critical groundwork for modern psychology was laid down. This focus will enable you to witness at close range the battle of ideas. The second section will describe in a broader fashion seven perspectives that have emerged in the modern day. For both levels of focus, you should allow yourself to imagine the intellectual passion with which the theories evolved. 🔍

Psychology's Historical Foundations

In 1908, **Hermann Ebbinghaus** (1858–1909), one of the first experimental psychologists, wrote "Psychology has a long past, but only a short history" (Ebbinghaus, 1908/1973). Scholars had long asked important questions about human nature—about how people perceive reality, the nature of consciousness, and the origins of madness—but they did not possess the means to answer them. Consider the fundamental questions posed in the

🔍 View the *Psychology Timeline* on **MyPsychLab**

Critical Thinking in Your Life

DOES "COMFORT FOOD" REALLY GIVE COMFORT?

An important goal of this text is to improve your ability to think critically: It should help you "reach intelligent decisions about what [you] should believe and how [you] should act" (Appleby, 2006, p. 61). To get started toward that goal, let's consider a real-world scenario. You're having a tough day, so you decide to indulge in some comfort food. Now take a step back. What evidence would you want to decide whether comfort food really makes you feel better? Let's see how researchers have approached this question.

If comfort food really gives comfort, people should consume more while experiencing emotional distress. To test that hypothesis, a team of researchers asked college women to watch a "brutal and violent" film excerpt (Evers et al., 2010). The researchers intended the excerpt to produce negative emotions—and it did. However, some of the women were told to suppress their emotional responses while they watched, "so that anybody looking at them would not be able to determine what kind of excerpt they were watching" (p. 797). A second group was not asked to hide their feelings. After watching the film, the students believed they were starting an unrelated study on taste. They were given the opportunity to eat both comfort food (for example, chocolate) and non-comfort food (for example, unsalted crackers). The women who had suppressed their emotions ate twice as much comfort food as the other group; they ate just about the same amount of non-comfort food. This pattern suggests that people actually do prefer comfort food when they are experiencing emotional turmoil.

But why does comfort food help with negative emotions? Another pair of researchers suggested that, across our lives, we mostly eat comfort food in the company of loved ones (Troisi & Gabriel, 2011). For that reason, we have associations built up in memory so that comfort food calls to mind the emotional warmth of those relationships. To test that hypothesis, the researchers assembled two groups of students: Some had previously reported that chicken soup was a comfort food; the second group did not have that association. At the start of the experiment, some students ate chicken soup and others did not. The students then completed a task in which they were given word fragments (for example, _li—_) that could be completed as relationship words (for example, _like_). The researchers demonstrated that the students who consumed chicken soup—when it counted as a comfort food—produced the most relationship words. For that group, the experience of eating chicken soup made relationship associations easily accessible in memory.

These projects suggest that the memories associated with the consumption of comfort food help people deal with negative emotions. Now, use your critical thinking skills. What else would you like to know before you indulge in your own comfort food binge? 👁

- In the first study, why might the researchers have kept their sample to just one sex?
- With respect to the researchers' theory, why would chicken soup not be comfort food for everyone?

4th and 5th centuries B.C. by the classical Greek philosophers **Plato** (427–347 B.C.) and **Aristotle** (384–322 B.C.): How does the mind work? What is the nature of free will? What is the relationship of individual citizens to their community or state? Although forms of psychology existed in ancient Indian Yogic traditions, Western psychology traces its origin to the writings of these philosophers. Plato and Aristotle defined opposing views that continue to have an impact on contemporary thinking. Consider how people come to know about the world. In the _empiricist_ view, people begin life with their mind as a blank tablet; the mind acquires information through experiences in the world. **John Locke** (1632–1704) articulated this position at length in the 17th century; its roots can be traced to Aristotle. In the _nativist_ view, people begin life with mental structures that provide constraints on how they experience the world. **Immanuel Kant** (1724–1804) fully developed this position in the 18th century; its roots can be traced to Plato. (This theoretical debate also takes place in the form of "nature versus nurture.") The French philosopher **René Descartes** (1596–1650) provided another important step toward contemporary psychology. Descartes proposed what, in his time, was a very new and very radical idea: The human body is an "animal machine" that can be understood scientifically—by discovering natural laws through empirical observation. Toward the end of the 19th century, psychology began to emerge as a discipline when researchers applied the laboratory techniques from other sciences—such as physiology and physics—to the study of such fundamental questions from philosophy.

A critical figure in the evolution of modern psychology was **Wilhelm Wundt**, who, in 1879 in Leipzig, Germany, founded the first formal laboratory devoted to experimental psychology. Although Wundt had been trained as a physiologist, over his research career his interest shifted from questions of body to questions of mind: He wished to understand basic processes of sensation and perception as well as the speed of simple mental processes. By the time he established his psychology laboratory, Wundt had already accomplished a range of research and published the first of several editions of _Principles of Physiological_

👁 **Watch** the **Video** _How to Be a Critical Thinker_ on **MyPsychLab**

In 1879, Wilhelm Wundt founded the first formal laboratory devoted to experimental psychology. Suppose you decided to found your own psychology laboratory. What one area in your life would you study if you could?

Psychology (King et al., 2009). Once Wundt's laboratory was established at Leipzig, he began to train the first graduate students specifically devoted to the emerging field of psychology. Those students often became founders of their own psychology laboratories around the world.

As psychology became established as a separate discipline, psychology laboratories began to appear in universities throughout North America, the first at Johns Hopkins University in 1883. These early laboratories often bore Wundt's impact. For example, after studying with Wundt, **Edward Titchener** became one of the first psychologists in the United States, founding a laboratory at Cornell University in 1892. However, at around the same time, a young Harvard philosophy professor who had studied medicine and had strong interests in literature and religion developed a uniquely American perspective. **William James**, brother of the great novelist Henry James, wrote a two-volume work, *The Principles of Psychology* (1890/1950), which many experts consider to be the most important psychology text ever written. Shortly after, in 1892, G. Stanley Hall founded the American Psychological Association. By 1900 there were more than 40 psychology laboratories in North America (Benjamin, 2007).

Almost as soon as psychology emerged, a debate arose about the proper subject matter and methods for the new discipline. This debate isolated some of the issues that still loom large in psychology. Let's consider the tension between structuralism and functionalism.

Structuralism: The Elements of the Mind Psychology's potential to make a unique contribution to knowledge became apparent when psychology became a laboratory science organized around experiments. In Wundt's laboratory, experimental participants made simple responses (saying yes or no, pressing a button) to stimuli they perceived under conditions varied by laboratory instruments. Because the data were collected through systematic, objective procedures, independent observers could replicate the results of these experiments. Emphasis

on the scientific method, concern for precise measurement, and statistical analysis of data characterized Wundt's psychological tradition.

When Titchener brought Wundt's psychology to the United States, he advocated that such scientific methods be used to study consciousness. Titchener's goal was to uncover the underlying structure of the human mind by defining the component elements of an individual's mental life. In fact, he conceived his research program in analogy to the work of chemists (1910, p. 49): "The psychologist arranges the mental elements precisely as the chemist classifies his elementary substances." Titchener's approach came to be known as **structuralism**, the study of the basic structural components of mind and behavior.

To discover the basic elements. Titchener relied on the technique of **introspection**, the systematic examination by individuals of their own thoughts and feelings about specific sensory experiences. Consider the domain of taste: Based on his introspections, Titchener suggested that all taste experiences emerge from combinations of the basic sensations of salty, sweet, sour, and bitter. Titchener's analysis was missing only one basic element, umami, later found by researchers. However, introspection functioned less well in other domains of human experience: Titchener and his followers identified more than 44,000 distinct elements of sensory experiences (Benjamin, 2007)! Structuralism attracted many critics because it was impossible to confirm that the products of each individual's introspections were general aspects of human psychology.

One important alternative to structuralism, pioneered by the German psychologist **Max Wertheimer**, focused on the way in which the mind understands many experiences as *gestalts*—organized wholes—rather than as the sums of simple parts: Your experience of a painting, for example, is more than the sum of the individual daubs of paint. **Gestalt psychology** continues to have an impact on the study of perception.

A second major opposition to structuralism came under the banner of *functionalism*.

Functionalism: Minds With a Purpose William James agreed with Titchener that consciousness was central to the study of psychology. However, James focused his attention not on the elements of mental processes, but on their purpose. James wished to understand the ways in which consciousness functions to help people adapt effectively to their environments. James's approach became known as **functionalism**.

For functionalists, the key question to be answered by research was "What is the function or purpose of any behavioral act?" For example, a structuralist might look at a *reflex* and try to identify its basic components. By contrast, a theorist like

structuralism The study of the structure of mind and behavior; the view that all human mental experience can be understood as a combination of simple elements or events.

introspection Individuals' systematic examination of their own thoughts and feelings.

Gestalt psychology A school of psychology that maintains that psychological phenomena can be understood only when viewed as organized, structured wholes, not when broken down into primitive perceptual elements.

functionalism The perspective on mind and behavior that focuses on the examination of their functions in an organism's interactions with the environment.

Classroom practices in the United States were changed through the efforts of the functionalist John Dewey. As a student, what classroom experiences have you experienced that encouraged your "intellectual curiosity"?

John Dewey focused on the functions of reflexes, which he described as "a continuously ordered sequence of acts, all adapted in themselves and in the order of their sequence, to reach a certain objective end, the reproduction of the species, the preservation of life, locomotion to a certain place" (1896, p. 366). Dewey's concern for the practical uses of mental processes led to important advances in education. His theorizing provided the impetus for *progressive education* in his own laboratory school and more generally in the United States: "Rote learning was abandoned in favor of learning by doing, in expectation that intellectual curiosity would be encouraged and understanding would be enhanced" (Kendler, 1987, p. 124).

Although James believed in careful observation, he put little value on the rigorous laboratory methods of Wundt. In James's psychology, there was a place for emotions, self, will, values, and even religious and mystical experience. His "warm-blooded" psychology recognized a uniqueness in each individual that could not be reduced to formulas or numbers from test results. For James, explanation rather than experimental control was the goal of psychology.

The Legacy of These Approaches Despite their differences, the insights of the practitioners of both structuralism and functionalism created an intellectual context in which contemporary psychology could flourish. Psychologists currently examine *both* the structure and the function of behavior. Consider the process of speech production. Suppose you want to invite a friend over to watch the Superbowl. To do so, the words you speak must serve the right function—*Superbowl, with me, today*—but also have the right structure: It wouldn't do to say, "Would watch Superbowl me the with today you to like?" To understand how speech production works, researchers study the way that speakers fit meanings (functions) to the grammatical structures of their languages (Bock, 1990). We will

emphasize both structure and function as we review both classic and contemporary research. Psychologists continue to employ a great variety of methodologies to study the general forces that apply to all humans as well as unique aspects of each individual.

Women as Pioneering Researchers

It probably won't surprise you to learn that, early in its history, research and practice in psychology were dominated by men. Even when they were still few in numbers, however, women made substantial contributions to the field (Benjamin, 2007). Let's consider four women who were pioneers in different areas of psychological research.

Mary Whiton Calkins (1863–1930) studied with William James at Harvard University. However, because she was a woman she was allowed to participate only as a "guest" graduate student. Although she completed all the requirements for a PhD with an exceptional record, the Harvard administration refused to grant a PhD to a woman. Despite this insult, Calkins established one of the first psychology laboratories in the United States and invented important techniques for studying memory. In 1905, she became the first woman president of the American Psychological Association.

In 1894, **Margaret Floy Washburn** (1871–1939) graduated from Cornell University to become the first woman to receive a PhD in psychology. She went on to write an influential early textbook, *The Animal Mind*, which was published in 1908. The book provided a review of research on perception, learning, and memory across animal species. In 1921, Washburn became the second woman to lead the American Psychological Association.

In 1894, Margaret Washburn became the first woman to receive a PhD in psychology. She went on to write an influential textbook, *The Animal Mind* (1908). What challenges might she have faced as a pioneer woman researcher?

Helen Thompson Wooley (1874–1947) accomplished some of the earliest research that examined differences between the sexes (Maracek et al., 2003; Milar, 2000). For her PhD research at the University of Chicago in 1900, Wooley compared the performance of 25 men and 25 women on a battery of tests, including tests of intelligence and emotions. The research led her to the conclusion that differences between the sexes arose not from natural ability but rather from differences in men and women's social experiences across their life spans. Wooley also offered a famous critique of "the flagrant personal bias, logic martyred in the cause of supporting a prejudice, unfounded assertions, and even sentimental rot and drivel" (Wooley, 1910, p. 340) that characterized research, largely by men, on differences between the sexes.

Leta Stetter Hollingworth (1886–1939) was inspired by Wooley to bring research data to bear on claims about gender differences (Maracek et al., 2003). In particular, Hollingworth attacked the claim that women were genetically inferior to men with respect to their levels of creativity and intelligence. Hollingworth also conducted some of the earliest research on children who tested at the extremes of intelligence—both those who had mental retardation and those who were gifted. She invented a curriculum to help nurture the talents of gifted children that she was able to implement in school settings in New York City.

Since the days in which these women were pioneers, the field of psychology has changed in the direction of far greater diversity. In fact, in recent years more women than men have earned PhDs in the field (National Science Foundation, 2010). As psychology continues to contribute to the scientific and human enterprise, more people—women and men, and members of all segments of society—are being drawn to its richness.

Perspectives on Psychology

Suppose your friend accepts the invitation to join you for the Superbowl. What *perspective* does each of you bring to your viewing of the game? Suppose one of you played football in high school, whereas the other did not. Or suppose one of you has rooted from birth for one of the competing teams, whereas the other has no prior commitments. You can see how these different perspectives would affect the way in which you evaluate the game as it unfolds.

In a similar fashion, psychologists' perspectives determine the way in which they examine behavior and mental processes. The perspectives influence what psychologists look for, where they look, and what research methods they use. This section defines seven perspectives—psychodynamic, behaviorist, humanistic, cognitive, biological, evolutionary, and sociocultural. As you read the section, note how each perspective defines the causes and consequences of behavior. 👁

....

👁 **Watch** the **Video** *The Basics: Diverse Perspectives* on **MyPsychLab**

psychodynamic perspective A psychological model in which behavior is explained in terms of past experiences and motivational forces; actions are viewed as stemming from inherited instincts, biological drives, and attempts to resolve conflicts between personal needs and social requirements.

A word of caution: Although each perspective represents a different approach to the central issues of psychology, you should come to appreciate why most psychologists borrow and blend concepts from more than one of these perspectives. Each perspective enhances the understanding of the entirety of human experience.

The Psychodynamic Perspective According to the **psychodynamic perspective**, behavior is driven, or motivated, by powerful inner forces. In this view, human actions stem from inherited instincts, biological drives, and attempts to resolve conflicts between personal needs and society's demands. Deprivation states, physiological arousal, and conflicts provide the power for behavior. According to this model, the organism stops reacting when its needs are satisfied and its drives reduced. The main purpose of action is to reduce tension.

Psychodynamic principles of motivation were most fully developed by the Viennese physician **Sigmund Freud** (1856–1939) in the late 19th and early 20th centuries. Freud's ideas grew out of his work with mentally disturbed patients, but he believed that the principles he observed applied to both normal and abnormal behavior. Freud's psychodynamic theory views a person as pulled and pushed by a complex network of inner and outer forces. Freud's model was the first to recognize that human nature is not always rational and that actions may be driven by motives that are not in conscious awareness.

Many psychologists since Freud have taken the psychodynamic model in new directions. Freud himself emphasized early childhood as the stage in which personality is formed. Neo-Freudian theorists have broadened psychodynamic theory to include social influences and interactions that occur over the individual's entire lifetime. Psychodynamic ideas have had a

Sigmund Freud, photographed with his daughter, Anna, on a trip to the Italian Alps in 1913. Freud suggested that behavior is often driven by motives outside of conscious awareness. What implications does that perspective have for the ways in which you make life choices?

great influence on many areas of psychology. You will encounter different aspects of Freud's contributions as you read about child development, dreaming, forgetting, unconscious motivation, personality, and psychoanalytic therapy.

The Behaviorist Perspective Those who take the **behaviorist perspective** seek to understand how particular environmental stimuli control particular kinds of behavior. First, behaviorists analyze the *antecedent* environmental conditions—those that precede the behavior and set the stage for an organism to make a response or withhold a response. Next, they look at the *behavioral response,* which is the main object of study—the action to be understood, predicted, and controlled. Finally, they examine the observable *consequences* that follow from the response. A behaviorist, for example, might be interested in the way in which speeding tickets of varying penalties (the consequences of speeding) change the likelihood that motorists will drive with caution or abandon (behavioral responses).

The behaviorist perspective was pioneered by **John Watson** (1878–1958), who argued that psychological research should seek the laws that govern observable behavior across species. **B. F. Skinner** (1904–1990) extended the influence of behaviorism by expanding its analyses to the consequences of behaviors. Both researchers insisted on precise definitions of the phenomena studied and on rigorous standards of evidence. Both Watson and Skinner believed that the basic processes

they investigated with nonhuman animals represented general principles that would hold true for humans as well.

Behaviorism has yielded a critical practical legacy. Its emphasis on the need for rigorous experimentation and carefully defined variables has influenced most areas of psychology. Although behaviorists have conducted much basic research with nonhuman animals, the principles of behaviorism have been widely applied to human problems. Behaviorist principles have yielded a more humane approach to educating children (through the use of positive reinforcement rather than punishment), new therapies for modifying behavior disorders, and guidelines for creating model utopian communities.

The Humanistic Perspective Humanistic psychology emerged in the 1950s as an alternative to the psychodynamic and the behaviorist models. According to the **humanistic perspective**, people are neither driven by the powerful, instinctive forces postulated by the Freudians nor manipulated by their environments, as proposed by the behaviorists. Instead, people are active creatures who are innately good and capable of choice. Humanistic psychologists study behavior, but not by reducing it to components, elements, and variables in laboratory experiments. Instead, they look for patterns in people's life histories.

The humanistic perspective suggests that the main task for humans is to strive for positive development. For example, **Carl Rogers** (1902–1987) emphasized that individuals have a natural tendency toward psychological growth and health—a process that is aided by the positive regard of those who surround them. **Abraham Maslow** (1908–1970) coined the term *self-actualization* to refer to each individual's drive toward the fullest development of his or her potential. In addition, Rogers, Maslow, and their colleagues defined a perspective that strives to deal with the whole person, practicing a *holistic* approach to human psychology. They believed that true understanding requires integrating knowledge of the individual's mind, body, and behavior with an awareness of social and cultural forces.

The humanistic approach expands the realm of psychology to include valuable lessons from the study of literature, history, and the arts. In this manner, psychology becomes a more complete discipline. Humanists suggest that their view is the yeast that helps psychology rise above its focus on negative forces and on the animal-like aspects of humanity. The humanistic perspective had a major impact on the development of new approaches to psychotherapy.

The Cognitive Perspective The cognitive revolution in psychology emerged as another challenge to the limits of behaviorism. The centerpiece of the **cognitive perspective** is human

John Watson was an important pioneer of the behaviorist perspective. Why did he find it necessary to research behaviors of both humans and nonhuman animals?

behaviorist perspective The psychological perspective primarily concerned with observable behavior that can be objectively recorded and with the relationships of observable behavior to environmental stimuli.

behaviorism A scientific approach that limits the study of psychology to measurable or observable behavior.

humanistic perspective A psychological model that emphasizes an individual's phenomenal world and inherent capacity for making rational choices and developing to maximum potential.

cognitive perspective The perspective on psychology that stresses human thought and the processes of knowing, such as attending, thinking, remembering, expecting, solving problems, fantasizing, and consciousness.

Michael Rougier/Time & Life Pictures/Getty Images

Carl Rogers provided foundational ideas for the humanistic perspective. Why did Rogers place an emphasis on positive regard?

thought and all the processes of knowing—attending, thinking, remembering, and understanding. From the cognitive perspective, people act because they think, and people think because they are human beings, exquisitely equipped to do so.

According to the cognitive model, behavior is only partly determined by preceding environmental events and past behavioral consequences, as behaviorists believe. Some of the most significant behavior emerges from totally novel ways of thinking, not from predictable ways used in the past. Consider how children learn their native language. In his book *Verbal Behavior* (1957), B. F. Skinner suggested that children acquire language through ordinary processes of learning. **Noam Chomsky** (b. 1928) helped originate the cognitive perspective by arguing forcefully against Skinner's claim. Chomsky asserted that even children are able to produce utterances that fall outside the bounds of their previous experience. In his own research with children, the Swiss researcher **Jean Piaget** (1896–1980) used a series of mental tasks to demonstrate qualitative changes over the course of cognitive development. To explain children's growing sophistication, Piaget made reference to children's inner cognitive states.

Cognitive psychologists study higher mental processes such as perception, memory, language use, thinking, problem solving, and decision making at a variety of levels. Cognitive psychologists view thoughts as both results and causes of overt actions. Feeling regret when you've hurt someone is an example of thought as a result. But apologizing for your actions after feeling regret is an example of thought as a cause of behavior.

Within the cognitive perspective, an individual responds to reality not as it is in the objective world of matter but as it is in the *subjective reality* of the individual's inner world of thoughts and imagination. Because of its focus on mental processes, many researchers see the cognitive perspective as the dominant approach in psychology today.

The Biological Perspective The **biological perspective** guides psychologists who search for the causes of behavior in the functioning of genes, the brain, the nervous system, and the endocrine system. An organism's functioning is explained in terms of underlying physical structures and biochemical processes. Experience and behaviors are largely understood as the result of chemical and electrical activities taking place within and between nerve cells.

Researchers who take the biological perspective generally assume that psychological and social phenomena can be ultimately understood in terms of biochemical processes: Even the most complex phenomena can be understood by analysis, or reduction, into ever smaller, more specific units. They might, for example, try to explain how you are reading the words of this sentence with respect to the exact physical processes in cells in your brain. According to this perspective, behavior is determined by physical structures and hereditary processes. Experience can modify behavior by altering these underlying biological structures and processes. Researchers might ask, "What changes in your brain occurred while you learned to read?" The task of psychobiological researchers is to understand behavior at the most precise level of analysis.

Many researchers who take the biological perspective contribute to the multidisciplinary field of **behavioral neuroscience**. Neuroscience is the study of brain function; behavioral neuroscience attempts to understand the brain processes underlying behaviors such as sensation, learning, and emotion. The advances in the brain-imaging techniques have led to dramatic breakthroughs in the field of **cognitive neuroscience**. Cognitive neuroscience trains a multidisciplinary research focus on the brain bases of higher cognitive functions such as memory and language. Brain-imaging techniques allow the biological perspective to be extended into a broad range of human experience. 👁

The Evolutionary Perspective The **evolutionary perspective** seeks to connect contemporary psychology to a central idea of the life sciences, Charles Darwin's theory of evolution by natural selection. The idea of natural selection is quite simple:

....

👁 Watch the Video *Developmental Cognitive Neuroscience: Adele Diamond* on MyPsychLab

biological perspective The approach to identifying causes of behavior that focuses on the functioning of genes, the brain, the nervous system, and the endocrine system.

behavioral neuroscience A multidisciplinary field that attempts to understand the brain processes that underlie behavior.

cognitive neuroscience A multidisciplinary field that attempts to understand the brain processes that underlie higher cognitive functions in humans.

evolutionary perspective The approach to psychology that stresses the importance of behavioral and mental adaptiveness, based on the assumption that mental capabilities evolved over millions of years to serve particular adaptive purposes.

Those organisms that are better suited to their environments tend to produce offspring (and pass on their genes) more successfully than those organisms with poorer adaptations. Over many generations, the species changes in the direction of the privileged adaptation. The evolutionary perspective in psychology suggests that *mental abilities* evolved over millions of years to serve particular adaptive purposes, just as physical abilities did.

To practice evolutionary psychology, researchers focus on the environmental conditions in which the human brain evolved. Humans spent 99 percent of their evolutionary history as hunter–gatherers living in small groups during the Pleistocene era (the roughly 2-million-year period ending 10,000 years ago). Evolutionary psychology uses the rich theoretical framework of evolutionary biology to identify the central adaptive problems that faced this species: avoiding predators and parasites, gathering and exchanging food, finding and retaining mates, and raising healthy children. After identifying the adaptive problems that these early humans faced, evolutionary psychologists generate inferences about the sorts of mental mechanisms, or psychological adaptations, that might have evolved to solve those problems.

Evolutionary psychology differs from other perspectives most fundamentally in its focus on the extremely long process of evolution as a central explanatory principle. Evolutionary psychologists, for example, attempt to understand the different sex roles assumed by men and women as products of evolution, rather than as products of contemporary societal pressures. Because evolutionary psychologists cannot carry out experiments that vary the course of evolution, they must be particularly inventive to provide evidence in favor of their theories.

The Sociocultural Perspective Psychologists who take a **sociocultural perspective** study *cross-cultural* differences in the causes and consequences of behavior. The sociocultural perspective is an important response to the criticism that psychological research has too often been based on a Western conception of human nature and had as its subject population mostly white middle-class Americans (Arnett, 2008; Gergen et al., 1996). A proper consideration of cultural forces may involve comparisons of groups within the same national boundaries. For example, researchers may look within the United States to compare the prevalence of eating disorders for women of different races. Cultural forces may also be assessed across nationalities, as in comparisons of media reports in the United States and Japan. Cross-cultural psychologists want to determine whether the theories researchers have developed apply to all humans, or only to more narrow, specific populations.

A cross-cultural perspective can be brought to bear on almost every topic of psychological research: Are people's perceptions of the world affected by culture? Do the languages people speak affect the way they experience the world? How does culture affect the way children develop toward adulthood? How do cultural attitudes shape the experience of old age? How

does culture affect our sense of self? Does culture influence an individual's likelihood to engage in particular behaviors? Does culture affect the way individuals express emotions? Does culture affect the rates at which people suffer from psychological disorders?

By asking these types of questions, the sociocultural perspective often yields conclusions that directly challenge those generated from the other perspectives. Researchers have claimed, for example, that many aspects of Freud's psychodynamic theories cannot apply to cultures that are very different from Freud's Vienna. This concern was raised as early as 1927 by the anthropologist Bronislaw Malinowski (1927), who soundly critiqued Freud's father-centered theory by describing the family practices of the Trobriand Islanders of New Guinea, for whom family authority resided with mothers rather than with fathers. The sociocultural perspective, therefore, suggests that some universal claims of the psychodynamic perspective are incorrect. The sociocultural perspective poses a continual, important challenge to generalizations about human experience that ignore the diversity and richness of culture.

Bronislaw Malinowski documented the important roles women play in the culture of the Trobriand Islands. Why is cross-cultural research critical to the search for universal psychological principles?

....

sociocultural perspective The psychological perspective that focuses on cross-cultural differences in the causes and consequences of behavior.

Table 1 • Comparison of Seven Perspectives on Psychology

Perspective	Focus of Study	Primary Research Topics
Psychodynamic	Unconscious drives Conflicts	Behavior as overt expression of unconscious motives
Behaviorist	Specific overt responses	Behavior and its stimulus causes and consequences
Humanistic	Human experience and potentials	Life patterns Values Goals
Cognitive	Mental processes Language	Inferred mental processes through behavioral indicators
Biological	Brain and nervous system processes	Biochemical basis of behavior and mental processes
Evolutionary	Evolved psychological adaptations	Mental mechanisms in terms of evolved adaptive functions
Sociocultural	Cross-cultural patterns of attitudes and behaviors	Universal and culture-specific aspects of human experience

Comparing Perspectives: Focus on Aggression   Each of the seven perspectives rests on a different set of assumptions and leads to a different way of looking for answers to questions about behavior. **Table 1** summarizes the perspectives. As an example, let's briefly compare how psychologists using these models might deal with the question of why people act aggressively. All of the approaches have been used in the effort to understand the nature of aggression and violence. For each perspective, here are examples of the types of claims researchers might make and experiments they might undertake:

- *Psychodynamic.* Analyze aggression as a reaction to frustrations caused by barriers to pleasure, such as unjust authority. View aggression as an adult's displacement of hostility originally felt as a child against his or her parents.
- *Behaviorist.* Identify reinforcements of past aggressive responses, such as extra attention given to a child who hits classmates or siblings. Assert that children learn from physically abusive parents to be abusive with their own children.
- *Humanistic.* Look for personal values and social conditions that foster self-limiting, aggressive perspectives instead of growth-enhancing, shared experiences.
- *Cognitive.* Explore the hostile thoughts and fantasies people experience while witnessing violent acts, noting both aggressive imagery and intentions to harm others. Study the impact of violence in films and videos, including pornographic violence, on attitudes toward gun control, rape, and war.
- *Biological.* Study the role of specific brain systems in aggression by stimulating different regions and then recording any destructive actions that are elicited. Also analyze the brains of mass murderers for abnormalities; examine female aggression as related to phases of the menstrual cycle.
- *Evolutionary.* Consider what conditions would have made aggression an adaptive behavior for early humans. Identify psychological mechanisms capable of selectively generating aggressive behavior under those conditions.
- *Sociocultural.* Consider how members of different cultures display and interpret aggression. Identify how cultural forces affect the likelihood of different types of aggressive behavior.

From this example of aggression, you can see how the different perspectives conspire to provide a full understanding of particular domains of psychological research. In contemporary psychology, most research is informed by multiple perspectives. New theories often emerge from combinations of different perspectives. In addition, technological advances have made it easier for researchers to combine perspectives. For example, innovative brain-imaging techniques allow researchers to bring a biological perspective to topics as varied as language processing and personality differences. Moreover, developments such as the Internet have made it easier for researchers to collaborate across the globe. They can bring a sociocultural perspective to topics as diverse as moral reasoning and people's body images. Psychology's diversity of perspectives helps researchers think creatively about core topics of human experience.

Stop *and* Review

1. What are the central concerns of the structuralist and functionalist approaches?
2. What conclusions did Helen Thompson Wooley draw about differences between the sexes?
3. How do the psychodynamic and behaviorist perspectives conceptualize the forces that shape people's actions?
4. What is the purpose of cognitive neuroscience?
5. How do the evolutionary perspective and sociocultural perspective complement each other?

✓•⸢**Study** and **Review** on **MyPsychLab**

WHAT PSYCHOLOGISTS DO

You now know enough about psychology to formulate questions that span the full range of psychological inquiry. If you prepared such a list of questions, you would be likely to touch on the areas of expertise of the great variety of individuals who call themselves psychologists. **Table 2** provides my own version of such questions and indicates what sort of psychologist might address each one.

As you examine the table, you will note the great many subfields within the profession of psychology. Some of the labels the field uses tell you about the major content of a psychologist's expertise. For example, *cognitive psychologists* focus on basic cognitive processes such as memory and language; *social psychologists* focus on the social forces that shape people's attitudes and behavior. Some of the labels identify the domains in which psychologists apply their expertise. For example, *industrial–organizational psychologists* focus their

Table 2 • The Diversity of Psychological Inquiry

The Question	Who Addresses It?	Focus of Research and Practice
How can people cope better with day-to-day problems?	Clinical psychologists Counseling psychologists Community psychologists Psychiatrists	Study the origins of psychological disorders and day-to-day problems to evaluate treatment options; provide diagnosis and treatment of psychological disorders and other issues of personal adjustment
How can I cope with the aftereffects of a stroke?	Rehabilitation psychologists	Provide assessment and counseling for people with illnesses or disabilities; offer coping strategies and education to affected individuals, caretakers, employers, and community members
How do memories get stored in the brain?	Biological psychologists Psychopharmacologists	Study the biochemical bases of behavior, feelings, and mental processes
How can you teach a dog to follow commands?	Experimental psychologists Behavior analysts	Use laboratory experiments, often with nonhuman participants, to study basic processes of learning, sensation, perception, emotion, and motivation
Why can't I always recall information I'm sure I know?	Cognitive psychologists Cognitive scientists	Study mental processes such as memory, perception, reasoning, problem solving, decision making, and language use
What makes people different from one another?	Personality psychologists Behavioral geneticists	Develop tests and theories to understand differences in personalities and behaviors; study the influence of genetics and environments on those differences
How does peer pressure work?	Social psychologists	Study how people function in social groups as well as the processes by which people select, interpret, and remember social information
What do babies know about the world?	Developmental psychologists	Study the changes that occur in the physical, cognitive, and social functioning of individuals across the life span; study the influence of genetics and environments on those changes
Why does my job make me feel so depressed?	Industrial–organizational psychologists Human factors psychologists	Study the factors that influence performance and morale in the general workplace or on particular tasks; apply those insights in the workplace
How should teachers deal with disruptive students?	Educational psychologists School psychologists	Study how to improve aspects of the learning process; help design school curricular, teaching–training, and child-care programs
Why do I get sick before every exam?	Health psychologists	Study how different lifestyles affect physical health; design and evaluate prevention programs to help people change unhealthy behaviors and cope with stress
Was the defendant insane when she committed the crime?	Forensic psychologists	Apply psychological knowledge to human problems in the field of law enforcement
Why do I always choke during important basketball games?	Sports psychologists	Assess the performance of athletes and use motivational, cognitive, and behavioral principles to help them achieve peak performance levels
How can I make sense of all the numbers people throw at me?	Quantitative psychologists Psychometricians	Develop and evaluate new statistical methods; construct and validate measurement tools
How accurately can psychologists predict how people will behave?	Mathematical psychologists	Develop mathematical expressions that allow for precise predictions about behavior and tests of contrasting psychological theories

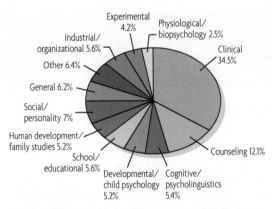

FIGURE 2 **Distribution of Degrees to Subfields of Psychology**

In 2009, roughly 3,500 people received PhDs in the many subfields of psychology (National Science Foundation, 2010). Although the largest percentage of those degrees went to individuals pursuing careers in clinical psychology, students also received advanced training in several other areas of basic and applied research.

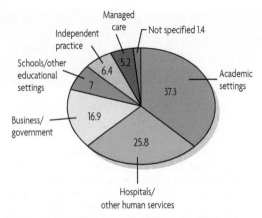

FIGURE 3 **Work Settings for Psychologists**

Shown are percentages of psychologists working in particular settings, according to a survey of American Psychological Association (APA) members holding doctoral degrees in psychology.

efforts on improving people's adjustment in the workplace; *school psychologists* focus on students' adjustment in educational settings.

Each type of psychologist achieves a balance between *research*—seeking new insights—and *application*—putting those insights to use in the world. There's a necessary relationship between those two types of activities. For example, we often think of *clinical psychologists* largely as individuals who apply psychological knowledge to better people's lives. However, clinical psychologists also have important research functions. Contemporary research continues to improve our understanding of the distinctions among psychological disorders and the treatments that best ease patients' distress. **Figure 2** provides information about the

numbers of people who pursue PhDs across psychology's many subfields.

Take a look back at Table 2. This list of questions illustrates why psychology has so many divisions. Did these questions capture your own concerns? If you have the time, make a list of your own questions. Cross off each question as you discover the answers answers it. ☀

Have you begun to wonder exactly how many practicing psychologists there are in the world? Surveys suggest the number is well over 500,000. **Figure 3** gives you an idea of the distribution of settings in which psychologists function. Although the percentage of psychologists in the population is greatest in Western industrialized nations, interest in psychology continues to increase in many countries. The International Union of Psychological Science draws together member organizations from 71 countries (Ritchie, 2010). The American Psychological Association (APA), an organization that includes psychologists from all over the world, has over 150,000 members. A second international organization, the Association for Psychological Science (APS), with about 23,000 members, focuses more on scientific aspects of psychology and less on the clinical, or treatment, side.

Stop *and* Review

① What is the relationship between research and application?

② In what two settings are most psychologists employed?

✔—Study and Review on MyPsychLab

Developmental psychologists may use puppets or other toys in their study of how children behave, think, or feel. Why might it be easier for a child to express his or her thoughts to a puppet than to an adult?

☀ Explore the Concept *Psychologists at Work* on MyPsychLab

Psychology in Your Life

IN WHAT WAYS DO PSYCHOLOGISTS PARTICIPATE IN THE LEGAL SYSTEM?

An important lesson of this text is that empirical research provides psychologists with a broad range of expertise. There are many opportunities to see how research results apply to important issues in everyday life. For instance, psychological expertise functions in the public forum. As an initial example, let's consider how *forensic psychologists* become involved in important legal decisions.

The legal system relies on forensic psychologists to provide assessments for both civil and criminal proceedings (Packer, 2008). On the civil side, for example, forensic psychologists provide evidence that influences decisions about child custody in divorce hearings. They might also testify about the potential psychological harm workers have sustained in a particular place of employment. On the criminal side, forensic psychologists evaluate people's capacity to understand the acts they have committed and their competence to stand trial. Forensic psychologists also assess whether individuals are a danger to themselves or others. Let's examine that last role more closely.

Suppose that a person is sent to prison for committing a violent crime. After having served some time, he or she arrives at a parole hearing. An important consideration at that hearing will be what lies in the prisoner's future. What is the likelihood that violent acts will occur again?

In recent years, psychologists have attempted to provide increasingly research-based answers to that question (Fabian, 2006). This research often begins with a theoretical analysis

of the life factors that make violence more or less likely. Researchers make an important distinction between *static* and *dynamic* factors (Douglas & Skeem, 2005). Static factors are those that are relatively stable over time (such as gender and age at first conviction); dynamic variables are those that may change over time (such as emotional control and substance abuse). The inclusion of dynamic factors suggests how risk changes over time. Past history alone does not provide a valid indication of how a person will behave in the future. It's also important to measure the trajectory of a person's life.

Researchers must provide evidence that risk assessment devices are successful at predicting future violence (Singh et al., 2011; Yang et al., 2010). To do so, researchers often follow groups of individuals over time. For example, Wong and Gordon (2006) evaluated 918 adult male offenders who were incarcerated in the Canadian provinces of Alberta, Saskatchewan, and Manitoba. Each participant was evaluated with the Violence Risk Scale (VRS), which measures six static and 20 dynamic variables. To evaluate the validity of the VRS, the researchers followed their participants over several years, to see how often they were convicted of new crimes after they had been released into the community. In both the short term (after 1 year) and the longer term (after 4.4 years), men who had obtained higher ratings on the VRS were more likely to be convicted of additional violent crimes.

Research results of this sort are quite important because they help forensic psychologists provide more accurate guidance for legal judgments.

HOW TO STUDY PSYCHOLOGY

Psychology is about understanding the seemingly mysterious processes that give rise to your thoughts, feelings, and actions. Some general strategies and specific suggestions for studying psychology follow in this section.

Study Strategies

1. *Set aside sufficient time* for your reading assignments and review of class notes. You will encounter much new technical information, many principles to learn, and a new

glossary of terms to memorize in the study of psychology. To master this material, you will need to set aside enough time for reading.

2. *Keep a record of your study time.* Plot the number of hours (in half-hour intervals) you study at each reading session. Chart your time investment on a cumulative graph. Add each new study time to the previous total on the left-hand axis of the graph and each study session on the base-line axis. The chart will provide visual feedback of your progress and show you when you have not been hitting the books as you should.

3. *Be an active participant.* Optimal learning occurs when you are actively involved with the learning materials. That means reading attentively, listening to lectures mindfully,

paraphrasing in your own words what you are reading or hearing, and taking good notes. In your textbooks, underline key sections, write notes to yourself in the margins, and summarize points that you think might be included on class tests.

4. *Space out your studying.* Research in psychology tells us that it is more effective to do your studying regularly rather than cramming just before tests. If you let yourself fall behind, it will be difficult to catch up with all the information included in introductory psychology at last-minute panic time.

5. *Get study-centered.* Find a place with minimal distractions for studying. Reserve that place for studying, reading, and writing course assignments—and do nothing else there. The place will come to be associated with study activities, and you will find it easier to work whenever you are seated at your study center.

Take the teacher's perspective, anticipating the kinds of questions she or he is likely to ask and then making sure you can answer them. Find out what kinds of tests you will be given in this course—essay, fill-in, multiple-choice, or true/false. That form will affect the extent to which you focus on the big ideas and/or on details. Essays and fill-ins ask for recall-type memory; multiple-choice and true/false tests ask for recognition-type memory.

Study Techniques

This section gives you specific advice about a technique you can use to learn material concerning psychology. The technique emerged from principles of human memory. It is called *PQ4R* from the initials of the six phases it suggests for effective study: Preview, Question, Read, Reflect, Recite, and Review (Thomas & Robinson, 1972).

1. *Preview.* Skim through the chapter to get a general sense of the topics the chapter will discuss. Make yourself aware of the organization and major topics. Read the section headings and scan the photos and figures. This will give you a clear sense of what the chapter covers.

2. *Question.* For each section, make up questions. You should use the section headings and key terms to help you. For example, you might transform the heading "The Goals of Psychology" into the question "What are the goals of psychology?" You might use the key term *biological perspective* to generate the question, "What is the major focus of the biological perspective?" These questions will help direct your attention as you read.

3. *Read.* Read the material carefully so that you are able to answer the questions you invented.

4. *Reflect.* As you read the text, reflect on it to relate the material to your prior knowledge about the topics. Think of extra examples to enrich the text. Try to link the ideas together across the subsections.

5. *Recite.* After you have read and reflected on a section, try to demonstrate your recall of the material as concretely as possible. For example, answer the questions you invented earlier by producing the material out loud. For later review, write down the ideas you find difficult to remember.

6. *Review.* After you have read the entire chapter, review the key points. If you are unable to recall important points, or you cannot answer the questions you invented, consult the book and repeat the earlier phases (read, reflect, and recite).

Take a moment now to use PQ4R for one of the earlier sections of this chapter to see how each phase works. It will take you some time to master the flow of PQ4R.

You are now prepared to study psychology!

Stop *and* Review

① What does it mean to be an active participant in a psychology course?

② What is the relationship between the *Question* and *Read* phases of PQ4R?

③ What is the purpose of the *Recite* phase of PQ4R?

✓• Study and Review on MyPsychLab

Recapping Main Points

What Makes Psychology Unique?

• Psychology is the scientific study of the behavior and the mental processes of individuals.

• The goals of psychology are to describe, explain, predict, and help control behavior.

The Evolution of Modern Psychology

• Structuralism emerged from the work of Wundt and Titchener. It emphasized the structure of the mind and behavior built from elemental sensations.

• Functionalism, developed by James and Dewey, emphasized the purpose behind behavior.

• Taken together, these theories created the agenda for modern psychology.

• Women made substantial research contributions in psychology's early history.

• Each of the seven perspectives on psychology differs in its view of human nature, the determinants of behavior, the focus of study, and the primary research approach.

- The psychodynamic perspective looks at behavior as driven by instinctive forces, inner conflicts, and conscious and unconscious motivations.
- The behaviorist perspective views behavior as determined by external stimulus conditions.
- The humanistic perspective emphasizes an individual's inherent capacity to make rational choices.
- The cognitive perspective stresses mental processes that affect behavioral responses.
- The biological perspective studies relationships between behavior and brain mechanisms.
- The evolutionary perspective looks at behavior as having evolved as an adaptation for survival in the environment.
- The sociocultural perspective examines behavior and its interpretation in cultural context.

What Psychologists Do

- Psychologists work in a variety of settings and draw on expertise from a range of specialty areas.
- Almost any question that can be generated about real-life experiences is addressed by some member of the psychological profession.

How to Study Psychology

- Devise concrete strategies for determining how much study time you need and how to distribute the time most efficiently.
- Take an active approach to your lectures and the text. The PQ4R method provides six phases—Preview, Question, Read, Reflect, Recite, and Review—for enhanced learning.

KEY TERMS

behavior
behavioral data
behavioral neuroscience
behaviorism
behaviorist perspective
biological perspective

cognitive neuroscience
cognitive perspective
evolutionary perspective
functionalism
Gestalt psychology
humanistic perspective

introspection
psychodynamic perspective
psychology
scientific method
sociocultural perspective
structuralism

Practice Test

1. The definition of psychology focuses on both
_____ and _____.
   a. behaviors; structures
   b. behaviors; mental processes
   c. mental processes; functions
   d. mental processes; structures

2. To what goal of psychology is "level of analysis" most relevant?
   a. explaining what happens
   b. describing what happens
   c. predicting what will happen
   d. controlling what happens

3. If you want to _____ what will happen, you first must be able to _____ what will happen.
   a. describe; explain   c. control; predict
   b. describe; control   d. explain; predict

4. While watching a horror film, Betty suppressed her emotions but Hilda did not. You would expect Betty to eat _____ comfort food than Hilda and _____ non-comfort food.
   a. more; the same amount of
   b. more; less
   c. the same amount of; more
   d. less; more

5. Who founded the first laboratory that was devoted to experimental psychology?
   a. William James   c. Max Wertheimer
   b. Wilhelm Wundt   d. John Dewey

6. A researcher tells you that her main goal is to understand mental experiences as the combination of basic components. It is most likely that she finds the historical roots of her research in
   a. functionalism.
   b. the humanist perspective.
   c. structuralism.
   d. the evolutionary perspective.

7. Who was the first woman to serve as president of the American Psychological Association?
   a. Margaret Washburn   c. Jane Goodall
   b. Anna Freud   d. Mary Calkins

8. Two professors at universities in Boston and Mumbai are collaborating on a research project to determine how their students in the United States and India respond to the same reasoning problems. It's likely that they take a _____ perspective in their research.
   a. humanistic   c. biological
   b. sociocultural   d. psychodynamic

9. The _____ perspective draws on the ways in which human mental abilities serve adaptive purposes.
   a. cognitive   c. evolutionary
   b. humanistic   d. sociocultural

10. When you're home with the flu, you spend a lot of time watching CourtTV. You weren't surprised to see a _____ psychologist testifying during a trial.
    a. health   c. forensic
    b. social   d. developmental

11. What type of question would a cognitive psychologist be likely to ask?
    a. Why do children sometimes have imaginary friends?
    b. Why do some students get sick every time they have a major exam?
    c. How can we design a keyboard for a computer that allows people to type more quickly?
    d. How are bilingual individuals able to switch between their two languages?

12. Which type of psychologist is *least* likely to focus on genetic aspects of human psychology?
    a. industrial–organizational psychologists
    b. developmental psychologists
    c. personality psychologists
    d. biological psychologists

13. Individuals with advanced degrees in psychology are most likely to be working in
    a. academic settings.
    b. hospitals and clinics.
    c. business and government.
    d. independent practice.

14. In assessments of violence risk, _____ counts as a dynamic factor.
    a. gender
    b. substance abuse
    c. stability of family upbringing
    d. age at first conviction

15. In what phase of P4QR should you try to relate the textbook material to your prior knowledge about a topic?
    a. Reflect   c. Review
    b. Recite   d. Question

ESSAY QUESTIONS

1. With respect to the goals of psychology, why is it appropriate to characterize psychologists as "rather optimistic"?

2. Why is it often good to consider the same research question from several of psychology's seven perspectives?

3. Why does the field of psychology include both research and application?

Stop and Review Answers

Stop and Review (What Makes Psychology Unique?)

1. Psychology is the *scientific* study of the *behavior* of *individuals* and their *mental* processes.
2. The four goals are to describe, explain, predict, and control behavior.
3. Researchers regularly try to explain behaviors by identifying underlying causes; successful causal explanations often allow accurate predictions.

Stop and Review (The Evolution of Modern Psychology)

1. Structuralism tries to understand mental experiences as the combination of basic components. Functionalism focuses on the purposes of behavioral acts.
2. Wooley argued that sex differences do not reflect natural ability but, rather, differences in men's and women's social experiences.
3. The psychodynamic perspective focuses on powerful, instinctive forces, and the behaviorist perspective focuses on how consequences shape behaviors.
4. Researchers in cognitive neuroscience combine the cognitive and biological perspectives to understand the brain bases of mental activities such as memory and language.

5. The evolutionary perspective focuses on the features that all people share as a consequence of human evolution. The socio-cultural perspective focuses on the differences brought about by cultures, against that shared evolutionary background.

Stop and Review (What Psychologists Do)

1. Research provides new insights that psychologists then try to apply in real-world settings.
2. Psychologists are most employed in academic settings (e.g., colleges and universities) and hospitals and other human services.

Stop and Review (How to Study Psychology)

1. You must be actively involved in the course by developing your own understanding of what you hear in lectures and read in the text.
2. In the *Question* phase you invent questions that direct your attention while you are reading; in the *Read* phase you read the material with an eye to answering your questions.
3. When you attempt to recite explicit answers to questions, you obtain concrete evidence of what you know and what you don't know.

Practice Test Answers

1. b	**5.** b	**9.** c	**13.** a
2. b	**6.** c	**10.** c	**14.** b
3. c	**7.** d	**11.** d	**15.** a
4. a	**8.** b	**12.** a	

References

Appleby, D. C. (2006). Defining, teaching, and assessing critical thinking in introductory psychology. In D. S. Dunn & S. L. Chew (Eds.), *Best practices for teaching introduction to psychology* (pp. 57–69). Mahwah, NJ: Erlbaum.

Arnett, J. J. (2008). The neglected 95%: Why American psychology needs to become less American. *American Psychologist, 63,* 602–614.

Benjamin, L. T., Jr. (2007). *A brief history of modern psychology.* Malden, MA: Blackwell.

Bock, K. (1990). Structure in language: Creating form in talk. *American Psychologist, 45,* 1221–1236.

Dewey, J. (1896). The reflex arc concept in psychology. *Psychological Review, 3,* 357–370.

Douglas, K. S., & Skeem, J. L. (2005). Violence risk assessment: Getting specific about being dynamic. *Psychology, Public Policy, and Law, 11,* 347–383.

Ebbinghaus, H. (1973). *Psychology: An elementary text-book.* New York: Arno Press. (Original work published 1908)

Evers, C., Stok, F. M., & de Ridder, D. T. D. (2010). Feeding your feelings: Emotion regulations strategies and emotional eating. *Personality and Social Psychology Bulletin, 36,* 792–804.

Fabian, J. M. (2006). A literature review of the utility of selected violence and sexual violence risk assessment instruments. *The Journal of Psychiatry & Law, 34,* 307–350.

Gergen, K. J., Gulerce, A., Lock, A., & Misra, G. (1996). Psychological science in a cultural context. *American Psychologist, 51,* 496–503.

Gordon 2006 [ED: cited in chapter but missing from Refs section]

James, W. (1950). *The principles of psychology* (2 vols.). New York: Holt, Rinehart & Wilson. (Original work published 1890)

Kendler, K. S., Kuhn, J. W., & Prescott, C. A. (2004). Childhood sexual abuse, stressful life events and risk for major depression in women. *Psychological Medicine, 34,* 1475–1482.

King, D. B., Viney, W., & Woody, W. D. (2009). *A History of psychology: Ideas and context* (4th ed.). Boston: Allyn & Bacon.

Malinowski, B. (1927). *Sex and repression in savage society.* London: Routledge & Kegan Paul.

Milar, K. S. (2000). The first generation of women psychologists and the psychology of women. *American Psychologist, 55,* 616–619.

National Science Foundation, Division of Science Resources Statistics. (2010). *Doctorate Recipients from U.S. Universities: 2009.* Special Report NSF 11-306. Arlington, VA. Available at http://www.nsf.gov/statistics/nsf11306/.

Packer, I. K. (2008). Specialized practice in forensic psychology: Opportunities and obstacles. *Professional Psychology: Research and Practice, 39,* 245–249.

Ritchie, P. L.-J. (2010). Annual report of the International Union of Psychological Science (IUPsyS). *International Journal of Psychology, 45,* 398–404.

Singh, J. P., Grann, M., & Fazel, S. (2011). A comparative study of violence risk assessment tools: A systematic review and metaregression analysis of 68 studies involving 25,980 participants. *Clinical Psychology Review, 31,* 599–513.

Skinner, B. F. (1957). *Verbal behavior.* New York: Appleton-Century-Crofts.

Thomas, E. L., & Robinson, H. A. (1972). *Improving reading in every class: A sourcebook for teachers.* Boston: Allyn & Bacon.

Titchener, E. B. (1910). *A textbook of psychology.* New York: Macmillan.

Troisi, J. D., & Gabriel, S. (2011). Chicken soup really is good for the soul: "Comfort food" fulfills the need to belong. *Psychological Science, 22,* 747–753.

Woolley, H. T. (1910). Psychological literature: A review of the recent literature on the psychology of sex. *Psychological Bulletin, 7,* 335–342.

Yang, C. Y., Kim, S. J., & Lee, S. G. (2011). Identification and field evaluation of the sex pheromone of *Synanthedon bicingulata* (Staudinger). *Journal of Chemical Ecology, 37,* 398–402.

Zimbardo, P. G., & Radl, S. L. (1999). *The shy child* (2nd ed.). Los Altos, CA: Malor Press.

The Biological and Evolutionary Bases of Behavior

The Biological and Evolutionary Bases of Behavior

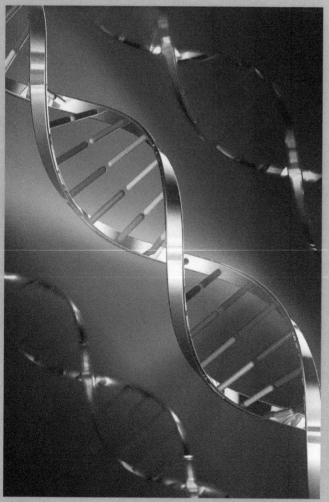

© Mads Abildgaard/iStockphoto.com

What makes you a unique individual? In this chapter we will focus on the biological aspects of your individuality. To help you understand what makes you different from the people around you, we will consider the role that heredity plays in shaping your life and in forming the brain that controls your experiences. Of course, you can appreciate these differences only against the background of what you have in common with all other people. You might, therefore, think of this as a chapter about biological potential: What possibilities for behavior define the human species, and how do those possibilities emerge for particular members of that species?

In a way, this chapter stands as proof of one remarkable aspect of your biological potential: Your brain is sufficiently complex to carry out a systematic examination of its own functions. Why is this so remarkable? The human brain is sometimes likened to a spectacular computer: At only 3 pounds, your brain contains more cells than there are stars in our entire galaxy—over 100 billion cells that communicate and store information with astonishing efficiency. But even the world's mightiest computer is incapable of reflecting on the rules that guide its own operation. Thus you are much more than a computer; your consciousness allows you to put your vast computational power to work, trying to determine your species' own rules for operation. The research we examine in this chapter arose from the special human desire for self-understanding.

The goal for this chapter is to help you to understand how biology contributes to the creation of unique individuals against a shared background potential. To approach this goal, I first describe how evolution and heredity determine your biology and behavior. You'll then see how laboratory and clinical research provide a view into the workings of the brain, the nervous system, and the endocrine system. Finally, we'll consider the basic mechanisms of communication among cells in your nervous system that produce the full range of complex human behaviors.

Psychologists often wish to understand the separate impact of nature and nurture on individuals' courses through life. Why might it be easier to observe the impact of environments versus the impact of heredity?

Because the features of environments can be directly observed, it is often easier to understand how they affect people's behavior. You can, for example, actually watch a parent acting aggressively toward a child and wonder what consequences such treatment might have on the child's later tendency toward aggression; you can observe the overcrowded and impoverished settings in which some children grow up and wonder whether these features of the environment lead to aggressive behaviors. The biological forces that shape behavior, by comparison, are never plainly visible to the naked eye. To make the biology of behavior more understandable to you, the chapter will begin by reviewing some of the basic elements of the theory of evolution—the principles that shape a species' potential repertory of behaviors. We'll then consider how behavioral variation is passed from generation to generation.

HEREDITY AND BEHAVIOR

One of the major goals of psychology is to discover the causes underlying the variety of human behavior. An important dimension of causal explanation within psychology is defined by the end points of *nature* versus *nurture,* or *heredity* versus *environment.* Consider the question of the roots of aggressive behavior. You might imagine that individuals are aggressive by virtue of some aspect of their biological makeup: They may have inherited a tendency toward violence from one of their parents. Alternatively, you might imagine that all humans are about equally predisposed to aggression and that the degree of aggression individuals display arises in response to features of the environment in which they are raised. The correct answer to this question has a profound impact on how society treats individuals who are overly aggressive—by focusing resources on changing certain environments or on changing aspects of the people themselves. You need to be able to discriminate the forces of heredity from the forces of environment.

Evolution and Natural Selection

In 1831, **Charles Darwin** (1809–1882), fresh out of college with a degree in theology, set sail from England on HMS *Beagle,* an ocean research vessel, for a five-year cruise to survey the coast of South America. During the trip, Darwin collected everything that crossed his path: marine animals, birds, insects, plants, fossils, seashells, and rocks. His extensive notes became the foundation for his books on topics ranging from geology to emotion to zoology. The book for which he is most remembered is *The Origin of Species,* published in 1859. In this work, Darwin set forth science's grandest theory: the evolution of life.

Natural Selection Darwin developed his theory of evolution by reflecting on the species of animals he had encountered while on his voyage. One of the many places *Beagle* visited was the Galápagos Islands, a volcanic archipelago off the west coast of South America. These islands are a haven for diverse forms of wildlife, including 13 species of finches, now known as Darwin's finches. Darwin wondered how so many different species of finches could have come to inhabit the islands. He reasoned that they couldn't have migrated from the mainland because

What observations ultimately led Charles Darwin to propose the theory of evolution?

In general, the theory of natural selection suggests that organisms well adapted to their environment, whatever it happens to be, will produce more offspring than those less well adapted. Over time, those organisms possessing traits more favorable for survival will become more numerous than those not possessing those traits. In evolutionary terms, an individual's success is measured by the number of offspring he or she produces.

Contemporary research has shown that natural selection can have dramatic effects, even in the short run. In a series of studies by **Peter** and **Rosemary Grant** (Grant & Grant, 2006, 2008), involving several species of Darwin's finches, records were kept of rainfall, food supply, and the population size of these finches on one of the Galápagos Islands. In 1976, the population numbered well over 1,000 birds. The following year brought a murderous drought that wiped out most of the food supply. The smallest seeds were the first to be depleted, leaving only larger and tougher seeds. That year the finch population decreased by more than 80 percent. However, smaller finches with smaller beaks died at a higher frequency than larger finches with thicker beaks. Consequently, as Darwin would have predicted, the larger birds became more numerous in the following years. Why? Because only they, with their larger bodies and thicker beaks, were fit enough to respond to the environmental change caused by the drought. Interestingly, in 1983, rain was plentiful, and seeds, especially the smaller ones, became abundant. As a result, smaller birds outsurvived larger birds, probably because their beaks were better suited for pecking the smaller seeds. The Grants' study shows that natural selection can have noticeable effects even over short periods. Researchers continue to document the impact of environments on natural selection in diverse species such as fruit flies, mosquitoes, flounders, and pygmy possums (Hoffmann & Willi, 2008).

Although Darwin provided the foundation for evolutionary theory, researchers continue to study mechanisms of evolutionary change that fell beyond the bounds of Darwin's ideas (Shaw & Mullen, 2011). For example, one important question that Darwin was unable to address fully was how populations with common ancestors evolve so that one species becomes two. As you have already seen in the Grants' research with Darwin's finches, species can change rapidly in response to local environments. One explanation for the appearance of new species is that they emerge when two populations from an original species become geographically separate—and

those species didn't exist there. He suggested, therefore, that the variety of species reflected the operation of a process he came to call **natural selection**.

Darwin's theory suggests that each species of finch emerged from a common set of ancestors. Originally, a small flock of finches found their way to one of the islands; they mated among themselves and eventually their number multiplied. Over time, some finches migrated to different islands in the archipelago. What happened next was the process of natural selection. Food resources and living conditions—*habitats*—vary considerably from island to island. Some of the islands are lush with berries and seeds, others are covered with cacti, and others have plenty of insects. At first, the populations on different islands were similar—there was *variation* among the groups of finches on each island. However, because food resources on the islands were limited, a bird was more likely to survive and reproduce if the shape of its beak was well suited to the food sources available on the island. For example, birds that migrated to islands rich in berries and seeds were more likely to survive and reproduce if they had thick beaks. On those islands, birds with thinner, more pointed beaks, unsuitable for crushing or breaking open seeds, died. The environment of each island determined which among the original population of finches would live and reproduce and which would more likely perish, leaving no offspring. Over time, this led to very different populations on each island and permitted the different species of Darwin's finches to evolve from the original ancestral group.

....

natural selection Darwin's theory that favorable adaptations to features of the environment allow some members of a species to reproduce more successfully than others.

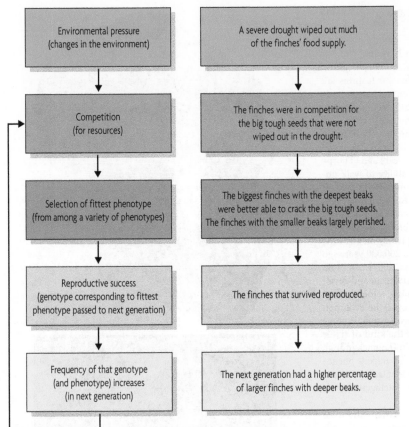

FIGURE 1 How Natural Selection Works

Environmental changes create competition for resources among species members. Only those individuals possessing characteristics instrumental in coping with these changes will survive and reproduce. The next generation will have a greater number of individuals possessing these genetically based traits.

therefore evolve in response to different environmental events. However, contemporary research on evolution has uncovered examples of new species that have emerged without that type of geographic isolation (Fitzpatrick et al., 2008). Researchers are pursuing a variety of explanations for how species arise under those circumstances. For example, some subsets of Darwin's finches are more likely to mate with finches that are physically similar to them. Such mating patterns may lead to the emergence of new species (Hendry et al., 2009).

Genotypes and Phenotypes Let's return our focus to the forces that bring about change within an existing species. The example of the ebb and flow of finch populations demonstrates why Darwin characterized the course of evolution as *survival of the fittest*. Imagine that each environment poses some range of difficulties for each species of living beings. Those members of the species who possess the range of physical and psychological attributes best adapted to the environment are most likely to survive. To the extent that the attributes that foster survival can be passed from one generation to another—and stresses in the environment endure over time—the species is likely to evolve.

To examine the process of natural selection in more detail, I must introduce some of the vocabulary of evolutionary theory. Let us focus on an individual finch. At conception, that finch inherited a **genotype**, or genetic structure, from its parents. In the context of a particular environment, this genotype determined the finch's development and behavior. The

outward appearance and repertoire of behaviors of the finch are known as its **phenotype**. For our finch, its genotype may have interacted with the environment to yield the phenotype of *small beak* and *ability to peck smaller seeds*.

If seeds of all types were plentiful, this phenotype would have no particular bearing on the finch's survival. Suppose, however, that the environment provided insufficient seeds to feed the whole population of finches. In that case, the individual finches would be in *competition* for resources. When species function in circumstances of competition, phenotypes help determine which individual members are better adapted to ensure survival. Recall our finch with a small beak. If only small seeds were available, our finch would be at a *selective advantage* with respect to finches with large beaks. If only large seeds were available, our finch would be at a disadvantage.

Only finches that survive can reproduce. Only those animals that reproduce can pass on their genotypes. Therefore, if the environment continued to provide only small seeds, over several generations the finches would probably come to have almost exclusively small beaks—with the consequence that they would be almost exclusively capable of eating only small seeds. In this way, forces in the environment can shape a species' repertory of possible behaviors. **Figure 1** provides a simplified

....

genotype The genetic structure an organism inherits from its parents.

phenotype The observable characteristics of an organism, resulting from the interaction between the organism's genotype and its environment.

model of the process of natural selection. Let us now apply these ideas to human evolution.

Human Evolution By looking backward to the circumstances in which the human species evolved, you can begin to understand why certain physical and behavioral features are part of the biological endowment of the entire human species. In the evolution of our species, natural selection favored two major adaptations—bipedalism and encephalization. Together, they made possible the rise of human civilization. *Bipedalism*, which refers to the ability to walk upright, emerged in our evolutionary ancestors 5 to 7 million years ago (Thorpe et al., 2007). As our ancestors evolved the ability to walk upright, they were able to explore new environments and exploit new resources. *Encephalization* refers to increases in brain size. Early human ancestors, who emerged about 4 million years ago (for example, *Australopithecus*), had brains roughly the same size as those of chimpanzees (see **Figure 2**). In the time from 1.9 million years ago *(Homo erectus)* to 200,000 years ago *(Homo sapiens),* brain size tripled (Gibbons, 2007). As brain size increased, our ancestors became more intelligent and developed capacities for complex thinking, reasoning, remembering, and planning (Sherwood et al., 2008). However, the evolution of a bigger brain did not guarantee that humans would become more intelligent—what was important was the kind of tissue that developed and expanded within the brain (Ramachandran, 2011). The genotype coding for mobile and intelligent phenotypes slowly squeezed out other, less well-adapted genotypes from the human gene pool, affording only intelligent bipeds the opportunity to reproduce.

After bipedalism and encephalization, perhaps the most important evolutionary milestone for our species was the advent of *language* (Sherwood et al., 2008). Think of the tremendous adaptive advantages that language conferred on early humans. Simple instructions for making tools, finding a good hunting or fishing spot, and avoiding danger would save time, effort, and lives. Instead of learning every one of life's lessons firsthand, by trial and error, humans could benefit from experiences shared by others. Conversation, even humor, would strengthen the social bonds among members of a naturally gregarious species. Most important, the advent of language would provide for the transmission of accumulated wisdom, from one generation to future generations.

Language is the basis for *cultural evolution,* which is the tendency of cultures to respond adaptively, through learning, to environmental change (Ramachandran, 2011). Cultural evolution has given rise to major advances in toolmaking, improved agricultural practices, and the development and refinement of industry and technology. Cultural evolution allows our species to make very rapid adjustments to changes in environmental conditions. Adaptations to the use of personal computers, for example, have arisen in only the past few decades. Even so, cultural evolution could not occur without genotype coding for the capacities to learn and to think abstractly. Culture—including art, literature, music, scientific knowledge, and philanthropic activities—is possible only because of the potential of the human genotype.

Variation in the Human Genotype

You have seen that the conditions in which humans evolved favored the evolution of important shared biological potential: for example, bipedalism and the capacity for thought and

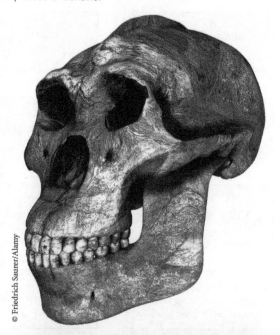

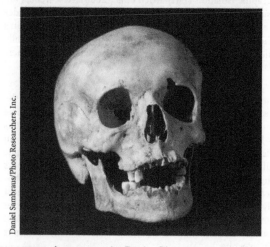

FIGURE 2 Increases in Brain Size across Human Evolution

Early in human evolution, brain size doubled from *Australopithecus* (top) to *Homo erectus* (middle). Over the course of evolution, increases continued so that the brains of modern humans, *Homo sapiens* (bottom), are three times larger than those of *Australopithecus.*

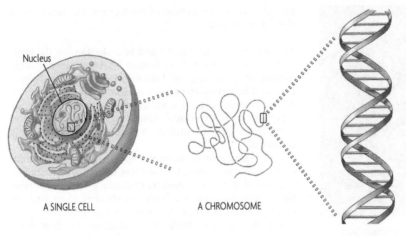

FIGURE 3 **Genetic Material**

The nucleus of each cell in your body contains a copy of the chromosomes that transmit your genetic inheritance. Each chromosome contains a long strand of DNA arranged in a double helix. Genes are segments of the DNA that contain instructions for the production of the proteins that guide your individual development.

From Lefton, Lester A.; Brannon, Linda, *Psychology*, 8th Edition, © 2003. Printed and electronically reproduced by permission of Pearson Education Inc., Upper Saddle River, New Jersey.

A SINGLE CELL

A CHROMOSOME

A SEGMENT OF DNA

language. There remains, however, considerable variation within that shared potential. Your mother and father have endowed you with a part of what their parents, grandparents, and all past generations of their family lines have given them, resulting in a unique biological blueprint and timetable for your development. The study of the mechanisms of **heredity**—the inheritance of physical and psychological traits from ancestors—is called **genetics** (Carlson, 2004).

The earliest systematic research exploring the relationship between parents and their offspring was published in 1866 by **Gregor Mendel** (1822–1884). Mendel's studies were carried out on the humble garden pea. He was able to demonstrate that the physical features of peas that emerged from different seeds—for example, whether the peas appeared *round* or *wrinkled*—could be predicted from the physical features of the plants from which the seeds had been obtained. Based on his observations, Mendel suggested that pairs of "factors"—one inherited from each parent—determined the properties of the offspring (Lander & Weinberg, 2000). Although Mendel's work originally received little attention from other scientists, modern techniques have allowed researchers to visualize and study Mendel's "factors," which we now call *genes*.

Much of this section will focus on **human behavior genetics,** a research field that unites genetics and psychology to explore the causal link between inheritance and behavior (Kim, 2009). The study of human behavior genetics most often focuses on the origins of individual differences: What factors in your individual genetic inheritance help to explain the way you think and behave? To complement human behavior genetics, two other fields have emerged that take a broader focus on how forces of natural selection affected the behavioral repertoire of humans and other species. Researchers in the field of **sociobiology** provide evolutionary explanations for the social behavior and social systems of humans and other animal species. Researchers in **evolutionary psychology** extend those evolutionary explanations to include other aspects of human experience, such as how the mind functions. This chapter focuses on individual differences. However, psychologists also consider instances in which the evolutionary perspective sheds light on shared human experience.

Examples range from partner choices in relationships to emotional expression.

Let's start with some basic principles of genetics.

Basic Genetics In the nucleus of each of your cells is genetic material called **DNA (deoxyribonucleic acid;** see **Figure 3)**. DNA is organized into tiny units, called **genes**. Genes contain the instructions for the production of proteins. These proteins regulate the body's physiological processes and the expression of phenotypic traits: body build, physical strength, intelligence, and many behavior patterns.

Genes are found on rodlike structures known as *chromosomes*. At the very instant you were conceived, you inherited from your parents 46 chromosomes—23 from your mother and 23 from your father. Each of these chromosomes contains thousands of genes—the union of a sperm and an egg results in only one of many billion possible gene combinations. The **sex chromosomes** are those that contain genes coding for development of male or female physical characteristics. You inherited an X chromosome from your mother and either an X or a Y chromosome from your father. An XX combination codes for development of female characteristics; an XY combination codes for development of male characteristics.

....

heredity The biological transmission of traits from parents to offspring.

genetics The study of the inheritance of physical and psychological traits from ancestors.

human behavior genetics The area of study that evaluates the genetic component of individual differences in behaviors and traits.

sociobiology A field of research that focuses on evolutionary explanations for the social behavior and social systems of humans and other animal species.

evolutionary psychology The study of behavior and mind using the principles of evolutionary theory.

DNA (deoxyribonucleic acid) The physical basis for the transmission of genetic information.

gene The biological unit of heredity; discrete section of a chromosome responsible for transmission of traits.

sex chromosome Chromosome that contains the genes that code for the development of male or female characteristics.

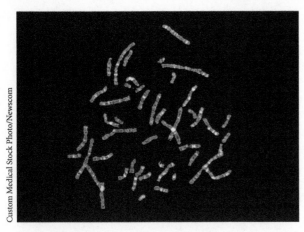

Custom Medical Stock Photo/Newscom

Human chromosomes—at the moment of conception, you inherited 23 from your mother and 23 from your father.

The pairs of genes you inherited—one from your mother and one from your father—provide the genetic starting point for most physical and psychological attributes. In many cases, there are different versions of a particular gene. Your phenotype is determined by the versions you inherited. Consider what happens when people come in contact with poison ivy: One version of a gene makes them immune to its allergic effects; the other version of the same gene will have them breaking out in a rash. However, the gene that makes people immune is the *dominant* version of the gene, whereas the gene that makes people susceptible is the *recessive* version. When people inherit different versions of a gene, the dominant gene wins out. If your skin responds badly to poison ivy, you likely inherited two recessive genes. A range of other physical traits (such as the color of your eyes and hair or the breadth of your lips) is determined by dominant and recessive genes.

As we begin to consider the genetic basis of more complex aspects of human experience, it is important to note that more than one pair of genes contributes to a particular attribute. These characteristics are known as **polygenic traits** because more than one gene influences the phenotype. An example is the genetic basis of psychological disorders. For each disorder, research suggests that more than one gene influences which individuals will be at risk (Keller & Miller, 2006).

Beginning in 1990, the U.S. government funded an international effort called the *Human Genome Project (HGP)*. The **genome** of an organism is the full sequence of genes found on the chromosomes with the associated DNA. In 2003, the HGP achieved the goal of providing a complete sequencing of the human genome. With that information in hand, researchers have now turned their attention to identifying all 20,500 human genes (Clamp et al., 2007). The ultimate goal is to

....

polygenic trait Characteristic that is influenced by more than one gene.

genome The genetic information for an organism, stored in the DNA of its chromosomes.

heritability The relative influence of genetics—versus environment—in determining patterns of behavior.

provide a complete account of the location and functions of that full set of genes.

Heritability To achieve the goal of understanding the functions of genes, research in human behavior genetics often focuses on estimating the **heritability** of particular human traits and behaviors. Heritability is measured on a scale of 0 to 1. If an estimate is near 0, it suggests that the attribute is largely a product of environmental influences; if an estimate is near 1, it suggests that the attribute is largely a product of genetic influences.

To separate environmental influences from genetic influences, researchers often use *adoption studies* or *twin studies*. For adoption studies, researchers obtain as much information as possible about the birth parents of children who are raised in adoptive homes. As the children develop, researchers assess the relative similarity of children to their birth families—representing genetics—and their adoptive families—representing environment.

In twin studies, researchers examine the extent to which *monozygotic (MZ)* twins (also called *identical twins*) and *dizygotic (DZ)* twins (also called *fraternal twins*) show similarity within pairs on particular traits or behaviors. MZ twins arise from a single fertilized egg. Historically, researchers believed that MZ twins share 100 percent of their genetic material. However, recent evidence suggests that factors both before and after birth often make "identical" twins less than genetically identical (Silva et al., 2011). Even so, MZ twins have more genetic overlap than DZ twins, who share roughly 50 percent of their genetic material. (DZ twins are no more genetically alike than any other pair of brothers and sisters.) Researchers compute heritability estimates by determining how much more alike MZ twins are than DZ twins on a particular attribute. Consider a twin study that assessed genetic impact on people's coffee consumption.

The study focused on a large sample of 2,252 MZ twins and 2,243 DZ twins from the Netherlands (Vink et al., 2009). The twins completed a survey that asked them to estimate the number of cups of caffeinated coffee they drank each day and also the number of cups of tea. The researchers found that MZ twins were more similar in the habits: For each comparison, the correlations were higher for MZ twins than for DZ twins. The researchers' statistical analyses yielded a "moderate" heritability estimate of 0.39 for coffee consumption. In addition, the twins' preference for coffee over tea yielded a "rather large" estimate of 0.62.

Featured Study

Are you part of a family that starts each day with a large cup of coffee—and can hardly stand the thought of tea? These data support the idea that some part of that behavior is explained by genes. In fact, researchers have begun to take the next step, to try to identify the actual genes that influence coffee consumption. Two independent studies have converged on the conclusion that important variation occurs among genes that affect individuals' ability to metabolize caffeine (Cornelis et al., 2011; Sulem et al., 2011). One group of researchers speculated that some gene variants might allow people to consume more coffee because their body eliminates caffeine more efficiently (Sulem et al., 2011). This example of the heritability of coffee consumption illustrates the evolution of contemporary research. Scientists try to move from a statement of fact (for example, "Coffee consumption is heritable") to an understanding of why that fact is true (for example, "Variation in particular genes affects individuals' ability to clear their bodies of caffeine").

The ability of researchers to associate genes with behavior points to some of the ethical issues that have arisen in the wake of the Human Genome Project's successes (Wilkinson, 2010). For example, a variety of techniques already allow prospective parents to choose to have a boy or a girl. Should they be willing and able to make that choice? How about choices with respect to a child's intelligence level, sports ability, or criminal inclinations? As the HGP and related efforts continue to yield new insights, such ethical questions will become increasingly prominent in debates over public policy.

You've learned that researchers are often able to estimate the heritability of important aspects of human experience. Let's now see why environments are critical as well.

Interactions of Genes and Environments This chapter began with a contrast between nature and nurture as causal forces in people's lives. However, researchers have increasingly come to document that both genetics and environments play critical roles to determine organisms' behaviors. Let's consider an example in which the circumstances in which children are raised have a major impact on the consequences of the genes they inherited.

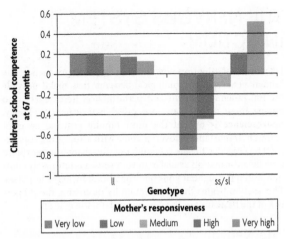

FIGURE 4 Genes and Environment Interact to Yield Children's School Competence

Children in this study inherited either two long versions (ll) of a gene or at least one short version (ss and sl). They also experienced varying levels of maternal responsiveness. The children's school competence is the product of both genetics and environment. For example, children with the ll genotype who experienced very low maternal responsiveness were equally as competent as children with an ss or sl genotype who experienced high maternal responsiveness.

Data from Grazyna Kochanska, Sanghag Kim, Robin A. Barry and Robert A. Philibert, Children's genotypes interact with maternal responsive care in predicting children's competence, *Development and Psychopathology*, May 23, 2011, pp. 605–616.

The study followed a group of children from ages 15 months to 67 months (Kochanska et al., 2011). With respect to genetics, the study assessed differences in a gene that affects the neurotransmitter serotonin (see discussion of neurotransmitters later in this chapter). The gene comes in short (s) and long (l) forms. The study contrasted children who inherited two long versions (ll) to children who acquired at least one short version (sl and ss). With respect to environments, the study assessed differences in the way the mothers treated their children. When the children were ages 15, 25, 38, and 52 months, the researchers observed them interacting with their mothers in a variety of naturalistic settings (for example, daily chores and play). The main measure was how responsive the mothers were to their children's needs in each setting. At age 67 months, the researchers assessed the children's school competence (combining measures such as reading and math ability). Figure 4 demonstrates the joint impact of genes and environment. For children born with at least one short variant of the gene, the mothers' responsiveness had a considerable impact: More maternal responsiveness led to greater school competence. However, for children born with two long variants of the gene, the mothers' responsiveness had virtually no impact on the children's outcomes.

Suppose you want to predict a child's school competence. As you look at Figure 4, make sure you understand why it wouldn't be enough to have information just about genetics or just about the environment.

From this example you can see why researchers seek to understand how and why certain environments allow genes to be expressed and certain genes affect the importance of the environment. Here are two examples of the important concept of the interactions of genes and environments: Genes and environments interact with respect to intellectual abilities; parenting and genes intereact to affect children's outcomes. As you encounter examples such as these, it should become increasingly clear to you that the answer is very rarely nature *or* nurture. Rather, you will see how behavior is often the joint product of nature *and* nurture.

Stop *and* Review

① How does the Grants' research on finches illustrate the role of genetic variation in the process of evolution?

② What is the difference between a genotype and a phenotype?

③ What were two evolutionary advances most critical in human evolution?

④ What is meant by heritability?

CRITICAL THINKING Consider the study that evaluated maternal responsiveness. Why might the researchers have sampled behavior at several points in time?

✓●─Study and Review on MyPsychLab

THE NERVOUS SYSTEM IN ACTION

Let's turn our attention now to the remarkable products of the human genotype: the biological systems that make possible the full range of thought and performance. Researchers who pursue these natural laws are called *neuroscientists*. Today, **neuroscience** is one of the most rapidly growing areas of research. Important discoveries come with astonishing regularity. The objective for the remainder of this chapter is to explore how the information available to your senses is ultimately communicated throughout your body and brain by nerve impulses. This section begins that exploration by discussing the properties of the basic unit of the nervous system, the neuron.

The Neuron

A **neuron** is a cell specialized to receive, process, and/or transmit information to other cells within the body. Neurons vary in shape, size, chemical composition, and function, but all neurons have the same basic structure (see **Figure 5**). There are between 100 billion and 1 trillion neurons in your brain.

Neurons typically take in information at one end and send out messages from the other. The part of the cell that receives incoming signals is a set of branched fibers called **dendrites**, which extend outward from the cell body. The basic job of the dendrites is to receive stimulation from sense receptors or other neurons. The cell body, or **soma**, contains the nucleus of the cell and the cytoplasm that sustains its life. The soma integrates information about the stimulation received from the dendrites (or in some cases received directly from another neuron) and passes it on to a single, extended fiber, the **axon**. In turn, the axon conducts this information along its length—which, in the spinal cord, can be several feet and, in the brain, less than a millimeter. At the other end of axons are swollen, bulblike structures called **terminal buttons**, through which the neuron is able to stimulate nearby glands, muscles, or other neurons. Neurons generally transmit information in only one direction: from the dendrites through the soma to the axon to the terminal buttons (see **Figure 6**). 👁

There are three major classes of neurons. **Sensory neurons** carry messages from sense receptor cells *toward* the central

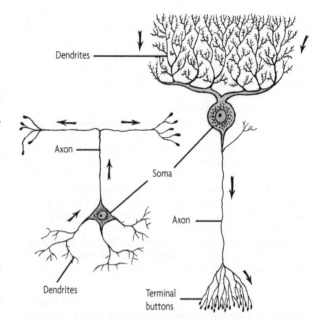

FIGURE 5 Two Types of Neurons

Note the differences in shape and dendritic branching. Arrows indicate directions in which information flows. Both cells are types of interneurons.

nervous system. Receptor cells are highly specialized cells that are sensitive, for example, to light, sound, and body position. **Motor neurons** carry messages *away* from the central nervous system toward the muscles and glands. The bulk of the neurons in the brain are **interneurons**, which relay messages from sensory neurons to other interneurons or to motor neurons. For every motor neuron in the body there are as many as 5,000 interneurons in the great intermediate network that forms the computational system of the brain.

As an example of how these three kinds of neurons work together, consider the pain withdrawal reflex (see **Figure 7**). When pain receptors near the skin's surface are stimulated by a sharp object, they send messages via sensory neurons to an

....

👁 **Watch the Video** *The Basics: How the Brain Works? Part 1* on MyPsychLab

neuroscience The scientific study of the brain and of the links between brain activity and behavior.

neuron A cell in the nervous system specialized to receive, process, and/or transmit information to other cells.

dendrite One of the branched fibers of neurons that receive incoming signals.

soma The cell body of a neuron, containing the nucleus and cytoplasm.

axon The extended fiber of a neuron through which nerve impulses travel from the soma to the terminal buttons.

terminal button A bulblike structure at the branched ending of an axon that contains vesicles filled with neurotransmitters.

sensory neuron Neuron that carries messages from sense receptors toward the central nervous system.

motor neuron Neuron that carries messages away from the central nervous system toward the muscles and glands.

interneuron Brain neuron that relays messages from sensory neurons to other interneurons or to motor neurons.

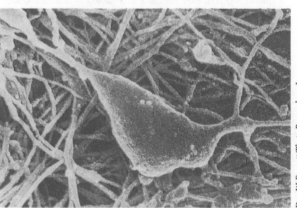

A neuron that affects contractions in the human intestine. What are the roles of the dendrites, soma, and axons in neural transmission?

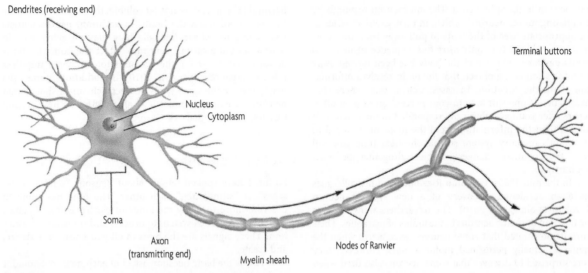

FIGURE 6 The Major Structures of the Neuron

The neuron receives nerve impulses through its dendrites. It then sends the nerve impulses through its axon to the terminal buttons, where neurotransmitters are released to stimulate other neurons.

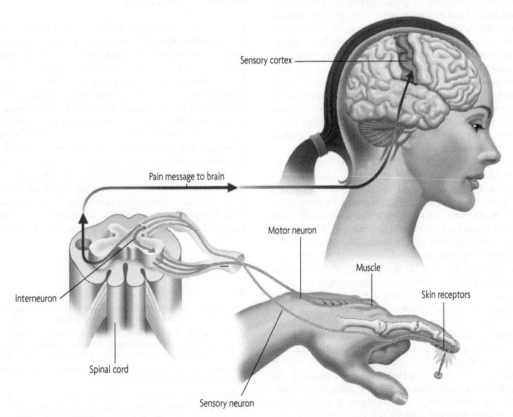

FIGURE 7 The Pain Withdrawal Reflex

The pain withdrawal reflex shown here involves only three neurons: a sensory neuron, a motor neuron, and an interneuron.

interneuron in the spinal cord. The interneuron responds by stimulating motor neurons, which, in turn, excite muscles in the appropriate area of the body to pull away from the pain-producing object. It is only *after* this sequence of neuronal events has taken place, and the body has been moved away from the stimulating object, that the brain receives information about the situation. In cases such as this, where survival depends on swift action, your perception of pain often occurs after you have physically responded to the danger. Of course, then the information from the incident is stored in the brain's memory system so that the next time you will avoid the potentially dangerous object altogether, before it can hurt you.

In the mid-1990s, **Giacomo Rizzolatti** and his colleagues made an accidental discovery of a new type of neuron (Rizolatti & Sinigaglia, 2010). The researchers were studying the function of motor neurons in the brains of macaques. Their work demonstrated that some neurons were active when the monkeys actually performed motor actions. However, they were surprised to discover that some neurons also fired when the monkeys only observed a researcher performing the same action! The researchers called these neurons **mirror neurons** because they respond when an individual observes another individual performing an action. Although the evidence is indirect (because researchers cannot conduct the same sorts of studies with humans that they conduct with monkeys), there is substantial evidence that mirror neurons are also at work in humans' brains. Mirror neurons may enable us to understand the *intentions* of other people's behavior. Imagine you see your friend Josh's hand moving toward a ball. As that happens, "your own ball-reaching neurons start firing. By running this virtual simulation of being Josh, you get the immediate impression that he is intending to reach for the ball" (Ramachandran, 2011, p. 128). Thus, mirror neurons allow you to use your own experiences to make sense of other people's behavior (Sinigaglia & Rizzolatti, 2011). These neurons may have afforded humans great ability to learn through imitation, which allowed for efficient cultural evolution. Such claims about the broad influence of mirror neurons on human achievement have led to an explosion of research.

Interspersed among the brain's vast web of neurons are about 5 to 10 times as many glial cells (**glia**). The word *glia* is derived from the Greek word for *glue*, which gives you a hint of one of the major duties performed by these cells: They hold neurons in place. In vertebrates, glial cells have several other important functions (Kettenmann & Verkhratsky, 2008). A first function applies during development. Glial cells help guide newborn neurons to appropriate locations in the brain. A second function is housekeeping. When neurons are damaged and die, glial cells in the area multiply and clean up the cellular junk left behind; they can also take up excess neurotransmitters and other substances at the gaps between neurons. A third function is insulation. Glial cells form an insulating cover, called a **myelin sheath**, around some types of axons. This fatty insulation greatly increases the speed of nerve signal conduction. A fourth function of glial cells is to prevent toxic substances in the blood from reaching the delicate cells of the brain. Specialized glial cells, called astrocytes, make up a *blood–brain barrier*, forming a continuous envelope of fatty material around the blood vessels in the brain. Substances that are not soluble in fat do not dissolve through this barrier, and because many poisons and other harmful substances are not fat soluble, they cannot penetrate the barrier to reach the brain. In addition, neuroscientists have come to believe that glia may play an active role in neural communication. Glia may affect the concentrations of ions that allow for the transmission of nerve impulses (Henneberger & Rusakov, 2010). In addition, some glia may generate the same types of electrochemical signals that neurons generate (Káradóttir et al., 2008). The next section discusses those signals. ✳

Action Potentials

So far, I have spoken loosely about neurons "sending messages" or "stimulating" each other. The time has come to describe more formally the kinds of electrochemical signals used by the nervous system to process and transmit information. These signals are the basis of all you know, feel, desire, and create.

This is the basic question asked of each neuron: Should it or should it not *fire*—produce a response—at some given time? In loose terms, neurons make this decision by combining the information arriving at their dendrites and soma (cell body) and determining whether those inputs are predominantly saying "fire" or "don't fire." More formally, each neuron will receive a balance of **excitatory**—fire!—and **inhibitory**—don't fire!—**inputs**. In neurons, the right pattern of excitatory inputs over time or space will lead to the production of an *action potential:* The neuron fires.

The Biochemical Basis of Action Potentials To explain how an **action potential** works, you need to appreciate the biochemical environment in which neurons draw together incoming information. All neural communication is produced by the flow of electrically charged particles, called *ions*, through the neuron's membrane, a thin "skin" separating the cell's internal and external environments. Think of a nerve fiber as a piece of macaroni, filled with salt water, floating in a salty soup. The soup and the fluid in the macaroni both contain ions—atoms of sodium ($Na+$), chloride ($Cl-$), and potassium ($K+$)—that have either positive ($+$) or negative ($-$) charges (see **Figure 8**). The membrane, or the surface of the macaroni, plays a critical role in keeping the ingredients of the two fluids in an appropriate balance. When a cell is inactive, or in a resting state, there is a greater concentration of potassium ions inside the axon and a greater concentration of sodium ions outside the

....

✳ Explore the Concept *Virtual Brain: Neural Conduction* on MyPsychLab

mirror neuron Neuron that responds when an individual observes another individual performing a motor action.

glia The cells that hold neurons together and facilitate neural transmission, remove damaged and dead neurons, and prevent poisonous substances in the blood from reaching the brain.

myelin sheath Insulating material that surrounds axons and increases the speed of neural transmission.

excitatory input Information entering a neuron that signals it to fire.

inhibitory input Information entering a neuron that signals it not to fire.

action potential The nerve impulse activated in a neuron that travels down the axon and causes neurotransmitters to be released into a synapse.

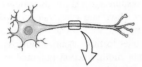

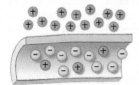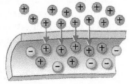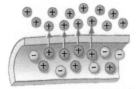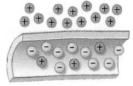

In a resting state, the fluid surrounding the axon has a different concentration of ions than the fluid inside the axon. For that reason, the fluid within the cell is *polarized* with respect to the exterior fluid, providing the neuron's resting potential.

When a nerve impulse arrives at a segment of the axon, positively charged sodium ions flow into the axon. The inflow of sodium causes the nerve cell to become *depolarized*. The nerve impulse is passed down the axon as each successive segment becomes depolarized.

Once the nerve impulse has been passed along, sodium ions flow back out of the axon to restore the resting potential.

Once the resting potential is restored, the segment of the axon is ready to transmit another impulse.

FIGURE 8 **The Biochemical Basis of Action Potentials**
Action potentials rely on an imbalance of the electrical charge of the ions present inside and outside of axons.

From Lefton, Lester A.; Brannon, Linda, *Psychology*, 8th Edition, © 2003. Printed and electronically reproduced by permission of Pearson Education Inc., Upper Saddle River, New Jersey.

axon. The membrane is not a perfect barrier; it "leaks" a little, allowing some sodium ions to slip in while some potassium ions slip out. To correct for this, nature has provided transport mechanisms within the membrane that pump out sodium and pump in potassium. Successful operation of these sodium-potassium pumps leaves the fluid inside a neuron with a slightly negative voltage (70/1,000 of a volt) relative to the fluid outside. This means that the fluid inside the cell is *polarized* with respect to the fluid outside the cell. This slight polarization is called the **resting potential**. It provides the electrochemical context in which a nerve cell can produce an action potential.

The nerve cell begins the transition from a resting potential to an action potential in response to the pattern of inhibitory and excitatory inputs. Each kind of input affects the likelihood that the balance of ions from the inside to the outside of the cell will change. They cause changes in the function of **ion channels**, excitable portions of the cell membrane that selectively permit certain ions to flow in and out. Inhibitory inputs cause the ion channels to work harder to keep the inside of the cell negatively charged—this will keep the cell from firing. Excitatory inputs cause the ion channels to begin to allow sodium ions to flow in—this will allow the cell to fire. Because sodium ions have a positive charge, their influx can begin to change the relative balance of positive and negative charges across the cell membrane. An action potential begins when the excitatory inputs are sufficiently strong with respect to inhibitory inputs to *depolarize* the cell from −70 millivolts to −55 millivolts: Sufficient sodium has entered the cell to effect this change.

Once the action potential begins, sodium rushes into the neuron. As a result, the inside of the neuron becomes positive relative to the outside, meaning the neuron has become fully depolarized. A domino effect now propels the action potential down the axon. The leading edge of depolarization causes ion channels in the adjacent region of the axon to open and allow sodium to rush in. In this way—through successive depolarization—the signal passes down the axon (see Figure 8).

How does the neuron return to its original resting state of polarization after it fires? When the inside of the neuron becomes positive, the channels that allow sodium to flow in close and the channels that allow potassium to flow out open. The outflow of potassium ions restores the negative charge of the neuron. Thus, even while the signal is reaching the far end of the axon, the portions of the cell in which the action potential originated are being returned to their resting balance, so that they can be ready for their next stimulation.

Properties of the Action Potential The biochemical manner in which the action potential is transmitted leads to several important properties. The action potential obeys the **all-or-none law:** The size of the action potential is unaffected by increases in the intensity of stimulation beyond the threshold level. Once excitatory inputs sum to reach the threshold level, a uniform action potential is generated. If the threshold is not

resting potential The polarization of cellular fluid within a neuron, which provides the capability to produce an action potential.

ion channel A portion of neurons' cell membranes that selectively permits certain ions to flow in and out.

all-or-none law The rule that the size of the action potential is unaffected by increases in the intensity of stimulation beyond the threshold level.

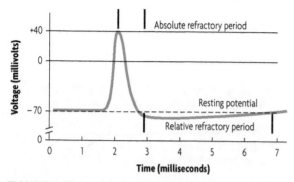

FIGURE 9 Timetable for Electrical Changes in the Neuron during an Action Potential

Sodium ions entering the neuron cause its electrical potential to change from slightly negative during its polarized, or resting, state to slightly positive during depolarization. Once the neuron is depolarized, it enters a brief refractory period during which further stimulation will not produce another action potential. Another action potential can occur only after the ionic balance between the inside and the outside of the cell is restored.

reached, no action potential occurs. An added consequence of the all-or-none law is that the size of the action potential does not diminish along the length of the axon. In this sense, the action potential is said to be *self-propagating;* once started, it needs no outside stimulation to keep itself moving. It's similar to a lit fuse on a firecracker.

Different neurons conduct action potentials along their axons at different speeds; the fastest have signals that move at the rate of 200 meters per second, the slowest plod along at 10 centimeters per second. The axons of the faster neurons are covered with a tightly wrapped myelin sheath—consisting, as noted earlier, of glial cells—making this part of the neuron resemble short tubes on a string. The tiny breaks between the tubes are called *nodes of Ranvier* (see Figure 6). In neurons having myelinated axons, the action potential literally skips along from one node to the next—saving the time and energy required to open and close ion channels at every location on the axon. Damage to the myelin sheath throws off the delicate timing of the action potential and causes serious problems. Multiple sclerosis (MS) is a devastating disorder caused by deterioration of the myelin sheath. It is characterized by double vision, tremors, and eventually paralysis. In MS, specialized cells from the body's immune system actually attack myelinated neurons, exposing the axon and disrupting normal synaptic transmission (Wu & Alvarez, 2011).

After an action potential has passed down a segment of the axon, that region of the neuron enters a **refractory period** (see **Figure 9**). During the *absolute refractory period,* further stimulation, no matter how intense, cannot cause another action potential to be generated; during the *relative refractory period,*

the neuron will fire only in response to a stimulus stronger than what is ordinarily necessary. Have you ever tried to flush the toilet while it is filling back up with water? There must be a critical level of water for the toilet to flush again. Similarly, for a neuron to be able to generate another action potential, it must "reset" itself and await stimulation beyond its threshold. The refractory period ensures, in part, that the action potential will travel in only one direction down the axon: It cannot move backward because "earlier" parts of the axon are in a refractory state.

Synaptic Transmission

When the action potential completes its leapfrog journey down the axon to a terminal button, it must pass its information along to the next neuron. But no two neurons ever touch: They are joined at a **synapse**, with a small gap between the *presynaptic membrane* (the terminal button of the sending neuron) and the *postsynaptic membrane* (the surface of a dendrite or soma of a receiving neuron). When the action potential reaches the terminal button, it sets in motion a series of events called **synaptic transmission**, which is the relaying of information from one neuron to another across the synaptic gap (see **Figure 10**). Synaptic transmission begins when the arrival of the action potential at the terminal button causes small round packets, called *synaptic*

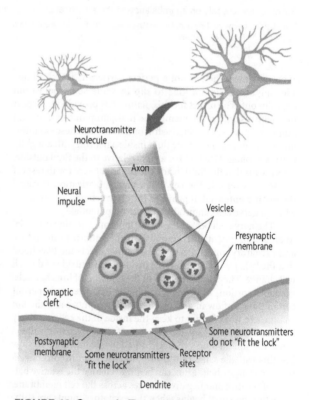

FIGURE 10 Synaptic Transmission

The action potential in the presynaptic neuron causes neurotransmitters to be released into the synaptic gap. Once across the gap, they stimulate receptor molecules embedded in the membrane of the postsynaptic neuron. Multiple neurotransmitters can exist within the same cell.

refractory period The period of rest during which a new nerve impulse cannot be activated in a segment of an axon.

synapse The gap between one neuron and another.

synaptic transmission The relaying information from one neuron to another across the synaptic gap.

vesicles, to move toward and affix themselves to the interior membrane of the terminal button. Inside each vesicle are **neurotransmitters**, biochemical substances that stimulate other neurons. The action potential also causes ion channels to open, allowing calcium ions into the terminal button. The influx of calcium ions causes the rupture of the synaptic vesicles and the release of whatever neurotransmitters they contain. Once the synaptic vesicles rupture, the neurotransmitters are dispersed rapidly across the *synaptic cleft*, the gap between the terminal button of one neuron and the cell membrane of the next. To complete synaptic transmission, the neurotransmitters attach to *receptor molecules* embedded in the postsynaptic membrane.

The neurotransmitters will bind to the receptor molecules under two conditions. First, no other neurotransmitters or other chemical substances can be attached to the receptor molecule. Second, the shape of the neurotransmitter must match the shape of the receptor molecule—as precisely as a key fits into a keyhole. If either condition is not met, the neurotransmitter will not attach to the receptor molecule. This means that it will not be able to stimulate the postsynaptic membrane. If the neurotransmitter does become attached to the receptor molecule, then it may provide "fire" or "don't fire" information to this next neuron. Once the neurotransmitter has completed its job, it detaches from the receptor molecule and drifts back into the synaptic gap. There it is either decomposed through the action of enzymes or reabsorbed into the presynaptic terminal button for quick reuse.

Depending on the receptor molecule, a neurotransmitter will have either an excitatory or an inhibitory effect. That is, the same neurotransmitter may be excitatory at one synapse but inhibitory at another. Each neuron integrates the information it obtains at synapses with between 1,000 and 10,000 other neurons to decide whether it ought to initiate another action potential. It is the integration of these thousands of inhibitory and excitatory inputs that allows all-or-none action potentials to provide the foundation for all human experience.

You may be wondering why we've taken this trip so deep into the nervous system. After all, this is a psychology course, and psychology is supposed to be about behavior and thinking and emotion. In fact, synapses are the biological medium in which all of these activities occur. If you change the normal activity of the synapse, you change how people behave, how they think, and how they feel. Understanding the functioning of the synapse has led to tremendous advances in the understanding of learning and memory, emotion, psychological disorders, drug addiction, and, in general, the chemical formula for mental health. You will use the knowledge you have acquired in this chapter throughout your study of psychology.

Neurotransmitters and Their Functions

Dozens of chemical substances are known or suspected to function as neurotransmitters in the brain. The neurotransmitters that have been studied most intensively meet a set of technical criteria. Each is manufactured in the presynaptic terminal button and is released when an action potential reaches that terminal. The neurotransmitter's presence in the synaptic cleft produces a biological response in the postsynaptic membrane; and, if its release is prevented, no subsequent responses can occur. To give you a sense of the effects different neurotransmitters have on the regulation of behavior, I will discuss a set

that has been found to play an important role in the daily functioning of the brain. This brief discussion will also enable you to understand many of the ways in which neural transmission can go awry. ◉

Acetylcholine *Acetylcholine* is found in both the central and peripheral nervous systems. Memory loss among patients suffering from Alzheimer's disease, a degenerative disease that is increasingly common among older persons, is believed to be caused by the deterioration of neurons that secrete acetylcholine (Craig et al., 2011). Acetylcholine is also excitatory at junctions between nerves and muscles, where it causes muscles to contract. A number of toxins affect the synaptic actions of acetylcholine. For example, botulinum toxin, often found in food that has been preserved incorrectly, poisons an individual by preventing release of acetylcholine in the respiratory system. This poisoning, known as *botulism*, can cause death by suffocation. Curare, a poison Amazon Indians use on the tips of their blowgun darts, paralyzes lung muscles by occupying critical acetylcholine receptors, preventing the normal activity of the transmitter.

GABA *GABA* (gamma-aminobutyric acid) is the most common inhibitory neurotransmitter in the brain. GABA may be used as a messenger in as many as a third of all brain synapses. Neurons that are sensitive to GABA are particularly concentrated in brain regions such as the thalamus, hypothalamus, and occipital lobes (see the discussion of the limbic system later in this chapter). GABA appears to play a critical role in some forms of psychopathology by inhibiting neural activity. When levels of this neurotransmitter in the brain become low, people may experience anxiety or depression (Croarkin et al., 2011; Kalueff & Nutt, 2007). Anxiety disorders are often treated with *benzodiazepine* drugs, such as *Valium* or *Xanax*, that increase GABA activity. The *benzodiazepine* drugs do not attach directly to GABA receptors. Instead they allow GABA itself to bind more effectively to postsynaptic receptor molecules.

Glutamate Glutamate is the brain's most common excitatory neurotransmitter. Because glutamate helps transmit information within the brain, it plays a critical role in processes of emotional response, learning, and memory (Morgado-Bernal, 2011). Learning proceeds more slowly when glutamate receptors are not functioning properly. In addition, disruptions of brain levels of glutamate have been associated with various psychological disorders, including schizophrenia (Bustillo et al., 2011). Glutamate also plays a role in addictions to drugs, alcohol, and nicotine. Researchers are beginning to explore the possibilities of treatments for these addictions that alter the brain's use of glutamate (Markou, 2007; Myers et al., 2011).

Dopamine, Norepinephrine, and Serotonin The *catecholamines* are a class of chemical substances that include two important neurotransmitters, *norepinephrine* and *dopamine*. Both have been shown to play prominent roles in psychological

···

◉ **Watch** the **Video** *In the Real World: Too Much, or Too Little, of a Good Thing* on **MyPsychLab**

neurotransmitter Chemical messenger released from a neuron that crosses the synapse from one neuron to another, stimulating the postsynaptic neuron.

Roughly 1.5 million people in the United States, including the actor Michael J. Fox, are impaired by Parkinson's disease. Research on the neurotransmitter dopamine has led to advances in understanding this disease. How does basic research in neuroscience allow for improved treatments?

disorders such as anxiety disorders, mood disorders, and schizophrenia (Goddard et al., 2010; Keshavan et al., 2011). Drugs that increase brain levels of norepinephrine elevate mood and relieve depression. Conversely, higher-than-normal levels of dopamine have been found in persons with schizophrenia. As you might expect, one way to treat people with this disorder is to give them a drug that decreases brain levels of dopamine.

All the neurons that produce *serotonin* are located in the brain stem (see the section "The Brain Stem, Thalamus, and Cerebellum" later in this chapter), which is involved in arousal and many autonomic processes. The hallucinogenic drug LSD (lysergic acid diethylamide) appears to produce its effects by suppressing the effects of serotonin neurons (Fantegrossi et al., 2008). These serotonin neurons normally inhibit other neurons, but the lack of inhibition produced by LSD creates vivid and bizarre sensory experiences, some of which last for hours. Abnormal levels of serotonin in the brain are associated with mood disorders. For example, reduced levels of serotonin may lead to depression. That's why many antidepressant drugs, such as *Prozac*, enhance the action of serotonin by preventing it from being removed from the synaptic cleft. 👁

....

👁 **Watch** the **Video** *What's In It For Me?: Your Brain on Drugs* on MyPsychLab

neuromodulator Any substance that modifies or modulates the activities of the postsynaptic neuron.

Endorphins   The *endorphins* are a group of chemicals that are usually classified as neuromodulators. A **neuromodulator** is any substance that modifies or modulates the activities of the postsynaptic neuron. Endorphins (short for *endogenous morphines*) play an important role in the control of emotional behaviors (anxiety, fear, tension, pleasure) and pain—drugs like opium and morphine bind to the same receptor sites in the brain. Endorphins have been called the "keys to paradise" because of their pleasure–pain controlling properties. Researchers have examined the possibility that endorphins are at least partially responsible for the pain-reducing effects of acupuncture and placebos (Han, 2011; Pollo et al., 2011). Such tests rely on the drug *naloxone*, whose only known effect is to block morphine and endorphins from binding to receptors. Any procedure that reduces pain by stimulating release of endorphins becomes ineffective when naloxone is administered. With the injection of naloxone, acupuncture and placebos do, in fact, lose their power—suggesting that, ordinarily, endorphins help them do their work.

Stop *and* Review

① What is the pattern of information flow through the major parts of each neuron?
② What is meant by the "all-or-none law"?
③ How do neurotransmitters pass from one neuron to the next?
④ What chemical substance is the most common inhibitory neurotransmitter in the brain?

✔•⌐**Study** and **Review** on **MyPsychLab**

BIOLOGY AND BEHAVIOR

You now have an understanding of the basic mechanisms that allow nerve cells to communicate. The time has come to assemble those neurons into the larger systems that guide your body and mind. This discussion begins with an overview of the techniques researchers use to hasten new discoveries. Next, we turn to a general description of the structure of the nervous system, followed by a more detailed look at the brain itself. I discuss the activity of the endocrine system, a second biological control system that works in cooperation with your nervous system and brain. Finally, we'll consider ways in which your life experiences continue to modify your brain.

Eavesdropping on the Brain

Neuroscientists seek to understand how the brain works at a number of different levels—from the operation of large structures visible to the naked eye to the properties of individual nerve cells visible only under powerful microscopes. The techniques researchers use are suited to their level of analysis. Here, you'll encounter the techniques that have been used most often to attribute functions and behaviors to particular regions of the brain.

Interventions in the Brain   Several research methods in neuroscience involve direct intervention with structures in

Psychology in Your Life

HOW DOES YOUR BRAIN DETERMINE TRUST?

Suppose a friend makes you a promise and says, "Trust me!" Should you? In recent years, researchers have begun to understand how your brain responds when you have to make decisions about trust. Much of that research has concentrated on the hormone *oxytocin*. Oxytocin first became the focus of researchers who were interested in the biological mechanisms that prompt nonhuman animals to form social bonds. Contemporary research suggests that the hormone plays a broad role in personal and social processes (IsHak et al., 2011). Let's consider trust.

To document the dramatic impact of oxytocin, a team of researchers recruited participants to play a game that focused on trust (Baumgartner et al., 2008). The game required two players to distribute a pool of "money units." In each round, the *investor* had to decide how many money units, out of 12, to invest. The experimenters provided the *trustee* with returns on those investments. The trustee then had the opportunity to share those returns fairly with the investor or not. In fact, halfway through the game, the investors all got the same feedback: The experimenters told them that they were getting their fair share only about half the time. The trustees could not be trusted!

What happened in the second half of the game depended on the investors' levels of oxytocin. Before the game started, half the investors received a dose of the hormone through a nasal spray. (Once it is absorbed, the hormone is able to cross into the brain.) The other participants received a placebo. For the first half of the game, it made little difference what investors had inhaled. The figure plots the average number of money units participants invested in each round. As you can see, before the feedback, oxytocin participants invested nearly the same amount as placebo participants. You might expect that the dramatic feedback—Don't trust this person!—would prompt participants to reduce their investments. That's exactly what the placebo group did. Their investments fell for the second half of the game. However, the oxytocin group didn't reduce their investments. In fact, the trend was in the opposite

direction. Apparently, the preexperimental dose of oxytocin prevented participants from acting on the information that the other players had violated their trust.

There's one more element to this project: While the investors were making their decisions they were undergoing fMRI scans. Those brain data enabled the researchers to determine what brain areas the dose of oxytocin affected. The scans revealed that oxytocin participants showed less activity in regions of the brain, such as the amygdala, that are involved in fear responses. The researchers suggested that, by dampening fear responses, oxytocin increases participants' ability "to trust in situations characterized by the risk of betrayal" (Baumgartner et al., 2008, p. 645).

After reading about this study, you might wonder whether your brain chemistry predisposes you to trust or distrust your friend. Researchers are starting to consider exactly that question of how individual differences in oxytocin function may have an important impact on social behavior (Bartz et al., 2011).

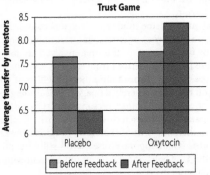

Data from J. A. Bartz & E. Hollander, The neuroscience of affiliation: Forging links between basic and clinical research on neuropeptides and social behavior, *Hormones and Behavior, 50*, pp. 518–528.

the brain. These methods find their historical roots in circumstances like the story of railroad foreman Phineas Gage, who in September 1848 suffered an accident in which a 3-foot, 7-inch-long pole was blown, as the result of an unexpected explosion, clear through his head. Gage's physical impairment was remarkably slight: He lost vision in his left eye, and the left side of his face was partially paralyzed, but his posture, movement, and speech were all unimpaired. Yet, psychologically, he was a changed man, as his doctor's account made clear:

> The equilibrium or balance, so to speak, between his intellectual faculties and animal propensities seems to

> have been destroyed. He is fitful, irreverent, indulging at times in the grossest profanity (which was not previously his custom), manifesting but little deference for his fellows, impatient of restraint or advice when it conflicts with his desires. . . . Previous to his injury, though untrained in schools, he possessed a well-balanced mind, and was looked upon by those who knew him as a shrewd, smart businessman, very energetic and persistent in executing all his plans of operation. In this regard his mind was radically changed, so decidedly that his friends and acquaintances said he was "no longer Gage." (Harlow, 1868, pp. 339–340)

Collection of Jack and Beverly Wilgus

Phineas Gage is shown holding the pole that caused his injury. Why were doctors so fascinated by Gage's changes in personality?

Gage's injury came at a time when scientists were just beginning to form hypotheses about the links between brain functions and complex behavior. The behavioral changes following the dramatic piercing of his brain prompted his doctor to hypothesize brain bases for aspects of personality and rational behavior.

At about the same time that Gage was convalescing from his injury, **Paul Broca** was studying the brain's role in language. His first research in this area involved an autopsy of a man whose name was derived from the only word he had been able to speak, "Tan." Broca found that the left front portion of Tan's brain had been severely damaged. This finding led Broca to study the brains of other persons who suffered from language impairments. In each case, Broca's work revealed similar damage to the same area of the brain, a region now known as **Broca's area**. Contemporary researchers still attempt to correlate patterns of behavior change or impairment with the sites of brain damage.

The problem with studying accidentally damaged brains, of course, is that researchers have no control over the location and extent of the damage. To produce a well-founded understanding of the brain and its relationship to behavioral and cognitive functioning, scientists need methods that allow them to specify precisely the brain tissue that has been incapacitated. Researchers have developed a variety of techniques to produce **lesions**, highly localized brain injuries. They may, for example, surgically remove specific brain areas, cut the neural connections to those areas, or destroy those areas through

Broca's area The region of the brain that translates thoughts into speech or signs.

lesion Injury to or destruction of brain tissue.

repetitive transcranial magnetic stimulation (rTMS) A technique for producing temporary inactivation of brain areas using repeated pulses of magnetic stimulation.

application of intense heat, cold, or electricity. As you would guess, experimental work with permanent lesions is carried out exclusively with nonhuman animals. (The ethics of this type of animal research has now come under heightened scrutiny.) Our conception of the brain has been radically changed as researchers have repeatedly compared and coordinated the results of lesioning experiments on animals with the growing body of clinical findings on the effects of brain damage on human behavior.

In recent years, scientists have developed a procedure called **repetitive transcranial magnetic stimulation (rTMS)** that uses pulses of magnetic stimulation to create temporary, reversible "lesions" in human participants—without any damage being done to tissue, brain regions can be briefly inactivated. This new technique enables researchers to address a range of questions that would not have been possible with nonhuman experiments (Sandrini et al., 2011). Consider an application of rTMS to study how your brain responds to nouns and verbs.

If you've spent any time studying languages, you're likely aware that nouns and verbs serve very different functions. A team of researchers used rTMS to test the hypothesis that different brain regions are at work when you produce the two parts of speech (Cappelletti et al., 2008). In the experiment, participants completed simple phrases presented by computer. For example, participants would read, "today I walk," and then complete, "yesterday I . . ." Similarly, they would read "one child," and then complete "many. . . ." Under ordinary circumstances, participants should be relatively quick to respond "walked" and "children." Suppose, however, that the researchers are able to use rTMS to "lesion" brain regions that help make these responses possible. Then, we'd expect participants' responses to be slowed down. In fact, the researchers identified one brain region (in the vicinity of Broca's area) that, when stimulated by rTMS, yielded slower performance for verbs but not for nouns. These data support the hypothesis that your brain processes make distinctions between nouns and verbs.

You can see why this experiment would not be possible with nonhuman participants: Humans are the only species that habitually produces nouns and verbs.

On other occasions, neuroscientists learn about the function of brain regions by directly *stimulating* them. For example, in the mid-1950s, **Walter Hess** (1881–1973) pioneered the use of electrical stimulation to probe structures deep in the brain. For example, Hess put electrodes into the brains of freely moving cats. By pressing a button, he could then send a small electrical current to the point of the electrode. Hess carefully recorded the behavioral consequences of stimulating each of 4,500 brain sites in nearly 500 cats. Hess discovered that, depending on the location of the electrode, sleep, sexual arousal, anxiety, or terror could be provoked by the flick of the switch—and turned off just as abruptly. For example, electrical stimulation of certain regions of the brain led the otherwise gentle cats to bristle with rage and hurl themselves on a nearby object.

Recording and Imaging Brain Activity Other neuroscientists map brain function by using electrodes to record the electrical activity of the brain in response to environmental stimulation. The brain's electrical output can be monitored at different levels of precision. At the most specific, researchers can insert ultrasensitive microelectrodes into the brain to record the electrical activity of a single brain cell. Such recordings can illuminate changes in the activity of individual cells in response to stimuli in the environment.

For human subjects, researchers often place a number of electrodes on the surface of the scalp to record larger, integrated patterns of electrical activity. These electrodes provide the data for an **electroencephalogram (EEG)**, or an amplified tracing of the brain activity. EEGs can be used to study the relationship between psychological activities and brain response. For example, in one experiment, researchers used EEGs to demonstrate that people's brains respond differently when they view emotionally charged images (Hajcak & Olvet, 2008). While their brain activity was being recorded, participants viewed a series of pleasant (e.g., smiling faces), neutral (e.g., household objects), and unpleasant (e.g., violent images) pictures on a computer screen. The EEGs revealed distinct patterns for the neutral versus emotional pictures: Participants appeared to devote more attention to the pleasant and unpleasant pictures, and that greater attention lingered even after the pictures left the computer screen.

Some of the most exciting technological innovations for studying the brain are machines originally developed to help neurosurgeons detect brain abnormalities, such as damage caused by strokes or diseases. These devices produce images of the living brain without invasive procedures that risk damaging brain tissue.

To obtain three-dimensional images of the brain, researchers may use **computerized axial tomography (CT or CAT)**. When an individual undergoes a CT scan, his or her head is placed in a doughnut-shaped ring that contains an X-ray source and an X-ray detector. During the scan, focused X-ray beams pass through the individual's head from several different angles. The computer assembles those separate X-ray images into coherent pictures of the brain. Researchers often

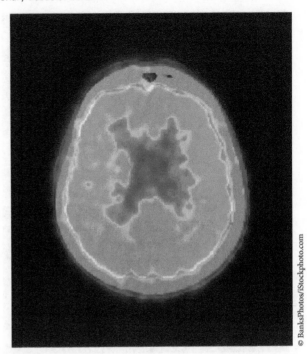

What can psychologists learn by looking at PET scans?

use CT scans to determine the location and extent of brain damage or brain abnormalities.

In research with **positron emission tomography**, or **PET**, subjects are given different kinds of radioactive (but safe) substances that eventually travel to the brain, where they are taken up by active brain cells. Recording instruments outside the skull can detect the radioactivity emitted by cells that are active during different cognitive or behavioral activities. This information is then fed into a computer that constructs a dynamic portrait of the brain, showing where different types of psychological activities are actually occurring.

Magnetic resonance imaging, or **MRI**, uses magnetic fields and radio waves to generate pulses of energy within the brain. As the pulse is tuned to different frequencies, some atoms line up with the magnetic field. When the magnetic pulse is turned off, the atoms vibrate (resonate) as they return to their original positions. Special radio receivers detect this resonance and channel information to a computer, which generates images of the locations of different atoms in areas of the brain. By looking at the image, researchers can link brain structures to psychological processes.

....

electroencephalogram (EEG) A recording of the electrical activity of the brain.

computerized axial tomography (CT or CAT) A technique that uses narrow beams of X-rays passed through the brain at several angles to assemble complete brain images.

positron emission tomography (PET) scan Brain image produced by a device that obtains detailed pictures of activity in the living brain by recording the radioactivity emitted by cells during different cognitive or behavioral activities.

magnetic resonance imaging (MRI) A technique for brain imaging that scans the brain using magnetic fields and radio waves.

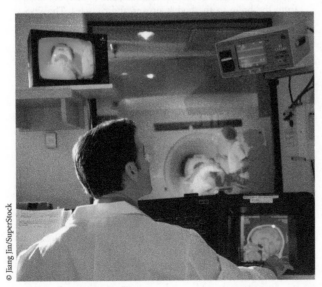

How have new imaging techniques expanded the range of questions researchers can ask?

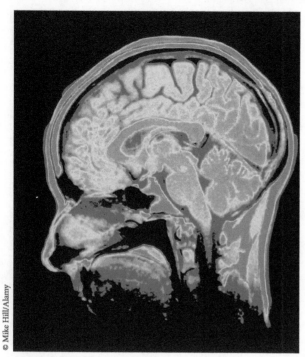

Magnetic resonance imaging (MRI) produces this color-enhanced profile of a normal brain. What is the purpose of trying to identify brain regions that underlie particular functions?

MRI is most useful for providing clear images of anatomical details; PET scans provide better information about function. A newer technique called **functional MRI**, or **fMRI**, combines some of the benefits of both techniques by detecting magnetic changes in the flow of blood to cells in the brain; fMRI allows more precise claims about both structure and function. Researchers have begun to use fMRI to discover the distributions of brain regions responsible for many of your most important cognitive abilities, such as attention, perception, language processing, and memory (Spiers & Maguire, 2007).

As you've just learned, cultural evolution has provided neuroscientists with the technology necessary to reveal some

....

functional MRI (fMRI) A brain-imaging technique that combines benefits of both MRI and PET scans by detecting magnetic changes in the flow of blood to cells in the brain.

central nervous system (CNS) The part of the nervous system consisting of the brain and spinal cord.

peripheral nervous system (PNS) The part of the nervous system composed of the spinal and cranial nerves that connect the body's sensory receptors to the CNS and the CNS to the muscles and glands.

somatic nervous system The subdivision of the peripheral nervous system that connects the central nervous system to the skeletal muscles and skin.

autonomic nervous system (ANS) The subdivision of the peripheral nervous system that controls the body's involuntary motor responses by connecting the sensory receptors to the central nervous system (CNS) and the CNS to the smooth muscle, cardiac muscle, and glands.

of your brain's most important secrets. The remainder of this chapter describes some of those secrets.

The Nervous System

The nervous system is composed of billions of highly specialized nerve cells, or *neurons*, that constitute the brain and the nerve fibers found throughout the body. The nervous system is subdivided into two major divisions: the **central nervous system (CNS)** and the **peripheral nervous system (PNS)**. The CNS is composed of all the neurons in the brain and spinal cord; the PNS is made up of all the neurons forming the nerve fibers that connect the CNS to the body. **Figures 11** and **12** show the relationship of the CNS to the PNS.

The job of the CNS is to integrate and coordinate all bodily functions, process all incoming neural messages, and send out commands to different parts of the body. The CNS sends and receives neural messages through the *spinal cord*, a trunk line of neurons that connects the brain to the PNS. The trunk line itself is housed in a hollow portion of the vertebral column called the spinal column. Spinal nerves branch out from the spinal cord between each pair of vertebrae in the spinal column, eventually connecting with sensory receptors throughout the body and with muscles and glands. The spinal cord coordinates the activity of the left and right sides of the body and is responsible for simple fast-action reflexes that do not involve the brain. For example, an organism whose spinal cord has been severed from its brain can still withdraw its limb from a painful stimulus. Although an intact brain would normally be notified of such action, the organism can complete the action without directions from above. Damage to the nerves of the spinal cord can result in paralysis of the legs or trunk, as seen in paraplegic individuals. The extent of paralysis depends on how high up on the spinal cord the damage occurred; higher damage produces greater paralysis.

Despite its commanding position, the CNS is isolated from any direct contact with the outside world. It is the role of the PNS to provide the CNS with information from sensory receptors, such as those found in the eyes and ears, and to relay commands from the brain to the body's organs and muscles. The PNS is actually composed of two sets of nerve fibers (see Figure 12). The **somatic nervous system** regulates the actions of the body's skeletal muscles. For example, imagine you are typing an e-mail. The movement of your fingers over the keyboard is managed by your somatic nervous system. As you decide what to say, your brain sends commands to your fingers to press certain keys. Simultaneously, the fingers send feedback about their position and movement to the brain. If you strike the wrong key (thw), the somatic nervous system informs the brain, which then issues the necessary correction, and, in a fraction of a second, you delete the mistake and hit the right key (the).

The other branch of the PNS is the **autonomic nervous system (ANS)**, which sustains basic life processes. This system is on the job 24 hours a day, regulating bodily functions that you usually don't consciously control, such as respiration, digestion, and arousal. The ANS must work even when you are asleep, and it sustains life processes during anesthesia and prolonged coma states.

The autonomic nervous system deals with survival matters of two kinds: those involving threats to the organism and those involving bodily maintenance. To carry out these functions, the autonomic nervous system is further subdivided into

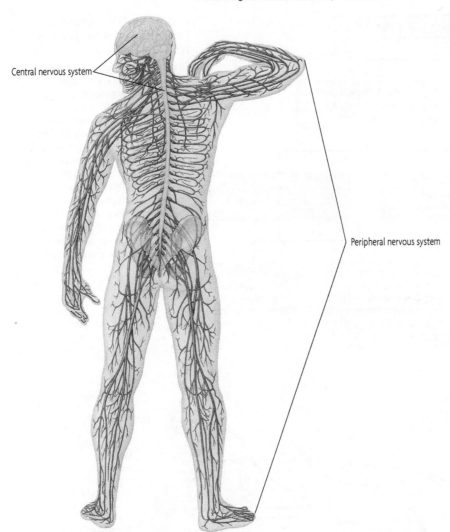

Central nervous system

Peripheral nervous system

FIGURE 11 Divisions of the Central and Peripheral Nervous Systems

The sensory and motor nerve fibers that constitute the peripheral nervous system are linked to the brain by the spinal cord.

Reprinted by permission of Richard McAnulty.

the sympathetic and parasympathetic nervous systems (see Figure 12). These divisions work in opposition to accomplish their tasks. The **sympathetic division** governs responses to emergency situations; the **parasympathetic division** monitors the routine operation of the body's internal functions. The sympathetic division can be regarded as a troubleshooter. In an emergency or stressful situation, it arouses the brain structures that prepare the organism either to fight the threat or flee from it—a pattern of activity called the *fight-or-flight response.* Digestion stops, blood flows away from internal organs to the muscles, oxygen transfer increases, and heart rate increases. After the danger is over, the parasympathetic division takes charge, and the individual begins to calm down. Digestion resumes, heartbeat slows, and breathing is relaxed. The parasympathetic division carries out the body's nonemergency housekeeping chores, such as elimination of bodily wastes, protection of the visual system (through tears and pupil constriction), and long-term conservation of body energy. The separate duties of the sympathetic and parasympathetic nervous systems are illustrated in **Figure 13**.

Brain Structures and Their Functions

The brain is the most important component of your central nervous system. The brains of human beings have three interconnected layers. In the deepest recesses of the brain, in a region called the *brain stem,* are structures involved primarily with autonomic processes such as heart rate, breathing, swallowing, and digestion. Enveloping this central core is the *limbic system,* which is involved with motivation, emotion, and memory processes. Wrapped around these two regions is the *cerebrum.* The universe of the human mind exists in this region. The cerebrum, and its surface layer, the *cerebral cortex,* integrates sensory information, coordinates your movements, and facilitates abstract thinking and reasoning (see **Figure 14**). Let's look

sympathetic division The subdivision of the autonomic nervous system that deals with emergency response and the mobilization of energy.

parasympathetic division The subdivision of the autonomic nervous system that monitors the routine operation of the body's internal functions and conserves and restores body energy.

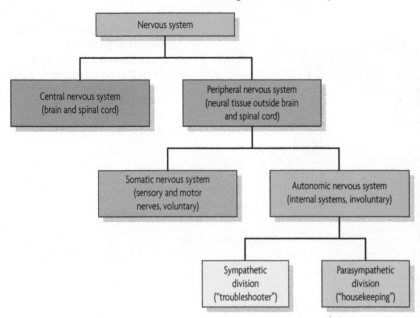

FIGURE 12 Hierarchical Organization of the Human Nervous System

The central nervous system is composed of the brain and the spinal cord. The peripheral nervous system is divided according to function: The somatic nervous system controls voluntary actions, and the autonomic nervous system regulates internal processes. The autonomic nervous system is subdivided into two systems: The sympathetic nervous system governs behavior in emergency situations, and the parasympathetic nervous system regulates behavior and internal processes in routine circumstances.

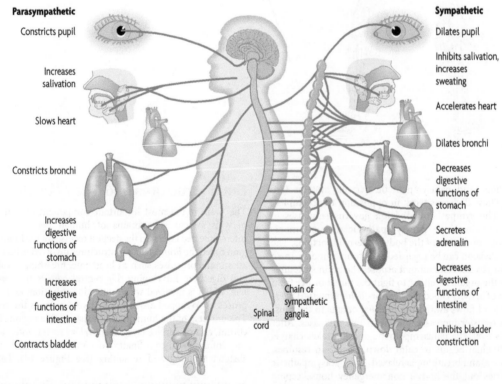

FIGURE 13 The Autonomic Nervous System

The parasympathetic nervous system, which regulates day-to-day internal processes and behavior, is shown on the left. The sympathetic nervous system, which regulates internal processes and behavior in stressful situations, is shown on the right. Note that on their way to and from the spinal cord, the nerve fibers of the sympathetic nervous system innervate, or make connections with, ganglia, which are specialized clusters of neuron chains.

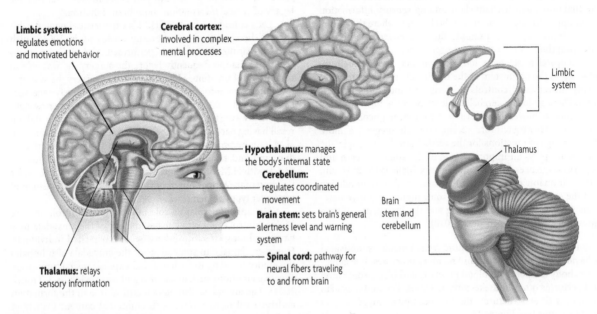

FIGURE 14 Brain Structures

The brain contains several major components, including the brain stem, cerebellum, limbic system, and cerebral cortex, all of which fit together in an intricate design.

more closely at the functions of the three major brain regions, beginning with the brain stem, thalamus, and cerebellum. 👁

The Brain Stem, Thalamus, and Cerebellum   The **brain stem** is found in all vertebrate species. It contains structures that collectively regulate the internal state of the body (see **Figure 15**). The **medulla**, located at the very top of the spinal cord, is the center for breathing, blood pressure, and the beating of the heart. Because these processes are essential for life, damage to the medulla can be fatal. Nerve fibers ascending from the body and descending from the brain cross over at the medulla, which means that the left side of the body is linked to the right side of the brain and the right side of the body is connected to the left side of the brain.

Directly above the medulla is the **pons,** which provides inputs to other structures in the brain stem and to the cerebellum (*pons* is the Latin word for *bridge*). The **reticular formation** is a dense network of nerve cells that serves as the brain's sentinel. It arouses the cerebral cortex to attend to new stimulation and keeps the brain alert even during sleep. Massive damage to this area often results in a coma.

....

👁 **Watch** the Video *The Basics: How the Brain Works Part 2* on MyPsychLab

brain stem The brain structure that regulates the body's basic life processes.

medulla The region of the brain stem that regulates breathing, waking, and heartbeat.

pons The region of the brain stem that connects the spinal cord with the brain and links parts of the brain to one another.

reticular formation The region of the brain stem that alerts the cerebral cortex to incoming sensory signals and is responsible for maintaining consciousness and awakening from sleep.

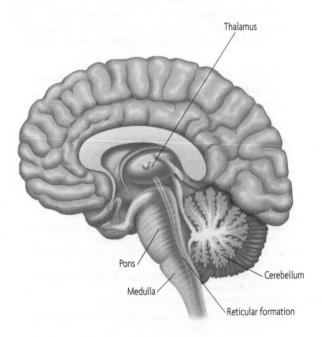

FIGURE 15 The Brain Stem, Thalamus, and Cerebellum

These structures are primarily involved in basic life processes: breathing, pulse, arousal, movement, balance, and simple processing of sensory information.

The reticular formation has long tracts of fibers that run to the **thalamus**, which channels incoming sensory information to the appropriate area of the cerebral cortex, where that information is processed. For example, the thalamus relays information from the eyes to cortical areas for vision.

Neuroscientists have long known that the **cerebellum**, attached to the brain stem at the base of the skull, coordinates bodily movements, controls posture, and maintains equilibrium. Damage to the cerebellum interrupts the flow of otherwise smooth movement, causing it to appear uncoordinated and jerky. However, more recent research suggests a more diverse range of functions for the cerebellum. For example, the cerebellum plays an important role in the ability to learn and perform sequences of body movements (Bellebaum & Daum, 2011; Timmann et al., 2010). Evidence is also accumulating that the cerebellum is involved in some higher cognitive functions such as language processing and the experience of pain (Moulton et al., 2010; Murdoch, 2010).

The Limbic System   The **limbic system** mediates motivated behaviors, emotional states, and memory processes. It also regulates body temperature, blood pressure, and blood-sugar level and performs other housekeeping activities. The limbic system comprises three structures: the hippocampus, amygdala, and hypothalamus (see **Figure 16**).

The **hippocampus**, which is the largest of the limbic system structures, plays an important role in the acquisition of memories (Wang & Morris, 2010). Considerable clinical evidence supports this conclusion, including the notable studies of a patient, H.M., perhaps psychology's most famous subject. When he was 27, H.M. underwent surgery in an attempt to reduce the frequency and severity of his epileptic seizures. During the operation, parts of his hippocampus were removed. As a result, H.M.'s memory performance was completely altered. H.M. served as a gracious participant for 50 years of

research. When he passed away in 2008, he left a remarkable legacy of critical information about brain function.

Let's consider aspects of H.M.'s experience. Long after his surgery, he continued to believe he was living in 1953, which was the year the operation was performed. If H.M. had encountered information frequently before the surgery, he was able to recall that information. However, after the surgery, he was able to acquire new information only if it was "massively repeated" (MacKay et al., 2007, p. 388). H.M. was able to acquire new skills (such as drawing figures from their mirror images) but he did not recall having participated in the training sessions. The damage to H.M.'s hippocampus also had consequences for his ability to produce and understand language (MacKay et al., 2011). Thus, research with H.M. provided extensive evidence about the broader function of the hippocampus beyond its role in the acquisition of particular types of memories.

The **amygdala** plays a role in emotional control. Because of this control function, damage to areas of the amygdala may have a calming effect on otherwise mean-spirited individuals. However, damage to some areas of the amygdala also impairs the ability to recognize when facial expressions communicate negative emotions such as sadness and fear (Adolphs & Tranel, 2004). The amygdala also plays a critical role in the formation and retrieval of memories with emotional content (Murty et al. 2011). For that reason, people with amygdala damage often have difficulty making correct decisions in situations that have an emotional component—such as responses to winning or losing money (Gupta et al., 2011).

The **hypothalamus** is one of the smallest structures in the brain, yet it plays a vital role in many of your most important daily actions. It is actually composed of several nuclei, small bundles of neurons that regulate physiological processes involved in motivated behavior (including eating, drinking, temperature regulation, and sexual arousal). The hypothalamus maintains the body's internal equilibrium, or **homeostasis**. When the body's energy reserves are low, the hypothalamus is involved in stimulating the organism to find food and to eat. When body temperature drops, the hypothalamus causes blood vessel constriction, or minute involuntary movements you commonly refer to as "shivering." The hypothalamus also regulates the activities of the endocrine system.

The Cerebrum   In humans, the **cerebrum** dwarfs the rest of the brain, occupying two thirds of its total mass. Its role is to regulate the brain's higher cognitive and emotional functions. The outer surface of the cerebrum, made up of billions of cells in a layer about a tenth of an inch thick, is called the **cerebral cortex**. The cerebrum is also divided into two almost symmetrical halves, the **cerebral hemispheres** (a later section of the chapter discusses the two hemispheres at length). The two hemispheres are connected by a thick mass of nerve fibers, collectively referred to as the **corpus callosum**. This pathway sends messages back and forth between the hemispheres.

Neuroscientists have mapped the brain to define four areas, or lobes, for each hemisphere (see **Figure 17**). The **frontal lobe**, involved in motor control and cognitive activities, such as planning, making decisions, and setting goals, is located above the lateral fissure and in front of the central sulcus.

thalamus The brain structure that relays sensory impulses to the cerebral cortex.

cerebellum The region of the brain attached to the brain stem that controls motor coordination, posture, and balance as well as the ability to learn control of body movements.

limbic system The region of the brain that regulates emotional behavior, basic motivational urges, and memory, as well as major physiological functions.

hippocampus The part of the limbic system that is involved in the acquisition of explicit memory.

amygdala The part of the limbic system that controls emotion, aggression, and the formation of emotional memory.

hypothalamus The brain structure that regulates motivated behavior (such as eating and drinking) and homeostasis.

homeostasis Constancy or equilibrium of the internal conditions of the body.

cerebrum The region of the brain that regulates higher cognitive and emotional functions.

cerebral cortex The outer surface of the cerebrum.

cerebral hemispheres The two halves of the cerebrum, connected by the corpus callosum.

corpus callosum The mass of nerve fibers connecting the two hemispheres of the cerebrum.

frontal lobe Region of the brain located above the lateral fissure and in front of the central sulcus; involved in motor control and cognitive activities.

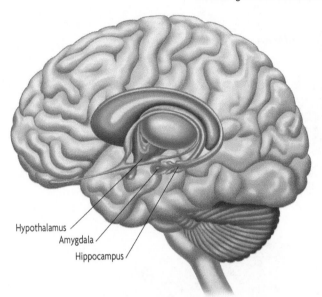

FIGURE 16 **The Limbic System**
The structures of the limbic system, which are present only in mammals, are involved in motivated behavior, emotional states, and memory processes.

Hypothalamus
Amygdala
Hippocampus

Accidents that damage the frontal lobes can have devastating effects on human action and personality. This was the location of the injury that brought about such a dramatic change in Phineas Gage (Macmillan, 2008). The frontal lobe also includes *Broca's area*, the region of the brain that Paul Broca identified from his research on patients with language disorders.

The **parietal lobe**, responsible for sensations of touch, pain, and temperature, is located directly behind the central sulcus. The **occipital lobe**, the final destination for visual information, is located at the back of the head. The **temporal lobe**, responsible for the processes of hearing, is found below the lateral fissure, on the sides of each cerebral hemisphere. The temporal lobe includes a region called **Wernicke's area**. In 1874, **Carl Wernicke** (1848–1905) discovered that patients who had damage to this region produced speech that was fluent but meaningless and had disrupted language comprehension.

It would be misleading to say that any lobe alone controls any one specific function. The structures of the brain perform their duties in concert, working smoothly as an integrated unit, similar to a symphony orchestra. Whether you are doing the dishes, solving a calculus problem, or carrying on a conversation with a friend, your brain works as a unified whole, each lobe interacting and cooperating with the others. Nevertheless, neuroscientists can identify areas of the four lobes of the cerebrum that are necessary for specific functions, such as vision,

hearing, language, and memory. When they are damaged, their functions are disrupted or lost entirely.

The actions of the body's voluntary muscles, of which there are more than 600, are controlled by the **motor cortex**, located just in front of the central sulcus in the frontal lobes. Recall that commands from one side of the brain are directed to muscles

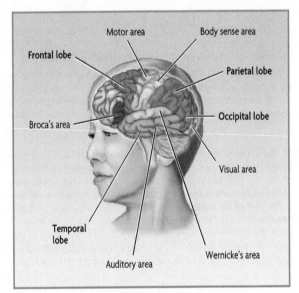

FIGURE 17 **The Cerebral Cortex**
Each of the two hemispheres of the cerebral cortex has four lobes. Different sensory and motor functions are associated with specific parts of each lobe

Lilienfeld, Scott O.; Lynn, Steven J.; Namy, Laura L.; Woolf, Nancy J, *Psychology: From Inquiry to Understanding,* 1st Edition, © 2009. Printed and electronically reproduced by permission of Pearson Education Inc., Upper Saddle River, New Jersey.

....

parietal lobe Region of the brain behind the frontal lobe and above the lateral fissure; contains somatosensory cortex.

occipital lobe Rearmost region of the brain; contains primary visual cortex.

temporal lobe Region of the brain found below the lateral fissure; contains auditory cortex.

Wernicke's area A region of the brain that allows fluent speech production and comprehension.

motor cortex The region of the cerebral cortex that controls the action of the body's voluntary muscles.

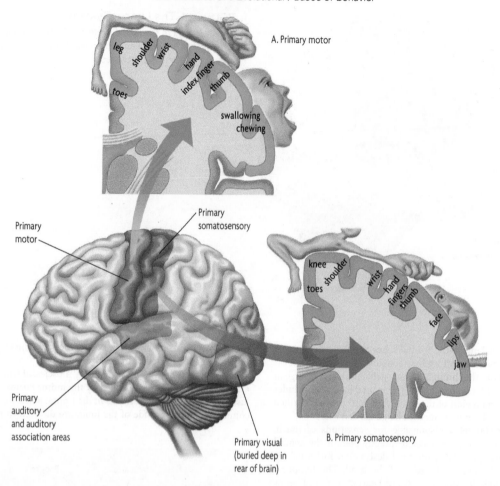

A. Primary motor

B. Primary somatosensory

FIGURE 18 Motor and Somatosensory Cortex

Different parts of the body are more or less sensitive to environmental stimulation and brain control. Sensitivity in a particular region of the body is related to the amount of space in the cerebral cortex devoted to that region. In this figure, the body is drawn so that the size of body parts is relative to the cortical space devoted to them. The larger the body part in the drawing, the greater its sensitivity to environmental stimulation and the greater the brain's control over its movement.

on the opposite side of the body. Also, muscles in the lower part of the body—for example, the toes—are controlled by neurons in the top part of the motor cortex. Muscles in the upper part of the body, such as the throat, are controlled by neurons in the lower part of the motor cortex. As you can see in **Figure 18**, the upper parts of the body receive far more detailed motor instructions than the lower parts. In fact, the two largest areas of the motor cortex are devoted to the fingers—especially the thumb—and to the muscles involved in speech. Their greater brain area

Watch the Video *The Big Picture: My Brain Made Me Do It* on MyPsychLab

somatosensory cortex The region of the parietal lobes that processes sensory input from various body areas.

auditory cortex The area of the temporal lobes that receives and processes auditory information.

visual cortex The region of the occipital lobes in which visual information is processed.

reflects the importance in human activity of manipulating objects, using tools, eating, and talking.

The **somatosensory cortex** is located just behind the central sulcus in the left and right parietal lobes. This part of the cortex processes information about temperature, touch, body position, and pain. Similar to the motor cortex, the upper part of the sensory cortex relates to the lower parts of the body, and the lower part to the upper parts of the body. Most of the area of the sensory cortex is devoted to the lips, tongue, thumb, and index fingers—the parts of the body that provide the most important sensory input (see Figure 18). And like the motor cortex, the right half of the somatosensory cortex communicates with the left side of the body, and the left half communicates with the right side of the body.

Auditory information is processed in the **auditory cortex**, which is in the two temporal lobes. The auditory cortex in each hemisphere receives information from *both* ears. Visual input is processed at the back of the brain in the **visual cortex**, located in the occipital lobes. Here the greatest area is devoted to input from the center part of the retina, at the back of the eye, the area that transmits the most detailed visual information.

Not all of the cerebral cortex is devoted to processing sensory information and commanding the muscles to action. In fact, the majority of it is involved in *interpreting* and *integrating* information. Processes such as planning and decision making are believed to occur in the **association cortex**. Association areas are distributed to several areas of the cortex—one region is labeled in Figure 18. The association cortex allows you to combine information from various sensory modalities to plan appropriate responses to stimuli in the environment.

We have now considered the many important structures in your nervous system. Recall that the discussion of the cerebrum noted that each cerebral structure is represented in both hemispheres of your brain. Let's turn now to differences between your brain's two hemispheres.

Hemispheric Lateralization

What types of information originally led researchers to suspect that the functions of the brain's two hemispheres differed? Recall that when Paul Broca carried out his autopsy on Tan, he discovered damage in the left hemisphere. As he followed up this original discovery, Broca found that other patients who showed similar disruption of their language abilities—a pattern now known as *Broca's aphasia*—also had damage on the *left* side of their brains. Damage to the same areas on the *right* side of the brain did not have the same effect. What should one conclude?

The chance to investigate hemispheric differences first arose in the context of a treatment for severe epilepsy in which

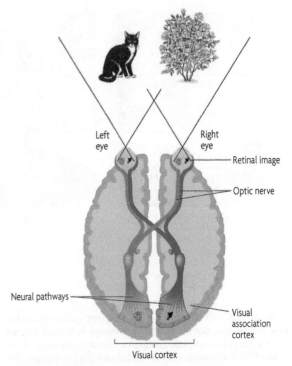

FIGURE 20 The Neural Pathways for Visual Information

The neural pathways for visual information coming from the inside portions of each eye cross from one side of the brain to the other at the corpus callosum. The pathways carrying information from the outside portions of each eye do not cross over. Severing the corpus callosum prevents information selectively displayed in the right visual field from entering the right hemisphere, and left visual field information cannot enter the left hemisphere.

surgeons sever the corpus callosum—the bundle of about 200 million nerve fibers that transfers information back and forth between the two hemispheres (see **Figure 19**). The goal of this surgery is to prevent the violent electrical activity that accompanies epileptic seizures from crossing between the hemispheres. The operation is usually successful, and a patient's subsequent behavior in most circumstances appears normal. Patients who undergo this type of surgery are often referred to as *split-brain* patients.

To test the capabilities of the separated hemispheres of epileptic patients, **Roger Sperry** (1968) and **Michael Gazzaniga** (1970) devised situations that could allow visual information to be presented separately to each hemisphere. Sperry and Gazzaniga's methodology relies on the anatomy of the visual system (see **Figure 20**). For each eye, information from the *right visual field* goes to the left hemisphere, and information from the *left visual field* goes to the right hemisphere. Ordinarily, information

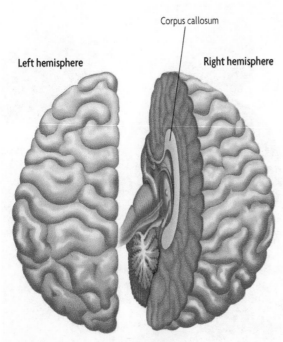

FIGURE 19 The Corpus Callosum

The corpus callosum is a massive network of nerve fibers that channels information between the two hemispheres. Severing the corpus callosum impairs this communication process.

....

association cortex The parts of the cerebral cortex in which many high-level brain processes occur.

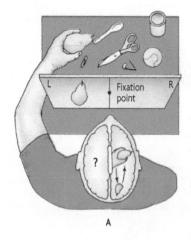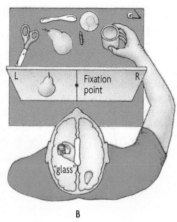

A B

FIGURE 21 Testing a Split-Brain Patient

When the split-brain patient uses his left hand to find a match to an object flashed briefly in the left visual field, he is successful because both the visual and tactile (touch) information are registered in the right hemisphere, as shown in A. Nevertheless, the patient cannot name the object, because speech is mainly a left-hemisphere function. Now consider the same patient asked to perform the same task with the right hand, as shown in B. In this case, he is unsuccessful in picking out the object by touch, because the visual information and the tactile information are processed in different hemispheres. In this test, however, the patient is able to name the object in his hand!

Zimbardo, Philip G.; Johnson, Robert L.; McCann, Vivian, *Psychology: Core Concepts*, 6th Edition, © 2009. Printed and electronically reproduced by permission of Pearson Education Inc., Upper Saddle River, New Jersey.

arriving from both hemispheres is shared very quickly across the corpus callosum. But because these pathways have been severed in split-brain patients, information presented to the right or left visual field may remain only in the left or right hemisphere (see **Figure 21**).

Because for most people speech is controlled by the left hemisphere, the left hemisphere could "talk back" to the researchers, whereas the right hemisphere could not. Communication with the right hemisphere was achieved by confronting it with manual tasks involving identification, matching, or assembly of objects—tasks that did not require the use of words. Consider the following demonstration of a split-brain subject using his left half brain to account for the activity of his left hand, which was being guided by his right half brain.

Featured Study

⊙► *A snow scene was presented to the right hemisphere and a picture of a chicken claw was simultaneously presented to the left hemisphere (Gazzaniga, 1985). The subject selected, from an array of objects, those that "went with" each of the two scenes. With his right hand, the patient pointed to a chicken head; with his left hand, he pointed to a shovel. The patient reported that the shovel was needed to clean out the chicken shed (rather than to shovel snow). Because the left brain was not privy to what the right brain "saw" due to the severed corpus callosum, it needed to explain why the left hand was pointing at a shovel when the only picture the left hemisphere was aware of seeing was a chicken claw. The left brain's cognitive system provided a theory to make sense of the behavior of different parts of its body.*

⊙► Simulate the Experiment *Hemispheric Specialization* on **MyPsychLab**

From a variety of research methods in addition to split-brain studies, we now know that, for most people, many language-related functions are *lateralized* to the left hemisphere. A function is considered lateralized when one cerebral hemisphere

plays the primary role in accomplishing that function. Speech—the ability to produce coherent spoken language—is perhaps the most highly lateralized of all functions. Neuroscientists have found that only about 5 percent of right-handers and 15 percent of left-handers have speech controlled by the right hemisphere; another 15 percent of left-handers have speech processes occurring in both sides of the brain (Rasmussen & Milner, 1977).

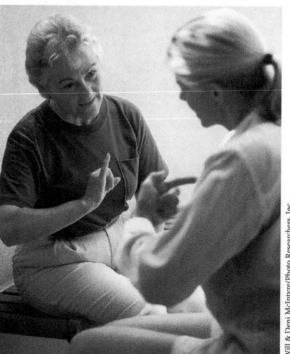

How have studies with individuals who use sign language influenced researchers' beliefs about the lateralization of brain function?

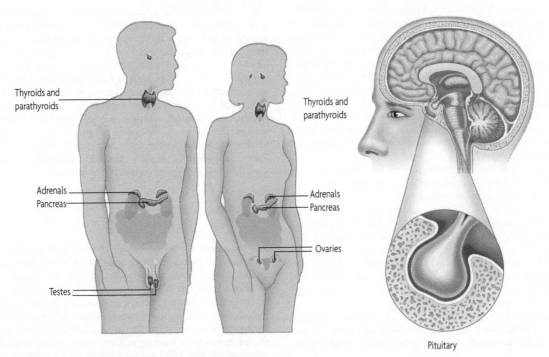

Thyroids and
parathyroids

Thyroids and
parathyroids

Adrenals
Pancreas

Adrenals
Pancreas

Ovaries

Testes

Pituitary

FIGURE 22 Endocrine Glands in Males and Females
The pituitary gland is shown at the far right; it is the master gland that regulates the glands shown at the left. The pituitary gland is under the control of the hypothalamus, an important structure in the limbic system.

For most people, therefore, speech is a left-hemisphere function. As a consequence, damage to the left side of most people's brains can cause speech disorders. What is interesting is that for users of languages like American Sign Language—which use systems of intricate hand positions and movements to convey meaning—left-brain damage is similarly disruptive (MacSweeney et al., 2008). What is lateralized, therefore, is not speech as such, but rather, the ability to produce the sequences of gestures—either vocal or manual—that encode communicative meaning.

You should not conclude that the left hemisphere is somehow better than the right hemisphere. Although the left hemisphere plays a dominant role for speech, the right hemisphere plays a dominant role for other tasks. For example, most people show greater right-hemisphere activity when they make judgments about spatial relationships and facial expressions (Badzakova-Trajkov et al., 2010). Still, it is the combined action of the right and left hemispheres that gives fullness to your experiences. For example, you might not be surprised to learn that the left hemisphere, with its greater endowment for language use, plays a key role in most forms of problem solving. However, the function of the right hemisphere becomes more apparent when problems require bursts of insight. Those individuals who show relatively greater activity in their right hemispheres are more likely to have those bursts of insight (Kounios et al., 2008).

This section reviewed the many important structures of your nervous system. Now we will consider the endocrine system, a bodily system that functions in close cooperation with the nervous system to regulate bodily functions.

The Endocrine System

The human genotype specifies a second highly complex regulatory system, the **endocrine system**, to supplement the work of the nervous system. The endocrine system is a network of glands that manufacture and secrete chemical messengers called **hormones** into the bloodstream (see **Figure 22**). Hormones are important in everyday functioning, although they are more vital at some stages of life and in some situations than others. Hormones influence body growth. They initiate, maintain, and stop development of primary and secondary sexual characteristics; influence levels of arousal and awareness; serve as the basis for mood changes; and regulate metabolism, the rate at which the body uses its energy stores. The endocrine system promotes the survival of an *organism* by helping fight infections and disease. It advances the survival of the *species* through regulation of sexual arousal, production of reproductive cells, and production of milk in nursing mothers. Thus you could not survive without an effective endocrine system.

Endocrine glands respond to the levels of chemicals in the bloodstream or are stimulated by other hormones or by nerve impulses from the brain. Hormones are then secreted into the blood and travel to distant target cells that have

....

endocrine system The network of glands that manufacture and secrete hormones into the bloodstream.

hormone One of the chemical messengers, manufactured and secreted by the endocrine glands, that regulate metabolism and influence body growth, mood, and sexual characteristics.

specific receptors; hormones exert their influence on the body's program of chemical regulation only at the places that are genetically predetermined to respond to them. In influencing diverse, but specific, target organs or tissue, hormones regulate an enormous range of biochemical processes. This multiple-action communication system allows for control of slow continuous processes such as maintenance of blood-sugar levels and calcium levels, metabolism of carbohydrates, and general body growth. But what happens during crises? The endocrine system also releases the hormone adrenaline into the bloodstream; adrenaline energizes your body so that you can respond quickly to challenges.

As you saw earlier, the brain structure known as the *hypothalamus* serves as a relay station between the endocrine system and the central nervous system. Specialized cells in the hypothalamus receive messages from other brain cells, commanding it to release a number of different hormones to the pituitary gland, where they either stimulate or inhibit the release of other hormones. Hormones are produced in several different regions of the body. These "factories" make a variety of hormones, each of which regulates different bodily processes, as outlined in **Table 1**. Let's examine the most significant of these processes.

The **pituitary gland** is often called the master gland, because it produces about 10 different kinds of hormones that influence the secretions of all the other endocrine glands, as well as a hormone that influences growth. The absence of this growth hormone results in dwarfism; its excess results in gigantic growth. In males, pituitary secretions activate the testes to secrete **testosterone**, which stimulates production of sperm. The pituitary gland is also involved in the development of male secondary sexual characteristics, such as facial hair, voice change, and physical maturation. Testosterone may even increase aggression and sexual desire. In females, a pituitary hormone stimulates production of **estrogen**, which is essential to the hormonal chain reaction that triggers the release of ova from a woman's ovaries, making her fertile. Certain birth control pills work by blocking the mechanism in the pituitary gland that controls this hormone flow, thus preventing the ova from being released.

Plasticity and Neurogenesis: Our Changing Brains

You now have a good basic idea of your nervous system at work: At all times, millions of neurons are communicating to do the essential work of your body and mind. What makes the brain even more interesting, however, is one consequence of all that neural communication: The brain itself changes over time. Do you want to take a moment to change your brain? Go back a few pages and memorize the definition of *action potential*. If you are successful at learning that definition—or any other new information—you will have brought about a modification of your brain. Researchers refer to changes in the performance of the brain as **plasticity**. A good deal of research in neuroscience focuses on the physical bases for plasticity. For example, researchers examine how learning arises from the formation of new synapses or from changes in communication across existing synapses (Miyashita et al., 2008). ◉

Because brain plasticity depends on life experiences, you won't be surprised to learn that brains show the impact of different environments and activities. One line of research, pioneered by **Mark Rosenzweig**, demonstrated the consequences for rats of being raised in impoverished or enriched environments (for reviews, see Rosenzweig, 1996, 1999). Early research demonstrated an advantage for young animals: The average cortex of rats reared in the enriched environments was heavier and thicker—positive attributes—than that of their impoverished littermates. Researchers have now demonstrated that environmental enrichment continues to have an impact on the brains of adult animals.

Table 1 • Major Endocrine Glands and the Functions of the Hormones They Produce

These Glands:	Produce Hormones That Regulate:
Hypothalamus	Release of pituitary hormones
Anterior pituitary	Testes and ovaries
	Breast milk production
	Metabolism
	Reactions to stress
Posterior pituitary	Water conservation
	Breast milk excretion
	Uterus contraction
Thyroid	Metabolism
	Growth and development
Parathyroid	Calcium levels
Gut	Digestion
Pancreas	Glucose metabolism
Adrenals	Fight-or-flight responses
	Metabolism
	Sexual desire in women
Ovaries	Development of female sexual traits
	Ova production
Testes	Development of male sexual traits
	Sperm production
	Sexual desire in men

....

◉ Watch the Video *Brain* on MyPsychLab

pituitary gland Located in the brain, the gland that secretes growth hormone and influences the secretion of hormones by other endocrine glands.

testosterone The male sex hormone, secreted by the testes, that stimulates production of sperm and is also responsible for the development of male secondary sex characteristics.

estrogen The female sex hormone, produced by the ovaries, that is responsible for the release of eggs from the ovaries as well as for the development and maintenance of female reproductive structures and secondary sex characteristics.

plasticity Changes in the performance of the brain; may involve the creation of new synapses or changes in the function of existing synapses.

Featured Study

At the age of one month, Long-Evans female rats were placed in either standard laboratory cages or an enriched environment (filled with a variety of objects, including tunnels, toys, and chains) (Harati et al., 2011). At 24 months (which counts as old age for rats), the rats underwent tests of spatial memory and attention. The rats that had been raised in enriched environments outperformed the rats from the standard environments on both types of tasks. The researchers also carried out analyses on the rats' brains. They discovered that the rats that had been raised in the enriched environments had more neurons in parts of the brain that were relevant to the tasks. Those brain results suggested that experience in the enriched environments had allowed for preservation or reduced loss of brain neurons.

With brain-imaging techniques, it is possible to measure very specific brain differences related to individuals' life experiences. Consider those musicians who play the violin. They are required to control the fingers of their left hands with an extremely delicate touch. If you refer back to Figure 18, you'll see that a good deal of sensory cortex is devoted to the fingers. Brain scans reveal that the representation of fingers of the left hand is even more enhanced for violin players, as compared to nonplayers (Elbert et al., 1995). No such increase is found for fingers of the right hand, which do not have as great a sensory role in violin playing. The extra representation of the left fingers was greatest for violinists who took up the instrument before age 12. The *Critical Thinking in Your Life* box explains how your cultural experience modifies your brain.

One important aspect of research on plasticity concerns circumstances in which humans or animals have sustained injuries to the brain or spinal cord, through strokes, degenerative diseases, or accidents. A good deal of clinical evidence confirms that the brain is sometimes able to heal itself. For example, patients who suffer from strokes that cause disruptions in language often recover over time. In some instances, the damaged brain areas themselves have enough lingering function that recovery is possible; in other cases other brain areas take over the functions of those that were damaged (Turkeltaub et al., 2011). Researchers have also begun to develop techniques to help the brain along in the healing process. In recent years, attention has focused on *stem cells*—unspecialized cells that, under appropriate conditions, can be prompted to function as new neurons (Li et al., 2008). Researchers hope that stem cells may ultimately provide a means to replace damaged tissue in the nervous system with new neural growth. Because the most flexible stem cells come from embryos and aborted fetuses, stem cell research has been subject to political controversy. Still, researchers believe that stem cell research could lead to cures for paralysis and other serious malfunctions in the nervous system. For that reason, the scientific community is highly motivated to discover ways to continue research within accepted societal norms.

Research on brain repair has accelerated in recent years in the face of important new data suggesting that **neurogenesis**—the production of new brain cells from naturally occurring stem cells—occurs in the brains of adult mammals, including humans (Leuner & Gould, 2010). For nearly 100 years, neuroscientists believed that the adult brains of mammals had their full supply of neurons—all that could happen over the adult years was that neurons could die out. However, the new data have challenged that view. Recall, for example, that the hippocampus is an important structure for the formation of certain types of memories. Now that researchers have documented neurogenesis in the adult hippocampus, they are trying to understand how newly born neurons provide a resource for the acquisition of new memories across the life span (Kempermann, 2008).

In this chapter, we have taken a brief peek at the marvelous 3-pound universe that is your brain. It is one thing to recognize that the brain controls behavior and your mental processes but quite another to understand how the brain serves all those functions. Neuroscientists are engaged in the fascinating quest to understand the interplay among brain, behavior, and environment. You now have the type of background that will allow you to appreciate new knowledge as it unfolds.

Stop and Review

① What are the advantages of fMRI over other brain-imaging techniques?
② What are the two major divisions of the autonomic nervous system?
③ What are some of the major functions of the amygdala?
④ For what activities do most people show more activity in the right hemisphere?
⑤ Why is the pituitary gland often called the master gland?
⑥ What is neurogenesis?

✓ [Study and Review on MyPsychLab

....

✷ Explore the Concept *Virtual Brain: Brain Damage and Neuroplasticity* on MyPsychLab

neurogenesis The creation of new neurons.

Critical Thinking in Your Life

HOW DOES CULTURE BECOME "EMBRAINED"?

You have probably had many opportunities to appreciate the impact of culture on people's behavior. Those cultural differences, of course, emerge from the activity of each individual's brain. In fact, researchers have suggested that, over the course of development, an individual's culture becomes "embrained" (Kitayama & Uskul, 2011). Let's explore that idea.

The process of embrainment begins as individuals are raised in an environment in which a particular set of values is transmitted. Those values have an impact on how people respond to a wide range of situations. For example, a good deal of cross-cultural research has demonstrated that people from Western cultures (such as the United States) most often conceptualize themselves as independent actors whereas people from Eastern cultures (such as Japan, China, and India) most often conceptualize themselves as being part of a larger group. This difference in conceptualization has a number of consequences for behavior.

Suppose, for example, you are given an ordinary coffee mug with your school logo. How painful would it be for you to part with it? Research suggests that the answer will depend on the culture in which you were nurtured (Maddux et al., 2010). For people from Western cultures, possessions become, in a sense, part of the self. Therefore, giving them up is like giving part of the self away. People from Eastern cultures don't have that relationship with their possessions. As such, they should experience less distress when they think about giving up a possession.

To obtain a measure of how much individuals valued a coffee mug, the researchers gave some experimental participants mugs as gifts and asked them how much someone would need to offer them before they would sell it. Other participants were shown the mugs and simply asked how much they would pay for them. Sellers from Western cultures wanted $3.24 more than what buyers thought the mug was worth. Sellers from Eastern cultures wanted just $1.60 more. This difference illustrates the way in which Western participants more highly value their possessions.

Think about all the moments in your life in which you came to acquire or give up possessions. In each case, cultural values prompt you to think about those possessions in a particular way. As those cases accumulate over time, your brain engages in repeated patterns of neural activity to execute your responses. When you read about brain plasticity, you probably weren't surprised that extensive experience with the violin changes players' brains (Elbert et al., 1995). The violinists' brains grow more efficient at carrying out the highly practiced activities. Violin playing becomes embrained. Similarly, as people repeat the behavioral responses that a culture makes available, the brain grows more efficient at producing those responses. Culture has become embrained.

- How might brain imaging techniques help you demonstrate that culture has become embrained?
- What might happen when someone grows up in a multicultural family?

Recapping Main Points

Heredity and Behavior

- Species originate and change over time because of natural selection.
- In the evolution of humans, bipedalism and encephalization were responsible for subsequent advances, including language and culture.
- The basic unit of heredity is the gene. Genes interact with environments to yield phenotypic traits.

The Nervous System in Action

- The neuron, the basic unit of the nervous system, receives, processes, and relays information to other cells, glands, and muscles.
- Neurons relay information from the dendrites through the cell body (soma) to the axon to the terminal buttons.

- Sensory neurons receive messages from specialized receptor cells and send them toward the CNS. Motor neurons direct messages from the CNS to muscles and glands. Interneurons relay information from sensory neurons to other interneurons or to motor neurons. Mirror neurons respond when an individual observes another individual performing a motor action.
- Once the summation of inputs to a neuron exceeds a specific threshold, an action potential is sent along the axon to the terminal buttons.
- All-or-none action potentials are created when the opening of ion channels allows an exchange of ions across the cell membrane.
- Neurotransmitters are released into the synaptic gap between neurons. Once they diffuse across the gap,

they lodge in the receptor molecules of the postsynaptic membrane.

- Whether these neurotransmitters excite or inhibit the membrane depends on the nature of the receptor molecule.

Biology and Behavior

- Neuroscientists use several methods to research the relation between brain and behavior: studying brain-damaged patients, producing lesions at specific brain sites, electrically stimulating the brain, recording brain activity, and imaging the brain with computerized devices.
- The brain and the spinal cord make up the central nervous system (CNS).
- The peripheral nervous system (PNS) is composed of all neurons connecting the CNS to the body. The PNS consists of the somatic nervous system, which regulates the body's skeletal muscles, and the autonomic nervous system (ANS), which regulates life-support processes.

- The brain consists of three integrated layers: the brain stem, limbic system, and cerebrum.
- The brain stem is responsible for breathing, digestion, and heart rate.
- The limbic system is involved in long-term memory, aggression, eating, drinking, and sexual behavior.
- The cerebrum controls higher mental functions.
- Some functions are lateralized to one hemisphere of the brain. For example, most individuals have speech localized in the left hemisphere.
- Although the two hemispheres of the brain work smoothly in concert, they play relatively greater roles for different tasks.
- The endocrine system produces and secretes hormones into the bloodstream.
- Hormones help regulate growth, primary and secondary sexual characteristics, metabolism, digestion, and arousal.
- New cell growth and life experiences reshape the brain after birth.

KEY TERMS

action potential
all-or-none law
amygdala
association cortex
auditory cortex
autonomic nervous system (ANS)
axon
brain stem
Broca's area
central nervous system (CNS)
cerebellum
cerebral cortex
cerebral hemispheres
cerebrum
computerized axial tomography (CT or CAT)
corpus callosum
dendrite
DNA (deoxyribonucleic acid)
electroencephalogram (EEG)
endocrine system
estrogen
evolutionary psychology
excitatory input
frontal lobe
functional MRI (fMRI)
gene
genetics
genome

genotype
glia
heredity
heritability
hippocampus
homeostasis
hormone
human behavior genetics
hypothalamus
inhibitory input
interneuron
ion channel
lesion
limbic system
magnetic resonance imaging (MRI)
medulla
mirror neuron
motor cortex
motor neuron
myelin sheath
natural selection
neurogenesis
neuromodulator
neuron
neuroscience
neurotransmitter
occipital lobe
parasympathetic division
parietal lobe

peripheral nervous system (PNS)
phenotype
pituitary gland
plasticity
polygenic trait
pons
positron emission tomography (PET) scan
refractory period
repetitive transcranial magnetic stimulation (rTMS)
resting potential
reticular formation
sensory neuron
sex chromosome
sociobiology
soma
somatic nervous system
somatosensory cortex
sympathetic division
synapse
synaptic transmission
temporal lobe
terminal button
testosterone
thalamus
visual cortex
Wernicke's area

Practice Test

✓•—Study and Review on MyPsychLab

1. When Peter and Rosemary Grant studied several species of Darwin's finches, they discovered that major climate changes affected which populations of finches survived. This is an example of
   a. heritability.
   b. the all-or-none law.
   c. natural selection.
   d. nature versus nurture.

2. Sharon is involved in a project in which she observes the behaviors of young children. She is most able to directly observe their
   a. genotypes.
   b. phenotypes.
   c. chromosomes.
   d. DNA.

3. Suppose you carried out a study to assess whether there is a genetic component to "sense of humor." To conclude that genetics plays a role, you would want to find that
   a. DZ twins are more similar in their sense of humor than MZ twins.
   b. DZ twins always have better senses of humor than MZ twins.
   c. MZ twins always have better senses of humor than DZ twins.
   d. MZ twins are more similar in their sense of humor than DZ twins.

4. One of the jobs of _____ is to receive stimulation from other neurons.
   a. axons
   b. terminal buttons
   c. synapses
   d. dendrites

5. After Jonas withdraws money from the bank, he has to wait two minutes before his card will work again. This sounds a lot like the _____ in neural transmission.
   a. all-or-none law
   b. action potential
   c. refractory period
   d. ion channels

6. Wilma is creating an illustration of neural transmission. She leaves a small gap between a terminal button on one neuron and the dendrite of the next. She should label that gap the
   a. ion channel.
   b. glia.
   c. node of Ranvier.
   d. synapse.

7. Bea has decided to undergo an acupuncture treatment to help her with her back pain. You explain that researchers believe that acupuncture leads to the release of _____ in the brain.
   a. GABA
   b. acetylcholine
   c. endorphins
   d. dopamine

8. Researchers suggest that culture becomes embrained because
   a. people in different cultures do not face the same problems.
   b. people's cultural values lead them to repeat the same patterns of neural responses.
   c. people from different cultures cannot produce the same neural responses.
   d. people's behavioral responses can only be predicted from cultural values.

9. Which technique allows researchers to create reversible "lesions"?
   a. fMRI
   b. rTMS
   c. PET scans
   d. EEG

10. The _____ nervous system processes incoming neural messages and sends commands to different parts of the body.
   a. central
   b. autonomic
   c. somatic
   d. peripheral

11. After he experienced damage to his _____, H.M. had difficulties acquiring new information.
   a. reticular formation
   b. thalamus
   c. hippocampus
   d. Broca's area

12. After Jeff inhales oxytocin through a nasal spray, you expect him to display _____ trust toward Mona due, in part, to _____ activity in his amygdala.
   a. more; reduced
   b. more; increased
   c. less; reduced
   d. less; increased

13. As you are chatting with Tejus, you noticed that she is right-handed. You think that it's most likely that her ability to produce speech is controlled by
   a. her left hemisphere.
   b. her right hemisphere.
   c. both the left and right hemispheres.
   d. neither the left nor the right hemisphere.

14. Which brain structure serves as a relay station between the brain and the endocrine system?
   a. the hippocampus
   b. the hypothalamus
   c. the pons
   d. the amygdala

15. Brain-imaging techniques reveal that the brain representation of the fingers of the left hand is enhanced for people who play the violin versus nonplayers. This result provides an example of
   a. neurogenesis.
   b. heritability.
   c. lateralization.
   d. brain plasticity.

ESSAY QUESTIONS

1. What important contrasts exist between research in human behavior genetics and research in evolutionary psychology?

2. Why does a neuron's behavior depend on the balance of excitatory and inhibitory inputs it receives?

3. What does research on enriched environments suggest about brain plasticity?

Stop and Review Answers

Stop and Review (Heredity and Behavior)

1. The Grants observed that, as a result of changes in the environment, sometimes big-beaked finches were able to survive and reproduce, whereas at other times small-beaked finches were able to survive and reproduce.
2. The genotype is the underlying genetic material that helps determine the phenotype, which is the observable characteristics of an organism.
3. Two critical advances were bipedalism and encephalization.
4. Heritability is a measure of the relative influence of genetics in determining an organism's constellation of traits and behaviors.

Stop and Review (The Nervous System in Action)

1. In general, the dendrites receive incoming signals. The soma integrates information from the many dendrites and passes that information along to the axon.
2. The all-or-none law suggests that, once the threshold for firing has been reached, the strength of an action potential is constant.
3. Neurotransmitters are released into synapses when synaptic vesicles rupture; the neurotransmitters then bind to receptor molecules on the receiving neuron.
4. GABA is the brain's most common inhibitory neurotransmitter.

Stop and Review (Biology and Behavior)

1. fMRI allows researchers to make claims about both structures and functions.
2. The autonomic nervous system is divided into the sympathetic and parasympathetic divisions.
3. The amygdala plays a role in emotional control and the formation of emotional memories.
4. Most people show greater right-hemisphere activity when they make judgments about spatial relationships and facial expressions.
5. The pituitary gland produces hormones that influence the activity of all the other endocrine glands.
6. Neurogenesis is the creation of new neurons.

Practice Test Answers

1. c	5. c	9. b	13. a
2. b	6. d	10. a	14. b
3. d	7. c	11. c	15. d
4. d	8. b	12. a	

References

Badzakova-Trajov, G., Häberling, I. S., Roberts, R. P., & Corballis, M. C. (2010). Cerebral asymmetries: Complementary and independent processes. *PLoS ONE, 5,* e9862.

Bartz, J. A., Zaki, J., Bolger, N., & Ochsner, K. N. (2011). Social effects of oxytocin in humans: Context and person matter. *Trends in Cognitive Sciences, 15,* 301–309.

Baumgartner, T., Heinrichs, M., Vonlanthen, A., Fischbacher, U., & Fehr, E. (2008). Oxytocin shapes the neural circuitry of trust and trust adaptation in humans. *Neuron, 58,* 639–650.

Bellebaum, C., & Daum, I. (2011). Mechanisms of cerebellar involvement in associate learning. *Cortex, 47,* 128–136.

Bustillo, J. R., Chen, H., Gasparovic, C., Mullins, P., Caprihan, A., Qualls, C., Apfeldorf, W., Lauriello, J., & Posse, S. (2011). Glutamate as a marker of cognitive function in schizophrenia: A proton spectroscopic imaging study at 4 Tesla. *Biological Psychiatry, 69,* 19–27.

Cappelletti, M., Fregni, F., Shapiro, K., Pascual-Leone, A., & Caramazza, A. (2008). Processing nouns and verbs in the left frontal cortex: A transcranial magnetic stimulation study. *Journal of Cognitive Neuroscience, 20,* 707–720.

Carlson, E. A. (2004). *Mendel's legacy: The origin of classical genetics.* Cold Spring Harbor, NY: Cold Spring Harbor Laboratory Press.

Clamp, M., Fry, B., Kamal, M., Xie, X., Cuff, J., Lin, M. F., Kellis, M., Lindblad-Toh, K., & Lander, E. S. (2007). Distinguishing protein-coding and noncoding genes in the human genome. *PNAS, 104,* 19428–19433.

Cornelis, M. C., Monda, K. L., Yu, K., Paynter, N., Azzato, E. M., Bennett, S. N., Berndt, S. I., Boerwinkle, E., Chanock, S., Chatterjee, N., Couper, D., Curhan, G., Heiss, G., Hu, F. B., Hunter, D. J., Jacobs, K., Jensen, M. K., Kraft, P., Landi, M. T., Nettleton, J. A., Purdue, M. P., Rajaraman, P., Rimm, E. B., Rose, L. M., Rothman, N., Silverman, D., Stolzenberg-Solomon, R., Subar, A., Yeager, M., Chasman, D. I., van Dam, R. M., & Caporaso, N. E. (2011). Genome-wide meta-analysis identifies regions on 7p21 (*AHR*) and 15q24 (*CYP1A2*) as determinants of habitual caffeine consumption. *PLoS Genetics, 7,* e10002033.

Craig, L. A., Hong, N. S., & McDonald, R. J. (2011). Revisiting the cholinergic hypothesis in the development of Alzheimer's disease. *Neuroscience and Biobehavioral Reviews, 35,* 1397–1409.

Croarkin, P. E., Levinson, A. J., & Daskalakis, Z. J. (2011). Evidence for GABA-ergic inhibitory deficits in major depressive disorder. *Neuroscience and Biobehavioral Reviews, 35,* 818–825.

Elbert, T., Pantev, C., Wienbruch, C., Rockstroh, B., & Taub, E. (1995). Increased cortical representation of the fingers of the left hand in string players. *Science, 270,* 305–307.

Fantegrossi, W. E., Murnane, K. S., & Reissig, C. J. (2008). The behavioral pharmacology of hallucinogens. *Biochemical Pharmacology, 75,* 17–33.

Fitzpatrick, B. M., Fordyce, J. A., & Gavrilets, S. (2008). What, if anything, is sympatric speciation? *Journal of Evolutionary Biology, 21,* 1452–1459.

Gazzaniga, M. (1970). *The bisected brain.* New York: Appleton-Century-Crofts.

Gazzaniga, M. S. (1985). *The social brain.* New York: Basic Books.

Gibbons, A. (2007). Food for thought. *Science, 316,* 1558–1560.

Goddard, A. W., Ball, S. G., Martinez, J., Robinson, M. J., Yang, C. R., Russell, J. M., & Shekhar, A. (2010). Current perspectives of the roles of the central norepinephrine system in anxiety and depression. *Depression and Anxiety, 27,* 339–250.

Grant, P. R., & Grant, B. R. (2006). Evolution of character displacement in Darwin's finches. *Science, 313,* 224–226.

Gupta, R. Koscik, T. R., Bechara, A., & Tranel, D. (2011). The amygdala and decision-making. *Neuropsychologia, 49,* 760–765.

Hajcak, G., & Olvet, D. M. (2008). The persistence of attention to emotion: Brain potentials during and after picture presentation. *Emotion, 8,* 250–255.

Han, J.-S. (2011). Acupuncture analgesia: Areas of consensus and controversy. *Pain, 152,* S41–S48.

Harati, H., Majchrzak, M., Cosquer, B., Galani, R., Kelche, C., Cassel, J.-C., & Barbelivien, A. (2011). Attention and memory in aged rats: Impact of lifelong environmental enrichment. *Neurobiology of Aging, 32,* 718–736.

Harlow, J. M. (1868). Recovery from the passage of an iron bar through the head. *Publications of the Massachusetts Medical Society, 2,* 327–347.

Hendry, A. P., Huber, S. K., De León, L. F., Herrel, A., & Podos, J. (2009). Disruptive selection in a bimodal population of Darwin's finches. *Proceedings of the Royal Society B, 276,* 753–759.

Henneberger, C., & Rusakov, D. A. (2010). Synaptic plasticity and Ca^{21} signaling in astrocytes. *Neuron Glia Biology, 6,* 141–146.

Hoffmann, A. A., & Willi, Y. (2008). Detecting genetic responses to environmental change. *Nature Reviews Genetics, 9,* 421–432.

IsHak, W. W., Kahloon, M., & Fakhry, H. (2011). Oxytocin role in enhancing well-being: A literature review. *Journal of Affective Disorders, 130,* 1–9.

Kalueff, A. V., & Nutt, D. J. (2007). Role of GABA in anxiety and depression. *Depression and Anxiety, 24,* 495–517.

Káradóttir, R., Hamilton, N. B., Bakiri, Y., & Attwell, D. (2008). Spiking and nonspiking classes of oligodendrocyte precursor glia in CNS white matter. *Nature Neuroscience, 11,* 450–456.

Keller, M. C., & Miller, G. (2006). Resolving the paradox of common, harmful, an heritable mental disorders: Which evolutionary genetic models work best? *Behavioral and Brain Sciences, 29,* 385–452.

Kempermann, G. (2008). The neurogenic reserve hypothesis: What is adult hippocampus neurogenesis good for? *Trends in Neurosciences, 31,* 163–169.

Keshavan, M. S., Nasrallah, H. A., & Tandon, R. (2011). Schizophrenia, "Just the facts" 6. Moving ahead with the schizophrenia concept: From the elephant to the mouse. *Schizophrenia Research, 127,* 3–13.

Kettenmann, H., & Verkhratsky, A. (2008). Neuroglia: The 150 years after. *Trends in Neuroscience, 31,* 653–659.

Kim, Y.-K. (Ed.) (2009). *Handbook of behavior genetics.* New York: Springer.

Kempermann, G. (2008). The neurogenic reserve hypothesis: What is adult hippocampus neurogenesis good for? *Trends in Neurosciences, 31,* 163–169.

Kitayama, S., & Uskul, A. K. (2011). Culture, mind, and the brain: Current evidence and future directions. *Annual Review of Psychology, 62,* 419–449.

Kochanska, G., Kim, S., Barry, R. A., & Philibert, R. A. (2011). Children's genotypes interact with maternal responsive care in predicting children's competence: Diathesis-stress or differential susceptibility? *Development and Psychopathology, 23,* 605–616.

Kounios, J., Fleck, J. I., Green, D. L., Payne, L., Stevenson, J. L., Bowdend, E. M., Jung-Beeman, M. (2008). The origins of insight in resting-state brain activity. *Neuropsychologia, 46,* 281–291.

Lander, E. S., & Weinberg, R. A. (2000). Genomics: Journey to the center of biology. *Science, 287,* 1777–1782.

Leuner, B., & Gould, E. (2010). Structural plasticity and hippocampal function. *Annual Review of Psychology, 61,* 111–140.

Li, J.-Y., Christophersen, M. S., Hall, V., Soulet, D., & Brundin, P. (2008). Critical issues of clinical human embryonic stem cell therapy for brain repair. *Trends in Neurosciences, 31,* 146–153.

MacKay, D. G., James, L. E., Taylor, J. K., & Marian, D. E. (2007). Amnesic H.M. exhibits parallel deficits and sparing in language and memory: Systems versus binding theory accounts. *Language and Cognitive Processes, 22,* 377–452.

Macmillan, M. (2008). Phineas Gage—Unravelling the myth. *Psychologist, 21,* 828–831.

MacSweeney, M., Capek, C. M., Campbell, R., & Woll, B. (2008). The signing brain: The neurobiology of sign language. *Trends in Cognitive Sciences, 12,* 432–440.

Maddux, W. W., Yang, H., Falk, C., Adam, H., Adair, W., Endo, Y., Carmon, Z., & Heine, S. J. (2010). For whom is parting with possessions more painful? Cultural differences in the endowment effect. *Psychological Science, 21,* 1910–1917.

Markou, A. (2007). Metabotropic glutamate receptor antagonists: Novel therapeutics for nicotine dependence and depression? *Biological Psychiatry, 61,* 17–22.

Miyashita, T., Kubik, S., Lewandowski, G., & Guzowski, J. F. (2008). Networks of neurons, networks of genes: An integrated view of memory consolidation. *Neurobiology of Learning and Memory, 89,* 269–284.

Morgado-Bernal, I. (2011). Learning and memory consolidation: Linking molecular and behavioral data. *Neuroscience, 176,* 12–19.

Moulton, E. A., Schmahmann, J. D., Becerra, L., & Borsook, D. (2010). The cerebellum and pain: Passive integrator or active participator? *Brain Research Reviews, 65,* 14–27.

Murdoch, B. E. (2010). The cerebellum and language: Historical perspective and review. *Cortex, 46,* 858–868.

Murty, V. P., Ritchey, M., Adcock, R. A., & LaBar, K. S. (2011). Reprint of: fMRI studies of successful emotional memory encoding: A quantitative meta-analysis. *Neuropsychologia, 49,* 695–705.

Myers, K. M., Carlezon, W. A., Jr., & Davis, M. (2011). Glutamate receptors in extinction and extinction-based therapies for psychiatric illness. *Neuropsychopharmacology, 36,* 274–293.

Pollo, A., Carlino, E., & Benedetti, F. (2011). Placebo mechanisms across different conditions: From the clinical setting to physical performance. *Philosophical Transactions of the Royal Society B, 366,* 1790–1798.

Ramachandran, V. S. (2011). *The tell-tale brain.* New York: Norton.

Rasmussen, T., & Milner, B. (1977). The role of early left-brain injury in determining lateralization of cerebral speech functions. *Annals of the New York Academy of Sciences, 299,* 355–369.

Rosenzweig, M. R. (1996). Aspects of the search for neural mechanisms of memory. *Annual Review of Psychology, 47,* 1–32.

Rosenzweig, M. R. (1999). Effects of differential experience on brain and cognition throughout the life span. In S. H. Broman & J. M. Fletcher (Eds.), *The changing nervous system: Neurobehavioral consequences of early brain disorders* (pp. 25–50). New York: Oxford University Press.

Sandrini, M., Umiltà, C., & Rusconi, E. (2011). The use of transcranial magnetic stimulation in cognitive neuroscience: A new synthesis of methodological issues. *Neuroscience and Biobehavioral Reviews, 35,* 516–536.

Shaw, K. L., & Mullen, S. P. (2011). Genes versus phenotypes in the study of speciation. *Genetica, 139,* 649–661.

Sherwood, C. C., Subiaul, F., & Zawidzki, T. W. (2008). A natural history of the human mind: Tracing evolutionary changes in brain and cognition. *Journal of Anatomy, 212,* 426–454.

Silva, S., Martins, Y., Matias, A., & Blickstein, I. (2011). Why are monozygotic twins different? *Journal of Perinatal Medicine, 39,* 195–202.

Sinigaglia, C., & Rizolatti, G. (2011). Through the looking glass: Self and others. *Consciousness and Cognition, 20,* 64–74.

Sperry, R. W. (1968). Mental unity following surgical disconnection of the cerebral hemispheres. *The Harvey Lectures,* Series 62. New York: Academic Press.

Spiers, H. J., & Maguire, E. A. (2007). Decoding human brain activity during real-world experiences. *Trends in Cognitive Sciences, 11,* 356–365.

Sulem, P., Gudbjartsson, D. F., Geller, F., Prokopenko, Feenstra, B., Aben, K. K. H., Franke, B., den Heijer, M., Kovacs, P., Stumvoll, M., Mägi, R., Yanek, L. R., Becker, L. C., Boyd, H. A., Stacey, S. N., Walters, G. B., Jonasdottir, A., Thorleifsson, G., Holm, H., Gudjonsson, S. A., Rafnar, T., Björnsdottir, G., Becker, D. M., Melbye, M., Kong, A., Tönjes, A., Thorgeirsson, T., Thorsteinsdottir, U., Kiemeney, L. A., & Stefansson, K. (2011). Sequence variants at CYP1A1–CYP1A2 and AHR associate with coffee consumption. *Human Molecular Genetics, 20,* 2071–2077.

Thorpe, S. K. S., Holder, R. L., & Crompton, R. H. (2007). Origin of human bipedalism as an adaptation for locomotion on flexible branches. *Science, 316,* 1328–1331.

Timmann, D., Drepper, J., Frings, M., Maschke, M., Richter, S., Gerwig, M., & Kolb, F. P. (2010). The human cerebellum contributes to motor, emotional and cognitive associative learning. A review. *Cortex, 46,* 845–857.

Turkeltaub, P. E., Messing, S., Norise, C., & Hamilton, R. H. (2011). Are networks for residual language function and recovery consistent across aphasic patients? *Neurology, 76,* 1726–1734.

Vink, J. M., Staphorsius, A. S., & Boomsma, D. I. (2009). A genetic analysis of coffee consumption in a sample of Dutch twins. *Twin Research and Human Genetics, 12,* 127–131.

Wang, S.-H., & Morris, R. G. M. (2010). Hippocampal-neocortical interactions in memory formation, consolidation, and reconsolidation. *Annual Review of Psychology, 61,* 49–79.

Wilkinson, S. (2010). *Choosing tomorrow's children: The ethics of selective reproduction.* Oxford: Oxford University Press.

Wu, G. F., & Alvarez, E. (2011). The immunopathophysiology of multiple sclerosis. *Neurologic Clinics, 29,* 257–278.

Memory

James Hardy/Altopress/Newscom

From Chapter 7 of *Psychology and Life*, 20th Edition. Richard J. Gerrig. Copyright © 2013 by Pearson Education, Inc.
All rights reserved.

As you begin this chapter on memory processes, please take a moment to call to mind your own earliest memory. How long ago did the memory originate? How vivid a scene do you recall? Has your memory been influenced by other people's recollections of the same event?

Now, a slightly different exercise. Please imagine what it would be like if you suddenly had no memory of your past—of the people you have known or of events that have happened to you. You wouldn't remember your best friend's face, or your 10th birthday, or your senior prom. Without such time anchors, how would you maintain a sense of who you are—of your self-identity? Or suppose you lost the ability to form any new memories. What would happen to your most recent experiences? Could you follow a conversation or untangle the plot of a TV show? Everything would vanish, as if events had never existed, as if you had never had any thoughts in mind. 👁

If you have never given much thought to your memory, it's probably because it tends to do its job reasonably well—you take it for granted, alongside other bodily processes, like digestion or breathing. But as with stomachaches or allergies, the times you notice your memory are likely to be the times when something goes wrong: You forget your car keys, an important date, lines in a play, or the answer to an examination question that you know you "really know." There's no reason you shouldn't find these occasions irritating, but you should also reflect for a moment on the estimate that the average human brain can store 100 trillion bits of information. The task of managing such a vast array of information is a formidable one. Perhaps you shouldn't be too surprised when an answer is sometimes not available when you need it!

The goal for this chapter is to explain how you usually remember so much and why you forget some of what you have known. We will explore how you get your everyday experiences into and out of memory. You will learn what psychology has discovered about different types of memories and about how those memories work. In the course of learning the many facts of memory, you're likely to gain an appreciation for how wonderful memory is.

One last thing: Because this is a chapter on memory, let's put your memory immediately to work. Please try to remember the number 51. Do whatever you need to do to remember 51. And yes, there will be a test!

WHAT IS MEMORY?

Memory is the capacity to encode, store, and retrieve information. In this chapter, we will consider memory to be a type of *information processing*. The bulk of our attention, therefore, will be trained on the flow of information in and out of your memory systems. Our examination of the processes that guide the acquisition and retrieval of information will enable you to refine your sense of what *memory* means.

Functions of Memory

When you think about memory, what is most likely to come to mind at first are situations in which you use your memory to recall (or try to recall) specific events or information: your favorite movie, the dates of World War II, or your student ID number.

How are actors and actresses able to remember all the different aspects—movements, expressions, and words—of their performances?

In fact, one of the important functions of memory is to allow you to have conscious access to the personal and collective past. But memory does much more for you than that. It also enables you to have effortless continuity of experience from one day to the next. When you walk through your neighborhood, for example, it is this second function of memory that makes the buildings along the way seem familiar. In defining types of memories, I will make plain to you how hard your memory works to fulfill these functions, often outside of conscious awareness.

Implicit and Explicit Memory   Consider **Figure 1**. What's wrong with this picture? It probably strikes you as unusual that there's a rabbit in the kitchen. But where does this feeling come from? You probably didn't go through the objects in the picture one by one and ask yourself, "Does the toaster belong?" "Do the cabinets belong?" Rather, the image of the rabbit jumps out at you as being out of place.

This simple example allows you to understand the difference between explicit and implicit uses of memory. For circumstances in which you engage conscious effort to encode or retrieve information, those are **explicit uses of memory.** When you encode or retrieve information without conscious effort, those are **implicit uses of memory.** Your discovery of

....

👁 Watch the Video *The Big Picture: The Woman Who Cannot Forget* on MyPsychLab

memory The mental capacity to encode, store, and retrieve information.

explicit use of memory Conscious effort to encode or recover information through memory processes.

implicit uses of memory Availability of information through memory processes without conscious effort to encode or recover information.

FIGURE 1 What's Wrong with This Picture?
Did you think right away, "What's a rabbit doing in the kitchen?" If the image of the rabbit immediately jumped out at you, it is because your memory processes performed an analysis of the scene outside of consciousness and delivered the rabbit as the odd element.

the rabbit is implicit because your memory processes brought past knowledge of kitchens to bear on your interpretation of the picture without any particular effort on your part. Suppose now I asked you, "What's missing from the picture?" To answer this second question, you probably have to put explicit memory to work. What appears in the typical kitchen? What's missing? (Did you think of the sink or the stove?) Thus, when it comes to using knowledge stored in memory, sometimes the use will be implicit—the information becomes available without any conscious effort—and sometimes it will be explicit—you make a conscious effort to recover the information.

The same distinction applies when it comes to the initial acquisition of memories. How do you know what should appear in a kitchen? Did you ever memorize a list of what appears there and what the appropriate configuration should be? Probably not. Rather, it's likely that you acquired most of this knowledge without conscious effort. By contrast, you probably learned the names of many of the objects in the room explicitly. To learn the association between words and experiences, your younger self needed to engage in explicit memory processes. You learned the word *refrigerator* because someone called your explicit attention to the name of that object.

The distinction between implicit and explicit memory greatly expands the range of questions researchers must address about memory processes (Roediger, 2008). Most early memory research focused on the explicit acquisition of information. Experimenters most frequently provided participants with new information to retain, and theories of memory were directed to explaining what participants could and could not remember under those circumstances. However, as you will see in this chapter, researchers have now devised methods for studying implicit memory as well. Thus you can obtain a more complete account of the variety of uses to which you put your memory. In fact, most circumstances in which you encode or

retrieve information represent a mix of implicit and explicit uses of memory. Let's turn now to a second dimension along which memories are distributed.

Declarative and Procedural Memory Can you whistle? Go ahead and try. Or if you can't whistle, try snapping your fingers. What kind of memory allows you to do these sorts of things? You probably remember having to learn these skills, but now they seem effortless. The earlier examples of implicit and explicit memories all involved the recollection of *facts* and *events*, which is called **declarative memory.** Now we see that you also have memories for *how to do things*, which is called **procedural memory.** Because the bulk of this chapter will be focused on how you acquire and use facts, let's take a moment now to consider how you acquire the ability to do things.

Procedural memory refers to the way you remember how things get done. With enough practice, you are able to acquire, retain, and employ procedural memories for perceptual, cognitive, and motor skills. Theories of procedural memory often concern themselves with how much practice you need and over what period of time: How do you go from a conscious list of declarative facts about some activity to unconscious, automatic performance of that same activity (Taatgen et al., 2008)? And why is it that after learning a skill, you often find it difficult to go back and talk about the component declarative facts?

We can see these phenomena at work in even the very simple activity of punching in a phone number that, over time, has become highly familiar. At first, you probably had to think

declarative memory Memory for information such as facts and events.

procedural memory Memory for how things get done; the way perceptual, cognitive, and motor skills are acquired, retained, and used.

Why does pretending to punch in a number help you to remember it?

your way through each digit, one at a time. You had to work through a list of declarative facts:

First, I must punch 2,
Next, I must punch 0,
Then I punch 7,
and so on.

However, when you began to punch in the number often enough, you could start to produce it as one unit—a swift sequence of actions on the touch-tone pad. The process at work is called *production compilation*: The mental commands that *produce* separate actions get *compiled* together (Taatgen & Lee, 2003). As a consequence of practice, you are able to carry out longer sequences of the activity without conscious intervention and mental effort (Stocco et al., 2010). But you also don't have conscious access to the content of these compiled units: Back at the telephone, it's not uncommon to find someone who can't actually remember the phone number without pretending to punch it in. In general, production compilation makes it hard to share your procedural knowledge with others. You may have noticed this if your parents tried to teach you to drive. Although they may be good drivers themselves, they may not have been very good at communicating the content of compiled good-driving procedures.

⦿ Watch the Video *The Basics: Do You Remember When . . . ?* on MyPsychLab

encoding The process by which a mental representation is formed in memory.

storage The retention of encoded material over time.

retrieval The recovery of stored information from memory.

You may also have noticed that production compilation can lead to errors. If you are a skilled typist, you've probably suffered from the *the* problem: As soon as you hit the *t* and the *h* keys, your finger may fly to the *e*, even if you're really trying to type *throne* or *thistle*. Once you have sufficiently committed the execution of *the* to procedural memory, you can do little else but finish the sequence. Without procedural memory, life would be extremely laborious—you would be doomed to go step by step through every activity. However, each time you mistakenly type *the*, you can reflect on the trade-off between efficiency and potential error. Let's continue now to an overview of the basic processes that apply to all these different types of memory.

An Overview of Memory Processes

No matter what the category of memory, being able to use knowledge at some later time requires the operation of three mental processes: encoding, storage, and retrieval. **Encoding** is the initial processing of information that leads to a representation in memory. **Storage** is the retention over time of encoded material. **Retrieval** is the recovery at a later time of the stored information. Simply put, encoding gets information in, storage holds it until you need it, and retrieval gets it out. Let's now expand on these ideas. ⦿

Encoding requires that you form *mental representations* of information from the external world. You can understand the idea of mental representations by analogy to representations outside your head. Imagine I wanted to know something about the best gift you got at your last birthday party. (Let's suppose it's not something you have with you.) What could you do to inform me about the gift? You might describe the properties of the object. Or you might draw a picture. Or you might pretend that you're using the object. In each case, these are representations of the original object. Although none of the representations is likely to be quite as good as having the real thing present, they should allow me to acquire knowledge of the most important aspects of the gift. Mental representations work much the same way. They preserve important features of past experiences in a way that enables you to *re-present* those experiences to yourself.

If information is properly encoded, it will be retained in *storage* over some period of time. Storage requires both short- and long-term changes in the structures of your brain. At the end of the chapter, we will see how researchers are attempting to locate the brain structures that are responsible for storing new and old memories. We will also see what happens in cases of extreme amnesia, where individuals become incapable of storing new memories.

Retrieval is the payoff for all your earlier effort. When it works, it enables you to gain access—often in a split second—to information you stored earlier. Can you remember what comes before storage: decoding or encoding? The answer is simple to retrieve now, but will you still be able to retrieve the answer as swiftly and confidently when you are tested on this chapter's contents days or weeks from now? Discovering how you are able to retrieve one specific bit of information from the vast quantity of information in your memory storehouse is a challenge facing psychologists who want to know how memory works.

Although it is easy to define encoding, storage, and retrieval as separate memory processes, the interaction among

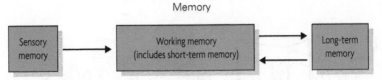

Memory

FIGURE 2 The Flow of Information In and Out of Long-Term Memory

Memory theories describe the flow of information to and from long-term memory. The theories address initial encodings of information in sensory and working memory, the transfer of information into long-term memory for storage, and the transfer of information from long-term memory to working memory for retrieval.

the three processes is quite complex. For example, to be able to encode the information that you have seen a tiger, you must first retrieve from memory information about the concept *tiger*. Similarly, to commit to memory the meaning of a sentence such as "He's as honest as Benedict Arnold," you must retrieve the meanings of each individual word, retrieve the rules of grammar that specify how word meanings should be combined in English, and retrieve cultural information that specifies exactly how honest Benedict Arnold (a famous Revolutionary War traitor) was.

We are now ready to look in more detail at the encoding, storage, and retrieval of information. The discussion will start with memory processes that preserve information for the short term such as sensory memory and working memory. We then move to the more permanent forms of long-term memory (see **Figure 2**). You will learn about how you remember and why you forget. The plan is to make you forever self-conscious about all the ways in which you use your capacity for memory. The hope is that your new knowledge will even allow you to improve some aspects of your memory skills.

Stop *and* Review

① What is the difference between explicit and implicit uses of memory?

② Suppose you are a skilled juggler. Does your skill rely more on declarative or procedural memory?

③ You suddenly can't remember the password for your e-mail account. Which memory process is most likely to be causing the difficulty?

✓•[Study and **Review** on **MyPsychLab**

MEMORY USE FOR THE SHORT TERM

Let's begin with a demonstration of the impermanence of some memories. **Figure 3** provides you with a reasonably busy visual scene. Please take a quick look at it—about 10 seconds—and then cover it up. Consider these questions about the scene:

1. What tool is the little boy at the bottom holding?
2. What is the middle man at the top doing?
3. In the lower right-hand corner, does the woman's umbrella handle hook to the left or to the right?

To answer these questions, wouldn't you be more comfortable if you could go back and have an extra peek at the picture?

This quick demonstration reminds you that much of the information you experience never lodges itself securely in your memory. Instead, you possess and use the information only for the short term. This section examines properties of three less permanent uses of memory: *iconic memory, short-term memory,* and *working memory.*

Iconic Memory

When you first covered up Figure 3, did you have the impression that you could briefly still "see" the whole picture? This extra peek at the picture is provided by your **iconic memory**—a memory system in the visual domain that allows large amounts of information to be stored for very brief durations (Neisser, 1967). Iconic memory is an example of a *sensory memory*: Researchers have speculated that each sensory system has a memory store that preserves representations of physical features of environmental stimuli for, at most, a few seconds (Radvansky, 2006). For example, people retain brief sensory representations of stimuli that have touched their fingertips (Auvray et al., 2011). We focus on iconic memory because it has received the most research attention.

A visual memory, or icon, lasts about half a second. Iconic memory was first revealed in experiments that required participants to retrieve information from visual displays that were exposed for only one-twentieth of a second.

George Sperling *(1960, 1963) presented participants with arrays of three rows of letters and numbers.*

7	1	V	F
X	L	5	3
B	4	W	7

Participants were asked to perform two different tasks. In a whole-report procedure, they tried to recall as many of the items in the display as possible. Typically, they could report only about four items. Other participants underwent a partial-report procedure, which required them to report only one row rather than the whole pattern. A signal of a high, medium, or low tone was sounded immediately after the presentation to indicate which row the participants were to report. Sperling found that regardless of which row he asked for, the participants' recall was quite high.

iconic memory Memory system in the visual domain that allows large amounts of information to be stored for very brief durations.

FIGURE 3 **How Much Can You Remember from This Scene?**

After viewing this scene for about 10 seconds, cover it up and try to answer the questions in the text. Under ordinary circumstances, iconic memory preserves a glimpse of the visual world for a brief time after the scene has been removed.

Because participants could accurately report any of the three rows in response to a tone, Sperling concluded that all of the information in the display must have gotten into iconic memory. That is evidence for its large capacity. At the same time, the difference between the whole- and partial-report procedures suggests that the information fades rapidly: The participants in the whole-report procedure were unable to recall all the information present in the icon. This second point was reinforced by experiments in which the identification signal was slightly delayed. **Figure 4** shows that as the delay interval increases from 0 seconds to 1 second, the number of items accurately reported declines steadily. Researchers have measured quite accurately the time course with which information must be transferred from the fading icon (Graziano & Sigman, 2008). To take advantage of the "extra peek" at the visual world, your memory processes must very quickly transfer information to more durable stores.

Note that iconic memory is not the same as the "photographic memory" that some people claim to have. The technical term for "photographic memory" is *eidetic imagery*: People who experience eidetic imagery are able to recall the details of

a picture, for periods of time considerably longer than iconic memory, as if they were still looking at a photograph. "People" in this case really means children: Researchers have estimated that roughly 8 percent of preadolescent children are eidetickers, but virtually no adults (Neath & Surprenant, 2003). No satisfactory theory has been proposed for why eidetic imagery fades over time. However, if you are reading this text as a high school or college student, you almost certainly have iconic memory but not eidetic images.

Short-Term Memory

Before you began to read this chapter, you may not have been aware that you had iconic memory. It is very likely, however, that you were aware that there are some memories that you possess only for the short term. Consider the common occurrence of consulting a Web page to find the start time for a movie. If you don't get to act on the information immediately, you often have to go right back to the Web. When you consider this experience, it's easy to understand why researchers

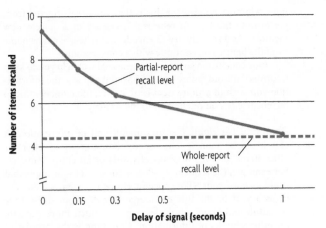

FIGURE 4 Recall by the Partial-Report Method
The solid line shows the average number of items recalled using the partial-report method, both immediately after presentation and at four later times. For comparison, the dotted line shows the number of items recalled by the whole-report method.
Adapted from Sperling, 1960.

have hypothesized a special type of memory called **short-term memory (STM)**.

You shouldn't think of short-term memory as a particular place that memories go to, but rather as a built-in mechanism for focusing cognitive resources on some small set of mental representations (Shiffrin, 2003). But the resources of STM are fickle. As even your experience with phone numbers shows, you have to take some special care to ensure that memories become encoded into more permanent forms.

The Capacity Limitations of STM Attentional resources are devoted to selecting the objects and events in the external world on which you will expend your mental resources. Just as there are limits on your capacity to attend to more than a small sample of the available information, there are limits on your ability to keep more than a small sample of information active in STM. The limited capacity of STM enforces a sharp focus of mental attention.

To estimate the capacity of STM, researchers at first turned to tests of *memory span*. At some point in your life, you have probably been asked to carry out a task like this one:

Read the following list of random numbers once, cover them, and write down as many as you can in the order they appear:

8 1 7 3 4 9 4 2 8 5

How many did you get correct?

Now read the next list of random letters and perform the same memory test:

J M R S O F L P T Z B

How many did you get correct?

If you are like most individuals, you probably could recall somewhere in the range of five to nine items. **George Miller** (1956) suggested that seven (plus or minus two) was the "magic number" that characterized people's memory performance on random lists of letters, words, numbers, or almost any kind of meaningful, familiar item. ◉▸

Tests of memory span, however, overestimate the true capacity of STM because participants are able to use other sources of information to carry out the task. When other sources of memory are factored out, researchers have estimated

the pure contribution of STM to your seven (or so) item memory span to be only between three and five items (Cowan, 2001). But if that's all the capacity you have to commence the acquisition of new memories, why don't you notice your limitations more often? Despite the capacity limitations of STM, you function efficiently for at least two reasons. As you will see

© Ocean/Corbis

What role does short-term memory play when you punch in your ATM password?

◉▸ Simulate the Experiment *Digit Span* on **MyPsychLab**

short-term memory (STM) Memory processes associated with preservation of recent experiences and with retrieval of information from long-term memory; short-term memory is of limited capacity and stores information for only a short length of time without rehearsal.

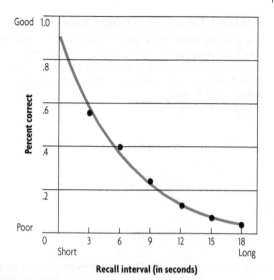

FIGURE 5 Short-Term Memory Recall without Rehearsal

When the interval between stimulus presentation and recall was filled with a distracting task, recall became poorer as the interval grew longer.

in the next two sections, the encoding of information in STM can be enhanced through rehearsal and chunking.

Rehearsal   You probably know that a good way to keep your movie time in mind is to keep repeating the digits in a cycle in your head. This memorization technique is called *maintenance rehearsal*. The fate of unrehearsed information was demonstrated in an ingenious experiment.

Participants heard three consonants, such as F, C, and V. After a delay of 3 to 18 seconds, the participants heard a signal that instructed them to recall the consonants (Peterson & Peterson, 1959). To prevent rehearsal, a distractor task was put between the stimulus input and the recall signal—the participants were given a three-digit number and told to count backward from it by 3s until the recall signal was presented. Many different consonant sets were given, and several short delays were used over a series of trials with a number of participants.

*As shown in **Figure 5**, recall became increasingly poorer as the time required to retain the information became longer. After even 3 seconds, there was considerable memory loss, and by 18 seconds, loss was nearly total. In the absence of an opportunity to rehearse the information, short-term recall was impaired with the passage of time.*

Performance suffered because information could not be rehearsed. It also suffered because of interference from the competing information of the distractor task. (We will consider interference as a cause of forgetting later in this chapter.) You may have noticed how often a new acquaintance says his or her name—and then you immediately forget it. One of the most common reasons for this is that you are distracted from performing the type of rehearsal necessary to acquire a new memory. As a remedy, try to encode and rehearse a new name carefully before you continue with a conversation.

Our conclusion so far is that rehearsal will help you to keep information from fading out of STM. But suppose the information you wish to acquire is, at least at first, too cumbersome to be rehearsed? You might turn to the strategy of chunking.

Chunking   A *chunk* is a meaningful unit of information. A chunk can be a single letter or number, a group of letters or other items, or even a group of words or an entire sentence. For example, the sequence 1–9–8–4 consists of four digits that could exhaust your STM capacity. However, if you see the digits as a year or the title of George Orwell's book *1984*, they constitute only one chunk, leaving you much more capacity for other chunks of information. **Chunking** is the process of reconfiguring items by grouping them on the basis of similarity or some other organizing principle, or by combining them into larger patterns (Cowan et al., 2010).

See how many chunks you find in this sequence of 20 numbers: 19411917186118121776. You can answer "20" if you see the sequence as a list of unrelated digits, or "5" if you break down the sequence into the dates of major wars in U.S. history. If you do the latter, it's easy for you to recall all the digits in proper sequence after one quick glance. It would be impossible for you to remember them all from a short exposure if you saw them as 20 unrelated items.

Your memory span can always be greatly increased if you can discover ways to organize an available body of information into smaller chunks. One famous subject, S.F., was an avid runner. He was able to memorize 84 random digits by using his knowledge of race results to find chunks in the strings of digits (Chase & Ericsson, 1981; Ericsson & Chase, 1982). Like S.F., you can structure incoming information according to its personal meaning to you (linking it to the ages of friends and relatives, for example); or you can match new stimuli with various codes that have been stored in your long-term memory. Even if you can't link new stimuli to rules, meanings, or codes in your long-term memory, you can still use chunking. You can simply group the items in a rhythmical pattern or temporal group (181379256460 could become 181, pause, 379, pause, 256, pause, 460). You know from everyday experience that this grouping principle works well for remembering telephone numbers.

Working Memory

Our focus so far has been on short-term memory, and specifically the role that STM plays in the explicit acquisition of new memories. However, you need more memory resources on a moment-by-moment basis than those that allow you to acquire facts. For example, you also need to be able to retrieve preexisting memories. At the start of this chapter, I asked you to commit a number to memory. Can you remember now what it was? If you can remember (if not, peek), you have made your

chunking The process of taking single items of information and recoding them on the basis of similarity or some other organizing principle.

How can you put chunking to good use while listening to a lecture?

mental representation of that memory active once more—that's another memory function. If you do something more complicated—suppose you try to count backward by 3s from 132 while you toss a ball from hand to hand—you'll put even more demands on your memory resources.

Based on an analysis of the memory functions you require to navigate through life, researchers have articulated theories of **working memory**—the memory resource that you use to accomplish tasks such as reasoning and language comprehension. Suppose you are trying to remember a movie time while you search for a pencil and pad to write it down. Whereas your short-term memory processes allow you to keep the number in mind, your more general working memory resource allows you to execute the mental operations to accomplish an efficient search. Working memory provides a foundation for the moment-by-moment fluidity of thought and action.

Alan Baddeley (2002, 2003) has provided evidence for four components of working memory:

- *A phonological loop.* This resource holds and manipulates speech-based information. The phonological loop overlaps most with short-term memory. When you rehearse a telephone number by "listening" to it as you run it through your head, you are making use of the phonological loop.
- *A visuospatial sketchpad.* This resource performs the same types of functions as the phonological loop for visual and spatial information. If, for example, someone asked you how many desks there are in your psychology classroom, you might use the resources of the visuospatial sketchpad to form a mental picture of the classroom and then estimate the number of desks from that picture.
- *The central executive.* This resource is responsible for controlling attention and coordinating information from the phonological loop and the visuospatial sketchpad. Any time you carry out a task that requires a combination of mental processes—imagine, for example, you are asked to describe a picture from memory—you rely on the central executive function to apportion your mental resources to different aspects of the task.

- *The episodic buffer* is a storage system with limited capacity that is controlled by the central executive. The episodic buffer allows you to retrieve information from long-term memory and combine it with information from the current situation. Most life events include a complex array of sights, sounds, and so on. The episodic buffer provides a resource to integrate those different types of perceptual stimulation with past experiences to provide a unified interpretation of each situation.

The incorporation of short-term memory into the broader context of working memory should help reinforce the idea that STM is not a place but a process. To do the work of cognition—to carry out cognitive activities like language processing or problem solving—you must bring a lot of different elements together in quick succession. You can think of working memory as short-term special focus on the necessary elements. If you wish to get a better look at a physical object, you can shine a brighter light on it; working memory shines a brighter mental light on your mental objects—your memory representations. Working memory also coordinates the activities required to take action with respect to those objects.

In everyday life, you often run up against the capacity limitations of working memory. Let's apply that insight in the academic domain.

Featured Study

What happens when you sit down to begin an exam? Often, thoughts rush in about how prepared you are for the exam, how hard it's likely to be, and so on. A pair of researchers wished to test the hypothesis that these anxious thoughts often exhaust students' working memory capacity—and, by doing so, make it difficult for the students to perform well on their exam (Ramirez & Beilock, 2011). To test that hypothesis, the researchers created a testing situation that put particular pressure on students (by promising them a monetary reward if they did well). The researchers assigned a subset of the students to a control group. Those students sat quietly for 10 minutes waiting for the exam to start. The other students experienced an intervention: They spent the same 10 minutes "writing about their thoughts and feelings regarding the math problems they were about to perform" (p. 212). The researchers argued that the thoughts and feelings, once expressed, would no longer compete for the students' working memory capacity once the exam began. In fact, students in the expressive writing group performed about 20 percent better than the control group on a series of math problems!

Next time you experience anxiety before an exam, consider spending a few minutes writing about your thoughts and feelings. By doing so, you could free up working memory capacity you need to excel on the exam.

Researchers have demonstrated that working memory capacity differs among individuals. They have devised several

---

working memory A memory resource that is used to accomplish tasks such as reasoning and language comprehension; consists of the phonological loop, visuospatial sketchpad, and central executive.

Table 1 • Sample Items for a Test
of Operation Span

Try to answer "yes" or "no" to each math problem and then memorize the words at the end of each problem. Once you're done with all four problems, cover them up and try to recall the four words.
IS (6 ÷ 2) − 2 = 2? SNOW
IS (8 × 1) − 5 = 3? TASTE
IS (9 × 2) − 6 = 12? KNIFE
IS (8 ÷ 4) + 3 = 6? CLOWN

procedures to measure those differences (Conway et al., 2005). Let's consider an example of one of those measures, which is called *operation span* (Turner & Engle, 1989). Take a look at **Table 1**. To determine operation span, researchers ask participants to read each math problem aloud and then answer "yes" or "no" to indicate whether the equation was correct. After solving each problem, participants try to memorize the word that comes after it. (In the real version of the test, participants get the words only after they've solved the problems, and they get the problems one at a time.) After completing a whole group of problems, participants try to recall all the words in the correct order. Try to get a feel for the task by working through Table 1. Operation span requires people to carry out one task (such as solving math problems) while maintaining a second task (such as remembering words). For that reason, it provides an index of individual differences in the efficiency of the central executive to apportion mental resources to different tasks.

Researchers use measures of working memory capacity (WMC) to predict performance on a variety of tasks. For example, in one study people tried to comprehend brief texts while irrelevant speech was played over headphones (Sörqvist et al., 2010). Because people with higher WMC are better able to focus their attention, their reading comprehension was less disrupted. Another project examined the impact of WMC on police officers' performance (Kleider et al., 2010). Police officers viewed a series of slides of armed and unarmed men. When the officers were experiencing negative emotions (after watching a disturbing video), those with lower WMC were more likely to shoot unarmed targets and less likely to shoot armed targets. The researchers suggested that negative emotions tax working memory resources. For officers with lower WMC, negative emotions leave them with insufficient resources to make accurate decisions.

A final note on working memory: Working memory helps maintain your psychological present. It is what sets a context for new events and links separate episodes together into a continuing story. It enables you to maintain and continually update your representation of a changing situation and to keep track of topics during a conversation. All of this is true because working memory serves as a conduit for information coming and going to long-term memory. Let's turn our attention now to the types of memories that can last a lifetime.

....

long-term memory (LTM) Memory processes associated with the preservation of information for retrieval at any later time.

retrieval cue Internally or externally generated stimulus available to help with the retrieval of a memory.

Stop *and* Review

① Why do researchers believe that the capacity of iconic memory is large?
② What is the contemporary estimate of the capacity of short-term memory?
③ What does it mean to *chunk* some group of items?
④ What are the components of working memory?

CRITICAL THINKING Recall the study that demonstrated the importance of rehearsal to maintain information in short-term memory. In that study, why were participants asked to count backward by 3s (for example, 167, 164, 161 . . .) rather than by 1s (167, 166, 165 . . .)?

✔—[Study and Review on MyPsychLab

LONG-TERM MEMORY: ENCODING AND RETRIEVAL

How long can memories last? At the chapter's outset, I asked you to recall your own earliest memory. How old is that memory? Fifteen years? Twenty years? Longer? When psychologists speak of *long-term memory,* it is with the knowledge that memories often last a lifetime. Therefore, whatever theory explains how memories are acquired for the long term must also explain how they can remain accessible over the life course. **Long-term memory (LTM)** is the storehouse of all the experiences, events, information, emotions, skills, words, categories, rules, and judgments that have been acquired from sensory and short-term memories. LTM constitutes each person's total knowledge of the world and of the self.

Psychologists know that it is often easier to acquire new long-term information when an important conclusion is stated in advance. With that conclusion in place, you have a framework for understanding the incoming information. For memory, here is the appropriate conclusion: Your ability to remember will be greatest when there is a good match between the circumstances in which you encoded information and the circumstances in which you attempt to retrieve it. You will see over the next several sections what it means to have a "good match."

Retrieval Cues

To begin the exploration of the match between encoding and retrieval, let's consider this general question: How do you "find" a memory? The basic answer is that you use retrieval cues. **Retrieval cues** are the stimuli available as you search for a particular memory. These cues may be provided externally, such as questions on a quiz ("What memory concepts do you associate with the research of Baddeley and Sperling?"), or generated internally ("Where have I met her before?"). Each time you attempt to retrieve an explicit memory, you do so for some purpose, and that purpose often supplies the retrieval cue. It won't surprise you that memories can be easier or harder to retrieve depending on the quality of the retrieval cue. If a friend asks you, "Who's the one Roman emperor I can't remember?"

In what ways is retrieval from long-term memory analogous to retrieval from a vast research library?

you're likely to be involved in a guessing game. If she asks instead, "Who was the emperor after Claudius?" you can immediately respond "Nero."

A good way for you to appreciate the importance of retrieval cues is by attempting to learn some word pairs. This procedure replicates classic memory experiments. Keep working at it until you can go through the six pairs three times in a row without an error.

    Apple–Boat
    Hat–Bone
    Bicycle–Clock
    Mouse–Tree
    Ball–House
    Ear–Blanket

Now that you've committed the pairs to memory, it's time to make the test more interesting. You need to have a *retention interval*—a period of time over which you must keep the information in memory. Let's spend a moment, therefore, discussing some of the procedures researchers might use to test your memory. You might assume that you either know something or you don't and that any method of testing what you know will give the same results. Not so. Let's consider two tests for explicit memory, recall and recognition. 👁

Recall and Recognition   When you **recall,** you reproduce the information to which you were previously exposed. "What are the components of working memory?" is a recall question. **Recognition** refers to the realization that a certain stimulus event is one you have seen or heard before. Here's a recognition question: "Which is the term for a visual sensory memory: (1) echo; (2) chunk; (3) icon; or (4) abstract code?" You can relate recall

....

👁 Watch the Video *Classic Footage of Assessment of Memory with the Stanford-Binet Intelligence Scale* on **MyPsychLab**

recall A method of retrieval in which an individual is required to reproduce the information previously presented.

recognition A method of retrieval in which an individual is required to identify stimuli as having been experienced before.

episodic memory Long-term memory for an autobiographical event and the context in which it occurred.

and recognition to your day-to-day experiences of explicit memory. When trying to identify a criminal, the police would be using a recall method if they asked the victim to describe, from memory, some of the perpetrator's distinguishing features: "Did you notice anything unusual about the attacker?" They would be using the recognition method if they showed the victim photos, one at a time, from a file of criminal suspects or if they asked the victim to identify the perpetrator in a police lineup.

Let's now use these two procedures to test you on the word pairs you learned a few moments ago. What words finished the pairs?

        Hat–?   Bicycle–?   Ear–?

Can you select the correct pair from these possibilities?

Apple–Baby	Mouse–Tree	Ball–House
Apple–Boat	Mouse–Tongue	Ball–Hill
Apple–Bottle	Mouse–Tent	Ball–Horn

Was the recognition test easier than the recall test? It should be. Let's try to explain this result with respect to retrieval cues.

Both recall and recognition require a search using cues. The cues for recognition, however, are much more useful. For recall, you have to hope that the cue alone will help you locate the information. For recognition, part of the work has been done for you. When you look at the pair *Mouse–Tree,* you only have to answer *yes* or *no* to "Did I have this experience?" By contrast, for *Mouse–?* You need to answer, "What was the experience I had?" In this light, you can see that I made the recognition test reasonably easy for you. Suppose you had viewed, instead, recombinations of the original pairs. Which of these are correct?

        Hat–Clock   Ear–Boat
        Hat–Bone   Ear–Blanket

Now you must recognize not just that you saw the word before, but that you saw it in a particular context. (We will return to the idea of context shortly.) If you are a veteran of difficult multiple-choice exams, you have come to learn how tough even recognition situations can be. However, in most cases, your recognition performance will be better than your recall because retrieval cues are more straightforward for recognition. Let's look at some other aspects of retrieval cues.

Episodic and Semantic Memories   The earlier discussion of the functions of memories made a distinction between declarative and procedural memories. Declarative memories themselves differ along another dimension with respect to the cues that are necessary to retrieve them from memory. Canadian psychologist **Endel Tulving** (1972) first proposed the distinction between *episodic* and *semantic* types of declarative memories (see **Figure 6**).

Episodic memories preserve, individually, the specific events that you have personally experienced. For example, memories of your happiest birthday or of your first kiss are stored in episodic memory. To recover such memories, you need retrieval cues that specify something about the time at which the event occurred and something about the content of the events. Depending on how the information has been encoded, you may or may not be able to produce a specific memory representation for an event. For example, do you have any specific memories to differentiate the 10th time ago you brushed your teeth from the 11th time ago?

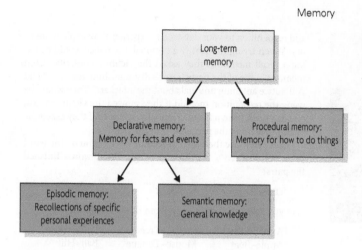

FIGURE 6 Dimensions of Long-Term Memory
Researchers have suggested that people store different types of memories.

Everything you know, you began to acquire in some particular context. However, there are large classes of information that, over time, you encounter in many different contexts. These classes of information come to be available for retrieval without reference to their multiple times and places of experience. These **semantic memories** are generic, categorical memories, such as the meanings of words and concepts. For most people, facts like the formula $E = MC2$ and the capital of France don't require retrieval cues that make reference to the episodes, the original learning contexts, in which the memory was acquired.

Of course, this doesn't mean that your recall of semantic memories is foolproof. You know perfectly well that you can forget many facts that have become dissociated from the contexts in which you learned them. A good strategy when you can't recover a semantic memory is to treat it like an episodic memory again. By thinking to yourself, "I know I learned the names of the Roman emperors in my Western civilization course," you may be able to provide the extra retrieval cues that will shake loose a memory.

Context and Encoding

To continue our exploration of encoding and retrieval, let's now consider a phenomenon that you might call "context shock." You see someone across a crowded room, and you know that you know the person but you just can't place her. Finally, after staring for longer than is absolutely polite, you remember who it is—and you realize you were having difficulty identifying her because you have never seen her in this particular context. What is the woman who delivers your mail doing at your best friend's party? Whenever you have this type of experience, you have rediscovered the principle of **encoding specificity**: Memories emerge most efficiently when the context of retrieval matches the context of encoding. Let's see how researchers have demonstrated that principle.

....

semantic memory Generic, categorical memory, such as the meaning of words and concepts.

encoding specificity The principle that subsequent retrieval of information is enhanced if cues received at the time of recall are consistent with those present at the time of encoding.

Encoding Specificity What are the consequences of learning information in a particular context? Endel Tulving and Donald Thomson (1973) first demonstrated the power of encoding specificity by reversing the usual performance relationship between recall and recognition.

Featured Study

Participants were asked to learn pairs of words like train–black, but they were told that they would be responsible for remembering only the second word of the pair. In a subsequent phase of the experiment, participants were asked to generate four free associates to words like white. Those words were chosen so that it was likely that the original to-be-remembered words (like black) would be among the associates. The participants were then asked to check off any words on their associates lists that they recognized as to-be-remembered words from the first phase of the experiment.

Events of personal importance, like seeing a good friend for the first time after a year's separation, are retained in *episodic* memory. What types of information from *semantic* memory might contribute to a reunion?

They were able to do so 54 percent of the time. However, when the participants were later given the first words of the pair, like train, and asked to recall the associate, they were 61 percent accurate.

Why was recall better than recognition? Tulving and Thomson suggested that what mattered was the change in context. After the participants had studied the word *black* in the context of *train,* it was hard to recover the memory representation when the context was changed to *white.* Given the significant effect of even these minimal contexts, you can anticipate that richly organized real-life contexts would have an even greater effect on your memory.

Researchers have provided several remarkable demonstrations of *context-dependent* memory. In one experiment, scuba divers learned lists of words either on a beach or under water. They were then tested for retention of those words, again in one of those two contexts. Performance was nearly 50 percent better when the context at encoding and recall matched—even though the material had nothing at all to do with water or diving (Godden & Baddeley, 1975). Researchers have demonstrated similar context-dependent memory effects for word lists when encoding and retrieval varied between the third and fifth floors of a psychology building (Unsworth et al., 2012). But it's not just word lists: Piano students performed a brief composition more accurately when they played it on the same piano on which they had first learned it (Mishra & Backlin, 2007).

In each of the examples so far, memories are encoded with respect to a context in the external environment—for example, the test room or the type of piano. However, encoding specificity also occurs based on people's internal states. For example, in one study participants drank either alcohol or a placebo before the study and test sessions for a free recall task

After receiving a traffic warning from this man, why might you not recognize him if you ran into him at a party?

(Weissenborn & Duka, 2000). In general, alcohol impaired memory performance. However, participants who drank alcohol at both study and test were able to retrieve information that eluded participants who drank alcohol at only study or test alone. When internal states provide the basis for encoding specificity, those effects are called *state-dependent memory.* Researchers have demonstrated that state-dependent memory occurs for other drugs such as marijuana and amphetamine. Also, if you take antihistamines for allergies, you might be interested to learn that they lead to state-dependent memory (Carter & Cassaday, 1998). How might you use that information when allergy season rolls around?

These various examples of encoding specificity point to the same conclusion. It's easiest to find your way back to information when you can reinstate the original context in which you encoded it.

The Serial Position Effect   Changes in context also explain one of the classic effects in memory research: the **serial position effect.** Suppose a professor required you to learn a list of unrelated words. If you tried to recall those words in order, your data would almost certainly conform to the pattern shown in **Figure 7**: You would do very well on the first few words (the **primacy effect**) and very well on the last few words (the **recency effect**) but rather poorly on the middle part of the list. Figure 7 shows the generality of this pattern when students are asked to try to remember word lists of varying lengths (6, 10, and 15 words) using either *serial recall* ("Recite the words in the order you heard them") or *free recall* ("Recite as many words as you can") (Jahnke, 1965). Researchers have found primacy and recency in a wide variety of test situations (Neath & Surprenant, 2003). What day is it today? Do you believe that you would be almost a second faster to answer this question at the beginning or end of the week than in the middle (Koriat & Fischoff, 1974)?

The role context plays in producing the shape of the serial position curve has to do with the **temporal distinctiveness** of different items on a list, different experiences in your life, and so on (Guérard et al., 2010; Neath et al., 2006). Temporal distinctiveness refers to the extent to which a particular item stands out from or is distinct from other items in time. It's easiest to understand the concept of temporal distinctiveness by analogy to distinctiveness in space. **Figure 8** provides that spatial analogy. Imagine, in Part A, that you are looking at train tracks. What you can see is that they look as if they clump together at the horizon—even though they are equally spaced apart. The early tracks are not distinctive; they blur together. By contrast, the nearest tracks stand out most; they are most distinctive.

Imagine now that you are trying to remember the last 10 movies you've seen. The movies are like the train tracks. Under most circumstances, you should remember the last movie best—giving you a recency effect—because it stands out most clearly in time. Meanwhile, this logic suggests that "middle" information will become more memorable if each item is

serial position effect A characteristic of memory retrieval in which the recall of beginning and end items on a list is often better than recall of items appearing in the middle.

primacy effect Improved memory for items at the start of a list.

recency effect Improved memory for items at the end of a list.

temporal distinctiveness The extent to which a particular item stands out from or is distinct from other items in time.

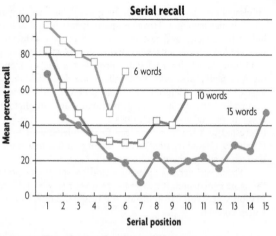

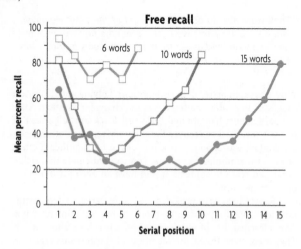

FIGURE 7 The Serial Position Effect

This figure shows the generality of the serial position effect. Students were asked to try to remember word lists of varying lengths (6, 10, and 15 words) using either *serial recall* ("Recite the words in the order you heard them") or *free recall* ("Recite as many words as you can"). Each curve shows better memory for both the beginning (the *primacy* effect) and end (the *recency* effect) of the list. ☞

made more distinctive. The idea with respect to the analogy, as shown in Part B of Figure 8, is to make the train tracks seem equally far apart.

To make the train tracks seem evenly spaced, engineers would have to make the more distant ones actually be farther apart. Researchers have used the same logic for a memory test, by exploiting the analogy between space and time (Neath & Crowder, 1990). They had participants try to learn lists of letters, but they manipulated how far apart in time the letters were made to seem. This manipulation was accomplished by asking participants to read out some number

of random digits that appeared on a computer screen between the letters. In the conventional condition (like Part A of Figure 8), each pair of letters was separated by two digits. In the proportional condition (like Part B), the first pair had four digits and the last pair had zero digits; this should have the effect of making the early digits more distinctive, just like moving distant train tracks farther apart. Participants, in fact, showed better memory for early items on the list when those items had been made more separate.

☞ Simulate the **Experiment** *Serial Position Effect* on **MyPsychLab**

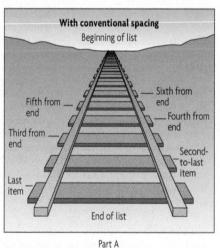

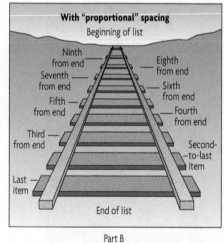

FIGURE 8 Temporal Distinctiveness

You can think of items you put into memory as train tracks. In Part A, you can imagine that memories farther back in time become blurred together, just like train tracks in the distance. In Part B, you see that one way to combat this effect is to make the earlier tracks physically farther apart, so the distances look proportional. Similarly, you can make early memories more distinctive by moving them apart psychologically.

This experiment suggests that the standard recency effect arises because the last few items are almost automatically distinctive. The same principle may explain primacy—each time you begin something new, your activity establishes a new temporal context. In that new context, the first few experiences are particularly distinctive. Thus you can think of primacy and recency as two views of the same set of train tracks—one from each end!

The Processes of Encoding and Retrieval

You have seen so far that a match between the context of encoding and of retrieval is beneficial to good memory performance. To refine that conclusion, we must consider the actual processes that are used to get information to and from long-term memory. This section will adopt a perspective called **transfer-appropriate processing**: The perspective suggests that memory is best when the type of processing carried out at encoding *transfers* to the processes required at retrieval (Roediger, 2008). Let's review research that illustrates this perspective.

Levels of Processing We'll begin with the idea that the type of processing you perform on information—the type of attention you pay to information at time of encoding—will have an influence on your memory for the information. **Levels-of-processing theory** suggests that the deeper the level at which information was processed, the more likely it is to be committed to memory (Craik & Lockhart, 1972; Lockhart & Craik, 1990). If processing involves more analysis, interpretation, comparison, and elaboration, it should result in better memory. ◉▶

The depth of processing is often defined by the types of judgments participants are required to make with respect to experimental materials. Consider the word *GRAPE*. You could make a physical judgment about this item—is the word in capital letters? Or a rhyme judgment—does the word rhyme with *tape*? Or a meaning judgment—does the word represent a type of fruit? Do you see how each of these questions requires you to think a little bit more deeply about *GRAPE*? In fact, the deeper the original processing participants carry out, the more words they remember (Lockhart & Craik, 1990).

Why does the depth of processing have an impact? One explanation is that the type of processing people do at "deeper" levels provides a better match to the processes that are required at retrieval (Roediger et al., 2002). When you use explicit memory processes to remember a word, you typically use information about its meaning (rather than, for example, its physical appearance). In that way, the meaning judgment at encoding provides a better match to processes of retrieval. This explanation makes the levels-of-processing effect a type of transfer-appropriate processing.

....

◉▶ Simulate the Experiment *Depth of Processing* on MyPsychLab

transfer-appropriate processing The perspective that suggests that memory is best when the type of processing carried out at encoding matches the processes carried out at retrieval.

levels-of-processing theory A theory that suggests that the deeper the level at which information was processed, the more likely it is to be retained in memory.

priming In the assessment of implicit memory, the advantage conferred by prior exposure to a word or situation.

Memory performance based on levels of processing confirms that the way in which information is committed to memory—the mental processes that you use to encode information—has an effect on whether you can retrieve that information later. However, so far we have looked at only explicit memory. We will now see that the match between processes at encoding and retrieval is particularly critical for implicit memory.

Processes and Implicit Memory Recall that the explicit versus implicit dimension applies both at encoding and at retrieval (Bowers & Marsolek, 2003). Under many circumstances, for example, you will retrieve implicitly memories that you originally encoded explicitly. This is true when you greet your best friend by name without having to expend any particular mental effort. Even so, implicit memories reveal the importance of the match between the processes at implicit encoding and the processes at implicit retrieval.

To explore the properties of implicit memory, researchers have often demonstrated that the same circumstances of encoding have quite a different impact on people's performance on explicit and implicit memory tasks. Consider a study that measured the memory performance of marathon runners (Eich & Metcalfe, 2009). Members of the *marathon* group had just completed the New York City marathon. Members of the *control* group were also marathoners, but they completed the memory tests one to three days before the marathon. Each group began the experiment by rating the pleasantness of a list of 26 words. The pleasantness ratings allowed participants to think about the meaning of a word without purposefully committing it to memory. Next, the participants completed a test of implicit memory known as *word stem completion*. In this task, participants see a stem, like *uni_____*, and write the first word that comes to mind. Suppose *unicorn* was on the original word list. People might write *unicorn* down in response to *uni_____* without being aware that they are experiencing the influence of the original list. Finally, the participants completed an explicit memory task in which they explicitly tried to recall the words they had rated earlier.

What affect should running a marathon have on memory performance? The researchers suggested that the stress of the run would make it more difficult for people to encode explicit information. For that reason, explicit memory should suffer post-marathon. However, the implicit memory task only relies on a *physical* match between the original stimulus and the information given at test. Whatever *perceptual* processes allowed people to encode *unicorn* as a physical stimulus should also make that physical reality available when they complete the stem *uni_____*. On this analysis, implicit memory should be unaffected by post-marathon stress. In fact, the researchers proposed that the marathoners' implicit memory might be even better than the control group's memory: The marathoners' post-run stress might have prompted them to focus more attention on the physical properties of the words than on the words' meaning.

Figure 9 presents the experiments' results. As you can see, the marathoners did, in fact, have worse explicit memory but better implicit memory. You are probably familiar with "proportion recalled" as a measure of explicit memory. The measure for implicit memory will be less familiar. It is known as **priming** because the first experience of the word *primes* memory for later experiences. This measure indicates

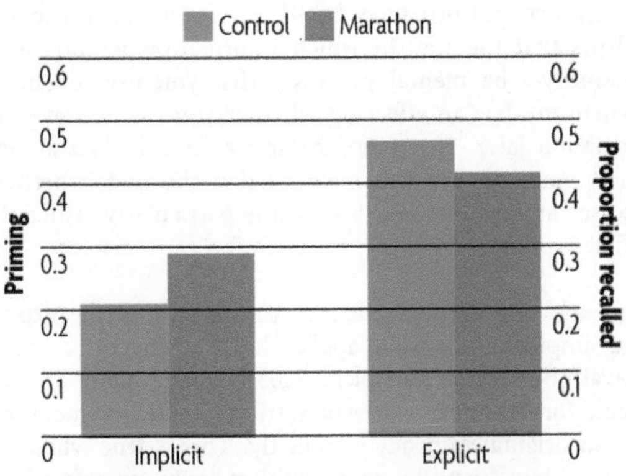

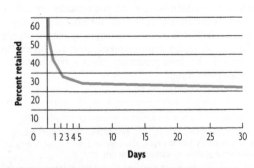

FIGURE 9 Comparison of Implicit and Explicit Memory Performance

People's explicit memory performance was worse after running a marathon. However, their implicit memory performance was better than that of members of the control group.

how much more likely participants were to provide *unicorn* in response to *uni*_____ if the word had appeared on the initial list. (For some participants, *unicorn* would not have been on the list.) Figure 9 shows priming for both the marathon and the control group, but more for the marathon group.

This experiment demonstrates priming based on perceptual processes that encode physical aspects of words. People also experience priming when conceptual processes function at encoding and retrieval.

A group of researchers wished to demonstrate that priming of conceptual information could last over a period of four to eight weeks (Thomson et al., 2010). Because they taught at a Canadian university, they used the names of U.S. states as their stimuli. Early in the semester, in several classes over a period of 10 years, the researchers introduced one U.S. state (which varied across years). They introduced the target state in the context of a lecture on memory retrieval. They suggested, one year, that a good strategy for remembering the states was to go through the alphabet. They noted, "when you come to the letter 'D,' you'll have a good chance of remembering Delaware" (p. 43). Each semester, a month or two later, the researchers asked students to write down all 50 states. By comparing across years, the researchers demonstrated that students were much more likely to remember a state when it had been mentioned in the earlier lecture.

You might think that participants were just able to remember the target state because they recalled their professors mentioning it in class. However, the researchers asked their students about their prior memories. Very few could recall what had happened earlier in the semester. Based on these responses, the researchers concluded that the conceptual priming of the particular state endured over the whole period of one to two months!

Are you impressed by the longevity of implicit memory? You should keep these results in mind as we turn to circumstances in which your memory processes fall short.

Why We Forget

Much of the time, your memory works just fine. You see a new acquaintance walking toward you, and you retrieve his name from memory without hesitation. Unfortunately, every once in a while, you end up greeting him in awkward silence—with that awful realization that you can't remember his name. How does that happen? Sometimes the answer will reside with the forces you've already learned. It could be the case, for example, that you're trying to recall the name in a context that's very different from the one in which you learned it. However, researchers have studied other explanations for forgetting. In fact, the earliest formal body of research on memory, published in 1885, focused directly on that topic. Let's begin with that work.

Ebbinghaus Quantifies Forgetting The study of forgetting was pioneered by by the German psychologist **Hermann Ebbinghaus** (1850–1909). Ebbinghaus served as his own subject. He began each study by reading through a list of nonsense syllables (e.g., *CEG* or *DAX*) one at a time. Then he read through the list again in the same order, and again, until he could recite all the items in the correct order. Next he distracted himself from rehearsing the original list by forcing himself to learn other lists. After this interval, Ebbinghaus measured his memory by seeing how many trials it took him to *relearn* the original list. If he needed fewer trials to relearn it than he had needed to learn it initially, information had been *saved* from his original study. (There is often a savings when animals relearn a conditioned response.)

For example, if Ebbinghaus took 12 trials to learn a list and 9 trials to relearn it several days later, his savings score for that elapsed time would be 25 percent (12 trials − 9 trials = 3 trials; 3 trials ÷ 12 trials = 0.25, or 25 percent). Using savings as his measure, Ebbinghaus recorded the memory retained after different time intervals. The curve he obtained is shown in **Figure 10**. As you can see, he found a rapid initial loss of memory. In fact, after one hour Ebbinghaus already had to spend half the original time to relearn the list. This initial period of rapid loss was followed by a gradually declining rate (Ebbinghaus, 1885/1964).

You have experienced the pattern revealed in Ebbinghaus's forgetting curve countless times in your life. Consider, for example, how reluctant you'd be to take an exam a week after

FIGURE 10 Ebbinghaus's Forgetting Curve

Ebbinghaus calculated his retention of nonsense syllables over a 30-day period using the savings method. The curve shows rapid forgetting and then reaches a plateau of little change.

you studied for it. You know from experience that much of what you learned will no longer be accessible. Similarly, you might find it easy to recall a name right after you've learned it, but if a week goes by when you don't use it, you might find yourself thinking, "I know I knew his name!"

Interference Why else might you forget a name that you knew a week ago? One important answer is that you didn't learn that name in isolation. Before you learned it, you had lots of other names in your head; after you learned it, you probably acquired a few more new ones. All those other names can have a negative impact on your ability to retrieve the one name you need in the moment. To make this point more formally, I want you to try to learn some new word pairs. Once again, keep working on these word pairs until you can repeat them three times in a row without an error.

> Apple–Robe
> Hat–Circle
> Bicycle–Roof
> Mouse–Magazine
> Ball–Baby
> Ear–Penny

How did it go? Examine the list. You can see what's happened—each old prompt is paired with a new response. Was it harder for you to learn these new pairs? Do you think it would now be harder for you to recall the old ones? (Give it a try.) The answer in both cases is typically "yes." This brief exercise should give you a sense of how memories can compete—or provide *interference*—with each other.

You already considered a real-life example of the problem of interference when you tried to differentiate your recollections of your episodes of toothbrushing. The specific memories interfere with each other. **Proactive interference** (*proactive* means "forward acting") refers to circumstances in which information you have acquired in the past makes it more difficult to acquire new information (see **Figure 11**). **Retroactive interference** (*retroactive* means "backward acting") occurs when the acquisition of new information makes it harder for you to remember older information. The word lists I provided demonstrate both of these types of interference. You've also experienced both proactive and retroactive interference if you've ever had to change your phone number. At first, you probably found it hard to remember the new number—the old one kept popping out (proactive interference). However, after finally being able to reliably reproduce the new one, you may have found yourself unable to remember the old number—even if you had used it for years (retroactive interference).

As with many other memory phenomena, Hermann Ebbinghaus was the first researcher to document interference rigorously through experiments. Ebbinghaus, after learning dozens of lists of nonsense syllables, found himself forgetting about 65 percent of the new ones he was learning. Fifty years later, students at Northwestern University who studied Ebbinghaus's lists had the same experience—after many trials with many lists, what the students had learned earlier interfered proactively with their recall of current lists (Underwood, 1948, 1949).

....

proactive interference Circumstances in which past memories make it more difficult to encode and retrieve new information.

retroactive interference Circumstances in which the formation of new memories makes it more difficult to recover older memories.

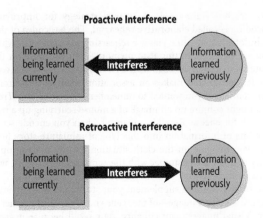

FIGURE 11 Proactive and Retroactive Interference
Proactive and retroactive interference help explain why it can be difficult to encode and retrieve memories. What you have learned in the past can make it more difficult for you to encode new information (proactive interference). What you are learning now can make it more difficult for you to retrieve old information (retroactive interference).

From Baron, Robert A., *Psychology*, 5th Edition, © 2001. Printed and electronically reproduced by permission of Pearson Education Inc., Upper Saddle River, New Jersey.

In this section, you've learned some reasons why you might forget information. It seems fitting that we move now to research that gives advice on how to make memory function better.

Improving Memory for Unstructured Information

After reading this whole section, you should have some concrete ideas about how you could improve your everyday memory performance—how you can remember more and forget less. (*The Critical Thinking in Your Life* box, later in the chapter, will help you solidify those ideas with respect to school work.) You know, especially, that you're best off trying to recover a piece of information in the same context, or by performing the same types of mental tasks, as when you first acquired it. But there's a slightly different problem with which you still need some help. It has to do with encoding unstructured or arbitrary collections of information.

For example, imagine that you are working as a clerk in a store. You must try to commit to memory the several items that each customer wants: "The woman in the green blouse wants hedge clippers and a garden hose. The man in the blue shirt wants a pair of pliers, six quarter-inch screws, and a paint scraper." This scenario, in fact, comes very close to the types of experiments in which researchers ask you to memorize paired associates. How did you go about learning the word pairs I presented earlier? The task probably was somewhat of a chore because the pairs were not particularly meaningful for you—and information that isn't meaningful is hard to remember. To find a way to get the right items to the right customer, you need to make associations seem less arbitrary. Let's explore *elaborative rehearsal* and *mnemonics*.

Elaborative Rehearsal A general strategy for improving encoding is called **elaborative rehearsal.** The basic idea of this technique is that while you are rehearsing information—while you are first committing it to memory—you elaborate on the material to enrich the encoding. One way to do this is to invent a relationship that makes an association seem less arbitrary. For example, if you wanted to remember the pair *Mouse–Tree,* you might conjure up an image of a mouse scurrying up a tree to look for cheese. Recall is enhanced when you encode separate bits of information into this type of miniature story line. Can you imagine, in the clerk situation, swiftly making up a story to link each customer with the appropriate items? (It will work with practice.) You may have already guessed that it is also often helpful to supplement your story line with a mental picture—a visual image—of the scene you are trying to remember. Visual imagery can enhance your recall because it gives you codes for both verbal and visual memories simultaneously (Paivio, 2006).

Elaborative rehearsal can also help save you from what has been called the *next-in-line effect:* When, for example, people are next in line to speak, they often can't remember what the person directly before them said. If you've ever had a circle of people each give his or her name, you're probably well acquainted with this effect. What was the name of the person directly in front of you? The origin of this effect appears to be a shift in attention toward preparing to make your own remarks or to say your own name (Bond et al., 1991). To counter this shift, you should use elaborative rehearsal. Keep your attention focused on the person in front of you and enrich your encoding of his or her name: *Judy—She's such a beauty.*

Mnemonics Another memory-enhancing option is to draw on special mental strategies called *mnemonics* (from the Greek word meaning "to remember"). **Mnemonics** are devices that encode a long series of facts by associating them with familiar and previously encoded information. Many mnemonics work by giving you ready-made retrieval cues that help organize otherwise arbitrary information. These mnemonics also encourage you to use visual imagery which, as noted earlier, provides effective elaboration as you rehearse new information.

Consider the *method of loci,* first practiced by ancient Greek orators. The singular of *loci* is *locus,* and it means "place." The method of loci is a means of remembering the order of a list of names or objects—or, for the orators, the individual sections of a long speech—by associating them with some sequence of places with which you are familiar. To remember a grocery list, you might mentally put each item sequentially along the route you take to get from home to school. To remember the list later, you mentally go through your route and find the item associated with each spot (see **Figure 12**).

The *peg-word method* is similar to the method of loci, except that you associate the items on a list with a series of cues rather than with familiar locations. Typically, the cues for the peg-word

How might a server use elaborative rehearsal or mnemonics to get the right meals to the right customers?

method are a series of rhymes that associate numbers with words. For example, you might memorize "one is a *bun,*" "two is a *shoe,*" "three is a *tree,*" and so on. Then you would associate each item on your list interacting with the appropriate cue. Suppose a history professor asked you to memorize, in order, the rulers of the Roman empire. You might have Augustus eating a platter of buns, Tiberius wearing oversized shoes, Caligula sitting in a tree, and so on. You can see that the key to learning arbitrary information is to encode the information in such a fashion that you provide yourself with efficient retrieval cues.

Metamemory

Suppose you're in a situation in which you'd really like to remember something. You're doing your best to use retrieval cues that reflect the circumstances of encoding, but you just can't get the bit of information to emerge. Part of the reason you're expending so much effort is that you're sure that you are in possession of the information. But are you correct to be so confident about the contents of your memory? Questions like this one—about how your memory works or how you know what information you possess—are questions of **metamemory.**

One major question on metamemory has been when and why *feelings-of-knowing*—the subjective sensations that you do have information stored in memory—are accurate. Research on feelings-of-knowing was pioneered by **J. T. Hart** (1965), who began his studies by asking students a series of general knowledge questions. Consider the question, "What planet is the largest in our solar system?" Do you know the answer? If you don't, how would you respond to this question: "Even though I don't remember the answer now, do I know the answer to the extent that I could pick the correct answer from among several wrong answers?" This was the question Hart put to his participants. He allowed them to give ratings from 1, to say they were quite sure they wouldn't choose correctly on the multiple choice, to 6, to say they were quite sure they would choose correctly. What would your rating be? Now here are your alternatives:

a. Mars
b. Venus
c. Earth
d. Jupiter

elaborative rehearsal A technique for improving memory by enriching the encoding of information.

mnemonic Strategy or device that uses familiar information during the encoding of new information to enhance subsequent access to the information in memory.

metamemory Implicit or explicit knowledge about memory abilities and effective memory strategies; cognition about memory.

Bread

Orange juice

Ice cream

Bananas

FIGURE 12 The Method of Loci

In the method of loci, you associate the items you wish to remember (such as the items on a grocery list) with locations along a familiar path (such as your route to and from school).

If you made an accurate feeling-of-knowing judgment, you should have been less likely to get the correct answer, d, if you gave a 1 rating than if you gave a 6. (Of course, to have a fair test you'd need to answer a long series of questions.) Hart found that when participants gave 1 ratings, they answered the questions correctly only 30 percent of the time, whereas 6 ratings predicted 75 percent success. That's pretty impressive evidence that feelings-of-knowing can be accurate.

You probably make another type of metamemory judgment, called a *judgment-of-learning* (JOL), each time you prepare for an exam. JOLs are your estimates of how well you have learned something. Research suggests that students use their JOLs to decide how to apportion their study time (Metcalfe, 2009). They spend more time reviewing material they believe they haven't already mastered. This real-world practice leads to an important question: Do JOLs allow people to predict their future performance on exams? You should want the answer to be "yes." If you *believe* that you've learned some information, you should want that to mean that you have, in fact, learned that material. However, as you might anticipate, the real answer to whether JOLs predict performance is "sometimes." Researchers have devoted a good deal of effort to try to understand when JOLs do and do not predict future performance

(Rhodes & Tauber, 2011; Undorf & Erdfelder, 2011). Much of that research focuses on how activities at encoding influence JOLs. For that reason, the most important question you can ask yourself is, "*Why*: Why do I believe I know (or don't know) this material?"

You have now learned quite a bit about how you get information in and out of memory. You know what is meant by a "good match" between the circumstances of encoding and of retrieval. The next section shifts focus from your memory processes to the content of your memories.

Stop *and* Review

① Do circumstances of recall or recognition generally provide more retrieval cues?

② At a party, why might you have the best recall of the first person to whom you spoke?

③ What does the perspective known as transfer-appropriate processing suggest?

④ For your English class, you memorize "The Raven." When you're done, you can no longer recite last

Critical Thinking in Your Life

HOW CAN MEMORY RESEARCH HELP YOU PREPARE FOR EXAMS?

One important use of critical thinking is to apply new knowledge to your life's important tasks. As you read about memory, you might ask yourself, "How will this research help me prepare for my next exam?" Let's see what advice can be generated from this type of critical thinking:

- *Encoding specificity.* As you'll recall, the principle of encoding specificity suggests that the context of retrieval should match the context of encoding. In school settings, "context" often will mean "the context of other information." If you always study material in the same context, you may find it difficult to retrieve it in a different context. As a remedy, change contexts even while you study. Ask yourself questions that mix different topics together. If you get stuck while you're taking an exam, try to generate as many retrieval cues as you can that reinstate the original context: "Let's see. We heard about this in the same lecture we learned about short-term memory. . . ."

- *Serial position.* The serial position curve suggests that, under very broad circumstances, information presented in the "middle" is least well remembered. In fact, college students fail more exam items on material from the middle of a lecture than on material from the start or end of the lecture (Holen & Oaster, 1976; Jensen, 1962). When you're listening to a lecture, remind yourself to pay special attention in the middle of the session. When it comes time to study, devote some extra time and effort to that material—and make sure not to study the material in the same order each time.

- *Elaborative rehearsal and mnemonics.* Sometimes when you study for exams, you will feel as if you are trying to acquire "unstructured information." You might, for example, be asked to memorize the dimensions of the five-factor model of personality. This feels just like a list with five items, so you need to find ways to provide structure yourself. Try to form visual images or make up sentences or stories that use the concepts in creative ways. For the five-factor model, I use the mnemonic OCEAN.

- *Metamemory.* Research on metamemory suggests that people generally have good intuitions about what they know and what they don't know. If you are in an exam situation in which there is time pressure, you should allow those intuitions to guide how you allocate your time. You might, for example, read the whole test over quickly and see which questions give you the strongest feelings-of-knowing.

As you read the basic facts from memory research, you might not have immediately seen how to put the information to use. Can you now see how critical thinking will allow you to apply psychological knowledge directly to your life?

- Why might it be a good idea to shuffle your notes before you study for an exam?
- What could a professor do to help students overcome the impact of serial position on lecture material?

---

week's assignment. Is this an example of proactive or retroactive interference?
⑤ How could you use the method of loci to remember the order of elements in the periodic table?
⑥ What is a judgment of learning?

CRITICAL THINKING Recall the experiment that tested implicit memory for U.S. states. Why did the researchers use a different state each time they replicated the experiment?

✔—Study and Review on MyPsychLab

STRUCTURES IN LONG-TERM MEMORY

Our focus so far has been on how you encode and later retrieve information from memory. This next section focuses on an important aspect of memory storage: the way in which the information you acquire over time becomes represented in large bodies of *organized knowledge*. Recall, for example, that I asked you to consider whether *grape* is a fruit. You could say *yes* very quickly. How about *porcupine*? Is it a fruit? How about *tomato*? In this section, we will consider how the difficulty of these types of judgments relates to the way information is structured in memory. You will also learn how memory organization allows you to make a best guess at the content of experiences you can't remember exactly.

Memory Structures

An essential function of memory is to draw together similar experiences, to enable you to discover patterns in your interactions with the environment. You live in a world filled with countless individual events, from which you must continually extract information to combine them into a smaller, simpler set that you can manage mentally. But apparently you don't need to expend any particular conscious effort to find structure in the world. It's unlikely that you ever formally thought to yourself something like, "Here's what belongs in a kitchen." It is through ordinary experience in the world that you have acquired mental structures to mirror environmental structures. Let's look at the types of memory structures you have formed in your moment-by-moment experience of the world.

Categories and Concepts Let's begin by discussing the mental effort a child must go through to acquire the meaning of a word, such as *doggie*. For this word to have meaning, the child must be able to store each instance in which the word *doggie* is used, as well as information about the context. In this way, the child finds out what common core experience—a furry creature with four legs—is meant by *doggie*. The child must acquire the knowledge that *doggie* applies not just to one particular animal, but to a *whole category* of creatures. This ability to categorize individual experiences—to take the same action toward them or give them the same label—is one of the most basic abilities of thinking organisms (Murphy, 2002).

The mental representations of the categories you form are called **concepts.** The concept *doggie*, for example, names the set of mental representations of experiences of dogs that a young child has gathered together in memory. (If the child hasn't yet refined his or her meaning for *doggie*, the concept might also include features that adults wouldn't consider to be appropriate.) You have acquired a vast array of concepts. You have categories for *objects* and *activities*, such as *barns* and *baseball*. Concepts may also represent *properties*, such as *red* or *large*; abstract ideas, such as *truth* or *love*; and *relations*, such as *smarter than* or *sister of*. Each concept represents a summary unit for your experience of the world.

As you consider the many categories you experience in the world, you will recognize that some category members are more or less typical. You can develop this intuition if you think about a category like *bird*. You would probably agree that a robin is a typical bird, whereas an ostrich or a penguin is atypical. The degree of typicality of a category member has real-life consequences. Classic research has shown, for example, that people respond more quickly to typical members of a category than to its more unusual ones. Your reaction time

to determine that a robin is a bird would be quicker than your reaction time to determine that an ostrich is a bird (Rosch et al., 1976). But what makes people consider a robin to be a typical bird, rather than an ostrich? Answers to this question have often focused on *family resemblance*—typical category members have attributes that overlap with many other members of the category (Rosch & Mervis, 1975). Robins have most of the attributes you associate with birds—they are about the right size, they fly, and so on. Ostriches, by contrast, are unusually large, and they do not fly. These examples suggest that family resemblance plays a role in judgments of typicality. However, recent research suggests that the most typical category members are also the *ideal* category members.

A team of researchers recruited individuals from two communities who had several decades of fishing experience: One group was Native American Menominee Indians from northern central Wisconsin; the second group was European Americans from roughly the same geographical location (Burnett et al., 2005). The experiment used these two groups because they differ with respect to the species of fish they consider to be most desirable or ideal. For example, the Menominee people consider sturgeon to be sacred. The researchers presented the participants with a group of 44 cards printed with the names of local fish. Participants sorted these cards into groups—the researchers used the participants' verbal justifications (for example, "good eating") for which fish they grouped together as an index of desirability. Also, the participants rated the extent to which each species was a good example of the "fish" category. The researchers found a 0.80 correlation between desirability and typicality. (Correlations can range from − 1.0 to + 1.0.) That's impressive evidence that the participants' notions of the "ideal" fish played a role in their judgments of typicality. In addition, the ratings were influenced by cultural differences in desirability. For example, the Menominee group rated sturgeon as even more typical than did the European American group.

If you don't have a lot of fishing experience, you might have less of a sense than these participants did about which fish are desirable. However, you can think about categories with which you have a lot of experience to see how your notions of what is ideal inform your judgments about what is typical.

Hierarchies and Basic Levels Concepts do not exist in isolation. As shown in **Figure 13**, concepts can often be arranged into meaningful organizations. A broad category like *animal* has several subcategories, such as *bird* and *fish,* which in turn contain exemplars such as *canary, ostrich, shark,* and *salmon.* The animal category is itself a subcategory of the still larger category of *living beings.* Concepts are also linked to other types of information: You store the knowledge that some birds are *edible,* some are *endangered,* some are *national symbols.*

There seems to be a level in such hierarchies at which people best categorize and think about objects. This has been called

How does the formation of categories—such as what constitutes a healthy head of lettuce, a sweet melon, or a flavorful tomato—help you make daily decisions like what to buy for dinner?

concepts Mental representation of a kind or category of items and ideas.

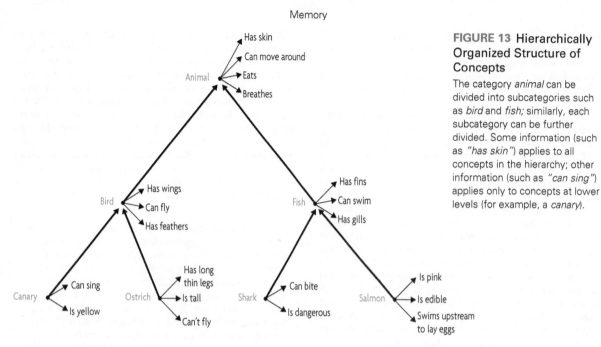

FIGURE 13 Hierarchically Organized Structure of Concepts

The category *animal* can be divided into subcategories such as *bird* and *fish;* similarly, each subcategory can be further divided. Some information (such as *"has skin"*) applies to all concepts in the hierarchy; other information (such as *"can sing"*) applies only to concepts at lower levels (for example, a *canary*).

the **basic level** (Rosch, 1973, 1978). For example, when you buy an apple at the grocery store, you could think of it as a *piece of fruit*—but that seems imprecise—or a *Golden Delicious*—but that seems too specific or narrow. The basic level is just *apple*. If you were shown a picture of such an object, that's what you'd be likely to call it. You would also be faster to say that it was an apple than that it was a piece of fruit (Rosch, 1978). The basic level emerges through your experience of the world. You are more likely to encounter the term *apple* than its more or less specific alternatives. If you became an apple grower, however, you might find yourself having daily conversations about *Cortlands* or *Granny Smiths*. With those experiences, your basic level would probably shift lower in the hierarchy.

Schemas   We have seen that concepts are the building blocks of memory hierarchies. They also serve as building blocks for more complex mental structures. Recall Figure 1. Why did you instantly know that the rabbit didn't belong in the kitchen? I suggested earlier that this judgment relied on implicit memory—but I didn't say what type of memory structure you were using. Clearly, what you need is some representation in memory that combines the individual concepts of a kitchen—your knowledge about ovens, sinks, and refrigerators—into a larger unit. We call that larger unit a schema. **Schemas** are conceptual frameworks, or clusters of knowledge, regarding objects, people, and situations. Schemas are "knowledge packages" that encode complex generalizations about your experience of the structure of the environment. You have schemas for kitchens and bedrooms, race car drivers and professors, surprise parties and graduations. A *script* is a more specific type

of memory representation that specifies how events unfold in time (Schank & Abelson, 1977). For example, you have likely encoded scripts that specify what happens when you go to a restaurant or visit a doctor's office.

Many types of schemas shape your day-to-day experiences. For example, the attachment relationships children form with their parents provide schemas for later social interactions. Also, you possess a *self-schema*—a memory structure that allows you to organize information about yourself.

One thing you may have guessed is that your schemas do not include all the individual details of all your varied experiences. A schema represents your average experience of situations in the environment. Thus your schemas are not permanent but shift with your changing life events. Your schemas also include only those details in the world to which you have devoted sufficient attention. For example, when asked to draw the information on the head sides of U.S. coins, college students virtually never filled in the word *Liberty,* although it appears on every coin (Rubin & Kontis, 1983). Check a coin! Thus your schemas provide an accurate reflection of what you've *noticed* about the world. Let's now look at all the ways in which you use your concepts and schemas.

Using Memory Representations   Let's consider some instances of memory structures in action. To begin, consider the picture in Part A of **Figure 14**. What is it? Although this is certainly an unusual member of the category, you probably reached the conclusion "It's a chair" with reasonable ease. However, to do so, you needed to draw on your memory representations of members of that category. You can say "It's a chair" because the object in the figure calls to mind your past experiences of chairs.

Researchers have provided two theories of how people use concepts in memory to categorize the objects they encounter in the world. One theory suggests that, for each concept

....

basic level The level of categorization that can be retrieved from memory most quickly and used most efficiently.

schema General conceptual framework, or cluster of knowledge, regarding objects, people, and situations; knowledge package that encodes generalizations about the structure of the environment.

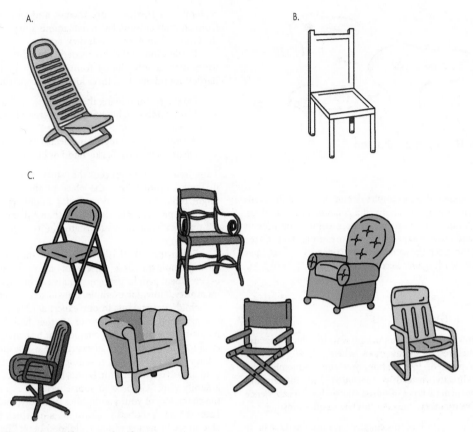

FIGURE 14 Theories of Categorization
A. What is this unusual object? B. One theory suggests that you categorize this object as a chair by comparing it to a single prototype stored in memory. C. An alternative theory suggests that you categorize this object by comparing it to the many exemplars you have in memory.

in memory, you encode a **prototype**—a representation of the most central or average member of a category (Rosch, 1978). On this view, you recognize objects by comparing them to prototypes in memory. Because the picture in Part A of Figure 14 matches many of the important attributes of the prototype in Part B, you can recognize the picture as a chair.

An alternative theory suggests that people retain memories of the many different **exemplars** they experience for each category. Part C of Figure 14 gives you a subset of the exemplars of chairs you might have seen. On the exemplar view, you recognize an object by comparing it to the exemplars you have stored in memory. You recognize the picture as a chair because it is similar to several of those exemplars. Researchers have conducted a large number of studies to contrast prototype and exemplar accounts of categorization. The data largely support the exemplar view: People appear to categorize the objects they encounter by comparing them to multiple representations in memory (Nosofsky, 2011; Voorspoels et al., 2008).

The picture in Figure 14 was meant to be an unusual chair but clearly a chair nonetheless. However, sometimes the world

provides ambiguous stimuli—and you use prior knowledge to help interpret those stimuli. Look at Figure 15. Do you see a duck or a rabbit? Let's suppose you have the expectation that you're going to see a duck. If you match the features of the picture against the features of a duck present in exemplars in memory, you're likely to be reasonably content. The same thing would happen if you were expecting a rabbit. You use information from memory to generate—and confirm—expectations.

As previously noted, memory representations also allow you to understand when something is unusual in the world. That's why you could quickly notice the anomalous rabbit in the center of Figure 1. Because the rabbit is inconsistent with your kitchen schema, you'd also be particularly likely to remember seeing it in the picture. That claim is supported by a study in which researchers filled a graduate student office with both typical objects (such as notebook, pencil) and atypical objects (such as harmonica, toothbrush) (Lampinen et al., 2001). Participants spent one minute in the room. Later in the experiment, the participants indicated which items on a list had been present in the room. Their memory was consistently more accurate for the atypical items than for the typical items. This study illustrates how memory structures direct your attention to unusual aspects of a scene.

....

prototype The most representative example of a category.

exemplar Member of a category that people have encountered.

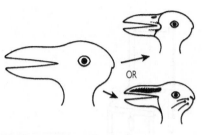

FIGURE 15 Recognition Illusion
Duck or rabbit?

Taken together, these examples demonstrate that the availability of memory representations influences the way you think about the world. Your past experiences color your present experiences and provide expectations for the future. You will see shortly that, for much the same reasons, concepts and schemas can sometimes work against accurate memory.

Remembering as a Reconstructive Process

Let's turn now to another important way in which you use memory structures. In many cases, when you are asked to remember a piece of information, you can't remember the information directly. Instead, you *reconstruct* the information based on more general types of stored knowledge. To experience **reconstructive memory,** consider this trio of questions:

- Did the first section of this chapter have the word *the* in it?
- Did 1991 contain the day July 7?
- Did you breathe yesterday between 2:05 and 2:10 P.M.?

You probably were willing to answer "Yes!" to each of these questions without much hesitation, but you almost certainly don't have specific, episodic memories to help you (unless, of course, something happened to fix these events in memory—perhaps July 7 is your birthday or you crossed out all the *the*'s in the first section of the chapter to curb your boredom). To answer these questions, you must use more general memories to reconstruct what is likely to have happened. Let's examine this process of reconstruction in a bit more detail.

The Accuracy of Reconstructive Memory If people reconstruct some memories, rather than recovering a specific memory representation for what happened, then you might expect that you could find occasions on which the reconstructed memory differed from the real occurrence—distortions. One of the most impressive demonstrations of memory distortions is also the oldest. In his classic book *Remembering: A Study in Experimental and Social Psychology* (1932), **Sir Frederic Bartlett** (1886–1969) undertook a program of research to demonstrate how individuals' prior knowledge influenced the way they remembered new information. Bartlett studied the way British undergraduates

. . . .

reconstructive memory The process of putting information together based on general types of stored knowledge in the absence of a specific memory representation.

remembered stories whose themes and wording were taken from another culture. His most famous story was "The War of the Ghosts," an American Indian tale.

Bartlett found that his readers' reproductions of the story were often greatly altered from the original. The distortions Bartlett found involved three kinds of reconstructive processes:

- *Leveling*—simplifying the story.
- *Sharpening*—highlighting and overemphasizing certain details.
- *Assimilating*—changing the details to better fit the participant's own background or knowledge.

Thus readers reproduced the story with words familiar in their culture taking the place of those unfamiliar: *Boat* might replace *canoe* and *go fishing* might replace *hunt seals*. Bartlett's participants also often changed the story's plot to eliminate references to supernatural forces that were unfamiliar in their culture.

Following Bartlett's lead, contemporary researchers have demonstrated a variety of memory distortions that occur when people use constructive processes to reproduce memories. How, for example, do you remember what you did as a child? Participants in one experiment were asked to indicate whether, before the age of 10, they had "Met and shook hands with a favorite TV character at a theme resort" (Braun et al., 2002, p. 7). After answering that question—as part of a larger life-experiences inventory—some of the participants read an advertisement for Disneyland that evoked the idea of a family visit: "Go back to your childhood . . . and remember the characters of your youth, Mickey, Goofy, and Daffy Duck." Later the ad described circumstances in which the visitor was able to shake hands with a childhood hero: "Bugs Bunny, the character you've idolized on TV, is only several feet away. . . . You [reach up] to grab his hand" (p. 6). After reading this type of ad, participants were now more likely to indicate—though they hadn't before—that they shook a character's hand. Moreover, they were more likely to report a specific memory that they had shaken Bugs Bunny's hand at Disneyland: 16 percent of the participants in this advertisement group remembered having done so versus 7 percent of the participants in a group that hadn't read the autobiographical ad. Of course, none of these memories can be accurate: Bugs Bunny isn't a Disney character!

This study suggests how even memories for your own life events are reconstructed from various sources. The study also illustrates the fact that people are not always accurate at recalling the original sources for various components of their memories (Mitchell & Johnson, 2009). In fact, researchers have demonstrated that individuals will sometimes come to believe that they actually carried out actions that they, in fact, only accomplished in their imaginations.

A group of 40 college students participated in an experiment that had three sessions (Seamon et al., 2006). In session 1, the students joined an experimenter for a one-hour walk around campus. The pair stopped 48 times during the walk. At each stop, the experimenter read an action statement such as "Check the Pepsi machine for change." After hearing each statement, the students did one of four things: They performed the actions themselves, they watched the experimenter perform the actions, they imagined that they were performing the actions, or they imagined that the experimenter was

Featured Study

Suppose, while you were at a party, someone told you the man you had just met was a millionaire. How would this affect your memories for his actions at the party? What if you had been told he only had delusions of being a millionaire?

performing them. In addition, half the actions were bizarre. For example, rather than "Check the Pepsi machine for change," half the students got "Get down on one knee and propose marriage to the machine." The experimenter and the participants took a second walk during session 2, which took place 24 hours later. On the second walk, the students imagined themselves or the experimenter performing some new and some old actions (both ordinary and bizarre) at locations that were also divided between new and old. In session 3, which took place two weeks after session 2, the students were asked to think back to the first session. They tried to recall whether each action had been performed or imagined. For both ordinary and bizarre actions, the same finding held true: Students often recalled that the actions they had only been asked to imagine had actually been performed by them or the experimenter. Thus, some participants agreed that they had actually proposed marriage to a Pepsi machine or patted a dictionary to ask how it was doing when they had only imagined doing so.

Can you find applications of this result in your own life? Suppose you keep reminding yourself to set your alarm clock before you go to bed. Each time you remind yourself, you form a picture in your head of the steps you must go through. If you imagine setting the clock often enough, you might mistakenly come to believe that you actually did so!

It is important to keep in mind, however, that just as with perceptual illusions, psychologists often infer the normal operation of processes by demonstrating circumstances in which the processes lead to errors. You can think of these memory distortions as the consequences of processes that usually work pretty well. In fact, a lot of the time, you don't need to remember the exact details of a particular episode. Reconstructing the gist of events will serve just fine.

Flashbulb Memories For most of your past life experiences, you would probably agree that you need to reconstruct the memories. For example, if someone asked you how you celebrated your birthday three years ago, you'd likely count backwards and try to reconstruct the context. However, there are some circumstances in which people believe that their memories remain completely faithful to the original events. These types of memories—which are called **flashbulb memories**—arise when people experience emotionally charged events: People's memories are so vivid that they seem almost to be photographs of the original incident. The first research on flashbulb memories focused on people's recollections of public events (Brown & Kulik, 1977). For example, the researchers asked participants if they had specific memories of how they first learned about the assassination of President John F. Kennedy. All but one of the 80 participants reported vivid recollections.

The concept of flashbulb memory applies to both private and public events. People might have vivid memories, for example, of an accident they experienced or how they learned about the September 11 attacks. However, research on flashbulb memories has largely focused on public events. To conduct these studies, researchers recruit participants and ask them to share their memories of emotionally resonant events. For different age groups, such events might be the *Challenger* explosion, the death of Princess Diana, or the attack on Pearl Harbor. The content of flashbulb memories reflects how people learned about the events. For example, people who acquired their information from the media tend to include more event facts in their memory reports than do people who acquired information from another individual (Bohannon et al., 2007). U.S. citizens had more specific recollections of the September 11 attacks than did citizens of other countries such as Italy, the Netherlands, and Japan (Curci & Luminet, 2006).

Research on these public events confirms that people acquire flashbulb memories. The question remains, however, whether these memories are as accurate as people believe them to be. To address the question of accuracy, researchers recruit participants directly after the events and then assess their memories at one or more points later in time. One such study began on September 12, 2001.

The day after the September 11 attacks, students provided answers to a series of questions, including "Where were you when you first heard the news?" and "Were there others with you and, if so, who?" (Talarico & Rubin, 2003). For purposes of comparison, the students also reported memories

Featured Study

flashbulb memories People's vivid and richly detailed memory in response to personal or public events that have great emotional significance.

for an everyday event (such as a party or sporting event) that occurred in the few days before the attack. The students answered the same types of questions for those everyday memories (for example, "Where were you physically?" and "Were there others present and, if so, who?"). The researchers called the students back to the laboratory 1, 6, or 32 weeks after the initial memory test. At each delay, the students answered the same series of memory questions they had answered on September 12. The researchers determined which details were consistent with the original reports and which were inconsistent. The students' memory performance showed no differences between September 11 memories and everyday memories. Their reports of consistent details fell from one day to 32 weeks after the event, but at much the same rate for flashbulb and everyday memories. Similarly, the students introduced inconsistent details at the same rate for both types of memories.

Why might the different words eyewitnesses use to describe an accident affect their later recall?

The researchers extended their project by inviting the original participants for another memory test after a full year had passed (Talarico & Rubin, 2007). The conclusions remained the same: In a pattern that was quite similar for both types of memories, the participants' ability to provide correct details decreased, whereas their tendency to introduce incorrect details increased. There was, however, one feature that set flashbulb memories apart from everyday memories: For their flashbulb memories, participants were considerably more confident that they were providing accurate memories.

In fact, researchers have suggested that people's trust in their flashbulb memories arises in part because the events on which the memories focus are socially important. For people of a certain age, it is crucial to remember how they learned about John F. Kennedy's assassination; for a younger cohort, September 11th has the same resonance. With respect to the terrorist attack, the researchers reached this conclusion: "The desire to 'never forget' results in overconfidence in the accuracy of our memory for hearing the news because the alternative is to admit being a callous observer and, in the case of the 11th September attacks, a poor patriot. Instead, we maintain vivid recollections and retell our stories in order to achieve social goals, not memorial ones" (Talarico & Rubin, 2007, p. 575).

The importance of memories of events such as September 11th indicates why it is often difficult for people to accept the results of research on flashbulb memories. How could memories that feel so vivid and true actually be inaccurate (or, at least, be no more accurate than other less vivid memories)? The same processes of reconstruction we saw earlier apply to flashbulb memories. However, people's desire to hold tight to their memories for particularly emotional events makes it quite difficult for them to consider the possibility that those memories might not be accurate.

Let's turn now to a domain in which people's overconfidence in their memories can have negative real-world consequences. In the domain of eyewitness testimony, people are always held responsible for reporting *exactly* what happened. ◉

Eyewitness Memory About a year ago, I was riding a train into New York City. An hour into the trip, I witnessed events that made me very uneasy. When the train stopped at a suburban station, a man who looked very agitated got on the train clutching a duffel bag. He stayed right inside the train doors until a buzzer rang to indicate that the doors were about to close. At that moment, he dropped the bag to the train floor

and sprinted off the train. As you might imagine, I quickly found a conductor to report what I had seen. It turned out that I wasn't the only passenger who had witnessed these events. The conductor asked us to describe exactly what had happened. Although there was reasonable overlap in our general account of the episode, it soon became clear that we differed with respect to our recollections of important details such as the man's age, height, and eye color. I suspect our collective eyewitness testimony would never have allowed the police to find the man who dropped the bag. (Are you wondering what the bag contained? As it turned out, it was filled with financial documents. How intriguing!)

Suppose the police had been able to arrest a suspect—who was then charged with corporate crimes. If I or one of my fellow passengers had been brought into the courtroom as a witness, we would have been charged "to tell the truth and nothing but the truth." Throughout this chapter, however, you have seen that whether a memory is accurate or inaccurate depends on the care with which it was encoded and the match of the circumstances of encoding and retrieval. Consider the cartoon of a crowd scene you examined earlier in the chapter, in Figure 3. Without looking back, try to write down or think through as much as you can about the scene. Now look again at Figure 3. How did you do? Was everything you recalled accurate? Because researchers understand that people may not be able to report "the truth," even when they genuinely wish to do so, they have focused a good deal of attention on the topic of *eyewitness memory*. The goal is to help the legal system discover the best methods for ensuring the accuracy of witnesses' memories.

Influential studies on eyewitness memory were carried out by **Elizabeth Loftus** (1979; Wells & Loftus, 2003) and her colleagues. The general conclusion from their research was that eyewitnesses' memories for what they had seen were quite vulnerable to distortion from *postevent information*. For example, participants in one study were shown a film of an automobile accident and were asked to estimate the speeds of the cars involved (Loftus & Palmer, 1974). However, some participants were asked, "How fast were the cars going when they smashed into each other?" while others were asked, "How fast were the cars going when they contacted each other?" *Smash* participants estimated the cars' speed to have been over 40 miles per hour; *contact* participants estimated the speed at 30 miles per hour. About a week later, all the eyewitnesses were

◉ **Watch** the **Video** *Thinking Like a Psychologist: Eyewitness Testimony* on **MyPsychLab**

Psychology in Your Life

HOW CAN YOU BENEFIT FROM THE "TESTING EFFECT"?

What strategies do you use when you want to learn important information? If you're like many students, your impulse might be to study the material as often as you can. However, a large body of research supports the existence of the *testing effect:* Students have better long-term retention of information when they take a test on the material rather than engaging in repeated study (Roediger & Butler, 2011).

Consider a project in which students read two brief science passages (Roediger & Karpicke, 2006). In the project's first phase, participants read one of the passages twice. That's the *Study, Study* condition. The participants read the second passage once and then immediately tried to recall its contents. That's the *Study, Test* condition. In the project's second phase, participants tried to recall both passages either five minutes, two days, or one week later. The figure presents the results. As you can see, when participants were tested after just five minutes, there was an advantage for repeated study. However, after either two days or one week, participants were much better off when they had engaged in study followed by a test.

Another project demonstrated the testing effect in the context of more elaborate study procedures. College undergraduates studied material from a science text (Karpicke & Blunt, 2011). In one condition, participants learned to create *concept maps* for the texts: "In concept mapping, students construct a diagram in which nodes are used to represent concepts, and links connecting the nodes represent relations among the concepts" (p. 772). You can imagine carrying out that exercise as a way to commit science concepts to memory. In another condition, participants obtained *retrieval practice:* They studied the text and then attempted to recall the information; they studied the text a second time and once again recalled it. One week later, the students returned to the laboratory to complete a short-answer test. Students who had engaged in concept mapping answered 45 percent of the questions correctly. Students who engaged in retrieval practice got 67 percent correct. That's quite a difference! (And

consider all the extra work the students carried out to create the concept maps.)

Do these studies suggest a plan of action? After you have studied material, you should give yourself a test! After you read this chapter, take the practice exam, consult the answer key, and then ensure you know why the right answer is, in fact, the right answer. You might also ask your professor to give you more exams. Researchers carried out a project in a middle-school science classroom in which students took a series of multiple-choice quizzes across a semester (McDaniel et al., 2011). The multiple-choice questions covered a subset of the material the teacher taught. On the end-of-semester exam, students got 79 percent of the questions right for material on which they had been quizzed. They got 72 percent correct on the material for which they hadn't previously been quizzed. Just taking the quizzes (which didn't count toward their grades) gave the students a 7 percent boost on the material those quizzes covered!

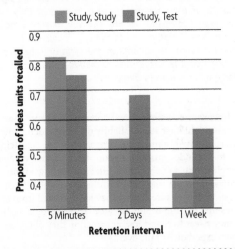

asked, "Did you see any broken glass?" In fact, no broken glass had appeared in the film. However, about a third of the *smash* participants reported that there had been glass, whereas only 14 percent of the *contact* eyewitnesses did so. Thus postevent information had a substantial effect on what eyewitnesses reported they had experienced.

This experiment represents what is probably the real-life experience of most eyewitnesses: After the events, they have a lot of opportunities to acquire new information that can interact with their original memories. In fact, Loftus and her colleagues demonstrated that participants often succumb to a *misinformation effect* (Frenda et al., 2011). For example, in

one study participants watched a slide show of a traffic accident. They were then asked a series of questions. For half of the participants, one question was, "Did another car pass the red Datsun while it was stopped at the stop sign?" For the other half, the question read, "Did another car pass the red Datsun while it was stopped at the yield sign?" The original slide show displayed a stop sign. Still, when participants were asked to recognize the original slide between options with a stop sign or a yield sign, those who had been asked about the stop sign were 75 percent correct, whereas those who had been asked about a yield sign were only 41 percent correct (Loftus et al., 1978). That's a large impact of misinformation.

Research on eyewitness memory has evolved to capture a broader range of the experiences of real eyewitnesses. For example, researchers have turned their attention to circumstances in which witnesses discuss events with other people who saw the same events, co-witnesses, before they provide testimony. Survey data confirm the importance of this question: In one sample, 86 percent of the individuals who had witnessed serious events such as physical assault and property vandalism had discussed the events with a co-witness (Paterson & Kemp, 2006). When people spoke to the police about the events, they were discouraged only 14 percent of the time from having such conversations. This is problematic because co-witnesses may serve as a source of information that taints the witnesses' own memories.

A team of researchers sought to demonstrate that people's memory performance can be harmed if they discuss events with co-witnesses (Paterson et al., 2011). Each participant watched one of two versions of a robbery video. The two versions differed in several details (for example, the thief called himself Joe versus James in the two versions). After watching a video, the participants were paired up to discuss what they'd seen. In some pairs, both participants had watched the same video. In other pairs, the participants had watched contrasting videos. That different-video condition should increase the probability that participants will acquire misinformation from their co-witness. One week later, the participants were interviewed to elicit their memories for the robbery. At the end of the interview, the participants signed transcripts of their statements to indicate that they were "accurate and complete" (p. 46). The researchers compared the participants' statements to the original videos they had watched. Of the participants in the different-video condition, 42 percent reported misinformation compared to only 19 percent in the same-video condition.

The interviewer actually warned some participants that their co-witness might have seen a slightly different video. However, that warning had almost no impact on the participants' ability to exclude misinformation from their statements. This experiment suggests that, after discussing events with co-witnesses, people may find it difficult to isolate their own eyewitness memories from what they have learned from others. Such results are important because when people testify in court, they swear to report just information they obtained from their own experience of the events.

We have now considered several important features of the encoding, storage, and retrieval of information. The final section of the chapter discusses the brain bases of these memory functions.

Stop *and* Review

① What is the relationship between categories and concepts?

② What claim is made by the exemplar theory of categorization?

③ On Frederic Bartlett's account, what three processes create distortions in reconstructive memory?

④ How did Elizabeth Loftus and her colleagues demonstrate misinformation effects?

CRITICAL THINKING Recall the study that investigated the typicality of fish. Why might the researchers have used two groups from the same geographical region?

✔ **Study** and **Review** on **MyPsychLab**

BIOLOGICAL ASPECTS OF MEMORY

The time has come, once again, for you to recall the number you committed to memory at the beginning of the chapter. Can you still remember it? What was the point of this exercise? Think for a minute about biological aspects of your ability to look at an arbitrary piece of information and commit it instantly to memory. How can you do that? To encode a memory requires that you instantly change something inside your brain. If you wish to retain that memory for at least the length of a chapter, the change must have the potential to become permanent. Have you ever wondered how memory storage is possible? My excuse for having you recall an arbitrary number was so that I could ask you to reflect on how remarkable the biology of memory really is. Let's take a closer look inside the brain.

Searching for the Engram

Let's consider your memory for the number 51 or, more specifically, your memory that the number 51 was the number you tried to remember. How could we determine where in your brain that memory resides? **Karl Lashley** (1929, 1950), who performed pioneering work on the anatomy of memory, referred to this question as the search for the **engram**, the physical memory representation. Lashley trained rats to learn mazes, removed varying-size portions of their cortexes, and then retested their memories for the mazes. Lashley found that memory impairment from brain lesioning was proportional to the amount of tissue removed. The impairment grew worse as more of the cortex was damaged. However, memory was not affected by *where* in the cortex the tissue was removed. Lashley concluded that the elusive engram did not exist in any localized regions but was widely distributed throughout the entire cortex.

Perhaps Lashley could not localize the engram partly because of the variety of types of memories that are called into play even in an apparently simple situation. Maze learning, in fact, involves complex interactions of spatial, visual, and olfactory signals. Neuroscientists now believe that memory for complex sets of information is distributed across many neural systems, even though discrete types of knowledge are separately processed and localized in limited regions of the brain (Nadel & Hardt, 2011).

Five major brain structures are involved in memory:

* The *cerebellum,* essential for procedural memory, memories acquired by repetition, and classically conditioned responses

....

engram The physical memory trace for information in the brain.

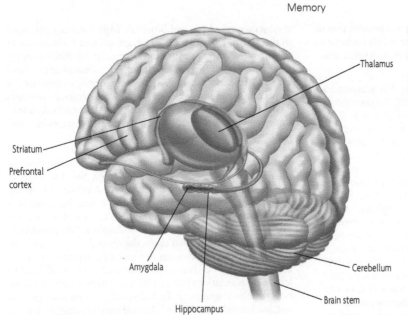

FIGURE 17 Brain Structures Involved in Memory
This simplified diagram shows some of the main structures of the brain that are involved in the formation, storage, and retrieval of memories.

- The *striatum*, a complex of structures in the forebrain; the likely basis for habit formation and for stimulus response connections
- The *cerebral cortex*, responsible for sensory memories and associations between sensations
- The *hippocampus*, largely responsible for declarative memory of facts, dates, and names, and the consolidation of spatial memories
- The *amygdala*, which plays a critical role in the formation and retrieval of memories with emotional significance

Other parts of the brain, such as the thalamus, the basal forebrain, and the prefrontal cortex, are involved also as way stations for the formation of particular types of memories (see **Figure 17**).

Here, let's take a look at the methods that neuroscientists use to draw conclusions about the role of specific brain structures for memory. This section examines two types of research. First, we consider the insights generated by "experiments of nature"—circumstances in which individuals who have suffered brain damage volunteer to further memory research. Second, we reflect on the ways in which researchers are applying new brain-imaging techniques to improve their understanding of memory processes in the brain.

Memory Disorders

In 1960, Nick A., a young Air Force radar technician, experienced a freak injury that permanently changed his life. Nick had been sitting at his desk while his roommate played with a miniature fencing foil. Then, suddenly, Nick stood up and turned around—just as his buddy happened to lunge with the sword. The foil pierced Nick's right nostril and continued to cut into the left side of his brain. The accident left Nick seriously disoriented. His worst problem was **amnesia,** the failure of memory over a prolonged period. Because of Nick's amnesia, he forgets many events immediately after they happen. After he reads a few paragraphs of writing, the first sentences slip

from his memory. He cannot remember the plot of a television show unless, during commercials, he actively thinks about and rehearses what he was just watching.

The particular type of amnesia from which Nick suffers is called **anterograde amnesia.** This means that Nick can no longer form explicit memories for events that occur after the time at which he suffered physical damage. One consequence of chronic alcoholism is *Korsakoff's syndrome,* for which anterograde amnesia is a prominent symptom. Other patients suffer from **retrograde amnesia.** In those cases, brain damage prevents access to memories that preceded the moment of injury. If you've ever had the misfortune of receiving a sharp blow to the head (during, for example, a car crash), you're likely to have experienced retrograde amnesia for the events leading up to the accident. ◉

Researchers are grateful to patients like Nick for allowing themselves to be studied as "experiments of nature." By relating the locus of brain injuries like Nick's to patterns of performance deficit, researchers have begun to understand the mapping between the types of memories reviewed in this chapter and regions of the brain (Squire & Wixted, 2011). Nick still remembers how to do things—his procedural knowledge appears to be intact even in the absence of declarative knowledge. So, for example, he remembers how to mix, stir, and bake the ingredients in a recipe, but he forgets what the ingredients are.

The selective impairment of explicit memory of the sort demonstrated by Nick is one of the major facts of the biology of memory: There is abundant evidence to support the conclusion

....

◉ **Watch** the Video *Special Topics: When Memory Fails* on **MyPsychLab**

amnesia A failure of memory caused by physical injury, disease, drug use, or psychological trauma.

anterograde amnesia An inability to form explicit memories for events that occur after the time of physical damage to the brain.

retrograde amnesia An inability to retrieve memories from the time before physical damage to the brain.

that different brain regions underlie explicit and implicit uses of memory (Voss & Paller, 2008). However, researchers continue to explore which exact functions are subsumed by each brain area.

A team of researchers tested people who had experienced damage to the hippocampus (Aly et al., 2010). The participants studied colored drawings of faces and lists of words. Then, they completed recognition memory tests for each type of stimulus. The participants indicated their recognition on a scale ranging from 1 (certain it is new) to 6 (certain it is old). The participants' recognition performance was much more impaired for words than for faces. The researchers wanted to understand that result, so that they could further pinpoint the hippocampus's role in recognition memory. Their analysis focused on the distinction between recollection and familiarity. Suppose you recognize a woman walking by you. If you have a concrete sense of how you know the woman, that's recollection. If you know that you know the woman, but you can't recall how or why, that's familiarity. The researchers suggested that faces are more likely to create experiences of familiarity than are words. On that view, the reason that the participants with hippocampal damage had greater recognition memory for faces than for words is because the hippocampus is necessary for recollection but not for familiarity. The data supported that hypothesis for the hippocampus's particular function.

This experiment demonstrates how research on people who have amnesia can provide a deeper understanding of the way that precise memory functions are distributed to particular brain structures.

The cases in which people lose the ability to recall past information or acquire new information are the most dramatic forms of memory disorders. However, people experience less extensive memory disruptions as a result of injury or disease. *Alzheimer's disease* is the most common disease that affects memory function. The disease affects about 13 percent of Americans ages 65 and older; it affects 43 percent of Americans 85 and older (Alzheimer's Association, 2011). Alzheimer's disease onset is deceptively mild—in early stages the only observable symptom may be memory impairment. However, its course is one of steady deterioration. Individuals with Alzheimer's disease may show gradual personality changes, such as apathy, lack of spontaneity, and withdrawal from social interactions. In advanced stages, people with Alzheimer's disease may become completely mute and inattentive, even forgetting the names of their spouse and children.

Human aging is accompanied by some ordinary changes in memory function. To make a timely diagnosis of Alzheimer's disease, doctors must determine whether older adults' memory impairments are something more than ordinary change. The symptoms of Alzheimer's disease were first described in 1906 by the German psychiatrist Alois Alzheimer. In those earliest investigations, Alzheimer noted that the brains of individuals who had died from the disease contained unusual tangles of neural tissue and sticky deposits called plaques. Still, Alzheimer could not determine whether those brain changes were the cause of the disease or its products. Contemporary researchers have provided evidence that plaques themselves cause the brain to deteriorate (Hardy & Selkoe, 2002). The plaques are formed from

Watch the **Video** *Memory Hazards and What Happens with Alzheimer's* on **MyPsychLab**

a substance called amyloid β-peptide (Aβ). Ordinary processes in the human brain that aid in the growth and maintenance of neurons create Aβ as a byproduct. Normally, Aβ dissolves in the fluid surrounding neurons, without any consequences. However, in Alzheimer's disease, Aβ becomes deadly to neurons: Aβ forms plaques and causes brain cells to self-destruct. Researchers study individuals who are at high risk for Alzheimer's disease to understand the biological basis for successive changes in memory function (Murphy et al., 2008).

Researchers often seek out people who have damage in particular brain regions to test specific theories about the biology of memory processes. Recall, for example, the discussion of metamemory which revealed that people's feeling-of-knowing judgments are often reasonably accurate. Researchers suggested that regions of the prefrontal cortex (PFC) (see Figure 17) provide the brain basis for those judgments (Modirrousta & Fellows, 2008). To test that claim, the researchers identified five individuals who had damage in those PFC regions. These individuals with PFC damage and matched controls all tried to learn new associations between faces and names. Even when the two participant groups performed equally well on a recognition test, the individuals with PFC damage were consistently less accurate on their feeling-of-knowing judgments. This experiment supports the claim that the prefrontal cortex plays a role in metamemory. It also provides an example of the value of research that examines more subtle forms of memory disorder.

Brain Imaging

Psychologists have gained a great deal of knowledge about the relationship between anatomy and memory from the amnesic patients who generously serve as participants in these experiments. However, the advent of brain-imaging techniques has enabled researchers to study memory processes in individuals without brain damage. For example, using positron emission tomography (PET), Endel Tulving and his colleagues (Habib et al., 2003) have identified a difference in activation between the two brain hemispheres in the encoding and retrieval of episodic information. Their studies parallel standard memory studies. For example, in the encoding phase of an experiment, participants might study lists of nouns such as "rabbit" and "sword." In the retrieval phase, participants receive a longer list of words and must indicate whether each word was on the earlier list (in which case they respond "old") or was absent from that list (in which case they respond "new"). To understand the brain bases of these processes, participants' cerebral blood flow is monitored through PET scans during encoding or retrieval. These researchers discovered disproportionately high brain activity in the left prefrontal cortex for encoding of episodic information and in the right prefrontal cortex for retrieval of episodic information. Thus the processes show some anatomical distinctions in addition to the conceptual distinctions made by cognitive psychologists.

In light of hemispheric lateralization results, the researchers considered the question of why the two hemispheres of the brain might have different specializations for these memory processes: "We might speculate that, earlier in evolution, mental functions were fewer than today and their cortical basis was bilateral. As more sophisticated mental capacities evolved there was a growing demand for cortical space. The solution to this problem was hemispheric specialization: new functions were taken over by one hemisphere, at the cost of displacing earlier functions which, however, were retained in the other hemisphere" (Habib et al., pp. 243-244).

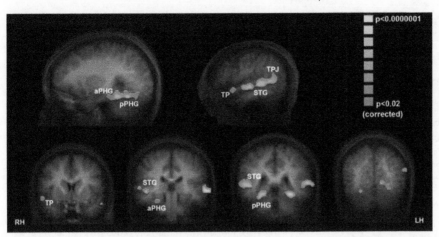

FIGURE 19 Brain Regions That Predict Successful Memory

When this set of brain regions was particularly active at time of encoding, people were more likely to remember details from their viewing of a sitcom. The areas are the right temporal pole (TP), superior temporal gyrus (STG), anterior parahippocampal cortex (aPHG), posterior parahippocampal gyrus (pPHG), and temporal parietal junction (TPJ). RH and LH refer to the right and left hemispheres.

Research with functional magnetic resonance imaging (fMRI) has also provided remarkable detail about the way that memory operations are distributed in the brain. For example, studies with fMRI have begun to identify the specific brain regions that are activated when new memories are formed. Consider a study in which participants underwent fMRI scans while watching an episode of the sitcom "Curb Your Enthusiasm" that was new to them (Hasson et al., 2008). Over the course of 27 minutes, the main character engaged in a series of events such as attending a dinner party and arguing with friends. Three weeks later, the participants returned to the laboratory to take a 77-question memory test on the episode. Each participant remembered some details but not others. The researchers analyzed the fMRI data to identify those brain regions that were particularly active when information was successfully encoded. As shown in **Figure 19**, several brain regions emerged from that analysis. Unless you pursue studies in cognitive neuroscience, you needn't worry why it is activity in exactly this set of structures that predicts later recall. Figure 19 should suggest to you that researchers are making progress toward the goal of witnessing the birth and consolidation of new memories.

Brain scans also provide information about how memory processes unfold in time. If you try to recall the capital of France, the answer might present itself to you (or not) rather quickly. However, if you try to recall what happened the first time you met someone from France, you'll likely need more time to retrieve and elaborate that memory. At first, you might recall the bare outline of the situation. In my case, I quickly remember that I heard a couple speaking French on a bus as I made my way toward Boston. As I think more about that day, I remember how diligently I was trying to use the French I'd learned in school to understand the conversation. The couple noticed that I was eavesdropping and, rather than getting angry, asked me for directions to Fenway Park. They have traveled from Paris, in part, to see an American baseball game! As I write these words, I can feel more and more aspects of the moment become vivid in memory. For those sorts of rich autobiographical memories, the role of different regions of the brain changes over time.

A team of researchers asked participants to retrieve autobiographical memories while undergoing fMRI scans (Daselaar et al., 2008). Participants heard a cue word, such as tree, and attempted to bring a specific event to mind that was associated with the word. Participants pushed a button on a response box to indicate when they had retrieved a memory. Because this process unfolded over several seconds, the researchers were able to determine how different brain areas became involved in different aspects of autobiographical memory. For example, early on, structures like the hippocampus were active as participants searched their episodic memories. As participants elaborated their memories, activity in other areas became more prominent. For example, participants' visual cortex became more active as they enriched their memories with visual images. When the visual cortex was particularly active, participants reported the strongest sense that they were actually reliving the memory.

Take a moment to retrieve your own memory in response to *tree*. Do you feel your recollection of the event become more elaborate over time? The fMRI scans provide a moment-by-moment account of where and how that elaboration occurs in your brain.

The results from imaging studies illustrate why researchers draw from different disciplines in the quest for a full understanding of memory processes. Classic memory research provides the fuel for neuropsychologists' detection of specialized brain structures. At the same time, the realities of physiology constrain psychologists' theories of the mechanisms of encoding, storage, and retrieval. Through shared effort, scientists in several fields of research provide great insight into the operation of memory processes.

Stop and Review

① What did Karl Lashley conclude about the location of the engram?

② What has been learned about the impairment of implicit memory for individuals with amnesia?

③ What have PET studies indicated about the brain bases of encoding and retrieval of episodic information?

CRITICAL THINKING Recall the study that looked at memory for sitcom details. Why was it important that participants hadn't seen the episode before?

✓ **Study** and **Review** on **MyPsychLab**

Recapping Main Points

What Is Memory?

- Cognitive psychologists study memory as a type of information processing.
- Memories involving conscious effort are explicit. Unconscious memories are implicit.
- Declarative memory is memory for facts; procedural memory is memory for how to perform skills.
- Memory is often viewed as a three-stage process of encoding, storage, and retrieval.

Memory Use for the Short Term

- Iconic memory has large capacity but very short duration.
- Short-term memory (STM) has a limited capacity and lasts only briefly without rehearsal.
- Maintenance rehearsal can extend the presence of material in STM indefinitely.
- STM capacity can be increased by chunking unrelated items into meaningful groups.
- The broader concept of working memory includes STM.
- The four components of working memory provide the resources for moment-by-moment experiences of the world.

Long-Term Memory: Encoding and Retrieval

- Long-term memory (LTM) constitutes your total knowledge of the world and of yourself. It is nearly unlimited in capacity.
- Your ability to remember information relies on the match between circumstances of encoding and retrieval.
- Retrieval cues allow you to access information in LTM.
- Episodic memory is concerned with memory for events that have been personally experienced. Semantic memory is memory for the basic meaning of words and concepts.
- Similarity in context between learning and retrieval aids retrieval.
- The serial position curve is explained by distinctiveness in context.
- Information processed more deeply is typically remembered better.

- For implicit memories, it is important that the processes of encoding and retrieval be similar.
- Ebbinghaus studied the time course of forgetting.
- Interference occurs when retrieval cues do not lead uniquely to specific memories.
- Memory performance can be improved through elaborative rehearsal and mnemonics.
- In general, feelings-of-knowing accurately predict the availability of information in memory.

Structures in Long-Term Memory

- Concepts are the memory building blocks of thinking. They are formed when memory processes gather together classes of objects or ideas with common properties.
- Concepts are often organized in hierarchies, ranging from general, to basic level, to specific.
- Schemas are more complex cognitive clusters.
- All these memory structures are used to provide expectations and a context for interpreting new information.
- Remembering is not simply recording but is a constructive process.
- People encode flashbulb memories in response to events with great emotional significance, but those memories may not be more accurate than everyday memories.
- New information can bias recall, making eyewitness memory unreliable when contaminated by postevent input.

Biological Aspects of Memory

- Difference brain structures (including the hippocampus, the amygdala, the cerebellum, the striatum, and the cerebral cortex) have been shown to be involved in different types of memories.
- Experiments with individuals with memory disorders have helped investigators understand how different types of memories are acquired and represented in the brain.
- Brain-imaging techniques have extended knowledge about the brain bases of memory encoding and retrieval.

KEY TERMS

amnesia	iconic memory	recognition
anterograde amnesia	implicit use of memory	reconstructive memory
basic level	levels-of-processing theory	retrieval
chunking	long-term memory (LTM)	retrieval cue
concept	memory	retroactive interference
declarative memory	metamemory	retrograde amnesia
elaborative rehearsal	mnemonic	schema
encoding	primacy effect	semantic memory
encoding specificity	priming	serial position effect
engram	proactive interference	short-term memory (STM)
episodic memory	procedural memory	storage
exemplar	prototype	temporal distinctiveness
explicit use of memory	recall	transfer-appropriate processing
flashbulb memory	recency effect	working memory

• Practice Test

1. At her school's talent show, Noa answers questions about politics while spinning basketballs on her fingers. The question and answering mostly require _____ memory, whereas the ball spinning mostly requires _____ memory.
   a. implicit; procedural
   b. declarative; procedural
   c. procedural; declarative
   d. implicit; declarative

2. To demonstrate the capacity of iconic memory, George Sperling showed that participants performed better with the _____ procedure.
   a. whole-report
   b. procedural memory
   c. partial-report
   d. implicit memory

3. Mark looks a number up in a phone book, but he forgets it before he has a chance to make the call. It sounds like Mark should have spent more effort on
   a. rehearsal.
   b. chunking.
   c. memory span.
   d. iconic memory.

4. Which of these is not a component of working memory?
   a. the iconic memory buffer
   b. the phonological loop
   c. the central executive
   d. the visuospatial sketchpad

5. Because of the usefulness of the retrieval cues, _____ is usually easier than _____.
   a. recall; episodic memory
   b. recognition; recall
   c. semantic memory; recognition
   d. recall; recognition

6. After Meghan meets a group of people, she can remember the name of only the last person she met. This is an example of a(n) _____ effect.
   a. primacy
   b. temporal distinctiveness
   c. encoding specificity
   d. recency

7. Consider the word *Mississippi*. Which of these questions asks you to process that word at the deepest level of processing?
   a. How many times does the letter *s* appear in the word?
   b. Is this word the name of a river?
   c. How many syllables does the word have?
   d. What is the word's first letter?

8. You've just memorized a list of nonsense words. You are going to try to recall the words every day for the next 30 days (without looking back at the list). You would expect to show the most forgetting between
   a. day 1 and day 2.
   b. day 3 and day 5.
   c. day 5 and day 10.
   d. day 10 and day 30.

9. Pavel needs to learn the order of the planets with respect to their distance from the sun. To begin, he imagines Mercury as a giant bun and Venus shaped like a shoe. It sounds like Pavel is using
   a. the method of loci.
   b. the peg-word method.
   c. metamemory.
   d. iconic memory.

10. At the start of each exam, Sarah reads over the full set of questions to determine which ones she feels pretty sure she'll get right. To make these judgments, Sarah is using
    a. encoding specificity.
    b. mnemonics.
    c. elaborative rehearsal.
    d. metamemory.

11. When you enter a restaurant to enjoy a meal, you'll probably put a memory structure known as a(n)_____ to good use.
    a. script
    b. exemplar
    c. prototype
    d. chunk

12. Your professor wants to give you advice based on the "testing effect." What is he likely to say?
    a. Quiz yourself after you finish reading each chapter!
    b. Study material from the middle of the chapter most carefully!
    c. Use your judgments-of-learning to decide what to study more!
    d. Try to study in the same room in which you're going to take the test!

13. Karl Lashley carried out his search for the engram by training rats on mazes and then removing different amounts of the
    a. cerebellum.
    b. cortex.
    c. striatum.
    d. amygdala.

14. Alois Alzheimer was able to demonstrate that
    a. plaques in the brain caused Alzheimer's disease.
    b. amyloid β-peptide caused Alzheimer's disease.
    c. people who died of Alzheimer's disease had plaques in their brains.
    d. plaques in the brain could be used to prevent Alzheimer's disease.

15. If you were asked to identify the brain bases of the encoding and retrieval of episodic memories, you should point to the
    a. striatum.
    b. cerebellum.
    c. amygdala.
    d. prefrontal cortex.

ESSAY QUESTIONS

1. What are the relationships among encoding, storage, and retrieval?

2. What are the primary functions of working memory?

3. In what ways have brain-imaging techniques helped confirm some of the theoretical distinctions made by memory researchers?Recapping Main Points

Stop and Review Answers

Stop and Review (What Is Memory?)

1. Explicit uses of memory involve conscious effort, whereas implicit uses of memory do not.
2. Your skill relies more on procedural memory.
3. Because you've previously encoded and stored your password, it's most likely your problem is with retrieval.

Stop and Review (Memory Use for the Short Term)

1. Comparisons of the whole- and partial-report procedures indicate that people have very brief access to all the information in a display.
2. Researchers believe that the capacity of STM is in the range of three to five items.
3. Chunking is the process of reconfiguring items into meaningful groups.
4. Working memory includes the phonological loop, the visuospatial sketchpad, the central executive, and the episodic buffer.

Stop and Review (Long-Term Memory: Encoding and Retrieval)

1. Recognition generally provides more retrieval cues.
2. This would be an example of the primacy effect in serial recall.
3. Transfer-appropriate processing suggests that memory is best when the type of processing carried out at encoding matches the type of processing carried out at retrieval.
4. These circumstances provide an example of retroactive interference because new information has made it harder to remember older information.

5. Beginning with hydrogen, you would associate each element with a position along a familiar route.
6. Judgments of learning are people's estimates of how well they have learned information.

Stop and Review (Structures in Long-Term Memory)

1. Concepts are the mental representations of the categories you form.
2. The exemplar theory claims that people categorize new objects by comparing them to the exemplars they have stored in memory.
3. Bartlett identified the processes of leveling, sharpening, and assimilating.
4. Loftus and her colleagues demonstrated that people will include incorrect postevent information when they attempt to remember events.

Stop and Review (Biological Aspects of Memory)

1. Lashley concluded that the engram did not exist in any localized regions but was widely distributed throughout the brain.
2. Research suggests that important aspects of implicit memory will often be spared for individuals who have amnesia for explicit memories.
3. PET scans reveal that different areas of the brain are disproportionately active for encoding and retrieval—left prefrontal cortex for encoding and right prefrontal cortex for retrieval.

Practice Test Answers

1. b	5. b	9. b	13. b
2. c	6. d	10. d	14. c
3. a	7. b	11. a	15. d
4. a	8. a	12. a	

References

Aly, M., Knight, R. T., & Yonelinas, A. P. (2010). Faces are special but not too special: Spared face recognition in amnesia is based on familiarity. *Neuropsychologia, 48*, 3941–3948.

Alzheimer's Association. (2011). *2011 Alzheimer's disease facts and figures.* Retrieved from www.alz.org/downloads/Facts_Figures_2011.pdf.

Auvray, M., Gallace, A., & Spence, C. (2011). Tactile short-term -memory for stimuli presented on the fingertips and across the rest of the -surface of the body. *Attention, Perception, & Psychophysics, 73*, 1227–1241.

Baddeley, A. D. (2002). Is working memory still working? *European Psychologist, 7*, 85–97.

Baddeley, A. D. (2003). Working memory: Looking back and looking forward. *Nature Reviews Neuroscience, 4*, 829–839.

Bartlett, F. C. (1932). *Remembering: A study in experimental and social psychology.* Cambridge, UK: Cambridge University Press.

Bohannon, J. N. III, Gratz, S., & Cross, V. S. (2007). The effects of affect and input source on flashbulb memories. *Applied Cognitive Psychology, 21*, 1023–1036.

Bond, C. F., Jr., Pitre, U., & van Leeuwen, M. D. (1991). Encoding operations and the next-in-line effect. *Personality and Social Psychology Bulletin, 17*, 435–441.

Braun, K. A., Ellis, R., & Loftus, E. F. (2002). Make my memory: How advertising can change our memories of the past. *Psychology & Marketing, 19*, 1–23.

Brown, R., & Kulik, J. (1977). Flashbulb memories. *Cognition, 5*, 73–99.

Burnett, R. C., Medin, D. L., Ross, N. O., & Blok, S. V. (2005). Ideal is typical. *Canadian Journal of Experimental Psychology, 59*, 3–10.

Carter, S. J., & Cassaday, H. J. (1998). State-dependent retrieval and chlorpheniramine. *Human Psychopharmacology, 13*, 513–523.

Chase, W. G., & Ericsson, K. A. (1981). Skilled memory. In J. R. Anderson (Ed.), *Cognitive skills and their acquisition*. Hillsdale, NJ: Erlbaum.

Conway, A. R., Kane, M. J., Bunting, M. F., Hambrick, D. Z., Wilhelm, O., & Engle, R. W. (2005). Working memory span tasks: A methodological review and user's guide. *Psychonomic Bulletin & Review, 12*, 769–786.

Craik, F. I. M., & Lockhart, R. S. (1972). Levels of processing: A framework for memory research. *Journal of Verbal Learning and Verbal Behavior, 11*, 671–684.

Curci, A., & Luminet, O. (2006). Follow-up of a cross-national comparison on flashbulb and event memory for the September 11th attacks. *Memory, 14*, 329–344.

Dselaar et al. 2008[ED: cited in chapter but not in Refs]

Ebbinghaus, H. (1964). *Memory: A contribution to experimental psychology*. New York: Dover. (Original work published 1885)

Eich, T. S., & Metcalfe, J. (2009). Effects of the stress of marathon running on implicit and explicit memory. *Psychonomic Bulletin & Review, 16*, 475–479.

Frenda, S. J., Nichols, R. M., & Loftus, E. F. (2011). Current issues and advances in misinformation research. *Current Directions in Psychological Science, 20*, 20–23.

Godden, D. R., & Baddeley, A. D. (1975). Context-dependent memory in two natural environments: On land and under water. *British Journal of Psychology, 66*, 325–331.

Graziano, M., & Sigman, M. (2008). The dynamics of sensory buffers: Geometric, spatial, and experience-dependent shaping of iconic memory. *Journal of Vision, 8*, 1–13. Neisser, U. (1967). *Cognitive psychology*. New York: Appleton-Century-Crofts.

Guérard, K., Neath, I., Surprenant, A. M., & Tremblay, S. (2010). Distinctiveness in serial memory for spatial information. *Memory & Cognition, 38*, 83–91.

Habib, R., Nyberg, L., & Tulving, E. (2003). Hemispheric asymmetries of memory: the HERA model revisited. *TRENDS in Cognitive Sciences, 7*, 241–245.

Hardy, J., & Selkoe, D. J. (2002). The amyloid hypothesis of Alzheimer's disease: Progress and problems on the road to therapeutics. *Science, 297*, 353–356.

Hart, J. T. (1965). Memory and the feeling-of-knowing experience. *Journal of Educational Psychology, 56*, 208–216.

Holen, M. C., & Oaster, T. R. (1976). Serial position and isolation effects in a classroom lecture simulation. *Journal of Educational Psychology, 68*, 723–725.

Jahnke, J. C. (1965). Primacy and recency effects in serial-position curves of immediate recall. *Journal of Experimental Psychology, 70*, 130–132. Kleider, H. M., Parrott, D. J., & King, T. Z. (2010). Shooting behaviour: How working memory and negative emotionality influence police officer shoot decisions. *Applied Cognitive Psychology, 24*, 707–717.

Jensen, A. R. (1962). Spelling errors and the serial position effect. *Journal of Educational Psychology, 53*, 105–109.

Karpicke, J. D., & Blunt, J. R. (2011). Retrieval practice produces more learning than elaborative studying with concept mapping. *Science, 331*, 772–775.

Koriat, A., & Fischhoff, B. (1974). What day is today? An inquiry into the process of time orientation. *Memory & Cognition, 2*, 201–205.

Lashley, K. S. (1929). *Brain mechanisms and intelligence*. Chicago: University of Chicago Press.

Lashley, K. S. (1950). In search of the engram. In *Physiological mechanisms in animal behavior: Symposium of the Society for Experimental Biology* (pp. 454–482). New York: Academic Press.

Lockhart, R. S., & Craik, F. I. M. (1990). Levels of processing: A retrospective commentary on a framework for memory research. *Canadian -Journal of Psychology, 44*, 87–122.

Loftus, E. F. (1979). *Eyewitness testimony*. Cambridge, MA: Harvard University Press.

Loftus, E. F., & Palmer, J. C. (1974). Reconstruction of automobile destruction: An example of the interaction between language and memory. *Journal of Verbal Learning and Verbal Behavior, 13*, 585–589.

Loftus, E. F., Miller, D. G., & Burns, H. J. (1978). Semantic integration of verbal information into a visual memory. *Journal of Experimental Psychology: Human Learning and Memory, 4*, 19–31.

McDaniel, M. A., Agarwal, P. K., Huelser, B. J., McDermott, K. B., & Roediger, H. L., III. (2011). Test-enhanced learning in a middle school science classroom: The effects of quiz frequency and placement. *Journal of Educational Psychology, 103*, 399–414.

Metcalfe, J. (2009). Metacognitive judgments and control of study. *Current Directions in Psychological Science, 18*, 159–163.

Miller, G. A. (1956). The magic number seven plus or minus two: Some limits in our capacity for processing information. *Psychological Review, 63*, 81–97.

Mishra, J., & Backlin, W. (2007). The effects of altering environmental and instrumental context on the performance of memorized music. *Psychology of Music, 35*, 1–20.

Mitchell, K. J., & Johnson, M. K. (2009). Source monitoring 15 years later: What have we learned from fMRI about the neural mechanisms of source memory? *Psychological Bulletin, 135*, 638–677.

Modirrousta, M., & Fellows, L. K. (2008). Medial prefrontal cortex plays a critical and selective role in "feeling of knowing" meta-memory judgments. *Neuropsychologia, 46*, 2958–2965.

Murphy, G. L. (2002). *The big book of concepts*. Cambridge, MA: MIT Press.

Murphy, K. J., Troyer, A. K., Levine, B., & Moscovitch, M. (2008). Episodic, but not semantic, autobiographical memory is reduced in amnestic mild cognitive impairment. *Neuropsychologia, 46*, 3116–3123.

Nadel, L., & Hardt, O. (2011). Update on memory systems and processes. *Neuropsychopharmacology, 36*, 251–273.

Neath, I., & Crowder, R. G. (1990). Schedules of presentation and temporal distinctiveness in human memory. *Journal of Experimental Psychology: Learning, Memory, and Cognition, 16*, 316–327.

Neath, I., & Surprenant, A. M. (2003). *Human memory: An introduction to research, data, and theory* (2nd ed.). Belmont, CA: Wadsworth.

Neath, I., Brown, G. D. A., McCormack, T., Chater, N., & Freeman, R. (2006). Distinctiveness models of memory and absolute identification: Evidence for local, not global, effects. *Quarterly Journal of Experimental Psychology, 59*, 121–135.

Nosofsky, R. M. (2011). The generalized context model: An exemplar model of classification. In E. M. Pothos & A. J. Wills (Eds.), *Formal approaches in categorization* (pp. 18–39). New York: Cambridge University Press.

Paivio, A. (2006). *Mind and its evolution: A dual coding theoretical interpretation*. Mahwah, NJ: Lawrence Erlbaum Associates, Inc.

Paterson, H. M., Kemp, R. I., & Ng, J. R. (2011). Combating co-witness contamination: Attempting to decrease the negative effects of discussion on eye-witness memory. *Applied Cognitive Psychology, 25*, 43–52.

Peterson, L. R., & Peterson, M. J. (1959). Short-term retention of individual verbal items. *Journal of Experimental Psychology, 58*, 193–198.

Radvansky, G. A. (2006). *Human memory*. Boston: Allyn & Bacon.

Ramirez, G., & Beilock, S. L. (2011). Writing about testing worries boosts exam performance in the classroom. *Science, 331*, 211–213.

Rhodes, M. G., & Tauber, S. K. The influence of delaying judgments of learning on metacognitve accuracy: A meta-analytic review. *Psychological Bulletin, 137*, 131–148.

Roediger, H. L., III. (2008). Relativity of remembering: Why the laws of memory vanished. *Annual Review of Psychology, 59*, 225–254.

Roediger, H. L., III., & Butler, A. C. (2011). The critical role of retrieval practice in long-term retention. *Trends in Cognitive Sciences, 15*, 20–27.

Roediger, H. L., III., & Karpicke, J. D. (2006). Test-enhanced learning: Taking memory tests improves long-term retention. *Psychological Science, 17*, 249–255.

Rosch, E. H. (1973). Natural categories. *Cognitive Psychology, 4,* 328–350.

Rosch, E. H. (1978). Principles of categorization. In E. Rosch & B. B. Lloyd (Eds.), *Cognition and categorization* (pp. 27–48). Hillsdale, NJ: Erlbaum.

Rosch, E., & Mervis, C. B. (1975). Family resemblances: Studies in the internal structure of categories. *Cognitive Psychology, 7,* 573–605.

Rosch, E. H., Mervis, C. B., Gray, W. D., Johnson, D. M., & Boyes-Braem, P. (1976). Basic objects in natural categories. *Cognitive Psychology, 8,* 382–439.

Rubin, D. C., & Kontis, T. C. (1983). A schema for common cents. *Memory & Cognition, 11,* 335–341.

Schank, R. C., & Abelson, R. P. (1977). *Scripts, plans, goals, and understanding.* Hillsdale, NJ: Erlbaum.

Seamon, J. G., Philbin, M. M., & Harrison, L G. (2006). Do you remember proposing marriage to the Pepsi machine? False recollections from a campus walk. *Psychonomic Bulletin & Review, 13,* 752–756.

Shiffrin, R. M. (2003). Modeling memory and perception. *Cognitive -Science, 27,* 341–378.

Sörqvist, P., Haling, N., & Hygge, S. (2010). Individual differences in susceptibility to the effects of speech on reading comprehension. *Applied Cognitive Psychology, 24,* 67–76.

Sperling, G. (1960). The information available in brief visual presentations. *Psychological Monographs, 74,* 1–29.

Sperling, G. (1963). A model for visual memory tasks. *Human Factors, 5,* 19–31.

Squire, L. R., & Wixted, J. T. (2011). The cognitive neuroscience of human memory since H. M. *Annual Review of Neuroscience, 34,* 259–288.

Stocco, A., Lebiere, C., & Anderson, J. R. (2010). Conditional routing of information in the cortex: A model of the basal ganglia's role in cognitive coordination. *Psychological Review, 117,* 541–574.

Taatgen, N. A., & Lee, F. J. (2003). Production compilation: A simple mechanism to model complex skill acquisition. *Human Factors, 45,* 61–76.

Taatgen, N. A., Huss, D., Dickison, D., & Anderson, J. R. (2008). The acquisition of robust and flexible cognitive skills. *Journal of Experimental Psychology: General, 137,* 548–565.

Talarico, J. M., & Rubin, D. C. (2003). Confidence, not consistency, characterizes flashbulb memories. *Psychological Science, 14,* 455–461.

Talarico, J. M., & Rubin, D. C. (2007). Flashbulb memories are special after all; in phenomenology, not accuracy. *Applied Cognitive Psychology, 21,* 527–578.

Thomson, D. R., Milliken, B., & Smilek, D. (2010). Long-term conceptual implicit memory: A decade of evidence. *Memory & Cognition, 38,* 42–46.

Tulving, E. (1972). Episodic and semantic memory. In E. Tulving & W. Donaldson (Eds.), *Organization of memory.* New York: Academic Press.

Turner, M. L., & Engle, R. W. (1989). Is working memory capacity task dependent? *Journal of Memory and Language, 28,* 127–154.

Underwood, B. J. (1948). Retroactive and proactive inhibition after five and forty-eight hours. *Journal of Experimental Psychology, 38,* 28–38.

Underwood, B. J. (1949). Proactive inhibition as a function of time and degree of prior learning. *Journal of Experimental Psychology, 39,* 24–34.

Undorf, M., & Erdfelder, E. (2011). Judgments of learning reflect encoding fluency: Conclusive evidence for the ease-of-processing hypothesis. *Journal of Experimental Psychology: Learning, Memory, and Cognition, 37,* 1264–1269.

Unsworth, N., Spillers, G. J., & Brewer, G. A. (2012). Dynamics of context-dependent recall: An examination of internal and external context change. *Journal of Memory and Language, 66,* 1–16.

Voorspoels, W., Vanpaemel, W., & Storms, G. (2008). Exemplars and prototypes in natural language concepts: A typicality-based evaluation. *Psychonomic Bulletin & Review, 15,* 630–637.

Voss, J. L., & Paller, K. A. (2008). Brain substrates of implicit and explicit memory: The importance of concurrently acquired neural signals of both memory types. *Neuropsychologia, 46,* 3021–3029.

Weissenborn, R., & Duka, T. (2000). State-dependent effects of alcohol on explicit memory: The role of semantic associations. *Psychopharmacology, 149,* 98–106.

Learning and Behavior Analysis

Learning and Behavior Analysis

Andersen Ross/Blend Images/Getty Images

Imagine that you are in a movie theater, watching a horror film. As the hero approaches a closed door, the music on the movie's sound track grows dark and menacing. You suddenly feel the urge to yell, "Don't go through that door!" Meanwhile, you find that your heart is racing. But why? If you think about this question formally, you might come to the answer, "I have learned an association between movie music and movie events—and that's what's making me nervous!" But had you ever thought about this relationship before? Probably not. Somehow, by virtue of sitting in enough movie theaters, you have learned the association without any particular thought. The main topic of this chapter is the types of associations that you acquire effortlessly in your day-to-day experience.

Psychologists have long been interested in *learning*, the ways in which organisms learn from experiences in the world. In just a moment, you will see a more precise definition of learning. We then consider particular types of learning: classical conditioning and operant conditioning. As you will see, each of these types of learning represents a different way in which organisms acquire and use information about the structure of their environments. For each of these types of learning, I describe both the basic mechanisms that govern its operation in the laboratory and applications to real-life situations.

This chapter also reflects on the way learning is similar and dissimilar across species. You will see that basic processes of conditioning are the same across a wide variety of species. However, you will also discover that some aspects of learning are constrained by species' particular genetic endowments. In particular, you will see how *cognition*—higher mental processes—affects learning processes in both humans and other species.

THE STUDY OF LEARNING

Our exploration of learning will begin with a definition of learning itself. We then consider two basic forms of learning. The section ends with a brief sketch of the history of psychological research on the topic.

What is Learning?

Learning is a process based on experience that results in a relatively consistent change in behavior or behavior potential. Let's look more closely at the three critical parts of this definition. 👁

A Process Based on Experience Learning can take place only through experience. Experience includes taking in information (and evaluating and transforming it) and making responses that affect the environment. Learning consists

....

👁 **Watch** the **Video** *The Big Picture: What Does It Mean to Learn?* on MyPsychLab

learning A process based on experience that results in a relatively permanent change in behavior or behavioral potential.

learning-performance distinction The difference between what has been learned and what is expressed in overt behavior.

of a response influenced by the lessons of memory. Learned behavior does not include changes that come about because of physical maturation or brain development as the organism ages, nor those caused by illness or brain damage. Some lasting changes in behavior require experience following maturational readiness. For example, consider the timetable that determines when an infant is ready to crawl, stand, walk, run, and be toilet trained. No amount of training or practice will produce those behaviors before the child has matured sufficiently. Psychologists are especially interested in discovering what aspects of behavior can be changed through experience and how such changes come about.

A Change in Behavior or Behavior Potential It is obvious that learning has taken place when you are able to demonstrate the results, such as when you send a text message or drive a car. You can't directly observe learning itself—meaning, you can't ordinarily see the changes in your brain—but learning is apparent from improvements in your *performance*. Often, however, your performance doesn't show everything that you have learned. Sometimes, too, you have acquired general attitudes, such as an *appreciation* of modern art or an *understanding* of Eastern philosophy, that may not be apparent in your measurable actions. In such instances, you have achieved a potential for behavior change because you have learned attitudes and values that can influence the kinds of books you read or the way you spend your leisure time. This is an example of the **learning-performance distinction**—the difference between what has been learned and what is expressed, or performed, in overt behavior.

A Relatively Consistent Change To qualify as learned, a change in behavior or behavior potential must be relatively consistent over different occasions. Thus, once you learn to swim, you will probably always be able to do so. Note that consistent changes are not always permanent changes. You may, for example, have become quite a consistent dart thrower when you practiced every day. If you gave up the sport, however, your skills might have deteriorated toward their original level. But if you have learned once to be a championship dart thrower, it ought to be easier for you to learn a second time. Something has been "saved" from your prior experience. In that sense, the change may be permanent.

© London Entertainment/Alamy

How does consistent form in ballet dancers fit the definition of learning?

Habituation and Sensitization To help you master the concept of learning, I will describe two of its most basic forms: *habituation* and *sensitization*. Imagine that you are examining a picture of a pleasant scene—an image, for example, of waterskiing or windsurfing. The first time you see it, you might have a fairly strong emotional response. However, if you view the same image repeatedly in short succession, your emotional response will become weaker over time (Leventhal et al., 2007). This is an example of **habituation**: You show a decrease in behavioral response when a stimulus is presented repeatedly. Habituation helps keep your focus on novel events in the environment—you don't expend behavioral effort to respond repeatedly to old stimuli.

Note how habituation fits the definition of learning. There's a change in behavior (your emotional response is weaker) that is based on experience (you've seen the image repeatedly), and that behavior change is consistent (you do not return to your original level of emotional response). However, the change in emotional response is unlikely to be permanent. If you see the same picture after sufficient time has passed, you might find it emotionally engaging once again.

When **sensitization** occurs, your response to a stimulus becomes stronger, rather than weaker, when it occurs repeatedly. Suppose, for example, you experience the same painful stimulus several times in short succession. Even if the intensity of the stimulus remained constant, you would report greater pain in response to the final stimulus in the series than you would in response to the first stimulus (Woolf, 2011). Once again, sensitization fits the definition of learning because experience in the world (repeated experiences of a painful stimulus) leads to a consistent change in behavioral response (reports that the pain is more intense). You might wonder what determines whether people will experience habituation or sensitization in response to different stimuli. In general, sensitization is more likely to occur when stimuli are intense or irritating.

Behaviorism and Behavior Analysis

Much of modern psychology's view of learning finds its roots in the work of **John Watson** (1878–1958). Watson founded the school of psychology known as *behaviorism*. For nearly 50 years, American psychology was dominated by the behaviorist tradition expressed in Watson's 1919 book, *Psychology from the Standpoint of a Behaviorist*. Watson argued that introspection—people's verbal reports of sensations, images, and feelings—was *not* an acceptable means of studying behavior because it was too subjective. How could scientists verify the accuracy of such private experiences? But once introspection has been rejected, what should the subject matter of psychology be? Watson's answer was *observable behavior*. In Watson's words, "States of consciousness, like the so-called phenomenon of spiritualism, are not objectively verifiable and for that reason can never become data for science" (Watson, 1919, p. 1). Watson also defined the chief goal of psychology as "the prediction and control of behavior" (Watson, 1913, p. 158).

B. F. Skinner (1904–1990) adopted Watson's cause and expanded his agenda. Skinner began the research that would lead him to formulate this position when, after reading Watson's 1924 book *Behaviorism*, he began his graduate study in psychology at Harvard. Over time, Skinner formulated a position known as *radical behaviorism*. Skinner embraced Watson's

B. F. Skinner expanded on Watson's ideas and applied them to a wide spectrum of behavior. Why did Skinner's psychology focus on environmental events rather than on internal states?

Sam Falk/Photo Researchers, Inc.

complaint against internal states and mental events. However, Skinner focused not so much on their legitimacy as data as on their legitimacy as *causes of behavior* (Skinner, 1990). In Skinner's view, mental events, such as thinking and imagining, do not cause behavior. Rather, they are examples of behavior that are caused by environmental stimuli.

Suppose that we deprive a pigeon of food for 24 hours, place it in an apparatus where it can obtain food by pecking a small disk, and find that it soon does so. Skinner would argue that the animal's behavior can be fully explained by environmental events—deprivation and the use of food as reinforcement. The subjective feeling of hunger, which cannot be directly observed or measured, is not a cause of the behavior but the result of deprivation. To explain what the bird does, you need not understand anything about its inner psychological states—you need only understand the principles of learning that allow the bird to acquire the association between behavior and reward. This is the essence of Skinner's brand of behaviorism.

This brand of behaviorism originated by Skinner served as the original philosophical cornerstone of **behavior analysis,** the area of psychology that focuses on discovering environmental determinants of learning and behavior (Cooper et al., 2007). In general, behavior analysts attempt to discover regularities in learning that are universal, occurring in all types of animal species, including humans, under comparable situations. That is why studies with nonhuman animals have been so critical to progress in this area. Complex forms of learning

habituation A decrease in a behavioral response when a stimulus is presented repeatedly.

sensitization An increase in behavioral response when a stimulus is presented repeatedly.

behavior analysis The area of psychology that focuses on the environmental determinants of learning and behavior.

represent combinations and elaborations of simpler processes and not qualitatively different phenomena. In the sections that follow, we consider classical conditioning and operant conditioning—two simple forms of learning that give rise to quite complex behaviors.

Stop *and* Review

① What is meant by the learning-performance distinction?
② What is the definition of habituation?
③ Why did Watson emphasize the study of observable behavior?
④ What is a major goal of behavior analysis?

✓●─[**Study** and **Review** on **MyPsychLab**

Physiologist Ivan Pavlov (shown here with his research team) observed classical conditioning while conducting research on digestion. What were some of Pavlov's major contributions to the study of this form of learning?

CLASSICAL CONDITIONING: LEARNING PREDICTABLE SIGNALS

Imagine once more that you are watching that horror movie. Why does your heart race when the sound track signals trouble for the hero? Somehow your body has learned to produce a physiological response (a racing heart) when one environmental event (for example, scary music) is associated with another (scary visual events). This type of learning is known as **classical conditioning,** a basic form of learning in which one stimulus or event predicts the occurrence of another stimulus or event. The organism learns a new *association* between two stimuli—a stimulus that did not previously elicit the response and one that naturally elicited the response. As you shall see, the innate capacity to quickly associate pairs of events in your environment has profound behavioral implications. ●

Pavlov's Surprising Observation

The first rigorous study of classical conditioning was the result of what may well be psychology's most famous accident. The Russian physiologist **Ivan Pavlov** (1849–1936) did not set out to study classical conditioning or any other psychological phenomenon. He happened on classical conditioning while conducting research on digestion, for which he won a Nobel Prize in 1904.

Pavlov had devised a technique to study digestive processes in dogs by implanting tubes in their glands and digestive organs to divert bodily secretions to containers outside their bodies so that the secretions could be measured and analyzed.

● Watch the Video *The Basics 1: Classical Conditioning and Learning Predictable Signals* on **MyPsychLab**

classical conditioning A type of learning in which a behavior (conditioned response) comes to be elicited by a stimulus (conditioned stimulus) that has acquired its power through an association with a biologically significant stimulus (unconditioned stimulus).

To produce these secretions, Pavlov's assistants put meat powder into the dogs' mouths. After repeating this procedure a number of times, Pavlov observed an unexpected behavior in his dogs—they salivated *before* the powder was put in their mouths! They would start salivating at the mere sight of the food and, later, at the sight of the assistant who brought the food or even at the sound of the assistant's footsteps. Indeed, any stimulus that regularly preceded the presentation of food came to elicit salivation. Quite by accident, Pavlov had observed that learning may result from two stimuli becoming associated with each other.

Fortunately, Pavlov had the scientific skills and curiosity to begin a rigorous attack on this surprising phenomenon. He ignored the advice of the great physiologist of the time, Sir Charles Sherrington, suggesting he give up his foolish investigation of "psychic" secretions. Instead, Pavlov abandoned his work on digestion and, in so doing, changed the course of psychology forever (Pavlov, 1928). For the remainder of Pavlov's life, he continued to search for the variables that influence classically conditioned behavior. Classical conditioning is also called *Pavlovian conditioning* because of Pavlov's discovery of the major phenomena of conditioning and his dedication to tracking down the variables that influence it.

Pavlov's considerable research experience allowed him to follow a simple and elegant strategy to discover the conditions necessary for his dogs to be conditioned to salivate. As shown in **Figure 1** dogs in his experiments were first placed in a restraining harness. At regular intervals, a stimulus such as a tone was presented, and a dog was given a bit of food. Importantly, the tone had no prior meaning for the dog with respect to food or salivation. As you might imagine, the dog's first reaction to the tone was only an *orienting response*—the dog pricked its ears and moved its head to locate the source of the sound. However, with repeated trials in which the tone preceded the food, the orienting response stopped and salivation began. What Pavlov had observed in his earlier research was no accident: The phenomenon could be replicated under controlled conditions. Pavlov demonstrated the generality of this effect by using a variety of other stimuli ordinarily neutral with respect to salivation, such as lights and ticking metronomes.

The main features of Pavlov's classical conditioning procedure are illustrated in **Figure 2**. At the core of

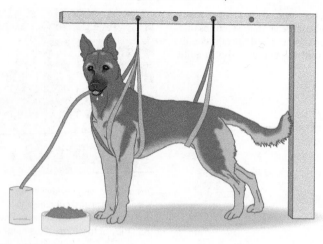

FIGURE 1 Pavlov's Original Procedure

In his original experiments, Pavlov used a variety of stimuli such as tones, bells, lights, and metronomes to serve as neutral stimuli. The experimenter presented one of these neutral stimuli and then the food powder. The dog's saliva was collected through a tube.

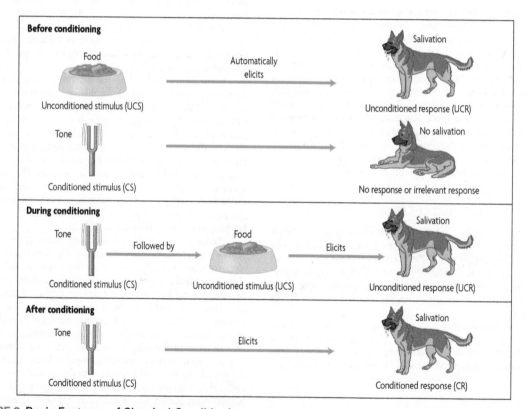

FIGURE 2 Basic Features of Classical Conditioning

Before conditioning, the unconditioned stimulus (UCS) naturally elicits the unconditioned response (UCR). A neutral stimulus, such as a tone, has no eliciting effect. During conditioning, the neutral stimulus is paired with the UCS. Through its association with the UCS, the neutral stimulus becomes a conditioned stimulus (CS) and elicits a conditioned response (CR) that is similar to the UCR.

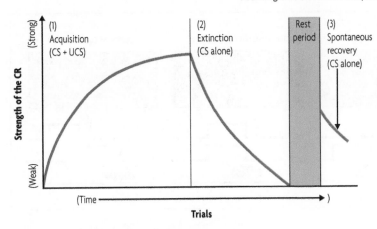

FIGURE 3 Acquisition, Extinction, and Spontaneous Recovery in Classical Conditioning

During acquisition (CS + UCS), the strength of the CR increases rapidly. During extinction, when the UCS no longer follows the CS, the strength of the CR drops to zero. The CR may reappear after a brief rest period, even when the UCS is still not presented. The reappearance of the CR is called spontaneous recovery.

classical conditioning are *reflex* responses such as salivation, pupil contraction, knee jerks, or eye blinking. A **reflex** is a response that is naturally triggered—*elicited*—by specific stimuli that are biologically relevant for the organism. Any stimulus, such as the food powder used in Pavlov's experiments, that naturally elicits a reflexive behavior is called an **unconditioned stimulus (UCS)** because learning is not a necessary condition for the stimulus to control the behavior. The behavior elicited by the unconditioned stimulus is called the **unconditioned response (UCR).**

In Pavlov's experiments, the stimuli such as lights and tones did not originally trigger the reflex response of salivation. However, over time each neutral stimulus was repeatedly paired with the unconditioned stimulus. This neutral stimulus is called the **conditioned stimulus (CS):** Its power to elicit behavior is *conditioned* on its association with the UCS. After several trials, the CS will produce a response called the **conditioned response (CR).** The conditioned response is whatever response the conditioned stimulus elicits as a product of learning—you will see several examples as this section unfolds. Let's review. Nature provides the UCS–UCR connections, but the learning produced by classical conditioning creates the CS–CR connection. The conditioned stimulus acquires some of the power to influence behavior that was originally limited to the unconditioned stimulus. Let's now look in more detail at the basic processes of classical conditioning. 👁

....

👁 Watch the Video *Classic Footage of Pavlov* on MyPsychLab

reflex An unlearned response elicited by specific stimuli that have biological relevance for an organism.

unconditioned stimulus (UCS) In classical conditioning, the stimulus that elicits an unconditioned response.

unconditioned response (UCR) In classical conditioning, the response elicited by an unconditioned stimulus without prior training or learning.

conditioned stimulus (CS) In classical conditioning, a previously neutral stimulus that comes to elicit a conditioned response.

conditioned response (CR) In classical conditioning, a response elicited by some previously neutral stimulus that occurs as a result of pairing the neutral stimulus with an unconditioned stimulus.

acquisition The stage in a classical conditioning experiment during which the conditioned response is first elicited by the conditioned stimulus.

Processes of Conditioning

Pavlov's original experiments inspired extensive study of how classically conditioned responses appear and disappear. In this section, we consider several important conclusions researchers have reached about the basic processes of classical conditioning. These conclusions have emerged from hundreds of different studies across a wide range of animal species.

Acquisition and Extinction **Figure 3** displays a hypothetical classical conditioning experiment. The first panel displays **acquisition,** the process by which the CR is first elicited and gradually increases in frequency over repeated trials. In general, the CS and UCS must be paired several times before the CS reliably elicits a CR. With systematic CS–UCS pairings, the CR is elicited with increasing frequency, and the organism may be said to have acquired a conditioned response.

In classical conditioning, as in telling a good joke, *timing* is critical. The CS and UCS must be presented closely enough in time to be perceived by the organism as being related. (We will describe an exception to this rule in a later section on *taste-aversion learning.*) Researchers have studied four temporal patterns between the two stimuli, as shown in **Figure 4** (Hearst, 1988). The most widely used type of conditioning is called *delay conditioning,* in which the CS comes on prior to and stays on at least until the UCS is presented. In *trace conditioning,* the CS is discontinued or turned off before the UCS is presented. *Trace* refers to the memory that the organism is assumed to have of the CS, which is no longer present when the UCS appears. In *simultaneous conditioning,* both the CS and UCS are presented at the same time. Finally, in the case of *backward conditioning,* the CS is presented after the UCS.

Conditioning is usually most effective in a delayed conditioning paradigm, with a short interval between the onsets of the CS and UCS. However, the exact time interval between the CS and the UCS that will produce optimal conditioning depends on several factors, including the intensity of the CS and the response being conditioned. Let's focus on the response being conditioned. For muscular responses, such as eye blinks, a short interval of a second or less is best. For visceral responses, such as heart rate and salivation, however, longer intervals of 5 to 15 seconds work best.

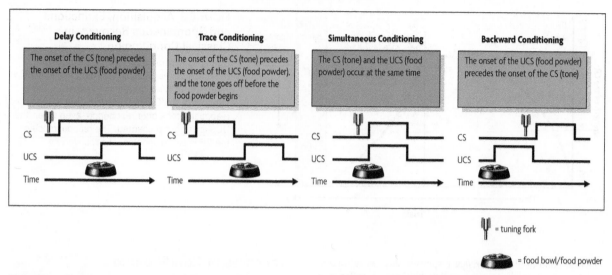

FIGURE 4 **Four Variations of the CS–UCS Temporal Arrangement in Classical Conditioning**
Researchers have explored the four possible timing arrangements between the CS and UCS. Conditioning is generally most effective in a delay conditioning paradigm with a short interval between the onsets of the CS and UCS.

From Baron, Robert A., *Psychology*, 5th Edition., © 2001. Printed and electronically reproduced by permission of Pearson Education Inc., Upper Saddle River, New Jersey.

Conditioning is generally poor with a simultaneous procedure and very poor with a backward procedure. Evidence of backward conditioning may appear after a few pairings of the UCS and CS but disappear with extended training as the animal learns that the CS is followed by a period free of the UCS. In both cases, conditioning is weak because the CS does not actually predict the onset of the UCS. (We will return to the importance of predictability, or *contingency*, in the next section.)

But what happens when the CS (for example, the tone) no longer predicts the UCS (the food powder)? Under those circumstances, the CR (salivation) becomes weaker over time and eventually stops occurring. When the CR no longer appears in the presence of the CS (and the absence of the UCS), the process of **extinction** is said to have occurred (see Figure 3, panel 2). Conditioned responses, then, are not necessarily a permanent aspect of the organism's behavioral repertoire. However, the CR will reappear in a weak form when the CS is presented alone again after extinction (see Figure 3, panel 3). Pavlov referred to this sudden reappearance of the CR after a rest period, or time-out, without further exposure to the UCS as **spontaneous recovery** after extinction.

When the original pairing is renewed, postextinction, the CR becomes rapidly stronger. This more rapid relearning is an instance of *savings:* Less time is necessary to reacquire the response than to acquire it originally. Thus some of the original conditioning must be retained by the organism even after experimental extinction appears to have eliminated the CR. In other words, extinction has only weakened performance, not wiped out the original learning. This is why the original definition of learning emphasized the distinction between learning and performance.

Stimulus Generalization Suppose we have taught a dog that presentation of a tone of a certain frequency predicts food powder. Is the dog's response specific to only that stimulus? If you think about this question for a moment, you will probably not be surprised that the answer is no. In general, once a CR has been conditioned to a particular CS, similar stimuli may also elicit the response. For example, if conditioning was to a high-frequency tone, a slightly lower tone could also elicit the response. A child bitten by a big dog is likely to respond with fear even to smaller dogs. This automatic extension of responding to stimuli that have never been paired with the original UCS is called **stimulus generalization.** The more similar the new stimulus is to the original CS, the stronger the response will be. When response strength is measured for each of a series of increasingly dissimilar stimuli along a given dimension, as shown in **Figure 5**, a *generalization gradient* is found.

The existence of generalization gradients should suggest to you the way classical conditioning serves its function in everyday experience. Because important stimuli rarely occur in exactly the same form every time in nature, stimulus generalization builds in a similarity safety factor by extending the range of learning beyond the original specific experience. With this feature, new but comparable events can be

extinction In conditioning, the weakening of a conditioned association in the absence of a reinforcer or unconditioned stimulus.

spontaneous recovery The reappearance of an extinguished conditioned response after a rest period.

stimulus generalization The automatic extension of conditioned responding to similar stimuli that have never been paired with the unconditioned stimulus.

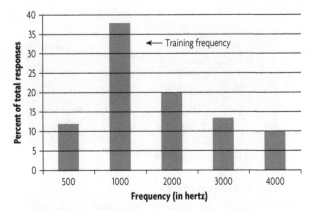

FIGURE 5 Stimulus Generalization Gradients

Rabbits were trained so that they produced a conditioned response (they closed their outer eyelid) when they heard a 1000 hertz tone (Siegel et al., 1968). During an extinction phase, the rabbits were tested on the training tone as well as tones that varied in distance from that tone. Tones more similar to the training tone produced more conditioned responses than those further away.

Data from Siegel, S., Hearst, E., George, N., & O'Neal, E. (1968). Generalization gradients obtained from individual subjects following classical conditioning. *Journal of Experimental Psychology, 78,* 171–174.

recognized as having the same meaning, or behavioral significance, despite apparent differences. For example, even when a predator makes a slightly different sound or is seen from a different angle, its prey can still recognize and respond to it quickly.

Stimulus Discrimination In some circumstances, however, it is important that a response be made to only a very small range of stimuli. An organism should not, for example, exhaust itself by fleeing too often from animals that are only superficially similar to its natural predators. **Stimulus discrimination** is the process by which an organism learns to respond differently to stimuli that are distinct from the CS on some dimension (for example, differences in hue or in pitch). An organism's discrimination among similar stimuli (tones of 1,000, 1,200, and 1,500 Hz, for example) is sharpened with discrimination training in which only one of them (1,200 Hz, for example) predicts the UCS and in which the others are repeatedly presented without it. Early in conditioning, stimuli similar to the CS will elicit a similar response, although not quite as strong. As discrimination training proceeds, the responses to the other, dissimilar stimuli weaken: The organism gradually learns which event-signal predicts the onset of the UCS and which signals do not.

stimulus discrimination A conditioning process in which an organism learns to respond differently to stimuli that differ from the conditioned stimulus on some dimension.

For an organism to perform optimally in an environment, the processes of generalization and discrimination must strike a balance. You don't want to be overselective—it can be quite costly to miss the presence of a predator. You also don't want to be overresponsive—if you are fearful of every shadow, you will waste time and energy to dispel your worry. Classical conditioning provides a mechanism that allows creatures to react efficiently to the structure of their environments.

Focus on Acquisition

In this section, we will examine more closely the conditions that are necessary for classical conditioning to take place. So far, I have *described* the acquisition of classically conditioned responses, but I have not yet *explained* it. Pavlov believed that classical conditioning resulted from the mere pairing of the CS and the UCS. In his view, if a response is to be classically conditioned, the CS and the UCS must occur close together in time—that is, be *temporally contiguous*. But as you will see next, contemporary research has modified that view.

Pavlov's theory dominated classical conditioning until the mid-1960s, when **Robert Rescorla** (1966) conducted a very telling experiment using dogs as subjects. Rescorla designed an experiment using a tone (the CS) and a shock (the UCS). For one group of animals the CS and UCS were merely contiguous—which, if Pavlov were correct, would be sufficient to produce classical conditioning. For the other group of animals, the tone reliably predicted the presence of the shock.

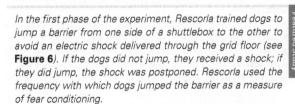

In the first phase of the experiment, Rescorla trained dogs to jump a barrier from one side of a shuttlebox to the other to avoid an electric shock delivered through the grid floor (see **Figure 6***). If the dogs did not jump, they received a shock; if they did jump, the shock was postponed. Rescorla used the frequency with which dogs jumped the barrier as a measure of fear conditioning.*

Why might a child who has been frightened by one dog develop a fear response to all dogs?

When the dogs were jumping across the barrier regularly, Rescorla divided his subjects into two groups and subjected them to another training procedure. To the random group, the UCS (the shock) was delivered randomly and independently of the CS (the tone) (see **Figure 7***). Although the CS and the UCS often occurred close together in time—they were, by chance, temporally contiguous—the UCS was as likely to be delivered in the absence of the CS as it was in its presence. Thus the CS had no predictive value. For the contingency group, however, the UCS always followed the CS. Thus, for this group, the sounding of the tone was a reliable predictor of the delivery of the shock.*

Once this training was complete, the dogs were put back into the shuttlebox, but this time with a twist. Now the tone used in the second training procedure occasionally sounded, signaling shock. What happened? **Figure 8***, indicates that dogs exposed to the contingent (predictable) CS–UCS relation jumped more frequently in the presence of the tone than did dogs exposed only to the contiguous (associated) CS–UCS relation. Contingency was critical for the signal to serve the dogs as a successful cue for the shock.*

FIGURE 6 **A Shuttlebox**
Rescorla used the frequency with which dogs jumped over a barrier as a measure of fear conditioning.

Thus, in addition to the CS being contiguous—occurring close in time—with the UCS, the CS must also *reliably predict* the occurrence of the UCS in order for classical conditioning to occur (Rescorla, 1988). This finding makes considerable sense. After all, in natural situations, where learning enables organisms to adapt to changes in their environment, stimuli come in clusters and not in neat, simple units, as they do in laboratory experiments.

There's one last requirement for a stimulus to serve as a basis for classical conditioning: It must be *informative* in the environment. Consider an experimental situation in which rats have learned that a tone predicts a shock. Now, a light is added into the situation so that both the light and tone precede the shock. However, when the light is subsequently presented alone, the rats do not appear to have learned that the light predicts the shock (Kamin, 1969). For these rats, the previous conditioning to the tone in the first phase of the experiment *blocked* any subsequent conditioning that could occur to the light. From the rat's point of view, the light may as well not have existed; it provided no additional information beyond that already given by the tone. The requirement of informativeness explains why conditioning occurs most rapidly when the CS stands out against the many other stimuli that may also be present in an environment. A stimulus is more readily noticed the more *intense* it is and the more it *contrasts* with other stimuli.

You can see that classical conditioning is more complex than even Pavlov originally realized. A neutral stimulus will become an effective CS only if it is both appropriately contingent and informative. But now let's shift your attention a bit. We want to identify real-life situations in which classical conditioning plays a role.

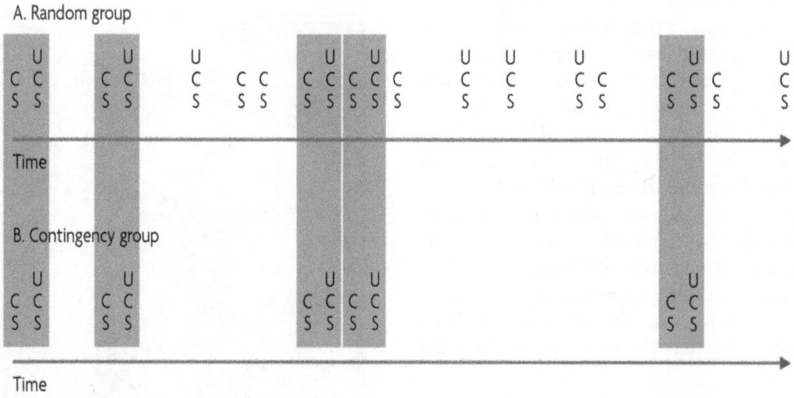

A. Random group

Time

B. Contingency group

Time

FIGURE 7 **Rescorla's Procedure for Demonstrating the Importance of Contingency**
For the random group, 5-second tones (the CS) and 5-second shocks (the UCS) were distributed randomly through the experimental period. For the contingency group, the dogs experienced only the subset of tones and shocks that occurred in a predictive relationship (the onset of the CS preceded the onset of the UCS by 30 seconds or less). Only the dogs in the contingency group learned to associate the CS with the UCS.

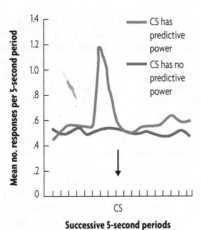

FIGURE 8 The Role of Contingency in Classical Conditioning

The arrow indicates the onset and offset of the 5-second CS tone. Rescorla demonstrated that dogs trained under the contingent CS–UCS relation showed more jumping (and thus conditioned fear) in the presence of the tone than did dogs trained under the contiguous but noncontingent CS–UCS relation.

Applications of Classical Conditioning

Your knowledge of classical conditioning can help you understand significant everyday behavior. In this section, we help you recognize some real-world instances of emotions and preferences as the products of this form of learning. We also explore the role classical conditioning plays in the unfolding of drug addiction.

Emotions and Preferences Earlier we asked you to think about your experience at a horror movie. In that case, you (unconsciously) learned an association between scary music (the CS) and certain likely events (the UCS—the kinds of things that happen in horror movies that cause reflexive revulsion). If you pay careful attention to events in your life, you will discover that there are many circumstances in which you can't quite explain why you are having such a strong emotional reaction or why you have such a strong preference about something. You might take a step back and ask yourself, "Is this the product of classical conditioning?"

Consider these situations (Rozin & Fallon, 1987; Rozin et al., 1986):

- Do you think you'd be willing to eat fudge that had been formed into the shape of dog feces?
- Do you think you'd be willing to drink a sugar-water solution if the sugar was drawn from a container that you knew was incorrectly labeled poison?
- Do you think you would be willing to drink apple juice into which a sterilized cockroach had been dipped?

If each of these situations makes you say "No way!" you are not alone. The classically conditioned response—feelings of disgust

....

👁 Watch the Video *Classic Footage of Little Albert* on MyPsychLab

or danger—wins out over the knowledge that the stimulus is really OK. Because classically conditioned responses are not built up through conscious thought, they are also hard to eliminate through conscious reasoning!

One of the most extensively studied real-world products of classical conditioning is *fear conditioning* (Hartley et al., 2011; Linnman et al., 2011). In the earliest days of behaviorism, John Watson and his colleague Rosalie Rayner sought to prove that many fear responses could be understood as the pairing of a neutral stimulus with something naturally fear provoking. To test their idea, they experimented on an infant who came to be called Little Albert.

Featured Study

👁 *Watson and Rayner (1920) trained Albert to fear a white rat he had initially liked, by pairing its appearance with an aversive UCS—a loud noise just behind him created by striking a large steel bar with a hammer. The unconditioned startle response and the emotional distress to the noxious noise formed the basis of Albert's learning to react with fear to the appearance of the white rat. His fear was developed in just seven conditioning trials. The emotional conditioning was then extended to behavioral conditioning when Albert learned to escape from the feared stimulus. The infant's learned fear then generalized to other furry objects, such as a rabbit, a dog, and even a Santa Claus mask!*

Albert's mother, a wet nurse at the hospital where the study was conducted, took him away before the researchers could try to treat the experimentally conditioned fear. Researchers in psychology are guided by important ethical principles. Those principles make them look back at Watson and Rayner's experiment with grave discomfort: No ethical researcher would ever replicate an experiment of this type.

Because Watson and Rayner never made Albert's true identity public, people have always wondered what happened to him in later life. One team of researchers carried out some detective work with archival materials (Beck et al., 2009). Based

How did John Watson and Rosalie Rayner condition Little Albert to fear small, furry objects?

Courtesy of Prof. Ben Harris, University of New Hampshire

on that work, they have argued that Albert was an infant whose actual name was Douglas Meritte who, quite unfortunately, died in 1925. However, other researchers remain unconvinced by that identification (Powell, 2011).

Fear conditioning has a powerful impact on people's lives. A single traumatic event can condition you to respond with strong physical, emotional, and cognitive reactions—perhaps for a lifetime. Therapists have designed treatments for these types of fears that are intended to counter the effects of classical conditioning.

We don't want to leave you with the impression that only negative responses are classically conditioned. In fact, we suspect that you will also be able to interpret responses of happiness or excitement as instances of classical conditioning. Certainly toilers in the advertising industry hope that classical conditioning works as a positive force. They strive, for example, to create associations in your mind between their products (for example, jeans, sports cars, and soft drinks) and passion. They expect that elements of their advertisements—"sexy" individuals or situations—will serve as the UCS to bring about the UCR—feelings of sexual arousal. The hope then is that the product itself will be the CS, so that the feelings of arousal will become associated with it. To find more examples of the classical conditioning of positive emotions, you should monitor your life for circumstances in which you have a rush of good feelings when you return, for instance, to a familiar location.

Learning to be a Drug Addict   Consider this scenario. A man's body lies in a Manhattan alley, a half-empty syringe dangling from his arm. Cause of death? The coroner called it an overdose, but the man had ordinarily shot up far greater doses than the one that had supposedly killed him. This sort of incident baffled investigators. How could an addict with high drug tolerance die of an overdose when he didn't even get a full hit?

Some time ago, Pavlov (1927) and later his colleague Bykov (1957) pointed out that tolerance to opiates can develop when an individual anticipates the pharmacological action of a drug. Contemporary researcher **Shepard Siegel** refined these ideas. Siegel suggested that the setting in which drug use occurs acts as a conditioned stimulus for a situation in which the body learns to protect itself by preventing the drug from having its usual effect. When people take drugs, the drug (UCS) brings about certain physiological responses to which the body responds with countermeasures intended to reestablish homeostasis. The body's countermeasures to the drug are the unconditioned response (UCR). Over time, this *compensatory response* also becomes the conditioned response. That is, in settings ordinarily associated with drug use (the CS), the body physiologically prepares itself (the CR) for the drug's expected effects. Tolerance arises because, in that setting, the individual must consume an amount of the drug that overcomes the compensatory response before starting to get

How do advertisers exploit classical conditioning to make you feel "passion" toward their products?

any "positive" effect. Increasingly larger doses are needed as the conditioned compensatory response itself grows.

Siegel tested these ideas in his laboratory by creating tolerance to heroin in laboratory rats.

In one study, Siegel and his colleagues classically conditioned rats to expect heroin injections (UCS) in one setting (CS_1) and dextrose (sweet sugar) solution injections in a different setting (CS_2) (Siegel et al., 1982). In the first phase of training, all rats developed heroin tolerance. On the test day, all animals received a larger-than-usual dose of heroin—nearly twice the previous amount. Half of them received it in the setting where heroin had previously been administered; the other half received it in the setting where dextrose solutions had been given during conditioning. Twice as many rats died in the dextrose-solution setting as in the usual heroin setting: 64 percent versus 32 percent!

Presumably, those receiving heroin in the usual setting were more prepared for this potentially dangerous situation because the context (CS_1) brought about a physiological response (CR) that countered the drug's typical effects.

To find out if a similar process might operate in humans, Siegel and a colleague interviewed heroin addicts who had come close to death from supposed overdoses. In 7 out of 10 cases, the addicts had been shooting up in a new and unfamiliar setting (Siegel, 1984). Although this natural experiment provides no conclusive data, it suggests that a dose for which an addict has developed tolerance in one setting may become an overdose in an unfamiliar setting. This analysis allows us to suggest that the addict we invoked at the beginning of this section might have died because he was shooting up in an unfamiliar setting.

Although we have mentioned research with heroin, classical conditioning is an important component to tolerance for a variety of drugs, including alcohol (S. Siegel, 2005). Thus the same principles Pavlov observed for dogs, bells, and salivation help explain some of the mechanisms underlying human drug addiction.

Biological Constraints

In the examples of classical conditioning you've seen so far, it seems that more or less any conditioned stimulus (such as a tuning fork) can work to signal more or less any unconditioned stimulus (such as food). However, some instances of conditioning depend not only on the relationship between stimuli and behavior but also on the way an organism is genetically predisposed toward stimuli in its environment. Animals appear to have encoded, within their genetic inheritance, the types of sensory cues—taste, smell, or appearance—that are most likely to signal dimensions of reward or danger. In those circumstances, researchers say that organisms have *biological preparedness*: A particular species has evolved so that the members require less learning experience than normal to acquire a conditioned response. Experimenters who try arbitrarily to break these genetic links will look forward to little success. Researchers believe that humans are biologically prepared to acquire intense fears—known as *phobias*—to stimuli such as snakes and spiders

that provided dangers over the course of human evolution. Here, we consider an important phenomenon called *taste-aversion learning* that provides an example of biological constraints on classical conditioning.

Imagine the strategy you might devise for tasting a variety of unfamiliar substances. If you had the genetic endowment of rats, you would be very cautious in doing so. When presented with a new food or flavor, rats take only a very small sample. Only if it fails to make them sick will they go back for more. To flip that around, suppose we include a substance with the new flavor that does make the rats ill—they'll never consume that flavor again. This phenomenon is known as **taste-aversion learning.** You can see why having this genetic capacity to sample and learn which foods are safe and which are toxic could have great survival value.

Taste-aversion learning is an enormously powerful mechanism. Unlike most other instances of classical conditioning, taste aversion is learned with only one pairing of a CS (the novel flavor) and its consequences (the result of the underlying UCS—the element that actually brings about the illness). This is true even with a long interval, 12 hours or more, between the time the rat consumes the substance and the time it becomes ill. Finally, unlike many classically conditioned associations that are quite fragile, this one is permanent after one experience. Again, to understand these violations of the norms of classical conditioning, consider how dramatically this mechanism aids survival.

John Garcia, the psychologist who first documented taste-aversion learning in the laboratory, and his colleague Robert Koelling used this phenomenon to demonstrate that, in general, animals are biologically prepared to learn certain associations. The researchers discovered that some CS–UCS combinations can be classically conditioned in particular species of animals, but others cannot.

In phase 1 of Garcia and Koelling's experiment, thirsty rats were first familiarized with the experimental situation in which licking a tube produced three CSs: saccharin-flavored water, noise, and bright light. In phase 2, when the rats licked the tube, half of them received only the sweet water and half received only the noise, light, and plain water. Each of these two groups was again divided: Half of each group was given electric shocks that produced pain, and half was given X-ray radiation that produced nausea and illness.

*The amount of water drunk by the rats in phase 1 was compared with the amount drunk in phase 2, when pain and illness were involved (see **Figure 9**). Big reductions in drinking occurred when flavor was associated with illness (taste aversion) and when noise and light were associated with pain. However, there was little change in behavior under the other two conditions—when flavor predicted pain or when the "bright-noisy water" predicted illness.*

The pattern of results suggests that rats have an inborn bias to associate particular stimuli with particular consequences (Garcia & Koelling, 1966).

taste-aversion learning A biological constraint on learning in which an organism learns in one trial to avoid a food whose ingestion is followed by illness.

Featured Study

Featured Study

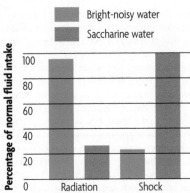

Bright-noisy water

Saccharine water

FIGURE 9 **Inborn Bias**
Results from Garcia and Koelling's study (1966) showed that rats possess an inborn bias to associate certain cues with certain outcomes. Rats avoided saccharin-flavored water when it predicted illness but not when it predicted shock. Conversely, rats avoided the "bright-noisy water" when it predicted shock but not when it predicted illness.

Researchers have put knowledge of the mechanisms of taste-aversion learning to practical use. To stop coyotes from killing sheep (and sheep ranchers from shooting coyotes), John Garcia and colleagues have put toxic lamb burgers wrapped in sheep fur on the outskirts of fenced-in areas of sheep ranches. The coyotes that eat these lamb burgers get sick, vomit, and develop an instant distaste for lamb meat. Their subsequent disgust at the mere sight of sheep makes them back away from the animals instead of attacking.

In the classic research on taste-aversion learning, researchers paired novel flavors with substances that made the rats feel ill. However, other aspects of gustatory experience also yield conditioned aversions, including the temperature of the food.

In a preliminary experiment, 20 rats had the opportunity to drink from two bottles containing water at either 50° F or 104° F (Smith et al., 2010). The rats showed a consistent preference for the cold water over the warm water. In the next experiment, 16 rats were split into two groups. After drinking cold water, one group was injected with a substance that made the rats ill; the other group received a saline injection that had no negative effect. The rats that became ill now showed a conditioned aversion to the cold

water. Despite their initial dislike for warm water, they now mostly drank water at that temperature. In later experiments, the researchers introduced the novel flavor of saccharin. Rats that got sick after drinking water that was both cold and sweet acquired an aversion to both components of the novel stimulus: They subsequently avoided both cold water and warm saccharin.

You can see how these experiments extend the concept of biological preparedness. Food has both taste and temperature. When illness is associated with either dimension, rats swiftly acquire conditioned aversions.

Stop *and* Review

① What is the role of reflexive behaviors in classical conditioning?
② What is the difference between the UCS and the CS?
③ What is meant by stimulus discrimination?
④ Why is contingency so important in classical conditioning?
⑤ What is the conditioned response when classical conditioning plays a role in drug addiction?
⑥ What makes taste-aversion learning unusual as a conditioned response?

✓●⌐**Study** and **Review** on **MyPsychLab**

CRITICAL THINKING Consider the experiment that demonstrated conditioned heroin tolerance in rats. Why were the rats given twice the normal dose of heroin on the test day?

OPERANT CONDITIONING: LEARNING ABOUT CONSEQUENCES

Let's return to the movie theater. The horror film is now over, and you peel yourself off your seat. Your companion asks you if you're hoping that a sequel will be made. You respond, "I've learned that I shouldn't go to horror films." You're probably right, but what kind of learning is this? Once again our answer begins around the turn of the 20th century.

How have researchers used taste-aversion conditioning to prevent coyotes from killing sheep?

Psychology in Your Life

HOW DOES CLASSICAL CONDITIONING AFFECT CANCER TREATMENT?

Medical researchers have made great strides in developing more effective treatments to combat cancers. Many of those treatments involve chemotherapy, drug treatments that kill or greatly weaken cancer cells. People who undergo chemotherapy often experience negative consequences such as fatigue and nausea. You might assume that those side effects would arise from the direct action of the chemotherapy drugs. Although that is partially the case, research suggests that processes of classical conditioning contribute greatly to the persistence of those side effects over time (Bovbjerg, 2006; Stockhorst et al., 2006).

Let's consider the concrete example of *anticipatory nausea*: Circumstances in which, over the course of cancer treatment, patients' nausea and vomiting begin even before they receive the chemotherapy drugs. Classical conditioning explains why this happens. The chemotherapy drugs serve as the unconditioned stimulus (UCS) producing posttreatment nausea as an unconditioned response (UCR). Distinctive features of the clinic environment serve as the conditioned stimulus (CS). Across visits to the clinic, the CS becomes paired with the UCS. The result is that patients experience anticipatory nausea as a conditioned response (CR) as soon as they arrived at the clinic. One study of 214 patients found that about 10 percent developed anticipatory nausea (Akechi et al., 2010). This situation had a measurable negative impact on their quality of life.

Classical conditioning might also explain why some of the aftereffects of chemotherapy endure well after the end of treatment. Researchers surveyed a group of 273 Hodgkin's disease survivors who ranged from 1 to 20 years beyond treatment (Cameron et al., 2001). The participants were asked to reflect over the past six months to indicate whether they "had noticed any smell or odor (anything [they had] seen / places [they had] gone to; any foods or drinks)" that had reminded them of treatment and made them "feel good or bad emotionally or physically" (p. 72). More than half of the participants—55 percent—reported lingering bad responses that were triggered by stimuli associated with their chemotherapy. The researchers suggest that these persistent responses were the result of classically conditioned associations between various aspects of the chemotherapy experience (the CS) and the drug infusions (the UCS).

As you've seen, research evidence strongly suggests that processes of classical conditioning amplify the negative effects of chemotherapy. The studies give researchers a context in which they can begin to design treatments. Some researchers have developed rat models of anticipatory nausea. Their goal is to develop drug treatments that will block the processes of classical conditioning, to prevent anticipatory nausea from developing (Chan et al., 2009; Ossenkopp et al., 2011). Other researchers have applied behavioral therapies (Roscoe et al., 2011). Those therapies use psychological interventions to counteract the initial classical conditioning. For example, patients might acquire techniques that enable them to experience deep relaxation—rather than nausea—in response to the conditioned stimulus. Interventions of this type couldn't eliminate the negative consequences of chemotherapy but they could help stop those negative consequences from enduring over time.

The Law of Effect

At about the same time that Pavlov was using classical conditioning to induce Russian dogs to salivate to the sound of a bell, **Edward L. Thorndike** (1874–1949) was watching American cats trying to escape from puzzle boxes (see **Figure 10**). Thorndike (1898) reported his observations and inferences about the kind of learning he believed was taking place in his subjects. The cats at first only struggled against their confinement, but once some "impulsive" action allowed them to open the door "all the other unsuccessful impulses [were] stamped out and the particular impulse leading to the successful act [was] stamped in by the resulting pleasure" (Thorndike, 1898, p. 13).

What had Thorndike's cats learned? According to Thorndike's analysis, learning was an association between stimuli in the situation and a response that an animal learned to make: a *stimulus–response (S–R) connection*. Thus the cats had learned to produce an appropriate response (for example, clawing at a button or loop) that in these stimulus circumstances (confinement in the puzzle box) led to a desired outcome (momentary freedom). Note that the learning of these S–R connections occurred gradually and automatically in a mechanistic way as the animal experienced the consequences of its actions through blind *trial and error*. Gradually, the behaviors that had satisfying consequences increased in frequency; they eventually became the dominant response when the animal was placed in the puzzle box. Thorndike referred to this relationship between behavior and its consequences as the **law of effect**: A response that is followed by satisfying consequences becomes more probable and a response that is followed by dissatisfying consequences becomes less probable.

---

law of effect A basic law of learning that states that the power of a stimulus to evoke a response is strengthened when the response is followed by a reward and weakened when it is not followed by a reward.

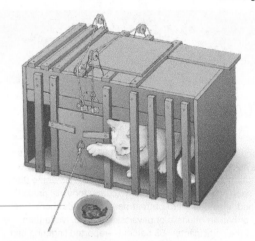

FIGURE 10 A Thorndike Puzzle Box

To get out of the puzzle box and obtain food, Thorndike's cat had to manipulate a mechanism to release a weight that would then pull the door open.

From Zimbardo/Johnson/McCann, *Psychology: Core Concepts*, © 2009. Reproduced by permission of Pearson Education, Inc.

Experimental Analysis of Behavior

B. F. Skinner embraced Thorndike's view that environmental consequences exert a powerful effect on behavior. Skinner outlined a program of research whose purpose was to discover, by systematic variation of stimulus conditions, the ways that various environmental conditions affect the likelihood that a given response will occur:

> *A natural datum in a science of behavior is the probability that a given bit of behavior will occur at a given time. An experimental analysis deals with that probability in terms of frequency or rate of responding. . . . The task of an experimental analysis is to discover all the variables of which probability of response is a function. (Skinner, 1966, pp. 213–214)*

Skinner's analysis was experimental rather than theoretical—theorists are guided by derivations and predictions about behavior from their theories, but empiricists, such as Skinner, advocate the bottom-up approach. They start with the collection and evaluation of data within the context of an experiment and are not theory driven.

To analyze behavior experimentally, Skinner developed **operant conditioning** procedures, in which he manipulated the *consequences* of an organism's behavior in order to see

what effect they had on subsequent behavior. An **operant** is any behavior that is *emitted* by an organism and can be characterized in terms of the observable effects it has on the environment. Literally, *operant* means *affecting the environment*, or operating on it (Skinner, 1938). Operants are *not elicited* by specific stimuli as classically conditioned behaviors are. Pigeons peck, rats search for food, babies cry and coo, some people gesture while talking, and others stutter. The probability of these behaviors occurring in the future can be increased or decreased by manipulating the effects they have on the environment. If, for example, a baby's coo prompts desirable parental contact, the baby will coo more in the future. Operant conditioning, then, modifies the probability of different types of operant behavior as a function of the environmental consequences they produce. 👁

To carry out his new experimental analysis, Skinner invented an apparatus that allowed him to manipulate the consequences of behavior, the *operant chamber*. **Figure 11** shows how the operant chamber works. When, after having produced an appropriate behavior defined by the experimenter, a rat presses a lever, the mechanism delivers a food pellet. This device allows experimenters to study the variables that allow rats to learn—or not to learn—the behaviors they define. For example, if a lever press produces a food pellet only after a rat has turned a circle in the chamber, the rat will swiftly learn (through a process called *shaping* that we will consider shortly) to turn a circle before pressing the lever.

In many operant experiments, the measure of interest is how much of a particular behavior an animal carries out in a period of time. Researchers record the pattern and total amount of behavior emitted in the course of an experiment. This methodology allowed Skinner to study the effect of reinforcement contingencies on animals' behavior. 👁

....

👁 Watch the Video *The Basics 2: Operant Conditioning and Learning About Consequences* on MyPsychLab

👁 Watch the Video *Classic Footage of B.F. Skinner and the Skinner Box* on MyPsychLab

operant conditioning Learning in which the probability of a response is changed by a change in its consequences.

operant Behavior emitted by an organism that can be characterized in terms of the observable effects it has on the environment.

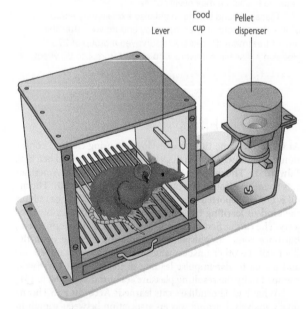

Lever   Food cup   Pellet dispenser

FIGURE 11 Operant Chamber

In this specially designed apparatus, typical of those used with rats, a press on the lever may be followed by delivery of a food pellet.

Reinforcement Contingencies

A **reinforcement contingency** is a consistent relationship between a response and the changes in the environment that it produces. Imagine, for example, an experiment in which a pigeon's pecking a disk (the response) is generally followed by the presentation of grain (the corresponding change in the environment). This consistent relationship, or reinforcement contingency, will usually be accompanied by an increase in the rate of pecking. For delivery of grain to increase *only* the probability of pecking, it must be contingent *only* on the pecking response—the delivery must occur regularly after that response but not after other responses, such as turning or bowing. Based on Skinner's work, modern behavior analysts seek to understand behavior in terms of reinforcement contingencies. Let's take a closer look at what has been discovered about these contingencies.

Positive and Negative Reinforcers Suppose you are now captivated by the idea of getting your pet rat to turn a circle in its cage. To increase the probability of circle-turning behavior, you would want to use a **reinforcer,** any stimulus that—when made contingent on a behavior—increases the probability of that behavior over time. *Reinforcement* is the delivery of a reinforcer following a response.

Reinforcers are always defined empirically, in terms of their effects on changing the probability of a response. If you look out at the world, you can probably find three classes of stimuli: those toward which you are neutral, those that you find *appetitive* (you have an "appetite" for them), and those

What environmental contingencies might cause babies to smile more often?

that you find *aversive* (you seek to avoid them). The compositions of these classes of stimuli clearly are not the same for all individuals: What is appetitive or aversive is defined by the behavior of the individual organism. Consider the strawberry. Although many people find strawberries quite delicious, I find strawberries virtually inedible. If you intend to use strawberries to change my behavior, it's important to know that I find them aversive rather than appetitive.

When a behavior is followed by the delivery of an appetitive stimulus, the event is called **positive reinforcement.** Your pet rat will turn circles if a consequence of circle turning is the delivery of desirable food. Humans will tell jokes if a consequence of their joke telling is a type of laughter they find pleasurable.

When a behavior is followed by the removal of an aversive stimulus, the event is called **negative reinforcement.** For example, I would be more likely to perform a behavior if it would allow me to cease eating strawberries. There are two general types of learning circumstances in which negative reinforcement applies. In **escape conditioning,** animals learn that a response will allow them to escape from an aversive stimulus. Raising an umbrella during a downpour is a common example of escape conditioning. You learn to use an umbrella to escape the aversive stimulus of getting wet. In **avoidance conditioning,** animals learn responses that allow them to avoid aversive stimuli before they begin. Suppose your car has a buzzer that sounds when you fail to buckle your seat belt. You will learn to buckle up to avoid the aversive noise.

To distinguish clearly between positive and negative reinforcement, remember the following: Both positive reinforcement and negative reinforcement *increase* the probability of the response that precedes them. Positive reinforcement increases response probability by the presentation of an appetitive stimulus following a response; negative reinforcement does the same in reverse, through the removal, reduction, or prevention of an aversive stimulus following a response.

Recall that for classical conditioning, when the unconditioned stimulus is no longer delivered, the conditioned response suffers extinction. The same rule holds for operant conditioning—if reinforcement is withheld, **operant extinction** occurs. Thus, if a behavior no longer produces predictable consequences, it returns to the level it was at before operant conditioning—it is extinguished. You can probably catch your own behaviors being reinforced and then *extinguished.* Have you ever had the experience of dropping a few coins into a

....

reinforcement contingency A consistent relationship between a response and the changes in the environment that it produces.

reinforcer Any stimulus that, when made contingent on a response, increases the probability of that response.

positive reinforcement A behavior is followed by the presentation of an appetitive stimulus, increasing the probability of that behavior.

negative reinforcement A behavior is followed by the removal of an aversive stimulus, increasing the probability of that behavior.

escape conditioning A form of learning in which animals acquire a response that will allow them to escape from an aversive stimulus.

avoidance conditioning A form of learning in which animals acquire responses that allow them to avoid aversive stimuli before they begin.

operant extinction When a behavior no longer produces predictable consequences, its return to the level of occurrence it had before operant conditioning.

soda machine and getting nothing in return? If you kicked the machine one time and your soda came out, the act of kicking would be reinforced. However, if the next few times, your kicking produced no soda, kicking would quickly be extinguished.

As with classical conditioning, *spontaneous recovery* is also a feature of operant conditioning. Suppose you had reinforced a pigeon by providing food pellets when it pecked a key in the presence of a green light. If you discontinued the reinforcement, the pecking behavior would extinguish. However, the next time you put the pigeon back in the apparatus with the green light on, the pigeon would likely spontaneously peck again. This is called spontaneous recovery. In human terms, you might kick the soda machine again with a time lag after your initial extinction experiences.

Positive and Negative Punishment   You are probably familiar with another technique for decreasing the probability of a response—punishment. A **punisher** is any stimulus that—when it is made contingent on a response—decreases the probability of that response over time. *Punishment* is the delivery of a punisher following a response. Just as we could identify positive and negative reinforcement, we can identify positive punishment and negative punishment. When a behavior is followed by the delivery of an aversive stimulus, the event is called **positive punishment** (you can remember *positive* because something is added to the situation). Touching a hot stove, for example, produces pain that punishes the preceding response so that you are less likely next time to touch the stove. When a behavior is followed by the removal of an appetitive stimulus, the event is referred to as **negative punishment** (you can remember *negative* because something is subtracted from the situation). Thus when a parent withdraws a child's allowance after she hits her baby brother, the child learns not to hit her brother in the future. Which kind of punishment explains why you might stay away from horror movies?

Although punishment and reinforcement are closely related operations, they differ in important ways. A good way to differentiate them is to think of each in terms of its effects on behavior. Punishment, by definition, always *reduces* the probability of a response occurring again; reinforcement, by definition, always *increases* the probability of a response recurring. For example, some people get severe headaches after drinking caffeinated beverages. The headache is the stimulus that positively punishes and reduces the behavior of drinking coffee. However, once the headache is present, people often take aspirin or another pain reliever to eliminate the headache. The aspirin's analgesic effect is the stimulus that negatively reinforces the behavior of ingesting aspirin.

....

punisher Any stimulus that, when made contingent on a response, decreases the probability of that response.

positive punishment A behavior is followed by the presentation of an aversive stimulus, decreasing the probability of that behavior.

negative punishment A behavior is followed by the removal of an appetitive stimulus, decreasing the probability of that behavior.

discriminative stimulus Stimulus that acts as a predictor of reinforcement, signaling when particular behaviors will result in positive reinforcement.

three-term contingency The means by which organisms learn that, in the presence of some stimuli but not others, their behavior is likely to have a particular effect on the environment.

Discriminative Stimuli and Generalization   You are unlikely to want to change the probability of a certain behavior at all times. Rather, you may want to change the probability of the behavior in a particular context. For example, you often want to increase the probability that a child will sit quietly in class without changing the probability that he or she will be noisy and active during recess. Through their associations with reinforcement or punishment, certain stimuli that precede a particular response—**discriminative stimuli**—come to set the context for that behavior. Organisms learn that, in the presence of some stimuli but not of others, their behavior is likely to have a particular effect on the environment. For example, in the presence of a green street light, the act of crossing an intersection in a motor vehicle is reinforced. When the light is red, however, such behavior may be punished—it may result in a traffic ticket or an accident. Skinner referred to the sequence of discriminative stimulus–behavior–consequence as the **three-term contingency** and believed that it could explain most human action (Skinner, 1953). **Table 1** describes how the three-term contingency might explain several different kinds of human behavior.

Under laboratory conditions, manipulating the consequences of behavior in the presence of discriminative stimuli can exert powerful control over that behavior. For example, a pigeon might be given grain after pecking a disk in the presence of a green light but not a red light. The green light is a discriminative stimulus that sets the occasion for pecking; the red is a discriminative stimulus that sets the occasion for not pecking. Organisms learn quickly to discriminate between these conditions, responding regularly in the presence of one stimulus and not responding in the presence of the other. By manipulating the components of the three-term contingency, you can constrain a behavior to a particular context.

Organisms also generalize responses to other stimuli that resemble the discriminative stimulus. Once a response has been reinforced in the presence of one discriminative stimulus, a similar stimulus can become a discriminative stimulus for that same response. For example, pigeons trained to peck a disk in the presence of a green light will also peck the disk in the presence of lights that are lighter or darker shades of green than the original discriminative stimulus. Similarly, you generalize to different shades of green on stop lights as a discriminative stimulus for your "resume driving" behavior.

Using Reinforcement Contingencies   Are you ready to put your new knowledge of reinforcement contingencies to work? Here are some considerations you might have:

- *How can you define the behavior that you would like to reinforce or eliminate?* You must always carefully target the specific behavior whose probability you would like to change. Reinforcement should be contingent on exactly that behavior. When reinforcers are presented so that they are not contingent, their presence has little effect on behavior. For example, if a parent praises poor work as well as good efforts, a child will not learn to work harder in school—but because of the positive reinforcement, other behaviors are likely to increase. (What might those be?)

- *How can you define the contexts in which a behavior is appropriate or inappropriate?* Remember that you rarely want to allow or disallow every instance of a behavior.

Table 1 • The Three-Term Contingency: Relationships among Discriminative Stimuli, Behavior, and Consequences

	Discriminative Stimulus	Emitted Response	Stimulus Consequence	
1. Positive reinforcement: A response in the presence of an effective signal produces the desired consequence. This response increases.	Soft-drink machine	Put coin in slot	Get drink	
2. Negative reinforcement (escape): An aversive situation is escaped from by an operant response. This escape response increases.	Heat	Fan oneself	Escape from heat	
3. Positive punishment: A response is followed by an aversive stimulus. The response is eliminated or suppressed.	Attractive matchbox	Play with matches	Get burned or get caught and spanked	
4. Negative punishment: A response is followed by the removal of an appetitive stimulus. The response is eliminated or suppressed.	Brussels sprouts	Refusal to eat them	No dessert	

Oleksiy Mark/Shutterstock.com

Katariina Järvinen/Shutterstock.com

Vlue/Shutterstock.com

Eric Gevaert/Shutterstock.com

We suggested earlier, for example, that you might want to increase the probability that a child will sit quietly in class without changing the probability that he or she will be noisy and active during recess. You must define the discriminative stimuli and investigate how broadly the desired response will be generalized to similar stimuli. If, for example, the child learned to sit quietly in class, would that behavior generalize to other "serious" settings?

• *Have you unknowingly been reinforcing some behaviors?* Suppose you want to eliminate a behavior. Try to determine whether you can identify reinforcers for that behavior. If so, you can try to extinguish the behavior by eliminating those reinforcers. Imagine, for example, that a young boy throws a large number of tantrums. You might ask yourself, "Have I been reinforcing those tantrums by paying the boy extra attention when he screams?" That extra attention would count as a *secondary gain* from the bad behavior (that is, the boy might have learned that when he throws the tantrum, he'll gain the extra attention). If this is the case, you can try to eliminate the tantrums by eliminating the reinforcement. Even better, you can combine extinction with positive reinforcement of more socially approved behaviors.

It's important to be aware that the reinforcers parents produce can make children's conduct problems, such as tantrums, more likely. In fact, parenting research has identified unknowing reinforcement as one cause of serious behavior problems in children. For example, Gerald Patterson and his colleagues

Copyright © Cindy Charles/PhotoEdit

How can parents use reinforcement contingencies to affect their children's behavior?

(Granic & Patterson, 2006) have outlined a *coercion model* for antisocial behavior. Family observations suggest that children are put at risk when their parents issue threats in response to small misbehaviors (such as whining, teasing, or yelling) without following through. At some moments, however, these parents would issue harsh or explosive discipline toward the same behaviors. The children appear to learn the lesson that relatively large acts of aggressive and coercive behavior are appropriate and necessary for achieving goals—leading to a cycle of increase in the severity of the children's antisocial behavior.

The coercion model suggests that parents' attempts to use punishment to affect children's behavior are often ineffective. There are other reasons that psychologists recommend against punishment. For example, an abundance of data suggests that physical punishment leads to negative child outcomes (Gershoff & Bitensky, 2007). For example, one study involving over 1,000 children examined the relationship between the amount of physical punishment the children received as 15-month-olds and the behavior problems they displayed as 36-month-olds and as first graders (Mulvaney & Mebert, 2007). To account for the fact that some children are more difficult than others—and, therefore, might be more likely to elicit punishment—the analyses focused on changes in each child's behavior. The study demonstrated that, for both "easy" and "difficult" children (as reported by their parents), the more the children had been spanked early in life the more likely they were to show increases in, for example, aggressive behaviors at both 36 months and in first grade. These types of data explain why experts advise that parents first try positive reinforcement rather than punishment: "Many undesirable behaviors can be completely suppressed by positive reinforcement of alternative and incompatible behaviors" (Benjet & Kazdin, 2003, p. 215). For example, you can praise a child for sitting quietly rather than spanking him for running around. Thus reinforcing children for behaving well is often a better long-term strategy than punishing them for behaving poorly. The *Critical Thinking in Your Life* box discusses "time outs" as another strategy to change children's behavior without using physical punishment.

One final thought. It's often the case that real-life situations will involve intricate combinations of reinforcement and punishment. Suppose, for example, parents use negative punishment by grounding a teenager for two weeks when he stays out past curfew. To soften up his parents, the teen helps more than usual around the house. Assuming his helping behavior appeals to the parents, the teen is trying to reinforce his parents' "reducing the sentence" behavior. If this strategy succeeds in changing the punishment to only one week, the teen's helping behavior will have been negatively reinforced—because helping led to the removal of the aversive stimulus of being grounded. Whenever the teen is grounded again (a discriminative stimulus), his helping behavior should be more likely. Do you see how all the contingencies fit together to change both the teen's and the parents' behaviors? 👁

Let's now take a look at the ways in which various objects and activities may come to function as reinforcers.

Properties of Reinforcers

Reinforcers are the power brokers of operant conditioning: They change or maintain behavior. Reinforcers have a number of interesting and complex properties. They can be learned through experience rather than be biologically determined and can be activities rather than objects. In some situations, even ordinarily powerful reinforcers may not be enough to change a dominant behavior pattern (in this case, we would say that the consequences were not actually reinforcers).

Conditioned Reinforcers When you came into the world, there were a handful of **primary reinforcers,** such as food and water, whose reinforcing properties were biologically determined. Over time, however, otherwise neutral stimuli have become associated with primary reinforcers and now function as **conditioned reinforcers** for operant responses. Conditioned reinforcers can come to serve as ends in themselves. In fact, a great deal of human behavior is influenced less by biologically significant primary reinforcers than by a wide variety of conditioned reinforcers. Money, grades, smiles of approval, gold stars, and various kinds of status symbols are among the many potent conditioned reinforcers that influence much of your behavior.

Virtually any stimulus can become a conditioned reinforcer by being paired with a primary reinforcer. In one experiment, simple tokens were used with animal learners.

With raisins as primary reinforcers, chimps were trained to solve problems (Cowles, 1937). Then tokens were delivered along with the raisins. When only the tokens were presented, the chimps continued working for their "money" because they could later deposit the hard-earned tokens in a "chimp-o-mat" designed to exchange tokens for the raisins.

Featured Study

Teachers and experimenters often find conditioned reinforcers more effective and easier to use than primary reinforcers because (1) few primary reinforcers are available in the classroom, whereas almost any stimulus event that is under control of a teacher can be used as a conditioned reinforcer; (2) they can be dispensed rapidly; (3) they are portable; and (4) their reinforcing effect may be more immediate because it depends only on the perception of receiving them and not on biological processing, as in the case of primary reinforcers.

In some institutions, such as psychiatric hospitals or drug treatment programs, *token economies* are set up based on these principles. Desired behaviors (grooming or taking medication, for example) are explicitly defined, and token payoffs are given by the staff when the behaviors are performed. These tokens can later be exchanged by the patients for a wide array of rewards and privileges (Dickerson et al., 2005; Matson & Boisjoli, 2009). These systems of reinforcement are especially effective in modifying patients' behaviors regarding self-care, upkeep of their environment, and, most important, frequency of their positive social interactions.

👁 Watch the Video *Thinking Like a Psychologist: Physical Punishment– You Decide!* on MyPsychLab

primary reinforcer Biologically determined reinforcer, such as food and water.

conditioned reinforcer In classical conditioning, a formerly neutral stimulus that has become a reinforcer.

Critical Thinking in Your Life

WHEN DO "TIME OUTS" CHANGE CHILDREN'S BEHAVIOR?

One of the classic threats that children receive is that if they don't "start behaving," they will be made to "go stand in a corner." This threat is one version of a strategy that experts call a *time out*. Here's an official definition: A time out is "the contingent withholding of the opportunity to earn reinforcement . . . from rewarding stimuli including attention from the parent, as a consequence of some form of misbehavior" (Morawska & Sanders, 2011, p. 2). You now know enough about operant conditioning to understand that definition! The important idea is that children learn that if they misbehave, they will lose access to rewarding stimuli. For that reason, time outs are a form of punishment.

Let's focus our attention on an imaginary boy named Timothy. To implement a time out, Timothy's parents make him sit on a kitchen chair. Will that work? Researchers have explored a number of variables that affect the likelihood that time outs will function effectively to change children's behavior (Everett et al., 2010). To begin, the contrast between "time in" and "time out" is very important (Morawska & Sanders, 2011). If Timothy doesn't actually find interactions with his parents rewarding, then a time out that suspends those interactions will not reduce his misbehavior (in fact, it's likely the time out will cause him to misbehave more).

Research also suggests that we should consider Timothy's age. Time outs are probably most effective for children ages 3 to 7 (Everett et al., 2010). Timothy's parents should choose a duration of one to five minutes. That should

be sufficient to create behavior change (Morawska & Sanders, 2011). Timothy's parents may want to explain to him why he is getting the time out. However, it's more important that they be the ones who decide when the time out is over. In that way, Timothy's parents can ensure that he has met the requirements for the time out (for example, three minutes without talking).

It's also very important that Timothy not learn that time outs allow him to escape from tasks he'd rather not perform (Everett et al., 2007). Suppose that Timothy's parents ask him to clean up his room. When he refuses to comply, they give him a time out. In that case, Timothy might very well prefer the time out to completing the chore—he will learn, more generally, that he can escape from aversive tasks if he is willing to weather a time out. Timothy's parents must ensure that they reaffirm their request once the time out period has passed.

As the text has noted, experts generally recommend that parents first try positive reinforcement when they ponder changing their children's behavior. However, when children behave in ways that make other strategies necessary, time outs provide a reliable alternative to reduce children's misbehavior.

- Why must parents understand what their children find rewarding before they implement a time out?
- How might parents detect when their children are accepting time outs to escape aversive tasks?

Response Deprivation and Positive Reinforcers Suppose you need to get a child to do something. You don't want to pay her or give her a gold star, so instead you strike this bargain: "When you finish your homework, you can play with your video game." Why might this tactic work? According to *response deprivation theory*, behaviors become preferred and, therefore, reinforcing when an animal is prevented from engaging in them (Klatt & Morris, 2001). For example, water-deprived rats learned to increase their running in an exercise wheel when their running was followed by an opportunity to drink. Conversely, exercise-deprived rats learned to increase their drinking when that response was followed by a chance to run (Premack, 1965). Can you see how the promise of video games after homework follows this same pattern? For a period of time, the child is video game–deprived—the rate at which the child would ordinarily play the video game is restricted below normal. To overcome that deprivation, she will learn to work on her homework.

This analysis suggests two important lessons. First, these examples remind you why you shouldn't assume that the same activity will function as a reinforcer for an animal at all

times. You need to know, for example, whether the animal is food-deprived before you attempt to use food as a reinforcer. Second, these examples suggest why virtually any activity can come to serve as a reinforcer. You can experience deprivation along any number of dimensions. In fact, if you didn't allow a child to do homework for a period of time, she would learn other behaviors to overcome homework-doing deprivation.

Schedules of Reinforcement

What happens when you cannot, or do not want to, reinforce your pet on every occasion when it performs a special behavior? Consider a story about the young B. F. Skinner. It seems that one weekend he was secluded in his laboratory with not enough of a food-reward supply for his hardworking rats. He economized by giving the rats pellets only after a certain interval of time—no matter how many times they pressed in between, they couldn't get any more pellets. Even so, the rats responded as much with this *partial reinforcement schedule* as they had with continuous reinforcement. And what do you

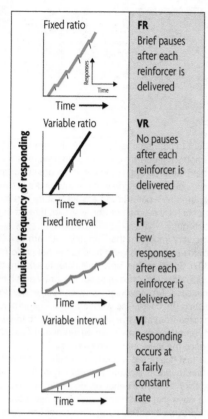

Fixed ratio	**FR** Brief pauses after each reinforcer is delivered
Variable ratio	**VR** No pauses after each reinforcer is delivered
Fixed interval	**FI** Few responses after each reinforcer is delivered
Variable interval	**VI** Responding occurs at a fairly constant rate

FIGURE 12 Reinforcement Schedules

These different patterns of behavior are produced by four simple schedules of reinforcement. The hash marks indicate when reinforcement is delivered.

predict happened when these animals underwent extinction training and their responses were followed by no pellets at all? The rats whose lever pressing had been partially reinforced continued to respond longer and more vigorously than did the rats who had gotten payoffs after every response. Skinner was on to something important!

The discovery of the effectiveness of partial reinforcement led to extensive study of the effects of different **schedules of reinforcement** on behavior (see **Figure 12**). You have experienced different schedules of reinforcement in your daily life. When you raise your hand in class, the teacher sometimes calls on you and sometimes does not; some slot machine players continue to put coins in the one-armed bandits even though the reinforcers are delivered only rarely. In real life or in the laboratory, reinforcers can be delivered according to either a *ratio schedule,* after a certain number of responses, or an *interval schedule,* after the first response following a specified interval of time. In each case, there can be either a constant, or *fixed,* pattern of reinforcement or an irregular, or *variable,* pattern of reinforcement, making four major types of schedules in all. So far you've learned about the **partial reinforcement effect:** Responses acquired under schedules of partial reinforcement are more resistant to extinction than those acquired with

continuous reinforcement. Let's see what else researchers have discovered about different schedules of reinforcement.

Fixed-Ratio Schedules   In **fixed-ratio (FR) schedules,** the reinforcer comes after the organism has emitted a fixed number of responses. When reinforcement follows only one response, the schedule is called an FR-1 schedule (this is the original continuous reinforcement schedule). When reinforcement follows only every 25th response, the schedule is an FR-25 schedule. FR schedules generate high rates of responding because there is a direct correlation between responding and reinforcement. A pigeon can get as much food as it wants in a period of time if it pecks often enough. Figure 12 shows that FR schedules produce a pause after each reinforcer. The higher the ratio, the longer the pause after each reinforcer. Stretching the ratio too thin by requiring a great many responses for reinforcement without first training the animal to emit that many responses may lead to extinction. Many salespeople are on FR schedules: They must sell a certain number of units before they can get paid.

Variable-Ratio Schedules   In a **variable-ratio (VR) schedule,** the average number of responses between reinforcers is predetermined. A VR-10 schedule means that, on average, reinforcement follows every 10th response, but it might come after only 1 response or after 20 responses. Variable-ratio schedules generate the highest rate of responding and the greatest resistance to extinction, especially when the VR value is large. Suppose you start a pigeon with a low VR value (for example, VR-5) and then move it toward a higher value. A pigeon on a VR-110 schedule will respond with up to 12,000 pecks per hour and will continue responding for hours even with no reinforcement. Gambling would seem to be under the control of VR schedules. The response of dropping coins in slot machines is maintained at a high, steady level by the payoff, which is delivered only after an unknown, variable number of coins has been deposited. VR schedules leave you guessing when the reward will come—you gamble that it will be after the next response, not many responses later.

Fixed-Interval Schedules   On a **fixed-interval (FI) schedule,** a reinforcer is delivered for the first response made after a fixed period of time. On an FI-10 schedule, the subject, after receiving reinforcement, has to wait 10 seconds before another response can be reinforced irrespective of the number of responses. Response rates under FI schedules show a scalloped pattern. Immediately after each reinforced response, the animal

....

schedule of reinforcement In operant conditioning, a pattern of delivering and withholding reinforcement.

partial reinforcement effect The behavioral principle that states that responses acquired under intermittent reinforcement are more difficult to extinguish than those acquired with continuous reinforcement.

fixed-ratio (FR) schedule A schedule of reinforcement in which a reinforcer is delivered for the first response made after a fixed number of responses.

variable-ratio (VR) schedule A schedule of reinforcement in which a reinforcer is delivered for the first response made after a variable number of responses whose average is predetermined.

fixed-interval (FI) schedule A schedule of reinforcement in which a reinforcer is delivered for the first response made after a fixed period of time.

makes few if any responses. As the payoff time approaches, the animal responds more and more. You experience an FI schedule when you reheat a slice of pizza. Suppose you set the oven's timer for 2 minutes. You probably won't check very much for the first 90 seconds, but in the last 30 seconds, you'll peek in more often.

Variable-Interval Schedules For **variable-interval (VI) schedules,** the average interval is predetermined. For example, on a VI-20 schedule, reinforcers are delivered at an average rate of 1 every 20 seconds. This schedule generates a moderate but very stable response rate. Extinction under VI schedules is gradual and much slower than under fixed-interval schedules. In one case, a pigeon pecked 18,000 times during the first 4 hours after reinforcement stopped and required 168 hours before its responding extinguished completely (Ferster & Skinner, 1957). You have experienced a VI schedule if you've taken a course with a professor who gave occasional, irregularly scheduled pop quizzes. Did you study your notes each day before class?

Shaping

As parts of experiments, we have spoken of rats pressing levers to get food. However, even lever pressing is a learned behavior. When a rat is introduced to an operant chamber, it is quite unlikely it will ever press the lever spontaneously; the rat has learned to use its paws in many ways, but it probably has never pressed a lever before. How should you go about training the rat to perform a behavior that it would rarely, if ever, produce on its own? You've settled on a reinforcer, food, and a schedule of reinforcement, FR-1—now what? To train new or complex behaviors, you will want to use a method called **shaping by successive approximations**—in which you reinforce any responses that successively approximate and ultimately match the desired response.

Here's how you'd do it. First, you deprive the rat of food for a day. (Without deprivation, food is not likely to serve as a reinforcer.) Then you systematically make food pellets available in the food hopper in an operant chamber so that the rat learns to look there for food. Now you can begin the actual shaping process by making delivery of food contingent on specific aspects of the rat's behavior, such as orienting itself toward the lever. Next, food is delivered only as the rat moves closer and closer to the lever. Soon the requirement for reinforcement is actually to touch the lever. Finally, the rat must depress the lever for food to be delivered. In small increments, the rat has learned that a lever press will produce food. Thus, for *shaping* to work, you must define what constitutes progress toward the target behavior and use *differential reinforcement* to refine each step along the way.

Let's look at another example, in which shaping was used to improve the performance of a Canadian pole vaulter who was an international competitor.

....

variable-interval (VI) schedule A schedule of reinforcement in which a reinforcer is delivered for the first response made after a variable period of time whose average is predetermined.

shaping by successive approximations A behavioral method that reinforces responses that successively approximate and ultimately match the desired response.

This woman is assisted by a monkey who has been operantly shaped to perform tasks such as getting food or drink, retrieving dropped or out-of-reach items, and turning lights on or off. For each of these behaviors, can you think through the successive approximations you would reinforce to arrive at the end point?

Rita Nannini/Photo Researchers, Inc.

A 21-year-old university pole vaulter sought a research team's assistance to help him correct a technical problem with his vaulting technique (Scott et al., 1997). The vaulter's particular problem was that he didn't sufficiently extend his arms (holding the pole) above his head before he planted the pole to lift himself off. At the beginning of the intervention, the vaulter's average hand-height at takeoff was calculated as 2.25 meters. The goal was set to use a shaping procedure to help him achieve his physical potential of 2.54 meters. A photoelectric beam was set up so that, when the vaulter achieved a desired extension, the beam was broken and equipment produced a beep. The beep served as a conditioned positive reinforcer. At first, the beam was set at 2.30 meters, but once the vaulter was able to reach that height with 90 percent success, the beam was moved to 2.35 meters. Further success brought further increments of 2.40, 2.45, 2.50, and 2.52 meters. In that way, the vaulter's behavior was successfully shaped toward the desired goal.

Featured Study

You can imagine how difficult it would have been for the vaulter to show spontaneous improvement of 0.27 meters. (That's about 10½ inches.) The shaping procedure allowed him to achieve that gain through successive approximations to the desired behavior.

Let's return to your rat. Recall that we suggested you might wish to teach it to turn circles in its cage. Can you devise a plan, using shaping, to bring about this behavior? Think about what each successive approximation would be. At the beginning, for example, you might reinforce the rat if it just turned its head in a particular direction. Next, you would let the rat obtain a food pellet only if it turned its whole body in the right direction. What might you do after that?

Operant conditioning has most often been studied with the assumption that processes of learning are consistent across all animals. In fact, we have cited examples from different species to show exactly such consistency. However, researchers have come to understand that learning may be modified by the particular biological capabilities of individual species. Next, let's examine that phenomenon.

Biological Constraints

You have no doubt seen animals performing tricks on television or in the circus. Some animals play baseball or Ping-Pong, and others drive tiny race cars. For years, **Keller Breland** and **Marion Breland** used operant conditioning techniques to train thousands of animals to perform a remarkable array of behaviors. The Brelands had believed that general principles derived from laboratory research using virtually any type of response could be directly applied to the control of animal behavior outside the laboratory.

At some point after training, though, some of the animals began to "misbehave." For example, a raccoon was trained pick up a coin, put it into a toy bank, and collect an edible reinforcer. However, when there were two coins to be deposited, conditioning broke down—the raccoon would not give up the coins. Instead, it would rub the coins together, dip them into the bank, and then pull them back out. But is this really so strange? Raccoons often engage in rubbing and washing behaviors as they remove the outer shells of a favorite food, crayfish. Similarly, when pigs were given the task of putting their hard-earned tokens into a large piggy bank, they instead would drop the coins onto the floor, root (poke at) them with their snouts, and toss them into the air. Again, should you consider this strange? Pigs root and shake their food as a natural part of their inherited food-gathering repertory.

These experiences convinced the Brelands that even when animals have learned to make operant responses perfectly, the "learned behavior drifts toward instinctual behavior" over time. They called this tendency **instinctual drift** (Breland & Breland, 1951, 1961). The behavior of their animals is not explainable by ordinary operant principles, but it is understandable if you consider biological constraints: The species-specific tendencies imposed by an inherited genotype. These tendencies override the changes in behavior brought about by operant conditioning.

....

instinctual drift The tendency for learned behavior to drift toward instinctual behavior over time.

How does instinctual drift affect the behaviors raccoons can learn to perform?

The bulk of traditional research on animal learning focused on arbitrarily chosen responses to conveniently available stimuli. The Brelands' theory and demonstration of instinctual drift make it evident that not all aspects of learning are under the control of the experimenters' reinforcers. Behaviors will be more or less easy to change as a function of an animal's normal, genetically programmed responses in its environment. Conditioning will be particularly efficient when you can frame a target response as biologically relevant. For example, what change might you make to get the pigs to place their tokens in a bank? You might consider pairing the token with a water reward for a thirsty pig. It would then not be rooted as food but would be deposited in the bank as a valuable commodity

You have now seen why modern behavior analysts must be attentive to the types of responses each species is best suited to learn. If you want to teach an old dog new tricks, you're best off adapting the tricks to the dog's genetic behavioral repertory! Our survey of learning is not complete, however, because we have not yet dealt with types of learning that might require more complex cognitive processes. We turn now to those types of learning.

Stop *and* Review

① What is the law of effect?
② How do reinforcement and punishment affect the probability of behaviors?
③ What is the role of discriminative stimuli in operant conditioning?
④ What is the difference between fixed-ratio and fixed-interval schedules of reinforcement?
⑤ What is meant by shaping?
⑥ What is instinctual drift?

CRITICAL THINKING In the experiment with chimps, why did the researcher start the training with raisins before moving to tokens?

✓•⌐**Study** and **Review** on **MyPsychLab**

COGNITIVE INFLUENCES ON LEARNING

The reviews of classical and operant conditioning have demonstrated that a wide variety of behaviors can be understood as the products of simple learning processes. You might wonder, however, if certain classes of learning require more complex, more cognitive types of processes. *Cognition* is any mental activity involved in the representation and processing of knowledge, such as thinking, remembering, perceiving, and language use. This section looks at forms of learning in animals and humans that cannot be explained only by principles of classical or operant conditioning. These phenomena suggest, therefore, that the behaviors are partially the product of cognitive processes.

Comparative Cognition

This chapter has emphasized that, species-specific constraints aside, rules of learning acquired from research on rats and pigeons apply as well to dogs, monkeys, and humans. Researchers who study **comparative cognition** consider even broader ranges of behavior to trace the development of cognitive abilities across species and the continuity of abilities from nonhuman to human animals (Wasserman & Zentall, 2006). This field is called *comparative cognition* because researchers often compare abilities across different species; because of the focus on nonhuman species, the field is also called *animal cognition*. In his original formulation of the theory of evolution, Charles Darwin suggested that cognitive abilities evolved along with the physical forms of animals. In this section, we will describe two impressive types of animal performance that indicate further continuity in the cognitive capabilities of nonhuman and human animals.

Cognitive Maps Edward C. Tolman (1886–1959) pioneered the study of cognitive processes in learning by inventing experimental circumstances in which mechanical one-to-one associations between specific stimuli and responses could not explain animals' observed behavior. Consider the maze shown in **Figure 13**. Tolman and his students demonstrated that, when an original goal path is blocked in a maze, a rat with prior experience in the maze will take the shortest detour around the barrier, even though that particular response was never previously reinforced (Tolman & Honzik, 1930). The rats, therefore, behaved as if they were responding to an internal **cognitive map**—a representation of the overall layout of the maze—rather than blindly exploring different parts of the maze through trial and error (Tolman, 1948). Tolman's results showed that conditioning involves more than the simple formation of associations between sets of stimuli or between responses and reinforcers. It includes learning and representing other facets of the total behavioral context (Lew, 2011).

....

comparative cognition The study of the development of cognitive abilities across species and the continuity of abilities from nonhuman to human animals.

cognitive map A mental representation of physical space.

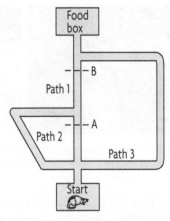

FIGURE 13 Use of Cognitive Maps in Maze Learning
Subjects preferred the direct path (Path 1) when it was open. With a block at A, they preferred Path 2. When a block was placed at B, the rats usually chose Path 3. Their behavior seemed to indicate that they had a cognitive map of the best way to get the food.

Research in Tolman's tradition has consistently demonstrated an impressive capacity for spatial memory in birds, bees, rats, humans, and other animals (for examples, see Joly & Zimmermann, 2011; Menzel et al., 2011). To understand the efficiency of spatial cognitive maps, consider the functions they serve (Poucet, 1993):

- Animals use spatial memory to recognize and identify features of their environments.
- Animals use spatial memory to find important goal objects in their environments.
- Animals use spatial memory to plan their route through an environment.

You can see these different functions of cognitive maps at work in the many species of birds that store food over a dispersed area but are able to recover that food with great accuracy when they need it. For example, pinyon jays bury thousands of pine seeds each fall and retrieve them four to seven months later to survive through the winter into the early spring (Stafford et al., 2006). By the time they are 8 months old, these birds appear to have the spatial memory they require to find their way back to their seeds. Other species use their spatial abilities to disperse seeds in ways that protect them against theft by other animals. Coal tits, for example, use their memories for the positions of their old seed caches to make decisions about proper locations for new caches (Male & Smulders, 2007). These seed-caching birds do not just roam their environments and come upon the seeds through good fortune. Only if their cognitive maps remain accurate can they later recover the seeds and survive to reproduce.

Conceptual Behavior We have seen that cognitive maps, in part, help animals preserve details of the spatial locations of objects in their environments. But what other cognitive processes can animals use to find structure in the diverse stimuli they encounter in their environments? Let's consider judgments

From left to right: Adult models aggression; boy imitates aggression; girl imitates aggression. What does this experiment demonstrate about the role models play in learning?

of *same* versus *different*. Take a moment to contemplate all the moments in a day in which you make these judgments: Does the milk you poured on your cereal taste funny? Will your friends realize you wore the same clothes two days in a row? Did you already watch this YouTube video? Researchers have begun to demonstrate that humans are not the only species that can make some judgments of same versus different (Wasserman & Young, 2010). Let's consider a study that documents pigeon's ability to detect changes in colored displays.

Pigeons viewed arrays that contained two colored circles (Wright et al., 2010). The arrays remained on view for five seconds. After a brief memory delay, a second array appeared in which one of the colors had changed (for example, from purple to orange). To get a reward, the pigeons needed to peck on the circle with the changed color. Pigeons were able to learn this response with trials using a set of colors on which they'd specifically been trained. Importantly, this pecking behavior also transferred to a new set of colors, for which they hadn't received explicit training. These results suggest that the pigeons had acquired the concept of same versus different colors.

Recall that a cornerstone of operant conditioning is that animals will repeat behaviors for which they have been reinforced. What makes these results particularly interesting is that pigeons learned to peck the new colors: the color that explicitly had not previously yielded reinforcement. Instead of responding to each individual color, the pigeons had acquired the higher-order concept of color change. This experiment that demonstrates concept acquisition in pigeons should convince you that humans are not the only species with impressive and useful cognitive capabilities.

Before we conclude this chapter, let's move to another type of learning that requires cognitive processes.

Observational Learning

To introduce this further type of learning, we'd like you to return for a moment to the comparison of rats' and humans' approaches to sampling new foods. The rats are almost certainly more cautious than you are, but that's largely because they are missing an invaluable source of information—input from other rats. When you try a new food, it's almost always in a context in which you have good reason to believe that other people have eaten and enjoyed the food. The probability of your

"food-eating behavior" is thus influenced by your knowledge of patterns of reinforcement for other individuals. This example illustrates your capacity to learn via *vicarious reinforcement* and *vicarious punishment*. You can use your cognitive capacities for memory and reasoning to change your own behaviors in light of the experience of others. 👁

In fact, much *social learning* occurs in situations where learning would not be predicted by traditional conditioning theory because a learner has made no active response and has received no tangible reinforcer. The individual, after simply watching another person exhibiting behavior that was reinforced or punished, later behaves in much the same way, or refrains from doing so. This is known as **observational learning.** Cognition often enters into observational learning in the form of expectations. In essence, after observing a model, you may think, "If I do exactly what she does, I will get the same reinforcer or avoid the same punisher." A younger child may be better behaved than his older sister because he has learned from the sister's mistakes.

This capacity to learn from watching as well as from doing is extremely useful. It enables you to acquire large integrated patterns of behavior without going through the tedious trial-and-error process of gradually eliminating wrong responses and acquiring the right ones. You can profit immediately from the mistakes and successes of others. Researchers have demonstrated that observational learning is not special to humans. Among other species, lemurs (Carlier & Jamon, 2006), ravens (Schwab et al., 2008), and chorus frog tadpoles (Ferrari & Chivers, 2008) are capable of changing their behavior after observing the performance of another member of their species.

A classic demonstration of human observational learning occurred in the laboratory of **Albert Bandura.** After watching adult models punching, hitting, and kicking a large plastic BoBo doll, the children in the experiment later showed a greater frequency of the same behaviors than did children in control conditions who had not observed the aggressive models (Bandura et al., 1963). Subsequent studies showed that children imitated such behaviors just from watching filmed

---

👁 **Watch** the **Video** *What's In It For Me?: Personal Behavior Modification* on **MyPsychLab**

observational learning The process of learning new responses by watching the behavior of another.

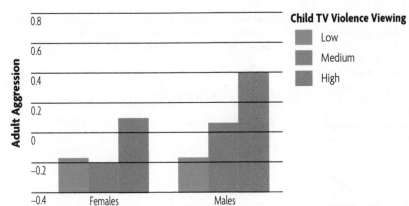

FIGURE 14 TV Violence and Aggression

For both men and women, those individuals who had viewed the most violent TV as children also displayed the most aggression as adults. The measure of aggression is a composite score that reflects the individuals' self-ratings and ratings of them by others. Higher scores indicate higher levels of aggression.

sequences of models, even when the models were cartoon characters.

There is little question now that we learn much—both prosocial (helping) and antisocial (hurting) behaviors—through observation of models, but there are many possible models in the world. What variables are important in determining which models will be most likely to influence you? Research suggests that there are four processes that determine when a model's observed behavior will be most influential (Bandura, 1977):

- *Attention.* The observer must pay attention to the model's behavior and its consequences. This is more likely when there are perceived similarities between features and traits of the model and the observer.
- *Retention.* The observer must store a representation of the model's behavior in memory.
- *Reproduction.* The observer must have the physical or mental ability to reproduce the model's behavior.
- *Motivation.* The observer must have a reason to reproduce the model's behavior. For example, the model's behavior could be seen as having reinforcing consequences.

Imagine yourself in modeling situations and see how each process on the list would apply. Suppose, for example, you were learning to perform surgery by observing an experienced doctor. How would each process affect your ability to learn?

Because people learn so efficiently from models, you can understand why a good deal of psychological research has been directed at the behavioral impact of television: Are viewers affected by what they see being rewarded and punished on TV? Attention has focused on the link between televised acts of violence—murder, rape, assault, robbery, terrorism, and suicide—and children's and adolescents' subsequent behavior. Does exposure to acts of violence foster imitation? Let's see what research has revealed.

The project began in 1977 when a team of researchers measured two years of television viewing for 557 children starting in either first or third grade. In particular, the researchers obtained measures of the extent to which the children watched TV shows with violent content. Fifteen years later, the researchers were able to conduct interviews with 329 of those

children, who were now 20 to 22 years old (Huesmann et al., 2003). The researchers sought to determine whether there would be a relationship between the amount of television violence the individuals viewed in childhood and their level of aggression as young adults. Their adult level of aggression was measured both through their own self-reports and through the reports of others, such as spouses. As shown in **Figure 14**, *the men and women who had watched the most violent TV as children also displayed the highest adult levels of aggression. These data suggest that early TV viewing of violence causes later aggression. You might wonder, however, if the causality works in the opposite direction: Could it be that the children destined to be aggressive were already more interested in violent content as children? Fortunately, the researchers collected data that allowed them to argue against this possibility. For example, the data found only a small relationship between childhood aggression and the individuals' viewing of TV violence as adults.*

This study argues strongly that children who watch violent TV are at risk to become overly aggressive as adults. 👁

Several decades of research have demonstrated three ways in which television violence has a negative impact on viewers' lives. First, as we have just seen, the viewing of television violence brings about, through the mechanisms of observational learning, increases in aggressive behavior. This causal association has particularly important implications for children: Aggressive habits borne of heavy television viewing early in life may serve as the basis for antisocial behavior later in life. Second, the viewing of television violence leads viewers to overestimate the occurrences of violence in the everyday world. Television viewers may be unduly afraid of becoming victims of real-world violence. Third, the viewing of television violence may bring about *desensitization,* a reduction in both emotional arousal and distress at viewing violent behavior.

Note that research has also shown that children can learn prosocial, helping behaviors when they watch television programs that provide prosocial behavioral models (Mares & Woodard, 2005). You should take seriously the idea that

👁 **Watch** the Video *In the Real World: Learned Aggression* on MyPsychLab

children learn from the television they watch. As a parent or caretaker, you may want to help children select appropriate televised models.

An analysis of observational learning acknowledges both that principles of reinforcement influence behavior and that humans have the capacity to use their cognitive processes to change behaviors with vicarious rewards and punishment. This approach to the understanding of human behavior has proven very powerful. Some successful programs of therapy have emerged from the cognitive modification of maladaptive patterns of behavior.

Let's close this chapter by calling back to mind a visit to a horror movie. How can behavior analysis explain your experiences? Suppose you went to the movie because of a friend's recommendation. You succumbed to vicarious reinforcement. Suppose you made it to the theater, despite having to forgo your normal route. That shows evidence of a cognitive map. Suppose the sound of scary music made you feel increasingly anxious. If the music was repeated over a short period of time, you felt the effects of sensitization. If the music was spread across the movie, that's more likely to be an effect of classical conditioning. Suppose your failure to enjoy the film made you vow never to see a horror movie again. You have discovered the effect a punisher has on your subsequent behavior!

Are you ready to return to the theater?

Stop and Review

① What conclusions did Tolman draw from his pioneering work?
② What evidence suggests that pigeons are able to learn the concepts of same versus different?
③ What is meant by vicarious reinforcement?
④ Why is it important to evaluate children's TV viewing in the context of observational learning?

CRITICAL THINKING   Consider the TV viewing study. What steps did the researchers take to assert that they had given the right causal explanation for the correlation revealed in their data?

✓• Study and Review on MyPsychLab

Recapping Main Points

The Study of Learning

- Learning entails a relatively consistent change in behavior or behavior potential based on experience.
- Behaviorists believe that much behavior can be explained by simple learning processes.
- They also believe that many of the same principles of learning apply to all organisms.

Classical Conditioning: Learning Predictable Signals

- In classical conditioning, first investigated by Pavlov, an unconditioned stimulus (UCS) elicits an unconditioned response (UCR). A neutral stimulus paired with the UCS becomes a conditioned stimulus (CS), which elicits a response, called the conditioned response (CR).
- Extinction occurs when the UCS no longer follows the CS.
- Stimulus generalization is the phenomenon whereby stimuli similar to the CS elicit the CR.
- Discrimination learning narrows the range of CSs to which an organism responds.
- For classical conditioning to occur, a contingent and informative relationship must exist between the CS and UCS.
- Classical conditioning explains many emotional responses and drug tolerance.
- Taste-aversion learning suggests that species are genetically prepared for some forms of associations.

Operant Conditioning: Learning about Consequences

- Thorndike demonstrated that behaviors that bring about satisfying outcomes tend to be repeated.

- Skinner's behavior analytic approach centers on manipulating contingencies of reinforcement and observing the effects on behavior.
- Behaviors are made more likely by positive and negative reinforcement. They are made less likely by positive and negative punishment.
- Contextually appropriate behavior is explained by the three-term contingency of discriminative stimulus–behavior–consequence.
- Primary reinforcers are stimuli that function as reinforcers even when an organism has not had previous experience with them. Conditioned reinforcers are acquired by association with primary reinforcers.
- Probable activities function as positive reinforcers.
- Behavior is affected by schedules of reinforcement that may be varied or fixed and delivered in intervals or in ratios.
- Complex responses may be learned through shaping.
- Instinctual drift may overwhelm some response–reinforcement learning.

Cognitive Influences on Learning

- Some forms of learning reflect more complex processes than those of classical or operant conditioning.
- Animals develop cognitive maps to enable them to function in a complex environment.
- Other species may be able to encode concepts such as same versus different.
- Behaviors can be vicariously reinforced or punished. Humans and other animals can learn through observation.

KEY TERMS

acquisition
avoidance conditioning
behavior analysis
classical conditioning
cognitive map
comparative cognition
conditioned reinforcers
conditioned response (CR)
conditioned stimulus (CS)
discriminative stimulus
escape conditioning
extinction
fixed-interval (FI) schedule
fixed-ratio (FR) schedule
habituation
instinctual drift

law of effect
learning
learning-performance distinction
negative punishment
negative reinforcement
observational learning
operant
operant conditioning
operant extinction
partial reinforcement effect
positive punishment
positive reinforcement
primary reinforcer
punisher
reflex
reinforcement contingency

reinforcer
schedule of reinforcement
sensitization
shaping by successive approximations
spontaneous recovery
stimulus discrimination
stimulus generalization
taste-aversion learning
three-term contingency
unconditioned response (UCR)
unconditioned stimulus (UCS)
variable-interval (VI) schedule
variable-ratio (VR) schedule

Practice Test

1. When Joan first moved to the city, she couldn't sleep because of the traffic noise. Now she hardly hears the traffic at all. This is an example of
   a. sensitization.
   b. habituation.
   c. consistency.
   d. classical conditioning.

2. You would *not* expect a close adherent to Skinner's ideas to focus on
   a. internal states as causes of behavior.
   b. forms of learning conserved across species.
   c. association between behaviors and rewards.
   d. the environmental stimuli that cause behaviors.

3. In Pavlov's experiments, _____ served as the unconditioned stimulus.
   a. salivation
   b. food powder
   c. the sight of the assistant
   d. tones

4. Six-year-old Pavel has a neighbor with a small dog who barks at him every day. Over time, Pavel has become frightened of all dogs. This is an example of
   a. stimulus discrimination.
   b. backward conditioning.
   c. spontaneous recovery.
   d. stimulus generalization.

5. Peter wishes to use classical conditioning in which a light will be the CS and an electric shock will be the UCS. You tell him that the light must _____ the shock.
   a. be temporally contiguous with
   b. reliably predict
   c. be in a blocking relationship with
   d. occur after

6. When classical conditioning contributes to drug tolerance, the conditioned stimulus is the
   a. setting in which individuals take the drugs.
   b. body's compensatory reaction to the drug.
   c. high the drugs give when individuals take them.
   d. individual's fear of an overdose.

7. One night after eating a hot dog you get very sick; now you shudder at the idea of eating a hot dog. A friend suggests that extinction trials will allow you to overcome this aversion. This means that you should
   a. associate hot dogs with foods you like.
   b. make yourself sick eating something else.
   c. eat some more hot dogs.
   d. use hot dogs as a reward.

8. For people undergoing chemotherapy, an unconditioned response would be
   a. anticipatory fatigue.
   b. the setting in which the individual receives the treatment.
   c. the infusion of drugs into their bodies.
   d. their bodies' reaction to the drugs.

9. In an operant conditioning experiment, you offer people expensive chocolate each time they perform a desired behavior. You think it's likely that the chocolate will be a _____ of the people.
   a. reinforcer for all
   b. reinforcer for none
   c. punisher for all
   d. reinforcer for some

10. Carlotta's parents haven't allowed her to watch television for three days. If she eats her brussels sprouts, she'll be allowed to watch TV that night. It sounds as if Carlotta's parents might be familiar with
    a. operant extinction.
    b. conditioned reinforcement.
    c. response deprivation theory.
    d. token economies.

11. In one study, the children who had received the most physical punishment as 15-month-olds showed _____ behavior problems at 36 months and _____ behavior problems in first grade then their less-punished peers.
    a. fewer; fewer.
    b. fewer; more
    c. more; fewer
    d. more; more

12. A time out may work best to change a child's behavior if the child is _____ years old and the time out lasts for _____ minutes.
    a. 10; 2
    b. 4; 4
    c. 10; 12
    d. 2; 3

13. In your new job, you get paid $2 every time you finish polishing 20 apples. This situation puts you on a _____ schedule.
    a. variable-interval
    b. variable-ratio
    c. fixed-ratio
    d. fixed-interval

14. Birds like Clark's nutcrackers are very successful at finding the seeds they have buried. This provides evidence for species-specific
    a. spatial memory.
    b. conditioning processes.
    c. applications of classical conditioning.
    d. shaping processes.

15. Zoe watches her older sister slip on ice and bruise her arm. After that, Zoe is very careful when she walks on ice. This is an example of
    a. observational learning.
    b. classical conditioning.
    c. operant extinction.
    d. sensitization.

ESSAY QUESTIONS

1. What information about classical conditioning might you share with someone who is about to undergo chemotherapy?

2. Why might you choose one schedule of reinforcement (that is, fixed interval versus variable interval) over another?

3. What mechanisms explain why viewing of TV violence might cause aggressive behavior?

Stop and Review Answers

Stop and Review (The Study of Learning)

1. The learning-performance distinction acknowledges that people's behaviors might not always reflect everything they have learned.
2. He argued that people's private experiences were too subjective to be studied with scientific rigor.
3. Behavior analysts attempt to discover regularities in learning that occur in all types of animal species.
4. Habituation is a decrease in an organism's behavioral response when a stimulus occurs repeatedly.

Stop and Review (Classical Conditioning: Learning Predictable Signals)

1. Classical conditioning begins with behaviors (such as salivation) that are reflex responses to unconditioned stimuli (such as the presentation of food powder).
2. The UCS is the unconditioned stimulus that produces a response prior to conditioning; the CS is the conditioned stimulus that produces a response as a result of conditioning.
3. Stimulus discrimination means that the organism has learned to produce a conditioned response to a more narrow range of conditioned stimuli than would otherwise be the case.
4. It's not enough for the CS and UCS to occur close together in time; the UCS must be contingent upon—be predictable from—the CS.
5. The CR is the body's compensatory response to the drug's effects.
6. Taste aversion will develop with only one pairing of the CS and UCS and with a long lag between the CS and UCS. It will often be permanent after one experience.

Stop and Review (Operant Conditioning: Learning about Consequences)

1. The law of effect states that a response followed by satisfying consequences becomes more probable and a response followed by dissatisfying consequences becomes less probable.
2. Reinforcement makes behaviors more likely; punishment makes behaviors less likely.
3. Animals learn that behaviors will have consequences (reinforcement or punishment) only in the context of particular stimuli—those stimuli are the discriminative stimuli.
4. In FR schedules, a reinforcer is delivered each time the organism has made a fixed number of responses. In FI schedules, a reinforcer is delivered when the organism makes the first response after a fixed amount of time.
5. Shaping is a method that allows an organism to learn a behavior through successive approximations.
6. Instinctual drift is the tendency, over time, for learned behaviors to drift toward instinctual behaviors.

Stop and Review (Cognitive Influences on Learning)

1. Tolman concluded that his rats developed cognitive maps for the layouts in the mazes.
2. Pigeons can learn to peck a circle on which a color had changed.
3. Vicarious reinforcement occurs when an individual's behavior becomes more probable after he or she observes other people's behaviors being reinforced.
4. Research suggests that children who observe a large number of aggressive acts may learn to be aggressive themselves.

Practice Test Answers

1. b	**5.** b	**9.** d	**13.** c
2. a	**6.** a	**10.** c	**14.** a
3. b	**7.** c	**11.** d	**15.** a
4. d	**8.** d	**12.** b	

References

Akechi, T., Okuyama, T., Endo, C., Sagawa, R., Uchida, M., Nakaguchi, T., Sakamoto, M., Komatsu, H., Ueda, R., Wada, M., & Furukawa, T. A. (2010). Anticipatory nausea among ambulatory cancer patients undergoing chemotherapy: Prevalence, associated factors, and impact on quality of life. *Cancer Science, 101*, 2596–2600.

Bandura, A. (1977). *Social learning theory.* Englewood Cliffs, NJ: Prentice-Hall.

Bandura, A., Ross, D., & Ross, S. A. (1963). Imitation of film-mediated aggressive models. *Journal of Abnormal and Social Psychology, 66*, 3–11.

Benjet, C., & Kazdin, A. E. (2003). Spanking children: The controversies, findings, and new directions. *Clinical Psychology Review, 23*, 197–224.

Bovbjerg, D. H. (2006). The continuing problem of post chemotherapy nausea and vomiting: Contributions of classical conditioning. *Autonomic Neuroscience: Basic and Clinical, 129*, 92–98.

Breland, K., & Breland, M. (1951). A field of applied animal psychology. *American Psychologist, 6*, 202–204.

Breland, K., & Breland, M. (1961). A misbehavior of organisms. *American Psychologist, 16*, 681–684.

Bykov, K. M. (1957). *The cerebral cortex and the internal organs.* New York: Academic Press.

Cameron, C. L., Cella, D. C., Herndon, E. E., II, Kornblith, A. B., Zucerkman, E., Henderson, E., Weiss, R. B., Cooper, M. R., Silver, R. T., Leone, L., Canellos, G. P., Peterson, B. A., & Holland, J. C. (2001). Persistent symptoms among survivors of Hodgkin's disease: An explanatory model based on classical conditioning. *Health Psychology, 20*, 71–75.

Chan, M. Y. T., Cross-Mellor, S. K., Kavaliers, M., & Ossenkopp, K.-P. (2009). Lipopolysaccharide (LPS) blocks the acquisition of LiCl-induced gaping in a rodent model of anticipatory nausea. *Neuroscience Letters, 450,* 301–305.

Cooper, J. O., Heron, T. E., & Heward, W. L. (2007). *Applied behavior analysis.* Upper Saddle River, NJ: Prentice-Hall.

Cowles, J. T. (1937). Food tokens as incentives for learning by chimpanzees. *Comparative Psychology Monographs, 74,* 1–96.

Dickerson, F. B., Tenhula, W. N., & Green-Paden, L. D. (2005). The token economy for schizophrenia: Review of the literature and recommendations for future research. *Schizophrenia Research, 75,* 405–416.

Everett, G. E., Olmi, D. J., Edwards, R. P., Tingstrom, D. H., Sterling-Turner, H. E., & Christ, T. J. (2007). An empirical investigation of time-out with and without escape extinction to treat escape-maintained noncompliance. *Behavior Modification, 31,* 412–434.

Ferrari, M. C. O., & Chivers, D. P. (2008). Cultural learning of predator recognition in mixed-species assemblages of frogs: The effect of tutor-to-observer ratio. *Animal Behaviour, 75,* 1921–1925.

Ferster, C. B., & Skinner, B. F. (1957). *Schedules of reinforcement.* New York: Appleton-Century-Crofts.

Garcia, J., & Koelling, R. A. (1966). The relation of cue to consequence in avoidance learning. *Psychonomic Science, 4,* 123–124.

Gershoff, E. T., & Bitensky, S. H. (2007). The case against corporal punishment for children: Converging evidence from social science research and international human rights law and implications for U. S. public policy. *Psychology, Public Policy, and Law, 13,* 231–272.

Granic, I., & Patterson, G. R. (2006). Toward a comprehensive model of antisocial development: A dynamic systems approach. *Psychological Review, 113,* 101–131.

Hartley, C. A., Fischl, B., & Phelps, E. A. (2011). Brain structure correlates of individual differences in the acquisition and inhibition of conditioned fear. *Cerebral Cortex 21,* 1954–1962.

Huesmann, L. R., Moise-Titus, J., Podolski, C. L., & Eron, L. D. (2003). Longitudinal relations between children's exposure to TV violence and their aggressive and violent behavior in young adulthood: 1977–1992. *Developmental Psychology, 39,* 201–221.

Joly, M., & Zimmermann, E. (2011). Do solitary foraging animals plan their routes? *Biology Letters, 7,* 638–640.

Kamin, L. J. (1969). Predictability, surprise, attention, and conditioning. In B. A. Campbell & R. M. Church (Eds.), *Punishment and aversive behavior* (pp. 279–296). New York: Appleton-Century-Crofts.

Klatt, K. P., & Morris, E. K. (2001). The Premack principle, response deprivation, and establishing operations. *The Behavior Analyst, 24,* 173–180.

Leventhal, A. M., Martin, R. L., Seals, R. W., Tapia, E., & Rehm, L. P. (2007). Investigating the dynamics of affect: Psychological mechanisms of affective habituation to pleasurable stimuli. *Motivation and Emotion, 31,* 145–157.

Lew, A. R. (2011). Looking beyond boundaries: Time to put landmarks back on the cognitive map? *Psychological Bulletin, 137,* 484–507.

Linnman, C., Rougemont-Bücking, A., Beucke, J. C., Zeffiro, T. A., & Milad, M. R. (2011). Unconditioned responses and functional fear networks in human classical conditioning. *Behavioural Brain Research, 221,* 237–245.

Lisanby, S. H. (2007). Electroconvulsive therapy for depression. *New England Journal of Medicine, 357,* 1939–1945.

Male, L. H., & Smulders, T. V. (2007). Memory for food caches: Not just retrieval. *Behavioral Ecology, 18,* 456–459.

Mares, M. L., & Woodard, E. (2005). Positive effects of television on children's social interactions: A meta-analysis. *Media Psychology, 7,* 301–322.

Matson, J. L., & Boisjoli, J. A. (2009). The token economy for children with intellectual disability and/or autism: A review. *Research in Developmental Disabilities, 30,* 240–248.

Menzel, R., Kirbach, A., Haass, W.-D., Fischer, B., Fuchs, J., Koblofsky, M., Lehmann, K., Reiter, L., Meyer, H., Nguyen, H., Jones, S., Norton, P., &

Greggers, U. (2011). A common frame of reference for learned and communicated vectors in honeybee navigation. *Current Biology, 21,* 645–650.

Morawska, A., & Sanders, M. (2011). Parental use of time out revisited: A useful or harmful parenting strategy. *Journal of Child and Family Studies, 20,* 1–8.

Mulvaney, M. K., & Mebert, C. J. (2007). Parental corporal punishment predicts behavior problems in early childhood. *Journal of Family Psychology, 21,* 389–397.

Ossenkopp, K.-P., Biagi, E., Cloutier, C. J., Chan, M. Y. T., Kavaliers, M., & Cross-Mellor, S. K. (2011). Acute corticosterone increases conditioned spontaneous orofacial behaviors but fails to influence dose related LiCl-induced conditioned "gaping" responses in a rodent model of anticipatory nausea. *European Journal of Pharmacology, 660,* 358–362.

Pavlov, I. P. (1927). *Conditioned reflexes* (G. V. Anrep, Trans.). London: Oxford University Press.

Pavlov, I. P. (1928). *Lectures on conditioned reflexes: Twenty-five years of objective study of higher nervous activity (behavior of animals)* (Vol. 1, W. H. Gantt, Trans.). New York: International Publishers.

Powell, R. A. (2011). Little Albert, lost or found: Further difficulties with the Douglas Merritte hypothesis. *History of Psychology, 14,* 106–107.

Premack, D. (1965). Reinforcement theory. In D. Levine (Ed.), *Nebraska symposium on motivation* (pp. 128–180). Lincoln: University of Nebraska Press.

Rescorla, R. A. (1966). Predictability and number of pairings in Pavlovian fear conditioning. *Psychonomic Science, 4,* 383–384.

Rescorla, R. A. (1988). Pavlovian conditioning: It's not what you think it is. *American Psychologist, 43,* 151–160.

Roscoe, J. A., Morrow, G. R., Aapro, M. S., Molassiotis, A., & Olver, I. (2011). Anticipatory nausea and vomiting. *Supportive Care in Cancer, 19,* 1533–1538.

Schwab, C., Bugnyar, T., Schloegl, C., & Kotrschal, K. (2008). Enhanced social learning between siblings in common ravens, *Corvus corax. Animal Behaviour, 75,* 501–508.

Scott, D., Scott, L. M., & Goldwater, B. (1997). A performance improvement program for an international-level track and field athlete. *Journal of Applied Behavior Analysis, 30,* 573–575.

Siegel, S. (1984). Pavlovian conditioning and heroin overdose: Reports by overdose victims. *Bulletin of the Psychonomic Society, 22,* 428–430.

Siegel, S. (2005). Drug tolerance, drug addiction, and drug anticipation. *Current Directions in Psychological Science, 14,* 296–300.

Siegel, S., Hinson, R. E., Krank, M. D., & McCully, J. (1982). Heroin "overdose" death: The contribution of drug-associated environmental cues. *Science, 216,* 436–437.

Skinner, B. F. (1938). *The behavior of organisms.* New York: Appleton-Century-Crofts.

Skinner, B. F. (1966). What is the experimental analysis of behavior? *Journal of the Experimental Analysis of Behavior, 9,* 213–218.

Skinner, B. F. (1990). Can psychology be a science of mind? *American Psychologist, 45,* 1206–1210.

Smith, P. L., Smith, J. C., & Houpt, T. A. (2010). Interactions of temperatures and taste in conditioned aversions. *Physiology & Behavior, 99,* 324–333.

Stafford, B. L., Balda, R. P., & Kamil, A. C. (2006). Does seed-caching experience affect spatial memory performance by pinyon jays? *Ethology, 112,* 1202–1208.

Stockhorst, U., Steingrueber, H.-J., Enck, P., & Klosterhalfen, S. (2006). Pavlovian conditioning of nausea and vomiting. *Autonomic Neuroscience: Basic and Clinical, 129,* 50–57.

Thorndike, E. L. (1898). Animal intelligence. *Psychological Review Monograph Supplement, 2*(4, Whole No. 8).

Tolman, E. C. (1948). Cognitive maps in rats and men. *Psychological Review, 55,* 189–208.

Tolman, E. C., & Honzik, C. H. (1930). "Insight" in rats. *University of California Publications in Psychology, 4,* 215–232.

Wasserman, E. A., & Young, M. E. (2010). Same-different discrimination: The keel and backbone of thought and reasoning. *Journal of Experimental Psychology: Animal Behavior Processes, 36,* 3–22.

Wasserman, E. A., & Zentall, T. R. (Eds.). (2006). *Comparative cognition: Experimental explorations of animal intelligence.* New York: Oxford University Press.

Watson, J. B. (1913). Psychology as the behaviorist views it. *Psychological Review, 20,* 158–177.

Watson, J. B. (1919). *Psychology from the standpoint of a behaviorist.* Philadelphia: Lippincott.

Watson, J. B., & Rayner, R. (1920). Conditioned emotional reactions. *Journal of Experimental Psychology, 3,* 1–14.

Wolf, H. (2011). Odometry and insect navigation. *The Journal of Experimental Biology, 214,* 1629–1641.

Wright, A. A., Katz, J. S., Magnotti, J., Elmore, L. C., Babb, S., & Alwin, S. (2010). Testing pigeon memory in a change detection task. *Psychonomic Bulletin & Review, 17,* 243–249.

Human Development across the Life Span

Human Development
across the Life Span

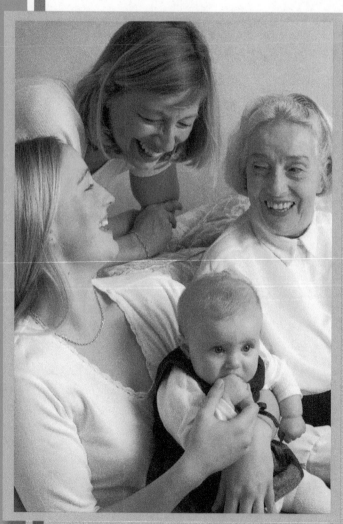

Mike Bluestone/Photo Researchers, Inc.

I magine you are holding a newborn baby. How might you predict what this child will be like as a 1-year-old? At 5 years? At 15? At 50? At 70? At 90? In this chapter, we consider theories that enable us to think systematically about the types of predictions we can make for the life course of a newborn child. **Developmental psychology** is the area of psychology that is concerned with changes in physical and psychological functioning that occur from conception across the entire life span. The task of developmental psychologists is to document and explain how mental functioning, social relationships, and other vital aspects of human nature develop and change throughout the entire life cycle. **Table 1** presents a rough guide to the major periods of the life span.

This chapter provides a general account of how researchers document development and the theories they use to explain patterns of change over time. The chapter divides your life experiences into different domains such as physical, cognitive, language, and social development and traces each domain across the life span. Let's begin with the question of what it means to study development.

STUDYING DEVELOPMENT

Suppose you try to make a list of all the ways in which you believe you have changed in the last year. What sorts of things would you put on the list? Have you undertaken a new physical fitness program? Or have you let an injury heal? Have you developed a range of new hobbies? Or have you decided to focus on just one interest? Have you developed a new circle of friends? Or have you become particularly close to one individual? This chapter will conceptualize development in terms of *change*. I've asked you to perform this exercise of thinking about your own changes to make the point that change almost always involves trade-offs.

Often people conceptualize the life span as mostly *gains*—changes for the better—in childhood and mostly *losses*—changes for the worse—over the course of adulthood. However, the perspective on development you'll see here emphasizes that *options*, and therefore gains and losses, are features of all development (Dixon, 2003; Lachman, 2004). When, for example, people choose a lifetime companion,

they give up variety but gain security. When people retire, they give up status but gain leisure time. It is also important that you not think of development as a *passive* process. You will see that many developmental changes require an individual's *active* engagement with his or her environment (Bronfenbrenner, 2004).

In this chapter, we consider research methods in psychology that are particularly relevant to developmental research. Ethics are extremely important in psychological research. Adults must give *informed consent* to indicate that they understand the procedures, risks, and benefits of their research participation. In most cases, parents or guardians must give permission for children under the age of 18 to participate in research. In addition, children over the age of 7 typically give *assent* to research participation. Researchers are required to write materials that describe procedures, risks, and benefits at age-appropriate levels. Children also retain all the rights of adult participants. They can, for example, withdraw from a study at any time. Because it is not always clear that young participants understand those rights, developmental researchers must be particularly careful to monitor for signs of particpants' discomfort or distress.

To document developmental change, a good first step is to determine what an average person is like—in physical appearance, cognitive abilities, and so on—at a particular age. **Normative investigations** seek to describe a characteristic of a specific age or developmental stage. By systematically testing individuals of different ages, researchers can determine developmental landmarks. These data provide *norms*, standard patterns of development or achievement, based on observation of many people.

Normative standards allow psychologists to make a distinction between chronological age—the number of months or years since a person's birth—and **developmental age**—the chronological age at which most people show the particular level of physical or mental development demonstrated by that child. A 3-year-old child who has verbal skills typical of most 5-year-olds is said to have a developmental age of 5 for verbal skills. Norms provide a standard basis for comparison both between individuals and between groups.

Developmental psychologists use several types of research designs to understand possible mechanisms of change. In a **longitudinal design,** the same individuals are repeatedly observed and tested over time, often for many years (see **Figure 1**). For example, one group of researchers tested children at ages 15, 25, 37, and 63 months to document the impact of children's home environment on the growth of their vocabulary (Rodriguez & Tamis-LeMonda, 2011). Longitudinal data collection allowed the researchers to draw

Table 1 • Stages in Life Span Development

Stage	Age Period
Prenatal	Conception to birth
Infancy	Birth at full term to about 18 months
Early childhood	About 18 months to about 6 years
Middle childhood	About 6 years to about 11 years
Adolescence	About 11 years to about 20 years
Early adulthood	About 20 years to about 40 years
Middle adulthood	About 40 years to about 65 years
Late adulthood	About 65 years and older

....

developmental psychology The branch of psychology concerned with interaction between physical and psychological processes and with stages of growth from conception throughout the entire life span.

normative investigation Research effort designed to describe what is characteristic of a specific age or developmental stage.

developmental age The chronological age at which most children show a particular level of physical or mental development.

longitudinal design A research design in which the same participants are observed repeatedly, sometimes over many years.

In a longitudinal design, observations are made of the same individual at different ages, often for many years. This well-known woman might be part of a longitudinal study of British children born in 1926. How might she be similar to and different from other children in that cohort?

strong conclusions about the long-term impact of features of the children's early environments. Researchers also often use longitudinal designs to study *individual differences.* To understand the life outcomes of different people, researchers may assess a range of potential causal factors early in life and see how those factors influence each individual's life course.

A general advantage of longitudinal research is that because the participants have lived through the same socioeconomic period, age-related changes cannot be confused with variations in differing societal circumstances. A disadvantage, however, is that some types of generalizations can be made only to the same

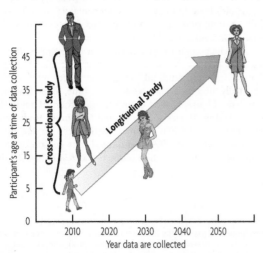

FIGURE 1 Longitudinal and Cross-Sectional Research

In longitudinal studies, researchers follow the same group of individuals over days, months, or years. In cross-sectional studies, researchers test individuals of different ages at the same moment in time.

cohort, the group of individuals born in the same time period as the research participants. Suppose, for example, we discovered that current 50-year-olds showed a gain in happiness in the years after their children left home. That result might not apply to a future cohort of 50-year-olds who grew up with different expectations about how long children would remain in their parents' homes. Also, longitudinal studies are costly because it is difficult to keep track of the participants over extended time, and data are easily lost because participants quit or disappear.

Much research on development uses a **cross-sectional design,** in which groups of participants, of different chronological ages, are observed and compared at one and the same time. A researcher can then draw conclusions about behavioral differences that may be related to age changes. For example, researchers who wanted to determine how people's ability to lie changes as they age tested samples of 8- through 16-year-old children (Evans & Lee, 2011). A disadvantage of cross-sectional designs comes from comparing individuals who differ by year of birth as well as by chronological age. Age-related changes are confounded by differences in the social or political conditions experienced by different birth cohorts. Thus a study comparing samples of 10- and 18-year-olds now might find that the participants differ from 10- and 18-year-olds who grew up in the 1970s, in ways related to their different eras as well as to their developmental stages.

Each methodology gives researchers the opportunity to document change from one age to another. Researchers use these methodologies to study development in each of several domains. As we now consider some of those domains—physical, cognitive, and social development—you'll come to appreciate and understand some of the vast changes you've already experienced.

cross-sectional design A research method in which groups of participants of different chronological ages are observed and compared at a given time.

A drawback of cross-sectional research is the cohort effect. What differences might exist between these two groups of women as a result of the eras in which they lived?

Stop *and* Review

① What is developmental age?
② Why are longitudinal designs often used to study individual differences?
③ What is the relevance of birth cohorts to cross-sectional designs?

✔• Study and Review on MyPsychLab

PHYSICAL DEVELOPMENT ACROSS THE LIFE SPAN

Many of the types of development we consider in this chapter require some special knowledge to detect. For example, you might not notice landmarks in social development until you read about them here. We will begin, however, with a realm of development in which changes are often plainly visible to the untrained eye: **physical development.** There is no doubt that you have undergone enormous physical change since you were born. Such changes will continue until the end of your life. Because physical changes are so numerous, the section will focus on the types that have an impact on psychological development.

Prenatal and Childhood Development

You began life with unique genetic potential: At the moment of conception a male's sperm cell fertilized a female's egg cell to form the single-cell **zygote;** you received half of the 46 chromosomes found in all normal human body cells from your mother and half from your father. This section begins with physical development in the *prenatal period,* from the moment of conception until the moment of birth. Next, we consider some of the sensory abilities children have obtained even before birth. Finally, we turn to important physical changes that you experienced during childhood.

Physical Development in the Womb   The first two weeks after formation of the zygote are known as the **germinal stage** of prenatal development. During this stage, cells begin to divide rapidly; after about one week a mass of microscopic cells attaches itself to the mother's uterine wall. The third through eighth week of prenatal development is called the **embryonic stage.** During this stage, rapid cell division continues, but the cells begin to become specialized to form different organs. As these organs develop, the first heartbeat occurs. Responses to stimulation have been observed as early as the sixth week, when the *embryo* is not yet an inch long. Spontaneous movements are observed by the seventh or eighth week (Stanojevic et al., 2011).

The **fetal stage** lasts from the end of the eighth week through the birth of the child. The mother will feel the *fetus* move in about the sixteenth week after conception. At this point, the fetus is about 7 inches long (the average length at birth is 20 inches). Most of the 100 billion neurons in the mature human brain are generated in utero (Stiles & Jernigan, 2010). In humans and many other mammals, most of this cell proliferation and migration of neurons to their correct locations take place before birth; the development of the branching processes of axons and dendrites largely occurs after birth. The sequence of brain development, from 30 days to 9 months, is shown in **Figure 2**. ✳

Over the course of pregnancy, environmental factors such as infection, radiation, or drugs can prevent the normal

....

✳ Explore the Concept *Virtual Brain: Development of the Brain* on MyPsychLab

physical development The bodily changes, maturation, and growth that occur in an organism starting with conception and continuing across the life span.

zygote The single cell that results when a sperm fertilizes an egg.

germinal stage The first two weeks of prenatal development following conception.

embryonic stage The second stage of prenatal development, lasting from the third through eighth weeks after conception.

fetal stage The third stage of prenatal development, lasting from the ninth week through birth of the child.

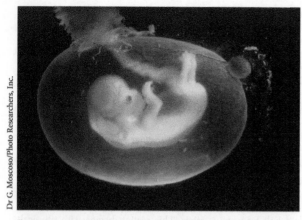

The brain grows rapidly in the developing fetus, accumulating billions of neurons by birth. What must the brain be prepared to do, as soon as the child enters the world?

formation of organs and body structures. Any environmental factor that causes structural abnormalities in the fetus is called a **teratogen.** For example, when mothers are infected with rubella (German measles), their children often suffer negative consequences such as mental retardation, eye damage, deafness, or heart defects. When the infection occurs

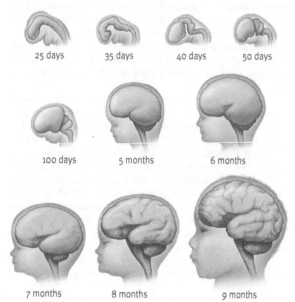

25 days 35 days 40 days 50 days

100 days 5 months 6 months

7 months 8 months 9 months

FIGURE 2 **The Development of the Human Brain**
During the nine months before birth, the brain reaches its complement of about 100 billion neurons.

Adapted from *The Brain* by R. Restak. Copyright © 1984. Bantam Books.

· ·

teratogen Environmental factors such as diseases and drugs that cause structural abnormalities in a developing fetus.

in the first six weeks after conception, the probability of birth defects may be 100 percent (De Santis et al., 2006). If exposure occurs later in the pregnancy, the probability of adverse effects becomes lower (for example, 50 percent in the fourth month; 6 percent in the fifth month). Mothers who consume alcohol during sensitive periods put their unborn children at risk for brain damage and other impairments (Bailey & Sokol, 2008). *Fetal alcohol syndrome* is the most serious consequence of a mother's alcohol consumption during pregnancy. Children with fetal alcohol syndrome often have small heads and bodies and facial abnormalities. Disruptions of the central nervous system cause cognitive and behavioral problems (Niccols, 2007).

Pregnant women who smoke also put their children at risk. Smoking during pregnancy increases the risk of miscarriage, premature births, and low-birth-weight babies (Salihu & Wilson, 2007). In fact, women who are exposed to secondhand smoke during pregnancy are also more likely to have babies with low birth weights (Crane et al., 2011). Finally, almost all illicit drugs cause damage to the fetus. Cocaine, for example, travels through the placenta and can affect fetal development directly. In adults, cocaine causes blood vessels to constrict; in pregnant women, cocaine restricts placental blood flow and oxygen supply to the fetus. If severe oxygen deprivation results, blood vessels in the fetus's brain may burst. Such prenatal strokes can lead to lifelong mental handicaps (Bennett et al., 2008; Singer et al., 2002). Research suggests that the brain systems most damaged by cocaine are those responsible for controlling attention: Children exposed to cocaine in the womb may spend their lives overcome by the distractions of irrelevant sights and sounds.

Babies Prewired for Survival What capabilities were programmed into your body and brain at birth? We are accustomed to thinking about newborns as entirely helpless. John Watson, the founder of behaviorism, described the human infant as "a lively, squirming bit of flesh, capable of making a few simple responses." If that sounds right, you might be surprised to learn that, moments out of the womb, infants reveal remarkable abilities. They might be thought of as *prewired for survival*, well suited to respond to adult caregivers and to influence their social environments.

To begin, infants are born with a repertory of reflexes that provide many of their earliest behavioral responses to the environment. A *reflex* is a response that is naturally triggered by specific stimuli that are biologically relevant for the organism. Consider two reflexes that quite literally prewire infants for survival. When something brushes against infants' cheeks, they turn their heads in that direction. This *rooting reflex* allows newborns to find their mothers' nipples. When an object is placed in their mouths, infants begin to suck. This *sucking reflex* allows infants to begin feeding. Reflexes of this sort keep infants alive in the early months of their lives.

For example, infants can hear even before birth. Researchers have demonstrated that what infants hear while in the womb has consequences. Newborns prefer to listen to their mothers' voices rather than the voices of other women (Spence & DeCasper, 1987; Spence & Freeman, 1996). In fact, research suggests that children recognize their mothers' voices even before they are born: In one study, the heart rate of fetuses increased

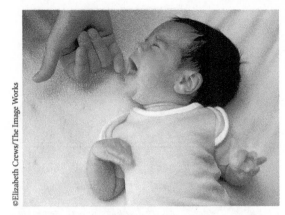

When something touches a newborn's cheek, the rooting reflex prompts the baby to seek something to suck. In what other ways are children prewired for survival?

in response to recordings of their mothers' voices and remained unchanged in response to strangers' voices (Kisilevsky et al., 2009). Newborns may find it relatively easy to learn to recognize their mothers' faces because they are associated with voices with which they are already familiar (Sai, 2005). Given these important results for mothers' voices, you might wonder whether children also respond more to their fathers' voices. Unfortunately, fetal heart rates do not change in a comparable pattern in response to fathers' voices, suggesting that fathers' voices do not become sufficiently familiar when children are in utero. In fact, newborns still show no preference for their fathers' voices (DeCasper & Prescott, 1984).

Most children begin to obtain visual experience during their last two months in utero (Del Giudice, 2011). They are able to perceive their own movements. Given this head start, it's not surprising that newborns put their visual systems to work almost immediately: A few minutes after birth, a newborn's eyes are alert, turning in the direction of a voice and searching inquisitively for the source of certain sounds. Even so, vision is less well developed than the other senses at birth. The visual acuity of adults is roughly 40 times better than the visual acuity of newborns (Sireteanu, 1999). However, visual acuity improves rapidly over the first six months of a baby's life. Newborns also are ill equipped to experience the world in three dimensions. You use a great variety of cues to experience depth. Researchers have begun to document the time course with which infants are able to interpret each type of cue. For example, at 4 months, infants start being able to use cues such as relative motion and interposition to infer three-dimensional structures from two-dimensional images of objects (Shuwairi et al., 2007; Soska & Johnson, 2008).

Even without perfect vision, however, children have visual preferences. Pioneering researcher **Robert Fantz** (1963) observed that babies as young as 4 months old preferred looking at objects with contours rather than those that were plain, complex ones rather than simple ones, and whole faces rather than faces with features in disarray. More recent research suggests that—by the age of 3 days—infants have a preference for *top-heavy patterns* (Macchi Cassia et al., 2004). To experience a top-heavy pattern, take a look at your face in a mirror—notice that your eyes, eyebrows, and so on, take up much more space than your lips. The fact that faces are top-heavy might explain why infants prefer to look at human faces versus other types of visual displays.

Once children start to move around in their environment, they quickly acquire other perceptual capabilities. For example, classic research by **Eleanor Gibson** and **Richard Walk** (1960) examined how children respond to depth information. This research used an apparatus called a *visual cliff*. The visual cliff had a board running across the middle of a solid glass surface. Checkerboard cloth was used to create a deep end and a shallow end. In their original research, Gibson and Walk demonstrated that children would readily leave the center board to crawl across the shallow end, but they were reluctant to crawl across the deep end. Subsequent research has demonstrated that fear of the deep end depends on crawling experience: Children who have begun to crawl experience fear of the deep end, whereas their noncrawling same-age peers do not (Campos et al., 1992; Witherington et al., 2005). Thus wariness of heights is not quite "prewired," but it develops quickly as children begin to explore the world under their own power. 👁

Growth and Maturation in Childhood Newborn infants change at an astonishing rate but, as shown in **Figure 4**, physical growth is not equal across all physical structures. You've probably noticed that babies seem to be all head. At birth, a baby's head is already about 60 percent of its adult size and measures a quarter of the whole body length (Bayley, 1956). An infant's body weight doubles in the first six months and triples by the first birthday; by the age of 2, a child's trunk is about half of its adult length. Genital tissue shows little change until the teenage years and then develops rapidly to adult proportions.

....

👁 **Watch** the **Video** *Classic Footage of Eleanor Gibson, Richard Walk, and the Visual Cliff* on **MyPsychLab**

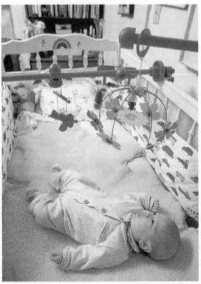

Early on, infants can perceive large objects that display a great deal of contrast. What visual experiences do newborns find particularly appealing?

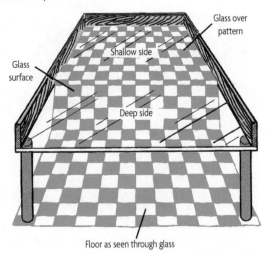

FIGURE 3 **The Visual Cliff**
Once children have gained experience crawling around their environment, they show fear of the deep side of the visual cliff.

For most children, physical growth is accompanied by the maturation of motor ability. **Maturation** refers to the process of growth typical of all members of a species who are reared in the species's usual habitat. The characteristic maturational sequences newborns experience are determined by the interaction of inherited biological boundaries and environmental inputs. To understand the impact of environmental inputs, developmental researchers make a distinction between *sensitive periods* and *critical periods*. A sensitive period is an optimal age range for children to have appropriate environmental experiences relevant to normal development. Development will proceed most smoothly if children have those experiences during the sensitive

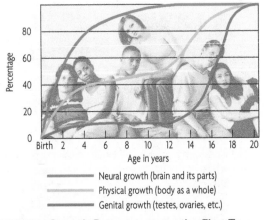

FIGURE 4 **Growth Patterns across the First Two Decades of Life**

Neural growth occurs very rapidly in the first year of life. It is much faster than overall physical growth. By contrast, genital maturation does not occur until adolescence.

....

maturation The continuing influence of heredity throughout development, the age-related physical and behavioral changes characteristic of a species.

period. However, if they have those experiences later in life, they will still be able to experience development—just with more difficulty. Critical periods impose stronger constraints on development: A critical period is an age range in which children must obtain appropriate environmental experiences. Without appropriate experiences during a crtical period, a child may not be able to develop a particular function.

Let's consider a particular example of motor development. In the sequence for locomotion, as shown in **Figure 5**, a child learns to walk without special training. Note that Figure 5 captures a sequence for an "average" child. Individual children often reach these motor milestones in their own particular orders (Adolph et al., 2010). In fact, some children skip stages like crawling altogether. Research on the development of walking also allows for an understanding of the importance of environmental inputs. Children who experience extra motor practice may reach motor milestones more quickly, whereas children whose motor experiences are restricted may develop more slowly. Still, within this individual variation, you can think of all unimpaired newborn children as possessing the same potential for physical maturation.

Children's physical development follows two general principles. The *cephalocaudal principle* states that development proceeds in a direction from head to foot. For example, children typically develop control of their arms before they develop control of their legs. The *proximodistal principle* states that parts of the body near the center develop before the extremities. For example, children's arms develop before their hands and their hands develop before their fingers. Finally, development typically proceeds from *gross* to *fine* motor skills. Gross motor skils involve larger muscles as when infants kick their legs or roll over. Fine motor skills require more presice coordination of smaller muscles. As they develop fine motor skills, infants become able to hold objects or put them in their mouths.

Physical Development in Adolescence

The first concrete indicator of the end of childhood is the *pubescent growth spurt*. At around age 10 for girls and age 12

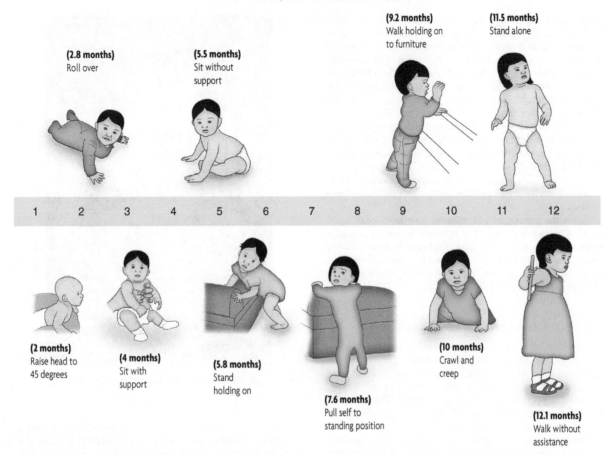

(2.8 months) Roll over

(5.5 months) Sit without support

(9.2 months) Walk holding on to furniture

(11.5 months) Stand alone

1 2 3 4 5 6 7 8 9 10 11 12

(2 months) Raise head to 45 degrees

(4 months) Sit with support

(5.8 months) Stand holding on

(7.6 months) Pull self to standing position

(10 months) Crawl and creep

(12.1 months) Walk without assistance

FIGURE 5 **Maturational Timetable for Locomotion**
The development of walking requires no special teaching. Physically capable members of our species pass through many of the same stages over the first year of life.

for boys, growth hormones flow into the bloodstream. For several years, the adolescent may grow 3 to 6 inches a year and gain weight rapidly as well. The adolescent's body does not reach adult proportions all at once. Hands and feet grow to full adult size first. The arms and legs come next, with the torso developing most slowly. Thus an individual's overall shape changes several times over the teenage years.

Another important process that occurs during adolescence is **puberty,** which brings about sexual maturity. (The Latin word *pubertas* means "covered with hair" and signifies the growth of hair on the arms and legs, under the arms, and in the genital area.) Puberty for males brings about the production of live sperm; for girls it leads to **menarche,** the onset of menstruation. In the United States, the average time for menarche is between the ages of 12 and 13, although the normal range extends from 11 to 15. For boys, the production of live sperm first occurs, on average, between the ages of 12 and 14,

but again there is considerable variation in this timing. These physical changes often bring about an awareness of sexual feelings.

Some other important physical changes happen inside adolescents' brains. Researchers once thought that most brain growth was over within the first few years of life. However, recent studies using brain-imaging techniques have demonstrated continuing development within the adolescent brain (Paus, 2005). Researchers have documented particularly important changes in the *limbic system*—which regulates emotional processes—and the *frontal lobes*—the areas responsible for planning and control of emotions. However, maturation of the limbic system precedes maturation of the frontal lobes. The relative timing of changes within those regions may explain one of most salient aspects of social development in adolescence: Adolescents tend to engage in risky behavior (Andrews-Hanna et al., 2011). 👁

We'll return to social aspects of risky behavior in the review of social development across the life span. For now, our focus is on physical development. Researchers speculate that maturation of the limbic system readies adolescents to go out into the world: "Evolutionarily speaking, adolescence is the period in which independence skills are acquired to increase

👁 **Watch** the **Video** *Special Topics: Risky Behavior and Brain Development* on **MyPsychLab**

puberty The process through which sexual maturity is attained.

menarche The onset of menstruation.

success upon separation from the protection of the family" (Casey et al., 2008, p. 70). In that evolutionary context, it makes sense that regions of the frontal cortex that inhibit and control the emotional drive toward independence would mature somewhat later in life. To survive apart from their families, adolescents would have to take some initial risks. The difficulty is that in contemporary times people no longer typically leave their families during adolescence. Thus, the evolutionary impulse toward novelty seeking and risk taking no longer has an adaptive function. Fortunately, as people develop from adolescence into adulthood, the frontal lobes achieve maturity (Steinberg, 2008). New connections form between the frontal lobes and limbic system. Those new connections enable individuals to exercise more cognitive control over their emotional impulses.

With the passing of adolescence, your body once again reaches a period of the life span in which biological change is comparatively minimal. You may affect your body in a variety of ways—by diet and exercise, for example—but the next striking set of changes that are consistent consequences of aging occurs in middle and late adulthood.

Physical Changes in Adulthood

Some of the most obvious changes that occur with age concern your physical appearance and abilities. As you grow older, you can expect your skin to wrinkle, your hair to thin and gray, and your height to decrease an inch or two. You can also expect some of your senses to become less acute. These changes do not appear suddenly at age 65. They occur gradually, beginning as soon as early adulthood. However, before we consider some common age-related changes, here's a more general point: Many physical changes arise not from aging but from *disuse;* research supports a general belief in the maxim "Use it or lose it." Older adults who maintain (or renew) a program of physical fitness may experience fewer of the difficulties that are often thought to be inevitable consequences of aging. Let's now look, however, at some changes that are largely unavoidable and frequently have an impact on the way adults think about their lives.

Vision Beginning at ages 40 to 50, most people begin experiencing changes in the function of their visual system: The lenses of their eyes become less flexible and the muscles that change the thickness of the lens become less effective. These changes can make seeing objects at close range difficult. Lens rigidity also affects dark adaptation, making night vision a problem for older people. Many of these normal visual changes can be aided with corrective lenses. With age, the lenses of people's eyes also become yellowed. The yellowing of the lens is thought to be responsible for diminished color vision experienced by some older people. Colors of lower wavelengths—violets, blues, and greens—are particularly hard for some older adults to discriminate. In one sample of 1,219 adults in the United States, 17 percent of adults reported visual impairments at age 45. This figure increased to 26 percent in adults 75 and older (Horowitz et al., 2005).

Hearing Hearing loss is common among those 60 and older. The average older adult has difficulty hearing high-frequency

Why do researchers give the advice "Use it or lose it"?

sounds (Mendelson & Rajan, 2011). Older adults can have a hard time understanding speech—particularly that spoken by high-pitched voices. (Oddly enough, with age, people's speaking voices increase in pitch due to stiffening of the vocal cords.) Deficits in hearing can be gradual and hard for an individual to notice until they are extreme. In addition, even when individuals become aware of hearing loss, they may deny it because it is perceived as an undesirable sign of aging. Some of the physiological aspects of hearing loss can be overcome with the help of hearing aids. You should also be aware, as you grow older or interact with older adults, that it helps to speak in low tones, enunciate clearly, and reduce background noise.

Reproductive and Sexual Functioning We saw that puberty marks the onset of reproductive functioning. In middle and late adulthood, reproductive capacity diminishes. Around age 50, most women experience *menopause,* the cessation of menstruation and ovulation. For men, changes are less abrupt, but the quantity of viable sperm falls off after age 40, and the volume of seminal fluid declines after age 60. Of course, these changes are relevant primarily to reproduction. Increasing age and physical change do not necessarily impair other aspects of sexual experience (DeLamater & Sill, 2005; Lindau et al., 2007). Indeed, sex is one of life's healthy pleasures that can enhance successful aging because it is arousing, provides aerobic exercise, stimulates fantasy, and is a vital form of social interaction.

You have had a brief review of the landmarks of physical development. Against that background, let's turn now to the ways in which you developed an understanding of the world around you.

Stop *and* Review

① How does experience with crawling influence children's performance on the visual cliff?

② What have recent studies demonstrated with respect to brain development in adolescence?

③ Why does increasing age often have an effect on color vision?

✓• Study and Review on MyPsychLab

COGNITIVE DEVELOPMENT ACROSS THE LIFE SPAN

How does an individual's understanding of physical and social reality change across the life span? **Cognitive development** is the study of the processes and products of the mind as they emerge and change over time. Because researchers have been particularly fascinated by the earliest emergence of cognitive capabilities, this section will largely focus on on the earliest stages of cognitive development. However, we will also consider some of the discoveries researchers have made about cognitive development across the adult years.

The discussion of cognitive development begins with the pioneering work of the late Swiss psychologist Jean Piaget.

Piaget's Insights into Mental Development

For nearly 50 years, **Jean Piaget** (1929, 1954, 1977) developed theories about the ways that children think, reason, and solve problems. Perhaps Piaget's interest in cognitive development grew out of his own intellectually active youth: Piaget published his first article at age 10 and was offered a post as a museum curator at age 14 (Brainerd, 1996). Piaget used simple demonstrations and sensitive interviews with his own children and with other children to generate complex theories about early mental development. His interest was not in the amount of information children possessed but in the ways their thinking and inner representations of physical reality changed at different stages in their development.

Building Blocks of Developmental Change Piaget gave the name **schemes** to the mental structures that enable individuals to interpret the world. Schemes are the building blocks of developmental change. Piaget characterized the infant's initial schemes as *sensorimotor intelligence*—mental structures or programs that guide sensorimotor sequences, such as sucking, looking, grasping, and pushing. With practice, elementary schemes are combined, integrated, and differentiated into ever-more-complex, diverse action patterns, as when a child pushes away undesired objects to seize a desired one behind him or her. According to Piaget, two basic processes work in tandem to achieve cognitive growth—assimilation and accommodation. **Assimilation** modifies new environmental information to fit into what is already known; the child accesses existing schemes to structure incoming sensory data. **Accommodation** restructures or modifies the child's existing schemes so that new information is accounted for more completely.

Consider the transitions a baby must make from sucking at a mother's breast, to sucking the nipple of a bottle, to sipping through a straw, and then to drinking from a cup. The initial sucking response is a reflex action present at birth, but it must be modified somewhat so that the child's mouth fits the shape and size of the mother's nipple. In adapting to a bottle, an infant still uses many parts of the sequence unchanged (assimilation) but must grasp and draw on the rubber nipple somewhat differently from before and learn to hold the bottle at an appropriate angle (accommodation). The steps from bottle to straw to cup require more accommodation but continue to rely on earlier skills. Piaget saw cognitive development as the result of exactly this sort of interweaving of assimilation and accommodation. The balanced application of assimilation and accommodation permits children's behavior and knowledge to become less dependent on concrete external reality, relying more on abstract thought.

Stages in Cognitive Development Piaget believed that children's cognitive development could be divided into a series of four ordered, discontinuous stages (see **Table 2**). All children are assumed to progress through these stages in the same sequence, although one child may take longer to pass through a given stage than does another.

Sensorimotor Stage The sensorimotor stage extends roughly from birth to age 2. In the early months, much of an infant's behavior is based on a limited array of inborn schemes, like sucking, looking, grasping, and pushing. During the first year, sensorimotor sequences are improved, combined, coordinated, and integrated (sucking and grasping, looking and manipulating, for example). They become more varied as infants discover that their actions have an effect on external events. 👁

The most important cognitive acquisition of the infancy period is the ability to form mental representations of absent objects—those with which the child is not in direct sensorimotor contact. **Object permanence** refers to children's understanding that objects exist and behave independently of their actions or awareness. In the first months of life, children follow objects with their eyes, but, when the objects disappear from view, they turn away as if the objects had also disappeared from their minds. At around 3 months of age, however, they keep looking at the place where the objects had disappeared.

....

👁 **Watch** the Video *Sensorimotor Development* on MyPsychLab

cognitive development The development of processes of knowing, including imagining, perceiving, reasoning, and problem solving.

scheme Piaget's term for a cognitive structure that develops as infants and young children learn to interpret the world and adapt to their environment.

assimilation According to Piaget, the process whereby new cognitive elements are fitted in with old elements or modified to fit more easily; this process works in tandem with accommodation.

accommodation According to Piaget, the process of restructuring or modifying cognitive structures so that new information can fit into them more easily; this process works in tandem with assimilation.

object permanence The recognition that objects exist independently of an individual's action or awareness; an important cognitive acquisition of infancy.

Table 2 • Piaget's Stages of Cognitive Development

Stage/Ages	Characteristics and Major Accomplishments
Sensorimotor (0–2)	Child begins life with small number of sensorimotor sequences.
	Child develops object permanence and the beginnings of symbolic thought.
Preoperational (2–7)	Child's thought is marked by egocentrism and centration.
	Child has improved ability to use symbolic thought.
Concrete operations (7–11)	Child achieves understanding of conservation.
	Child can reason with respect to concrete, physical objects.
Formal operations (11→)	Child develops capacity for abstract reasoning and hypothetical thinking.

Between 8 and 12 months, children begin to search for those disappearing objects. By age 2 years, children have no remaining uncertainty that "out of sight" objects continue to exist (Flavell, 1985).

Preoperational Stage The preoperational stage extends roughly from 2 to 7 years of age. The big cognitive advance in this developmental stage is an improved ability to represent mentally objects that are not physically present. Except for this development, Piaget characterizes the preoperational stage

....

egocentrism In cognitive development, the inability of a young child at the preoperational stage to take the perspective of another person.

centration Preoperational children's tendency to focus their attention on only one aspect of a situation and disregard other relevant aspects.

according to what the child *cannot* do. For example, Piaget believed that young children's preoperational thought is marked by **egocentrism,** the child's inability to take the perspective of another person. You have probably noticed egocentrism if you've heard a 2-year-old's conversations with other children. Children at this age often seem to be talking to themselves rather than interacting.

Preoperational children also experience **centration**—they tend to focus (center) their attention on only one aspect of a situation and disregard other relevant aspects. Centration is illustrated by Piaget's classic demonstration of a child's inability to understand that the amount of a liquid does not change as a function of the size or shape of its container.

When an equal amount of lemonade is poured into two identical glasses, children of ages 5 and 7 report that the glasses contain the same amount. When, however, the lemonade from one glass is poured into a tall, thin glass, their opinions diverge. The 5-year-olds know that the lemonade in the tall glass is the same lemonade, but they report that it now is more. The 7-year-olds correctly assert that there is no difference between the amounts.

In Piaget's demonstration, the younger children center on a single, perceptually noticeable dimension—the height of the lemonade in the glass. The older children take into account both height and width and correctly infer that appearance is not reality.

Concrete Operations Stage The concrete operations stage goes roughly from 7 to 11 years of age. At this stage, the child has become capable of mental operations, actions performed in the mind that give rise to logical thinking. The preoperational and concrete operations stages are often put in contrast because children in the concrete operation stage are now capable of what they failed earlier on. Concrete operations allow children to replace physical action with mental action. For example, if a child sees that Adam is taller than Zara and, later, that Zara is taller than Tanya, the child can reason that Adam is the tallest of the three—without physically manipulating the three individuals. However, the child still cannot draw the

Piaget observed that the typical 6-month-old will attend to an attractive toy (left) but will quickly lose interest if a screen blocks the toy from view (right). What understanding about objects will the child achieve by age 2?

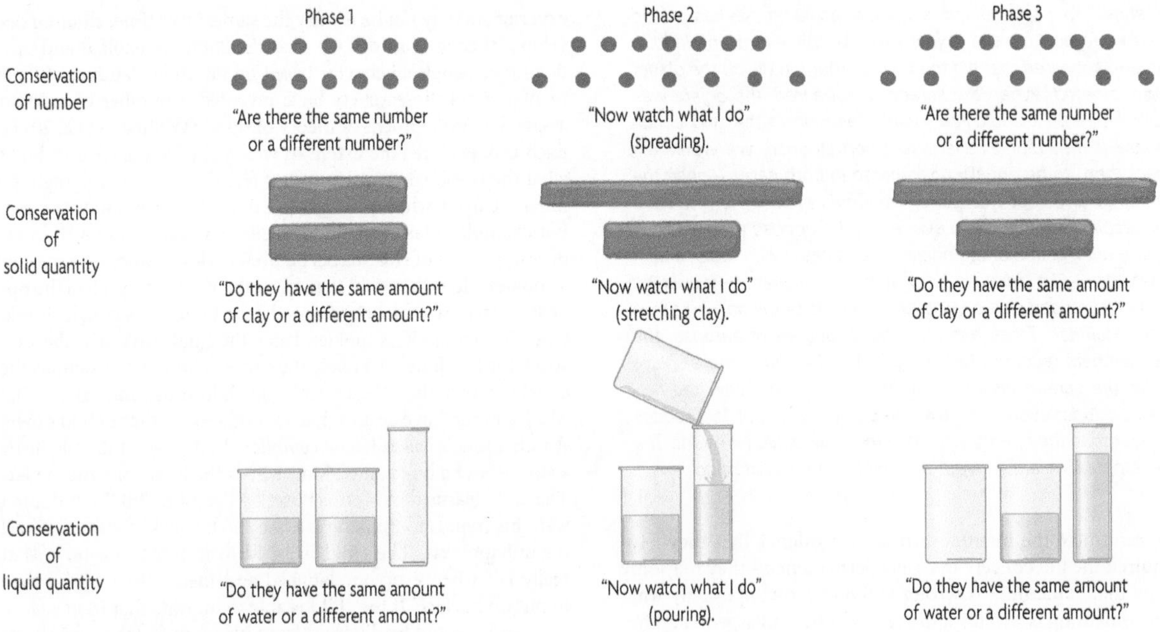

Phase 1   Phase 2   Phase 3

Conservation of number

"Are there the same number or a different number?"   "Now watch what I do" (spreading).   "Are there the same number or a different number?"

Conservation of solid quantity

"Do they have the same amount of clay or a different amount?"   "Now watch what I do" (stretching clay).   "Do they have the same amount of clay or a different amount?"

Conservation of liquid quantity

"Do they have the same amount of water or a different amount?"   "Now watch what I do" (pouring).   "Do they have the same amount of water or a different amount?"

FIGURE 6 Tests of Conservation

appropriate inference ("Adam is tallest") if the problem is just stated with a verbal description. Children only become able to solve problems of this sort with abstract thought when they arrive at the stage of concrete operations.

The lemonade study illustrates another hallmark of the concrete operations period. The 7-year-olds have mastered what Piaget called **conservation**: They know that the physical properties of objects do not change when nothing is added or taken away, even though the objects' appearances change. **Figure 6** presents examples of Piaget's tests of conservation for different dimensions. One of the newly acquired operations children can bring to bear on conservation tasks is reversibility. *Reversibility* is the child's understanding that both physical actions and mental operations can be reversed: The child can reason that the amount of lemonade *couldn't* have changed because when the physical action is reversed—when the lemonade is poured back into the original glass—the two volumes will once again look identical. 👁

Formal Operations Stage The formal operations stage covers a span roughly from age 11 on. In this final stage of cognitive growth, thinking becomes abstract. Adolescents can see how their particular reality is only one of several imaginable realities, and they begin to ponder deep questions of truth, justice, and existence. They seek answers to problems in a systematic fashion: Once they achieve formal operations, children can start to play the role of scientist, trying each of a series of

possibilities in careful order. Adolescents also begin to be able to use types of advanced deductive logic. Unlike their younger siblings, adolescents have the ability to reason from abstract premises ("If *A*, then *B*" and "not *B*") to their logical conclusions ("not *A*").

Contemporary Perspectives on Early Cognitive Development

Piaget's theory remains the classic reference point for the understanding of cognitive development (Feldman, 2004; Flavell, 1996). However, contemporary researchers have come up with more flexible ways of studying the development of the child's cognitive abilities.

Infant Cognition You've already met some of the tasks Piaget used to draw conclusions about cognitive development. However, contemporary researchers have developed innovative techniques that have allowed them to reevaluate some of Piaget's conclusions. Consider object permanence, which Piaget suggested was the major accomplishment of the 2-year-old child. Contemporary research techniques suggest that infants as young as 3 months old have already developed aspects of this concept. This important finding has been shown with different tasks devised by researcher **Renée Baillargeon** and her colleagues.

In one study, 4-month-old infants watched while an experimenter lowered a wide rectangular object (Wang et al., 2004). In one condition, the path of the object would put it behind a wide occluder—a barrier wide enough to hide the rectangular object completely. In the other condition, the object was

conservation According to Piaget, the understanding that physical properties do not change when nothing is added or taken away, even though appearances may change.

destined to pass behind a narrow occluder—a barrier too narrow to occlude the object fully. As this event unfolded, a screen appeared that hid the final moment in which the object was lowered. When the screen disappeared, the object was fully hidden. How did the infants respond in the two conditions? If they didn't have object permanence, we would expect them to be equally unbothered in both cases—once the rectangular object was gone, we would expect them to have no recollection that it had ever existed. Suppose they did have some recollection of the object. In that case, we would expect that they—like adults who watched the events—would be rather surprised that a wide object could be hidden by a narrow occluder. To assess the infants' degree of surprise, the researchers recorded how long infants looked at the displays after the screen disappeared. The infants who saw the narrow occluder event looked at the display for about 16 seconds longer than their peers who saw the wide occluder event. The rectangular object was out of sight but not out of mind.

We can't take the infants' surprise as evidence that they have acquired the full concept of object permanence—they may only know that something is wrong without knowing exactly what that something is. Even so, the research by Baillargeon and her colleagues suggests that event very young children have acquired important knowledge of the physical world.

The innovative methods researchers have developed to penetrate infants' minds continue to transform our understanding of what infants know and how they know it. Consider the development of perceptual processes. We saw earlier that children come into the world "prewired for survival." Still, experience in the world expands their perceptual and conceptual abilities. For example, as an adult you are easily able to recognize that a two-dimensional drawing provides a representation of a three-dimensional object. When did this ability first emerge? Using a measure of looking time (similar to the methods used by Baillargeon and her colleagues), researchers demonstrated that 9-month-olds could recognize that, for example, a line drawing of a sheep corresponded to a three-dimensional stuffed animal (Jowkar-Baniani & Schmuckler, 2011). Let's consider a second example that shows how infants piece together the workings of the world. Suppose you watched a video clip in which either a living creature or a moving ball caused a jumble of blocks to become neatly ordered. As an adult you know that non-living objects don't typically make the world more orderly. For that reason, you'd likely be more surprised by the clip with the ball. As measured by looking times, 12-month-old infants showed the same type of surprise (Newman et al., 2010). However, 7-month-olds looked equally as long at the clips that used living agents and balls. Thus, an understanding of the causal properties of living and non-living entities develops past the middle of the first year of life.

As you read the material in this section, did you find yourself surprised? It's easy to gaze down at infants in their cribs and imagine that their agenda is little more than to eat and to sleep. However, you've just seen that a growing body of research reveals that, even in the earliest months of their lives, children are hard at work trying to understand the world around them.

Theory of Mind Even as children's own cognitive abilities develop, they also come to understand that other people have cognitive experiences of the world—and that those cognitive

experiences may not be exactly the same. Over time, children develop a **theory of mind,** which is the ability to explain and predict other people's behavior based on an understanding of their mental states. Researchers have invented a number of tasks to assess the development of theory of mind (Wellman et al., 2011). Each task explores the extent to which children understand that what they desire, believe, know, or feel about the world might be different from what other people desire, believe, know, or feel. For example, a task called *Diverse desires* begins with a child indicating which of two snacks he prefers (for example, a carrot or a cookie). He is then told that an adult, Mr. Jones, prefers the opposite snack. So, if the child says that he prefers a carrot, he is told that Mr. Jones prefers cookies. Later, the child is asked to choose a snack for Mr. Jones. To make the correct choice (for example, the cookies rather than the carrot), the child must understand that Mr. Jones can have desires that are different from the child's own. Another task is called *Hidden emotion*. In this task, the child hears a story about a boy named Matt who is the target of a mean joke. The child learns that Matt is upset by the joke. Still, Matt doesn't want his friends to think he is a baby so he doesn't want to reveal his unhappiness. The child is asked to indicate first how Matt really felt when everyone laughed and then what look he tried to put on his face. If the child is able to indicate that Matt's facial expression would be different from his inner feelings, she shows that she has developed that aspect of theory of mind. You may be thinking, "These tasks are easy!" That thought should give you a sense of how easily you now understand other people's mental states. In fact, children acquire different aspects of theory of mind at different times. For most children in the United States, there's a fairly steady sequence from an understanding of others' desires to an understanding of their beliefs, knowledge, and then emotions from ages 2 to 6. For example, it's very likely that children will be able to understand diverse desires before they are able to understand hidden emotions.

Still, researchers have documented how some aspects of theory of mind emerge even in infancy. Consider the relationship between actions and goals (people's intentions). As an adult, you are accustomed to inferring people's goals when you watch them perform actions. For example, if you see someone pull out a set of keys, you easily infer that he or she needs to unlock something. When did you start to understand how actions relate to goals? Research suggests that 7-month-olds have begun to divide the world up into actions that are goal-directed and those that are not (Hamlin et al., 2008). As a second example, consider how you respond when a friend points at an object. As an adult, you infer your friend's behavior is guided by an intention: You are meant to shift your attention in the direction of the gesture. Similarly, 12-month-old infants are able to use pointing gestures produced by adults to find a hidden toy (Behne et al., 2012). These studies illustrate how carefully infants attend to the world around them to develop an understanding of the mental states that underlie other people's behaviors.

Social and Cultural Influences on Cognitive Development
Another focus of contemporary research is on the role of social interactions in cognitive development. Much of this research has its origins in the theories of Russian psychologist

---

theory of mind The ability to explain and predict other people's behavior based on an understanding of their mental states.

Lev Vygotsky. Vygotsky argued that children develop through a process of **internalization:** They absorb knowledge from their social context that has a major impact on how cognition unfolds over time.

The social theory that Vygotsky pioneered has found support in cross-cultural studies of development (Gauvain et al., 2011). As Piaget's theory initially seized the attention of developmental researchers, many of them sought to use his tasks to study the cognitive achievements of children in diverse cultures (Maynard, 2008). These studies began to call into question the universality of Piaget's claims because, for example, people in many cultures failed to show evidence that they had acquired formal operations. Late in his life, Piaget himself began to speculate that the specific achievements he characterized as formal operations may rely more on the particular type of science education children obtain rather than on an unfolding of biologically predetermined stages of cognitive development (Lourenço & Machado, 1996).

Vygotsky's concept of internalization helps explain the effect culture has on cognitive development. Children's cognition develops to perform culturally valued functions (Fleer & Hedegaard, 2010; Serpell, 2000). Piaget, for example, invented tasks that reflected his own preconceptions about appropriate and valuable cognitive activities. Other cultures prefer their children to excel in other ways. If Piaget's children had been evaluated with respect to their understanding of the cognitive complexities of weaving, they probably would have appeared to be retarded in their development relative to Mayan children in Guatemala (Rogoff, 1990). Cross-cultural studies of cognitive development have quite often demonstrated that type of schooling plays a large role in determining children's achievement on Piagetian tasks (Rogoff & Chavajay, 1995). Psychologists must use these types of findings to sort out the nature and nurture of cognitive development.

The developmental changes we've considered so far are very dramatic. It's easy to tell that a 12-year-old has all sorts of cognitive capabilities unknown to a 1-year-old. We now shift to the more subtle changes that take place throughout adulthood.

Cognitive Development in Adulthood

As we have traced cognitive development across childhood into adolescence, "change" has usually meant "change for the better." When we arrive at the period of late adulthood, though, cultural stereotypes suggest that "change" means "change for the worse" (Parr & Siegert, 1993). However, even when people believe that the course of adulthood brings with it general decline, they still anticipate certain types of gains very late into life (Dixon & de Frias, 2004). We will consider intelligence and memory to see the interplay of losses and gains.

Intelligence There is little evidence to support the notion that general cognitive abilities decline among the healthy elderly. Only about 5 percent of the population experiences major losses in cognitive functioning. When age-related decline in cognitive functioning occurs, it is usually limited to only some abilities. When intelligence is separated into the components that make up your verbal abilities *(crystallized intelligence)* and those that are part of your ability to learn quickly and thoroughly *(fluid intelligence)*, fluid intelligence shows the greater decline with age (Hertzog, 2011). Much of the decrease in fluidity has been attributed to a general slowing down of processing speed: Older adults' performance on intellectual tasks that require many mental processes to occur in small amounts of time is greatly impaired (Sheppard & Vernon, 2008).

Researchers who study cognitive performance have been quite interested in determining what older adults might do to minimize declines with age. Much research attention has considered the maxim "Use it or lose it." One study, for example, focused on a group of older adults whose average age was 69 (Bielak et al., 2007). The adults whose everyday lives had the highest levels of social, physical, and intellectual activities also showed the fastest processing speed on cognitive tasks. These results appear to support "use it or lose it." However, interpretation of results of this sort is muddied by a specific concern: Correlation is not causation (Salthouse, 2006). The result *could* indicate that a high level of activity causes processing speed to remain relatively high. However, we must also consider the possibility that a smaller decline in processing speed allows some older adults to remain more active.

Even if it proves difficult to demonstrate that "using it" prevents "losing it," researchers have provided evidence that "using it more" can bring about better intellectual functioning (Hertzog et al., 2008). Let's consider evidence that frequent computer use works against intellectual decline.

Participants whose ages ranged from 32 to 84 provided information about the frequency of their computer use (Tun & Lachman, 2010). In addition, the 2,671 participants completed a battery of cognitive tests. The data showed positive correlations between computer use and cognitive ability: More computer use was associated with greater ability. For example, one cognitive task assessed participants' ability to respond to stimuli by switching quickly between two different rules. Participants who used computers more performed better on this task. The benefit of this particular task was especially large for participants who otherwise showed lower intellectual ability.

Featured Study

The researchers acknowledged that these results are correlational: They raise the possibility that people with more cognitive ability may choose to use computers more. However, they argue that the particular pattern of benefits favors the explanation that computer use prevents people from "losing it." To understand this claim, try to contemplate the multiple cognitive activities in which you engage the next time you navigate through cyberspace.

It's important to note that there's one intelligence measure on which people show improvement over the life span. Psychologists have demonstrated age-related gains in **wisdom**— expertise in the fundamental practices of life (Staudinger & Glück, 2011). **Table 4** presents some of the types of knowledge

---

internalization According to Vygotsky, the process through which children absorb knowledge from the social context.

Many prominent figures, such as Nelson Mandela, continue to make important professional contributions through their 70s and beyond. How can some aspects of intellectual performance be kept from decline through late adulthood?

that define wisdom (Smith & Baltes, 1990). You can see that each type of knowledge is best acquired over a long and thoughtful life.

Memory   A common complaint among the elderly is the feeling that their ability to remember things is not as good as it used to be. On a number of tests of memory, adults over 60 *do* perform worse than young adults in their 20s (Hess, 2005). Aging does *not* seem to diminish elderly individuals' ability to access their general knowledge store and personal information about events that occurred long ago. In a study of name and face recognition, middle-aged adults could identify 90 percent of their high school classmates in yearbooks 35 years after graduation; older adults were still able to recognize 70 to 80 percent of their

Table 4 • Features of Wisdom

- *Rich factual knowledge.* General and specific knowledge about the conditions of life and its variations
- *Rich procedural knowledge.* General and specific knowledge about strategies of judgment and advice concerning life matters
- *Life span contextualism.* Knowledge about the contexts of life and their temporal (developmental) relationships
- *Uncertainty.* Knowledge about the relative indeterminacy and unpredictability of life and ways to manage it

wisdom Expertise in the fundamental pragmatics of life.

classmates some 50 years later (Bahrick et al., 1975). However, aging affects the processes that allow new information to be effectively organized, stored, and retrieved (Buchler & Reder, 2007).

As yet, researchers have been unable to develop a wholly adequate description of the mechanisms that underlie memory impairment in older adults—perhaps because the impairment has multiple sources (Hess, 2005). Some theories focus on differences between older and younger people in their efforts to organize and process information. Other theories point to elderly people's reduced ability to pay attention to information. Another type of theory looks to neurobiological changes in the brain systems that produce the physical memory traces (Charlton et al., 2010). Note that these brain changes are not the same as the abnormal tangles of neural tissue and plaques that cause the memory loss of Alzheimer's disease. Researchers also believe that older adults' performance may be impaired by their very belief that their memory will be poor (Hess & Hinson, 2006). Researchers continue to evaluate the relative contributions of each of these factors.

Let's now narrow our focus from general cognitive development to the more specific topic of the acquisition of language.

Stop *and* Review

① In Piaget's theory, what is the relationship between assimilation and accommodation?
② What does it mean when a child is able to overcome centration?
③ How has contemporary research modified conclusions about object permanence?
④ What was the major emphasis of Lev Vygotsky's theory?
⑤ What happens to processing speed across the life span?

CRITICAL THINKING   Recall the experiment that looked at object permanence in 4-month-olds. Why was looking time an appropriate measure to test the researchers' hypothesis?

✔•⌐Study and Review on MyPsychLab

ACQUIRING LANGUAGE

Here's a remarkable fact: By the time they are 6 years old, children can analyze language into its units of sound and meaning, use the rules they have discovered to combine sounds into words and words into meaningful sentences, and take an active part in coherent conversations. Children's remarkable language accomplishments have prompted most researchers to agree that the ability to learn language is biologically based—that you are born with an innate language capacity (Tomasello, 2008). Even so, depending on where a child happens to be born, he or she may end up as a native speaker of any one of the world's

4,000 different languages. In addition, children are prepared to learn both spoken languages and gestural languages, like American Sign Language. This means that the innate predisposition to learn language must be both quite strong and quite flexible (Schick et al., 2006). 👁

To explain how it is that infants are such expert language learners, we will consider evidence that supports the claim of an innate language capacity. But we will also acknowledge the role that the environment plays—after all, children learn the particular languages that are being used in the world around them. **Table 5** outlines the various types of knowledge children must acquire for their particular signed or spoken language. Adults put all of these types of knowledge to use in fluent conversation.

Perceiving Speech and Perceiving Words

Imagine you are a newborn child, hearing a buzz of noise all around you. How do you start to understand that some of those sounds are relevant to communicating with other people? A child's first step in acquiring a particular language is to take note of the sound contrasts that are used meaningfully in that language. (For signed languages, the child must attend to contrasts in hand positions, for example.) Each spoken language samples from the set of possible distinctions that can be produced by the human vocal tract; no language uses all of the speech–sound contrasts that can be made. The minimal meaningful units of speech that allow people to distinguish one word from another are called **phonemes**. There are about

Table 5 • The Structure of Language

Grammar is the field of study that seeks to describe the way language is structured and used. It includes several domains:

Phonology—the study of the sounds that are put together to form words.

A **phoneme** is the smallest unit of speech that distinguishes between any two utterances. For example, *b* and *p* distinguish *bin* from *pin*.

Phonetics is the study and classification of speech sounds.

Syntax—the way in which words are strung together to form sentences. For example, subject *(I)* + verb *(like)* + object *(you)* is standard English word order.

A **morpheme** is the minimum distinctive unit of grammar that cannot be divided without losing its meaning. The word *bins* has two morphemes, *bin* and *s*, indicating the plural.

Semantics—the study of the meanings of words and their changes over time.

Lexical meaning is the dictionary meaning of a word. Meaning is sometimes conveyed by the *context* of a word in a sentence ("Run *fast*" versus "Make the knot *fast*") or the *inflection* with which it is spoken (try emphasizing different words in *white house cat*).

Pragmatics—rules for participation in conversations; social conventions for communicating, sequencing sentences, and responding appropriately to others.

45 distinct phonemes in English. Imagine you heard someone speak the words *right* and *light*. If you are a native speaker of English, you would have no trouble hearing the difference—/r/ and /l/ are different phonemes in English. If your only language experience was with Japanese, however, you would not be able to hear the difference between these two words because /r/ and /l/ are not distinct phonemes in Japanese. Do English speakers acquire the ability to make this distinction, or do Japanese speakers lose it?

To answer this type of question, researchers needed to develop methods to obtain linguistic information from prelinguistic children.

Using principles of operant conditioning, researchers condition infants to turn their heads toward a sound source when they detect a change from one speech sound to another. The reward that reinforces this behavior is an illuminated box that contains a clapping and drumming toy animal. The procedure ensures that, if the children detect changes, they are very likely to turn toward the sound source. To measure the children's ability to perceive a distinction, researchers monitor how frequently the children turn their heads when a change is present.

Janet Werker *and her colleagues (Werker, 1991; Werker & Lalond, 1988) have used this technique to examine the innate basis of speech perception abilities, a version of the /r/–/l/ question I posed earlier. Werker studied sound distinctions that are used in Hindi, but not in English—distinctions that make it difficult for adult English speakers to learn Hindi. Werker and her colleagues measured the ability of infants learning English or Hindi, as well as adults who spoke English or Hindi, to hear the differences between the Hindi phonemes. She found that all the infants, regardless of which language they were learning, could hear the differences until the age of 8 months. However, of the infants older than 8 months and of the adults, only the Hindi speakers or speakers-to-be could hear the Hindi contrasts.*

Research of this type strongly suggests that you started out with an innate ability to perceive sound contrasts that are important for spoken languages. However, you swiftly lose the ability to perceive some of the contrasts that are not present in the language you begin to acquire (Werker & Tees, 1999).

Along with this biological head start for speech perception, many children also get an environmental head start. When adults in many cultures speak to infants and young children, they use a special form of language that differs from language addressed to adults. For example, when talking to infants and children, adults tend to slow down their rate of speech and use an exaggerated, high-pitched intonation; they tend to produce utterances that are shorter and have simpler structures (Soderstrom, 2007). Depending on the age of the child,

👁 **Watch** the **Video** *Language Development* on **MyPsychLab**

phoneme Minimal unit of speech in any given language that makes a meaningful difference in speech and production and reception; *r* and *l* are two distinct phonemes in English but variations of one in Japanese.

researchers call the forms of speech either **infant-directed speech** or **child-directed speech.** The features that define infant- and child-directed speech appear in many but not all cultures (Kitamura et al., 2002; Lee & Davis, 2010). Researchers suggest that these special forms of speech provide infants and children with information that makes them better able to acquire phonemes and words from the language being used around them (Song et al., 2010; Thiessen et al., 2005).

At what age are children able to perceive the repetition of patterns of sounds—words—within the stream of speech directed to them? This is the first big step toward acquiring language: You can't learn that *doggie* has something to do with the shaggy thing in the corner until you recognize that the sound pattern *doggie* seems to recur in that shaggy thing's presence. Infants, on average, appear to gain the insight that repeated sounds have significance somewhere between ages 6 and 7 months (Jusczyk, 2003; Jusczyk & Aslin, 1995). For one special word, however, the breakthrough comes a couple of months early: Children at age 4 months already show a recognition preference for their own names (Mandel et al., 1995)!

Learning Word Meanings

Once you could detect the co-occurrence of sounds and experiences, you were prepared to start learning word meanings. There's no denying that children are excellent word learners. At around 18 months, children's word learning often takes off at an amazing rate. Researchers have called this phase the *naming explosion* because children begin to acquire new words, especially names for objects, at a rapidly increasing rate (see **Figure 7**). By the age of 6, the average child is estimated to understand 14,000 words (Templin, 1957). Assuming that most of these words are learned between the ages of 18 months and 6 years, this works out to about nine new words a day or almost one word per waking hour (Carey, 1978). Children have an ability that researchers call *fast mapping*: They are able to learn the meanings of new words with minimal experience—sometimes with only a single exposure to a word and its referent (Gershkoff-Stowe & Hahn, 2007). How is this possible?

Imagine a straightforward situation in which a child and her father are walking through a park and the father points and says, "That's a doggie." The child must decide to which piece of the world *doggie* applies. This is no easy feat (Quine, 1960). Perhaps *doggie* means "any creature with four legs" or "the animal's fur" or "the animal's bark" or any of the other large set of meanings that will be true each time someone points toward a dog. Given all the possibilities, how are children able to fix the meanings of individual words?

Researchers suggest that children act like scientists—developing *hypotheses* about what each new word might mean. You can, for example, see children's scientific minds actively at

work when they *overextend* words, using them incorrectly to cover a wide range of objects. They may use the word *doggie* to refer to all animals or the word *moon* to refer to all round objects, including clocks and coins. Other times, children might *underextend* a word—believing, for example, that *doggie* refers only to their own family dog.

The view that children form hypotheses, however, does not explain how children acquire particular meanings in particular contexts. Researchers have suggested that children's hypotheses are guided by expectations such as the *principle of contrast*. This principle suggests that differences in *forms* signal differences in *meaning*: When children hear new words, they should look for meanings that contrast with those for the words they already know (Clark, 2003). Suppose, for example, a father and daughter are watching a TV scene in which a kangaroo is jumping. The child knows the word *jump* but not the word *kangaroo*. Suppose the parent says, "Kangaroo!" What might happen next? Because the child knows *jump*, she supposes that her parent would just say *jump* if *kangaroo* just meant "jump"—different forms should signal contrasts in meaning. The child can now hypothesize that *kangaroo* must label the object rather than the action. She is on her way to acquiring a meaning for *kangaroo*. If you've spent time around small children, you've probably noticed the principle of contrast at work. For example, a child will often become upset if his mother calls his fire *engine* a fire *truck*!

Acquiring Grammar

To explain how children acquire meanings, I characterized children as scientists whose hypotheses are constrained by innate principles. The same analogy describes how children acquire the rules by which units of meaning are combined into larger units—in other words, grammar. The challenge

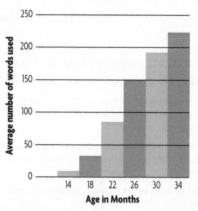

FIGURE 7 Children's Growth in Vocabulary
Soon after their first words occur, children's vocabulary increases rapidly. These longitudinal data show the number of different words that children used while engaged in 90 minutes of ordinary activities with their caregivers.

Source: Data from Huttenlocher, J., Waterfall, H., Vasilyeva, M., Vevea, J., & Hedges, L. V. (2010). Sources of variability in children's language growth. *Cognitive Psychology, 61,* 343–365.

---

infant-directed speech A form of speech addressed to infants that includes slower speed, distinctive intonation, and structural simplifications.

child-directed speech A form of speech addressed to children that includes slower speed, distinctive intonation, and structural simplifications.

Children develop linguistic fluency by listening to the speech patterns of those around them. What evidence suggests that they have a biological head start on acquiring grammar?

© DPA/The Image Works

for the child is that different languages follow different rules. For example, in English the typical ordering of units in a sentence is subject-verb-object, but in Japanese the ordering is subject-object-verb. Children must discover what order is present in the language being used around them. How do they do that?

Most researchers now believe that a large part of the answer resides in the human genome. Linguist **Noam Chomsky** (1965, 1975), for example, argued that children are born with mental structures that facilitate the comprehension and production of language. Some of the best evidence for such a biological basis for grammar comes from children who acquire complete grammatical structure in the absence of well-formed input. For example, researchers have studied deaf children whose hearing loss was sufficiently severe that they could not acquire spoken language but whose parents did not expose them to full-fledged signed languages such as American Sign Language (Franklin et al., 2011; Goldin-Meadow, 2003). These children began to invent signing systems of their own and—despite the lack of environmental support for these invented languages—the gestural systems came to have regular, grammatical structure: "With or without an established language as a guide, children appear to be 'ready' to seek structure at least at word and sentence levels when developing systems for communication" (Goldin-Meadow & Mylander, 1990, p. 351).

But how can researchers go about specifying exactly what knowledge is innately given? The most productive approach to this question is to study language acquisition across many languages—*cross-linguistically*. By examining what is hard and what is easy for children to acquire across the world's many languages, researchers can determine what aspects of grammar are most likely to be supported by innate predispositions.

Here we arrive back at the child as scientist. Children bring innate constraints to the task of learning a particular language. **Dan Slobin** has defined these guidelines as a set of *operating principles* that together constitute the child's

language-making capacity. According to Slobin's (1985) theory, the operating principles take the form of directives to the child. Here, for example, is an operating principle that helps children discover the words that go together to form a grammatical unit: "store together ordered sequences of word classes and functor classes that co-occur in the expression of a particular proposition type, along with a designation of the proposition type" (p. 1252). In simpler language, this operating principle suggests that children must keep track of the relationship between the order in which words appear and the meanings they express. Slobin derived the operating principles by summarizing across the data provided by a large number of other researchers, who examined a variety of different languages. I will use English examples to demonstrate the principles at work.

Consider what English-speaking children can do when they begin, at about age 2, to use combinations of words—the *two-word stage*. Children's speech at this point has been characterized as *telegraphic* because it is filled with short, simple sequences using mostly nouns and verbs. Telegraphic speech lacks function words, such as *the, and,* and *of,* which help express the relationships between words and ideas. For example, "Allgone milk" is a telegraphic message.

For adults to understand two-word utterances, they must know the context in which the words are spoken. "Tanya ball," for example, could mean, among other things, "Tanya wants the ball" or "Tanya throws the ball." Even so, children at the two-word stage show evidence that they have already acquired some knowledge of the grammar of English. Operating principles allow them to discover that word order is important in English and that the three critical elements are actor-action-object (subject-verb-object), arranged in that order. Evidence for this "discovery" comes when children misinterpret a sentence such as "Mary was followed by her little lamb to school" as *Mary* (actor) *followed* (action) *her lamb* (object) (see **Figure 8**). Over time, children must apply other operating principles to discover that there are exceptions to the actor-action-object rule.

Consider now an operating principle, which Slobin calls *extension,* that requires children to try to use the same unit of meaning, or *morpheme,* to mark the same concept. Examples of such concepts are possession, past tense, and continuing action. In English, each of these concepts is expressed by adding a grammatical morpheme to a content word, such as -*'s* (as in Maria*'s*), -*ed* (as in call*ed*), and -*ing* (as in laugh*ing*). Note how the addition of each of these sounds to a noun or verb changes its meaning.

Children use operating principles like extension to form hypotheses about how these morphemes work. Because this principle requires that the child try to mark all cases in the same way, however, the error of **overregularization** often results. For example, once children learn the past-tense rule (adding -*ed* to the verb), they add -*ed* to all verbs, forming words such as *doed* and *breaked*. As children learn the rule for plurals (adding the sound -*s* or -*z* to the end of a word), they

language-making capacity The innate guidelines or operating principles that children bring to the task of learning a language.

overregularization A grammatical error, usually appearing during early language development, in which rules of the language are applied too widely, resulting in incorrect linguistic forms.

FIGURE 8 Acquiring Grammar
Many toddlers would interpret "Mary was followed by the lamb" and "Mary followed the lamb" to have identical meanings.

again overextend the rule, creating words such as *foots* and *mouses*. Overregularization is an especially interesting error because it usually appears *after* children have learned and used the correct forms of verbs and nouns. The children first use the correct verb forms (for example, *came* and *went*), apparently because they learned them as separate vocabulary items; but when they learn the general rule for the past tense, they extend it even to verbs that are exceptions to the rule—words that they previously used correctly. Over time, children use other operating principles to overcome this temporary overapplication.

Children's acquisition of language has a major impact on their ability to participate in social interactions. Keep them in mind as we shift our focus now to social development across the life span.

Stop *and* Review

① What are some ways in which infant- and child-directed speech differ from adult-directed speech?
② Why do children overextend word meanings?
③ How does research with deaf children support the idea that aspects of grammar are innate?
④ How would you notice when a child is overregularizing English past-tense constructions?

CRITICAL THINKING Consider the study on children's ability to perceive sound distinctions. Why was it important to compare English-speaking adults with infants who are English-speakers-to-be?

✓•─Study and Review on MyPsychLab

SOCIAL DEVELOPMENT ACROSS THE LIFE SPAN

We have seen so far how radically you change as a physical and cognitive being from birth to older adulthood. This section of the chapter explores **social development:** how individuals' social interactions and expectations change across the life span. You will see that the social and cultural environment interacts with biological aging to provide each period of the life span with its own special challenges and rewards.

As you ponder social development, it is particularly important for you to consider the way in which culture and environment affect certain aspects of our lives. For example, people who live in circumstances of economic hardship undergo types of stresses that are absent from the "normal" course of development (Conger et al., 2010; Edin & Kissane, 2010). Current trends in the United States and in other countries throughout the world make it imperative for developmental psychologists to consider the difficult circumstances in which many children, adolescents, and adults are forced to live—circumstances that continually put their sanity, safety, and survival at risk. U.S. culture also enforces different outcomes for men and for women and for individuals who belong to minority groups. For example, in 2007 12 percent of women over 65 were living in poverty compared to 7 percent of men in this age range; 27 percent of African American women over 65 were living in poverty compared to 9 percent of White women over 65 (Federal Interagency Forum on Aging-Related Statistics, 2010). These differences are direct products of structural inequities in contemporary U.S. society.

When I draw conclusions about the "average" life course, keep in mind that culture dictates that some individuals will depart from this average; as I describe the psychological challenges facing the "ordinary" individual, bear in mind that many individuals face extraordinary challenges. It is the role of researchers to document the impact of contemporary problems—and to design interventions to alleviate their harshest consequences.

As you read the remainder of this chapter, keep in mind how the tasks of life are jointly determined by a biological accumulation of years and a social accumulation of cultural experiences. This discussion of social development begins with Erik Erikson's life span theory, which makes explicit the challenges and rewards in each of life's major periods.

Erikson's Psychosocial Stages

Erik Erikson (1902–1994), who was trained by Sigmund Freud's daughter, Anna Freud, proposed that every individual must successfully navigate a series of **psychosocial stages,** each of which presented a particular conflict or crisis. Erikson (1963)

....

social development The ways in which individuals' social interactions and expectations change across the life span.

psychosocial stage Proposed by Erik Erikson, one of the successive developmental stages that focus on an individual's orientation toward the self and others; these stages incorporate both the sexual and social aspects of a person's development and the social conflicts that arise from the interaction between the individual and the social environment.

Psychology in Your Life

WHAT HAPPENS WHEN CHILDREN BECOME BILINGUAL?

The section on language acquisition focused on the processes that allow children to learn a single language. However, across the globe many children become *bilingual* at an early age—they learn more than one language at the same time. You might wonder how that works. For example, how do children cope when their environment provides two words that have the same meaning, such as *dog* in English and *perro* in Spanish? One possibility might be that children unite both languages into one big mental dictionary. However, that does not seem to be the case. Remarkably, from the earliest moments of bilingual acquisition, children seem to keep two or more vocabularies separate (Montanari, 2010). They quickly become able to produce the appropriate word in the appropriate language context.

Still, there are potential costs for bilingual children. Essentially, they need to spread the same time for language-learning across two different languages. One consequence is that bilingual children tend to know less vocabulary in each language than their monolingual peers. For example, one study looked at the ability of 1,738 children between ages 3 and 10 to understand words in either one or two languages (Bialystok et al., 2010). Although some bilingual children had larger vocabularies than their monolingual peers, the average was lower for bilingual children all the way across the 7-year age range.

Before you decide never to let a child become an early bilingual, here's an important clarification: This difference in vocabulary size and skill is the only consistent negative consequence of bilingualism (Bialystok & Craik, 2010). In fact, researchers have demonstrated that bilingualism has a number of positive consequences. Consider a study in which 6-year-old monolingual and bilingual children viewed four ambiguous figures (Bialystok & Shapero, 2005). One of the stimuli was the duck-rabbit that appears on p. 196. The researchers assessed the ease with which the children were able to perceive the two different interpretations of each figure. The bilingual children consistently outperformed the monolingual children. But why? The researchers suggested that the "processing advantage most likely stems from the constant need [for bilingual children] to manage two active language systems in order to use one of them fluently" (p. 596).

The more general claim is that bilingual children are better able to control their cognitive resources in tasks that require selective attention and cognitive flexibility. This ability is known as *executive control*. Bilinguals as young as 24 months demonstrate better executive control than their monolingual age-mates (Poulin-Dubois et al., 2011). In addition, because of the benefit for executive control, lifelong bilingualism may protect people from some forms of the cognitive decline that accompany aging (Bialystok & Craik, 2010).

You can see that bilingualism presents interesting circumstances. People who become early bilinguals may have lifelong reductions in their vocabularies in each language. At the same time, they are likely to maintain better performance in the very wide range of tasks that require executive control. Does that sound like an acceptable trade-off?

---

identified eight stages in the life cycle. At each stage, a particular crisis comes into focus, as shown in **Table 6**. Although each conflict never completely disappears, it needs to be sufficiently resolved at a given stage if an individual is to cope successfully with the conflicts of later stages.

Trust vs. Mistrust In Erikson's first stage, an infant needs to develop a basic sense of *trust* in the environment through interaction with caregivers. Trust is a natural accompaniment to a strong attachment relationship with a parent who provides food, warmth, and the comfort of physical closeness. But a child whose basic needs are not met, who experiences inconsistent handling, lack of physical closeness and warmth, and the frequent absence of a caring adult, may develop a pervasive sense of mistrust, insecurity, and anxiety.

Autonomy vs. Self-Doubt With the development of walking and the beginnings of language, there is an expansion of a child's exploration and manipulation of objects (and sometimes people). With these activities should come a comfortable sense of *autonomy*, or independence, and of being a capable and worthy person. Excessive restriction or criticism at this second stage may lead instead to self-doubts, whereas demands beyond the child's ability, as in too-early or too-severe toilet training, can discourage the child's efforts to persevere in mastering new tasks.

Initiative vs. Guilt Toward the end of the preschool period, a child who has developed a basic sense of trust, first in the immediate environment and then in himself or herself, can now *initiate* both intellectual and motor activities. The ways that parents respond to the child's self-initiated activities either encourage the sense of freedom and self-confidence needed for the next stage or produce guilt and feelings of being an inept intruder in an adult world.

Competence vs. Inferiority During the elementary school years, the child who has successfully resolved the crises of the earlier stages is ready to go beyond random exploring and testing to the systematic development of *competencies*. School and

Table 6 • Erikson's Psychosocial Stages

Crisis	Age	Challenge
Trust vs. mistrust	Birth to 1 year	Developing a sense that the world is safe and good
Autonomy vs. self-doubt	1 to 3 years	Realizing that one is an independent person with the ability to make decisions
Initiative vs. guilt	3 to 6 years	Developing a willingness to try new things and to handle failure
Competence vs. inferiority	6 years to adolescence	Learning competence in basic skills and to cooperate with others
Identity vs. role confusion	Adolescence	Developing a coherent, inteargated sense of inner self
Intimacy vs. isolation	Young adulthood	Establishing ties to another in a trusting, loving relationship
Generativity vs. stagnation	Middle adulthood	Finding meaning in career, family, and community via productive work
Ego integrity vs. despair	Late life	Viewing one's life as satisfactory and worth living

From Morris, Charles G.; Maisto, Albert A., *Understanding Psychology*, 9th Ed., © 2010. Reprinted the Electronically reproduced by permission of Pearson Education, Inc., Upper Saddle River, New Jersey.

sports offer arenas for learning intellectual and motor skills, and interaction with peers offers an arena for developing social skills. Successful efforts in these pursuits lead to feelings of competence. Some youngsters, however, become spectators rather than performers or experience enough failure to give them a sense of inferiority, leaving them unable to meet the demands of the next life stages.

Identity vs. Role Confusion   Erikson believed that the essential crisis of adolescence is discovering one's true *identity* amid the confusion created by playing many different roles for the different audiences in an expanding social world. Resolving

Erik Erikson's psychosocial stage model is a widely used tool for understanding human development over the life span. What crisis did Erikson suggest dominates individuals of your age?

this crisis helps the individual develop a sense of a coherent self; failing to do so adequately may result in a self-image that lacks a central, stable core.

Intimacy vs. Isolation   The essential crisis for the young adult is to resolve the conflict between *intimacy* and *isolation*—to develop the capacity to make full emotional, moral, and sexual commitments to other people. Making that kind of commitment requires that the individual compromise some personal preferences, accept some responsibilities, and yield some degree of privacy and independence. Failure to resolve this crisis adequately leads to isolation and the inability to connect to others in psychologically meaningful ways. ◉

Generativity vs. Stagnation   The next major opportunity for growth, which occurs during adult midlife, is known as *generativity*. People in their 30s and 40s move beyond a focus on self and partner to broaden their commitments to family, work, society, and future generations. Those people who haven't resolved earlier developmental tasks are still self-indulgent, question past decisions and goals, and pursue freedom at the expense of security.

Ego integrity vs. Despair   The crisis in later adulthood is the conflict between *ego integrity* and *despair*. Resolving the crises at each of the earlier stages prepares the older adult to look back without regrets and to enjoy a sense of wholeness. When previous crises are left unresolved, aspirations remain unfulfilled, and the individual experiences futility, despair, and self-depreciation.

You will see that Erikson's framework is very useful for tracking individuals' progress across the life span. Let's begin with childhood.

Social Development in Childhood

Children's basic survival depends on forming meaningful, effective relationships with other people. **Socialization** is

⊙ Watch the Video *Classic Footage of Erik Erikson* on MyPsychLab

socialization The lifelong process whereby an individual's behavioral patterns, values, standards, skills, attitudes, and motives are shaped to conform to those regarded as desirable in a particular society.

the lifelong process through which an individual's behavior patterns, values, standards, skills, attitudes, and motives are shaped to conform to those regarded as desirable in a particular society. This process involves many people—relatives, friends, teachers—and institutions—schools, houses of worship—that exert pressure on the individual to adopt socially approved values and standards of conduct. The family, however, is the most influential shaper and regulator of socialization. The concept of family itself is being transformed to recognize that many children grow up in circumstances that include either less (a single parent) or more (an extended household) than a mother, father, and siblings. Whatever the configuration, though, the family helps the individual form basic patterns of responsiveness to others—and these patterns, in turn, become the basis of the individual's lifelong style of relating to other people.

Temperament Even as infants begin the process of socialization, they do not all start at the same place. Children begin life with differences in **temperament**—biologically based levels of emotional and behavioral response to the environment (Thomas & Chess, 1977). Researcher **Jerome Kagan** and his colleagues have demonstrated that some infants are "born shy" and others are "born bold" (Kagan & Snidman, 2004). These groups of children differ in sensitivity to physical and social stimulation: The shy or *inhibited* babies are consistently "cautious and emotionally reserved when they confront unfamiliar persons or contexts"; the bold or *uninhibited* babies are consistently "sociable, affectively spontaneous, and minimally fearful in the same unfamiliar situations" (Kagan & Snidman, 1991, p. 40). In one sample, about 10 percent of the infants were inhibited and about 25 percent were uninhibited; the rest of the infants fell in between those end points (Kagan & Snidman, 1991). Researchers have begun to explore the genetic and brain bases of differences in temperament (LoBue et al., 2011; Rothbart, 2007).

Longitudinal studies have demonstrated the long-term impact of early temperament. For example, one study followed a group of children from ages 4 months to 5 years (Degnan et al., 2011). The researchers measured the extent to which the children, as 4-month-olds, showed a pattern of sociability and positive emotional reactions toward new experiences—a pattern the researchers called *exuberance*. The children's levels of low or high exuberance were quite stable when they were measured at 9, 24, and 36 months. At 5 years of age, the more exuberant children displayed greater competence when they interacted with unfamiliar peers. At the same time, when they became frustrated, the more exuberant children were likely to engage in disruptive behaviors.

Infant temperament sets the stage for later aspects of social development. Next, we consider the *attachment* bonds children form as their first social relationships.

Attachment Social development begins with the establishment of a close emotional relationship between a child and a mother, father, or other regular caregiver. This intense, enduring, social–emotional relationship is called **attachment.** Because children are incapable of feeding or protecting themselves, the earliest function of attachment is to ensure survival. In some species, the infant automatically becomes

Why is it important for a child to develop a secure attachment to a parent or other caregiver?

Photo by Nina Leen/Time Life Pictures/Getty Images

imprinted on the first moving object it sees or hears (Bolhuis & Honey, 1998). **Imprinting** occurs rapidly during a critical period of development and cannot easily be modified. The automaticity of imprinting can sometimes be problematic. Ethologist **Konrad Lorenz** demonstrated that young geese raised by a human imprint on the human instead of on one of their own kind. In nature, fortunately, young geese mostly see other geese first.

You won't find human infants imprinting on their parents. Even so, **John Bowlby** (1973), an influential theorist on human attachment, suggested that infants and adults are biologically predisposed to form attachments. That attachment relationship has broad consequences. Beginning with Bowlby (1973), theorists have suggested that the experiences that give rise to an attachment relationship provide individuals with a lifelong schema for social relationships called an *internal working model* (Dykas & Cassidy, 2011). An internal

⦿ Watch the Video *In the Real World: Socialization* on MyPsychLab

temperament A child's biologically based level of emotional and behavioral response to environmental events.

attachment Emotional relationship between a child and the regular caregiver.

imprinting A primitive form of learning in which some infant animals physically follow and form an attachment to the first moving object they see and/or hear.

working model is a memory structure that gathers together a child's history of interactions with his or her caretakers, the interactions that yielded a particular pattern of attachment. The internal working model provides a template that an individual uses to generate expectations about future social interactions.

One of the most widely used research procedures for assessing attachment is the *Strange Situation Test,* developed by **Mary Ainsworth** and her colleagues (Ainsworth et al., 1978). In the first of several standard episodes, the child is brought into an unfamiliar room filled with toys. With the mother present, the child is encouraged to explore the room and to play. After several minutes, a stranger comes in, talks to the mother, and approaches the child. Next, the mother exits the room. After this brief separation, the mother returns, there is a reunion with her child, and the stranger leaves. The researchers record the child's behaviors at separation and reunion. Researchers have found that children's responses on this test fall into three general categories (Ainsworth et al., 1978):

- *Securely attached* children show some distress when the parent leaves the room; seek proximity, comfort, and contact upon reunion; and then gradually return to play.
- *Insecurely attached–avoidant* children seem aloof and may actively avoid and ignore the parent upon her return.
- *Insecurely attached–anxious/ambivalent* children become quite upset and anxious when the parent leaves; at reunion, they cannot be comforted, and they show anger and resistance to the parent but, at the same time, express a desire for contact.

In samples from several different countries, about 65 percent of babies are classified as securely attached; among the insecurely attached children, about 20 percent are classified as avoidant and 15 percent as anxious (Ein-Dor et al., 2010). 👁

Categorizations based on the Strange Situation Test have proven to be highly predictive of a child's later behavior in a wider variety of settings, particularly the overall division between children who are securely and insecurely attached. For example, children who were securely attached at 12 months played more comfortably with their mothers at 24 months than did their insecurely attached peers (Donovan et al., 2007). Similarly, research has revealed that children who showed secure or insecure behavior in the Strange Situation at 15 months differed widely in their school behavior at age 8 to 9 years (Bohlin et al., 2000). Those children who had been securely attached at 15 months were more popular and less socially anxious than their peers who had been insecurely attached. Similar continuity from the quality of attachment to later years has been demonstrated in 10-year-olds (Urban et al., 1991) and adolescents (Weinfield et al., 1997). Researchers have also developed measures that assess attachment beyond infancy. Those measures also predict an individual's social functioning (Shmueli-Goetz et al., 2008). Researchers also use attachment measures to predict the quality of adults' loving relationships.

Attachment relationships are quite important in young lives. Secure attachment to adults who offer dependable social support enables the child to learn a variety of prosocial behaviors, to take risks, to venture into novel situations, and to seek and accept intimacy in personal relationships.

Parenting Styles As you saw earlier, children bring individual temperaments to their interactions with their parents. Children's temperaments may make parents' best (or worst) efforts at parenting have unexpected consequences. Researchers recognize that children's temperaments and parents' behaviors each influence the other to yield developmental outcomes such as the quality of attachment relationships: As much as parents change their children, children change their parents (Collins et al., 2000).

Even so, researchers have located a **parenting style** that is generally most beneficial. This style resides at the intersection of the two dimensions of *demandingness* and *responsiveness* (Maccoby & Martin, 1983): "Demandingness refers to the parent's willingness to act as a socializing agent, whereas responsiveness refers to the parent's recognition of the child's individuality" (Darling & Steinberg, 1993, p. 492). As shown in **Figure 9**, *authoritative* parents make appropriate demands on their children—they demand that their children conform to appropriate rules of behavior—but are also responsive to their children. They keep channels of communication open to foster their children's ability to regulate themselves (Gray & Steinberg, 1999). This authoritative style is most likely to produce an effective parent–child bond. The contrast, as seen in Figure 9, is to parenting styles that are *authoritarian*—parents apply discipline with little attention to the child's autonomy—or *indulgent*—parents are responsive, but they fail to help children learn about the structure of social rules in which they must live—or *neglecting*—parents neither apply discipline nor are they responsive to their children's individuality.

Konrad Lorenz, the researcher who pioneered the study of imprinting, graphically demonstrates what can happen when young animals become imprinted on someone other than their mother. Why is imprinting important for many animal species?

👁 Watch the Video *Separation Anxiety* on MyPsychLab

parenting style The manner in which parents rear their children; an authoritative parenting style, which balances demandingness and responsiveness, is seen as the most effective.

FIGURE 9 A Classification
of Parenting Styles

Parent's Responsiveness

		Accepting Responsive Child-centered	Rejecting Unresponsive Parent-centered
Parent's Demandingness	Demanding, controlling	Authoritative-reciprocal High in bidirectional communication	Authoritarian Power assertive
	Undemanding, low in control attempts	Indulgent	Neglecting, ignoring, indifferent, uninvolved

Parenting styles can be classified with respect to the two dimensions of demandingness—the parent's willingness to act as a socializing agent—and responsiveness—the parent's recognition of the child's individuality. The authoritative style is most likely to produce an effective parent–child bond.

As you might expect, parenting styles have an impact on children's attachment relationships. Children whose parents use an authoritative style are more likely to be securely attached through childhood into adolescence (Karavasilis et al., 2003). Still, the impact of parenting may depend, in part, on a child's particular genetic make-up.

A team of researchers assessed 601 children to determine which versions of the mineralocorticoid receptor (MR) gene they had inherited (Luijk et al., 2011). When the children were, on average, 14.7 months old, their attachment security was evaluated using the Strange Situation Test. During the same visit to the laboratory, observers watched the mothers' behavior toward their children. The observations yielded two measures of the mothers' behavior: maternal sensitive responsiveness reflected a mother's sensitivity toward and cooperation with her child; maternal extreme insensitivity reflected a mother's harsh behaviors, including withdrawal from and neglect of the child. The data indicated that both genes and environment mattered. For children who inherited at least one copy of the "minor" version of the MR gene, sensitive responsiveness led to greater attachment security and extreme insensitivity led to lower attachment security. Attachment security was unaffected by maternal behaviors for children who did not inherit a "minor" version of the gene.

Other research suggests that children's outcomes can improve when parenting improves. For example, one study followed over 1,000 children and their mothers from when the children were 15 months old until they began first grade (NICHD Early Child Care Research Network, 2006). The researchers assessed the children's attachment relationships at 15 months in the Strange Situation. Evaluations of the mothers' parenting styles were based on videotapes of their interactions with their children. The researchers analyzed the videotapes to see whether the mothers' parenting styles changed over the course of the three-year project. Changes in mothers' parenting style had an impact on the fates of the insecurely attached children: When parenting quality improved, children's outcomes were

consistently better than when parenting quality decreased. Results of this sort encourage researchers to design interventions to improve parenting practices (Van Zeijl et al., 2006). As we have seen, those interventions should also be responsive to children's particular genetic inheritance.

A close interactive relationship with loving adults is a child's first step toward healthy physical growth and normal socialization. As the original attachment to the primary caregiver extends to other family members, they too become models for new ways of thinking and behaving. From these early attachments, children develop the ability to respond to their own needs and to the needs of others.

Contact Comfort and Social Experience What do children obtain from the attachment bond? Sigmund Freud and other psychologists argued that babies become attached to their parents because the parents provide them with food—their most basic physical need. This view is called the *cupboard theory* of attachment. If the cupboard theory were correct, children should thrive as long as they are adequately fed. Does this seem right?

Harry Harlow (1958) did not believe that the cupboard theory explained the importance of attachment. He set out to test the cupboard theory against his own hypothesis that infants might also attach to those who provide **contact comfort** (Harlow & Zimmerman, 1958). Harlow separated macaque monkeys from their mothers at birth and placed them in cages, where they had access to two artificial "mothers": a wire one and a terry cloth one. Harlow found that the baby monkeys nestled close to the terry cloth mother and spent little time on the wire one. They did this even when only the wire mother gave milk! The baby monkeys also used the cloth mother as a source of comfort when frightened and as a base of operations when exploring new stimuli. When a fear stimulus (for example, a toy bear beating a drum) was introduced, the baby monkeys would run to the cloth mother. When novel and intriguing stimuli were introduced, the baby monkeys would

....

contact comfort Comfort derived from an infant's physical contact with the mother or caregiver.

gradually venture out to explore and then return to the terry cloth mother before exploring further.

Further studies by Harlow and his colleagues found that the monkeys' formation of a strong attachment to the mother substitute was not sufficient for healthy social development. At first, the experimenters thought the young monkeys with terry cloth mothers were developing normally, but a very different picture emerged when it was time for the female monkeys who had been raised in this way to become mothers. Monkeys who had been deprived of chances to interact with other responsive monkeys in their early lives had trouble forming normal social and sexual relationships in adulthood.

Let's see now what lessons research with monkeys holds for human deprivation.

Human Deprivation Tragically, human societies have sometimes created circumstances in which children are deprived of contact comfort. Many studies have shown that a lack of close, loving relationships in infancy affects physical growth and even survival. In 1915, a doctor at Johns Hopkins Hospital reported that, despite adequate physical care, 90 percent of the infants admitted to orphanages in Baltimore

How did Harlow demonstrate the importance of contact comfort for normal social development?

....

◉ Watch the Video *Classic Footage of Harlow's Monkeys: Contact Comfort* on MyPsychLab

died within the first year. Studies of hospitalized infants over the next 30 years found that, despite adequate nutrition, the children often developed respiratory infections and fevers of unknown origin, failed to gain weight, and showed general signs of physiological deterioration (Bowlby, 1969; Spitz & Wolf, 1946).

Contemporary studies continue to demonstrate patterns of disruption. For example, one study compared attachment outcomes for children raised at home to those for children largely (90 percent of their lives) raised in institutions (Zeanah et al., 2005). The researchers found that 74 percent of the home-reared children had secure attachments; for institution-reared children, only 20 percent had secure attachments. Moreover, a lack of normal social contact may have a long-lasting effect on children's brain development. One study measured children's brain responses to pictures of faces displaying happy, angry, fearful, and sad expressions (Moulson et al., 2009). By comparison to children being reared by their families, children who were living in institutions showed disruptions in their brain responses to emotional expressions.

Unfortunately, no matter what the setting in which children live, there is a potential for abuse. In a recent analysis, the U.S. government found that about 125,000 children experienced physical abuse in a single year, and roughly 66,700 experienced sexual abuse (U.S. Department of Health and Human Services, 2010). One study looked at the psychological well-being of 2,759 adults who had been sexually abused as children (Cutajar et al., 2010). Of that group, 23 percent had sought mental health services compared to 8 percent of a control sample that was matched for sex and age. Instances of child abuse provide psychologists with a very important agenda: to determine what types of interventions are in the best interest of the child. In the United States, roughly 424,000 children and youths were living in some type of foster care (such as a foster home or group residence) (Child Welfare Information Gateway, 2011. Are these children always happy to be removed from their abusive homes? The answer is complex because even abused children have often formed an attachment to their caretakers: The children may remain loyal to their natural family and hope that everything could be put right if they were allowed to return. This is one reason that much research attention is focused on designing intervention programs to reunite families (Miller et al., 2006).

In this section, you have seen how experiences during childhood have an impact on later social development. Let's now shift our focus to later periods of life, beginning with adolescence.

Social Development in Adolescence

Earlier in the chapter, adolescence was defined by physical changes. In this section, those changes will serve as background to social experiences. Because the individual has reached a certain level of physical and mental maturity, new social and personal challenges present themselves. We will first consider the general experience of adolescence and then turn to the individual's changing social world.

The Experience of Adolescence The traditional view of adolescence predicts a uniquely tumultuous period of life, characterized by extreme mood swings and unpredictable,

Martin Rogers/Getty Images

difficult behavior: "storm and stress." This view can be traced back to romantic writers of the late 18th and early 19th centuries, such as Goethe. The storm-and-stress conception of adolescence was strongly propounded by **G. Stanley Hall,** the first psychologist of the modern era to write at length about adolescent development (1904). Following Hall, the major proponents of this view have been psychoanalytic theorists working within the Freudian tradition (for example, Blos, 1965; Freud, 1946, 1958). Some of them have argued that not only is extreme turmoil a normal part of adolescence but that failure to exhibit such turmoil is a sign of arrested development. **Anna Freud** wrote that "to be normal during the adolescent period is by itself abnormal" (1958, p. 275).

Two early pioneers in cultural anthropology, **Margaret Mead** (1928) and **Ruth Benedict** (1938), argued that the storm-and-stress theory is not applicable to many non-Western cultures. They described cultures in which children gradually take on more and more adult responsibilities without any sudden stressful transition or period of indecision and turmoil. Contemporary research has confirmed that the experience of adolescence differs across cultures (Arnett, 1999). Those cross-cultural differences argue against strictly biological theories of adolescent experience. Instead, researchers focus on the transitions children are expected to make in different cultures.

Most researchers reject "storm and stress" as a biologically programmed aspect of development. Nonetheless, people typically do experience more extreme emotions and more conflict as they pass from childhood into adolescence. The discussion of physical development noted that brain areas that control emotional responses show growth during adolescence. That brain maturation may explain why adolescents experience both extreme positive and extreme negative emotions (Casey et al., 2008; Steinberg, 2008).

Identity Formation Recall Erikson's claim that the essential task of adolescence is to weather a crisis to discover one's true identity. **James Marcia** (1966, 1980) expanded on Erikson's analysis to claim that each adolescent can be classified according to an *identity status*:

- *Identity diffusion*: An individual has not yet gone through an identity crisis or made commitments to goals and values.
- *Foreclosure*: An individual has never gone through an identity crisis because he or she committed, for example, to parental values.
- *Moratorium*: An individual is actively involved in exploring different identities but has not yet made a commitment.
- *Identity achievement*: An individual has explored different identities and made a tentative commitment to one.

Longitudinal analyses of adolescents' experiences suggest that indivudals often follow a progression that starts with identity diffusion and ends with identity achievement (Meeus, 2011). In addition, adolescents who have achieved more mature identities tend to experience greater well-being. 👁

Adolescents' quest to achieve identity helps explain the conflicts they have with their parents. For cultures like the

....

👁 **Watch** the **Video** *What's In It For Me?: Identity* on MyPsychLab

majority culture in the United States, one consequence is that children attempt to achieve *independence* from their parents. Parents and their adolescent children must weather a transition in their relationship from one in which a parent has unquestioned authority to one in which the adolescent seeks reasonable autonomy to make important decisions (Daddis, 2011). Consider the results of a study that followed 1,330 adolescents from age 11 to age 14 (McGue et al., 2005). As 14-year-olds, these adolescents reported greater conflict with their parents than they had at age 11. At age 14, the adolescents' parents were less involved in their lives; the adolescents had less positive regard for their parents and they believed that their parents had less positive regard for them. These data illustrate some of the relationship costs that arise when children strive for independence.

Still, adolescents' conflicts with their parents often do not lead to harmful outcomes. Most adolescents at most times are able to use their parents as ready sources of practical and emotional support (Smetana et al., 2006). For that reason, many adolescents have conflicts with their parents that leave their basic relationship unharmed. When conflict occurs in the context of otherwise positive relationships, there may be few negative consequences. However, in the context of negative relationships, adolescent conflict can lead to other problems such as social withdrawal and delinquency (Adams & Laursen, 2007). Thus, family contexts may explain why some adolescents experience unusual levels of "storm and stress."

Peer Relationships Much of the study of social development in adolescence focuses on the changing roles of family (or adult caretakers) and friends (Smetana et al., 2006). We have already seen that attachments to adults form soon after birth. Children also begin to have friends at very young ages. Adolescence, however, marks the first period in which peers appear to compete with parents to shape a person's attitudes and behaviors. Adolescents participate in peer relations at the three levels of friendships, cliques, and crowds (Brown & Klute, 2003). Over the course of these years, adolescents come to count increasingly on their one-on-one *friendships* to provide them with help and support (Bauminger et al., 2008; Branje et al., 2007). *Cliques* are groups that most often consist of 6 to 12 individuals. Membership in these groups may change over time, but they tend to be drawn along lines of, for example, age and race (Smetana et al., 2006). Finally, *crowds* are the larger groups such as "jocks" or "nerds" that exist more loosely among individuals of this age. Through interaction with peers at these three levels, adolescents gradually define the social component of their developing identities, determining the kinds of people they chose to be and the kinds of relationships they choose to pursue.

The peer relationships that adolescents form are quite important to social development. They give individuals opportunities to learn how to function in what can often be demanding social circumstances. In that sense, peer relationships play a positive role in preparing adolescents for their futures. At the same time, parents often worry—with reasonable cause—about negative aspects of peer influence (Brechwald & Prinstein, 2011; Dishion & Tipsord, 2011). In fact, adolescents are more likely to engage in risky behavior when they are under the influence of their peers.

Critical Thinking in Your Life

HOW DOES DAY CARE AFFECT CHILDREN'S DEVELOPMENT?

If you plan to have both children and a career, you're likely to face a difficult question: Is it wise to put your children in day care? Fortunately, psychological research can be brought to bear on this important question.

A team of researchers has been studying a group of 1,364 children since they were 1 month old; the children are now in their late teens (Vandell et al., 2010). Some children in the sample were tended by their mothers for the whole period before they started school; many others experienced various types of day care for small or large parts of each day. The research team's earliest publications focused on day care's impact on children's attachment security. The data indicated that children who attended day care were at risk for insecure attachments but only if it was also true that their mothers were insensitive to their needs (NICHD Early Child Care Research Network, 1997). Otherwise, children who attended day care had equally secure attachments as their peers who remained at home.

As the children have gotten older, the research team has measured their intellectual and social development. Those studies have confirmed both positive and negative consequences of time spent in day care. On the positive side, the children who experienced day care have often performed better on standardized tests of, for example, memory and vocabulary (Belsky et al., 2007). On the negative side, the children who experienced day care have often had more social and behavior problems in their classrooms. However, the likelihood of social problems depends on the exact type of day care. Children's outcomes were better when they experienced quality day care (Belsky et al., 2010). But what does "quality" mean?

Alison Clarke-Stewart (1993; Clarke-Stewart & Alhusen, 2005), an expert on day care, has summarized the research literature to provide guidelines for quality day care. Some recommendations relate to the physical comfort of the children:

- The day care center should be physically comfortable and safe.
- There should be at least one caretaker for every six or seven children (more for children under age 3).

Other recommendations cover educational and psychological aspects of the day care curriculum:

- Children should have a free choice of activities intermixed with explicit lessons.
- Children should be taught social problem-solving skills.

Clarke-Stewart has also suggested that day care providers should share the qualities of good parents:

- Caregivers should be responsive to the children's needs and actively involved in their activities.
- Caregivers should not put undue restrictions on the children.
- Caregivers should have sufficient flexibility to recognize differences among the needs of individual children.

If these guidelines are followed, quality day care can be provided to all children whose parents work outside the home.

- If you are trying to compare outcomes for children who do and do not participate in day care, on what dimensions should you try to match the children?
- How might you assess whether day care providers interact with children in appropriate ways?

A team of researchers wished to examine the impact of adults and peers on teenagers' driving (Simons-Morton et al., 2011). To do so, the researchers outfitted the cars of newly licensed drivers (with a mean age of 16.4 years) with equipment that recorded the details of the teens' driving. The equipment allowed the researchers to determine when the teens' driving had resulted in crashes or near crashes. The cars also had video cameras that enabled the researchers to determine whether the teens' passengers were adults or friends. The teens provided ratings to indicate which of them had risk-taking friends. In the 18-month period of the study, the teens had 37 crashes and 242 near crashes. When the teens had an adult passenger, their crash/near crash rates were 75 percent lower than when they did not. Meanwhile, among teens with risk-taking friends, the crash/near crash rate was 96 percent higher!

This study confirms a general tendency for peer influence to shift adolescents toward riskier behaviors. However, some adolescents are more susceptible to peer influence than others—and that susceptibility has consequences. In a longitudinal study, students who were more susceptible to their close friends' influence at the study's outset were more likely to have problems with drugs and alcohol one year later (Allen et al., 2006). Note, once again, that adolescence need not be a time of storm and stress. However, research of this type indicates the patterns of behavior that put some adolescents at risk.

Social Development in Adulthood

Erikson defined two tasks of adulthood as intimacy and generativity. Freud identified the needs of adulthood as *Lieben und Arbeiten*, or love and work. Abraham Maslow (1968, 1970) described the needs of this period of life as love and belonging,

What might happen when an adolescent driver has risk-taking friends as his passengers?

which, when satisfied, develop into the needs for success and esteem. Other theorists label these needs as affiliation or social acceptance and achievement or competence needs. The shared core of these theories is that adulthood is a time in which both social relationships and personal accomplishments take on special priority. This section will track these themes across the breadth of adulthood.

Intimacy   Erikson described **intimacy** as the capacity to make a full commitment to another person. Intimacy, which can occur in both friendships and romantic relationships, requires openness, courage, ethical strength, and usually some compromise of one's personal preferences. Research has consistently confirmed Erikson's supposition that social intimacy is a prerequisite for a sense of psychological well-being across the adult life stages (Kesebir & Diener, 2008). There are forces that affect people's particular choices for friends, romantic partners, and sexual partners, but here, the focus is on the role intimate relationships play in social development.

Young adulthood is the period in which many people enter into marriages or other stable relationships. In 2010, 13.6 percent of 20- to 24-year-olds were married; among 25- to 29-year-olds that figure increased to 38.2 percent (U.S. Census Bureau, 2011). In addition, many other individuals live with partners to whom they are not married. In 2007, 4.9 percent of U.S. households had opposite-sex partners, and 0.7 percent of households had same-sex partners (U.S. Census Bureau, 2008). In recent years, some states have allowed same-sex couples to enter into civil commitments or legal marriages. Researchers try to understand the consequences of all these types of relationships for social development in adulthood. For example, research attention has focused on differences and similarities between heterosexual and homosexual couples (Balsam et al., 2008; Roisman et al., 2008). Studies suggest that the strategies heterosexuals and homosexuals use to maintain relationships over time have much in common: Both types of couples try to remain close by, for example, sharing tasks and activities together (Haas & Stafford, 2005).

intimacy The capacity to make a full commitment—sexual, emotional, and moral—to another person.

However, heterosexual couples obtain more societal support for their relationships (Herek, 2006). To combat a lack of social acceptance, homosexual couples often take special measures to maintain relationships, such as being publicly "out" as a couple.

Each of these types of relationships increases the role of family in adults' social lives. Families also grow when individuals decide to include children in their lives. What may surprise you, however, is that the birth of children can often pose a threat to the overall happiness of a couple (Lawrence et al., 2007; Twenge et al., 2003). Why might that be? Researchers have focused on differences in the way that men and women make the transition to parenthood in heterosexual relationships (Cowan & Cowan, 2000; Dew & Wilcox, 2011). In contemporary Western society, marriages are more often founded on notions of equality between men and women than was true in the past. However, children's births can have the effect of pushing husbands and wives in the direction of more traditional gender roles. The wife may feel too much of the burden of child care; the husband may feel too much pressure to support a family. The net effect may be that, following the birth of a child, the marriage changes in ways that both spouses find to be negative. In recent years, researchers have begun to study gay male and lesbian couples raising children. As you might expect, homosexual relationships are less troubled by concerns about gender roles in the context of parenting (Goldberg & Perry-Jenkins, 2007; Patterson, 2002). Even so, in parallel to results for heterosexual couples, a study of lesbian couples found decreasing love and increasing conflict across the transition to parenthood (Goldberg & Sayer, 2006).

For many couples, satisfaction with the marriage continues to decline because of conflicts as the child or children

What factors have an impact on marital happiness and the likelihood that couples will stay together?

pass through their adolescent years. Contrary to the cultural stereotype, many parents look forward to the time when their youngest child leaves home and leaves them with an "empty nest" (Gorchoff et al., 2008). Parents may enjoy their children most when they are no longer under the same roof. Are you discouraged from having children? I certainly hope not! The goal, as always, is to make you aware of research that can help you anticipate and interpret the patterns in your own life.

You've now learned that marriages are happier, on the whole, when the spouses reach late adulthood. However, you're certainly aware that many marriages end in divorce long before late adulthood arrives. Researchers would like to be able to determine which couples are fundamentally mismatched and which couples could avoid divorce (Amato, 2010). Studies that follow couples over time have identified a number of factors that put marriages at risk, including frequent conflict, infidelity, and low levels of love and trust.

Let's conclude this section where we began, with the idea that social intimacy is a prerequisite for psychological well-being. What matters most is not the quantity of social interaction but the quality. As you grow into older adulthood, you will begin to protect your need for intimacy by selecting those individuals who provide the most direct emotional support.

Let's turn now to a second aspect of adult development, generativity.

Generativity Those people who have established an appropriate foundation of intimate relationships are most often able to turn their focus to issues of **generativity.** This is a commitment beyond oneself to family, work, society, or future generations—typically a crucial step in development in one's 30s and 40s (Whitbourne et al., 2009). An orientation toward the greater good allows adults to establish a sense of psychological well-being that offsets any longing for youth. Let's consider an example of how generativity functions in an academic setting.

Featured Study

Many professors play an important role as mentors for younger colleagues. A team of researchers wished to demonstrate that professors' individual levels of generativity would help predict how successful they would be in their mentorship roles (Zacher et al., 2011). A research assistant to each of 128 professors provided information about each professor's level of generativity by responding to questions like, "My supervisor devotes more energy to building up the next generation of scientists than to getting ahead him-/herself" (p. 244). The research assistants also evaluated the professors' success as mentors. The data suggested that professors higher in generativity were able to remain successful as mentors later in life than professors with lower generativity.

This study illustrates how people with greater generativity continue to pass along their wisdom to future generations.

....

generativity A commitment beyond one's self and one's partner to family, work, society, and future generations; typically, a crucial state in development in one's 30s and 40s.

sex difference One of the biologically based characteristics that distinguish males from females.

Note also that in a sample of 2,507 adults between the ages of 35 and 74, higher generativity was associated with greater reports of well-being along dimensions such as self-acceptance and personal growth (Rothrauff & Cooney, 2008).

Late adulthood is a time when goals are shifted; priorities change when the future does not apparently flow as freely. Across that change in priorities, however, older adults preserve their sense of the value of their lives. Erikson defined the last crisis of adulthood to be the conflict between ego integrity and despair. The data suggest that few adults look back over their lives with despair. In fact, people report more emotional well-being as they age (Carstensen et al., 2011). Most older adults review their lives—and look to the future—with a sense of wholeness and satisfaction.

We have worked our way through the life span by considering social and personal aspects of childhood, adolescence, and adulthood. To close out the chapter, let's consider two particular domains in which experience changes over time, the domains of sex and gender differences and moral development.

Stop *and* Review

① At what life stage did Erik Erikson suggest people navigate the crisis of intimacy versus isolation?
② What long-term consequences have been demonstrated for children's early attachment quality?
③ What dimensions define parenting styles?
④ In what levels of peer relationships do adolescents engage?
⑤ What impact does the birth of a child often have on marital satisfaction?

CRITICAL THINKING   Recall the study that examined risk taking by teenage drivers. Why might the researchers focused on newly licensed drivers?

✓•【**Study** and **Review** on **MyPsychLab**

SEX AND GENDER DIFFERENCES

One type of information most children begin to acquire in the first few months in life is that there are two categories of people in their social world: males and females. Over time, children learn that there are many respects in which the psychological experiences of males and females are quite similar. However, when differences do occur, children acquire an understanding that some of those differences arise from biology and others arise from cultural expectations. Biologically based characteristics that distinguish males and females are referred to as **sex differences.** These characteristics include different reproductive functions and differences in hormones and anatomy. However, the first differences children perceive are entirely social: They begin to sense differences between males and females well before they understand anything about anatomy. In contrast to biological sex, **gender** is a psychological phenomenon referring to learned sex-related behaviors and attitudes. Cultures vary in how strongly gender is linked to daily activities and in the amount of tolerance for what is perceived as cross-gender behavior. In this section, we consider both sex differences and gender development: the nature and nurture of children's sense of maleness or femaleness.

Sex Differences

Starting at about six weeks after conception, male fetuses begin to diverge from female fetuses when the male testes develop and begin to produce the hormone *testosterone*. The presence or absence of testosterone plays a critical role in determining whether a child will be born with male or female anatomy. Prenatal exposure to testerone also plays an important role in establishing sex-typical behaviors and characteristics (Hines, 2011). Researchers have carried out studies in which they determine the level of testosterone in the amniotic fluid of each individual participant. The researchers have correlated those fetal testosterone levels with, for example, the quality of each boy's or girl's social relationships when they were 4 years old (Knickmeyer et al., 2005). In general, boys had higher levels of fetal testosterone than girls. Against that background, individuals' higher levels of fetal testosterone were associated with poorer social relationships for both boys and girls. These results suggest that the extent to which individuals conform to expectations for male and female behavior may depend, in part, on their prenatal hormonal environment (Morris et al., 2004).

Brain scans have revealed consistent structural differences between men's and women's brains. Men typically have bigger brains than women (Lenroot & Giedd, 2010). Appropriate comparisons across the sexes adjust for that overall variation. The differences that remain after those adjustments are intriguing with respect to behavioral dissimilarities between men and women. For example, MRI scans reveal that the regions of the frontal lobe that play an important role in regulating social behavior and emotional functioning are relatively bigger in women than in men (Welborn et al., 2009). To confirm that sex differences of this type are biological—rather than the product of a lifetime of experience as men or women in particular cultural roles—researchers have undertaken similar studies with children and adolescents (Lenroot et al., 2007). Those studies confirm that sex differences emerge in the brain as a part of ordinary biological development.

Other analyses of sex differences focus on the distinct ways in which men's and women's brains accomplish cognitive and emotional tasks (Canli et al., 2002). Consider the brain processes engaged when the two sexes view humorous pictures.

Featured Study

Fifteen men and 14 women underwent fMRI scans while viewing 80 funny and 80 neutral pictures (Kohn et al., 2011). After viewing each image for 7 seconds, the participants answered "How funny was this picture?" on a scale of 1 to 5. Overall, women found more humor in the funny pictures than did the men (with average ratings of 3.79 versus 3.48). The women's and men's patterns of brain activities suggested an origin for the difference in these judgments: Women showed relatively more activity in regions of the brain, such as the amygdala, that play a role in emotional responses. The relatively lower activity of men's emotion areas may have resulted in less appreciation of the humor.

Further studies of the brain at work confirm sex differences in the encoding and recognition of emotionally laden stimuli (Cahill et al., 2004; Derntl et al., 2010). These studies suggest that some of the behavioral differences that set men and women apart can be traced to biological differences rather than to cultural roles.

Gender Identity and Gender Stereotypes

You have just seen that important aspects of men's and women's behavior are shaped by biological differences. However, cultural expectations also have an important impact on **gender identity**—an individual's sense of maleness or femaleness. Very early in life, children start to understand that the world is divided into two genders (Martin & Ruble, 2010). For example, 10- to 14-month-old children already demonstrate a preference for a video showing the abstract movements of a child of the same sex (Kujawski & Bower, 1993). In their earliest years, children begin to understand that they are either boys or girls—they settle into their gender identity. At the same time, they acquire knowledge of **gender stereotypes,** which are beliefs about attributes and behaviors regarded as appropriate for males and females in a particular culture.

Researchers have documented the time course with which most children acquire those gender stereotypes (Martin & Ruble, 2010). Through the preschool years, children's experience in the world provides them with knowledge about cultural expectations for men and women. Between ages 5 and 7, children consolidate that knowledge into gender stereotypes. In fact, those are the years of the children's greatest rigidity with respect to those stereotypes. For example, one study assessed children's gender stereotypes by asking them to indicate which children "like to play toy shop" or "are cruel and hurt others on purpose" (Trautner et al., 2005). For each statement, children dropped cards into different boxes that represented *only males, more males than females, equal numbers of males and females, more females than males,* or *only females.* Children of ages 5 to 7 gave the most "only" responses, indicating the strongest gender stereotypes. Older children showed more flexibility in their thinking about gender and behavior. That is, they were more likely to indicate that both males and females engage in a variety of behaviors. Thus, by around age 8, children have begun to understand that there are also similarities between boys and girls.

gender A psychological phenomenon that refers to learned sex-related behaviors and attitudes of males and females.

gender identity One's sense of maleness or femaleness; usually includes awareness and acceptance of one's biological sex.

gender stereotype Belief about attributes and behaviors regarded as appropriate for males and females in a particular culture.

How do children acquire the information that leads to gender identity and gender stereotypes? Parents provide one ready source. Parents dress their sons and daughters differently, give them different kinds of toys to play with, and communicate with them differently. When parents play with their children, they consider some toys to be "masculine" and some to be "feminine." When they play with their children, they are more likely to choose gender-appropriate toys—though that preference may be stronger for play with boys than for play with girls (Wood et al., 2002). In general, children receive encouragement from their parents to engage in sex-typed activities (McHale et al., 2003).

Peers provide another important sources of gender socialization. **Eleanor Maccoby** (2002) argues, for example, that young children are segregationists—they seek out peers of the same sex even when adults are not supervising them or in spite of adult encouragement for mixed-group play. Maccoby believes that many of the differences in gender behavior among children are the results of peer relationships. In fact, boys and girls show consistent differences in their patterns of social interaction. For example, at least by the age of 6, boys prefer to interact in groups, whereas girls prefer one-on-one interactions (Benenson et al., 1997; Benenson & Heath, 2006). Girls are more likely to engage in social conversations and disclose information about themselves; boys are more likely to engage in rough-and-tumble play (Rose & Rudolph, 2006). These differences continue as children grow older. The friendships of adolescent girls are likely to display greater intimacy and more self-disclosure; the friendships of adolescent boys are likley to display more competition and excitement (Perry & Pauletti, 2011).

We have been considering factors that affect gender development across all children. However, as with other domains of development, it's important to acknowledge individual differences among children. Consider a study that examined children's gender-typed behaviors over a six-year period.

The mothers of 5,501 children provided information about their gender-typed behaviors when the children were age 2 (Golombok et al., 2008). The mothers completed the Preschool Activities Inventory (PSAI), *which asked them to indicate, for example, how often their children had played with jewelry or engaged in fighting in the last month. The mothers provided PSAI ratings again when their children were 3 and 5 years old. When the children were 8, they reported their own behavior by completing the* Children's Activities Inventory (CAI). *For this inventory, children listened to pairs of statements that described different types of children: "Some children play with jewelry. . . . but other children don't play with jewelry" (p. 1586). The children indicated how similar they felt to the two types of children. Based on these longitudinal assessments, the researchers concluded that the likelihood that individual children will engage in gender-typed behavior remains very stable over time.*

Why is the children's behavior so stable? The researchers pointed to both nature and nurture. With respect to nature, the researchers suggested that children may experience prenatal environments that cause their brains to be relatively more

How do parents and peers influence children's acquisition of gender roles?

masculine or feminine. With respect to nurture, the researchers considered differences among the behaviors of both parents and peers. Parents who have less flexible gender stereotypes may also have children who produce more gender-typed behavior. In addition, children may seek friends who are similar to them with respect to their levels of gender-typed behavior—creating a context for those behaviors to be stable over time.

We have briefly considered how and why it is that boys and girls experience social development in different fashions. Let's now consider moral development.

Stop *and* Review

① What is the distinction between sex differences and gender differences?
② What does research suggest about differences in brain activity between men and women for the processing of humorous pictures?
③ In what ways are young children "segregationists"?

CRITICAL THINKING   Recall the study on the stability of gender-typed behaviors. Why might the researchers have switched to self-reports from the children at age 8?

✓●⌐**Study** and **Review** on **MyPsychLab**

MORAL DEVELOPMENT

So far we have seen, across the life span, how important it is to develop close social relationships. Let's now consider another aspect of what it means to live as part of a social group: On many occasions you must judge your behavior according to the needs of society, rather than just according to your own needs. This is the basis of *moral behavior.* **Morality** is a system of

morality A system of beliefs and values that ensures that individuals will keep their obligations to others in society and will behave in ways that do not interfere with the rights and interests of others.

beliefs, values, and underlying judgments about the rightness or wrongness of human acts.

Take a moment to think about the types of moral judgments that you make on a day-to-day basis. As I was preparing to revise this section of *Psychology and Life*, I spent some time compiling a list of moments that I thought were interesting with respect to my own engagement with moral issues. For example, I recently watched a movie that showed a bad guy on the telephone trying to con a helpless elderly woman. The scam was so amusing that I couldn't help but root for the con man to succeed. However, as I thought back on the scene I realized that my enjoyment was morally suspect. How could I want the bad guy to win, and against such an innocent victim? Two other items from my list of moral issues emerged in a visit to a grocery store. When I got to the store, the parking lot was very crowded. The only empty spaces were far from the entrance. Still, no one (including me) cheated and parked in the spaces designated for people with handicaps. Why not? Meanwhile, once I got in the store, I witnessed an argument between a customer and the store manager. The manager had caught the customer feeding grapes to her son, before she had paid for them. The mother was arguing both that "Everyone does it" and that "Stores expect people to do it, which is why their prices are so high." As the argument drew a crowd, it became clear that there were individual differences in people's responses. About equal numbers were siding with the customer and with the manager. This episode makes it clear why studies of moral development often focus on individual differences.

Before we consider how moral development unfolds for each individual, we want to consider the question for the whole human species: How did morality evolve? To answer that question, contemporary researchers have built on Charles Darwin's foundational observations about how humans function as a social species (Krebs, 2008). From an evolutionary perspective, moral behaviors are consequences of adaptive solutions to situations that have recurred across human history. For example, many early human endeavors (such as killing large game or defending territory) required cooperation among large groups of people. Thus, it was adaptive for humans to evolve a disposition "to resolve fundamental social dilemmas in cooperative ways" (Krebs, p. 154): "Although two self-serving individuals who have little to gain by resolving their differences may reach an impasse or end up in a fight, it is in the interest of those who have a lot to gain to resolve their conflicts in mutually acceptable ways and to be receptive to fair, balanced, and reversible solutions" (Krebs, p. 163). In contemporary times, moral questions often have a dimension of self-interested versus cooperative behavior: Should a person drive his or her car less so that everyone can breathe cleaner air? The evolutionary perspective suggests that our reflexive responses to such questions is part of our genetic inheritance (Haidt, 2007).

However, even if people share some evolved moral responses, what constitutes moral and immoral behavior in particular situations can become a matter of heated public debate. Perhaps it is no coincidence, therefore, that the study of moral development has also proved to be controversial. The controversy begins with the foundational research of Lawrence Kohlberg.

Kohlberg's Stages of Moral Reasoning

Lawrence Kohlberg (1964, 1981) founded his theory of moral development by studying *moral reasoning*—the judgments people make about what courses of action are correct or incorrect in particular situations. Kohlberg's theory was shaped by the earlier insights of Jean Piaget (1965), who sought to tie the development of moral judgment to a child's general cognitive development. Piaget developed his theory by telling children pairs of stories. He asked the children to explain why they thought one of the children was naughtier than the other. Here's an example of contrasting stories (Piaget, 1965, p. 122):

A. A little boy who is called John is in his room. He is called to dinner. He goes into the dining room. But behind the door there was a chair, and on the chair there was a tray with fifteen cups on it. John couldn't have known that there was all this behind the door. He goes in, the door knocks against the tray, bang go the fifteen cups and they all get broken!

B. Once there was a little boy whose name was Henry. One day when his mother was out he tried to get some jam out of the cupboard. He climbed up on to a chair and stretched out his arm. But the jam was too high up and he couldn't reach it and have any. But while he was trying to get it he knocked over a cup. The cup fell down and broke.

As an adult, do you think John or Henry has committed the naughtier act? Younger children generally choose John. To the preoperational child, someone who breaks 15 cups accidentally is naughtier than someone who breaks one cup intentionally. In Piaget's view, as the child progresses through the stages of cognitive growth, he or she assigns differing relative weights to the *consequences* of an act and to the actor's *intentions*. As the child gets older, the actor's intentions weigh more heavily in the judgment of morality.

Kohlberg expanded Piaget's view to define stages of moral development. Each stage is characterized by a different basis for making moral judgments (see **Table 7**). The lowest level of moral reasoning is based on self-interest; higher levels center on social good, regardless of personal gain. To document these stages, Kohlberg used a series of dilemmas that pit different moral principles against one another:

In one dilemma, a man named Heinz is trying to help his wife obtain a certain drug needed to treat

Table 7 • Kohlberg's Stages of Moral Reasoning

Levels and Stages	Reasons for Moral Behavior
I Preconventional morality	
Stage 1 Pleasure/pain orientation	To avoid pain or not to get caught
Stage 2 Cost–benefit orientation; reciprocity—an eye for an eye	To get rewards
II Conventional morality	
Stage 3 Good-child orientation	To gain acceptance and avoid disapproval
Stage 4 Law and order orientation	To follow rules, avoid censure by authorities
III Principled morality	
Stage 5 Social contract orientation	To promote the society's welfare
Stage 6 Ethical principle orientation	To achieve justice and avoid self-condemnation
Stage 7 Cosmic orientation	To be true to universal principles and feel oneself part of a cosmic direction that transcends social norms

her cancer. An unscrupulous druggist will only sell it to Heinz for ten times more than what the druggist paid. This is much more money than Heinz has and more than he can raise. Heinz becomes desperate, breaks into the druggist's store, and steals the drug for his wife. Should Heinz have done that? Why? An interviewer probes the participant for the reasons for the decision and then scores the answers.

The scoring is based on the *reasons* the person gives for the decision, not on the decision itself. For example, someone who says that the man should steal the drug because of his obligation to his dying wife or that he should not steal the drug because of his obligation to uphold the law (despite his personal feelings) is expressing concern about meeting established obligations and is scored at Stage 4.

Four principles govern Kohlberg's stage model: (1) An individual can be at only one stage at a given time; (2) everyone goes through the stages in a fixed order; (3) each stage is more comprehensive and complex than the preceding; and (4) the same stages occur in every culture. Kohlberg inherited much of this stage philosophy from Piaget, and, in fact, the progression from Stages 1 to 3 appears to match the course of normal cognitive development. The stages proceed in order, and each can be seen to be more cognitively sophisticated than the preceding. Almost all children reach Stage 3 by the age of 13.

Much of the controversy with Kohlberg's theory occurs beyond Stage 3. In Kohlberg's original view, people would continue their moral development in a steady progression beyond level 3. However, not all people attain Stages 4 to 7. In fact, many adults never reach Stage 5, and only a few go beyond it. The content of Kohlberg's later stages appears to be subjective, and it is hard to understand each successive stage as more comprehensive and sophisticated than the preceding. For example, "avoiding self-condemnation," the basis for moral judgments at Stage 6, does not seem obviously more sophisticated than "promoting society's welfare," the basis for Stage 5. Furthermore, Kohlberg's own research ultimately demonstrated that the higher stages are not

found in all cultures (Gibbs et al., 2007). Let's turn now to contemporary research that enlarges Kohlberg's theory to include considerations of gender and culture.

Gender and Cultural Perspectives on Moral Reasoning

Most critiques of Kohlberg's theory take issue with his claims of universality: Kohlberg's later stages have been criticized because they fail to recognize that adult moral judgments may reflect different, but equally moral, principles. In a well-known critique, **Carol Gilligan** (1982) argued that Kohlberg overlooked potential differences between the habitual moral judgments of men and women. Gilligan proposed that women's moral development is based on a standard of *caring for others* and progresses to a stage of self-realization, whereas men base their reasoning on a standard of *justice*. Research has confirmed that concerns about caring and justice are relevant to moral reasoning—but not that these concerns are found especially in women or in men (Jaffee & Hyde, 2000). Although Gilligan's specific proposals have received limited support, men and women do appear to differ in some aspects of moral reasoning. For example, women tend to display more awareness of how their actions affect other people, an ability that is called *moral sensitivity* (You et al., 2011). In addition, men and women show differences in brain activity when they view images (for example, an injured child) that cause an emotional response of compassion (Mercadillo et al., 2011). These brain differences likely relate to the more general sex differences in emotional processing you encountered earlier in the chapter.

Cross-cultural research has also expanded researchers' understanding about the range of concerns that contribute to moral reasoning (Gibbs et al., 2007; Sachdeva et al., 2011). One analysis has identified three types of concern (Jensen, 2008). The first set of concerns relates to *autonomy*: "A focus on people who have needs, desires, and preferences"; "the moral goal is to recognize" people's right "to the fulfillment of these needs and desires" (Jensen, 2008, p. 296). The second set of concerns relates to *community*: A focus on people "as members of social groups such as family, school, and nation"; the moral goal is "the fulfillment of role-based duties to others, and the protections and positive functioning of social groups." The third set of concerns relates to *divinity*: A focus "on people as spiritual or religious entities"; "the moral goal is for the self to become increasingly connected to . . . [the] pure or divine."

If you think through these three types of concerns you can see how their importance might vary cross-culturally. Consider this situation: You see a stranger at the side of the road with a flat tire. Should you stop to help? Suppose you say no. Is that immoral? If you have grown up in the United States, you probably think helping, under these circumstances, is a matter of personal choice, so it isn't immoral. But if you had grown up in India, in a culture that puts considerably more emphasis on interdependence and mutual assistance, you probably *would* view a failure to help as immoral (Miller et al., 1990).

It's also important to recognize that people's life experiences will have an impact on their judgments. Consider individuals who have grown up in circumstances of great violence.

> *The researchers recruited a group of children and adolescents from a highly impoverished area in Bogotá, Columbia (Posada & Wainryb, 2008). A large majority of the participants (88 percent) had witnessed or experienced some severe type of violence: They had, for example, seen people shot at, shot, or killed. The researchers first asked the participants to share their moral judgments in the abstract. The participants answered questions like, "Is it okay or not okay to take other people's things?" On such abstract questions, all the participants presented responses based on norms of justice. They indicated, for example, that it would not be okay to steal. However, the pattern changed when the participants made similar judgments in concrete contexts. For example, the participants read a scenario in which 15-year-old Julio had the opportunity to steal a bicycle from one of "the people who hurt his father and his brother and forced his family to move" (p. 886). After hearing that scenario, participants often indicated their belief that Julio would steal the bicycle. In addition, despite their general aversion to stealing, many participants approved of that behavior in this concrete instance.*

The researchers note that the participants' violent life experiences have not completely overwhelmed ordinary moral development: "Even the impoverished environments of war and displacement present youths with opportunities for reflecting on the intrinsic features of actions that harm others" (p. 896). Still, the researchers speculate that, because of their impact on moral judgments, "contexts underscoring revenge might give rise to cycles of violence" (p. 896). The same behavior that seems very wrong framed against one set of moral concerns may look very right framed against another.

We have now visited several domains in which people undergo developmental change. The final section of the chapter offers some thoughts for your future.

Stop *and* Review

① What are the three major levels of moral reasoning in Kohlberg's theory?

② What distinction did Carol Gilligan believe separates the moral reasoning of men and women?

③ What are three types of concerns people may bring to circumstances of moral reasoning?

CRITICAL THINKING Consider the study that looked at moral judgments by children and adolescents in Columbia. Why might the researchers have chosen scenarios that involved revenge?

✓•⸢ **Study** and **Review** on **MyPsychLab**

LEARNING TO AGE SUCCESSFULLY

Let's now review some of the themes of this chapter, to form a prescription for successful aging. Early in the chapter, I encouraged you to think of development as a type of change that always brings with it gains and losses. In this light, the trick to prospering across the life span is to solidify one's gains and minimize one's losses. Many of the changes that are stereotypically associated with aging are functions of disuse rather than decay. The fundamental advice is straightforward: Keep at it!

How can older adults cope successfully with whatever changes inevitably accompany increasing age? Successful aging might consist of making the most of gains while minimizing the impact of the normal losses that accompany aging. This strategy for successful aging, proposed by psychologists **Paul Baltes** and **Margaret Baltes,** is called **selective optimization with compensation** (Baltes et al., 1992; Freund & Baltes, 1998). *Selective* means that people scale down the number and extent of their goals for themselves. *Optimization* refers to people exercising or training themselves in areas that are of highest priority to them. *Compensation* means that people use alternative ways to deal with losses—for example, choosing age-friendly environments. Let's consider an example:

> *When the concert pianist [Arthur] Rubinstein was asked, in a television interview, how he managed to remain such a successful pianist in his old age, he mentioned three strategies: (1) In old age he performed fewer pieces, (2) he now practiced each piece more frequently, and (3) he produced more ritardandos [slowings of the tempo] in his playing before fast segments, so that the playing speed sounded faster*

selective optimization with compensation A strategy for successful aging in which one makes the most gains while minimizing the impact of losses that accompany normal aging.

than it was in reality. These are examples of selection (fewer pieces), optimization (more practice), and compensation (increased use of contrast in speed). (Baltes, 1993, p. 590)

This example provides a template for how you might think about your own life. Although the selective optimization perspective originated in research on the aging process, it is a good way to characterize the choices you must make throughout your life span. You should always try to select the goals most important to you, optimize your performance with respect to those goals, and compensate when progress toward those goals is blocked. That's the final bit of advice about life span development. I hope you will age wisely and well!

Recapping Main Points

Studying Development

- Researchers collect normative, longitudinal, and cross-sectional data to document change.

Physical Development across the Life Span

- Environmental factors can affect physical development while a child is still in the womb.
- Newborns and infants possess a remarkable range of capabilities: They are prewired for survival.
- Through puberty, adolescents achieve sexual maturity.
- Some physical changes in late adulthood are consequences of disuse, not inevitable deterioration.

Cognitive Development across the Life Span

- Piaget's key ideas about cognitive development include development of schemes, assimilation, accommodation, and the four-stage theory of discontinuous development. The four stages are sensorimotor, preoperational, concrete operational, and formal operational.
- Many of Piaget's theories are now being altered by ingenious research paradigms that reveal infants and young children to be more competent than Piaget had thought.
- Children develop a theory of mind, which is the ability to explain and predict other people's behavior based on an understanding of their mental states.
- Cross-cultural research has questioned the universality of cognitive developmental theories.
- Age-related declines in cognitive functioning are typically evident in only some abilities.

Acquiring Language

- Many researchers believe that humans have an inborn language-making capacity. Even so, interactions with adult speakers is an essential part of the language acquisition process.
- Like scientists, children develop hypotheses about the meanings and grammar of their language. These hypotheses are often constrained by innate principles.

Social Development across the Life Span

- Social development takes place in a particular cultural context.
- Erik Erikson conceptualized the life span as a series of crises with which individuals must cope.
- Children begin the process of social development with different temperaments.
- Socialization begins with an infant's attachment to a caregiver.
- Failure to make this attachment leads to numerous physical and psychological problems.
- Adolescents must develop a personal identity by forming comfortable social relationships with parents and peers.
- The central concerns of adulthood are organized around the needs of intimacy and generativity.
- People become less socially active as they grow older because they selectively maintain only those relationships that matter most to them emotionally.
- People assess their lives, in part, by their ability to contribute positively to the lives of others.

Sex and Gender Differences

- Research has revealed biologically based sex differences between the brains of men and women.
- Children's gender stereotypes are most rigid between ages 5 and 7.
- Beginning at birth, parents and peers help bring about the socialization of gender roles.

Moral Development

- Kohlberg defined stages of moral development.
- Subsequent research has evaluated gender and cultural differences in moral reasoning.

Learning to Age Successfully

- Successful cognitive aging can be defined as people optimizing their functioning in select domains that are of highest priority to them and compensating for losses by using substitute behaviors.

KEY TERMS

accommodation
assimilation
attachment
centration
child-directed speech
cognitive development
conservation
contact comfort
cross-sectional design
developmental age
developmental psychology
egocentrism
embryonic stage
fetal stage
gender
gender identity

gender stereotype
generativity
germinal stage
imprinting
infant-directed speech
internalization
intimacy
language-making capacity
longitudinal design
maturation
menarche
morality
normative investigation
object permanence
overregularization
parenting style

phoneme
physical development
psychosocial stage
puberty
scheme
selective optimization
  with compensation
sex difference
social development
socialization
temperament
teratogen
theory of mind
wisdom
zygote

Practice Test

1. Rachel just turned 4, but she has the language ability of a 6-year-old. For language ability, Rachel's _____ age is greater than her _____ age.
   a. chronological; normative
   b. developmental; cross-sectional
   c. developmental; chronological
   d. chronological; developmental

2. Your friend Pat says, "I'm sure Caroline recognized my voice as soon as she was born." If Pat is Caroline's _____, Pat's claim is probably correct.
   a. mother   c. mother or father
   b. father   d. sister

3. Jack and Jill are twins. Under most circumstances, you would expect that Jack would begin his pubescent growth spurt _____ Jill.
   a. at the same time as   c. a year before
   b. earlier than   d. later than

4. Tamara is a child whose thought is marked by egocentrism and centration. With respect to Piaget's theory, you infer that Tamara is in the _____ stage.
   a. sensorimotor
   b. preoperational
   c. concrete operations
   d. formal operations

5. You are testing 20-year-old Keith and his 45-year-old father, Matthew. If they are both average members of their age groups, you'd expect Keith to show more _____ and Matthew to show more _____.
   a. crystallized intelligence; fluid intelligence
   b. wisdom; crystallized intelligence
   c. wisdom; fluid intelligence
   d. fluid intelligence; wisdom

6. You are examining data from an experiment on speech perception. Participant 27 was able to hear a sound distinction that is used in Hindi but not in English. You conclude the Participant 27 is *least* likely to be an
   a. adult who is an English speaker.
   b. infant in a Hindi-language environment.
   c. adult who is a Hindi speaker.
   d. infant in an English-language environment.

7. If Siyun believes that "mommy" applies to all women, that is an _____. If she believes that "mommy" applies only to her own mother, that is an _____.
   a. contrast; overextension
   b. underextension; hypothesis
   c. hypothesis; contrast
   d. overextension; underextension

8. Mona and Bianca are both 6-year-olds. Mona speaks English. Bianca speaks both English and Turkish. You expect that _____ will have a bigger vocabulary in English and that _____ will show better executive control.
   a. Mona; Mona
   b. Bianca; Mona
   c. Mona; Bianca
   d. Bianca; Bianca

9. According to Erik Erikson, the major crisis of age 6 to puberty is
   a. autonomy versus self-doubt.
   b. identity versus role confusion.
   c. generativity versus stagnation.
   d. competence versus inferiority.

10. As a mother, Lisbeth is high on the dimension of demandingness and low on the dimension of responsiveness. This combination would be described as a(n) _____ style of parenting.
    a. indulgent   c. neglecting
    b. authoritative   d. authoritarian

11. Which of these statements was *not* mentioned as a recommendation for quality day care?
    a. Children should be taught social problem-solving skills.
    b. Children should have similar levels of intellectual development.
    c. Caregivers should not put undue restrictions on the children.
    d. Children should have a free choice of activities intermixed with explicit lessons.

12. Whereas _____ differences are affected by culture, _____ differences are affected by biology.
    a. gender; sex   c. sex; identity
    b. generativity; gender d. sex; gender

13. You are asked to guess whether 6-year-old Chris is a girl or boy. Which observation would most lead you to believe that Chris is a girl?
    a. Chris enjoys rough-and-tumble play.
    b. Chris doesn't like to engage in social conversations.
    c. Chris most enjoys one-on-one relationships.
    d. Chris prefers to have social interactions in groups.

14. For moral behavior, Gracie is most concerned about following rules and avoiding the censure of authorities. She is at the stage of _____ morality.
    a. principled   c. preconventional
    b. cultural   d. conventional

15. Carol Gilligan criticized Kohlberg's theory by arguing that women are more focused on the standard of _____, whereas men are more focused on the standard of _____.
    a. caring for others; avoiding pain
    b. caring for others; justice
    c. justice; caring for others
    d. avoiding self-condemnation; justice

ESSAY QUESTIONS

1. What types of abilities signal that children are acquiring a theory of mind?

2. Why do deprivation and abuse have consequences for social development?

3. Why is it sometimes difficult to discriminate between sex differences and gender differences?

Stop and Review Answers

Stop and Review (Studying Development)

1. Developmental age is the chronological age at which most people are able to achieve a particular physical or mental accomplishment.
2. To study individual differences, researchers often measure variation (on some dimension) among people at one age and then reexamine the same participants later in life to examine the consequences of that variation.
3. For some cross-sectional analyses, researchers have to rule out the possibility that what appear to be age-related changes are really differences brought about by the time at which individuals were born.

Stop and Review (Physical Development across the Life Span)

1. Compared to their noncrawling peers, children who have begun to crawl experience fear on the "deep" end of the visual cliff.
2. Recent studies indicate that the brain continues to mature during adolescence, particularly in areas such as the frontal lobes.
3. As people age, the lenses in their eyes often become yellowed, which is thought to be responsible for diminished color vision.

Stop and Review (Cognitive Development across the Life Span)

1. Assimilation allows children to fit new information to old schemes; accommodation changes schemes to fit new information.
2. A child who can overcome centration is able to ignore surface aspects of a problem to show deeper understanding of a domain such as number or liquid quantity.
3. By inventing more subtle measures of infants' knowledge, researchers have been able to demonstrate that children show evidence of object permanence by age 4 months.
4. Vygotsky emphasized the importance of the social context in the way that children's cognitive development unfolds.
5. Research suggests that people's processing speed slows down as they age.

Stop and Review (Acquiring Language)

1. When talking to infants and children, adults tend to slow down, use exaggerated, high-pitched intonation, and produce shorter utterances with simpler structures.

2. Children form hypotheses for the meanings of new words. On some occasions, their hypotheses are broader than the adult category.
3. Deaf children who have not been exposed to either a spoken language or a formal signed language will sometimes begin to use their own signed languages that share structural features with real languages.
4. If a child is overregularizing English past-tense constructions, you would expect to hear him or her say words like *doed* and *breaked* rather than *did* and *broke*.

Stop and Review (Social Development across the Life Span)

1. Erikson suggested that the crisis of intimacy versus isolation comes into focus during early adulthood.
2. Research suggests that children who have secure attachments at early ages are, for example, more popular and less socially anxious later in life.
3. Parenting styles are defined by the dimensions of the parent's demandingness and the parent's responsiveness.
4. Adolescents experience peer relationships at the levels of friendships, cliques, and crowds.
5. The birth of a child often has a negative impact on marital satisfaction.

Stop and Review (Sex and Gender Differences)

1. Sex differences emerge from biological differences between men and women; gender differences emerge from cultural constructions of different roles for men and women.
2. Research suggests that women show more activity in brain areas related to the processing of emotion.
3. Young children prefer the company of peers of the same sex.

Stop and Review (Moral Development)

1. The three major levels are preconventional morality, conventional morality, and principled morality.
2. Gilligan argued that men are more focused on justice, whereas women are more focused on caring for others.
3. People may bring concerns related to autonomy, community, and divinity.

Practice Test Answers

1. c	**5.** d	**9.** d	**13.** c
2. a	**6.** a	**10.** d	**14.** d
3. d	**7.** d	**11.** b	**15.** b
4. b	**8.** c	**12.** a	

References

Adams, R. E., & Laursen, B. (2007). The correlates of conflict: Disagreement is not necessarily detrimental. *Journal of Family Psychology, 21*, 445–458.

Adolph, K. E., Karasik, L. B., & Tamis-LeMonda, C. S. (2010). Motor skill. In M. Bornstein (Ed.), *Handbook of cultural developmental science* (pp. 61–88). New York: Psychology Press.

Ainsworth, M. D. S., Blehar, M., Waters, E., & Wall, S. (1978). *Patterns of attachment.* Hillsdale, NJ: Erlbaum.

Allen, J. P., Porter, M. R., & McFarland, F. C. (2006). Leaders and followers in adolescent close relationships: Susceptibility to peer influence as a predictor of risky behavior, friendship instability, and depression. *Development and Psychopathology, 18*, 155–172.

Amato, P. R. (2010). Research on divorce: Continuing trends and new developments. *Journal of Marriage and Family, 72*, 650–666.

Andrews-Hanna J. R., Mackiewicz Seghete, K. L., Claus, E. D., Burgess, G. C., Ruzic, L., & Banich, M. T. (2011). Cognitive control in adolescence: Neural underpinnings and relation to self-report behaviors. *PLoS ONE, 6*, e21598.

Arnett, J. J. (1999). Adolescent storm and stress reconsidered. *American Psychologist, 54*, 317–326.

Bahrick, H. P., Bahrick, P. O., & Wittlinger, R. P. (1975). Fifty years of memory for names and faces: A cross-sectional approach. *Journal of Experimental Psychology: General, 104*, 54–75.

Bailey, B. A., & Sokol, R. J. (2008). Pregnancy and alcohol use: Evidence and recommendations for prenatal care. *Clinical Obstetrics and Gynecology, 51*, 436–444.

Balsam, K. F., Beauchaine, T. P., Rothblum, E. D., & Solomon, S. E. (2008). Three-year follow-up of same-sex couples who had civil unions in Vermont, same-sex couples not in civil unions, and heterosexual married couples. *Developmental Psychology, 44*, 102–116.

Baltes, P. B. (1993). The aging mind: Potential and limits. *The Gerontologist, 33*, 580–594.

Baltes, P. B., Smith, J., & Staudinger, U. M. (1992). Wisdom and successful aging. In T. B. Sonderegger (Ed.), *The Nebraska Symposium on Motivation: Vol. 39. The psychology of aging* (pp. 123–167). Lincoln: University of Nebraska Press.

Bauminger, N., Finzi-Dottan, R., Chason, S., & Har-Even, D. (2008). Intimacy in adolescent friendship: The roles of attachment, coherence, and self-disclosure. *Journal of Social and Personal Relationships, 25*, 409–428.

Bayley, N. (1956). Individual patterns of development. *Child Development, 27*, 45–74.

Behne, T., Liszkowski, U., Carpenter, M., & Tomasello, M. (2012). Twelve-month-olds' comprehension and production of pointing. *British Journal of Developmental Psychology*, in press.

Belsky, J., Vandell, D. L., Burchinal, M., Clarke-Stewart, K. A., McCartney, K., Owen, M. T., & The NICHD Early Child Care Research Network. (2007). Are there long-term effects of early child care? *Child Development, 78*, 681–701.

Benedict, R. (1938). Continuities and discontinuities in cultural conditioning. *Psychiatry, 1*, 161–167.

Benenson, J. F., & Heath, A. (2006). Boys withdraw from one-on-one interactions, whereas girls withdraw more in groups. *Developmental Psychology, 42*, 272–282.

Benenson, J. F., Apostoleris, N. H., & Parnass, J. (1997). Age and sex differences in dyadic and group interaction. *Developmental Psychology, 33*, 538–543.

Bialystok, E., & Craik, F. I. M. (2010). Cognitive and linguistic processing in the bilingual mind. *Current Directions in Psychological Science, 19*, 19–23.

Bialystok, E., & Shapero, D. (2005). Ambiguous benefits: The effect of bilingualism on reversing ambiguous figures. *Developmental Science, 8*, 595–604.

Bialystok, E., Luk, G., Peets, K. F., & Yang, S. (2010). Receptive vocabulary differences in monolingual and bilingual children. *Bilingualism: Language and Cognition, 13*, 525–531.

Bielak, A. A. M., Hughes, T. F., Small, B. J., & Dixon, R. A. (2007). It's never too late to engage in lifestyle activities: Significant concurrent but not change relationships between lifestyle activities and cognitive speed. *Journal of Gerontology: Psychological Sciences, 62B*, P331–P339.

Bennett, D. S., Bendersky, M., & Lewis, M. (2008). Children's cognitive ability from 4 to 9 years old as a function of prenatal cocaine exposure, environmental risk, and maternal verbal intelligence. *Developmental Psychology, 44*, 919–928.

Blos, P. (1965). *On adolescence: A psychoanalytic interpretation.* New York: The Free Press.

Bolhuis, J. J., & Honey, R. C. (1998). Imprinting, learning and development: From behaviour to brain and back. *Trends in Neurosciences, 21*, 306–311.

Bowlby, J. (1969). *Attachment and loss, Vol 1. Attachment.* New York: Basic Books.

Bowlby, J. (1973). *Attachment and loss, Vol 2. Separation, anxiety and anger.* London: Hogarth.

Brainerd, C. J. (1996). Piaget: A centennial celebration. *Psychological Science, 7*, 191–195.

Branje, S. J. T., Frijns, T., Finkenaer, C., Engels, R., & Meeus, W. (2007). You are my best friend: Commitment and stability in adolescents' same-sex friendships. *Personal Relationships, 14*, 587–603.

Brechwald, W. A., & Prinstein, M. J. (2011). Beyond homophily: A decade of advances in understanding peer influence processes. *Journal of Research on Adolescence, 21*, 166–179.

Bronfenbrenner, U. (Ed.) (2004). *Making human beings human: Bioecological perspectives on human development.* Thousand Oaks, CA: Sage Publications.

Brown, F. B., & Klute, C. (2003). Friendships, cliques, and crowds. In G. R. Adams & M. D. Berzonsky (Eds.), *Blackwell handbooks of developmental psychology* (pp. 330–348). Malden, MA: Blackwell Publishing.

Buchler, N. E. G., & Reder, L. M. (2007). Modeling age-related memory deficits: A two-parameter solution. *Psychology and Aging, 22*, 104–121.

Cahill, L., Uncapher, M., Kilpatrick, L., Alkire, M. T., & Turner, J. (2004). Sex-related hemispheric lateralization of amygdala function in emotionally influenced memory: An fMRI investigation. *Learning & Memory, 11*, 261–266.

Canli, T., Desmond, J. E., Zhao, Z., & Gabrieli, J. D. E. (2002). Sex differences in the neural basis of emotional memories. *Proceedings of the National Academy of Sciences, 99*, 10789–10794.

Carey, S. (1978). The child as word learner. In M. Hale, J. Bresnan, & G. A. Miller (Eds.), *Linguistic theory and psychological reality* (pp. 265–293). Cambridge, MA: MIT Press.

Carstensen, L. L., Turan, B., Scheibe, S., Ram, N., Ersner-Hershfield, H., Samanez-Larkin, G. R., Brooks, K. P., & Nesselroade, J. R. (2011). Emotional experience improves with age: Evidence based on over 10 years of experience sampling. *Psychology and Aging, 26*, 21–33.

Casey, B. J., Getz, S., & Galvan, A. (2008). The adolescent brain. *Developmental Review, 28*, 62–77.

Charlton, R. E., Barrick, T. R., Markus, H. S., & Morris, R. G. (2010). The relationship between episodic long-term memory and white matter integrity in normal aging. *Neuropsychologia, 48*, 114–122.

Child Welfare Information Gateway. (2011). *Foster Care Statistics 2009.* Retrieved from www.childwelfare.gov/pubs/factsheets/foster.pdf.

Chomsky, N. (1965). *Aspects of a theory of syntax.* Cambridge, MA: MIT Press.

Chomsky, N. (1975). *Reflections on language.* New York: Pantheon Books.

Clark, E. V. (2003). *First language acquisition.* Cambridge, UK: Cambridge University Press.

Clarke-Stewart, A., & Alhusen, V. D. (2005). *What we know about childcare.* Cambridge, MA: Harvard University Press.

Clarke-Stewart, K. A. (1993). *Daycare.* Cambridge, MA: Harvard University Press.

Collins, W. A., Maccoby, E. E., Steinberg, L., Hetherington, E. M., & Bornstein, M. H. (2000). Contemporary research on parenting: The case for nature and nurture. *American Psychologist, 55,* 218–232.

Conger, R. D., Conger, K. J., & Martin, M. J. (2010). Socioeconomic status, family processes, and individual development. *Journal of Marriage and Family, 72,* 685–704.

Cowan, C. P., & Cowan, P. (2000). *When partners become parents: The big life change for couples.* Mahwah, NJ: Erlbaum.

Crane, J., Keough, M., Murphy, P., Burrage, & L., Hutchens, D. (2011). Effects of environmental tobacco smoke on perinatal outcomes: A retrospective cohort study. *BJOG, 118,* 865–871.

Cutajar, M. C., Mullen, P. E., Ogloff, J. R. P., Thomas, S. D., Wells, D. L., & Spataro, J. (2010). Psychopathology in a large cohort of sexually abused children followed up to 43 years. *Child Abuse & Neglect, 34,* 813–822.

Daddis, C. (2011). Desire for increased autonomy and adolescents' perceptions of peer autonomy: "Everyone else can; why can't I?" *Child Development, 82,* 1310–1326.

Darling, N., & Steinberg, L. (1993). Parenting style as context: An integrative model. *Psychological Bulletin, 113,* 487–496.

De Santis, M., Cavaliere, A. F., Straface, G., & Caruso, A. (2006). Rubella infection in pregnancy. *Reproductive Toxicology, 21,* 390–398.

DeCasper, A. J., & Prescott, P. A. (1984). Human newborns' perception of male voices: Preference, discrimination, and reinforcing value. *Developmental Psychology, 17,* 481–491.

Degnan, K. A., Hane, A. A., Henderson, H. A., Moas, O. L., Reeb-Sutherland, B. C., & Fox, N. A. (2011). Longitudinal stability of temperamental exuberance and social-emotional outcomes in early childhood. *Developmental Psychology, 47,* 765–780.

Del Giudice, M. (2011). Alone in the dark? Modeling the conditions for visual experience in human fetuses. *Developmental Psychobiology, 53,* 214–219.

DeLamater, J. D., & Sill, M. (2005). Sexual desire in later life. *The Journal of Sex Research, 42,* 138–149.

Derntl, B., Finkelmeyer, A., Eickhoff, S., Kellermann, T., Falkenberg, D. I., Schneider, F., & Habel, U. (2010). Multidimensional assessment of empathic abilities: Neural correlates and gender differences. *Psychoneuroendocrinology, 35,* 67–82.

Dew, J., & Wilcox, W. B. (2011). If momma ain't happy: Explaining declines in marital satisfaction among new mothers. *Journal of Marriage and Family, 73,* 1–12.

Dishion, T. J., & Tipsord, J. M. (2011). Peer contagion in child and adolescent social and emotional development. *Annual Review of Psychology, 62,* 189–214.

Dixon, R. A., & de Frias, C. M. (2004). The Victoria longitudinal study: From characterizing cognitive aging to illustrating changes in memory compensation. *Aging Neuropsychology and Cognition, 11,* 346–376.

Donovan, W., Leavitt, L., Taylor, N., & Broder, J. (2007). Maternal sensitivity, mother-infant 9-month interaction, infant attachment status: Predictors of mother-toddler interaction at 24 months. *Infant Behavior & Development, 30,* 336–352.

Dykas, M. J., & Cassidy, J. (2011). Attachment and the processing of social information across the life span: Theory and evidence. *Psychological Bulletin, 137,* 19–46.

Edin, K., & Kissane, R. J. (2010). Poverty and the American family: A decade in review. *Journal of Marriage and Family, 72,* 460–479.

Ein-Dor, T., Mikulincer, M., Doron, G., & Shaver, P. R. (2010). The attachment paradox: How can so many of (the insecure ones) have no adaptive advantages? *Perspectives on Psychological Science, 5,* 123–141.

Erikson, E. (1963). *Childhood and society.* New York: Norton.

Evans, A. D., & Lee, K. (2011). Verbal deception from late childhood to middle adolescence and its relation to executive functioning skills. *Developmental Psychology, 47,* 1108–1116.

Fantz, R. L. (1963). Pattern vision in newborn infants. *Science, 140,* 296–297.

Federal Interagency Forum on Aging-Related Statistics. (2010). *Older Americans 2010: Key indicators of well-being.* Retrieved from www.agingstats.gov/agingstatsdotnet/Main_Site/Data/2010_Documents/Docs/OA_2010.pdf.

Feldman, D. H. (2004). Piaget's stages: The unfinished symphony of cognitive development. *New Ideas in Psychology, 22,* 175–231.

Flavell, J. H. (1985). *Cognitive development* (2nd ed.). Englewood Cliffs, NJ: Prentice Hall.

Flavell, J. H. (1996). Piaget's legacy. *Psychological Science, 7,* 200–203.

Fleer, M., & Hedegaard, M. (2010). Children's development as participation in everyday practices across different institutions. *Mind, Culture, and Activity, 17,* 149–168.

Freud, A. (1946). *The ego and the mechanisms of defense.* New York: International Universities Press.

Freud, A. (1958). Adolescence. *Psychoanalytic Study of the Child, 13,* 255–278.

Freund, A. M., & Baltes, P. B. (1998). Selection, optimization, and compensation as strategies of life management: Correlations with subjective indicators of successful aging. *Psychology and Aging, 13,* 531–543.

Gauvain, M., Beebe, H., & Zhao, S. (2011). Applying the cultural approach to cognitive development. *Journal of Cognition and Development, 12,* 121–133.

Gibbs, J. C., Basinger, K. S., Grime, R. L., & Snarey, J. R. (2007). Moral judgment development across culture: Revisiting Kohlberg's universality claims. *Developmental Review, 27,* 443–500.

Gibson, E. J., & Walk, R. D. (1960). The "visual cliff." *Scientific American, 202,* 64–71.

Gilligan, C. (1982). *In a different voice: Psychological theory and women's development.* Cambridge, MA: Harvard University Press.

Goldberg, A. E., & Perry-Jenkins, M. (2007). The division of labor and perceptions of parental roles: Lesbian couples across the transition to parenthood. *Journal of Social and Personal Relationships, 24,* 297–318.

Goldberg, A. E., & Sayer, A. (2006). Lesbian couples' relationship quality across the transition to parenthood. *Journal of Marriage and Family, 68,* 87–100.

Goldin-Meadow, S. (2003). *The resilience of language: What gesture creation in deaf children can tell us about how all children learn language.* New York: Psychology Press.

Goldin-Meadow, S., & Mylander, C. (1990). Beyond the input given: The child's role in the acquisition of language. *Language, 66,* 323–355.

Golombok, S., Rust, J., Zervoulis, K., Croudace, T., Golding, J., & Hines, M. (2008). Developmental trajectories of sex-typed behavior in boys and girls: A longitudinal general population study of children aged 2.5–8 years. *Child Development, 79,* 1583–1593.

Gorchoff, S. M., John, O. P., & Helson, R. (2008). Contextualizing change in marital satisfaction during middle age: An 18-year longitudinal study. *Psychological Science, 19,* 1194–1200.

Gray, M. R., & Steinberg, L. (1999). Unpacking authoritative parenting: Reassessing a multidimensional construct. *Journal of Marriage and the Family, 61,* 574–587.

Haidt, J. (2007). The new synthesis in moral psychology. *Science, 316,* 998–1002.

Hall, G. S. (1904). *Adolescence: Its psychology and its relations to physiology, anthropology, sociology, sex, crime, religion and education* (Vols. 1 and 2). New York: D. Appleton.

Hamlin, J. K., Hallinan, E. V., & Woodward, A. L. (2008). Do as I do: 7-month-old infants selectively reproduce other's goals. *Developmental Science, 11,* 487–494.

Harlow, H. F. (1958). The nature of love. *American Psychologist, 13,* 673–685.

Harlow, H. F., & Zimmerman, R. R. (1958). The development of affectional responses in infant monkeys. *Proceedings of the American Philosophical Society, 102,* 501–509.

Haas, S. M., & Stafford, L. (2005). Maintenance behaviors in same-sex and marital relationships: A matched sample comparison. *Journal of Family Communication, 5,* 43–60.

Herek, G. M. (2006). Legal recognition of same-sex relationships in the United States: A social science perspective. *American Psychologist, 61,* 607–621.

Hertzog, C. (2011). Intelligence in adulthood. In R. J. Sternberg & S. B. Kaufman (Eds.), *The Cambridge handbook of intelligence* (pp. 174–190). New York: Cambridge University Press.

Hertzog, C., Kramer, A. F., Wilson, R. S., & Lindenberger, U. (2008). Enrichment efforts on adult cognitive development: Can the functional capacity of older adults be preserved and enhanced? *Psychological Science in the Public Interest, 9,* 1–49.

Hess, T. M. (2005). Memory and aging in context. *Psychological Bulletin, 131,* 383–406.

Hess, T. M., & Hinson, J. T. (2006). Age-related variation in the influences of aging sterotypes on memory in adulthood. *Psychology and Aging, 21,* 621–625.

Hines, M. (2011). Gender development and the human brain. *Annual Review of Neuroscience, 34,* 69–88.

Horowitz, A., Brennan, M., & Reinhardt, J. P. (2005). Prevalence and risk factors for self-reported visual impairment among middle-aged and older adults. *Research on Aging, 27,* 307–326.

Jaffee, S., & Hyde, J. S. (2000). Gender differences in moral orientation: A meta-analysis. *Psychological Bulletin, 126,* 703–726.

Jensen, L A. (2008). Through two lenses: A cultural-developmental approach to moral psychology. *Developmental Review, 28,* 289–315.

Jowkar-Baniani, F., & Schmuckler, M. A. (2011). Picture perception in infants: Generalization from two-dimensional to three-dimensional displays. *16,* 211–226.

Jusczyk, P. W. (2003). Chunking language input to find patterns. In D. H. Rakison & L. M. Oakes (Eds.), *Early category and concept development.* London: Oxford University Press.

Jusczyk, P. W., & Aslin, R. N. (1995). Infants' detection of the sound patterns of words in fluent speech. *Cognitive Psychology, 29,* 1–23.

Kagan, J., & Snidman, N. (1991). Infant predictors of inhibited and uninhibited profiles. *Psychological Science, 2,* 40–44.

Karavasilis, L., Doyle, A. B., & Markiewicz, D. (2003). Associations between parenting style and attachment to mother in middle childhood and adolescence. *International Journal of Behavioral Development, 27,* 153–164.

Kesebir, P., & Diener, E. (2008). In pursuit of happiness: Empirical answers to philosophical questions. *Perspectives on Psychological Science, 3,* 117–125.

Kisilevsky, B. S., Hains, S. M. J., Brown, C. A., Lee, C. T., Cowperthwaite, B., Stutzman, S. S., Swansburg, M. L., Lee, L., Xie, X., Huang, H., Ye, H.-H., Zhang, K., & Wang, Z. (2009). Fetal sensitivity to properties of maternal speech and language. *Infant Behavior and Development, 32,* 59–71.

Kitamura, C., Thanavishuth, C., Burnham, D., & Luksaneeyanawin, S. (2002). Universality and specificity in infant-directed speech: Pitch modifications as a function of infant age and sex in a tonal and non-tonal language. *Infant Behavior & Development, 24,* 372–392.

Knickmeyer, R., Baron-Cohen, S., Raggatt, P., & Taylor, K. (2005). Foetal testosterone, social relationships, and restricted interests in children. *Journal of Child Psychology and Psychiatry, 46,* 198–210.

Kohlberg, L. (1964). Development of moral character and moral ideology. In M. L. Hoffman & L. W. Hoffman (Eds.), *Review of child development research* (Vol. 1). New York: Russell Sage Foundation.

Kohlberg, L. (1981). *The philosophy of moral development.* New York: Harper & Row.Kohn, N., Kellermann, T., Gur, R. C., Schneider, F., & Habel, U. (2011). Gender differences in the neural correlates of humor processing: Implications for different processing modes. *Neuropsychologia, 49,* 888–897.

Krebs, D. L. (2008). Morality: An evolutionary account. *Perspectives on Psychological Science, 3,* 149–172.Kujawski, J. H., & Bower, T. G. R. (1993). Same-sex preferential looking during infancy as a function of abstract representation. *British Journal of Developmental Psychology, 11,* 201–209.

Lawrence, E., Nylen, K., & Cobb, R. J. (2007). Prenatal expectations and marital satisfaction over the transition to parenthood. *Journal of Family Psychology, 21,* 155–164.

Lee, S. A. S., & Davis, B. L. (2010). Segmental distribution patterns of English infant- and adult-directed speech. *Journal of Child Language, 37,* 767–791.

Lenroot, R. K., & Giedd, J. N. (2010). Sex differences in the adolescent brain. *Brain and Cognition, 72,* 46–55.

Lenroot, R. K., Gogtay, N., Greenstein, D. K., Wells, E. M., Gregory L. Wallace, G. L., Clasen, L. V., Blumenthal, J. D., Lerch, J., Zijdenbos, A. P., Evans, A. C., Thompson, P. M., & Giedda, J. N. (2007). Sexual dimorphism of brain developmental trajectories during childhood and adolescence. *NeuroImage, 36,* 1065–1073.

Lindau, S. T., Schumm, L. P., Laumann, E. O., Levinson, W., O'Muircheartaigh, C. A., & Waite, L. J. (2007). A study of sexuality and health among older adults in the United States. *The New England Journal of Medicine, 357,* 762–775.

LoBue, V., Coan, J. A., Thrasher, C., & DeLoache, J. S. (2011). Prefrontal asymmetry and parent-rated temperament in infants. *PLOSone, 6,* e22694.

Lourenço, O., & Machado, A. (1996). In defense of Piaget's theory: A reply to 10 common criticisms. *Psychological Review, 103,* 143–164.

Luijk, M. P. C. M., Tharner, A., Bakermans-Kranenburg, M. J., van IJzendoorn, M. H., Jaddoe, V. W. V., Hofman, A., Verhulst, F. C., & Tiemeier, H. (2011). The association between parenting and attachment security is moderated by a polymorphism of the mineralocorticoid receptor gene: Evidence for differential susceptibility. *Biological Psychology, 88,* 37–40.

Macchi Cassia, V., Turati, C., & Simion, F. (2004). Can a nonspecific bias toward top-heavy patterns explain newborns' face preference? *Psychological Science, 15,* 379–383.

Maccoby, E. E. (2002). Gender and group processes: A developmental perspective. *Current Directions in Psychological Science, 11,* 54–58.

Maccoby, E. E., & Martin, J. A. (1983). Socialization in the context of the family: Parent–child interaction. In E. M. Hetherington (Ed.), *Handbook of child psychology: Vol. 4. Socialization, personality, and social development* (pp. 1–101). New York: Wiley.

Mandel, D. R., Jusczyk, P. W., & Pisoni, D. B. (1995). Infants' recognition of the sound patterns of their own names. *Psychological Science, 5,* 314–317.

Marcia, J. E. (1966). Development and validation of ego-identity status. *Journal of Personality and Social Psychology, 3,* 551–558.

Marcia, J. E. (1980). Identity in adolescence. In J. Adelson (Ed.), *Handbook of adolescent psychology* (pp. 159–187). New York: Wiley.

Martin, C. L., & Ruble, D. N. (2010). Patterns of gender development. *Annual Review of Psychology, 61,* 353–381.

Maslow, A. H. (1968). *Toward a psychology of being* (2nd ed.). Princeton, NJ: Van Nostrand.

Maslow, A. H. (1970). *Motivation and personality* (rev. ed.). New York: Harper & Row.

Maynard, A. E. (2008). What we thought we knew and how we came to know it: Four decades of cross-cultural research from a Piagetian point of view. *Human Development, 51*, 56–65.

McGue, M., Elkins, I., Walden, B., & Iacono, W. G. (2005). Perceptions of the parent-adolescent relationship: A longitudinal investigation. *Developmental Psychology, 41*, 971–984.

McHale, S. M., Crouter, A. C., & Whiteman, S. D. (2003). The family contexts of gender development in childhood and adolescence. *Social Development, 12*, 125–148.

Mead, M. (1928). *Coming of age in Samoa.* New York: Morrow.

Meeus, W. (2011). The study of adolescent identity formation 2000–2010: A review of longitudinal research. *Journal of Research on Adolescence, 21*, 75–94.

Mendelson, J. R., & Rajan, R. (2011). Cortical effects of aging and hearing loss. In J. A. Winer & C. E. Schreiner (Eds.), *The auditory cortex* (pp. 493–501). New York: Springer.

Mercadillo, R. E., Díaz, J. L., Pasaye, E. H., & Barrios, F. A. (2011). Perception of suffering and compassion experience: Brain gender disparities. *Brain and Cognition, 76*, 5–14.

Miller, J. G., Bersoff, D. M., & Harwood, R. L. (1990). Perceptions of social responsibilities in India and in the United States: Moral imperatives or personal decisions? *Journal of Personality and Social Psychology, 58*, 33–47.

Miller, K. A., Fisher, P. A., Fetrow, B., & Jordan, K. (2006). Trouble on the journey home: Reunification failures in foster care. *Children and Youth Services Review, 28*, 260–274.

Montanari, S. (2010). Translation equivalents and the emergence of multiple lexicons in early trilingual development. *First Language, 30*, 102–125.

Morris, J. A., Jordan, C. L., & Breedlove, S. M. (2004). Sexual differentiation of the vertebrate nervous system. *Nature Neuroscience, 7*, 1034–1039.

Moulson, M. C., Fox, N. A., Zeanah, C. H., & Nelson, C. A. (2009). Early adverse experiences and the neurobiology of facial emotion processing. *Developmental Psychology, 45*, 17–30.

Newman, G. E., Keil, F. C., Kuhlmeier, V. A., & Wynn, K. (2010). Early understandings of the link between agents and order. *PNAS, 107*, 17140–17145.

Niccols, A. (2007). Fetal alcohol syndrome and the developing socio-emotional brain. *Brain and Cognition, 65*, 135–142.

NICHD Early Child Care Research Network. (1997). The effects of infant child care on infant-mother attachment security: Results of the NICHD Study of Early Child Care. *Child Development, 68*, 860–879.

NICHD Early Child Care Research Network. (2006). Infant-mother attachment classification: Risk and protection in relation to changing maternal caregiving quality. *Developmental Psychology, 42*, 38–58.

Parr, W. V., & Siegert, R. (1993). Adults' conceptions of everyday memory failures in others: Factors that mediate the effects of target age. *Psychology and Aging, 8*, 599–605.

Paus, T. (2005). Mapping brain maturation and cognitive development during adolescence. *Trends in Cognitive Sciences, 9*, 60–68.

Perry, D. G., & Pauletti, R. E. (2011). Gender and adolescent development. *Journal of Research on Adolescence, 21*, 61–74.

Piaget, J. (1929). *The child's conception of the world.* New York: Harcourt, Brace.

Piaget, J. (1954). *The construction of reality in the child.* New York: Basic Books.

Piaget, J. (1965). *The moral judgment of the child* (M. Gabain, Trans.). New York: Macmillan.

Piaget, J. (1977). *The development of thought: Equilibrium of cognitive structures.* New York: Viking Press.

Posada, R., & Wainryb, C. (2008). Moral development in a violent society: Columbian children's judgments in the context of survival and revenge. *Child Devleopment, 79*, 882–898.

Poulin-Dubois, D., Blaye, A., Coutya, J., & Bialystok, E. (2011). The effects of bilingualism on toddlers' executive functioning. *Journal of Experimental Child Psychology, 108*, 567–579.

Quine, W. V. O. (1960). *Word and object.* Cambridge, MA: The MIT Press.

Rodriguez, E. T., & Tamis-LeMonda, C. S. (2011). Trajectories of the home learning environment across the first 5 years: Associations with children's vocabulary and literacy skills at prekindergarten. *Child Development, 82*, 1058–1075.

Rogoff, B. (1990). *Apprenticeship in thinking: Cognitive development in social context.* New York: Oxford University Press.

Roisman, G. I., Clausell, E., Holland, A., Fortuna, K., & Elieff, C. (2008). Adult romantic relationships as contexts of human development: A multimethod comparison among same-sex couples with opposite-sex dating, engaged, and married dyads. *Developmental Psychology, 44*, 91–101.

Rose, A. J., & Rudolph, K. D. (2006). A review of sex- differences in peer relationship processes: Potential trade-offs for the emotional and behavioral development of girls and boys. *Psychological Bulletin, 132*, 98–131.

Rothbart, M. K. (2007). Temperament, development, and personality. *Current Directions in Psychological Science, 16*, 207–212.

Rothrauff, T., & Cooney, T. M. (2008). The role of generativity in psychological well-being: Does it differ for childless adults and parents? *Journal of Adult Development, 15*, 148–159.

Sachdeva, S., Singh, P., & Medin, D. (2011). Culture and the quest for universal principles of moral reasoning. *International Journal of Psychology, 46*, 161–176.

Sai, F. Z. (2005). The role of the mother's voice in developing mother's face preference: Evidence for intermodal perceptional at birth. *Infant and Child Development, 14*, 29–50.

Salihu, H. M., & Wilson, R. E. (2007). Epidemiology of prenatal smoking and perinatal outcomes. *Early Human Development, 83*, 713–720.

Salthouse, T. A. (2006). Mental exercise and mental aging: Evaluating the validity of the "use it or lose it" hypothesis. *Perspectives on Psychological Science, 1*, 68–87.

Schick, B., Marschark, M., & Spencer, P. E. (Eds.) (2006). *Advances in the sign language development of deaf children.* New York: Oxford University Press.

Serpell, R. (2000). Intelligence and culture. In R. J. Sternberg (Ed.), *Handbook of intelligence* (pp. 549–577). Cambridge, UK: Cambridge University Press.

Sheppard, L. D., & Vernon, P. A. (2008). Intelligence and speed of information-processing: A review of 50 years of research. *Personality and Individual Differences, 44*, 535–551.

Shmueli-Goetz, Y., Target, M., Fonagy, P., & Datta, A. (2008). The child attachment interview: A psychometric study of reliability and discriminant validity. *Developmental Psychology, 44*, 939–956.

Shuwairi, S. M., Albert, M. K., & Johnson, S. P. (2007). Discrimination of possible and impossible objects in infancy. *Psychological Science, 18*, 303–307.

Simons-Morton, B. G., Ouimet, M. C., Zhang, Z., Klauer, S. E., Lee, S. E., Wang, J., Chen, R., Albert, P., & Dingus, T. A. (2011). The effect of passengers and risk-taking friends on risky driving and crashes/near crashes among novice teenagers. *Journal of Adolescent Health, 49*, 587–593.

Singer, L. T., Arendt, R., Minnes, S., Farkas, K., Salvator, A., Kirchner, H. L., & Kliegman, R. (2002). Cognitive and motor outcomes of cocaine-exposed infants. *Journal of the American Medical Association, 287*, 1952–1960.

Sireteanu, R. (1999). Switching on the infant brain. *Science, 286*, 59–61.

Slobin, D. I. (1985). Crosslinguistic evidence for the language-making capacity. In D. Slobin (Ed.), *The crosslinguistic study of language acquisition: Vol. 2. Theoretical issues* (pp. 1157–1256). Hillsdale, NJ: Erlbaum.

Smetana, J. G., Campione-Barr, N., & Metzger, A. (2006). Adolescent development in interpersonal and societal contexts. *Annual Review of Psychology, 57*, 255–284.

Smith, J., & Baltes, P. B. (1990). Wisdom-related knowledge: Age/cohort differences in response to life-planning problems. *Developmental Psychology, 26*, 494–505.

Soderstrom, M. (2007). Beyond babytalk: Re-evaluating the nature and content of speech input to preverbal infants. *Developmental Review, 27,* 501–532.

Song, J. Y., Demuth, K., & Morgan, J. (2010). Effects of the acoustic properties of infant-directed speech on infant word recognition. *Journal of the Acoustical Society of America, 128,* 389–400.

Soska, K. C., & Johnson, S. P. (2008). Development of three-dimensional object completion in infancy. *Child Development, 79,* 1230–1236.

Spence, M. J., & DeCasper, A. J. (1987). Prenatal experience with low-frequency maternal-voice sounds influences neonatal perception of maternal voice samples. *Infant Behavior and Development, 10,* 133–142.

Spence, M. J., & Freeman, M. S. (1996). Newborn infants prefer the maternal low-pass filtered voice, but not the maternal whispered voice. *Infant Behavior and Development, 19,* 199–212.

Spitz, R. A., & Wolf, K. (1946). Anaclitic depression. *Psychoanalytic Study of Children, 2,* 313–342.

Stanojevic, M., Kurjak, A., Salihagić-Kadić, A., Vasilj, O., Miskovic, B., Shaddad, A. N., Ahmed, B., & Tomasović, S. (2011). Neurobehavioral continuity from fetus to neonate. *Journal of Perinatal Medicine, 39,* 171–177.

Staudinger, U. M., & Glück, J. (2011). Psychological wisdom research: Commonalities and differences in a growing field. *Annual Review of Psychology, 62,* 215–241.

Steinberg, L. (2008). A social neuroscience perspective on adolescent risk-taking. *Developmental Review, 28,* 78–106.

Stiles, J., & Jernigan, T. L. (2010). The basics of brain development. *Neuropsychology Review, 20,* 327–348.

Templin, M. (1957). Certain language skills in children: Their development and interrelationships. *Institute of Child Welfare Monograph,* Series No. 26. Minneapolis: University of Minnesota Press.

Thiessen, E. D., Hill, E. A., & Saffran, J. R. (2005). Infant-directed speech facilitates word segmentation. *Infancy, 7,* 53–71.

Thomas, A., & Chess, S. (1977). *Temperament and development.* New York: Brunner/Mazel.

Tomasello, M. (2008). *Origins of human communication.* Cambridge, MA: MIT Press.

Trautner, H. M., Ruble, D. N., Cyphers, L., Kirsten, B., Behrendt, R., & Hartmann, P. (2005). Rigiditiy and flexibility of gender stereotypes in childhood: Developmental or differential? *Infant and Child Development, 14,* 365–381.

Tun, P. A., & Lachman, M. E. (2010). The association between computer use and cognition across adulthood: Use it so you won't lose it? *Psychology and Aging, 25,* 560–568.

Twenge, J. M., Campbell, W. K., & Foster, C. A. (2003). Parenthood and marital satisfaction: A meta-analytic review. *Journal of Marriage and Family, 65,* 574–583.

Urban, J., Carlson, E., Egeland, B., & Stroufe, L. A. (1991). Patterns of individual adaptation across childhood. *Development and Psychopathology, 3,* 445–460.

U.S. Census Bureau (2008). *2007 American community survey.* Retrieved from www.census.gov/acs/www/index.html.

U.S. Census Bureau (2011). *America's families and living arrangements: 2010.* Retrieved from www.census.gov/population/www/socdemo/hh-fam/cps2010.html.

U.S. Department of Health and Human Services. (2010). *Child maltreatment 2009.* Retrieved from www.acf.hhs.gov/programs/cb/pubs/cm09/cm09.pdf.

U.S. Department of Health and Human Services. (2010). *Trends in the prevalence of sexual behaviors.* Retrieved from www.cdc.gov/HealthyYouth/yrbs/pdf/us_sexual_trend_yrbs.pdf.

Van Zeijl, J., Mesman, J., Van IJzendoorn, M. H., Bakermans-Kranenburg, M. J., Juffer, F., Stolk, M. N., Koot, H. M., & Alink, L. R. A. (2006). Attachment-based intervention for enhancing sensitive discipline in mothers of 1- to 3-year-old children at risk for externalizing behavior problems: A randomized controlled trial. *Journal of Consulting and Clinical Psychology, 74,* 994–1005.

Vandell, D. L., Belsky, J., Burchinal, M., Steinberg, L., Vandergrift, N., & NICHD Early Child Care Research Network. (2010). Do effects of early child care extend to age 15 years? Results from the NICHD study of early child care and youth development. *Child Development, 81,* 737–756.

Weinfield, N. S., Ogawa, J. R., & Sroufe, L. A. (1997). Early attachment as a pathway to adolescent peer competence. *Journal of Research on Adolescence, 7,* 241–265.

Welborn, B. L., Papademetris, X., Reis, D. L., Rajeevan, N., Bloise, S. M., & Gray, J. R. (2009). Variation in orbitofrontal cortex volume: Relation to sex, emotion regulation and affect. *Social Cognitive and Affective Neuroscience, 4,* 328–339.

Wellman, H. M., Fang, F., & Peterson, C. C. (2011). Sequential progressions in a theory-of-mind scale: Longitudinal perspectives. *Child Development, 82,* 780–792.

Werker, J. F. (1991). The ontogeny of speech perception. In I. G. Mattingly & M. Studdert-Kennedy (Eds.), *Modularity and the motor theory of speech perception* (pp. 91–109). Hillsdale, NJ: Erlbaum.

Werker, J. F., & Lalond, F. M. (1988). Cross-language speech perception: Initial capabilities and developmental change. *Developmental Psychology, 24,* 672–683.

Werker, J. F., & Tees, R. C. (1999). Influences on infant speech processing: Toward a new synthesis. *Annual Review of Psychology, 50,* 509–535.

Whitbourne, S. K., Sneed, J. R., & Sayer, A. (2009). Psychological development from college through midlife: A 34-year sequential study. *Developmental Psychology, 45,* 1328–1340.

Witherington, D. C., Campos, J. J., Anderson, D. I., Lejeune, L., & Seah, E. (2005). Avoidance of heights on the visual cliff in newly walking infants. *Infancy, 7,* 285–298.

Wood, E., Desmarais, S., & Gugula, S. (2002). The impact of parenting experience of gender stereotyped toy play of children. *Sex Roles, 47,* 39–49.

You, D., Maeda, Y., & Bebeau, M. J. (2011). Gender differences in moral sensitivity: A meta-analysis. *Ethics & Behavior, 21,* 262–282.

Zacher, H., Rosing, K., Henning, T., & Frese, M. (2011). Establishing the next generation at work: Leader generativity as a moderator of the relationship between leader age, leader-member exchange, and leadership success. *Psychology and Aging, 26,* 241–252.

Zeanah, C. H., Smyke, A. T., Koga, S. F., & Carlson, E. (2005). Attachment in institutionalized and community children in Romania. *Child Development, 76,* 1015–1028.

Intelligence and Intelligence Assessment

© Image Source/Alamy

From Chapter 9 of *Psychology and Life*, 20th Edition. Richard J. Gerrig. Copyright © 2013 by Pearson Education, Inc.

Suppose you were asked to define the word *intelligence*. What types of behaviors would you include in your definition? Think back on your own experiences. What was it like when you first started school? What was it like when you labored at your first job? It's very likely that you heard your behaviors labeled as intelligent or unintelligent—smart or not so smart—in those and other situations. When those labels are applied in casual conversation, they have relatively few consequences. However, there are many settings in which it matters whether your behaviors are considered intelligent or not. For example, if you grew up in the United States, it is likely that your "potential" was measured at an early age. In most school districts, teachers and administrators attempt, very early in your life, to measure your *intelligence*. The goal, most often, is to match students with classroom work that makes appropriate demands. However, as you've almost certainly observed, people's lives often seem to be affected by intelligence testing in areas well outside the classroom.

This chapter examines the foundations and uses of intelligence assessment. It will review the contributions psychologists have made to the understanding of individual differences in the areas of intelligence. We will also consider the types of controversies that almost inevitably arise when people begin to interpret these differences. The focus will be on how intelligence tests work, what makes any test useful, and why they do not always do the job they were intended to do. The chapter will conclude by considering the role of psychological assessment in society.

Let's begin with a brief overview of the general practice of psychological assessment.

WHAT IS ASSESSMENT?

Psychological assessment is the use of specified testing procedures to evaluate the abilities, behaviors, and personal qualities of people. Psychological assessment is often referred to as the measurement of *individual differences* because the majority of assessments specify how an individual is different from or similar to other people on a given dimension. Let's begin with a brief history of assessment. This historical overview will help you to understand both the uses and limitations of assessment, as well as prepare you to appreciate some current controversies.

History of Assessment

The development of formal tests and procedures for assessment is a relatively new enterprise in Western psychology, coming into wide use only in the early 1900s. However, long before Western psychology began to devise tests to evaluate people, assessment techniques were commonplace in ancient China. In fact, China employed a sophisticated program of civil service testing over 4,000 years ago—officials were required to demonstrate their competence every third year at an oral examination. Two thousand years later, during the Han Dynasty, written civil service tests were used to measure competence in

the areas of law, the military, agriculture, and geography. During the Ming Dynasty (A.D. 1368–1644), public officials were chosen on the basis of their performance at three stages of an objective selection procedure. During the first stage, examinations were given at the local level. The 4 percent who passed these tests had to endure the second stage: 9 days and nights of essay examinations on the classics. The 5 percent who passed the essay exams were allowed to complete a final stage of tests conducted at the nation's capital.

China's selection procedures were observed and described by British diplomats and missionaries in the early 1800s. Modified versions of China's system were soon adopted by the British and later by the Americans for the selection of civil service personnel (Wiggins, 1973).

The key figure in the development of Western intelligence testing was an upper-class Englishman, **Sir Francis Galton** (1822–1911). His book *Hereditary Genius,* published in 1869, greatly influenced subsequent thinking on the methods, theories, and practices of testing. Galton, a half cousin to Charles Darwin, attempted to apply Darwinian evolutionary theory to the study of human abilities. He was interested in how and why people differ in their abilities. He wondered why some people were gifted and successful—like him—while many others were not.

Galton was the first to postulate four important ideas about the assessment of intelligence. First, differences in intelligence were *quantifiable* in terms of degrees of intelligence. In other words, numerical values could be assigned to distinguish among different people's levels of intelligence. Second, differences among people formed a *bell-shaped curve,* or *normal distribution.* On a bell-shaped curve, most people's scores cluster in the middle, and fewer are found toward the two extremes of genius and mental deficiency (we'll return to the bell-shaped curve later in the chapter). Third, intelligence, or mental ability, could be measured by objective tests, tests on which each question had only one "right" answer. And fourth, the precise extent to which two sets of test scores were related could be determined by a statistical procedure he called *co-relations,* now known as *correlations.* These ideas proved to be of lasting value.

What important ideas about the assessment of intelligence are credited to Sir Francis Galton (1822–1911)?

---

psychological assessment The use of specified procedures to evaluate the abilities, behaviors, and personal qualities of people.

Unfortunately, Galton postulated a number of ideas that proved considerably more controversial. He believed, for example, that genius was inherited. In his view, talent, or eminence, ran in families; nurture had only a minimal effect on intelligence. In his view, intelligence was related to Darwinian species' fitness and, somehow, ultimately to one's moral worth. Galton attempted to base public policy on the concept of genetically superior and inferior people. He started the *eugenics* movement, which advocated improving the human species by applying evolutionary theory to encouraging biologically superior people to interbreed while discouraging biologically inferior people from having offspring. Galton wrote, "There exists a sentiment, for the most part quite unreasonable, against the gradual extinction of an inferior race" (Galton, 1883/1907, p. 200). You'll see later in the chapter that remnants of these elitist ideas are still being proposed today.

Sir Francis Galton's work created a context for contemporary intelligence assessment. Let's now see what features define circumstances of formal assessment.

Basic Features of Formal Assessment

To be useful for classifying individuals or for selecting those with particular qualities, a **formal assessment** procedure should meet three requirements. The assessment instrument should be (1) reliable, (2) valid, and (3) standardized. If it fails to meet these requirements, we cannot be sure whether the conclusions of the assessment can be trusted. Although this chapter focuses on intelligence assessment, formal assessment procedures apply to all types of psychological testing. To ensure that you'll understand the broad application of these principles, I will draw on examples both from intelligence testing and other domains of psychological assessment.

Reliability *Reliability* is the extent to which an assessment instrument can be trusted to give consistent scores. If you stepped on your bathroom scale three times in the same morning and it gave you a different reading each time, the scale would not be doing its job. You would call it *unreliable* because you could not count on it to give consistent results. Of course, if you ate a big meal in between two weighings, you wouldn't expect the scale to produce the same result. That is, a measurement device can

be considered reliable or unreliable only to the extent that the underlying concept it is measuring should remain unchanged.

One straightforward way to find out if a test is reliable is to calculate its **test–retest reliability**—a measure of the correlation between the scores of the same people, on the same test, given on two different occasions. A perfectly reliable test will yield a correlation coefficient of +1.00. This means that the identical pattern of scores emerges both times. The same people who got the highest and lowest scores the first time do so again. A totally unreliable test results in a 0.00 correlation coefficient. That means there is no relationship between the first set of scores and the second set. Someone who initially got the top score gets a completely different score the second time. As the correlation coefficient moves higher (toward the ideal of +1.00), the test is increasingly reliable. Another measure of reliability is the **internal consistency** of responses on a single test. For example, we can compare a person's score on the odd-numbered items of a test with the score on the even-numbered items. A reliable test yields the same score for each of its halves.

The researchers who develop and administer assessment devices work hard to ensure reliability. Did you take the SAT I exam for college admissions? You may not know this, but one section of the exam you took did not have an impact on your score. The questions on this unscored section were most likely being considered for future exams. The researchers who develop the exam can compare performance on the scored questions to performance on the unscored questions to ensure that people's scores on future exams are comparable to the scores on the exam that you took. For that reason, if you took the SAT I, you provided some of the information that helps to make the test reliable.

Validity The *validity* of a test is the degree to which it measures what an assessor intends it to measure. A valid test of intelligence measures that trait and predicts performance in situations where intelligence is important. Scores on a valid measure of creativity reflect actual creativity, not drawing ability or moods. In general, then, validity reflects a test's ability to make accurate predictions about behaviors or outcomes related to the purpose or design of the test. The conditions under which a test is valid may be very specific, so it is always important to ask about a test, "For what purpose is it valid?" Three important types of validity are *content validity, criterion-related validity,* and *construct validity.*

A test has **content validity** if it measures the full range of the domain of interest. Suppose you wanted to assess people's satisfaction with their lives. It wouldn't be enough to focus, for example, on success in school. To develop a measure that had content validity, you'd want to sample broadly from the

How would you feel if someone used your adult height to assess intelligence? The measure would be reliable, but would it be valid?

formal assessment The systematic procedures and measurement instruments used by trained professionals to assess an individual's functioning, aptitudes, abilities, or mental states.

test–retest reliability A measure of the correlation between the scores of the same people on the same test given on two different occasions.

internal consistency A measure of reliability; the degree to which a test yields similar scores across its different parts, such as odd versus even items.

content validity The extent to which a test adequately measures the full range of the domain of interest.

different domains of people's lives. You would ask people if they were satisfied with their jobs, their relationships, and so on.

To assess **criterion-related validity,** psychologists compare a person's score on the test with his or her score on some other standard, or *criterion,* associated with what the test measures. For example, if a test is designed to predict success in college, then college grades would be an appropriate criterion. If the test scores correlate highly with college grades, then the test has criterion-related validity. A major task of test developers is to find appropriate, measurable criteria. Let's see how researchers demonstrated the criterion-related validity of a measure of juror bias.

When people become members of juries they are supposed to consider the evidence without any biases. A pair of researchers sought to demonstrate the validity of a measurement device—the Pretrial Juror Attitude Questionnaire (PJAQ)—that would enable them to identify potential jurors who could not meet that unbiased standard (Lecci & Myers, 2008). The PJAQ consists of a series of 29 statements (for example, "If a suspect runs from police, then he probably committed the crime," "Many accident claims filed against insurance companies are phony"). People who take the PJAQ indicate their agreement to each statement on a 5-point scale ranging from strongly disagree to strongly agree. To assess the criterion-related validity of the PJAQ, the researchers asked 617 participants to complete the measure. Next, they had the same group of participants read summaries of trials for murder, rape, and armed robbery cases. The participants indicated what verdict they thought was appropriate for each case. When participants arrive at more guilty verdicts than the majority of their peers, that pattern suggests that some prior bias may be at work. The PJAQ successfully predicted which participants were likely to provide a high number of guilty verdicts.

Once criterion-related validity has been demonstrated for an assessment device, researchers feel confident using the device to make future predictions.

For many personal qualities of interest to psychologists, no ideal criterion exists. No single behavior or objective measure of performance can indicate, for example, how anxious,

depressed, or aggressive a person is overall. Psychologists have theories, or *constructs,* about these abstract qualities—what causes them, how they affect behavior, and how they relate to other variables. The **construct validity** of a test is the degree to which it adequately measures the underlying construct. For example, a new measure of depression has construct validity if the scores it produces correlate highly with valid measures of the features that define the construct of depression. In addition, the new measure should not show relationships with features that fall outside the construct of depression.

Consider for a moment the relationship between validity and reliability. Whereas reliability is measured by the degree to which a test correlates with itself (administered at different times or using different items), validity is measured by the degree to which the test correlates with something external to it (another test, a behavioral criterion, or judges' ratings). Usually, a test that is not reliable is also not valid because a test that cannot predict itself will be unable to predict anything else. For example, if your class took a test of aggressiveness today and scores were uncorrelated with scores from a parallel form of the test tomorrow (demonstrating unreliability), it is unlikely that the scores from either day would predict which students had fought or argued most frequently over a week's time: After all, the two sets of test scores would not even make the same prediction! Conversely, it is quite possible for a test to be highly reliable without being valid. Suppose, for example, we decided to use your current height as a measure of intelligence. Do you see why that would be reliable but not valid?

Norms and Standardization   So we have a reliable and valid test, but we still need *norms* to provide a context for interpreting different test scores. Suppose, for example, you get a score of 18 on a test designed to reveal how depressed you are. What does that mean? Are you a little depressed, not at all depressed, or about averagely depressed? To find out what your score means, you would want to compare your individual score with typical scores, or statistical **norms,** of other students. You would check the test norms to see what the usual range of scores is and what the average is for students of your age and sex. That would provide you with a context for interpreting your depression score.

You probably encountered test norms when you received your scores on aptitude tests, such as the SAT I. The norms told you how your scores compared with those of other students and helped you interpret how well you had done relative to that *normative population.* Group norms are most useful for interpreting individual scores when the comparison group shares important qualities with the individuals tested, such as age, social class, culture, and experience.

For norms to be meaningful, everyone must take the same test under standardized circumstances. **Standardization** is the administration of a testing device to all persons, in the same way,

How would you test the validity of a measure of juror attitudes?

criterion-related validity The degree to which test scores indicate a result on a specific measure that is consistent with some other criterion of the characteristic being assessed.

construct validity The degree to which a test adequately measures an underlying construct.

norm Standard based on measurement of a large group of people; used for comparing the scores of an individual with those of others within a well-defined group.

standardization A set of uniform procedures for treating each participant in a test, interview, or experiment, or for recording data.

under the same conditions. The need for standardization sounds obvious, but it does not always occur in practice. Some people may be allowed more time than others, be given clearer or more detailed instructions, be permitted to ask questions, or be motivated by a tester to perform better. When procedures do not include explicit instructions about the way to administer a test or the way to score the results, it is difficult to interpret what a given test score means or how it relates to any comparison group.

You have now seen some of the concerns researchers have when they construct a test and find out whether it is indeed testing what they wish to test. They must assure themselves that the test is reliable and valid. They must also specify the standard conditions under which it should be administered, so that resulting norms have meaning. Therefore, you should evaluate any test score you get in terms of the test's reliability and validity, the norms of performance, and the degree of standardization of the circumstances in which you took the test.

We are now ready to turn to the measurement of intelligence.

Stop and Review

① What overarching ideas did Sir Francis Galton contribute to the study of intelligence?

② How would a researcher determine whether a measure has criterion-related validity?

③ Why is it important to have norms for measures?

CRITICAL THINKING Recall the study that assessed the criterion-related validity of the Pretrial Juror Attitude Questionnaire. How might you assess the PJAQ's validity in the context of real-world trials?

✔●─[Study and **Review** on **MyPsychLab**

INTELLIGENCE ASSESSMENT

How intelligent are you or your friends? To answer this question, you must begin by defining **intelligence.** Doing so is not an easy task, but a group of 52 intelligence researchers concurred on this general definition: "Intelligence is a very general mental capability that, among other things, involves the ability to reason, plan, solve problems, think abstractly, comprehend complex ideas, learn quickly and learn from experience" (Gottfredson, 1997, p. 13). Given this range of capabilities, it should be clear immediately why controversy has almost always surrounded how intelligence is measured. The way in which theorists conceptualize intelligence and higher mental functioning greatly influences the way they try to assess it.

....

👁 Watch the Video *The Big Picture: What is Intelligence?* on **MyPsychLab**

intelligence The global capacity to profit from experience and to go beyond given information about the environment.

mental age In Binet's measure of intelligence, the age at which a child is performing intellectually, expressed in terms of the average age at which normal children achieve a particular score.

chronological age The number of months or years since an individual's birth.

Some psychologists believe that human intelligence can be quantified and reduced to a single score. Others argue that intelligence has many components that should be separately assessed. Still others say that there are actually several distinct kinds of intelligence, across different domains of experience. 👁

In this section, you'll learn how tests of intelligence mesh with these different conceptions of intelligence. Let's begin by considering the historical context in which interest in intelligence and intelligence testing first arose.

The Origins of Intelligence Testing

The year 1905 marked the first published account of a workable intelligence test. **Alfred Binet** (1857–1911) had responded to the call of the French minister of public instruction for the creation of more effective teaching methods for developmentally disabled children. Binet and his colleague **Theodore Simon** (1873–1961) believed that measuring a child's intellectual ability was necessary for planning an instructional program. Binet attempted to devise an objective test of intellectual performance that could be used to classify and separate developmentally disabled from normal schoolchildren. He hoped that such a test would reduce the school's reliance on the more subjective, and perhaps biased, evaluations of teachers.

To *quantify*—measure—intellectual performance, Binet designed age-appropriate problems or test items on which many children's responses could be compared. The problems on the test were chosen so that they could be scored objectively as correct or incorrect, could vary in content, were not heavily influenced by differences in children's environments, and assessed judgment and reasoning rather than rote memory (Binet, 1911).

Children of various ages were tested, and the average score for normal children at each age was computed. Each individual child's performance was then compared with the average for other children of his or her age. Test results were expressed in terms of the average age at which normal children achieved a particular score. This measure was called the **mental age.** For instance, when a child's score equaled the average score of a group of 5-year-olds, the child was said to have a *mental age* of 5, regardless of his or her actual **chronological age,** the number of years since birth.

Why did Binet's measure of intelligence compare chronological age and mental age?

Binet's successful development of an intelligence test had great impact in the United States. A unique combination of historical events and social-political forces had prepared the United States for an explosion of interest in assessing mental ability. At the beginning of the 20th century, the United States was a nation in turmoil. As a result of global economic, social, and political conditions, millions of immigrants entered the country. New universal education laws flooded schools with students. Some form of assessment was needed to identify, document, and classify immigrant adults and schoolchildren (Brysbaert & Rastle, 2009). When World War I began, millions of volunteers marched into recruiting stations. Recruiters needed to determine who of these many people had the ability to learn quickly and benefit from special leadership training. New nonverbal, group-administered tests of mental ability were used to evaluate over 1.7 million recruits. A group of prominent psychologists, including Lewis Terman, Henry Goddard, and Robert Yerkes, responded to the wartime emergency and designed these tests in only one month's time (Thorne & Henley, 2005).

One consequence of this large-scale testing program was that the American public came to accept the idea that intelligence tests could differentiate people in terms of leadership ability and other socially important characteristics. This acceptance led to the widespread use of tests in schools and industry. Assessment was seen as a way to inject order into a chaotic society and as an inexpensive, democratic way to separate those who could benefit from education or military leadership training from those who could not. To facilitate the wide-scale use of intelligence testing, researchers strove for more broadly applicable testing procedures. 👁

IQ Tests

Although Binet began the standardized assessment of intellectual ability in France, U.S. psychologists soon took the lead. They also developed the IQ, or intelligence quotient. The IQ was a numerical, standardized measure of intelligence. Two families of individually administered IQ tests are used widely today: the Stanford–Binet scales and the Wechsler scales.

The Stanford–Binet Intelligence Scale Stanford University's **Lewis Terman**, a former public school administrator, appreciated the importance of Binet's method for assessing intelligence. He adapted Binet's test questions for U.S. schoolchildren, he standardized the administration of the test, and he developed age-level norms by giving the test to thousands of children. In 1916, he published the Stanford Revision of the Binet Tests, commonly referred to as the *Stanford–Binet Intelligence Scale* (Terman, 1916).

With his new test, Terman provided a base for the concept of the **intelligence quotient, or IQ** (a term coined by William Stern, 1914). The IQ was the ratio of mental age to chronological age multiplied by 100 to eliminate decimals:

$$IQ = \text{mental age} \div \text{chronological age} \times 100$$

A child with a chronological age of 8 whose test scores revealed a mental age of 10 had an IQ of 125 (10 ÷ 8 × 100 = 125), whereas a child of that same chronological age who performed at the level of a 6-year-old had an IQ of 75 (6 ÷ 8 × 100 = 75). Individuals who performed at the mental age equivalent to their chronological age had IQs of 100. Thus the score of 100 was considered to be the average IQ.

The new Stanford–Binet test soon became a standard instrument in clinical psychology, psychiatry, and educational counseling. The Stanford–Binet contains a series of subtests, each tailored for a particular mental age. Since it was first introduced, the Stanford–Binet has undergone a series of revisions (Terman & Merrill, 1937, 1960, 1972; Thorndike et al., 1986). Through those revisions, the range of the test has been extended to measure the IQ of very young children and very intelligent adults. In addition, the revisions have provided updated norms for age-appropriate average scores. The most recent, fifth edition of the Stanford–Binet test provides IQ estimates for individuals in the normal range of performance as well as for those individuals who are either mentally impaired or mentally gifted (Roid, 2003). 👁

The Wechsler Intelligence Scales **David Wechsler** of Bellevue Hospital in New York set out to correct the dependence on verbal items in the assessment of adult intelligence. In 1939, he published the Wechsler–Bellevue Intelligence Scale, which combined verbal subtests with nonverbal, or performance, subtests. Thus, in addition to an overall IQ score, people were given separate estimates of verbal IQ and nonverbal IQ. After a few changes, the test was retitled the *Wechsler Adult Intelligence Scale*—the WAIS—in 1955. Today, you would take the WAIS-IV (Wechsler, 2008).

The WAIS-IV has 10 core subtests and five supplemental subtests that span several aspects of IQ. **Table 1** provides examples of the types of questions you would find on the test. As you can see in the table, the WAIS-IV organizes the subtests into four scales that measure verbal comprehension, perceptual reasoning, working memory, and processing speed. If you were to take the WAIS-IV, you could receive an overall, or Full Scale, IQ as well as separate measures for each of the four scales.

The WAIS-IV is designed for people age 16 years and older, but similar tests have been developed for children (see **Figure 1**). *The Wechsler Intelligence Scale for Children—Fourth Edition* (WISC-IV; Wechsler, 2003) is suited for children ages 6 to 16, and the *Wechsler Preschool and Primary Scale of Intelligence—Third Edition* (WPPSI-III; Wechsler, 2002) for children ages 2½ to 7¼ years. The revisions of both tests have made the materials more colorful, more contemporary, and more enjoyable for children. However researchers continue to strive for improvements: Testing for a new WPPSI-IV began in 2011.

The WAIS-IV, the WISC-IV, and the WPPSI-III form a family of intelligence tests that yield Full Scale IQ scores at all age levels. In addition, they provide comparable subtest scores that allow researchers to track the development over time of more specific intellectual abilities. For this reason, the Wechsler scales are particularly valuable when the same individual is to be tested at different ages—for example, when a child's progress in response to different educational programs is monitored.

....

👁 Watch the Video *Special Topics: Intelligence Testing, Then and Now* on MyPsychLab

👁 Watch the Video *Classic Footage of Assessment of Memory with the Stanford-Binet Intelligence Scale* on MyPsychLab

intelligence quotient (IQ) An index derived from standardized tests of intelligence; originally obtained by dividing an individual's mental age by chronological age and then multiplying by 100; now directly computed as an IQ test score.

Table 1 • Questions and Problems Similar to Those on the WAIS-IV

Verbal Comprehension Scale	
Similarities	In what ways are airplanes and submarines alike?
Vocabulary	What does *emulate* mean?
Perceptual Reasoning Scale	
Block Design	The test taker uses patterned blocks to reproduce designs provided by the examiner.
Picture Completion	The test taker examines a picture and says what is missing (for example, a horse without a mane).
Working Memory Scale	
Digit Span	Repeat the following numbers: 3 2 7 5 9.
Arithmetic	If you paid $8.50 for a movie ticket and $2.75 for popcorn, how much change would you have left from a $20 bill?
Processing Speed Scale	
Symbol Search	The test taker tries to determine whether one of two abstract symbols (such as Θ, A) appears on a longer list of symbols.
Cancellation	The test taker looks at visual displays and carries out the examiner's instructions (for example, "Draw a line through each blue square and green triangle").

Extremes of Intelligence

IQ scores are no longer derived by dividing mental age by chronological age. If you took the test today, your score would be added up and directly compared with the scores of other people your age. An IQ of 100 is "average" and would indicate that 50 percent of those your age had earned lower scores. **Figure 2** shows the distribution of IQ scores as measured by the WAIS. In this section, we consider the individuals whose IQ scores are below 70 and above 130. As you can see in Figure 2, those scores are quite rare.

Intellectual Disability and Learning Disorders When individuals below the age of 18 obtain valid IQ scores that are approximately two standard deviations below the mean on an intelligence test, they meet one criterion for a classification of **intellectual disability.** For the WAIS, that criterion would represent an IQ score of 70. However, as shown in **Table 2,**

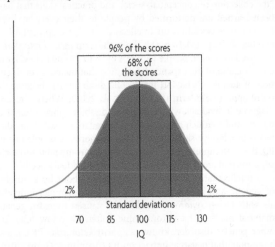

FIGURE 2 Distribution of IQ Scores in the General Population

IQ scores are normed so that a score of 100 is the population average (as many people score below 100 as score above 100). Scores between 85 and 115 are labeled average. Scores above 130 may indicate that an individual is gifted; scores below 70 contribute to a diagnosis of intellectual disability.

From Craig, Grace J.; Dunn, Wendy L., *Understanding Human Development*, 2nd Edition, © 2010. Printed and electronically reproduced by permission of Pearson Education Inc., Upper Saddle River, New Jersey.

....

intellectual disability Condition in which individuals have IQ scores of 70 to 75 or below and also demonstrate limitations in the ability to bring adaptive skills to bear on life tasks.

FIGURE 1 Intelligence Testing

A psychologist administers an intelligence test to a 4-year-old child. The performance part of the test includes sorting an array of colored candy. Why is performance an important component of an IQ assessment?

From Craig, Grace J.; Dunn, Wendy L., Understanding Human Development, 2nd Edition, © 2010. Printed and electronically reproduced by permission of Pearson Education Inc., Upper Saddle River, New Jersey.

Table 2 • Diagnosis of Intellectual Disability

Intellectual disability is diagnosed if:
• The individual's IQ is approximately two standard deviations below the mean on an intelligence test.
• The individual demonstrates limitations in adaptive behavior, such as
Conceptual skills
Language use
Reading and writing
Money concepts
Social skills
Follow rules/obey laws
Social responsibility
Avoid victimization
Practical skills
Personal care
Health care
Occupational skills
• The age of onset is below 18.

Source: Excerpted from American Association on Mental Retardation, 2010, p. 44.

to be considered intellectually disabled, individuals must also demonstrate limitations in adaptive behavior, which is defined as "the collection of conceptual, social, and practical skills that have been learned are performed by people in their everyday lives" (American Association on Intellectual and Developmental Disabilities, 2010, p. 15). In earlier times, the term *mental retardation* was used to refer to people with IQs of 70 to 75 and below. However, because of the expanded definition that includes consideration of adaptive behavior, intellectual disability has become the more appropriate term (Schalock et al., 2007). When clinicians diagnose individuals with intellectual disability, they attempt to understand as much as possible what limitations each individual has with adaptive skills. Rather than categorizing people just on IQ, the contemporary goal is to provide environmental and social supports that are closely matched to each individual's needs.

Intellectual disability can be brought about by a number of genetic and environmental factors. For example, individuals with *Down syndrome*—a disorder caused by extra genetic material on the 21st chromosome—often have low IQs. Another genetic disorder, known as *phenylketonuria* (PKU), also has a potential negative impact on IQ (Brumm & Grant, 2010). However, through strict adherence to a special diet, people can control the negative effects of PKU if it is diagnosed in infancy. Family studies suggest that genetic inheritance likely plays a role for intellectual disability only in the IQ range of 55 to 70 (Plomin & Spinath, 2004). The more severe forms of disability appear to be caused by the occurrence of spontaneous genetic abnormalities in an individual's development that are not heritable. The environment that is most often critical for intellectual disability is the prenatal environment. Pregnant women who suffer diseases such as rubella and syphilis are at risk for

having children with intellectual disabilities. In addition, pregnant women who consume alcohol or other drugs, particularly during the early weeks of pregnancy, also increase the likelihood of having children with cognitive deficits (Bennett et al., 2008; Huizink & Mulder, 2006).

Historically, individuals with intellectual disabilities were educated—to the extent that they were educated—almost entirely in separate facilities. However, evidence accumulated that these separate programs were not effective. In 1975, the U.S. government passed legislation requiring that students with disabilities be educated to the greatest extent possible in general classrooms (McLeskey et al., 2011). The law recognizes that some levels of impairment still require students to receive separate instruction. However, educational practice has changed over the decades so that increasing numbers of students diagnosed with an intellectual disability spend some or much of each school day in classrooms with their peers.

IQ scores give general information about how well people are able to perform—with respect to age-appropriate norms—on a variety of verbal and nonverbal tasks. In some instances, there is cause for concern when IQ scores and performance fail to match up. People who present a sufficiently large discrepancy between their achievement and their measured IQ might be diagnosed with a learning disorder. Before clinicians diagnose a **learning disorder,** they need to rule out other factors that can lead to poor performance, such as low motivation, mediocre teaching, or physical problems (such as visual deficits). Many schools provide special assistance to students who have been diagnosed with learning disorders.

Giftedness Individuals are most likely to be labeled as *gifted* if they have an IQ score above 130. However, as with the definition of intellectual disability, researchers have suggested that the conception of giftedness is not adequately captured just by IQ. For example, **Joseph Renzulli** (2005) has argued in favor of a "three-ring" conception of giftedness that characterizes giftedness along the dimensions of ability, creativity, and task commitment (see **Figure 3**). On this view, individuals can be considered gifted with IQs that are

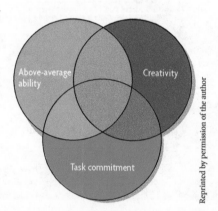

FIGURE 3 The Three-Ring Conception of Giftedness

According to the three-ring conception, gifted individuals are found at the intersection of above-average ability, high levels of creativity, and high levels of task commitment.

Reprinted by permission of the author.

....

learning disorder A disorder defined by a large discrepancy between individuals' measured IQ and their actual performance.

Critical Thinking in Your Life

WHY DO INTELLIGENT PEOPLE HAVE LONGER LIVES?

Let's begin with a fact: People with higher IQs tend to live longer lives (Deary et al., 2010b). Consider a study that examined the mortality of 1,181 people born in Scotland in 1936 (Deary et al., 2008). Their intelligence was measured as children, in 1947, using a standard IQ test. The researchers determined who had died in the period from 1968 to 2003. When the researchers related IQ to mortality, they discovered a strong pattern: For each standard deviation increase in IQ score (see Figure 2), there was "a 30% reduced hazard of dying" (p. 876). This pattern of greater longevity for people with higher IQs has been replicated across several national samples (Deary et al., 2010b).

This fact about IQ and mortality has given rise to four explanations (Deary, 2008):

- Lower IQ scores in childhood might arise, in part, from circumstances in the pre- of postnatal environment that caused an individual's brain not to function at full potential. The same brain deficiencies that lead to lower IQ might also hasten death.

- Some people might possess not just more efficient brains but a whole "well-put-together system" (Deary, 2008, p. 176) that extends to the whole body. That well-put-together system might yield both higher IQ and greater physical health.

- People with higher IQs typically obtain more education and, as a consequence, pursue more professional careers. Higher IQs might, therefore, ultimately allow people to lead lives in environments that provide fewer potential dangers to their health.

- People with higher IQs might engage in fewer behaviors that are dangerous to their health. In fact, evidence suggests that "people with higher intelligence in early life are more likely to have better diets, take more exercise, avoid accidents, give up smoking, engage in less binge drinking and put on less weight in adulthood" (Deary, 2008, p. 176).

Note that these explanations are not mutually exclusive. That is, each of them could contribute to the correlation between IQ and longevity.

Let's focus on the idea that people with higher IQs engage in fewer unhealthy behaviors. Two researchers examined data from over 10,000 Wisconsin high school students (Hauser & Palloni, 2011). They found a strong relationship between IQ and survival. However, they found an even stronger relationship between class rank and survival. Students who had ranked at the top of their class greatly outlived their peers at the bottom. Based on these results, the researchers called attention to the students' attitudes and behaviors: They suggested that the same qualities that led the students to excel in high school helped assure them longer lives. This conclusion is important because people don't need high IQs to make intelligent decisions about school, work, and healthful lifestyles.

- The relationship between IQ and longevity provides a strong example of correlation not being causation. How does each explanation attempt to identify the factors that contribute to the correlation?

- Which explanations give people the opportunity to change the relationship between their own IQ and their potential longevity?

---

above average but not necessarily superior. In addition, they need to show high levels of creativity and exert high levels of commitment to particular problems or domains of performance. This expanded definition of giftedness explains why people often are not gifted across the academic spectrum (Sternberg, 2010). Abilities, creativity, and task commitment may all differ, for example, between verbal and mathematical domains.

What qualities do gifted children generally possess? The formal study of gifted children began in 1921 when Lewis Terman (1925) began a long-term study of a group of over 1,500 boys and girls who tested in the top 1 percent of their school populations. This group of individuals was followed all the way into their 80s (Holahan & Sears, 1995). Terman and his successors wanted to see how these children fared as they made their way through life. The questions Terman asked continue to shape the research agenda. For example, Terman explored the myth that gifted children have problems with social and emotional adjustment. Terman concluded just the opposite: He found his sample to be better adjusted than their less gifted peers. Contemporary research comparing the personality attributes of gifted and non-gifted students continues to contradict the stereotype that gifted students are less well-adjusted than their peers (Martin et al., 2010; Zeidner & Shani-Zinovich, 2011). In fact, gifted students may have some advantages, such as lower levels of anxiety.

Terman also documented that the gifted children were largely successful in life. This is not surprising because IQ is a good predictor of occupational status and income. Thus the concern about gifted individuals is not that they aren't doing well. The concern, instead, is that they don't receive sufficient educational support to allow them to develop their gifts fully (Reis & Renzulli, 2010). When giftedness is recognized as a multidimensional construct, gifted education must also have the flexibility to address individual students' particular talents.

Stop *and* Review

① What measures were originally used to compute the intelligence quotient?

② What type of subtests did David Wechsler introduce to the measurement of IQ?

③ What factors contribute to the diagnosis of intellectual disability?

④ What dimensions define giftedness in the "three-ring" conception?

✔•⌐Study and Review on MyPsychLab

THEORIES OF INTELLIGENCE

So far, we have seen some of the ways in which intelligence has been measured. You are now in a position to ask yourself: Do these tests capture everything that is meant by the word *intelligence*? Do these tests capture all abilities you believe constitute your own intelligence? To help you to think about those questions, I now review theories of intelligence. As you read about each theory, ask yourself whether its proponents would be comfortable using IQ as a measure of intelligence. ◉

Psychometric Theories of Intelligence

Psychometric theories of intelligence originated in much the same philosophical atmosphere that gave rise to IQ tests. **Psychometrics** is the field of psychology that specializes in mental testing in any of its facets, including personality assessment, intelligence evaluation, and aptitude measurement. Thus psychometric approaches are intimately related to methods of testing. These theories examine the *statistical relationships* between different measures of ability, such as the 14 subtests of the WAIS-III, and then make inferences about the nature of human intelligence on the basis of those relationships. The technique used most frequently is called *factor analysis*, a statistical procedure that detects a smaller number of dimensions, clusters, or factors within a larger set of independent variables. The goal of factor analysis is to identify the basic psychological dimensions of the concept being investigated. Of course, a statistical procedure only identifies statistical regularities; it is up to psychologists to suggest and defend interpretations of those regularities.

Charles Spearman carried out an early and influential application of factor analysis in the domain of intelligence. Spearman discovered that the performance of individuals on each of a variety of intelligence tests was highly correlated. From this pattern he concluded that there is a factor of *general*

....

◉ Watch the Video *The Basics: Theories of Intelligence* on MyPsychLab
· **psychometrics** The field of psychology that specializes in mental testing.
g According to Spearman, the factor of general intelligence underlying all intelligent performance.
crystallized intelligence The facet of intelligence involving the knowledge a person has already acquired and the ability to access that knowledge; measures by vocabulary, arithmetic, and general information tests.
fluid intelligence The aspect of intelligence that involves the ability to see complex relationships and solve problems.

intelligence, or *g*, underlying all intelligent performance (Spearman, 1927). Each individual domain also has associated with it specific skills that Spearman called *s*. For example, a person's performance on tests of vocabulary or arithmetic depends both on his or her general intelligence and on domain-specific abilities.

Raymond Cattell (1963), using more advanced factor analytic techniques, determined that general intelligence can be broken down into two relatively independent components, which he called crystallized and fluid intelligence. **Crystallized intelligence** involves the knowledge a person has already acquired and the ability to access that knowledge; it is measured by tests of vocabulary, arithmetic, and general information. **Fluid intelligence** is the ability to see complex relationships and solve problems; it is measured by tests of block designs and spatial visualization in which the background information needed to solve a problem is included or readily apparent. Crystallized intelligence allows you to cope well with your life's recurring, concrete challenges; fluid intelligence helps you attack novel, abstract problems.

Since Cattell, many psychologists have broadened their conceptions of intelligence to include much more than performance on traditional IQ tests. Let's now examine two types of theories that go beyond IQ.

Sternberg's Triarchic Theory of Intelligence

Robert Sternberg (1999) also stresses the importance of cognitive processes in problem solving as part of his more general theory of intelligence. Sternberg outlines a triarchic—three-part—theory. His three types of intelligence, analytical, creative, and practical, all represent different ways of characterizing effective performance. Sternberg suggests that *successful intelligence* reflects performance in all three domains.

Analytical intelligence provides the basic information-processing skills that people apply to life's many familiar tasks. This type of intelligence is defined by the components, or mental processes, that underlie thinking and problem solving. Sternberg identifies three types of components that are central to information processing: (1) knowledge acquisition components, for learning new facts; (2) performance components, for problem-solving strategies and techniques; and (3) metacognitive components, for selecting strategies and monitoring progress toward success. To put some of your analytical intelligence to work, you can try the exercise in **Table 3**.

How did you do on the anagrams? To solve these anagrams, you mostly needed to use performance components and metacognitive components. The performance components are what allowed you to manipulate the letters in your head; the metacognitive components are what allowed you to have strategies for finding solutions. Consider T-R-H-O-S. How did you mentally transform that into SHORT? A good strategy to get started is to try consonant clusters that are probable in English—such as S-H and T-H. Selecting strategies requires metacognitive components; carrying them out requires performance components. Note that a good strategy will sometimes fail. Consider T-N-K-H-G-I. What makes this anagram hard for many people is that K-N is not a very likely combination to start a word, whereas T-H is. Did you stare at this anagram for a while, trying to turn it into a word beginning with T-H?

Table 3 • Using Analytical Intelligence

The following is a list of *anagrams*—scrambled words. As quickly as possible, try to find a solution for each anagram

1. H-U-L-A-G	_____
2. P-T-T-M-E	_____
3. T-R-H-O-S	_____
4. T-N-K-H-G-I	_____
5. T-E-W-I-R	_____
6. L-L-A-O-W	_____
7. R-I-D-E-V	_____
8. O-C-C-H-U	_____
9. T-E-N-R-E	_____
10. C-I-B-A-S	_____

The solutions are listed in "Recapping Main Points."

From Sternberg, R. J. 1986. *Intelligence applied.* San Diego: Harcourt Brace Jovanovich. Reprinted by permission of the author.

By breaking down various tasks into their components, researchers can pinpoint the processes that differentiate the performance outcomes of individuals with different IQs. For example, researchers might discover that the metacognitive components of high-IQ students prompt them to select different strategies to solve a particular type of problem than do their lower-IQ peers. The difference in strategy selection accounts for the high-IQ students' greater problem-solving success.

Creative intelligence captures people's ability to deal with novel problems. Sternberg (2006) suggests that "creative intelligence involves skills used to create, invent, discover, imagine, suppose, or hypothesize" (p. 325). Suppose, for example, a group of individuals found themselves stranded after an accident. You would credit with intelligence the person in the group who could most quickly help the group find its way home.

Practical intelligence is reflected in the management of day-to-day affairs. It involves your ability to *adapt* to new and different environments, *select* appropriate environments, and effectively *shape* your environment to suit your needs. Practical intelligence is bound to particular contexts. To measure practical intelligence, researchers must immerse themselves in those contexts to develop appropriate measures.

A team of researchers wanted to assess the importance of practical intelligence for executives in the printing and graphics industry (Baum et al., 2011). They developed a measure of practical intelligence that comprised scenarios relevant to the industry (for example, company sales have fallen). The participants who completed the measure—all of whom were leaders of companies in the industry—then read a list of 10 possible actions to address the situation. Their task was to put the actions in sequence from "most important to do first" to "least important to do first" (p. 413). To calculate practical intelligence, the researchers compared each leader's responses to the rankings of 50 industry experts. The researchers assessed the relationship between practical intelligence and the growth of each business in the four years after the assessment took place. Among leaders who indicated that they wished their companies to grow,

greater practical intelligence was associated with higher growth.

You can see from this example why practical intelligence requires different measures for different contexts. However, the general idea remains the same: People can bring more or less practical intelligence to bear on their day-to-day tasks.

Critics of Sternberg's theory have typically wondered whether measures of creative and practical intelligence can be meaningfully separated from more classic concepts like *g* (Brody, 2003; Gottfredson, 2003). The underlying question is whether Sternberg's anlaysis of successful intelligence actually predicts success better than classic IQ measures. To counter these criticisms, Sternberg has created real-world applications of his theory. For example, he and his collaborators have measured the theory's broader range of intellectual skills with the goal of improving the college admissions process (Sternberg, 2010). Sternberg asserts that the combined measures of successful intelligence allow for better predictions of students' academic performance in their first year of college.

Gardner's Multiple Intelligences and Emotional Intelligence

Howard Gardner (1999, 2006) has also proposed a theory that expands the definition of intelligence beyond those skills covered on an IQ test. Gardner identifies numerous intelligences that cover a range of human experience. The value of any of the abilities differs across human societies, according to what is needed by, useful to, and prized by a given society. As shown in **Table 4** Gardner identified eight intelligences.

Gardner argues that Western society values logical–mathematical and linguistic intelligence, whereas non-Western societies often value other types of intelligence. For example, in the Caroline Island of Micronesia, sailors must be able to navigate long distances without maps, using only their spatial intelligence and bodily kinesthetic intelligence. Such abilities count more in that society than the ability to write a term paper. In Bali, where artistic performance is part of everyday life, musical intelligence and talents involved in coordinating intricate dance steps are highly valued. Interpersonal intelligence is more central to collectivist societies such as Japan, where cooperative action and communal life are emphasized, than it is in individualistic societies such as the United States (Triandis, 1990).

Many people have embraced Gardner's theory because it suggests that people can excel in domains that are not recognized by traditional conceptions of intelligence. However, Gardner's theory has not been without critics. To begin, research suggests that there is overlap among people's functioning on what Gardner argues are separate types of intelligence (Almeida et al., 2010; Visser et al., 2006). For example, measures of Linguistic, Logial/Mathematical, Spatial, Naturalistic, and Interpersonal intelligence all show strong correlations with *g*. These correlations suggest that Gardner might just be relabeling different aspects of traditional conceptions of intelligence. Other critiques have focused on particular intelligences. For example, research evidence argues against the idea that language learning ability reflects an innate talent (Mercer, 2012).

Explore the Concept *Gardner's Multiple Intelligences* on MyPsychLab

Table 4 • Gardner's Multiple Intelligences

Form of Intelligence	Definition	Examples of Professions in Which the Form Is Important
Logical-mathematical	The ability to manipulate abstract symbols	Science, computer programming
Linguistic	The ability to use language well	Journalism, law
Naturalist	The ability to observe aspects of the natural environment carefully	Forest conservation
Musical	The ability to compose and understand music	Audio engineering, music
Spatial	The ability to reason well about spatial relations	Architecture, surgery
Bodily-kinesthetic	The ability to plan and understand sequences of movements	Dance, athletics
Interpersonal	The ability to understand other people and social interactions	Politics, teaching
Intrapersonal	The ability to understand yourself	Ministry
Existential (tentative; Gardner, 1999)	The ability to address "the big questions" about existence	Philosophy professor

From Kosslyn, Stephen M.; Rosenberg, Robin S., *Introducing psychology: Brain, Person, Group,* 4th Edition, © 2011. Reprinted and Electronically reproduced by permission of Pearson Education, Inc., Upper Saddle River, New Jersey.

In recent years, researchers have begun to explore a type of intelligence—*emotional intelligence*—that is related to Gardner's concepts of *interpersonal* and *intrapersonal* intelligence (see Table 4). On one prominent view, **emotional intelligence** has four major components (Mayer et al., 2008a, 2008b):

- The ability to perceive, appraise, and express emotions accurately and appropriately
- The ability to use emotions to facilitate thinking
- The ability to understand and analyze emotions and to use emotional knowledge effectively
- The ability to regulate one's emotions to promote both emotional and intellectual growth

This definition reflects a view of the positive role of emotion as it relates to intellectual functioning—emotions can make thinking more intelligent, and people can think intelligently about their emotions and those of others.

Researchers have begun to demonstrate that emotional intelligence has important consequences for everyday life. Consider the emotional experiences of athletes as they anticipate and participate in sports events. Greater emotional intelligence may help athletes cope with stressors.

Featured Study

A team of researchers hypothesized that athletes who were high in emotional intelligence (EI) would be better able to control their emotions in response to stressful competition-related stimuli (Laborde et al., 2011). The researchers recruited 30 male handball players and measured their EI. To provide the players with a stressful experience, the researchers had them listen to a 20-minute audio tape that featured negative statements (for example, "Your motivation is leaving you," p. 24) as well as the sound of a hissing crowd. The researchers assessed the impact of this stressful experience by measuring the players' heart rates before and after they heard the tape. Players with low EI showed changes in their heart rate that indicated that the tape caused them to experience stress. By contrast, players with high EI showed very little impact of the stressful experience on their heart rates.

This study illustrates how players high in emotional intelligence are able to use their ability to understand and regulate emotions to cope with stressors. You can imagine how that ability might be useful in the heat of competition!

This review of intelligence testing and theories of intelligence sets the stage for a discussion of the societal circumstances that make the topic of intelligence so controversial.

Stop and Review

① Why did Spearman come to believe in *g*, general intelligence?

② What are the three types of intelligence in Sternberg's triarchic theory?

③ In Gardner's theory, what kind of intelligence might determine whether someone could be a successful sculptor?

emotional intelligence Type of intelligence defined as the abilities to perceive, appraise, and express emotions accurately and appropriately, to use emotions to facilitate thinking, to understand and analyze emotions, to use emotional knowledge effectively, and to regulate one's emotions to promote both emotional and intellectual growth.

CRITICAL THINKING   Consider the study relating practical intelligence to business growth. Why was it useful to to assess the impact of practical intelligence over a period of four years?

✓●─[Study and Review on MyPsychLab

THE POLITICS OF INTELLIGENCE

We have seen that contemporary conceptions of intelligence reject the narrow linking of a score on an IQ test with a person's intelligence. Even so, IQ tests remain the most frequent measure of "intelligence" in Western society. Because of the prevalence of IQ testing and the availability of IQ scores, it becomes easy to compare different groups according to their "average" IQ. In the United States, such ethnic and racial group comparisons have often been used as evidence for the innate genetic inferiority of members of minority groups. This section will briefly examine the history of this practice of using IQ test scores to index the alleged mental inferiority of certain groups. Then we will look at current evidence on the nature and nurture of intelligence and IQ test performance. You will see that this is one of the most politically volatile issues in psychology because public policies about immigration quotas, educational resources, and more may be based on how group IQ data are interpreted. ●

The History of Group Comparisons

In the early 1900s, psychologist **Henry Goddard** (1866–1957) advocated mental testing of all immigrants and the *selective exclusion* of those who were found to be "mentally defective." Such views may have contributed to a hostile national climate against admission of certain immigrant groups (Zenderland, 1998). Indeed, Congress passed the 1924 Immigration Restriction Act, which made it national policy to administer intelligence tests to immigrants as they arrived at Ellis Island in New York Harbor. Vast numbers of Jewish, Italian, Russian, and immigrants of other nationalities were classified as "morons" on the basis of IQ tests. Some psychologists interpreted these statistical findings as evidence that immigrants from Southern and Eastern Europe were genetically inferior to those from the hardy Northern and Western European stock (see Ruch, 1937). However, these "inferior" groups were also least familiar with the dominant language and culture, embedded in the IQ tests, because they had immigrated most recently. (Within a few decades, these group differences completely disappeared from IQ tests, but the theory of racially inherited differences in intelligence persisted.)

The argument for genetic inferiority advanced by Goddard (1917) and others was reinforced by World War I Army Intelligence tests on which African Americans and

....
● Watch the Video *In the Real World: Intelligence Tests and Stereotypes* on MyPsychLab

other racial minorities scored lower than the White majority. Louis Terman, whom as we saw promoted IQ testing in the United States, commented in this unscientific manner on the data he had helped collect on U.S. racial minorities:

> *Their dullness seems to be racial. . . . There seems no possibility at present of convincing society that they should not be allowed to reproduce, although from a eugenics point of view, they constitute a grave problem because of their unusually prolific breeding.*
> (Terman, 1916, pp. 91–92)

The names have changed, but the problem remains the same. In the United States today, African Americans and Latinos score, on average, lower than Asian Americans and Whites on standardized intelligence tests. Of course, there are individuals in all groups who score at the highest (and the lowest) extremes of the IQ scale. How should these group differences in IQ scores be interpreted? One tradition has been to attribute these differences to genetic inferiority (nature). After this section discusses the evidence for genetic differences in IQ, we will consider a second possibility, that differences in environments (nurture) exert a significant impact on IQ. The validity of either explanation, or some combination of them, has important social, economic, and political consequences.

Heredity and IQ

How can researchers assess the extent to which intelligence is genetically determined? Any answer to this question requires that the researcher choose some measure as an index of intelligence. Thus the question becomes not whether "intelligence," in the abstract, is influenced by heredity but, in most cases, whether IQs are similar within family trees. To answer this more limited question, researchers need to tease apart the effects of shared genes and shared environment. One method

Why were IQ tests given to immigrants as they arrived at Ellis Island? How were these tests used to draw conclusions about genetic inferiority?

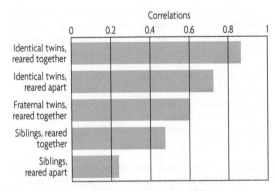

FIGURE 4 IQ and Genetic Relationship

This figure presents the correlations between the IQ scores of identical (monozygotic), fraternal (dizygotic) twins, and other sibling pairs. The data demonstrate the importance of both genetic factors and environmental factors. For example, identical twins show higher correlations between their IQs than do fraternal twins or other sibling pairs—a genetic influence. However, the correlations are also higher when the twins and other sibling pairs were raised together—an environmental influence.

Data from Bouchard, T. J., & McGue, M. (1981). Familial studies of intelligence: A review. *Science, 212,* 1055–1059.

is to compare functioning in identical twins (monozygotic), fraternal twins (dizygotic), and relatives with other degrees of genetic overlap. **Figure 4** presents correlations between IQ scores of individuals on the basis of their degree of genetic relationship (Bouchard & McGue, 1981). As you can see, the greater the genetic similarity, the greater the IQ similarity. (Note in these data that the impact of environment is also revealed in the greater IQ similarities among those who have been reared together.) 🌼

Researchers use results of this sort to try to estimate the *heritability* of IQ. A **heritability estimate** of a particular trait, such as intelligence, is based on the proportion of the variability in test scores on that trait that can be traced to genetic factors. The estimate is found by computing the variation in all the test scores for a given population (college students or psychiatric patients, for example) and then identifying what portion of the total variance is due to genetic or inherited factors. This is done by comparing individuals who have different degrees of genetic overlap. Researchers who have reviewed the variety of studies on heritability of IQ conclude that about 30 to 80 percent of the variance in IQ scores is due to genetic makeup (Deary et al., 2010a).

That range in heritability estimates arises, in part, because heritability *increases* across the life span: To document this increase, researchers have often assessed twins' IQ repeatedly over several years (van Soelen et al., 2011). Let's consider a study that took 13 years to complete.

....

🌼 Explore the Concept *Correlations Between IQ Scores of Persons of Varying Relationships* on MyPsychLab

heritability estimate A statistical estimate of the degree of inheritance of a given trait or behavior, assessed by the degree of similarity between individuals who vary in their extent of genetic similarity.

Featured Study

A team of researchers began their study by recruiting 209 pairs of 5-year-old twins (Hoekstra et al., 2007). At age 5, the children completed an IQ test that provided estimates for both verbal and nonverbal IQ. The researchers measured the twins' IQs again at ages 7, 10, 12, and 18 years. Given the duration of the study, you won't be surprised that some twins dropped out over time. However, the researchers were able to obtain IQs for 115 pairs at all five ages. The data analyses showed that the twins' IQs were reasonably stable over time. Across all the twin pairs, the correlations between scores at age 5 and scores at age 18 were 0.51 for verbal IQ and 0.47 for nonverbal IQ. To estimate heritability, the researchers compared the correlations between MZ and DZ twins at each age. For verbal IQ, the heritability estimate was 46 percent at age 5 and increased to 84 percent at age 18. For nonverbal IQ, the heritability estimate was 64 percent at age 5 and increased to 74 percent at age 18.

Many people are surprised by a result of this sort, because it seems that environments should have more, not less, of an effect as people get older. Here's how researchers explain such counterintuitive findings: "It is possible that genetic dispositions nudge us toward environments that accentuate our genetic propensities, thus leading to increased heritability throughout the life span" (Plomin & Petrill, 1997, p. 61).

Let's return now to the point at which genetic analysis becomes controversial: test score differences between African Americans and White Americans. Several decades ago, the gap between the scores of Whites and Blacks was roughly 15 IQ points. However, researchers estimated that the gap closed by 4 to 7 points in the 30 years from 1972 to 2002 (Dickens &

This photo shows Nobel Prize–winning chemist Marie Curie with her daughters Irene (on the left) and Eve (on the right). Irene also won a Nobel Prize in chemistry, and Eve became a famous author. Why do families like this one encourage researchers to attempt to understand the impact of heredity and environment on IQ?

© INTERFOTO/Alamy

Flynn, 2006). Although the close in the gap suggests environmental influences, the lingering difference has prompted many people to suggest that there are unbridgeable genetic differences between the races (Hernnstein & Murray, 1994). However, even if IQ is highly heritable, does this difference reflect genetic inferiority of individuals in the lower-scoring group? The answer is no. Heritability is based on an estimate *within* one given group. It cannot be used to interpret differences *between* groups, no matter how large those differences are on an objective test.

Heritability estimates pertain only to the average in a given population of individuals. We know, for instance, that the heritability estimate for height is quite high—in the range of 0.93 to 0.96 (Silventoinen et al., 2006). Still, you cannot determine how much of your height is due to genetic influences. The same argument is true for IQ; despite high heritability estimates, we cannot determine the specific genetic contribution to any individual's IQ or to mean IQ scores among groups. The fact that on an IQ test one racial or ethnic group scores lower than another group does not mean that the difference between these groups is genetic in origin, even if the heritability estimate for IQ scores is high as assessed within a group (Hunt & Carlson, 2007).

Another point of controversy is the concept of race itself. When people assert that an IQ gap is caused by genetics, they make the strong assumption that genetic analysis permits clear distinctions among races. Researchers on IQ generally acknowledge that race is both a *biological* and a *social* construct. For example, the social convention in the United States is typically to call people who have any African ancestry Black. Consider the remarkable golfer Tiger Woods, who has often been labeled—and discriminated against—as African American even though his actual heritage is much more complex (his ancestors were White, Black, Thai, Chinese, and Native American). Woods provides an excellent example of circumstances in which social judgments do not follow biological reality. Even so, some intelligence researchers argue that there are sufficient differences among races that meaningful comparisons can be made (Daley & Onwuegbuzie, 2011; Hunt & Carlson, 2007). Other researchers argue just as strenuously that the concept of race is so driven by social circumstances that group comparisons are useless (Sternberg & Grigorenko, 2007; Sternberg et al., 2005).

Surely genetics plays a sizable role in influencing individuals' scores on IQ tests, as it does on many other traits and abilities. We have seen, however, that heredity does not constitute an adequate explanation for IQ differences between racial and ethnic groups. It has a necessary, but not sufficient, role in our understanding of such performance effects. Let's turn now to the role the environment may play in creating the IQ gap.

Environments and IQ

Because heritability estimates are less than 1.0, we know that genetic inheritance is not solely responsible for anyone's IQ. Environments must also affect IQ. But how can we assess what aspects of the environment are important influences on IQ? What features of your environment affect your potential to score well on an IQ test (Kristensen & Bjerkedal, 2007; van der Sluis et al., 2008)? Environments are complex stimulus packages that vary on many dimensions, both physical and social, and may be experienced in different ways by those within them. Even children in the same family setting do not necessarily share the same critical, psychological environment. Think back to growing up in your family. If you had siblings, did they

Tiger Woods has ancestors who were White, African American, Thai, Chinese, and Native American. What does that suggest about the construct of race in the United States?

all get the same attention from your parents? Did conditions of stress change over the course of time? Did your family's financial resources change? Did your parents' marital status change? It is obvious that environments are made up of many components that are in a dynamic relationship and that change over time. So it becomes difficult for psychologists to say what kinds of environmental conditions—attention, stress, poverty, health, war, and so on—actually have an impact on IQ.

Researchers have most often focused on more global measures of environment, like the socioeconomic status (SES) of the family. Children who come from more privileged, high-SES backgrounds are likely to have higher IQs than their less privileged, low-SES peers (Daley & Onwuegbuzie, 2011; Hackman et al., 2010). Why does SES affect IQ? Wealth versus poverty can affect intellectual functioning in many ways, health and educational resources being two of the most obvious. Poor health during pregnancy and low birth weight are solid predictors of a child's lowered mental ability. Furthermore, impoverished homes may suffer from a lack of books, written media, computers, and other materials that add to one's mental stimulation. The "survival orientation" of poor parents, especially in single-parent families, that leaves parents little time or energy to play with and intellectually stimulate their children is detrimental to performance on tasks such as those on standard IQ tests.

We have seen that both nature and nurture have an impact on people's intellectual functioning. However, researchers increasingly focus their attention on interactions of genes and environments. To demonstrate such an interaction for intelligence, a team of researchers followed

The personal attention children receive can affect their intelligence. In the "separate but equal" schoolroom of 1940s, African American children received little attention. In contrast, the parent shown below is deeply involved in her child's education. How do these types of environmental differences affect IQ?

750 twin pairs from ages 10 months to 2 years (Tucker-Drob et al., 2011). The children performed tests of mental abilities at both those ages. We know from research on the heritibility of intelligence that the children will have inherited genes that would predict a range of intellectual performance. However, at 10 months the children's mental ability showed very little impact of genes. This was true for children from both high- and low-SES homes. By 2 years, a different pattern emerged. Now, the children raised in high-SES homes showed levels of mental

ability that were greatly influenced by their genes. By contrast, the mental ability of children from low-SES homes still failed to show an impact of genes. This pattern suggests that the environments in which low-SES children were reared did not allow them to experience their full genetic potential.

Researchers have spent the past 40 years developing programs intended to counteract the effects of impoverished environments. The Head Start program was first funded by the federal government in 1965 to address the "physical health, developmental, social, educational, and emotional needs of low-income children and to increase the capacity of the families to care for their children, through empowerment and supportive services" (Kassebaum, 1994, p. 123). The idea of Head Start and similar programs was not to move children to privileged environments but to improve the environments into which they were born. Children are exposed to special preschool education, they receive decent daily meals, and their parents are given advice on health and other aspects of child rearing.

Consider a program started in 1962 at the High/Scope Perry preschool in Ypsilanti, Michigan (Schweinhart, 2004). The program focused on a group of 3- and 4-year-old low-income African American children who had been evaluated as being at risk for school failure. The High/Scope Perry program provided the children with a classroom environment that focused on *participatory education*—children were encouraged to initiate and plan their own activities and activities for the classroom group. In addition, the program involved parents in the children's educations through home visits and parent group meetings. The researchers followed the students who participated in the program for the next 40 years. **Figure 5** compares the outcomes of participants to a group of students from the same population who did not participate. As you can see, High/Scope Perry students had higher IQs at age 5 than their peers outside the program. They were also considerably more likely to graduate from a regular high school and have higher-paying jobs at age 40.

Assessments of early intervention programs often provide encouraging results. A project that reviewed the impact of Head Start on 2,803 children from 18 U.S. cities found consistent improvements in the childrens' cognitive development and social competence (Zhai et al., 2011). Another project evaluated the experiences of a different sample of 1,260 children (Lee, 2011). Some of the children were classified as "high risk" because their family environments included factors such as parents who were unemployed, prone to violence, or substance abusers. Children with more family risk factors benefited the most from the Head Start program. In addition, when children started at age 3, and therefore were able to spend two years in the program, they demonstrated more improvements in academic outcomes than children who started at age 4. These studies provide strong evidence for the importance of

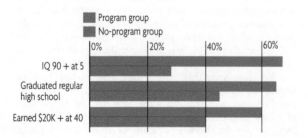

FIGURE 5 The Impact of a Preschool Intervention

Students who participated in the High/Scope Perry preschool program had better outcomes than students who were not participants.

From *Lifetime Effects: The High/Scope Perry Preschool Study Through Age 40* (p. 196) by Lawrence J. Schweinhart, JU. Montie, Z. Xiang, W.S. Barnett, C.R. Belfield & M. Nores, Ypsilanti, MI: HighScope Press. © 2005 HighScope Educational Research Foundation. Used with permission.

the environment for intellectual development. They also provide concrete models for programs that can change the lives of children who are at risk.

Culture and the Validity of IQ Tests

People would probably care much less about IQ scores if they didn't allow for such useful predictions: Extensive research shows that IQ scores are valid predictors of school grades from elementary school through college, of occupational status, and of performance in many jobs (Gottfredson, 2002; Nettelbeck & Wilson, 2005). These patterns of results suggest that IQ tests validly measure intellectual abilities that are very basic and important toward the types of success that are valued in Western cultures—intelligence, as measured by IQ, directly affects success. IQ distinctions can also affect academic and job performance indirectly by changing one's motives and beliefs. Those with higher IQ scores are likely to have had more success experiences in school, become more motivated to study, develop an achievement orientation, and become optimistic about their chances of doing well. Also, children scoring low on IQ tests may get "tracked" into schools, classes, or programs that are inferior and may even be stigmatizing to the students' sense of self-competence. In this way, IQ can be affected by environment and, in turn, can create new environments for the child—some better, some worse. IQ assessment may thus become destiny—whatever the child's underlying genetic endowment for intelligence. ◉

Even though IQ tests have proven to be valid for mainstream uses, many observers still question their validity for comparisons among different cultural and racial groups (Greenfield, 1997; Serpell, 2000). To make meaningful comparisons, researchers must use tests that have been validated for each separate group (Hunt & Carlson, 2007). However, critics have often argued that there are systematic biases in IQ tests that make them invalid across cultures. For example, questions on IQ tests that assess verbal comprehension presuppose that certain types of knowledge will have been accessible to all test takers (see Table 2). In reality, people from different cultures often have quite different background knowledge that affects the difficulty of those questions (Fagan & Holland, 2007). In addition, forms of tests and testing may not match cultural notions of intelligence or appropriate behavior (Sternberg, 2007). Consider one case of negative evaluations in the classroom:

> When children of Latino immigrant parents go to school, the emphasis on understanding rather than speaking, on respecting the teacher's authority rather than expressing one's own opinions leads to negative academic assessment. . . . Hence, a valued mode of communication in one culture—respectful listening—becomes the basis for a rather sweeping negative evaluation in the school setting where self-assertive speaking is the valued mode of communication. (Greenfield, 1997, p. 1120)

These immigrant children must learn how they must behave in U.S. classrooms to make their teachers understand the extent of their intelligence. ◉

Although concerns about cross-cultural comparisons often focus on the *content* of tests, major problems also lie in the *context* of intelligence testing. **Claude Steele** (1997; Steele & Aronson, 1995, 1998) has argued that people's performance on ability tests is influenced by **stereotype threat**—the threat of being at risk for confirming a negative stereotype of one's group. Research suggests that a person's belief that a negative stereotype is relevant in a situation can function to bring about the poor performance encoded in the stereotype. Let's consider an example of stereotype threat at work.

---

*The study focused on first- and second-generation immigrants from the West Indies (Deaux et al., 2007). The researchers hypothesized that first-generation immigrants, who were born in the West Indies, would not generally have had enough U.S. cultural experience to acquire the negative stereotypes about their intellectual abilities. By contrast, the researchers expected that second-generation immigrants, who had been born in the United States, would possess these stereotypes. That prediction was upheld when groups of students who were first- and second-generation immigrants completed scales that assessed their knowledge of the stereotypes. To demonstrate the consequences of this distribution of knowledge, the researchers had both types of immigrants complete a series of questions from the verbal portion of a GRE practice test. The researchers led half the students to believe that their performance was diagnostic of their verbal abilities. The researchers told the other half that they were only answering the questions to assist with test development. As you can see in **Figure 6**, for the second-generation immigrants who possessed the negative stereotype, performance was impaired in the diagnostic condition: When the situation made the stereotype relevant, stereotype threat had a negative impact. However, because the first-generation immigrants didn't possess the stereotype, they didn't suffer the effects of stereotype threat.*

(Featured Study)

Let me emphasize again that what affected the performance of the second-generation immigrants was how they defined the situation. Only when people believe the situation is relevant to the stereotype—because, for example, they believe that the test measures their intelligence—does knowledge of the stereotype impair performance. Given results of this type, do you think it would be possible to measure IQ without invoking stereotype threat?

Why does stereotype threat have a negative impact? Researchers have identified three mechanisms that disrupt performance (Schmader et al., 2008). First, stereotype threat produces a physiological stress response that has a negative impact on people's ability to focus their attention. Second, stereotype threat leads people to monitor their performance more closely in ways that can lead, for example, to more cautious and less creative responses. Third, when people experience stereotype threat they have to expend mental resources to suppress negative thoughts and feelings.

· ·

◉ **Watch** the **Video** *Thinking Like a Psychologist: Intelligence Tests and Success* on **MyPsychLab**

◉ **Watch** the **Video** *Cultural Influences on Intelligence: Robert Sternberg* on **MyPsychLab**

stereotype threat The threat associated with being at risk for confirming a negative stereotype of one's group.

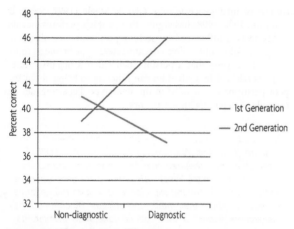

FIGURE 6 Stereotype Threat

The study contrasted second-generation immigrants—who possessed a negative stereotype about their group's intellectual ability—with first-generation immigrants—who did not possess that stereotype. Because the second-generation immigrants possessed the stereotype, their performance was impaired when they believed a test was diagnostic of their intellectual ability.

Based on Kay Deaux, Nida Bikmen, Alwyn Gilkes, Ana Ventuneac, Yvanne Joseph, Yasser A. Payne and Claude M. Steele, Becoming American: Stereotype threat effects in Afro-Caribbean immigrant groups, *Social Psychological Quarterly*, 70, pages 384-404, copyright © 2007 by the American Sociological Association.

The net effect of stereotype threat is to overwhelm test takers' working memory resources—leaving them less able to succeed on the problems at hand.

You have now learned some of the ways in which psychologists assess and interpret individual differences in intelligence. You have a good understanding of how researchers have tried to measure and understand this difficult concept. In this chapter's final section, we will consider why psychological assessment can sometimes generate controversy.

Stop *and* Review

① Under what circumstances did Goddard and others begin to make IQ comparisons among groups?

② Why is it inappropriate to use heritability estimates to make claims about racial differences in IQ?

③ What aspects of people's lives are affected by preschool interventions?

CRITICAL THINKING   Consider the study on stereotype threat. In what ways do real-life test-givers create the belief that tests are diagnostic?

✔︎ Study and Review on MyPsychLab

....

◉ Watch the Video *Are Intelligence Tests Valid: Robert Guthrie* on MyPsychLab

ASSESSMENT AND SOCIETY

The primary goal of psychological assessment is to make accurate assessments of people that are as free as possible of errors of assessors' judgments. This goal is achieved by replacing subjective judgments of teachers, employers, and other evaluators with more objective measures that have been carefully constructed and are open to critical evaluation. This is the goal that motivated Alfred Binet in his pioneering work. Binet and others hoped that testing would help democratize society and minimize decisions based on arbitrary criteria of sex, race, nationality, privilege, or physical appearance. However, despite these lofty goals, there is no area of psychology more controversial than assessment. Three ethical concerns that are central to the controversy are the fairness of test-based decisions, the utility of tests for evaluating education, and the implications of using test scores as labels to categorize individuals.

Critics concerned with the fairness of testing practices argue that the costs or negative consequences may be higher for some test takers than for others (Helms, 2006; Hosp et al., 2011). The costs are quite high, for example, when tests on which minority groups receive low scores are used to keep them out of certain jobs. Sometimes, minority group members test poorly because their scores are evaluated relative to inappropriate norms. To address these issues, researchers have studied methods of personnel selection that combine assessments of an array of cognitive and noncognitive skills (Newman & Lyon, 2009). The goal is to predict job success with composite measures that recognize group differences in test scores.

A second ethical concern is that testing not only helps evaluate students; it may also play a role in the shaping of education. The quality of school systems and the effectiveness of teachers are frequently judged on the basis of how well their students score on standardized achievement tests (Crocco & Costigan, 2007). Local support of the schools through tax levies, and even individual teacher salaries, may ride on test scores. The high stakes associated with test scores may lead to cheating. For example, one study analyzed standardized test scores for public elementary schools in Chicago. The researchers estimated that serious cases of administrator or teacher

When schools are rewarded for high scores on standardized tests, are teachers likely to place more emphasis on test-taking skills than on broader learning goals?

Psychology in Your Life

WHAT BRAIN DIFFERENCES ACCOMPANY HIGHER INTELLIGENCE?

As you've learned in this chapter, psychometricians have been measuring differences in intelligence for about 150 years. Contemporary imaging techniques have allowed researchers to examine the brain bases of these differences. Those analyses have led to conclusions both about the structure and function of different brains.

Let's begin with structural differences. Research points to the conclusion that "bigger is better" (Deary et al., 2010a). Consider a study in which individuals completed the WAIS and then underwent MRI scans to identify the brain basis for *g*. The brain scans identified several regions in which people who were relatively high on general intelligence had more brain tissue than people who were lower (Haier et al., 2004). Note, however, that this conclusion that "bigger is better" is the product of brain development. One study assessed the relationship between IQ and thickness of cortex (assessed with MRI scans) for children who ranged in age from 7 to 19 (Shaw et al., 2006). For the youngest children, there was a negative correlation between IQ and cortical thickness (that is, the children with the highest IQs were likely to have the lowest thickness). However, over the period of adolescence, the correlation reversed so that children with higher IQs ended up with thicker cortexes. Thus, what made the brains of high-IQ children special was the extremely rapid rate at which their brains grew over time. This pattern led the researchers to conclude that "intelligence is related to dynamic properties of cortical maturation" (p. 678).

Let's turn to brain function. The basic conclusion is that more intelligent people use their brain resources more efficiently when they perform cognitive tasks. In particular, they are likely to demonstrate better performance with less overall activity in the frontal cortex (Neubauer & Fink, 2009). The frontal cortex plays a critical role in many higher cognitive activities. For example, one study demonstrated the importance of the frontal cortex when people solve spatial analogies (Preusse et al., 2011). (Participants had to discover the relationship between two geometrical figures and determine whether a second pair preserved the same relationship.) The researchers divided their participants into a group that was high in fluid intelligence and a group that was average in fluid intelligence. Participants with average fluid intelligence were less accurate on the task. In addition, as shown by fMRI scans, people with average fluid intelligence showed increases in frontal activity as the problems grew harder; people with high fluid intelligence did not show similar increases. This pattern supports the conclusion that those with high fluid intelligence were making more efficient use of the frontal cortex: They were getting better results with less activity. Note that an exception to the rule of greater efficiency occurs when tasks are particularly difficult. Under those circumstances, more intelligent people tend to expand more brain resources whereas less intelligent people tend to give up on the task.

You can see how contemporary research has begun to explain the brain underpinnings of differences in intelligence.

---

cheating occur in at least 4 to 5 percent of the classrooms (Jacob & Levitt, 2003). In 2011, the state of Georgia released a report documenting extensive cheating in Atlanta's school system (Severson, 2011). The state's investigation found cheating at 44 schools involving 178 teachers and principals. The district first came under scrutiny because it had reported improvements in test scores that were statistically improbable. Many teachers confessed that they had felt pressure to cheat. These circumstances illustrate how damaging it can be when test scores are taken to matter more than education.

A third ethical concern is that test outcomes can take on the status of unchangeable labels. People too often think of themselves as being an IQ of 110 or a B student, as if the scores were labels stamped on their foreheads. Such labels may become barriers to advancement as people come to believe that their mental and personal qualities are fixed and unchangeable—that they cannot improve their lot in life. For those who are negatively assessed, the scores can become self-imposed motivational limits that lower their sense of self-efficacy and restrict the challenges they are willing to tackle. That is another dangerous consequence of pronouncements about group deficiencies in IQ.

Those stigmatized publicly in this way come to believe what the "experts" are saying about them, and so disidentify with schools and education as means to improve their lives.

This chapter has reviewed important aspects of intelligence. You've learned how researchers have defined and redefined intelligence to recognize important aspects of human performance. You've also seen why the measure of IQ remains controversial. People must give careful consideration of the broader context in which people take tests before they make claims about the abilities of particular individuals and groups.

Stop and Review

① Why might assessment have negative consequences for particular groups of individuals?

② Why might assessment play a role in shaping education?

③ Why might test scores become labels that have broad consequences?

✔ Study and Review on MyPsychLab

Recapping Main Points

What Is Assessment?

- Psychological assessment has a long history, beginning in ancient China. Many important contributions were made by Sir Francis Galton.
- A useful assessment tool must be reliable, valid, and standardized. A reliable measure gives consistent results. A valid measure assesses the attributes for which the test was designed.
- A standardized test is always administered and scored in the same way; norms allow a person's score to be compared with the averages of others of the same age, sex, and culture.

Intelligence Assessment

- Binet began the tradition of objective intelligence testing in France in the early 1900s. Scores were given in terms of mental ages and were meant to represent children's current level of functioning.
- In the United States, Terman created the Stanford–Binet Intelligence Scale and popularized the concept of IQ.
- Wechsler designed intelligence tests for adults, children, and preschoolers.
- The definitions of both intellectual disability and giftedness focus both on IQ scores and day-to-day performance.

Theories of Intelligence

- Psychometric analyses of IQ suggest that several basic abilities, such as fluid and crystallized aspects of intelligence, contribute to IQ scores.
- Contemporary theories conceive of and measure intelligence very broadly by considering the skills and insights people use to solve the types of problems they encounter.

- Sternberg differentiates analytical, creative, and practical aspects of intelligence.
- Gardner identifies eight types of intelligence that both include and go beyond the types of intelligence assessed by standard IQ measures. Recent research has focused on emotional intelligence.

The Politics of Intelligence

- Almost from the outset, intelligence tests have been used to make negative claims about ethnic and racial groups.
- Because of the reasonably high heritability of IQ, some researchers have attributed the lower scores of some racial and cultural groups to innate inferiority.
- Environmental disadvantages and stereotype threat appear to explain the lower scores of certain groups. Research shows that group differences can be affected through environmental interventions.

Assessment and Society

- Though often useful for prediction and as an indication of current performance, test results should not be used to limit an individual's opportunities for development and change.
- When the results of an assessment will affect an individual's life, the techniques used must be reliable and valid for that individual and for the purpose in question.

Solutions to the anagrams in Table 3:

1. laugh
2. tempt
3. short
4. knight
5. write
6. allow
7. drive
8. couch
9. enter
10. basic

KEY TERMS

chronological age
construct validity
content validity
criterion-related validity
crystallized intelligence
emotional intelligence
fluid intelligence
formal assessment

g
heritability estimate
intellectual disability
intelligence
intelligence quotient (IQ)
internal consistency
learning disorder
mental age

norm
psychological assessment
psychometrics
standardization
stereotype threat
test–retest reliability

Practice Test

1. Which of these was *not* one of the ideas Sir Francis Galton formulated about intelligence assessment?
a. Differences in intelligence are quantifiable.
b. Intelligence can be measured by objective tests.
c. Intelligence scores follow a bell-shaped curve.
d. Intelligence scores change over the life span.

2. When Poindexter took IQ tests on the Internet, he took four tests at the same site and obtained scores of 116, 117, 129, and 130. Given these scores, you conclude that the IQ tests are
a. neither reliable nor valid.
b. both reliable and valid.
c. reliable but not valid.
d. valid but not reliable.

3. Martin filled out a test to measure his happiness. He got a score of 72. To interpret that score, Martin needs to consult the _____ the test.
a. test–retest reliability
b. norms for
c. standardization of
d. criterion-related validity of

4. Deborah is 10 years old, but she has a mental age of 12. Using the original method for calculating IQ, you conclude that Deborah has an IQ of
a. 90.   c. 150.
b. 100.   d. 120.

5. Which cause of intellectual disability is easiest to treat?
a. Down syndrome
b. PKU
c. The mother's prenatal consumption of alcohol
d. The mother's prenatal consumption of cocaine

6. Which of these qualities is *not* part of the "three-ring" conception of giftedness?
a. creativity   c. task commitment
b. mathematical genius   d. high ability

7. At age 9, Don and Betty both had their IQs tested. Don scored 103 and Betty scored 118. Based on just that information you predict that
a. Betty will live 15 years longer than Don.
b. Don is likely to live longer than Betty.
c. Betty is likely to live longer than Don.
d. Don and Betty are likely to live roughly the same number of years.

8. _____ intelligence is defined as the knowledge a person has already acquired.
a. Crystallized   c. Fluid
b. Analytical   d. Creative

9. Felix is applying for chef school. He takes an entrance exam that poses a series of questions on food preparation. This sounds most like a test of _____ intelligence.
a. fluid   c. practical
b. analytic   d. creative

10. Julian is rarely aware when the people around him are upset. You suspect that Julian is not very high on _____ intelligence.
a. naturalist
b. emotional
c. spatial
d. bodily kinesthetic

11. Goneril and Regan are sisters. You would expect them to have the most similar IQs if they
a. are identical twins.
b. are fraternal twins.
c. grew up in the same home.
d. were adopted before age 2.

12. Studies of the impact of socioeconomic status (SES) on mental ability suggest that
a. SES only has an impact on IQ scores for particular racial groups.
b. SES has no overall impact on mental ability.
c. individuals with lower SES do not benefit from preschool programs.
d. individuals with higher SES generally demonstrate more mental ability.

13. Stereotype threat has an impact on people's test performance when they believe that
a. the stereotype is widespread in a culture.
b. the testing situation is unfair to certain ethnic groups.
c. the testing situation is relevant to the stereotype.
d. stereotypes change over time.

14. Brain research on intelligence differences suggests that, by comparison to people with lower IQs, people with higher IQs
a. acquire greater cortical thickness across adolescence.
b. always have greater cortical thickness.
c. never have greater cortical thickness.
d. have greater cortical thickness as young children.

15. When Cyrus was 12, he was told he was a genius. As an adult, he never feels as if he is living up to his potential. This is a good example of circumstances in which assessment has
a. generated an incorrect outcome.
b. yielded a label that has personal implications.
c. shaped the educational experiences of an individual.
d. had negative consequences for Cyrus's group.

ESSAY QUESTIONS

1. Why can a test be reliable but not valid?

2. What is the goal of Howard Gardner's theory of multiple intelligences?

3. How have Head Start and other early intervention programs demonstrated the impact of environments on IQ?

Stop and Review Answers

Stop and Review (What Is Assessment?)

1. Galton suggested that differences in intelligence could be measured objectively.
2. The researcher should determine whether scores on the measure allow for accurate predictions of relevant future outcomes.
3. Norms enable researchers to understand the scores of particular individuals in the context of a broader population's scores.

Stop and Review (Intelligence Assessment)

1. The original measure of IQ was mental age divided by chronological age.
2. Wechsler added performance subtests to his IQ measure.
3. Diagnosis of intellectual disability focuses on both IQ and adaptive skills.
4. The three dimensions are ability, creativity, and task commitment.

Stop and Review (Theories of Intelligence)

1. Because Spearman demonstrated that people's performance on a variety of intelligence tests was highly correlated, he concluded that there was a factor of general intelligence.
2. Sternberg proposed that people have analytical, creative, and practical intelligence.

3. Gardner defined "spatial" intelligence as the ability to perceive the visual–spatial world and transform one's initial perceptions—these abilities are relevant to sculpture.

Stop and Review (The Politics of Intelligence)

1. Goddard and others suggested that IQ tests be used to exclude some immigrants as mentally inferior.
2. Heritability estimates do not allow for comparisons between groups of individuals.
3. Research has demonstrated that people who experience quality preschool programs have higher measured IQs and are more likely to graduate from regular high schools and have better-paying jobs.

Stop and Review (Assessment and Society)

1. If members of particular groups generally test less well than others, that pattern might prevent equal access to jobs.
2. In many school districts, support is based on test scores—forcing teachers to cover only material that will be tested.
3. When tests are used without flexibility to label people as belonging to certain academic or social tracks, those labels can have broad consequences.

Practice Test Answers

1. d	5. b	9. c	13. c
2. a	6. b	10. b	14. a
3. b	7. c	11. a	15. b
4. d	8. a	12. d	

References

Almeida, L. S., Prieto, M. D., Ferreira, A. I., Bermejo, M. R., Ferrando, M., & Ferrándiz, C. (2010). Intelligence assessment: Gardner multiple intelligence theory as an alternative. *Learning and Individual Differences, 20,* 225–230.

American Association on Intellectual and Developmental Disabilities. (2010). *Intellectual disability: Definition, classification, and systems of supports* (11th ed.). Washington, DC: American Association on Intellectual and Developmental Disabilities.

Baum, J. R., Bird, B. J., & Singh, S. (2011). The practical intelligence of entrepreneurs: Antecedents and a link with new venture growth. *Personnel Psychology, 64,* 397–425.

Bennett, D. S., Bendersky, M., & Lewis, M. (2008). Children's cognitive ability from 4 to 9 years old as a function of prenatal cocaine exposure, environmental risk, and maternal verbal intelligence. *Developmental Psychology, 44,* 919–928.

Binet, A. (1911). *Les idées modernes sur les enfants.* Paris: Flammarion.

Brody, N. (2003). Construct validation of the Sternberg Triarchic Abilities Test: Comment and reanalysis. *Intelligence, 31,* 319–329.

Brumm, V. L., & Grant, M. L. (2010). The role of intelligence in phenylketonuria: A review of research and management. *Molecular Genetics and Metabolism, 99,* S18–S21.

Brysbaert, M., & Rastle, K. (2009). *Historical and conceptual issues in psychology.* Harlow, England: Pearson.

Cattell, R. B. (1963). Theory of fluid and crystallized intelligence: A critical experiment. *Journal of Educational Psychology, 54,* 1–22.

Crocco, M. S., & Costigan, A. T. (2007). The narrowing of curriculum and pedagogy in the age of accountability: Urban educators speak out. *Urban Education, 42,* 512–535.

Daley, C. E., & Onwuegbuzie, A. J. (2011). Race and intelligence. In R. J. Sternberg & S. B. Kaufman (Eds.), *The Cambridge handbook of intelligence* (pp. 293–306). New York: Cambridge University Press.

Deary, I. J., Batty, G. D., Pattie, A., & Gale, C. R. (2008). More intelligent, more dependable children live longer: A 55-year longitudinal study of a representative sample of the Scottish nation. *Psychological Science, 19,* 874–880.

Deary, I. J., Penke, L., & Johnson, W. (2010a). The neuroscience of human intelligence differences. *Nature Reviews Neuroscience, 11,* 201–211.

Deary, I. J., Weiss, A., & Batty, G. D. (2010b). Intelligence, personality, and health outcomes. *Psychological Science in the Public Interest, 11,* 53–79.

Deaux, K., Bikmen, N., Gilkes, A., Ventuneac, A., Joseph, Y., Payne, Y. A., & Steele, C. A. (2007). Becoming American: Stereotype threat effects in

Afro-Caribbean immigrant groups. *Social Psychology Quarterly, 70,* 384–404.

Dickens, W. T., & Flynn, J. R. (2006). Black Americans reduce the racial IQ gap: Evidence from standardization samples. *Psychological Science, 17,* 913–920.

Fagan, J. F., & Holland, C. R. (2007). Racial equality in intelligence: Predictions from a theory of intelligence as processing. *Intelligence, 35,* 319–334.

Galton, F. (1907). *Inquiries into human faculty and its development.* London: Dent Publishers. (Original work published 1883)

Gardner, H. (1999). *The disciplined mind.* New York: Simon & Schuster.

Gardner, H. (2006). *Multiple intelligences: New Horizons.* New York: Basic books.

Gottfredson, L. S. (1997). Mainstream science on intelligence: An editorial with 52 signatories, history, and bibliography. *Intelligence, 24,* 13–23.

Gottfredson, L. S. (2002). Where and why *g* matters: Not a mystery. *Human Performance, 15,* 25–46.

Gottfredson, L. S. (2003). Dissecting practical intelligence theory: Its claims and evidence. *Intelligence, 31i,* 343–397.

Greenfield, P. M. (1997). You can't take it with you: Why ability assessments don't cross cultures. *American Psychologist, 52,* 1115–1124.

Hackman, D. A., Farah, M. J., & Meaney, M. J. (2010). Socioeconomic status and the brain: Mechanistic insights from human and animal research. *Nature Reviews Neuroscience, 11,* 651–659.

Haier, R. J., Jung, R. E., Yeo, R. A., Head, K., & Alkire, M. T. (2004). Structural variation and general intelligence. *NeuroImage, 23,* 425–433.

Hauser, R. M., & Palloni, A. (2011). Adolescent IQ and survival in the Wisconsin longitudinal study. *The Journals of Gerontology: Series B, 66,* i91–i101.

Helms, J. E. (2006). Fairness is not validity or cultural bias in racial-group assessment: A quantitative perspective. *American Psychologist, 61,* 845–859.

Hernnstein, R. J., & Murray, C. (1994). *The bell curve.* New York: The Free Press.

Hoekstra, R. A., Bartels, M., & Boomsma, D. I. (2007). Longitudinal genetic study of verbal and nonverbal IQ from early childhood to young adulthood. *Learning and Individual Differences, 17,* 97–114.

Holahan, C. K., & Sesrs, R. R. (1995). The gifted group in later maturity. Stanford, CA: Stanford University Press.

Hosp, J. L., Hosp, M. A., & Dole, J. K. (2011). Potential bias in predictive validity of universal screening measures across disaggregation subgroups. *School Psychology Review, 40,* 108–131.

Huizink, A. C., & Mulder, E. J. H. (2006). Maternal smoking, drinking or cannabis use during pregnancy and neurobehavioral and cognitive functioning in human offspring. *Neuroscience and Biobehavioral Reviews, 30,* 24–41.

Hunt, E., & Carlson, J. (2007). Considerations relating to the study of group differences in intelligence. *Perspectives on Psychological Science, 2,* 194–213.

Jacob, B. R., & Levitt, S. D. (2003). Rotten apples: An investigation of the prevalence and predictors of teacher cheating. *The Quarterly Journal of Economics, 118,* 843–877.

Kassebaum, N. L. (1994). Head Start: Only the best for America's children. *American Psychologist, 49,* 1123–1126.

Kristensen, P., & Bjerkedal, T. (2007). Explaining the relation between birth order and intelligence. *Science, 316,* 1717.

Laborde, S., Brüll, A., Weber, J., & Anders, L. S. (2011). Trait emotional intelligence in sports: A protective role against stress through heart rate variability? *Personality and Individual Differences, 51,* 23–27.

Lecci, L., & Myers, B. (2008). Individual differences in attitudes relevant to juror decision making: Development and validation of the Pretrial Juror Attitude Questionnaire (PJAQ). *Journal of Applied Social Psychology, 38,* 2010–2038.

Lee, K. (2011). Impacts of the duration of head start enrollment on children's academic outcomes: Moderation effects of family risk factors and early outcomes. *Journal of Community Psychology, 39,* 698–716.

Martin, L. T., Burns, R. M., & Schonlau, M. (2010). Mental disorders among gifted and nongifted youth. A selected review of the epidemiologic literature. *Gifted Child Quarterly, 54,* 31–41.

Mayer, J. D., Roberts, R. D., & Barsade, S. G. (2008a). Human abilities: Emotional intelligence. *Annual Review of Psychology, 59,* 507–536.

Mayer, J. D., Salovey, P., & Caruso, D. R. (2008b). Emotional intelligence: New ability or eclectic traits. *American Psychologist, 63,* 503–517.

McLeskey, J., Landers, E., Williamson, P., & Hoppey, D. (2011). Are we moving toward educating students with disabilities in less restrictive settings? *Journal of Special Education, 26,* 60–66.

Mercer, S. (2012). Dispelling the myth of the natural-born linguist. *ELT Journal, 66,* 22–29.

Nettelbeck, T., & Wilson, C. (2005). Intelligence and IQ: What teachers should know. *Educational Psychology, 25,* 609–630.

Neubauer, A. C., & Fink, A. (2009). Intelligence and neural efficiency. *Neuroscience and Biobehavioral Reviews, 33,* 1004–1023.

Newman, D. A., & Lyon, J. S. (2009). Recruitment efforts to reduce adverse impact: Targeted recruiting for personality, cognitive ability, and diversity. *Journal of Applied Psychology, 94,* 298–317.

Plomin, R., & Petrill, S. A. (1997). Genetics and intelligence: What's new? *Intelligence, 24,* 53–77.

Plomin, R., & Spinath, F. M. (2004). Intelligence: Genetics, genes, and genomics. *Journal of Personality and Social Psychology, 86,* 112–129.

Preusse, F., van der Meer, E., Deshpande, G., Krueger, F., & Wartenburger, I. (2011). Fluid intelligence allows flexilble recruitment of the parieto-frontal network in analogical reasoning. *Frontiers in Human Neuroscience, 5,* Article 22.

Reis, S. M., & Renzulli, J. S. (2010). Is there still a need for gifted education? An examination of current research. *Learning and Individual Differences, 20,* 308–317.

Renzulli, J. S. (2005). The three-ring conception of giftedness: A developmental model for promoting creative productivity. In R. J. Sternberg & J. E. Davidson (Eds.), *Conceptions of giftedness* (2nd ed., pp. 246–279). New York: Cambridge University Press.

Roid, G. (2003). *Stanford-Binet intelligence scale* (5th ed.). Itasca, IL: Riverside Publishing.

Schalock, R. L., Luckasson, R. A., & Shogren, K. A. (2007). The renaming of *mental retardation*: Understanding the change to the term *intellectual disability. Intellectual and Developmental Disabilities, 45,* 116–124.

Schmader, T., Johns, M., & Forbes, C. (2008). An integrated process model of stereotype threat effects on performance. *Psychological Review, 115,* 336–356.

Schweinhart, L. J. (2004). *The High/Scope Perry preschool study through age 40: Summary, conclusions, and frequently asked questions.* Retrieved from www.highscope.org/Research/PerryProject/PerryAge40SumWeb.pdf.

Serpell, R. (2000). Intelligence and culture. In R. J. Sternberg (Ed.), *Handbook of intelligence* (pp. 549–577). Cambridge, UK: Cambridge University Press.

Severson, K. (2011, July 6). Systematic cheating is found in Atlanta's school system. *The New York Times,* p. A13.

Shaw, P., Greenstein, D., Lerch, J., Clasen, L. Lenroot, R., Gogtay, N., Evans, A., Rapoport, J., & Giedd, J. (2006). Intellectual ability and cortical development in children and adolescents. *Nature, 440,* 676–679.

Silventoinen, K., Posthuma, D., van Beijsterveldt, T., Bartels, M., Boomsma, D. I. (2006). Genetic contributions to the association between height and intelligence: Evidence from Dutch twin data from childhood to middle age. *Genes, Brain and Behavior, 5,* 585–595.

Spearman, C. (1927). *The abilities of man.* New York: Macmillan.

Steele, C. M. (1997). A threat in the air: How stereotypes shape intellectual identity and performance. *American Psychologist, 6,* 613–629.

Steele, C. M., & Aronson, J. (1995). Stereotype threat and the intellectual test performance of African Americans. *Journal of Personality and Social Psychology, 69,* 797–811.

Steele, C. M., & Aronson, J. (1998). Stereotype threat and the test performance of academically successful African Americans. In C. Jencks & M. Phillips (Eds.), *The Black–White test score gap* (pp. 401–427). Washington, DC: Brookings Institution Press.

Sternberg, R. J. (1999). The theory of successful intelligence. *Review of General Psychology, 3,* 292–316.

Sternberg, R. J. (2007). Who are the bright children? The cultural context of being and acting intelligent. *Educational Researcher, 36,* 148–155.

Sternberg, R. J. (2010). Assessment of gifted students for identification purposes: New techniques for a new millennium. *Learning and Individual Differences, 20,* 327–336.

Sternberg, R. J., & Grigorenko, E. L. (2007). The difficulty of escaping preconceptions in writing an article about the difficulty of escaping preconceptions: Commentary on Hunt and Carlson (2007). *Perspectives on Psychological Science, 2,* 221–226.

Sternberg, R. J., Grigorenko, E. L., & Kidd, K. K. (2005). Intelligence, race, and genetics. *American Psychologist, 60,* 46–59.

Terman, L. M. (1916). *The measurement of intelligence.* Boston: Houghton Mifflin.

Terman, L. M., & Merrill, M. A. (1937). *Measuring intelligence.* Boston: Houghton Mifflin.

Terman, L. M., & Merrill, M. A. (1960). *The Stanford-Binet intelligence scale.* Boston: Houghton Mifflin.

Terman, L. M., & Merrill, M. A. (1972). *Stanford-Binet intelligence scale—manual for the third revision, Form L-M.* Boston: Houghton Mifflin.

Thorndike, R. L., Hagen, E. P., & Sattler, J. M. (1986). *Stanford-Binet intelligence scale* (4th ed.). Chicago: Riverside.

Thorne, B. M., & Henley, T. B. (2005). *Connections in the history and systems of psychology* (3rd ed.). Boston: Houghton Mifflin.

Triandis, H. C. (1990). Cross-cultural studies of individualism and collectivism. In J. Berman (Ed.), *Nebraska Symposium on Motivation, 1989* (pp. 41–133). Lincoln: University of Nebraska Press.

Tucker-Drob, E., Rhemtulla, M., Harden, K. P., Turkheimer, E., & Fask, D. (2011). Emergence of a gene x socioeconomic status on infant mental ability between 10 months and 2 years. *Psychological Science, 22,* 125–133.

van der Sluis, S., Willemsen, G., de Geus, E. J. C., Boomsma, D. I., & Posthuma, D. (2008). Gene-environment interaction in adults' IQ scores: Measures of past and present environment. *Behavior Genetics, 38,* 348–360.

van Soelen, I. L. C., Brouwer, R. M., van Leeuwen, M., Kahn, R. S., Hulshoff Pol, H. E., & Boomsma, D. I. (2011). Heritability of verbal and performance intelligence in a pediatric longitudinal sample. *Twin Research and Human Genetics, 14,* 119–128.

Visser, B. A., Ashton, M. C., & Vernon, P. A. (2006). Beyond *g*: Putting multiple intelligences theory to the test. *Intelligence, 34,* 487–502.

Wechsler, D. (2002). *WPPSI-III manual.* San Antonio, TX: Psychological Corporation.

Wechsler, D. (2003). *WISC-IV manual.* San Antonio, TX: Psychological Corporation.

Wechsler, D. (2008). *Wechsler Adult Intelligence Scale—Fourth Edition.* San Antonio, TX: Pearson.

Wiggins, J. S. (1973). *Personality and prediction: Principles of personality assessment.* Reading, MA: Addison-Wesley.

Zeidner, M., & Shani-Zinovich, I. (2011). Do academically gifted and nongifted students differ on the Big-Five and adaptive status? Some recent data and conclusions. *Personality and Individual Differences, 51,* 566–570.

Zenderland, L. (1998). *Measuring minds: Henry Herbert Goddard and the origins of American intelligence testing.* Cambridge, UK: Cambridge University Press.

Zhai, F., Brooks-Gunn, J., & Waldfogel, J. (2011). Head Start and urban children's school readiness: A birth cohort study in 18 cities. *Developmental Psychology, 47,* 134–152.

Understanding Human Personality

From Chapter 13 of *Psychology and Life*, 20th Edition. Richard J. Gerrig. Copyright © 2013 by Pearson Education, Inc. All rights reserved.

Understanding
Human Personality

© Oliver Furrer/Alamy

Please take a moment to compare and contrast your two closest friends. In what ways are they similar? In what ways are they different? It seems likely that your analysis would very quickly come to focus on your friends' *personalities*. You might, for example, assert that one is friendlier than the other or that one has more self-confidence. Assertions of this sort would suggest that you've brought your own personality theory to bear on your relationships—you have your own system for appraising personality.

Psychologists define **personality** as the complex set of psychological qualities that influence an individual's characteristic patterns of behavior across different situations and over time. In this chapter, you'll encounter several theories of personality. Theories of personality are hypothetical statements about the structure and functioning of individual personalities. Each theory has two major goals. First, the theories try to understand the *uniqueness* of each individual with respect to the structure, origins, and correlates of personality. Second, they attempt to understand how each unique personality yields *characteristic patterns of behavior*. Different theories make different predictions about the way people will respond and adapt to life events.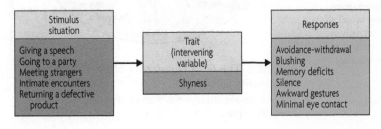

Before we meet some of the major theoretical approaches, we should ask why there are so many different (often competing) theories. Theorists differ in their approaches to personality by varying their starting points and sources of data and by trying to explain different types of phenomena. Some are interested in the structure of individual personality and others in how that personality developed and will continue to grow. Some are interested in what people do, either in terms of specific behaviors or important life events; others study how people feel about their lives. Finally, some theories try to explain the personalities of people with psychological problems, whereas others focus on healthy individuals. Thus each theory can teach something about personality, and together they can teach much about human nature.

The goal for this chapter is to provide you with a framework for understanding your everyday experience of personality. As we begin, consider this series of questions: If psychologists studied *you*, what portrait of your personality would they draw? What early experiences might they identify

as contributing to the way you now act and think? What conditions in your current life exert strong influences on your thoughts and behaviors? What makes you different from other individuals who are functioning in many of the same situations as you? This chapter should help you formulate specific answers to these questions.

TRAIT PERSONALITY THEORIES

One of the oldest approaches to personality involves scaling the degree to which people can be described by *different traits*. There seems to be a natural tendency for people to classify their own and others' behavior along different dimensions. Let's examine the formal theories psychologists have developed to capture these intuitions.

Describing with Traits

Traits are enduring qualities or attributes that predispose individuals to behave consistently across situations. For example, you may demonstrate honesty on one day by returning a lost wallet and on another day by not cheating on a test. Some trait theorists think of traits as *predispositions* that cause behavior, but more conservative theorists use traits only as *descriptive dimensions* that simply summarize patterns of observed behavior. Let's examine prominent trait theories.

Allport's Trait Approach **Gordon Allport** (1897–1967) viewed traits as the building blocks of personality and the source of individuality. According to Allport (1937, 1961, 1966), traits produce coherence in behavior because they connect and unify a person's reactions to a variety of stimuli. Traits may act as *intervening variables*, relating sets of stimuli and responses that might seem, at first glance, to have little to do with each other (see **Figure 1**).

Allport identified three kinds of traits: cardinal traits, central traits, and secondary traits. *Cardinal traits* are traits around which a person organizes his or her life. For Mother Teresa, a cardinal trait might have been self-sacrifice for the good of others. However, not all people develop such overarching cardinal traits. Instead, *central traits* are traits that represent major characteristics of a person, such as honesty or optimism. *Secondary traits* are specific personal features that help predict an individual's behavior but are less useful for understanding an individual's personality. Food or dress preferences are examples of secondary traits. Allport was interested in discovering the

....

Watch the Video *The Big Picture: What is Personality?* on **MyPsychLab**

Watch the Video *The Basics: Personality Theories* on **MyPsychLab**

personality The psychological qualities of an individual that influence a variety of characteristic behavior patterns across different situations and over time.

trait Enduring personal quality or attribute that influences behavior across situations.

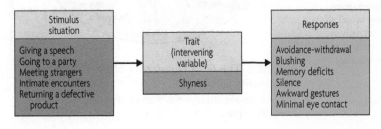

FIGURE 1 Shyness as a Trait
Traits may act as intervening variables, relating sets of stimuli and responses that might seem, at first glance, to have little to do with each other.

In the absence of personality test results, traits can be inferred from observed behavior. For example, Martin Luther King Jr. (left) would be thought to have the cardinal trait of peacefully resisting injustice; honesty would be one of Abraham Lincoln's (center) central traits; and Lady Gaga's (right) predilection for changeable styles would be a secondary trait. What do you think may be your cardinal, central, and secondary traits?

unique combination of these three types of traits that make each person a singular entity and championed the use of case studies to examine these unique traits. 👁

Allport saw *personality structures*, rather than *environmental conditions*, as the critical determiners of individual behavior. "The same fire that melts the butter hardens the egg" was a phrase he used to show that the same stimuli can have different effects on different individuals. Many contemporary trait theories have followed in Allport's tradition.

Identifying Universal Trait Dimensions   In 1936, a dictionary search by Gordon Allport and his colleague H. S. Odbert found 17,953 adjectives in the English language to describe individual differences. Researchers since that time have attempted to identify the fundamental dimensions that underlie that enormous trait vocabulary. They have tried to determine how many dimensions exist and which ones will allow psychologists to give a useful, universal characterization of all individuals.

Raymond Cattell (1979) used Allport and Odbert's list of adjectives as a starting point in his quest to uncover the appropriate small set of basic trait dimensions. His research led him to propose that 16 factors underlie human personality. Cattell called these 16 factors *source traits* because he believed they provide the underlying source for the surface behaviors we think of as personality. Cattell's 16 factors included important behavioral oppositions such as *reserved* versus *outgoing, trusting* versus *suspicious*, and *relaxed* versus *tense*. Even so, contemporary trait theorists argue that even fewer dimensions than 16 capture the most important distinctions among people's personalities.

Hans Eysenck (1973, 1990) derived just three broad dimensions from personality test data: *extraversion* (internally versus externally oriented), *neuroticism* (emotionally stable versus emotionally unstable), and *psychoticism* (kind and considerate versus aggressive and antisocial). As shown in **Figure 2**, Eysenck plotted the two dimensions of extraversion and neuroticism to form a circular display. Individuals can fall anywhere around the circle, ranging from very introverted to very extraverted and from very unstable (neurotic) to very stable. The traits listed around the circle describe people with combinations of these two dimensions. For example, a person who is very extraverted and somewhat unstable is likely to be impulsive.

FIGURE 2 **The Four Quadrants of Eysenck's Personality Circle**
The two dimensions of extraversion and neuroticism yield a circular display.

....

👁 **Watch** the **Video** *Classic Footage of Gordon Allport on Personality Traits* on **MyPsychLab**

Table 1 • The Five-Factor Model

Factor	End Points of the Dimension
Extraversion	Talkative, energetic, and assertive versus quiet, reserved, and shy
Agreeableness	Sympathetic, kind, and affectionate versus cold, quarrelsome, and cruel
Conscientiousness	Organized, responsible, and cautious versus careless, frivolous, and irresponsible
Neuroticism	Stable, calm, and contented versus anxious, unstable, and temperamental
Openness to experience	Creative, intellectual, and open-minded versus simple, shallow, and unintelligent

Five-factor Model Research evidence supports many aspects of Eysenck's theory. However, in recent years, a consensus has emerged that five factors, which overlap imperfectly with Eysenck's three dimensions, best characterize personality structure. The five dimensions are very broad because each brings into one large category many traits that have unique connotations but a common theme. These five dimensions of personality are now called the **five-factor model,** or, more informally, the *Big Five* (McCrae & Costa, 2008). The five factors are summarized in **Table 1**. You'll notice again that each dimension has two poles—terms that are similar in meaning to the name of the dimension describe the high pole, and terms that are opposite in meaning describe the low pole. ✸

The movement toward the five-factor model represented attempts to find structure among the large list of traits that Allport and Odbert (1936) had extracted from the dictionary. The traits were boiled down into about 200 synonym clusters that were used to form trait dimensions that have a high pole and a low pole, such as *responsible* versus *irresponsible*. Next, people were asked to rate themselves and others on the bipolar dimensions, and the ratings were subjected to statistical procedures to determine how the synonym clusters were interrelated. Using this method, several independent research teams came to the same conclusion: that there are only *five basic dimensions* underlying the traits people use to describe themselves and others (Norman, 1963, 1967; Tupes & Christal, 1961).

To demonstrate the universality of the five-factor model, researchers have broadened their studies beyond the English language: The five-factor structure has been replicated in 56 different nations (Schmitt et al., 2007). The five factors are not meant to replace the many specific trait terms that carry their own nuances and shades of meaning. Rather, they outline a taxonomy—a classification system—that allows you to give a description of all the people you know in ways that capture the important dimensions on which they differ.

As you've seen, the five-factor model originally emerged from statistical analyses of clusters of trait terms rather than from a theory that said, "These are the factors that must exist" (Ozer & Reise, 1994). However, researchers have started

to demonstrate that there are differences in the ways that individuals' brains function that correspond to trait differences in the five-factor model.

A brain structure called the amygdala plays an important role in the processing of emotional stimuli. However, researchers had begun to suspect that not all amygdalas—and, therefore, not all people—responded to stimuli in the same way. To test this idea, a team of researchers recruited 15 participants who differed in their level of extraversion (Canli et al., 2002b). The researchers predicted that extraversion would have an impact on emotional processing because that trait captures important aspects of people's emotional lives. To look for individual differences, the researchers had the participants view fearful, happy, and neutral faces while they underwent fMRI scans. **Figure 3** *displays the correlation between participants' self-reports of extraversion and activity in the left and right amygdalas: The areas in red are those areas for which high levels of extraversion were associated with high levels of brain activity. As you can see, extraversion was not correlated with the brains' responses to fearful faces (that is, there are no areas in red). In fact, fearful faces activated both the left and right amygdalas, but more or less equally across all levels of extraversion. By contrast, for happy faces the highly extraverted individuals showed abundant activity in the left amygdala.*

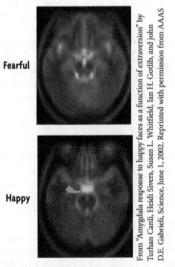

Fearful

Happy

From "Amygdala response to happy faces as a function of extraversion" by Turhan Canli, Heidi Sivers, Susan L. Whitfield, Ian H. Gotlib, and john D.E. Gabrieli, Science, June 1, 2002. Reprinted with permission from AAAS.

FIGURE 3 Extraversion Affects the Function of the Left Amygdala

Participants viewed fearful and happy faces. The figure displays in red those areas of the brain for which there was a positive correlation between extraversion and amygdala activity. For the fearful faces, there was no correlation. However, for happy faces, the most extraverted participants also showed the highest levels of activity in their left amygdalas.

From "Amygdala response to happy faces as a function of extraversion" by Turhan Canli, Heidi Sivers, Susan L. Whitfield, Ian H. Gotlib, and John D. E. Gabrieli, *Science*, June 1, 2002. Reprinted with permission from AAAS.

✸ Explore the Concept *The Five Factor Mode* on MyPsychLab

five-factor model A comprehensive descriptive personality system that maps out the relationships among common traits, theoretical concepts, and personality scales; informally called the Big Five.

Researchers have characterized emotions as either *approach-related* or *withdrawal-related*. This study suggests that people who are most content to approach other people—that's what makes them extraverted—have more activation in brain regions that support approach-related emotions.

Evolutionary Perspectives on Trait Dimensions   Supporters of the five-factor model have tried to explain why exactly these five dimensions emerge by looking to evolution: They try to relate the five dimensions to consistent types of interactions that people had with each other and with the external world over the course of human evolution (Buss, 2009; Michalski & Shackelford, 2010). Because, for example, humans are essentially a social species, we can view variation on the five dimensions as answers to fundamental social questions: "who is good company (Extraversion), who is kind and supportive (Agreeableness), who puts in sustained effort (Conscientiousness), who is emotionally undependable (Neuroticism), and who has ideas that pan out (Openness [to experience])" (Bouchard & Loehlin, 2001, p. 250). This evolutionary analysis would help explain the universality of the five factors across diverse cultures (Yamagata et al., 2006).

Researchers who take this evolutionary approach have also considered why there is such great variation along these dimensions (Penke et al., 2007). Consider extraversion. As I just noted, humans are a highly social species. For that reason, it might seem maladaptive for an individual to be unsociable and reserved rather than sociable and active. However, we need to factor in differences among environments. People who are highly extraverted are more likely to engage in risky behaviors than those who are not (Nettle, 2006). In particularly dangerous environments, people who were relatively more cautious about social interactions would be more likely to survive. The diversity of environments over human evolution explains why people embody both low and high values on each of the five dimensions. If this explanation is correct, we might also expect that, like other aspects of human experience that have been shaped by evolution, traits can be passed from one generation to the next. We turn now to that claim.

Traits and Heritability

You've probably heard people say things such as "Jim's artistic, like his mother" or "Mary's as stubborn as her grandfather." Or maybe you've felt frustrated because the characteristics that you find irritating in your siblings are those you would like to change in yourself. Let's look at the evidence that supports the heritability of personality traits.

Recall that *behavioral genetics* is the study of the degree to which personality traits and behavior patterns are inherited. To determine the effect of genetics on personality, researchers study the personality traits of family members who share different proportions of genes and who have grown up in the same or different households. For example, if a personality characteristic such as *sociability* is passed on genetically, then sociability should correlate more highly between identical, *monozygotic* (MZ) twins (who share close to 100 percent of their genes) than between fraternal, *dizygotic* (DZ) twins or other siblings (who share, on average, 50 percent of their genes). 👁

Heritability studies show that almost all personality traits are influenced by genetic factors (McCrae et al., 2010; Munafò & Flint, 2011). The findings are the same with many different

Research with identical twins demonstrates the heritability of personality traits. Are there personality traits you believe run in your family?

measurement techniques, whether they measure broad traits, such as extraversion and neuroticism, or specific traits, such as self-control or sociability. Let's consider one sample study.

To study the importance of heritability for personality, a team of researchers followed samples of 696 monozygotic twin pairs and 387 dizygotic twin pairs for a period of 13 years (Kandler et al., 2010). Across those years, the researchers obtained the twins' self-reports of personality as well as personality evaluations by the twins' peers. Comparisons of the MZ and DZ twins suggested that personality stability over time relied on genetic factors, whereas change over time was produced by environmental factors. However, on the whole, genetic factors were more powerful. The researchers suggested that their data were consistent with a set-model of personality, in which "environmental fluctuations are assumed to affect short-term changes (a few days, weeks, or even several months) in personality, whereas genetic factors determine individual set-points to which individuals will regress on a long-term basis" (p. 995).

These data illustrate the general conclusion that genetics have a strong impact on personality. Look back to Table 1. Which poles of the five factors seem to apply best to you? Can you find similarities between you and your parents?

Do Traits Predict Behaviors?

Suppose a professor asks you to choose some trait terms that you believe apply particularly well to yourself. You might say, for example, that you are *very friendly*. What does your professor now know? If personality theories allow for predictions about behaviors, what can your professor predict from knowing that you rate yourself as being very friendly? How can he or she determine the validity of your belief? Let's explore this question.

👁 Watch the Video *Special Topics: Twins and Personality* on MyPsychLab

One idea you might have is that knowing that a person can be characterized by a particular trait would enable you to predict his or her behavior across different *situations*. Thus, we would expect you to produce friendly behaviors in all situations. However, in the 1920s, several researchers who set out to observe trait-related behaviors in different situations were surprised to find little evidence that behavior was consistent across situations. For example, two behaviors presumably related to the trait of honesty—lying and cheating on a test—were only weakly correlated among schoolchildren (Hartshorne & May, 1928). Similar results were found by other researchers who examined the *cross-situational consistency* for other traits such as introversion or punctuality (Dudycha, 1936; Newcomb, 1929).

If trait-related behaviors are not cross-situationally consistent—that is, if people's behavior changes in different situations—why do you perceive your own and others' personalities to be relatively stable? Even more puzzling, the personality ratings of observers who know an individual from one situation correlate with the ratings of observers who know the individual from another situation. The observation that personality ratings across time and among different observers *are consistent,* whereas behavior ratings of a person across situations *are not consistent,* came to be called the **consistency paradox** (Mischel, 1968).

The identification of the consistency paradox led to a great deal of research (Mischel, 2004). Over time, the consensus emerged that the appearance of behavioral inconsistency arose, in large part, because situations had been categorized in the wrong way: The paradox fades away once theorists can provide an appropriate account of the *psychological features* of situations (Mischel & Shoda, 1995, 1999). Suppose, for example, you

....

consistency paradox The observation that personality ratings across time and among different observers are consistent while behavior ratings across situations are not consistent.

want to try to assess behavioral consistency by determining if a friend acts in much the same way at every party she attends. You're likely to discover that her behavior varies widely if your level of analysis is just "parties." What you need to determine is what psychologically relevant features separate parties into different categories. Perhaps your friend feels uncomfortable in situations in which she is expected to disclose personal information to strangers. As a consequence, she might seem very unfriendly at some parties (where she is expected to disclose personal information) but quite friendly at others (where she is not). Meanwhile, other situations that require her to be disclosing—such as job interviews—might also bring out negative behaviors. Thus we find consistency in the way that features of situations elicit people's distinctive responses.

Researchers have described the knowledge people have of the relationships between dispositions and situations as *if . . . then . . . personality signatures: If* an individual brings a particular disposition to a specific situation *then* he or she will behave in a particular way (Mischel, 2004). This perspective suggests that we understand other people, in part, by acquiring knowledge of their particular if-then patterns. Consider a study that demonstrated the consequences of if-then knowledge for close relationships.

The researchers hypothesized that people who have a better understanding of how their friends will respond in different situations would have less conflict with those friends (Friesen & Kammrath, 2011). To test this hypothesis, the researchers asked pairs of friends to complete the if-then trigger profile questionnaire. The questionnaire presents participants with types of behaviors. They were asked to imagine, for example, that they were responding to someone who was being "overly skeptical of information that he/she receives" (p. 568). For each behavior, the participants indicated to what extent the behavior was likely to serve as a "trigger" for strong negative emotions. Participants

Assuming you could afford either one, which of these vacations would you prefer? What might that tell us about the ways in which personality traits interact with features of situations?

Psychology in Your Life

DO YOU BELIEVE THAT PERSONALITY CAN CHANGE?

In this chapter, you will encounter a diverse set of theories psychologists have originated to explore human personality. However, it's likely that there's one aspect of personality about which you already have a theory of your own—the extent to which personality can change. Take a moment to contemplate these two statements: "Everyone is a certain kind of person, and there is not much that can be done to really change that"; "Everyone can change even their most basic qualities" (Plaks et al., 2009, p. 1070). Do you agree more strongly with one of those two sentiments?

The statements capture two different theories that ordinary people have about personality change (Dweck, 1999). The first theory is an *entity theory,* which suggests that personality traits are essentially fixed; people change little over time. The second theory is an *incremental theory,* which suggests that personality traits are malleable; people are capable of change over time. In samples of college and elementary schoolchildren, about 80 percent of people can be firmly categorized as holding an entity theory or an incremental theory (Plaks et al., 2009). Let's look at some consequences of people's theories.

Consider what it means to be shy, from the perspective of the two theories. Shy people who are entity theorists believe that there's not much they can do to overcome their shyness; shy people who are incremental theorists are more likely to think that they can change, so they view social situations as learning opportunities (Beer, 2002). In one study, both types

of shy people experienced three five-minute interactions with strangers. As you would guess, early in the sessions all the shy participants expressed discomfort in these social interactions. However, as the sessions unfolded, the entity theorists continued to experience high levels of anxiety, whereas the incremental theorists grew less uncomfortable (Beer, 2002). Each individual's theory about the potential for change had a major impact on his or her behavior.

As a second example, think about times in which someone has done something to upset you. How did you respond to the events? People with entity theories tend to believe that wrong-doers cannot change and, therefore, they must be punished; people with incremental theories are more likely to believe that people are not inescapably bad and, therefore, punishment is not always required (Yeager et al., 2011). In one study, adolescents recalled recent events in which acquaintances had upset them. They then indicated the extent to which they were interested in revenge by responding how much they felt like "hurting this person" and "finding a way to punish this person" (Yeager et al., p. 1094). The adolescents who qualified as entity theorists were much more interested in revenge than their incremental theorist peers.

So, let's return to the question posed in this box's title: Do you believe that personality can change? These research examples should convince you that holding an entity theory or an incremental theory can have a broad impact on how people get through their lives.

---

completed the measure both for themselves ("How much does this behavior trigger you?") and their friends ("How much does this behavior trigger your friend?"). Based on these two sets of scores, the researchers were able to derive a measure of accuracy indicating how much the pairs knew about each others' if-then behaviors. The participants also completed a measure of the amount of conflict in the relationship. The researchers found that pairs with the highest if-then accuracy were likely to have the least conflict in their relationships.

Take a moment to consider the if-then knowledge for your friends. Do you see why it would be helpful to understand "*if* this situation occurs, *then* they are likely to respond negatively"?

Evaluation of Trait Theories

We have seen that trait theories allow researchers to give concise descriptions of different people's personalities. These theories have been criticized, however, because they do not generally explain how behavior is generated or how personality develops;

they identify and describe only characteristics that are correlated with behavior. Although contemporary trait theorists have begun to address these concerns, trait theories typically portray a *static,* or at least stabilized, view of *personality structure* as it currently exists. By contrast, psychodynamic theories of personality, to which we next turn, emphasize conflicting forces within the individual that lead to change and development.

Stop *and* Review

① What are the end points of the trait dimension of neuroticism?
② How have researchers assessed the heritability of traits?
③ What is the consistency paradox?

CRITICAL THINKING Recall the study that looked at personality stability over time. Why might the researchers have used both self- and peer-ratings to assess personality?

✔●Study and Review on MyPsychLab

PSYCHODYNAMIC THEORIES

Common to all **psychodynamic personality theories** is the assumption that powerful inner forces shape personality and motivate behavior. Sigmund Freud, the originator of psychodynamic theories, was characterized by his biographer Ernest Jones as "the Darwin of the mind" (1953). Freud's theory of personality boldly attempts to explain the origins and course of personality development, the nature of mind, aspects of abnormal personality, and the way personality can be changed by therapy. The focus here will only be on normal personality. After we explore Freud, we will consider some criticisms and reworkings of his theories.

Freudian Psychoanalysis

According to psychoanalytic theory, at the core of personality are events within a person's mind *(intrapsychic events)* that motivate behavior. Often, people are aware of these motivations; however, some motivation also operates at an unconscious level. The *psychodynamic* nature of this approach comes from its emphasis on these inner wellsprings of behavior, as well as the clashes among these internal forces. For Freud, *all behavior was motivated.* No chance or accidental happenings cause behavior; all acts are determined by motives. Every human action has a cause and a purpose that can be discovered through analysis of thought associations, dreams, errors, and other behavioral clues to inner passions. The primary data for Freud's hypotheses about personality came from clinical observations and in-depth case studies of individual patients in therapy. He developed a theory of normal personality from his intense study of those with mental disorders. Let's look at some of the most important aspects of Freud's theory.

Drives and Psychosexual Development Freud's medical training as a neurologist led him to postulate a common biological basis for the behavioral patterns he observed in his patients. He ascribed the source of motivation for human actions to *psychic energy* found within each individual. Each person was assumed to have inborn instincts or drives that were *tension systems* created by the organs of the body. These energy sources, when activated, could be expressed in many different ways.

Freud postulated two basic drives. One he saw as involved with *self-preservation* (meeting such needs as hunger and thirst). The other he called *Eros,* the driving force related to sexual urges and preservation of the species. Freud greatly expanded the notion of human sexual desires to include not only the urge for sexual union but all attempts to seek pleasure or to make physical contact with others. He used the term **libido** to identify the source of energy for sexual urges—a psychic energy that drives us toward sensual pleasures of all types. Sexual urges demand immediate satisfaction, whether through direct actions or through indirect means such as fantasies and dreams.

According to Freud, Eros, as a broadly defined sexual drive, does not suddenly appear at puberty but operates from birth. Eros is evident, he argued, in the pleasure infants derive from physical stimulation of the genitals and other sensitive areas, or *erogenous zones.* Freud's five stages of *psychosexual development* are shown in **Table 2**. Freud believed that the physical source of sexual pleasure changed in this orderly progression. One of the major obstacles of psychosexual development, at least for boys, occurs in the phallic stage. Here, the 4- or 5-year-old child must overcome the *Oedipus complex.* Freud named this complex after the mythical figure Oedipus, who unwittingly killed his father and married his mother. Freud believed that every young boy has an innate impulse to view his father as a sexual rival for his mother's attentions. Because the young boy cannot displace his father, the Oedipus complex is generally resolved when the boy comes to *identify* with his father's power. (Freud was inconsistent with respect to his theoretical account of the experiences of young girls.) ✹

According to Freud, either too much gratification or too much frustration at one of the early stages of psychosexual

. . . .

✹ Explore the Concept *Freud's Five Psychosexual Stages of Personality Development* on MyPsychLab

psychodynamic personality theory Theory of personality that shares the assumption that personality is shaped by and behavior is motivated by inner forces.

libido The psychic energy that drives individuals toward sensual pleasures of all types, especially sexual ones.

Table 2 • Freud's Stages of Psychosexual Development

Stage	Age	Erogenous Zones	Major Developmental Task (Potential Source of Conflict)	Some Adult Characteristics of Children Who Have Been Fixated at This Stage
Oral	0–1	Mouth, lips, tongue	Weaning	Oral behavior, such as smoking, overeating; passivity and gullibility
Anal	2–3	Anus	Toilet training	Ordeliness, parsimoniousness, obstinacy, or the opposite
Phallic	4–5	Genitals	Oedipus complex	Vanity, recklessness, or the opposite
Latency	6–12	No specific area	Development of defense mechanisms	None: Fixation does not normally occur at this stage
Genitals	13–18	Mature sexual intimacy		Adults who have successfully integrated earlier stages should emerge with a sincere interest in others and a mature sexuality

Why did Freud believe that eating is motivated not only by the self-preservation drive to satisfy hunger but also by the "erotic" drive to seek oral gratification?

development leads to **fixation,** an inability to progress normally to the next stage of development. As shown in Table 2, fixation at different stages can produce a variety of adult characteristics. The concept of fixation explains why Freud put such emphasis on early experiences in the continuity of personality. He believed that experiences in the early stages of psychosexual development had a profound impact on personality formation and adult behavior patterns.

Psychic Determinism   The concept of fixation gives us a first look at Freud's belief that early conflicts help *determine* later behaviors. **Psychic determinism** is the assumption that all mental and behavioral reactions (symptoms) are determined by earlier experiences. Freud believed that symptoms were not arbitrary. Rather, symptoms were related in a meaningful way to significant life events.

Freud's belief in psychic determinism led him to emphasize the **unconscious**—the repository of information that is unavailable to conscious awareness (see **Figure 4**). Other writers had discussed this construct, but Freud put the concept of the unconscious determinants of human thought, feeling, and action at center stage in the human drama. According to Freud, behavior can be motivated by drives of which a person is not

fixation   A state in which a person remains attached to objects or activities more appropriate for an earlier stage of psychosexual development.

psychic determinism   The assumption that mental and behavioral reactions are determined by previous experiences.

unconscious   The domain of the psyche that stores repressed urges and primitive impulses.

aware. You may act without knowing why or without direct access to the true cause of your actions. There is a *manifest* content to your behavior—what you say, do, and perceive—of which you are fully aware, but there is also a concealed, *latent* content. The meaning of neurotic (anxiety-based) symptoms, dreams, and slips of the pen and tongue is found at the unconscious level of thinking and information processing. Many psychologists today consider this concept of the unconscious to be Freud's most important contribution to the science of psychology. Much modern literature and drama, as well, explores the implications of unconscious processes for human behavior.

According to Freud, impulses within you that you find unacceptable still strive for expression. A *Freudian slip* occurs when an unconscious desire is betrayed by your speech or behavior. For example, I once felt obligated to write a thank-you note although I hadn't much enjoyed a weekend I'd spent at a friend's home. I intended to write, "I'm glad we got to spend a chunk of time together." However, in a somewhat testy phone call, the friend informed me that I'd actually written "I'm glad we got to spend a *junk* of time together." Do you see how the substitution of *junk* for *chunk* could be the expression of an unconscious desire? The concept of unconscious motivation adds a new dimension to personality by allowing for greater complexity of mental functioning.

You've now learned some basic aspects of Freud's theory. Let's see how they contribute to the structure of personality.

FIGURE 4 Freud's Conception of the Human Mind
Freudian theory likens the human mind to an iceberg. The tip of the iceberg, which you can see, represents consciousness. The unconscious is the vast bulk of the iceberg, which remains hidden beneath the water.

The Structure of Personality In Freud's theory, personality differences arise from the different ways in which people deal with their fundamental drives. To explain these differences, Freud pictured a continuing battle between two antagonistic parts of the personality—the *id* and the *superego*—moderated by a third aspect of the self, the *ego*. Although it might sound almost as if these aspects of self are separate creatures, keep in mind that Freud believed them all to be just different mental *processes*. He did not, for example, identify specific brain locations for the id, ego, and superego. 🗲

The **id** is the storehouse of the fundamental drives. It operates irrationally, acting on impulse and pushing for expression and immediate gratification without considering whether what is desired is realistically possible, socially desirable, or morally acceptable. The id is governed by the *pleasure principle*, the unregulated search for gratification—especially sexual, physical, and emotional pleasures—to be experienced here and now without concern for consequences.

The **superego** is the storehouse of an individual's values, including moral attitudes learned from society. The superego corresponds roughly to the common notion of *conscience*. It develops as a child comes to accept as his or her own values the prohibitions of parents and other adults against socially undesirable actions. It is the inner voice of *oughts* and *should nots*. The superego also includes the *ego ideal*, an individual's view of the kind of person he or she should strive to become. Thus the superego is often in conflict with the id. The id wants to do what feels good, whereas the superego insists on doing what is right.

The **ego** is the reality-based aspect of the self that arbitrates the conflict between id impulses and superego demands. The ego represents an individual's personal view of physical and social reality—his or her conscious beliefs about the causes and consequences of behavior. Part of the ego's job is to choose actions that will gratify id impulses without undesirable consequences. The ego is governed by the *reality principle*, which puts reasonable choices before pleasurable demands. Thus the ego would block an impulse to cheat on an exam because of concerns about the consequences of getting caught, and it would substitute the resolution to study harder the next time or solicit the teacher's sympathy. When the id and the superego are in conflict, the ego arranges a compromise that at least partially satisfies both. However, as id and superego pressures intensify, it becomes more difficult for the ego to work out optimal compromises.

Repression and Ego Defense Sometimes this compromise between id and superego involves "putting a lid on the id." Extreme desires are pushed out of conscious awareness into the privacy of the unconscious. **Repression** is the psychological process that protects an individual from experiencing extreme anxiety or guilt about impulses, ideas, or memories that are unacceptable and/or dangerous to express. The ego remains unaware of both the mental content that is censored and the process by which repression keeps information out of consciousness. Repression is considered to be the most basic of the various ways in which the ego defends against being overwhelmed by threatening impulses and ideas.

Ego defense mechanisms are mental strategies the ego uses to defend itself in the daily conflict between id impulses that seek expression and the superego's demand to deny them (see **Table 3**). In psychoanalytic theory, these mechanisms are considered vital to an individual's psychological coping

with powerful inner conflicts. By using them, a person is able to maintain a favorable self-image and to sustain an acceptable social image. For example, if a child has strong feelings of hatred toward his father—which, if acted out, would be

Table 3 • Major Ego Defense Mechanisms

Denial of reality	Protecting self from unpleasant reality by refusing to perceive it
Displacement	Discharging pent-up feelings, usually of hostility, on objects less dangerous than those that initially aroused the emotion
Fantasy	Gratifying frustrated desires in imaginary achievements ("daydreaming" is a common form)
Identification	Increasing feelings of worth by identifying self with another person or institution, often of illustrious standing
Isolation	Cutting off emotional charge from hurtful situations or separating incompatible attitudes into logic-tight compartments (holding conflicting attitudes that are never thought of simultaneously or in relation to each other); also called compartmentalization
Projection	Placing blame for one's difficulties on others or attributing one's own "forbidden" desires to others
Rationalization	Attempting to prove that one's behavior is "rational" and justifiable and thus worthy of the approval of self and others
Reaction formation	Preventing dangerous desires from being expressed by endorsing opposing attitudes and types of behavior and using them as "barriers"
Regression	Retreating to earlier developmental levels involving more childish responses and usually a lower level of aspiration
Repression	Pushing painful or dangerous thoughts out of consciousness, keeping them unconscious; this is considered to be the most basic of the defense mechanisms
Sublimation	Gratifying or working off frustrated sexual desires in substitutive nonsexual activities socially accepted by one's culture

....

🗲 **Explore** the **Concept** *The Id, Ego, and Superego* on **MyPsychLab**

id The primitive, unconscious part of the personality that represents the internalization of society's values, standards, and morals.

superego The aspect of personality that represents the internalization of society's values, standards, and morals.

ego The aspect of personality involved in self-preservation activities and in directing instinctual drives and urges into appropriate channels.

repression The basic defense mechanism by which painful or guilt-producing thoughts, feelings, or memories are excluded from conscious awareness.

ego defense mechanism Mental strategy (conscious or unconscious) used by the ego to defend itself against conflicts experienced in the normal course of life.

dangerous—repression may take over. The hostile impulse is then no longer consciously pressing for satisfaction or even recognized as existing. However, although the impulse is not seen or heard, it is not gone; these feelings continue to play a role in personality functioning. For example, by developing a strong *identification* with his father, the child may increase his sense of self-worth and reduce his unconscious fear of being discovered as a hostile agent. ✳

In Freudian theory, **anxiety** is an intense emotional response triggered when a repressed conflict is about to emerge into consciousness. Anxiety is a danger signal: Repression is not working! Red alert! More defenses needed! This is the time for a second line of defense, one or more additional ego defense mechanisms that will relieve the anxiety and send the distressing impulses back down into the unconscious. For example, a mother who does not like her son and does not want to care for him might use *reaction formation,* which transforms her unacceptable impulse into its opposite: "I hate my child" becomes "I love my child. See how I smother the dear little thing with love?" Such defenses serve the critical coping function of alleviating anxiety.

If defense mechanisms defend you against anxiety, why might they still have negative consequences for you? Useful as they are, ego mechanisms of defense are ultimately self-deceptive. When overused, they create more problems than they solve. It is psychologically unhealthy to spend a great deal of time and psychic energy deflecting, disguising, and rechanneling unacceptable urges in order to reduce anxiety. Doing so leaves little energy for productive living or satisfying human relationships. Freud argued that some forms of mental illness result from excessive reliance on defense mechanisms to cope with anxiety.

Evaluation of Freudian Theory

This chapter has devoted a great deal of space to outlining the essentials of psychoanalytic theory because Freud's ideas have had an enormous impact on the way many psychologists think about normal and abnormal aspects of personality. However, there probably are more psychologists who criticize Freudian concepts than who support them. What is the basis of some of their criticisms?

First, psychoanalytic concepts are vague and not operationally defined; thus much of the theory is difficult to evaluate scientifically. Because some of its central hypotheses cannot be disproved, even in principle, Freud's theory remains questionable. How can the concepts of libido, the structure of personality, and repression of infantile sexual impulses be studied in any direct fashion?

A second, related criticism is that Freudian theory is good history but bad science. It does not reliably *predict* what will occur; it is applied *retrospectively*—after events have occurred. Using psychoanalytic theory to understand personality typically involves historical reconstruction, not scientific

construction of probable actions and predictable outcomes. In addition, by overemphasizing historical origins of current behavior, the theory directs attention away from the current stimuli that may be inducing and maintaining the behavior.

There are three other major criticisms of Freudian theory. First, it is a developmental theory, but it never included observations or studies of children. Second, it minimizes traumatic experiences (such as child abuse) by reinterpreting memories of them as fantasies (based on a child's desire for sexual contact with a parent). Third, it has an *androcentric* (male-centered) bias because it uses a male model as the norm without trying to determine how females might be different.

Some aspects of Freud's theory, however, continue to gain acceptance as they are modified and improved through empirical scrutiny. For example, the concept of the unconscious is being systematically explored by contemporary researchers (McGovern & Baars, 2007). This research reveals that much of your day-to-day experience is shaped by processes outside of your awareness. These results support Freud's general concept but weaken the link between unconscious processes and psychopathology: Little of your unconscious knowledge will cause you anxiety or distress.

Researchers have also found evidence for some of the habits of mind Freud characterized as defense mechanisms. We saw earlier that individuals are most likely to use defense mechanisms when they are experiencing anxiety. Researchers have tested this hypothesis in a variety of ways.

One study focused on a group of 9- to 11-year-old girls (Sandstrom & Cramer, 2003). The researchers carried out interviews with their peers to determine who among the group of 50 girls was relatively popular and who was relatively unpopular. Each of the 50 girls underwent a laboratory experience in which they were rejected by another young girl. The researchers reasoned that—because of their history of negative social interactions—the unpopular girls would experience more anxiety than the popular girls in the face of this rejection. The researchers suggested that, to cope with that anxiety, the unpopular girls would show evidence for more frequent use of defense mechanisms. To test this hypothesis, the researcher asked the girls to tell stories based on cards from the Thematic Apperception Test. The stories were analyzed for evidence of the defense mechanisms denial and projection (see Table 3). These analyses supported the hypothesis: The unpopular girls used more defense mechanisms than the popular girls after the episode of peer rejection.

Featured Study

Some styles for coping with stress fall within the general category of defense mechanisms. For example, inhibiting the thoughts and feelings associated with personal traumas or guilty or shameful experiences can take a devastating toll on mental and physical health (Pennebaker, 1997; Petrie et al., 2004). These findings echo Freud's beliefs that repressed psychic material can lead to psychological distress.

Freud's theory is the most complex, comprehensive, and compelling view of normal and abnormal personality functioning—even when its predictions prove wrong. However, like any other theory, Freud's is best treated as one that must be

✳ Explore the Concept *Defense Mechanisms* on MyPsychLab

anxiety An intense emotional response caused by the preconscious recognition that a repressed conflict is about to emerge into consciousness.

confirmed or disconfirmed element by element. Freud retains his influence on contemporary psychology because some of his ideas have been widely accepted. Others have been abandoned. Some of the earliest revisions of Freud's theory arose from within his own original circle of students. Let's see how they sought to amend Freud's views.

Extending Psychodynamic Theories

Some of those who came after Freud retained his basic representation of personality as a battleground on which unconscious primal urges conflict with social values. However, many of Freud's intellectual descendants made major adjustments in the psychoanalytic view of personality. In general, these post-Freudians have made the following changes:

- They put greater emphasis on ego functions, including ego defenses, development of the self, conscious thought processes, and personal mastery.
- They view social variables (culture, family, and peers) as playing a greater role in shaping personality.
- They put less emphasis on the importance of general sexual urges, or libidinal energy.
- They extended personality development beyond childhood to include the entire life span.

We will now see how these themes emerged in the theories of Alfred Adler, Karen Horney, and Carl Jung.

Alfred Adler (1870–1937) rejected the significance of Eros and the pleasure principle. Adler (1929) believed that as helpless, dependent, small children, people all experience feelings of *inferiority*. He argued that all lives are dominated by the search for ways to overcome those feelings. People compensate to achieve feelings of adequacy or, more often, overcompensate in an attempt to become *superior*. Personality is structured around this underlying striving; people develop lifestyles based on particular ways of overcoming their basic, pervasive feelings of inferiority. Personality conflict arises from incompatibility between external environmental pressures and internal strivings for adequacy, rather than from competing urges within the person.

Karen Horney (1885–1952) was trained in the psychoanalytic school but broke from orthodox Freudian theory in

Why might a person's enthusiasm for boxing suggest the use of displacement as an ego defense mechanism?

Jung recognized creativity as a means to release images from both the personal and collective unconscious. Why did Jung believe in the two types of unconscious?

several ways. She challenged Freud's phallocentric emphasis on the importance of the penis, hypothesizing that male envy of pregnancy, motherhood, breasts, and suckling is a dynamic force in the unconscious of boys and men. This "womb envy" leads men to devalue women and to overcompensate by unconscious impulses toward creative work. Horney also placed greater emphasis than did Freud on cultural factors and focused on present character structure rather than on infantile sexuality (Horney, 1937, 1939). Because Horney also had influence on the development of humanistic theories, we will return to her ideas in the next section.

Carl Jung (1875–1961) greatly expanded the conception of the unconscious. For Jung (1959), the unconscious was not limited to an individual's unique life experiences but was filled with fundamental psychological truths shared by the whole human race, a **collective unconscious.** The collective unconscious explains your intuitive understanding of primitive myths, art forms, and symbols, which are the universal archetypes of existence. An **archetype** is a primitive symbolic representation of a particular experience or object. Each archetype is associated with an instinctive tendency to feel and think about it or experience it in a special way. Jung postulated many archetypes that give rise to myths and symbols: the sun god, the hero, the earth mother. *Animus* was the male archetype, *anima* was the female archetype, and all men and women experienced both archetypes in varying degrees. The archetype of the self is the *mandala,* or magic circle; it symbolizes striving for unity and wholeness (Jung, 1973).

Jung saw the healthy, integrated personality as balancing opposing forces, such as masculine aggressiveness and feminine sensitivity. This view of personality as a constellation of compensating internal forces in dynamic balance was called **analytic psychology.** In addition, Jung rejected the primary importance of libido so central to Freud's own theory. Jung

....

collective unconscious The part of an individual's unconscious that is inherited, evolutionarily developed, and common to all members of the species.

archetype A universal, inherited, primitive, and symbolic representation of a particular experience or object.

analytic psychology A branch of psychology that views the person as a constellation of compensatory internal forces in a dynamic balance.

added two equally powerful unconscious instincts: the need to create and the need to become a coherent, whole individual. In the next section on humanist theories, we will see this second need paralleled in the concept of *self-actualization*.

Stop and Review

① According to Freud's theory, what behaviors might arise if an individual became fixated at the oral stage of development?

② How is the ego guided by the reality principle?

③ Although Leon is highly aggressive, he always blames others for starting fights. What defensive mechanism might be at work here?

④ According to Alfred Adler's view, what drive motivates much of people's behavior?

CRITICAL THINKING Recall the study on the use of defense mechanisms. Why might the researchers have specifically used a rejection episode to produce anxiety?

✓—⌐Study and Review on MyPsychLab

HUMANISTIC THEORIES

Humanistic approaches to understanding personality are characterized by a concern for the integrity of an individual's personal and conscious experience and growth potential. In this section, you will see how humanistic theorists have developed concepts related to the self. You will learn, in addition, what additional features set humanistic theories apart from other types of personality theories.

Features of Humanistic Theories

For **Carl Rogers** (1902–1987), the *self* is a central concept for personality. Rogers suggested that we develop a **self-concept**, a mental model of our typical behaviors and unique qualities. Rogers believed that, as we go through life, we strive to experience congruence between our self-concept and our actual life experiences. Rogers's emphasis on the self signals a key feature of all humanistic theories, which is an emphasis on the drive toward self-actualization. **Self-actualization** is a constant striving to realize one's inherent potential. **Abraham Maslow** placed self-actualization at the pinnacle of his hierarchy of needs. The striving toward self-fulfillment is a constructive, guiding force

....

self-concept A person's mental model of his or her typical behaviors and unique qualities.

self-actualization A concept in personality psychology referring to a person's constant striving to realize his or her potential and to develop inherent talents and capabilities.

unconditional positive regard Complete love and acceptance of an individual by another person, such as a parent for a child, with no conditions attached.

© Corbis Premium RF/Alamy

Why did Carl Rogers emphasize parents' unconditional positive regard for their children?

that moves each person toward generally positive behaviors and enhancement of the self.

The drive for self-actualization at times comes into conflict with the need for approval from the self and others, especially when the person feels that certain obligations or conditions must be met in order to gain approval. For example, Rogers (1947, 1951, 1977) stressed the importance of **unconditional positive regard** in raising children. By this, he meant that children should feel they will always be loved and approved of, in spite of their mistakes and misbehavior—that they do not have to earn their parents' love. He recommended that, when a child misbehaves, parents should emphasize that it is the behavior they disapprove of, not the child. Unconditional positive regard is important in adulthood, too, because worrying about seeking approval interferes with self-actualization. As an adult, you need to give to and receive unconditional positive regard from those to whom you are close. Most important, you need to feel unconditional positive *self-regard*, or acceptance of yourself, in spite of the weaknesses you might be trying to change.

Although not often given due credit, Karen Horney was another major theorist whose ideas created the foundation of humanistic psychology (Frager & Fadiman, 1998). Horney came to believe that people have a "real self" that requires favorable environmental circumstances to be actualized, such as an atmosphere of warmth, the goodwill of others, and parental love of the child as a "particular individual" (Horney, 1945, 1950). In the absence of those favorable nurturing conditions, the child develops a basic anxiety that stifles spontaneity of expression of real feelings and prevents effective relations with others. To cope with their basic anxiety, individuals resort to interpersonal or intrapsychic defenses. Interpersonal defenses produce movement toward others (through excessive compliance and self-effacing actions), against others (by aggressive, arrogant, or narcissistic solutions), and away from others (through detachment). Intrapsychic defenses operate to develop for some people an unrealistic idealized self-image that generates a "search for glory" to justify it and a pride system that operates on rigid rules of conduct to live up to a grandiose self-concept. Such people often live by the "tyranny of shoulds," self-imposed obligations, such as "I should be perfect, generous, attractive, brave," and so forth. Horney believed that the goal of a humanistic therapy was to help the individual achieve the joy of self-realization and promote the inherent constructive forces in human nature that support a striving for self-fulfillment.

As you have seen, humanistic theories emphasize self-actualization or progress toward the real self. In addition, humanistic theories have been described as being holistic, dispositional, and phenomenological. Let's see why.

Humanistic theories are *holistic* because they explain people's separate acts in terms of their entire personalities; people are not seen as the sum of discrete traits that each influence behavior in different ways. Maslow believed that people are intrinsically motivated toward the upper levels of the hierarchy of needs, unless deficiencies at the lower levels weigh them down.

Humanistic theories are *dispositional* because they focus on the innate qualities within a person that exert a major influence over the direction behavior will take. Situational factors are seen as constraints and barriers (like the strings that tie down balloons). Once freed from negative situational conditions, the actualizing tendency should actively guide people to choose life-enhancing situations. However, humanistic theories are not dispositional in the same sense as trait theories or psychodynamic theories. In those views, personal dispositions are recurrent themes played out in behavior again and again. Humanistic dispositions are oriented specifically toward creativity and growth. Each time a humanistic disposition is exercised, the person changes a little, so that the disposition is never expressed in the same way twice. Over time, humanistic dispositions guide the individual toward self-actualization, the purest expression of these motives.

Humanistic theories are *phenomenological* because they emphasize an individual's frame of reference and subjective view of reality—not the objective perspective of an observer or of a therapist. Thus a humanistic psychologist always strives to see each person's unique point of view. This view is also a present-oriented view; past influences are important only to the extent that they have brought the person to the present situation, and the future represents goals to achieve. Thus, unlike psychodynamic theories, humanistic theories do not see people's present behaviors as unconsciously guided by past experiences.

The upbeat humanist view of personality was a welcome treat for many psychologists who had been brought up on a diet of bitter-tasting Freudian medicine. Humanistic approaches focus directly on improvement—on making life more palatable—rather than dredging up painful memories that are sometimes better left repressed. The humanist perspective emphasizes each person's ability to realize his or her fullest potential.

Evaluation of Humanistic Theories

Freud's theory was often criticized for providing the too-pessimistic view that human nature develops out of conflicts, traumas, and anxieties. Humanistic theories arose to celebrate the healthy personality that strives for happiness and self-actualization. It is difficult to criticize theories that encourage and appreciate people, even for their faults. Even so, critics have complained that humanistic concepts are fuzzy and difficult to explore in research. They ask, "What exactly is

self-actualization? Is it an inborn tendency, or is it created by the cultural context?" Humanistic theories also do not traditionally focus on the particular characteristics of individuals. They are more theories about human nature and about qualities all people share than about the individual personality or the basis of differences among people. Other psychologists note that, by emphasizing the role of the self as a source of experience and action, humanistic psychologists neglect the important environmental variables that also influence behavior.

Despite these limitations, a type of contemporary research can be traced in part to the humanist tradition that focuses directly on individual *narrative identities* or *life stories* (McAdams & Olson, 2010). The tradition of using psychological theory to understand the details of an individual's life—to produce a *psychobiography*—can be traced back to Freud's analysis of Leonardo da Vinci (Freud, 1910/1957; see Elms, 1988, for a critique of Freud's work). **Psychobiography** is defined as "the systematic use of psychological (especially personality) theory to transform a life into a coherent and illuminating story" (McAdams, 1988, p. 2). Consider the great artist Pablo Picasso. Picasso suffered a series of traumas as a young child, including a serious earthquake and the death of a young sister. A psychobiography might attempt to explain some of Picasso's vast artistic creativity as the lifelong residue of his responses to these early traumas (Gardner, 1993). When a well-known or historical figure is the subject of a psychobiography, a researcher may turn to published work, diaries, and letters as sources of relevant data. For more ordinary individuals, researchers may directly elicit narratives of life experiences. The request might be, for example, for participants to reflect on key events in their lives: "Why do you think that this [was] an important event in your life story? What does this event say about who you are, who you were, who you might be, or how you have developed over time?" (McAdams et al., 2006, p. 1379). The characteristic themes that emerge over a series of narrative accounts support the holistic and phenomenological version of personality that was put forth by the early humanists: People construct their identities by weaving life stories out of the strands of narrative. Personal accounts provide a window on people's views of themselves and interpersonal relationships.

Humanistic theorists emphasized each individual's drive toward self-actualization. This group recognized, however, that people's progress toward this goal is determined, in part, by realities of their environments. We turn now to theories that directly examine how individuals' behaviors are shaped by their environments.

Stop *and* Review

① What is self-actualization?
② In what ways are humanistic theories dispositional?
③ What is a psychobiography?

✔•⎡Study and Review on MyPsychLab

....

psychobiography The use of psychological (especially personality) theory to describe and explain an individual's course through life.

SOCIAL-LEARNING AND COGNITIVE THEORIES

Common to all the theories you've seen so far is an emphasis on hypothesized inner mechanisms—traits, instincts, impulses, tendencies toward self-actualization—that propel behavior and form the basis of a functioning personality. What most of these theories lacked, however, was a solid link between personality and particular behaviors. Psychodynamic and humanistic theories, for example, provide accounts of the total personality but do not predict specific actions. Another tradition of personality theory emerged from a more direct focus on individual differences in behavior. Much of a person's behavior can be predicted from contingencies in the environment. Psychologists with a *learning theory* orientation look to the environmental circumstances that control behavior. Personality is seen as the sum of the overt and covert responses that are reliably elicited by an individual's *reinforcement history*. Learning theory approaches suggest that people are different because they have had different histories of reinforcement.

This next set of theories has as a shared starting point that behavior is influenced by environmental contingencies. However, these contemporary social-learning and cognitive theories go one step further to emphasize the importance of cognitive processes as well as behavioral ones. Those researchers who have proposed cognitive theories of personality point out that there are important individual differences in the way people think about and define any external situation. Like humanistic theories, cognitive theories emphasize that you participate in creating your own personality. For example, you actively *choose* your own environments to a great extent; you do not just react passively. You weigh alternatives and select the settings in which you act and are acted upon—you choose to enter situations that you expect to be reinforcing and to avoid those that are unsatisfying and uncertain.

Let's look now at more concrete embodiments of these ideas. We visit the theories of Julian Rotter, Walter Mischel, and Albert Bandura.

Rotter's Expectancy Theory

Julian Rotter (1954) focused his theory on **expectancy,** which is the extent to which people believe that their behaviors in particular situations will bring about rewards. Suppose, for example, that you need to decide how much to practice before a presentation in class. You'd like to get at least a *B*. Having a high expectancy means that you think it's very likely that extra practice will lead to a *B* or better; having a low expectancy means that you're not at all confident that extra practice will help with your grade. Your expectancies arise, in part, because of your own history of reinforcement: If practice has led to rewards in the past, you'll have a stronger expectancy that it will lead to a reward again. Rotter also emphasized *reward*

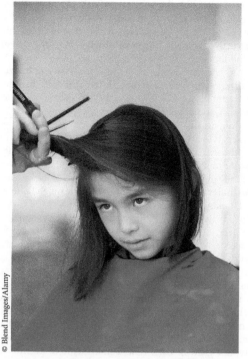

© Blend Images/Alamy

If your parents complimented you every time you got a new haircut, how might that affect your confidence about your appearance and grooming as an adult? Suppose they were regularly critical. What effect could that have?

value—the value that an individual assigns to a particular reward. If you've had a tough semester, a *B* might have more value to you than it would in a different context. On Rotter's view, you can only begin to predict people's behavior if you can assess both their expectancy with respect to a reward and the extent to which they value a reward.

Rotter emphasized that people bring specific expectancies to the many situations they face in life. However, Rotter also believed that people develop a more general expectancy about the extent to which they can control the rewards they obtain. Rotter (1966) defined a dimension of **locus of control:** Some people—known as *internals*—believe more strongly that the outcomes of their actions are contingent on what they do; other people—known as *externals*—believe that the outcomes of their actions are contingent on environmental factors. In **Table 4,** you'll see sample items from Rotter's *Internal-External Scale.* To complete the scale, you choose (a) or (b) from each item as the statement you believe to be more accurate. These examples should give you a sense of some differences in the ways that internals and externals generate expectancies about life outcomes. Researchers have consistently demonstrated the importance of people's locus of control orientations. For example, one study examined the relationship between people's locus of control orientation at age 10 and their mental and physical health at age 30 (Gale et al., 2008). The 30-year-olds who had been more internally oriented as children were, on the whole, in better health. They were, for example, at lower risk for obesity, high blood pressure, and psychological distress. The

---

expectancy The extent to which people believe that their behaviors in particular situations will bring about rewards.

locus of control People's general expectancy about the extent to which the rewards they obtain are contingent on their own actions or on environmental factors.

Table 4 • Sample Items from the Internal–External Scale

1. a. In the long run people get the respect they deserve in the world.
   b. Unfortunately, an individual's worth often passes unrecognized no matter how hard he tries.

2. a. Without the right breaks, one cannot be an effective leader.
   b. Capable people who fail to become leaders have not taken advantage of their opportunities.

3. a. Most people don't realize the extent to which their lives are controlled by accidental happenings.
   b. There really is no such thing as "luck."

4. a. What happens to me is my own doing.
   b. Sometimes I feel that I don't have enough control over the direction my life is taking.

Note: 1a, 2b, 3b, and 4a indicate a more internal locus of control orientation.

From J. B. Rotter, Generalized expectancies for internal versus external locus of control of reinforcement, Table 1. *Psychological Monographs*, *80* (1):11–12. Copyright © 1966 by the American Psychological Association. Adapted with permission.

researchers suggested that people with external orientations might be in poorer shape because they believe that their health is outside their control—and therefore they take few actions to better their health.

Mischel's Cognitive–affective Personality Theory

Walter Mischel developed an influential theory of the cognitive basis of personality. Mischel emphasizes that people actively participate in the cognitive organization of their interactions with the environment. His approach emphasizes the importance of understanding how behavior arises as a function of interactions between persons and situations (Mischel, 2004). Consider this example:

> John's unique personality may be seen most clearly in that he is always very friendly when meeting someone for the first time, but that he also predictably becomes rather abrupt and unfriendly as he begins to spend more time with that person. Jim, on the other hand, is unique in that he is typically shy and quiet with people who he does not know well but becomes very gregarious once he begins to know someone well. (Shoda et al., 1993a, p. 1023)

If we were to average John's and Jim's overall friendliness, we would probably get about the same value on this trait—but that would fail to capture important differences in their behavior. According to Mischel (1973, 2004), how you respond to a specific environmental input depends on the variables defined in **Table 5**. Do you see how each variable listed would affect the way in which a person would behave in particular situations? Try to invent a situation in which you would produce behavior different from the characters listed in the table because you contrast on the particular variable. You may wonder what determines the nature of these variables for a specific individual. Mischel believes that they result from his or her history of observations and interactions with other people and with inanimate aspects of the physical environment (Mischel, 1973).

I want to provide you with a concrete example of how the variables in Mischel's theory explain differences with respect to the particular behaviors people produce in the same situations. Let's consider a study that documented how interactions of competencies and self-regulatory plans (see Table 5) interact to predict aggressive behavior among 10-year-old boys.

The study focused on 59 boys who were attending a summer camp (Ayduk et al., 2007). To measure their competencies, the researchers gave each boy a test of verbal intelligence. To measure their self-regulatory abilities, the researchers had each boy engage in a task that measured his capacity to delay his gratification. The boys were brought into a room with a small and large pile of food of a type they particularly enjoyed (for example, M&M candies). To obtain the larger pile, the boys had to wait 25 minutes without ringing a bell to call a researcher back—if they used the bell, they got only the small pile. To endure the 25-minute wait, the boys needed to be able to regulate their own behavior. In particular, to make the time pass more easily,

Featured Study

Table 5 • Person Variables in Mischel's Cognitive–Affective Personality Theory

Variable		
Encodings	The way you categorize information about yourself, other people, events, and situations	As soon as Bob meets someone, he tries to figure out how wealthy he or she is.
Expectancies and beliefs	Your beliefs about the social world and likely outcomes for given actions in particular situations; your beliefs about your ability to bring outcomes about	Greg invites friends to the movies, but he never expects them to say "yes."
Affects	Your feelings and emotions, including physiological responses	Cindy blushes very easily.
Goals and values	The outcomes and affective states you do and do not value; your goals and life projects	Peter wants to be president of his college class.
Competencies and self-regulatory plans	The behaviors you can accomplish and plans for generating cognitive and behavioral outcomes	Jan can speak English, French, Russian, and Japanese and expects to work for the United Nations.

they needed to be able to divert their attention from the candy and the bell. For that reason, the researchers used the boys' ability to control their attention as a measure of self-regulatory ability. Finally, to measure aggression, the researchers obtained multiple assessments from the camp counselors about the boys' verbal and physical aggression during group activities. As you can see in **Figure 5,** *to predict the boys' levels of aggression it's important to know both about competencies and self-regulatory abilities. In particular, boys with high verbal intelligence but low ability to control their attention were substantially more aggressive than their peers who had both high intelligence and high ability to control their attention.*

Copyright © Michael Newman/PhotoEdit

You might expect that more intelligent boys would have knowledge that would allow them to function in social environments without resorting to aggression. This study demonstrates that knowledge alone is not sufficient—the boys also need to have the ability and motivation to perform alternative behaviors. The results allow you to understand why Mischel's personality theory focuses on the interactions among several different types of variables.

As you can see in Table 5, Mischel's theory also considers the role that people's goals have in defining their responses to particular situations. Research suggests that people differ both in their choice of life goals and the strategies they use to implement those goals (Cantor & Kihlstrom, 1987; Kihlstrom & Cantor, 2000). Can you see how choices and skills with respect to goals could produce the different patterns of behavior you would recognize as personality? For example, some people have *intimacy* as an important goal—they strongly seek to foster

Would you feel comfortable making personality judgments about these boys from this one snapshot? Why might you want to know their patterns of behavior across different types of situations?

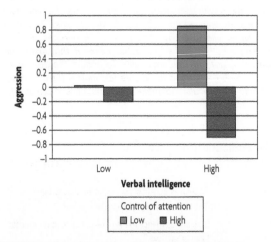

FIGURE 5 Boys' Levels of Aggressive Behavior

Boys' levels of aggressive behavior at a summer camp reflected an interaction between their verbal intelligence and their ability to control their attention to delay gratification.

Data from O. Ayduk, M. L. Rodriguez, W. Mischel, Y. Shoda, & J. Wright. Verbal intelligence and self-regulatory competencies, *Journal of Research in Personality (41)*: 374–388, Copyright © 2007.

interdependence and engage in self-disclosure—whereas other people don't bring those needs to friendships. These goals influence behavior: People with strong intimacy goals work harder in relationships to minimize conflicts (Sanderson et al., 2005). In this case, you recognize personality in the consistent way in which people's goals lead them to behave.

Bandura's Cognitive Social-learning Theory

Through his theoretical writing and extensive research with children and adults, Albert Bandura (1986, 1999) has been an eloquent champion of a social-learning approach to understanding personality (he also studied aggressive behavior in children). This approach combines principles of learning with an emphasis on human interactions in social settings. From a social-learning perspective, human beings are not driven by inner forces, nor are they helpless pawns of environmental influence. The social-learning approach stresses the cognitive processes that are involved in acquiring and maintaining patterns of behavior and, thus, personality.

Bandura's theory points to a complex interaction of individual factors, behavior, and environmental stimuli. Each can influence or change the others, and the direction of change is rarely one way—it is *reciprocal*. Your behavior can

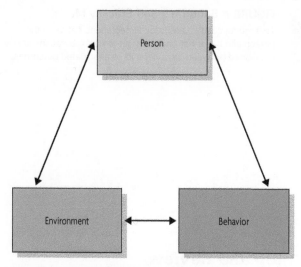

FIGURE 6 Reciprocal Determinism

In reciprocal determinism, the individual, the individual's behavior, and the environment all interact to influence and modify the other components.

be influenced by your attitudes, beliefs, or prior history of reinforcement as well as by stimuli available in the environment. What you do can have an effect on the environment, and important aspects of your personality can be affected by the environment or by feedback from your behavior. This important concept, **reciprocal determinism,** implies that you must examine all components if you want to completely understand human behavior, personality, and social ecology (Bandura, 1999; see **Figure 6**). So, for example, if you don't generally think of yourself as an athlete, you may not choose to be active in track-and-field events, but if you live near a pool, you may nonetheless spend time swimming. If you are outgoing, you'll talk to others sitting around the pool and thereby create a more sociable atmosphere, which, in turn, makes it a more enjoyable environment. This is one instance of reciprocal determinism among person, place, and behavior.

Bandura's social-learning theory emphasizes observational learning as the process by which a person changes his or her behavior based on observations of another person's behavior. Through observational learning, children and adults acquire an enormous range of information about their social environment. Through observation, you learn what is appropriate and gets rewarded and what gets punished or ignored. Because you can use memory and think about external events, you can foresee the possible consequences of your actions without having to actually experience them. You may acquire skills, attitudes, and beliefs simply by watching what others do and the consequences that follow.

As his theory developed, Bandura (1997) elaborated self-efficacy as a central construct. **Self-efficacy** is the belief that one can perform adequately in a particular situation. Your sense of self-efficacy influences your perceptions, motivation, and performance in many ways. You don't even try to do things or take chances when you expect to be ineffectual. You avoid situations

when you don't feel adequate. Even when you do, in fact, have the ability—and the desire—you may not take the required action or persist to complete the task successfully, if you think you lack what it takes.

Beyond actual accomplishments, there are three other sources of information for *self-efficacy judgments:*

- vicarious experience—your observations of the performance of others
- persuasion—others may convince you that you can do something, or you may convince yourself
- monitoring of your emotional arousal as you think about or approach a task—for example, anxiety suggests low expectations of efficacy; excitement suggests expectations of success

Self-efficacy judgments influence how much effort you expend and how long you persist when faced with difficulty in a wide range of life situations (Bandura, 1997, 2006).

Let's consider the impact of self-efficacy in academic settings. Research suggests, for example, that how vigorously and persistently you study this chapter may depend more on your sense of self-efficacy than on actual ability.

A group of 1,291 sophomores from five California State University campuses participated in a study that examined the impact of self-efficacy beliefs on college performance (Vuong et al., 2010). Each student completed measures of self-efficacy that related to his or her college experience: self-efficacy in academic coursework and self-efficacy for social interactions with faculty, counselor, and peers. They used a 10-point scale ranging from "Not confident" to "Extremely confident" to indicate how they felt about completing various tasks such as "Asking questions in class" and "Making friends at school" (Zajacova et al., 2005, p. 700). The sophomores also reported their GPAs and how likely they were to persist with their education. Self-efficacy for academic coursework predicted both the students' GPAs and persistence (Vuong et al., 2010). However, self-efficacy for social interactions was unrelated to the measures of academic performance.

This study illustrates how people have self-efficacy for different domains of life experience. In fact, we'd expect that people would often have different amounts of self-efficacy in different domains. What might the researchers have measured to assess the importance of self-efficacy for social interactions in the sophomores' college experiences?

Bandura's theory of self-efficacy also acknowledges the importance of the environment. Expectations of failure or

reciprocal determinism A concept of Albert Bandura's social-learning theory that refers to the notion that a complex reciprocal interaction exists among the individual, his or her behavior, and environmental stimuli and that each of these components affects the others.

self-efficacy A belief that one can perform adequately in a particular situation.

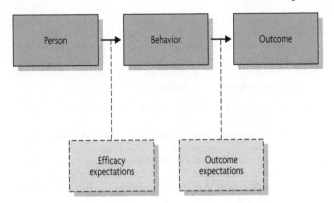

FIGURE 7 Bandura's Self-Efficacy Model

This model positions efficacy expectations between the person and his or her behavior; outcome expectations are positioned between behavior and its anticipated outcomes.

success—and corresponding decisions to stop trying or to persevere—may be based on perceptions of the supportiveness or unsupportiveness of the environment, in addition to perceptions of one's own adequacy or inadequacy. Such expectations are called *outcome-based expectancies*. **Figure 7** displays how the parts of Bandura's theory fit together. Behavioral outcomes depend both on people's perceptions of their own abilities and their perceptions of the environment.

Evaluation of Social-Learning and Cognitive Theories

One set of criticisms leveled against social-learning and cognitive theories is that they often overlook emotion as an important component of personality. In psychodynamic theories, emotions like anxiety play a central role. In social-learning and cognitive theories, emotions are perceived merely as by-products of thoughts and behavior or are just included with other types of thoughts rather than being assigned independent importance. For those who feel that emotions are central to the functioning of human personality, this is a serious flaw. Cognitive theories are also attacked for not fully recognizing the impact of unconscious motivation on behavior and affect.

A second set of criticisms focuses on the vagueness of explanations about the way personal constructs and competencies are created. Cognitive theorists have often had little to say about the developmental origins of adult personality; their focus on the individual's perception of the current behavior setting obscures the individual's history.

Despite these criticisms, cognitive personality theories have made major contributions to current thinking. Mischel's awareness of the situation has brought about a better understanding of the interaction between what a person brings to a behavior setting and what that setting brings out of the person. Bandura's ideas have led to improvements in the way teachers educate children and help them achieve as well as new treatments in the areas of health, business, and sports performance.

Do these cognitive personality theories provide you with insights about your own personality and behaviors? You can start to see how you define yourself in part through interactions with the environment. Let's turn now to theories that can add even further to your definition of self.

Stop *and* Review

① In Julian Rotter's theory, what does it mean to have an external locus of control orientation?

② In Walter Mischel's theory, what five types of variables explain individual differences?

③ What three components are involved in Albert Bandura's theory of reciprocal determinism?

CRITICAL THINKING Recall the study that examined boys' aggression in summer camp. Why was it important that the researchers obtained multiple assessments of the boys' levels of aggression?

✓•—⎣**Study** and **Review** on **MyPsychLab**

SELF THEORIES

We have arrived now at theories of personality that are most immediately personal: They deal directly with how each individual manages his or her sense of *self*. What is your conception of your *self*? Do you think of your *self* reacting consistently to the world? Do you try to present a consistent *self* to your friends and family? What impact do positive and negative experiences have on the way you think about your *self*? Let's begin our consideration of these questions with a brief historical review.

The concern for analysis of the self found its strongest early advocate in William James (1892). James identified three components of self-experience: the *material me* (the bodily self, along with surrounding physical objects), the *social me* (your awareness of how others view you), and the *spiritual me* (the self that monitors private thoughts and feelings). James believed that everything that you associate with your identity becomes, in some sense, a part of the self. This explains why people may react defensively when their friends or family members—a part of the self—have been attacked. The concept of self was also central to psychodynamic theories. Self-insight was an important part of the psychoanalytic cure in Freud's theory, and Jung stressed that to fully develop the self, one must integrate and accept all aspects of one's conscious and unconscious life. Finally for this historical review, you already learned that Carl Rogers had the self as the cornerstone of his humanistic theory of personality development.

How has the self been treated in contemporary theory? We will first consider cognitive aspects of self-concepts. We then visit the concept of self-esteem and the steps people take to preserve self esteem. Finally, we'll look at the important topic of how views of the self differ across cultures.

Self-Concepts and Self-Esteem

The self-concept is a dynamic mental structure that motivates, interprets, organizes, mediates, and regulates intrapersonal and interpersonal behaviors and processes. The self-concept includes many components. Among them are your memories about yourself; beliefs about your traits, motives, values, and abilities; the ideal self that you would most like to become; the possible selves that you contemplate enacting; positive or negative evaluations of yourself (self-esteem); and beliefs about what others think of you (Chen et al., 2006). *Schemas* can be thought of as "knowledge packages" that embody complex generalizations about the structure of the environment. Your self-concept contains schemas about the self—*self-schemas*—that allow you to organize information about yourself, just as other schemas allow you to manage other aspects of your experience. However, self-schemas influence more than just the way you process information about yourself. Research indicates that these schemas, which you frequently use to interpret your own behavior, influence the way you process information about other people as well (Krueger & Stanke, 2001; Mussweiler & Bodenhausen, 2002). Thus you interpret other people's actions in terms of what you know and believe about yourself.

A person's **self-esteem** is a *generalized* evaluation of the self. People differ in their levels of self-esteem. Because I have described the importance of genetics for other aspects of personality, you may not be surprised to learn that individual differences in self-esteem have a genetic component: People inherit a tendency toward high or low self-esteem (Neiss et al., 2006). However, environmental factors also have important effects. For example, people's satisfaction or dissatisfaction with their physical appearance has a major impact on their reports of self-esteem (Donnellan et al., 2007). Self-esteem also varies with respect to people's perceptions of their ability to navigate in the social world. People who are high in self-esteem typically feel that they will function well in social relationships; people with low self-esteem have doubts about their social value (Anthony et al., 2007).

Self-esteem can strongly influence people's thoughts, moods, and behavior (Swann et al., 2007). In fact, researchers have linked a number of negative outcomes to low levels of self-esteem. For example, among adolescents and college students, low self-esteem was related to aggression and antisocial behavior (Donnellan et al., 2005). Similarly, people who reported low self-esteem as adolescents had poorer mental and physical health as well as more financial problems as adults (Orth et al., 2008; Trzeniewski et al., 2006). These results suggest that having low self-esteem can undermine people's ability to set goals for positive outcomes and cope with negative life events.

Some people clearly experience low self-esteem. However, evidence suggests that most people go out of their way to maintain self-esteem and to sustain the integrity of their self-concept

(Vignoles et al., 2006). To preserve their self-image, people engage in a variety of forms of *self-enhancement*: People take steps to view their own actions and behaviors as consistently positive (Sedikides & Gregg, 2008). For example, when people doubt their ability to perform a task, they may engage in **self-handicapping** behavior. They deliberately sabotage their performance! The purpose of this strategy is to have a ready-made excuse for failure that does not imply *lack of ability* (McCrae & Hirt, 2001). Thus, a student might party with friends instead of studying for an important exam. That way, if he doesn't succeed, he can blame his failure on low effort rather than low aptitude. Note that my use of "he" in this example is deliberate. Research suggests that men consistently engage in more self-handicapping than do women.

*Before taking an intelligence test, male and female psychology students were given the opportunity to work through 18 practice items (McCrae et al., 2008). The researchers gave half the students practice matters instructions: Those students were told that without appropriate practice their intelligence tests scores would not be valid. The other students received practice does not matter instructions: Those students were told that practice would likely have no effect on their test scores. Suppose you were in the practice matters condition. If you wanted to have a ready excuse for your (potentially) low intelligence score, you might choose not to practice very much. As you can see in **Figure 8**, that's, on average, what the men chose to do. Women who were told that practiced mattered, practiced quite a bit. Men who had the same instructions practiced least of all. To understand this difference, the researchers asked the participants to complete a scale that had items such as "I try to devote my full effort to every class I take" and "I pride myself in being a hard worker" (p. 309). The women consistently agreed more with such statements than did their male peers.*

These results support the researchers' claim that women put too much value on effort to engage in self-handicapping. The effort women expend is an important contributor to their self-esteem.

In recent years, researchers have provided support for a theory that places self-esteem in a broader perspective. **Terror management theory** proposes that self-esteem helps people cope with the inevitability of death (Greenberg, 2008). Terror management theory suggests that people wish to achieve *symbolic immortality* which "is conferred by cultural institutions that enable people to feel part of something larger, more significant, and more eternal than their own individual lives through connections and contributions to their families, nations, professions, and ideologies" (Pyszczynski et al., 2004, p. 436).

self-esteem A generalized evaluative attitude toward the self that influences both moods and behavior and that exerts a powerful effect on a range of personal and social behaviors.

self-handicapping The process of developing, in anticipation of failure, behavioral reactions and explanations that minimize ability deficits as possible attributions for the failure.

terror management theory A theory proposing that self-esteem helps people cope with the inevitability of death.

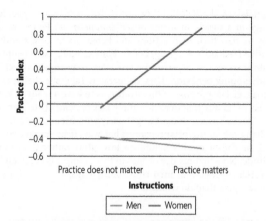

FIGURE 8 Men's and Women's Self-Handicapping

The *practice index* combined the number of practice items a student completed and the amount of time he or she spent practicing into a single measure. Positive scores indicate more than average practice; negative scores indicate less than average practice. When instructions suggested that practice didn't matter, the difference between men's and women's practice was small. However, when students believed their practice did matter, women practiced considerably more than the men.

Data from S. M. McCrae, E. R. Hirt, & B. J. Milner, She works hard for the money, *Journal of Experimental Social Psychology (44)*: 292–311, © 2008.

People attain self-esteem when they believe that they have made valuable contributions that provide a route to symbolic immortality. To support terror management theory, researchers have demonstrated many ways in which people's behavior changes when their attention is called to the inevitability of death. For example, one project instilled *mortality salience* in a subset of participants by asking them to "Jot down, as specifically as you can, what you think will happen to you as you physically die and once you are physically dead" (Greenberg et al., 2010, p. 5). Members of the control group did not complete this exercise. Later in the experimental session, the participants answered questions like "How much would you like to become famous?" and "How famous do you think you will become in the future?" Participants for whom mortality was made salient reported themselves to be more interested in pursuing and achieving fame than their peers who had not contemplated death. Can you see how expectations of fame relate to self-esteem and symbolic immortality?

This section has emphasized that people engage in behaviors such as self-handicapping to maintain a high sense of self-esteem. For that reason, you might not be surprised to learn that people's global ratings of self-esteem are often not a good predictor of their performance across domains (Baumeister et al.,

independent construal of self Conceptualization of the self as an individual whose behavior is organized primarily by reference to one's own thoughts, feelings, and actions, rather than by reference to the thoughts, feelings, and actions of others.

2003). Instead, people's self-views with respect to more specific domains of performance (such as particular academic subjects) provide better predictive information about their likely performance (Swann et al., 2007). Similarly, programs to boost self-esteem are best targeted toward particular domains in which people can learn strategies that actually change performance.

The Cultural Construction of Self

The discussion so far has focused on constructs relevant to the self, such as self-esteem and self-handicapping, that apply quite widely across individuals. However, researchers on the self have also begun to study the way in which self-concepts and self-development are affected by differing cultural constraints. If you have grown up in a Western culture, you are likely to be pretty comfortable with the research reviewed so far: The theories and constructs match the ways that Western cultures conceptualize the *self*. However, the type of culture from which the Western self emerges—an *individualistic* culture—is in the minority with respect to the world's population, which includes about 70 percent *collectivist* cultures. Individualistic cultures emphasize individuals' needs, whereas collectivist cultures emphasize the needs of the group (Triandis, 1994, 1995). This overarching emphasis has important implications for how each member of these cultures conceptualizes his or her *self*: Hazel Markus and Shinobu Kitayama (1991; Kitayama et al., 1995; Markus et al., 1997) have argued that each culture gives rise to different interpretations of the meaning of self—or different *construals* of self:

- Individualistic cultures encourage **independent construals of self**—"Achieving the cultural goal of independence requires construing oneself as an individual whose behavior is organized and made meaningful primarily by reference to one's own internal repertoire of thoughts, feelings, and action, rather than by reference to the thoughts, feelings, and actions of others" (Markus & Kitayama, 1991, p. 226).

Self-handicapping behavior in action: Instead of studying for tomorrow's exam, you fall asleep in the library, thereby enabling yourself to say, "Well, I didn't really study" if you don't ace the test. Are there situations in which you resort to self-handicapping?

- Collectivist cultures encourage **interdependent construals of self**—"Experiencing interdependence entails seeing oneself as part of an encompassing social relationship and recognizing that one's behavior is determined, contingent on, and, to a large extent organized by what the actor perceives to be the thoughts, feelings, and actions of *others* in the relationship" (Markus & Kitayama, 1991, p. 227).

Researchers have documented the reality and implications of these distinctions in a number of ways (Cross et al., 2011).

One type of cross-cultural research on the self has used a measurement device called the *Twenty Statements Test* (TST) (Kuhn & McPartland, 1954). When they take this test, participants are asked to give 20 different answers to the question "Who am I?" Take a moment to reflect on that question. As shown in **Table 6**, responses typically fall into six different categories. Culture has an impact on the categories that are most likely for people's responses. For example, one study had roughly 300 students from the United States and India perform the TST procedure (Dhawan et al., 1995). In keeping with their independent sense of self, about 65 percent of the responses of U.S. women and 64 percent of the responses of U.S. men fell into the category of *self-evaluations*. For the Indian students, 33 percent of women's responses and 35 percent of men's responses fell into this category. Thus the Indian students were about half as likely to produce self-evaluations. Note that differences between men and women overall were rather small—culture mattered more.

You might wonder how the export of Western culture affects the self-concepts of members of collectivist cultures. One study compared the TST responses of Kenyans who had virtually no exposure to Western culture—members of pastoral Samburu and Maasai tribes—to those who had moved to the Westernized capital city of Nairobi. Roughly 82 percent of the tribe members' responses on the TST were social responses; workers in Nairobi gave only 58 percent social responses, and students at the University of Nairobi gave only 17 percent social responses (Ma & Schoeneman, 1997). This pattern

Table 6 • Categories of Twenty Statements Test Responses

Category	Examples
Social identity	I'm a student. I'm a daughter.
Ideological beliefs	I believe that all human beings are good. I believe in God.
Interests	I like playing the piano. I enjoy visiting new places.
Ambitions	I want to become a doctor. I want to learn more psychology.
Self-evaluations	I am honest and hardworking. I am a tall person. I worry about the future.
Other	I have noisy friends. I own a dog.

suggests that when a nation imports Western products, it may also import a Western sense of self.

These studies illustrate that the cultures to which people belong have a strong impact on the way they construe their selves. For example, there are differences in how people from different cultures assess causal forces in the world. For now, let's consider a study that relates back to terror management theory and mortality salience. Recall that mortality salience generally makes people wish to bolster their self. However, that impulse has different outcomes for people with different construals of self.

At the start of a study, European American and Asian American students were randomly assigned to a mortality salience group or a control group (Ma-Kellams & Blascovich, 2011). Students in the mortality salience group wrote down thoughts about their death whereas students in the control group wrote about dental pain. Next, the students read a scenario that described a serious car accident in which a university employee named Steve had been the victim. After reading the scenario, participants completed an Assignment of Blame Scale (ABS) to indicate how much they held Steve responsible. As you can see in **Figure 9**, *mortality salience pushed European American and Asian American responses in different directions. Perhaps to protect their independent construals of self from the fear of being accident victims, European Americans blamed Steve more when they were experiencing mortality salience. By contrast, Asian Americans who were experiencing mortality salience appeared to include Steve within their interdependent construals of self and, as a consequence, blamed him less.*

Featured Study

In what ways is an individual's sense of self different when he or she is a member of a culture with an interdependent construal of self rather than an independent construal of self?

© paul prescott/Alamy

....

interdependent construal of self Conceptualization of the self as part of an encompassing social relationship; recognizing that one's behavior is determined, contingent on, and, to a large extent, organized by what the actor perceived to be the thoughts, feelings, and actions of others.

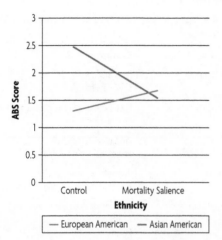

FIGURE 9 Culture and Mortality Salience

European American and Asian American students assigned blame (on the Assignment of Blame Scale, ABS) to Steve, who had been the victim of a serious car accident. Mortality salience affected the students' ratings quite differently, as a product of their cultural construal of self.

Data from Christine Ma-Kellams and Jim Blascovich, "Culturally divergent responses to mortality salience," *Psychological Science*, August 1, 2011, copyright © 2011 Association for Psychological Science.

Over the next few days, you might try to experience both construals of self by trying to attend to how the events that happen around you have an impact both on your self as an individual and your self as a member of a larger social structure.

Evaluation of Self Theories

Self theories succeed at capturing people's own concepts of their personalities and the way they wish to be perceived by others. Furthermore, examinations of cross-cultural construals of the self have had great influence on the way psychologists assess the universality of their theories. However, critics of self theory approaches to personality argue against their limitless boundaries. Because so many things are relevant to the self and to the self-concept, it is not always clear which factors are most important for predicting behavior. In addition, the emphasis on the self as a social construct is not entirely consistent with evidence that some facets of personality may be inherited. As with other theories, self theories capture some but not all of what you think of as personality.

Stop *and* Review

① What is self-esteem?
② What is self-handicapping?
③ What does it mean to have an interdependent construal of self?

CRITICAL THINKING   Recall the study that demonstrated gender differences in self-handicapping. Why was it important that participants completed the worker scale before they had the opportunity to practice?

✔●—[Study and **Review** on **MyPsychLab**

COMPARING PERSONALITY THEORIES

There is no unified theory of personality that a majority of psychologists can endorse. Several differences in basic assumptions have come up repeatedly in this survey of the various theories. It may be helpful to recap five of the most important differences in assumptions about personality and the approaches that advance each assumption: ✱

1. *Heredity versus environment.* This difference is also referred to as *nature versus nurture.* What is more important to personality development: genetic and biological factors or environmental influences? Trait theories have been split on this issue; Freudian theory depends heavily on heredity; humanistic, social-learning, cognitive, and self theories all emphasize either environment as a determinant of behavior or interaction with the environment as a source of personality development and differences.

2. *Learning processes versus innate laws of behavior.* Should emphasis be placed on the view that personalities are modified through learning or on the view that personality development follows an internal timetable? Again, trait theories have been divided. Freudian theory has favored the inner determinant view, whereas humanists postulate an optimistic view that experience changes people. Social-learning, cognitive, and self theories clearly support the idea that behavior and personality change as a result of learned experiences.

3. *Emphasis on past, present, or future.* Trait theories emphasize past causes, whether innate or learned; Freudian theory stresses past events in early childhood; social-learning theories focus on past reinforcements and present contingencies; humanistic theories emphasize present reality or future goals; and cognitive and self theories emphasize past and present (and the future if goal setting is involved).

4. *Consciousness versus unconsciousness.* Freudian theory emphasizes unconscious processes; humanistic, social-learning, and cognitive theories emphasize conscious processes. Trait theories pay little attention to this distinction; self theories are unclear on this score.

5. *Inner disposition versus outer situation.* Social-learning theories emphasize situational factors; traits play up dispositional factors; and the others allow for an interaction between person-based and situation-based variables.

Each type of theory makes different contributions to the understanding of human personality. Trait theories provide a catalog that describes parts and structures. Psychodynamic theories add a powerful engine and the fuel to get the vehicle moving. Humanistic theories put a person in the driver's seat. Social-learning theories supply the steering wheel, directional signals, and other regulation equipment. Cognitive theories add reminders that the way the trip is planned, organized,

✱ Explore the Concept *Psychodynamic, Behavioral, Trait and Type, Humanistic and Cognitive Approaches to Personality* on MyPsychLab

Critical Thinking in Your Life

HOW IS PERSONALITY CONVEYED IN CYBERSPACE?

Let's start with a straightforward question: Does your e-mail address allow people to make accurate guesses about your personality? To address that question, a team of researchers used a web-based survey to obtain e-mail addresses and self-reports of personality from 599 individuals (Back et al., 2008). Next, the researchers asked a different group of 100 students to make personality judgments based only on the e-mail addresses. Consider the researchers' example, honey.bunny77@hotmail.de. How aggreeable and conscientious would you imagine the person with that e-mail address to be?

The researchers found that personality ratings based on just the e-mail addresses were quite consistent among the group of 100 raters. The researchers also found positive correlations between the raters' assessments and the e-mail users' self-reports on most of the personality dimensions. The raters were able to make reasonably valid personality judgments based on just the e-mail addresses! The raters appeared to be responding to a number of features of the addresses. For example, the raters gave higher conscientiousness ratings to addresses with a larger number of characters; they gave lower conscientiousness ratings to addresses with a larger number of digits.

Of course, if you are like many students, your e-mail address is only one of a very large number of decisions you need to make to determine your exact presence in cyberspace. Suppose you have a page on Facebook. To manage the impression you make, you need to make decisions about any number of variables, including how many friends you allow, how much personal detail you provide, and what types of photos you upload (Krämer & Winter, 2008). These variables contribute to visitors' perceptions. For example, one study varied the number of friends (102, 302, 502, 702, or 902) on a mock Facebook page (Tong et al., 2008). Participants rated the *social attractiveness* of the page's owner. Those ratings were highest for 302 friends: Too few and too many friends counted against the owner. Why 302? The participants reported that they had a median number of 300 friends. Perhaps participants gave the highest ratings when they thought the page owner was similar to them.

Another study examined how Facebook photographs contributed to judgments on the particular personality trait of *narcissism* (Buffardi & Campbell, 2008). People who are narcissistic have an overly positive self-image. How might that trait be expressed through Facebook photos? The researchers found that participants rated page owners as being particularly narcissistic when the main photo on their Facebook pages was attractive and self-promoting (that is, the photo seemed dedicated to "persuading others about [the page owner's] own positive qualities," p. 1307). In addition, there was a positive correlation between raters' judgments and the page owner's self-reports of narcissism: The Facebook pages communicated valid information on this trait!

Do these results make you rethink how you present yourself in cyberspace?

- Why might people be comfortable making personality judgments based on Facebook content?
- How might you determine other circumstances in which similarity has an impact on people's judgments of Facebook pages?

and remembered will be affected by the mental map the driver chooses for the journey. Finally, self theories remind the driver to consider the image his or her driving ability is projecting to backseat drivers and pedestrians.

To complete this review of personality, we will now consider personality assessment. You will see some of the ways in which psychologists obtain information about the range of personality attributes that make each individual unique.

Stop *and* Review

① In what ways do personality theories differ on the dimension of heredity versus environment?
② Does Freud's theory of personality focus most directly on the past, present, or future?
③ Which dimension of personality theories refers to people's awareness of the forces that shape their behaviors?

✔ Study and Review on MyPsychLab

ASSESSING PERSONALITY

Think of all the ways in which you differ from your best friend. Psychologists wonder about the diverse attributes that characterize an individual, set one person apart from others, or distinguish people in one group from those in another (for example, shy people from outgoing or depressed individuals from happy). Two assumptions are basic to these attempts to understand and describe human personality: first, that there are personal characteristics of individuals that give coherence to their behavior and, second, that those characteristics can be assessed or measured. Personality tests must meet the standards of reliability and validity. In addition, clinicians and researchers receive thorough training to administer and interpret the tests. We will consider *objective* and *projective* personality tests. Psychologists often combine different measures to obtain a full understanding of an individual's personality. 👁

Objective Tests

Objective tests of personality are those in which scoring and administration are relatively simple and follow well-defined rules. Some objective tests are scored by computer programs. The final score is usually a single number, scaled along a single dimension (such as *adjustment* versus *maladjustment*), or a set of scores on different traits (such as impulsiveness, dependency, or extraversion) reported in comparison with the scores of a normative sample.

A *self-report inventory* is an objective test in which individuals answer a series of questions about their thoughts, feelings, and actions. One of the first self-report inventories, the *Woodworth Personal Data Sheet* (written in 1917) asked questions such as "Are you often frightened in the middle of the night?" (see DuBois, 1970). Today, a person taking a **personality inventory** reads a series of statements and indicates whether each one is true or typical for him- or herself. Let's consider two prominent personality inventories, the *Minnesota Multiphasic Personality Inventory,* or MMPI, and the *NEO Personality Inventory* (NEO-PI).

The MMPI The MMPI was developed at the University of Minnesota during the 1930s by psychologist Starke Hathaway and psychiatrist J. R. McKinley (Hathaway & McKinley, 1940, 1943). Its basic purpose is to diagnose individuals according to a set of psychiatric labels. The first test consisted of 550 items, which individuals determined to be either true or false for themselves or to which they responded, "Cannot say." From that item pool, scales were developed that were relevant to the kinds of problems patients showed in psychiatric settings.

The MMPI scales were unlike other existing personality tests because they were developed using an *empirical* strategy rather than the intuitive, theoretical approach that dominated at the time. Items were included on a scale only if they clearly distinguished between two groups—for example, patients with schizoprehnia and a normal comparison group. Each item had to demonstrate its validity by being answered similarly by members within each group but differently between the two groups. Thus the items were not selected on a theoretical basis (what the content seemed to mean to experts) but on an empirical basis (did they distinguish between the two groups?).

The MMPI has 10 *clinical scales,* each constructed to differentiate a special clinical group (such as individuals with schizophrenia) from a normal comparison group. The test also includes *validity scales* that detect suspicious response patterns, such as blatant dishonesty, carelessness, defensiveness,

....

👁 **Watch** the **Video** *In the Real World: Putting Popular Personality Assessments to the Test* on **MyPsychLab**

personality inventory A self-report questionnaire used for personality assessment that includes a series of items about personal thoughts, feelings, and behaviors.

Table 7 • MMPI-2 Clinical Scales

Hypochondriasis (Hs): Abnormal concern with bodily functions
Depression (D): Pessimism; hopelessness; slowing of action and thought
Conversion hysteria (Hy): Unconscious use of mental problems to avoid conflicts or responsibility
Psychopathic deviate (Pd): Disregard for social custom; shallow emotions; inability to profit from experience
Masculinity–femininity (Mf): Differences between men and women
Paranoia (Pa): Suspiciousness; delusions of grandeur or persecution
Psychasthenia (Pt): Obsessions; compulsions; fears; guilt; indecisiveness
Schizophrenia (Sc): Bizarre, unusual thoughts or behavior; withdrawal; hallucinations; delusions
Hypomania (Ma): Emotional excitement; flight of ideas; overactivity
Social introversion (Si): Shyness; disinterest in others; insecurity

or evasiveness. When an MMPI is interpreted, the tester first checks the validity scales to be sure the test is valid and then looks at the rest of the scores. The pattern of the scores— which are highest, how they differ—forms the "MMPI profile." Individual profiles are compared with those common for particular groups, such as felons and gamblers.

In the mid-1980s, the MMPI underwent a major revision, and it is now called the *MMPI-2* (Butcher et al., 2001). The MMPI-2 has updated language and content to better reflect contemporary concerns, and new populations provided data for norms. The MMPI-2 also adds 15 new *content scales* that were derived using, in part, a theoretical method. For each of 15 clinically relevant topics (such as anxiety or family problems), items were selected on two bases: if they seemed theoretically related to the topic area and if they statistically formed a *homogeneous scale,* meaning that each scale

Table 8 • MMPI-2 Content Scales

Anxiety Practices	
Fears	Type A (workaholic)
Obsessiveness	Low self-esteem
Depression	Social discomfort
Health concerns	Family problems
Bizarre mentation (thoughts)	Work interference
Anger and cynicism	Negative treatment indicators (negative attitudes about doctors and treatment)

measures a single, unified concept. The clinical and content scales of the MMPI-2 are given in **Table 7** and **Table 8**. You'll notice that most of the clinical scales measure several related concepts and that the names of the content scales are simple and self-explanatory.

Because the MMPI-2 plays such a critical role in clinical research and practice, researchers continue to assess the test's reliability and validity to make appropriate clinical judgments. Important aspects of that research were incorporated into the MMPI-2-RF (for "revised form"), which appeared in 2008 (Tellegen & Ben-Porath, 2008). The MMPI-2-RF features revised clinical scales that supplement the MMPI-2 clinical scales. The goal of these revised scales is to allow better discrimination among people with different types of psychological disorders. The revised clinical scales have begun to undergo tests of reliability and validity that will allow psychologists to put the MMPI-2-RF to appropriate uses (Forbey et al., 2010; Rouse et al., 2008).

The NEO-PI Recall that the MMPI was designed to assess individuals with clinical problems. By contrast, the NEO Personality Inventory (NEO-PI) was designed to assess personality characteristics in nonclinical adult populations. It measures the five-factor model of personality you met earlier. If you took the NEO-PI, you would receive a profile sheet that showed your standardized scores relative to a large normative sample on each of the five major dimensions: Neuroticism, Extraversion, Openness, Agreeableness, and Conscientiousness (Costa & McCrae, 1985). The recent NEO-PI-3 assesses 30 separate traits organized within the five major factors (McCrae et al., 2005). For example, the Neuroticism dimension is broken down into six facet scales: Anxiety, Angry hostility, Depression, Self-consciousness, Impulsiveness, and Vulnerability. Much research has demonstrated that the NEO-PI dimensions show good reliability and validity (McCrae et al., 2004, 2011). The NEO-PI is being used to study personality stability and change across the life span as well as the relationship of personality characteristics to physical health and various life events, such as career success or early retirement.

Projective Tests

As you just saw, objective tests take one of two forms: Either they provide test takers with a series of statements and ask them to give a simple response (such as "true," "false," or "cannot say") or they ask test takers to rate themselves with respect to some dimension (such as "anxious" versus "nonanxious"). Thus the respondent is constrained to choose one of the predetermined responses. *Projective tests*, by contrast, have no predetermined range of responses. In a **projective test,** a person is given a series of stimuli that are purposely ambiguous, such as abstract patterns, incomplete pictures, or drawings that can be interpreted in many ways. The person may be asked to describe the patterns, finish the pictures, or tell stories about the drawings. Projective tests were first used by psychoanalysts, who hoped that such tests would reveal their patients' unconscious personality dynamics. Because the stimuli are ambiguous, responses to them are determined partly by what the person brings to the situation—namely, inner feelings, personal motives, and conflicts from prior life experiences. These personal, idiosyncratic aspects, which are *projected* onto the stimuli, permit the personality assessor to make various interpretations.

Projective tests are among the assessment devices most commonly used by psychological practitioners (Butcher, 2010; Musewicz et al., 2009). However, because projective tests are so widespread, critics have often worried that they are used in ways that are not valid. The next sections review two of the most common projective tests, the Rorschach test and the Thematic Apperception Test, and includes discussion of those issues of validity.

The Rorschach In the Rorschach test, developed by Swiss psychiatrist **Hermann Rorschach** in 1921, the ambiguous stimuli are symmetrical inkblots (Rorschach, 1942). Some are black and white, and some are colored (see **Figure 10**). During the test, a respondent is shown an inkblot and asked, "What might this be?" Respondents are assured that there are no right or wrong answers (Exner, 1974). Testers record verbatim what people say, how much time they take to respond, the total time they take per inkblot, and the way they handle the inkblot card. Then, in a second phase called an *inquiry,* the respondent is reminded of the previous responses and asked to elaborate on them.

The responses are scored on three major features: (1) the *location,* or part of the card mentioned in the response—whether the respondent refers to the whole stimulus or to part of it and the size of the details mentioned; (2) the *content* of the response—the nature of the object and activities seen; and (3) the *determinants*—which aspects of the card (such as its color or shading) prompted the response. Scorers may also note whether responses are original and unique or popular and conforming.

You might think that ambiguous inkblots would give rise to an uninterpretable diversity of responses. In fact, researchers have devised a comprehensive scoring system for Rorschach responses that allows for meaningful comparisons among different test takers (Exner, 2003; Exner & Weiner, 1994). For example, the scoring system specifies content categories that frequently appear in people's responses. Those categories include *whole human* (the response mentions or implies a whole human form) and *blood* (the response mentions blood, either human or animal). Researchers have developed training

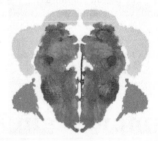

FIGURE 10 An Inkblot Similar to Those Used in the Rorschach Test

What do you see? Does your interpretation of this inkblot reveal anything about your personality?

projective test A method of personality assessment in which an individual is presented with a standardized set of ambiguous, abstract stimuli and asked to interpret their meanings; the individual's responses are assumed to reveal inner feelings, motives, and conflicts.

FIGURE 11 **The Type of Image Used on the TAT Test**

What story do you want to tell? What does your story reveal about your personality?

procedures to ensure that clinicians can learn to use the comprehensive scoring system reliably (Hilsenroth et al., 2007). In addition, researchers have undertaken formal studies to determine whether the results from the scoring system make it possible to diagnose specific psychological disorders such as posttraumatic stress disorder (Arnon et al., 2011). However, practitioners also make diagnoses based on people's Rorschach responses without any formal evidence that supports the validity of the practitioners' inferences. For that reason, the Rorschach test remains controversial (Garb et al., 2005).

The TAT In the Thematic Apperception Test (TAT), developed by **Henry Murray** in 1938, respondents are shown pictures of ambiguous scenes and asked to generate stories about them, describing what the people in the scenes are doing and thinking, what led up to each event, and how each situation will end (see **Figure 11**). The person administering the TAT evaluates the structure and content of the stories as well as the behavior

● Watch the Video *Thinking Like a Psychologist: Testing Personality* on MyPsychLab

of the individual telling them, in an attempt to discover some of the respondent's major concerns, motivations, and personality characteristics. For example, an examiner might evaluate a person as conscientious if his or her stories concerned people who lived up to their obligations and if the stories were told in a serious, orderly way. As with the Rorschach test, critics have suggested that the TAT is often used for purposes for which its validity remains uncertain (Lilienfeld et al., 2001). One use of the TAT has received research support: The TAT has often been used to reveal individual differences in dominant needs, such as needs for power, affiliation, and achievement (McClelland, 1961). Researchers have also used the TAT to investigate group differences, such as changes across generations in the dominant needs of students entering medical school (Borges et al., 2010).

As you learned about these personality assessment devices, did you see the relationship between them and the theories of personality you encountered earlier? Earlier, you saw that each of the types of theories illuminated test different aspects of human experience. Here, the same conclusion applies for personality tests: Each has the potential to provide unique insights into an individual's personality. Clinicians most often use a combination of tests when they carry out a personality assessment. ●

To close the chapter, please consider a series of questions in light of what you have just learned: If psychologists studied you, what portrait of your personality would they draw? Which early experiences might they identify as contributing to how you now act and think? What conditions in your current life exert strong influences on your thoughts and behaviors? What makes you different from other individuals who are functioning in many of the same situations as you? You now can see that each type of personality theory provides a framework against which you can begin to form your answers to these questions. Suppose the time has really come to paint your psychological portrait. Where would you begin?

Stop *and* Review

① What is the purpose of the MMPI's 10 clinical scales?
② What is the purpose of the NEO Personality Inventory (NEO-PI)?
③ What three major features do clinicians use to interpret Rorschach responses?

✓ Study and Review on MyPsychLab

Recapping Main Points

Trait Personality Theories

- Some theorists view traits—attributes along continuous dimensions—as the building blocks of personality.
- The five-factor model is a personality system that maps out the relationships among common trait words, theoretical concepts, and personality scales.
- Twin and adoption studies reveal that personality traits are partially inherited.
- People display behavioral consistency when situations are defined with respect to relevant psychological features.

Psychodynamic Theories

- Freud's psychodynamic theory emphasizes instinctive biological energies as sources of human motivation.
- Basic concepts of Freudian theory include psychic energy as powering and directing behavior, early experiences as key determinants of lifelong personality, psychic determinism, and powerful unconscious processes.
- Personality structure consists of the id, the superego, and the reconciling ego.

- Unacceptable impulses are repressed and ego defense mechanisms are developed to lessen anxiety and bolster self-esteem.
- Post-Freudians like Adler, Horney, and Jung put greater emphasis on ego functioning and social variables and less on sexual urges. They saw personality development as a lifelong process.

Humanistic Theories

- Humanistic theories focus on self-actualization—the growth potential of the individual.
- These theories are holistic, dispositional, and phenomenological.
- Contemporary theories in the humanist tradition focus on individuals' life stories.

Social-Learning and Cognitive Theories

- Social-learning theorists focus on understanding individual differences in behavior and personality as a consequence of different histories of reinforcement.
- Cognitive theorists emphasize individual differences in perception and subjective interpretation of the environment.
- Julian Rotter emphasized people's expectancies about rewards, including general internal or external locus of control orientations.
- Walter Mischel explored the origins of behaviors as interactions of persons and situations.
- Albert Bandura described the reciprocal determinism among people, environments, and behaviors.

Self Theories

- Self theories focus on the importance of the self-concept for a full understanding of human personality.
- People engage in behaviors such as self-handicapping to maintain self-esteem.
- Terror management theory suggests that self-esteem helps people cope with thoughts about death.
- Cross-cultural research suggests that individualistic cultures give rise to independent construals of self, whereas collectivist cultures give rise to interdependent construals of self.

Comparing Personality Theories

- Personality theories can be contrasted with respect to the emphasis they put on heredity versus environment; learning processes versus innate laws of behavior; the past, present, or future; consciousness versus unconsciousness; and inner dispositions versus outer situations.
- Each theory makes different contributions to the understanding of human personality.

Assessing Personality

- Personality characteristics are assessed by both objective and projective tests.
- The most common objective test, the MMPI-2, is used to diagnose clinical problems.
- The NEO-PI is an objective test that measures five major dimensions of personality.
- Projective tests of personality ask people to respond to ambiguous stimuli.
- Two important projective tests are the Rorschach test and the TAT.

KEY TERMS

analytic psychology	independent construal of self	repression
anxiety	interdependent construal of self	self-actualization
archetype	libido	self-concept
collective unconscious	locus of control	self-efficacy
consistency paradox	personality	self-esteem
ego	personality inventory	self-handicapping
ego defense mechanism	projective test	superego
expectancy	psychic determinism	terror management theory
five-factor model	psychobiography	trait
fixation	psychodynamic personality theory	unconditional positive regard
id	reciprocal determinism	unconscious

Practice Test

1. Sheldon doesn't like movies that make him cry. This is an example of a(n)_____ trait.
   a. cardinal
   b. secondary
   c. central
   d. peripheral

2. Which of these factors is *not* a trait dimension in the five-factor model?
   a. creativeness
   b. neuroticism
   c. agreeableness
   d. extraversion

3. You overhear Rick say, "Bad people must be punished!" Based just on that evidence, you begin to suspect that Rick may believe in a(n) _____ theory of personality.
   a. incremental
   b. humanistic
   c. entity
   d. collectivist

4. According to Freud, at ages 4 to 5 children are in the _____ stage of development.
   a. genital
   b. oral
   c. phallic
   d. anal

5. You attend a lecture that is focusing on archetypes in the collective unconscious. The lecture seems to be about the ideas of
   a. Carl Jung.
   b. Sigmund Freud.
   c. Karen Horney.
   d. Alfred Adler.

6. One of the most important claims of humanistic theories of personality is that people strive for
   a. superiority.
   b. zones.
   c. self-preservation.
   d. self-actualization.

7. Humanistic theories are _____ because they emphasize an individual's subjective view of reality.
   a. holistic
   b. deterministic
   c. phenomenological
   d. dispositional

8. With respect to Walter Mischel's personality theory, which of these statements relates to the variable of goals and values?
   a. Bart wants to graduate from college before he turns 30.
   b. Reese thinks she can persuade her brother to lend her his car.
   c. Piper sweats a lot before she takes an exam.
   d. Vito can do multiplication without a calculator.

9. Jason's best friend Buffy is trying to convince him that he can get a new job. If Buffy is successful, that could have an impact on Jason's sense of
   a. self-efficacy.
   b. self-regulation.
   c. reciprocal determinism.
   d. libido.

10. Brian spends the whole night before he is going to compete in a triathalon reviewing the notes for his philosophy class. This might be an example of
    a. self-efficacy.
    b. psychic determinism.
    c. self-handicapping.
    d. neuroticism.

11. Because Miriam lives in a _____ culture she is likely to have a(n) _____ construal of self.
    a. collectivist; dependent
    b. collectivist; interdependent
    c. individualistic; interdependent
    d. collectivist; independent

12. Which features of Facebook pages were *not* related to judgments of narcissism?
    a. The number of funny quotations.
    b. The attractiveness of the main photograph.
    c. The self-promotion of the main photograph.
    d. The owner's amount of social interaction.

13. Chad and Jeremy are both personality theorists. Chad believes that personalities are largely determined before birth. Jeremy believes that personalities arise from life experiences. The dimension on which they disagree is
    a. learning processes versus innate laws of behavior.
    b. consciousness versus unconsciousness.
    c. inner disposition versus outer situation.
    d. heredity versus environment.

14. The personality test that most directly assesses the dimensions of the five-factor model is the
    a. Rorschach.
    b. NEO-PI.
    c. TAT.
    d. MMPI-2.

15. If you wanted to measure need for achievement, your first choice might be the
    a. Rorschach.
    b. TAT.
    c. MMPI-2.
    d. NEO-PI.

ESSAY QUESTIONS

1. How do traits and situations interact to affect predictions of behaviors?

2. How do humanistic theories give rise to a focus on life stories and psychobiography?

3. What theoretical ideas led to the development of projective personality tests?

Stop and Review Answers

Stop and Review (Type and Trait Personality Theories)

1. Neuroticism is defined as a dimension from stable, calm, and contented versus anxious, unstable, and temperamental.
2. To assess the heritability of traits, researchers have conducted studies that compare the trait similarity of monozygotic and dizygotic twins.
3. The consistency paradox refers to finding that people often give consistent personality descriptions for individuals even though the individuals' behavior is not consistent across situations.

Stop and Review (Psychodynamic Theories)

1. The individual might engage in oral behaviors such as smoking or overeating; the individual might be overly passive or gullible.
2. The ego is guided by the reality principle to put reasonable choices before the id's demands for pleasure.
3. Leon might be using the defense mechanism of projection—he projects his own motives onto other people.
4. Adler suggested that people are driven to overcome feelings of inferiority.

Stop and Review (Humanistic Theories)

1. Self-actualization is a person's constant striving to reach his or her inherent potential.
2. Humanistic theories focus on people's innate qualities, which influence their behaviors.
3. A psychobiography uses psychological theories to give a coherent account of the way in which an individual's life unfolds.

Stop and Review (Social-Learning and Cognitive Theories)

1. People who have an external locus of control orientation believe that rewards are largely contingent on environmental factors.

2. Mischel's theory focuses on encodings, expectancies and beliefs, affects, goal and values, and competencies and self-regulatory plans.
3. According to Bandura, the individual's characteristics, the individual's behavior, and the environment all interact to influence and modify the other components.

Stop and Review (Self Theories)

1. Self-esteem is a generalized evaluation of the self.
2. Self-handicapping applies to circumstances in which people engage in behaviors that allow them to attribute their failures to causes besides lack of ability.
3. People who have interdependent construals of self experience themselves as one element of a larger social structure.

Stop and Review (Comparing Personality Theories)

1. Some theories explain individual differences by focusing on each person's genetic endowment, whereas other theories make reference to the life experiences that have shaped individual personalities.
2. Freud's theory stresses the way in which events in early childhood—the past—affect an adult's personality.
3. The relevant dimension of personality theories is consciousness versus unconsciousness.

Stop and Review (Assessing Personality)

1. Each of the MMPI's 10 clinical scales is intended to differentiate people who have a specific clinical disorder from those who do not.
2. The NEO-PI measures the five personality traits defined by the five-factor model of personality.
3. Clinicians assess Rorschach responses for location, content, and determinants.

Practice Test Answers

1. b	5. a	9. a	13. d
2. a	6. d	10. c	14. b
3. c	7. c	11. b	15. b
4. c	8. a	12. a	

References

Adler, A. (1929). *The practice and theory of individual psychology.* New York: Harcourt, Brace & World.

Allport, G. W. (1937). *Personality: A psychological interpretation.* New York: Holt, Rinehart & Winston.

Allport, G. W. (1961). *Pattern and growth in personality.* New York: Holt, Rinehart & Winston.

Allport, G. W. (1966). Traits revisited. *American Psychologist, 21,* 1–10.

Allport, G. W., & Odbert, H. S. (1936). Trait-names, a psycholexical study. *Psychological Monographs, 47*(1, Whole No. 211).

Anthony, D. B., Holmes, J. G., & Wood, J. V. (2007). Social acceptance and self-esteem: Tuning the sociometer to interpersonal value. *Journal of Personality and Social Psychology, 92,* 1024–1039.

Arnon, Z., Maoz, G., Gazit, T., & Klein, E. (2011). Rorschach indicators of PTSD: A retrospective study. *Rorschachiana, 32,* 5–26.

Ayduk, O., Rodriguez, M. L., Mischel, W., Shoda, Y., & Wright, J. (2007). Verbal intelligence and self-regulatory competencies: Joint predictors of boys' aggression. *Journal of Research in Personality, 41,* 374–388.

Back, M. D., Schmukle, S. C., & Egloff, B. (2008). How extraverted is honey. bunny77@hotmail.de? *Journal of Research in Personality, 42,* 1116–1122.

Bandura, A. (1986). *Social foundations of thought and action: A social cognitive theory.* Englewood Cliffs, NJ: Prentice-Hall.

Bandura, A. (1997). *Self-efficacy: The exercise of control.* New York: Freeman.

Bandura, A. (1999). Social cognitive theory of personality. In L. A. Pervin & O. P. John (Eds.), *Handbook of personality: Theory and research* (2nd ed., pp. 154–196). New York: Guilford Press.

Bandura, A. (2006). Toward of psychology of human agency. *Perspectives on Psychological Science, 1,* 164–180.

Baumeister, R. F., Campbell, J. D., Krueger, J. I., & Vohs, K. D. (2003). Does high self-esteem cause better performance, interpersonal success, happiness, or healthy lifestyles? *Psychological Science in the Public Interest, 4,* 1–44.

Beer, J. S. (2002). Implicit self-theories of shyness. *Journal of Personality and Social Psychology, 83,* 1009–1024.

Borges, N. J., Manuel, R. S., Elam, C. L., & Jones, B. J. (2010). Differences in motives between Millennial and Generation X medical students. *Medical Education, 44,* 570–576.

Bouchard, T. J. Jr., & Loehlin, J. C. (2001). Genes, evolution, and personality. *Behavior Genetics, 31,* 243–273.

Buffardi, L. E., & Campbell, W. K. (2008). Narcissism and social networking web sites. *Personality and Social Psychology Bulletin, 34,* 1303–1314.

Buss, D. M. (2009). How can evolutionary psychology successfully explain personality and individual differences? *Perspectives on Psychological Science, 4,* 359–366.

Butcher, J. N. (2010). Personality assessment from the nineteenth to the early twenty-first century: Past achievements and contemporary challenges. *Annual Review of Clinical Psychology, 6,* 1–20.

Butcher, J. N., Graham, J. R., Ben-Porath, Y. S., Tellegen, A., Dahlstrom, W. G., & Kaemmer, B. (2001). *Minnesota Multiphasic Personality Inventory-2 (MMPI-2): Manual for administration and scoring* (2nd ed.). Minneapolis: University of Minnesota Press.

Canli, T., Sivers, H., Whitfield, S. L., Gotlib, I. H., & Gabrieli, J. D. E. (2002b). Amygdala response to happy faces as a function of extraversion. *Science, 296,* 2191.

Cantor, N., & Kihlstrom, J. R. (1987). *Personality and social intelligence.* Englewood Cliffs, NJ: Prentice Hall.

Cattell, R. B. (1979). *Personality and learning theory.* New York: Springer.

Chan, M. Y. T., Cross-Mellor, S. K., Kavaliers, M., & Ossenkopp, K.-P. (2009). Lipopolysaccharide (LPS) blocks the acquisition of LiCl-induced gaping in a rodent model of anticipatory nausea. *Neuroscience Letters, 450,* 301–305.

Costa, P. T. Jr., & McCrae, R. R. (1985). *The NEO Personality Inventory manual.* Odessa, FL: Psychological Assessment Resources.

Cross, S. E., Hardin, E. E., & Gercek-Swing, B. (2011). The what, how, why, and where of self-construal. *Personality and Social Psychology Review, 15,* 142–179.

Dhawan, N., Roseman, I. J., Naidu, R. K., Thapa, K., & Rettek, S. I. (1995). Self-concepts across two cultures: India and the United States. *Journal of Cross-Cultural Psychology, 26,* 606–621.

Donnellan, M. B., Trzesniewski, K. H., Robins, R. W., Moffitt, T. E., & Caspi, A. (2005). Low self-esteem is realted to aggression, antisocial behavior, and delinquency. *Psychological Science, 16,* 328–335.

Donnellan, M. B., Trzesniewski, K. H., Conger, K. J., & Conger, R. D. (2007). A three-wave longitudinal study of self-evaluations during young adulthood. *Journal of Research in Personality, 41,* 453–472.

DuBois, P. H. (1970). *A history of psychological testing.* Boston: Allyn & Bacon.

Dudycha, G. J. (1936). An objective study of punctuality in relation to personality and achievement. *Archives of Psychology, 204,* 1–53.

Elms, A. C. (1988). Freud as Leonardo: Why the first psychobiography went wrong. *Journal of Personality, 56,* 19–40.

Exner, J. E. Jr. (1974). *The Rorschach: A comprehensive system.* New York: Wiley.

Exner, J. E. Jr. (2003). *The Rorschach: A comprehensive system* (4th ed.). New York: Wiley.

Exner, J. E. Jr., & Weiner, I. B. (1994). *The Rorschach: A comprehensive system: Vol. 3. Assessment of children and adolescents* (2nd ed.). New York: Wiley.

Eysenck, H. J. (1973). *The inequality of man.* London: Temple Smith.

Eysenck, H. J. (1990). Biological dimensions of personality. In L. A. Pervin (Ed.), *Handbook of personality theory and research* (pp. 244–276). New York: Guilford Press.

Forbey, J. D., Lee, T. T. C., & Handel, R. W. (2010). Correlates of the MMPI-2 in a college setting. *Psychological Assessment, 22,* 737–744.

Frager, R., & Fadiman, J. (1998). *Personality and personal growth.* New York: Longman.

Freud, S. (1957). Leonardo da Vinci and a memory of his childhood. In J. Strachey (Ed. and Trans.), *The standard edition of the complete psychological works of Sigmund Freud* (Vol. 11, pp. 59–137). London: Hogarth Press. (Original work published 1910)

Friesen, C. A., & Kammrath, L. K. (2011). What it pays to know about a close other: The value of if-then personality knowledge in close relationships. *Psychological Science, 22,* 567–571.

Gale, C. R., Batty, G. D., & Deary, I. J. (2008). Locus of control at age 10 years and health outcomes and behaviors at age 30 years: The 1970 British Cohort Study. *Psychosomatic Medicine, 70,* 397–403.

Garb, H. N., Wood, J. M., Lilienfeld, S. O., & Nezworski, M. T. (2005). Roots of the Rorschach controversy. *Clinical Psychology Review, 25,* 97–118.

Greenberg, J. (2008). Understanding the vital human quest for self-esteem. *Perspectives on Psychological Science, 3,* 48–55.

Greenberg, J., Kosloff, S., Solomon, S., Cohen, F., & Landau, M. (2010). Toward understanding the fame game: The effect of mortality salience on the appeal of fame. *Self and Identity, 9,* 1–18.

Hartshorne, H., & May, M. A. (1928). *Studies in the nature of character: Vol. 1. Studies in deceit.* New York: Macmillan.

Hathaway, S. R., & McKinley, J. C. (1940). A multiphasic personality schedule (Minnesota): I. Construction of the schedule. *Journal of Psychology, 10,* 249–254.

Hathaway, S. R., & McKinley, J. C. (1943). *Minnesota Multiphasic Inventory manual.* New York: Psychological Corporation.

Hilsenroth, M. J., Charnas, J. W., Zodan, J., & Streiner, D. L. (2007). Criterion-based training for Rorschach scoring. *Training and Education in Professional Psychology, 1,* 125–134.

Horney, K. (1937). *The neurotic personality of our time.* New York: Norton.

Horney, K. (1939). *New ways in psychoanalysis.* New York: Norton.

Horney, K. (1945). *Our inner conflicts: A constructive theory of neurosis.* New York: Norton.

Horney, K. (1950). *Neurosis and human growth.* New York: Norton.

James, W. (1892). *Psychology.* New York: Holt.

Jones, E. (1953). *The life and works of Sigmund Freud.* New York: Basic Books.

Jung, C. G. (1959). The concept of the collective unconscious. In *The archetypes and the collective unconscious, collected works* (Vol. 9, Part 1, pp. 54–74.). Princeton, NJ: Princeton University Press. (Original work published 1936)

Jung, C. G. (1973). *Memories, dreams, reflections* (rev. ed., A. Jaffe, Ed.). New York: Pantheon Books.

Kandler, C., Bleidorn, W., Riemann, R., Spinath, F. M., Thiel, W., & Angleitner, A. (2010). Sources of cumulative continuity in personality: A longitudinal multiple-rater twin study. *Journal of Personality and Social Psychology, 98,* 995–1008.

Kihlstrom, J. F., & Cantor, N. (2000). Social intelligence. In R. J. Sternberg (Ed.), *Handbook of intelligence* (pp. 359–369). New York: Cambridge University Press.

Kitayama, S., Markus, H. R., & Lieberman, C. (1995). The collective construction of self-esteem: Implications for culture, self, and emotion. In J. A. Russell, J. Fernandez-Dols, T. Manstead, & J. Wellenkamp (Eds.), *Everyday conceptions of emotion* (pp. 523–550). Dordrecht: Kluwer.

Krämer, N. C., & Winter, S. (2008). Impression management 2.0: The relationship of self-esteem, extraversion, self- efficacy, and self-presentation within social networking sites. *Journal of Media Psychology, 20*, 106–116.

Krueger, J., & Stanke, D. (2001). The role of self-referent and other-referent knowledge in perceptions of group characteristics. *Personality & Social Psychology Bulletin, 27*, 878–888.

Kuhn, M. H., & McPartland, T. S. (1954). An empirical investigation of self-attitudes. *American Sociological Review, 19*, 68–76.

Lilienfeld, S. O., Wood, J. M., & Garb, H. N. (2001). The scientific status of projective techniques. *Psychological Science in the Public Interest, 1*, 27–66.Ma, V., & Schoeneman, T. J. (1997). Individualism versus collectivism: A comparison of Kenyan and American self-concepts. *Basic and Applied Social Psychology, 19*, 261–273.

Markus, H. R., & Kitayama, S. (1991). Culture and the self: Implications for cognition, emotion, and motivation. *Psychological Review, 98*, 224–253.

Markus, H. R., Mullally, P. R., & Kitayama, S. (1997). Selfways: Diversity in modes of cultural participation. In U. Neisser & D. A. Jopling (Eds.), *The conceptual self in context* (pp. 13–61). Cambridge, UK: Cambridge University Press.

McAdams, D. P. (1988). Biography, narrative, and lives: An introduction. *Journal of Personality, 56*, 1–18.

McAdams, D. P., Bauer, J. J., Sakaeda, A. R., Anyidoho, N. A., Machado, M. A., Magrino-Failla, K., White, K. W., & Pals, J. L. (2006). Continuity and change in the life story: A longitudinal study of autobiographical memories in emerging adulthood. *Journal of Personality, 74*, 1371–1400.

McAdams, D. P., & Olson, B. D. (2010). Personality development: Continuity and change over the life course. *Annual Review of Psychology, 61*, 517–542.

McCrae, R. R., & Costa, P. T., Jr. (2008). The five-factor theory of personality. In O. P. John, R. W. Robins, & L. A. Pervin (Eds.), *The handbook of personality: Theory and research* (3rd ed., 159–181). New York: Guilford Press.

McClelland, D. C. (1961). *The achieving society.* Princeton, NJ: Van Nostrand.

McCrae, R. R., Costa, P. T. Jr., & Martin, T. A. (2005). The NEO-PI-3: A more readable revised NEO Personality Inventory. *Journal of Personality Assessment, 84*, 261–270.

McCrae, R. R., Costa, P. T. Jr., Martin, T. A., Oryol, V. E., Rukavishnikov, A. A., Senin, I. G., Hřebíčková, M., & Urbánek, T. (2004). Consensual validation of personality traits across cultures. *Journal of Research in Personality, 38*, 179–201.

McCrae, R. R., Kurtz, J. E., Yamagata, S., & Terracciano, A. (2011). Internal consistency, retest reliability, and their implications for personality scale validity. *Personality and Social Psychology Review, 15*, 28–50.

McCrae, R. R., Scally, M., Terracciano, A., Abecasis, G. R., & Costa, P. T., Jr. (2010). An alternative to the search for single polymorphisms: Toward molecular personality scales for the five-factor model. *Journal of Personality and Social Psychology, 99*, 1014–1024.

McCrae, S. M., & Hirt, E. R. (2001). The role of ability judgments in self-handicapping. *Personality & Social Psychology Bulletin, 27*, 1378–1389.

McCrae, S. M., Hirt, E. R., & Milner, B. J. (2008). She works hard for the money: Valuing effort underlies gender differences in behavioral self-handicapping. *Journal of Experimental Social Psychology, 44*, 292–311.

McGovern, K., & Baars, B. J. (2007). Cognitive theories of consciousness. In P. D. Zelazo, M. Moscovitch, & E. Thompson (Eds.), *The Cambridge handbook of consciousness* (pp. 177–205). New York: Cambridge University Press.

Michalski, R. L., & Shackelford, T. K. (2010). Evolutionary personality psychology: Reconciling human nature and individual differences. *Personality and Individual Differences, 48*, 509–516.

Mischel, W. (1968). *Personality and assessment.* New York: Wiley.

Mischel, W. (2004). Toward an integrative science of the person. *Annual Review of Psychology, 55*, 1–22.

Mischel, W., & Shoda, Y. (1995). A cognitive-affective system theory of personality: Reconceptualizing situations, dispositions, dynamics, and invariance in personality structure. *Psychological Review, 102*, 246–268.

Mischel, W., & Shoda, Y. (1999). Integrating dispositions and processing dynamics within a unified theory of personality: The cognitive-affective personality system. In L. A. Pervin & O. P. John (Eds.), *Handbook of personality: Theory and research* (2nd ed., pp. 197–218). New York: Guilford Press.

Munafò, M. R., & Flint, J. (2011). Dissecting the genetic architecture of human personality. *Trends in Cognitive Sciences, 15*, 395–400.

Musewicz, J., Marczyk, G., Knauss, L., & York, D. (2009). Current assessment practice, personality measurement, and Rorschach usage by psychologists. *Journal of Personality Assessment, 91*, 453–461.

Nettle, D. (2006). The evolution of personality variation in humans and other animals. *American Psycholgist, 61*, 622–631.

Newcomb, T. M. (1929). *The consistency of certain extrovert-introvert behavior traits in 50 problem boys* (Contributions to Education, No. 382). New York: Columbia University Press.

Neiss, M. B., Sedikides, C., & Stevenson, J. (2006). Genetic influences on level and stability of self-esteem. *Self and Identity, 5*, 247–266.

Norman, W. T. (1963). Toward an adequate taxonomy of personality attributes: Replicated factor structure in peer nomination personality ratings. *Journal of Abnormal and Social Psychology, 66*, 574–583.

Norman, W. T. (1967). *2,800 personality trait descriptors: Normative operating characteristics for a university population* (Research Rep. No. 083101-T). Ann Arbor: University of Michigan Press.

Orth, U., Robins, R. W., & Roberts, B. W. (2008). Low self-esteem prospectively predicts depression in adolescence and young adulthood. *Journal of Personality and Social Psychology, 95*, 695–708.

Ozer, D. J., & Reise, S. P. (1994). Personality assessment. *Annual Review of Psychology, 45*, 357–388.

Penke, L., Denissen, J. J. A., & Miller, G. F. (2007). The evolutionary genetics of personality. *European Journal of Personality, 21*, 549–587.

Pennebaker, J. W. (1997). Writing about emotional experiences as a therapeutic process. *Psychological Science, 8*, 162–166.

Petrie, K. J., Fontanilla, I., Thomas, M. G., Booth, R. J., & Pennebaker, J. W. (2004). Effect of written emotional expression on immune function in patients with human immunodeficiency virus infection: A randomized trial. *Psychosomatic Medicine, 66*, 272–275.

Plaks, J., Levy, S. R., & Dweck, C. (2009). Lay theories of personality: Cornerstones of meaning in social cognition. *Social and Personality Psychology Compass, 3*, 1069–1081.

Pyszczynski, T., Greenberg, J., Solomon, S., Arndt, J., & Schimel, J. (2004). Why do people need self-esteem? A theoretical and empirical review. *Psychological Bulletin, 130*, 435–468.

Rogers, C. R. (1947). Some observations on the organization of personality. *American Psychologist, 2*, 358–368.

Rogers, C. R. (1951). *Client-centered therapy: Its current practice, implications and theory.* Boston: Houghton Mifflin.

Rogers, C. R. (1977). *On personal power: Inner strength and its revolutionary impact.* New York: Delacorte.

Rorschach, H. (1942). *Psychodiagnostics: A diagnostic test based on perception.* New York: Grune & Stratton.

Rotter, J. B. (1966). Generalized expectancies for internal versus external locus of control of reinforcement. *Psychological Monographs, 80* (Whole No. 609).

Rouse, S. V., Greene, R. L., Butcher, J. N., Nichols, D. S., & Williams, C. L. (2008). What do the MMPI-2 Restructured Clinical Scales reliably measure? Answers from multiple research settings. *Journal of Personality Assessment, 90*, 435–442.

Sandstrom, M. J., & Cramer, P. (2003). Girls' use of defense mechanisms following peer rejection. *Journal of Personality, 71,* 605–627.

Schmitt, D. P., Allik, J., McCrae, R. R., & Benet-Martinez, V. (2007). The geographic distribution of Big Five personality traits: Patterns and profiles of human self-description across 56 nations. *Journal of Cross-Cultural Psychology, 38,* 173–212.

Sedikides, C., & Gregg, A. P. (2008). Self-enhancement: Food for thought. *Perspectives on Psychological Science, 3,* 102–116.

Swann, W. B., Chang-Schneider, C., & McClarty, K. L. (2007). Do people's self-views matter? Self-concept and self-esteem in everyday life. *American Psychologist, 62,* 84–94.

Tellegen, A. & Ben-Porath, Y. S. (2008). *MMPI-2-RF Technical Manual.* Minneapolis: University of Minnesota Press.

Tong, S. T., Van Der Heide, B., Langwell, L., & Walther, J. B. (2008). Too much of a good thing? The relationship between number of friends and interpersonal impressions on Facebook. *Journal of Computer-Mediated Communication, 13,* 531–549.

Triandis, H. C. (1994). *Culture and social behavior.* New York: McGraw-Hill.

Triandis, H. C. (1995). *Individualism and collectivism.* Boulder, CO: Westview.

Trzesniewski, K. H., Donnellan, M. B., Moffitt, T. E., Robins, R. W., Poulton, R., & Caspi, A. (2006). Low self-esteem during adolescence predicts poor health, criminal behavior, and limited economic prospects during adulthood. *Developmental Psychology, 42,* 381–390.

Tupes, E. G., & Christal, R. C. (1961). *Recurrent personality factors based on trait ratings* (Tech. Rep. No. ASD-TR-61-97). Lackland Air Force Base, TX: U.S. Air Force.

Vignoles, V. L., Regalia, C., Manzi, C., Golledge, J., & Scabini, E. (2006). Beyond self-esteem: Influence of multiple motives on identity construction. *Journal of Personality and Social Psychology, 90,* 308–333.

Vuong, M., Brown-Welty, S., & Tracz, S. (2010). The effects of self-efficacy on academic success of first-generation college sophomore students. *Journal of College Student Development, 51,* 50–64.

Yaeger, D. S., Trzesniewski, K. H., Tirri, K., Nokelainen, P., & Dweck, C. S. (2011). Adolescents' implicit theories predict desire for vengeance after peer conflict: Correlational and experimental evidence. *Developmental Psychology, 47,* 1090–1107.

Yamagata, S., Suzuki, A., Ando, J., Ono, Y., Kijima, N., Yoshimura, K., Osendorf, F., Angleitner, A., Riemann, R., Spinath, F. M., Livesley, W. J., & Jang, K. L. (2006). Is the genetic structure of human personality universal? A cross-cultural twin study from North America, Europe, and Asia. *Journal of Personality and Social Psychology, 90,* 987–998.

Zajacova, A., Lynch, M. S., & Espenshade, J. T. (2005). Self-efficacy, stress, and academic success in college. *Research in Higher Education, 46,* 677–706.

Emotion, Stress, and Health

From Chapter 12 of *Psychology and Life*, 20th Edition. Richard J. Gerrig. Copyright © 2013 by Pearson Education, Inc. All rights reserved.

Emotion, Stress, and Health

© FogStock/Alamy

uppose you walk into class and a friend asks, "How are you feeling?" How would you answer that question? There are at least three different types of information you might provide. First, you might reveal the mood you are in—the *emotions* you are feeling. Are you happy because you know you can finish reading this chapter in time to go to a party? Are you angry because your boss just yelled at you over the telephone? Second, you might say something more general about the amount of *stress* you are experiencing. Do you feel as if you can cope with all the tasks you have to get done? Or are you feeling a bit overwhelmed? Third, you might report on your psychological or physical *health*. Do you feel some illness coming on? Or do you feel an overall sense of wellness?

This chapter will explore interactions among these three ways in which you might answer the question "How are you feeling?"—in relation to your emotions, stress, and health. *Emotions* are the touchstones of human experience. They give richness to your interactions with people and nature, and significance to your memories. This chapter will discuss the experience and functions of emotions. But what happens if the emotional demands on your biological and psychological functioning are too great? You may become overwhelmed and unable to deal with the stressors of your life. This chapter will also examine how *stress* affects you and how you can combat it. Finally, the focus will broaden to consider psychology's contributions to the study of health and illness. *Health psychologists* investigate the ways in which environmental, social, and psychological processes contribute to the development of disease. Health psychologists also use psychological processes and principles to help treat and prevent illness while also developing strategies to enhance personal wellness.

We begin now by looking at the content and meaning of emotions.

EMOTIONS

Just imagine what your life would be like if you could think and act but not feel. Would you be willing to give up the capacity to experience fear if you would also lose the passion of a lover's kiss? Would you give up sadness at the expense of joy? Surely these would be bad bargains, promptly regretted. We will soon see that emotions serve a number of important functions. Let's begin, however, by offering a definition of emotion and by describing the roots of your emotional experiences.

Although you might be tempted to think of emotion as only a feeling—"I feel happy" or "I feel angry"—we need a more inclusive definition of this important concept that involves both the body and the mind. Contemporary psychologists define **emotion** as a complex pattern of bodily and mental changes that includes physiological arousal, feelings, cognitive processes, visible expressions (including face and posture), and specific behavioral reactions made in response to a situation perceived as personally significant. To see why

....

◉ Watch the Video *Thinking Like a Psychologist: Affective Forecasting* on MyPsychLab

emotion A complex pattern of changes, including physiological arousal, feelings, cognitive processes, and behavioral reactions, made in response to a situation perceived to be personally significant.

all of these components are necessary, you should imagine a situation in which you would feel a surge of happiness. Your physiological arousal might include a gently beating heart. Your feeling would be positive. The associated cognitive processes include interpretations, memories, and expectations that allow you to label the situation as happy. Your overt behavioral reactions might be expressive (smiling) and/or action-oriented (embracing a loved one).

Before I provide an account that unites arousal, feelings, thoughts, and actions, you need to learn the distinction between emotions and moods. As you've just seen, emotions are specific responses to specific events—in that sense, emotions are typically relatively short lived and relatively intense. By contrast, *moods* are often less intense and may last several days. There's often a weaker connection between moods and triggering events. You might be in a good or bad mood without knowing exactly why. Keep this distinction between emotions and moods in mind as you meet the theories that explain them.

Basic Emotions and Culture

Suppose you could gather together in one room representatives from a great diversity of human cultures. What would be common in their experiences of emotion? For an initial answer, you might look to Charles Darwin's book *The Expression of Emotions in Man and Animals* (1872/1965). Darwin believed that emotions evolve alongside other important aspects of human and nonhuman structures and functions. He was interested in the *adaptive* functions of emotions, which he thought of not as vague, unpredictable, personal states but as highly specific, coordinated modes of operation of the human brain. Darwin viewed emotions as inherited, specialized mental states designed to deal with a certain class of *recurring situations* in the world (Hess & Thibault, 2009). Suppose, for example, you find yourself in a situation in which another individual is making it impossible for you to achieve your goals. Our evolutionary ancestors might have undertaken combat to resolve the situation. Now, a facial expression of anger communicates your mental state and signals your readiness to take action. Communication through emotions may avert direct conflict.

Over the history of our species, humans have been attacked by predators, fallen in love, given birth to children, fought each other, confronted their mates' sexual infidelity, and witnessed the death of loved ones—innumerable times. We might expect, therefore, that certain types of emotional responses would emerge in all members of the human species. Researchers have tested this claim of the *universality of emotions* by looking at the emotional responses of newborn children as well as the consistency of facial expressions across cultures.

Are Some Emotional Responses Innate? If the evolutionary perspective is correct, we would expect to find much the same patterns of emotional responses in children all over the world. **Silvan Tomkins** (1911–1991) was one of the first psychologists to emphasize the pervasive role of immediate, unlearned affective (emotional) reactions. Tomkins (1962, 1981) pointed out that, without prior learning, infants respond to loud sounds with fear or with difficulties in breathing. They seem "prewired" to respond to certain stimuli with an emotional response general enough to fit a wide range of circumstances. ◉

Charles Darwin was one of the first to use photographs in the study of emotion. These plates are from *The Expression of Emotions in Man and Animals* (1872/1965). Why did Darwin believe that emotions were the product of evolution?

Early accounts of emotional development focused on their facial expressions and suggested that infants produce facial expressions to convey specific emotions (Izard, 1994). However, contemporary research suggests that infants start life with facial expressions that are just broadly positive and negative (Camras & Shutter, 2010). For example, 11-month-old infants from the United States, Japan, and China produce the same facial expression when they are experiencing fear and anger (Camras et al., 2007). Apparently, children's ability to display distinct facial expressions for negative emotions emerges after the first year of life. Note, however, that infants' emotional responses are not restricted to facial expressions; they can indicate emotions through other types of motor activity. For example, 11-month-olds are more likely to increase their breathing rate as an indication of fear versus anger (Camras et al., 2007). That behavioral response was similar for infants from the United States, Japan, and China. These results suggest that infants may begin to differentiate emotions through other behavioral means, before they mark the emotions clearly with facial expressions.

Infants may nonetheless have an innate ability to interpret the facial expressions of others. In one experiment, 5-month-old infants habituated—they showed decreasing interest—to repeated presentations of an adult face showing smiles of different intensities (Bornstein & Arterberry, 2003). The infants were subsequently shown two new photographs: One photograph showed the same adult with a novel smile (that is, a smile with a different intensity); the second photograph showed the same adult with a fearful expression. The infants consistently spent more time looking at the fearful expression—suggesting both that they experienced the fearful expression as something new and also that they sorted the different smiles into the same category. Other research has demonstrated that patterns of brain activity for 7-month-old infants are different in response to angry and fearful expressions (Kobiella et al., 2008). Thus, infants have distinctive responses to facial expressions that, as we just saw for 11-month-olds, they are not yet able to produce.

Are Facial Expressions Universal? We have seen that infants are able to interpret standard emotional expressions. If that is so, we might also expect to find adult members of even vastly different cultures showing reasonable agreement in the way they believe emotion is communicated by facial expressions.

According to **Paul Ekman,** the leading researcher on the nature of facial expressions, all people share an overlap in "facial language" (Ekman, 1984, 1994). Ekman and his associates have demonstrated what Darwin first proposed—that a set of emotional expressions is universal to the human species, presumably because they are innate components of our evolutionary heritage. Before you read on, take a look at **Figure 1** to see how well you can identify these seven universally recognized expressions of emotion (Ekman & Friesen, 1986).

There is considerable evidence that these seven expressions are recognized and produced worldwide in response to the emotions of happiness, surprise, anger, disgust, fear, sadness, and contempt. Cross-cultural researchers have asked people from a variety of cultures to identify the emotions associated with expressions in standardized photographs. Individuals are generally able to identify the expressions associated with the seven emotions.

In one study, members of a preliterate culture in New Guinea (the Fore culture), who had had almost no exposure to Westerners or to Western culture prior to this experiment, accurately identified the emotions expressed in the White faces shown in Figure 1. They did so by referring to situations in which they had experienced the same emotion.

Featured Study

Why do researchers believe that some emotional responses are innate?

 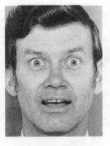 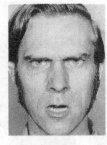 

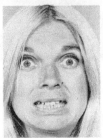 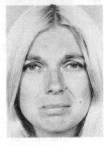 

FIGURE 1 Judgments of Emotional Expressions

Match these seven emotion terms with the faces shown at left: fear, disgust, happiness, surprise, contempt, anger, and sadness. The answers are given at the end of the chapter (see "Recapping Main Points").

For example, photo 5 (fear) suggested being chased by a wild boar when you didn't have your spear, and photo 6 (sadness) suggested your child had died. Their only confusion came in distinguishing surprise, photo 2, from fear, perhaps because these people are most fearful when taken by surprise.

Next, researchers asked other members of the culture (who had not participated in the first study) to model the expressions that they used to communicate six of the emotions (excluding contempt). When U.S. college students viewed videotapes of the facial expressions of the Fore people, they were able to identify their emotions accurately—with one exception. Not surprisingly, the Americans had difficulty distinguishing between the Fore poses of fear and surprise, the same emotions that the Fore had confused in the Western poses (Ekman & Friesen, 1971).

Other research has compared judgments of facial expressions across individuals in Hungary, Japan, Poland, Sumatra, the United States, and Vietnam—high agreement was found across these diverse populations (Biehl et al., 1997). Still, Japanese adults were worse at identifying anger than were U.S., Hungarian, Polish, and Vietnamese adults. Vietnamese adults were worse at identifying disgust than the participants from all the other countries.

These cross-cultural differences support the hypothesis that cultures have different *dialects* for facial expressions (Dailey et al., 2010; Elfenbein et al., 2007). For languages, dialects are regional or social variation in, for example, pronunciation and word use. Within the domain of emotions, proponents of a dialect theory argue for similar cultural variation in the production of facial expressions. In fact, there are consistent cross-cultural differences in the specific movements of facial muscles people perform to create different facial expressions. Furthermore, people find it easier to recognize facial expressions when they are produced by members of their own culture (Dailey et al., 2010; Elfenbein et al., 2007). Culture also has an impact on the way in which people gather information when

they view a face: People from Eastern cultures are more likely to focus attention on the eyes whereas people from Western cultures spread their attention across the whole face (Jack et al., 2009). These habitual differences in examining faces may lead people from different cultures to have different expectations for how faces will look when they are conveying particular emotional expressions (Jack et al., 2012).

How Does Culture Constrain Emotional Expression?
We've just seen that some aspects of emotional expression may remain constant across cultures. Even so, different cultures have different standards for how emotion should be managed. Some forms of emotional response, even facial expressions, are unique to each culture. Cultures establish social rules for when people may show certain emotions and for the social appropriateness of certain types of emotional displays by given types of people in particular settings (Mesquita & Leu, 2007). Let's look at three examples of cultures that express emotions in manners different from the Western norm.

The Wolof people of Senegal live in a society where status and power differences among people are rigidly defined. High-caste members of this culture are expected to show great restraint in their expressions of emotionality; low-caste individuals are expected to be more volatile, particularly a caste called the *griots*. The griots, in fact, are often called upon to express the "undignified" emotions of the nobility:

> *One afternoon, a group of women (some five nobles and two griots) were gathered near a well on the edge of town when another woman strode over to the well and threw herself down it. All the women were shocked at the apparent suicide attempt, but the noblewomen were shocked in silence. Only the griot women screamed, on behalf of all.* (Irvine, 1990, p. 146)

Can you imagine how you would respond in this situation? It might be easier to put yourself in the place of the griots rather than in the place of the noblewomen: How could you help but

In what ways do cultures constrain emotional expressions in situations like funerals?

scream? The answer, of course, is that the noblewomen have acquired cultural norms for emotional expression that require them not to show any overt response.

As a second example, consider the practice of Mĕbengokre women in Central Brazil (Lea, 2004). When the women experience loss they engage in ceremonial wailing. The wailing uses a particular high-pitched tone but also special words that are not used in other circumstances. As you might imagine, the women wail in response to family deaths. However, wailing occurs in other circumstances as well: "The theme uniting all situations that give rise to wailing is the feeling of separation and loss that is canonically associated with death" (p. 114). So, for example, Mĕbengokre women wail when a close relative is leaving on an extended trip.

For a third example, let's turn to a cross-cultural difference in norms for emotional displays related to pain. Psychological context has a major impact on the extent to which people experience pain. Similarly, the cultural context has an impact on the extent to which it is considered appropriate for people to perform behaviors that reveal they are experiencing pain. For example, one study demonstrated a contrast between what people in the United States and Japan consider proper behavioral displays for pain (Hobara, 2005). Participants in both cultures completed the Appropriate Pain Behavior Questionnaire (APBQ) that includes such items as "Women should be able to tolerate pain in most circumstances" and "It is acceptable for men to cry when in pain." In general, Japanese participants provided lower scores on the APBQ: They indicated less approval for open emotional expressions of pain. In addition, both cultural groups suggested more approval for women's emotional displays than men's displays. The researcher attributed the cultural difference to the "traditional stoicism . . . of many Asian cultures" (Hobara, 2005, p. 392).

When you think about the types of emotional patterns that may have evolved over the course of human experience, always bear in mind that culture may have the last word. Western notions of what is necessary or inevitable in emotional expression are as bound to U.S. culture as those of any other societies. Can you see how different standards for emotional expression could cause misunderstandings between people of different cultural origins?

Let's turn now to theories that explore the link between different aspects of emotions.

Theories of Emotion

Theories of emotion generally attempt to explain the relationship between physiological and psychological aspects of the experience of emotion. This section begins by discussing the responses your body gives in emotionally relevant situations. It then reviews theories that explore the way these physiological responses contribute to your psychological experience of emotion.

Physiology of Emotion   What happens when you experience a strong emotion? Your heart races, your respiration goes up, your mouth dries, your muscles tense, and maybe you even shake. In addition to these noticeable changes, many others occur beneath the surface. All these responses are designed to mobilize your body for action to deal with the source of the emotion. Let's look at their origins.

The *autonomic nervous system* (ANS) prepares the body for emotional responses through the action of both its sympathetic and parasympathetic divisions. The balance between the divisions depends on the quality and intensity of the arousing stimulation. With mild, *unpleasant* stimulation, the *sympathetic* division is more active; with mild, *pleasant* stimulation, the *parasympathetic* division is more active. With more intense stimulation of either kind, both divisions are increasingly involved. Physiologically, strong emotions such as fear or anger activate the body's *emergency reaction system,* which swiftly and silently prepares the body for potential danger. The sympathetic nervous system takes charge by directing the release of hormones (epinephrine and norepinephrine) from the adrenal glands, which in turn leads the internal organs to release blood sugar, raise blood pressure, and increase sweating and salivation. To calm you after the emergency has passed, the parasympathetic nervous system inhibits the release of the activating hormones. You may remain aroused for a while after an experience of strong emotional activation because some of the hormones continue to circulate in your bloodstream.

Particular emotional experiences give rise to distinct patterns of activity in the autonomic nervous system (Friedman, 2010). Consider a cross-cultural study in which a team of researchers measured autonomic responses such as heart rate and skin temperature while men and women from the United States and Minangkabau men from West Sumatra generated

How does the brain respond differently to experiences of puppies and spiders?

emotions and emotional expressions. Members of the Minang-kabau culture are socialized not to display negative emotions. Would they, even so, show the same underlying autonomic patterns for negative emotions as did the U.S. participants? The data revealed a high level of similarity across the two cultures, leading the researchers to suggest that patterns of autonomic activity are "an important part of our common evolved biological heritage" (Levenson et al., 1992, p. 986).

Let's move now from the autonomic nervous system to the central nervous system. Integration of both the hormonal and the neural aspects of arousal is controlled by the *hypothalamus* and the *limbic system,* control systems for emotions and for patterns of attack, defense, and flight. Neuroanatomy research has particularly focused on the *amygdala* as a part of the limbic system that acts as a gateway for emotion and as a filter for memory. The amygdala does this by attaching significance to the information it receives from the senses. It plays an especially strong role in attaching meaning to negative experiences—the amygdala serves as a "threat detector" to make us aware of dangers in our environment (Kim et al., 2011).

The *cortex* is involved in emotional experiences through its internal neural networks and its connections with other parts of the body. The cortex provides the associations, memories, and meanings that integrate psychological experience and biological responses. Research using brain-scanning techniques has begun to map particular responses for different emotions. For example, positive and negative emotions are not just opposite responses in the same portions of the cortex. Rather, opposite emotions lead to greatest activity in quite different parts of the brain. Consider a study in which participants underwent fMRI scans while viewing positive pictures (such as puppies, brownies, and sunsets) and negative pictures (angry people, spiders, and guns). The scans showed greater activity in the brain's left hemisphere for positive pictures and in the right hemisphere for negative pictures (Canli et al., 1998). In fact, researchers have suggested that there are two distinct systems in the brain that handle

approach-related and *withdrawal-related* emotional responses (Davidson et al., 2000; Maxwell & Davidson, 2007). Consider puppies and spiders. It is likely that most people would want to approach the puppies but withdraw from the spiders. Research suggests that different brain circuits—apportioned to the different hemispheres of the brain—underlie those responses.

We have seen so far that your body provides many responses to situations in which emotions are relevant. But how do you know which feeling goes with which physiological response? Let's now consider three theories that attempt an answer to this question.

James–Lange Theory of Body Reaction   You might think, at first, that everyone would agree that emotions precede responses: For example, you yell at someone (response) because you feel angry (emotion). However, over 100 years ago, William James argued, as Aristotle had much earlier, that the sequence was reversed—you feel *after* your body reacts. As James put it, "We feel sorry because we cry, angry because we strike, afraid because we tremble" (James, 1890/1950, p. 450). This view that emotion stems from *bodily feedback* became known as the **James–Lange theory of emotion** (Carl Lange was a Danish scientist who presented similar ideas the same year as James). According to this theory, perceiving a stimulus causes autonomic arousal and other bodily actions that lead to the experience of a specific emotion (see **Figure 2**). The James–Lange theory is considered a *peripheralist* theory because it assigns the most prominent role in the emotion chain to visceral reactions, the actions of the autonomic nervous system that are peripheral to the central nervous system.

....

James–Lange theory of emotion A peripheral-feedback theory of emotion stating that an eliciting stimulus triggers a behavioral response that sends different sensory and motor feedback to the brain and creates the feeling of a specific emotion.

271

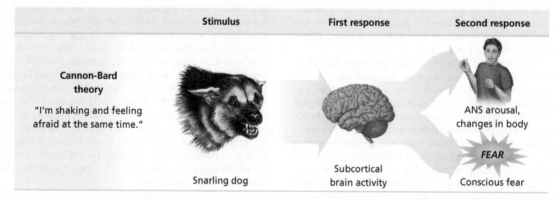

Stimulus   **First response**   **Second response**

James–Lange theory

"I'm afraid because I'm shaking."

Snarling dog

ANS arousal, changes in body

FEAR

Conscious fear

FIGURE 2 The James–Lange Theory of Emotion

In the James–Lange theory, events trigger both autonomic arousal and behavioral action, which are perceived and then result in a specific emotional experience.

Cannon–Bard Theory of Central Neural Processes Physiologist Walter Cannon (1927, 1929) rejected the peripheralist theory in favor of a *centralist* focus on the action of the central nervous system. Cannon (and other critics) raised a number of objections to the James–Lange theory (Leventhal, 1980). They noted, for example, that visceral activity is irrelevant for emotional experience—experimental animals continue to respond emotionally even after their viscera are separated surgically from the CNS. They also argued that ANS responses are typically too slow to be the source of split-second elicited emotions. According to Cannon, emotion requires that the brain intercede between the input stimulation and the output response.

Another physiologist, Philip Bard, also concluded that visceral reactions were not primary in the emotion sequence. Instead, an emotion-arousing stimulus has two simultaneous effects, causing both bodily arousal via the sympathetic nervous system and the subjective experience of emotion via the cortex. The views of these physiologists were combined in the **Cannon–Bard theory of emotion.** This theory states that an emotion stimulus produces two concurrent reactions, arousal and experience of emotion, that do not cause each other (see **Figure 3**). If something makes you angry, your heartbeat increases at the same time as you think "I'm ticked off!"—but neither your body nor your mind dictates the way the other responds.

The Cannon–Bard theory predicts independence between bodily and psychological responses. We will see next that contemporary theories of emotion reject the claim that these responses are necessarily independent.

Cognitive Appraisal Theories of Emotion Because arousal symptoms and internal states are similar for many different emotions, it is possible to confuse them at times when they are experienced in ambiguous or novel situations. **Stanley Schachter** (1922–1997) originated the **two-factor theory of emotion** to explain how people deal with such uncertainty. According to Schachter (1971a), the experience of emotion is the joint effect of the two factors of physiological arousal and cognitive appraisal. Both parts are necessary for an emotion to occur. In this view, all arousal is assumed to be general and undifferentiated, and arousal is the first step in the emotion sequence. You appraise your physiological arousal in an effort to discover what you are feeling, what emotional label best fits,

Cannon–Bard theory of emotion A theory stating that an emotional stimulus produces two co-occurring reactions—arousal and experience of emotion—that do not cause each other.

two-factor theory of emotion The theory that emotional experiences arise from autonomic arousal and cognitive appraisal.

Stimulus   **First response**   **Second response**

Cannon–Bard theory

"I'm shaking and feeling afraid at the same time."

Snarling dog

Subcortical brain activity

ANS arousal, changes in body

FEAR

Conscious fear

FIGURE 3 The Cannon–Bard Theory of Emotion

In the Cannon–Bard theory, events are first processed at various centers in the brain, which then direct the simultaneous reactions of arousal, behavioral action, and emotional experience.

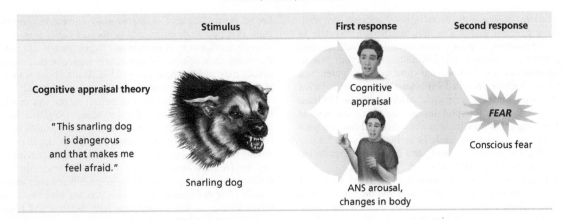

FIGURE 4 The Cognitive Appraisal Theory of Emotion

In the cognitive appraisal theory, both stimulus events and physiological arousal are cognitively appraised at the same time using situational cues and contextual factors. The emotional experience results from the appraisal of the arousal.

and what your reaction means in the particular setting in which it is being experienced.

Richard Lazarus (1922–2002) was another leading proponent of the importance of cognitive appraisal. Lazarus (1991, 1995; Lazarus & Lazarus, 1994) maintained that "emotional experience cannot be understood solely in terms of what happens in the person or in the brain, but grows out of ongoing transactions with the environment that are evaluated" (Lazarus, 1984a, p. 124). Lazarus also emphasized that appraisal often occurs without conscious thought. When you have past experiences that link emotions to situations—here comes that bully I've clashed with before!—you need not explicitly search the environment for an interpretation of your arousal. This position has become known as the **cognitive appraisal theory of emotion** (see **Figure 4**).

To test this theory, experimenters have sometimes created situations in which environmental cues were available to provide a label for an individual's arousal.

An attractive female researcher interviewed male participants who had just crossed one of two bridges in Vancouver, Canada (Dutton & Aron, 1974). One bridge was a safe, sturdy bridge; the other was a wobbly, precarious bridge. The researcher pretended to be interested in the effects of scenery on creativity and asked the men to write brief stories about an ambiguous picture that included a woman. She also invited them to call her if they wanted more information about the research. Those men who had just crossed the dangerous bridge wrote stories with more sexual imagery, and four times as many of those men called the female researcher than did those who had crossed the safe bridge. To show that arousal was the independent variable influencing the emotional misinterpretation, the research team also arranged for another group of men to be interviewed 10 minutes or more after crossing the dangerous bridge, enough time for their physical arousal symptoms to be reduced. These nonaroused men did not show the signs of sexual response that the aroused men did.

In this situation, we can see that the main source of arousal is the danger the men feel from the wobbly bridge. However, when the men themselves appraised the situation to assess the source of their arousal, they made a *misattribution*: They believed it was caused by the attractive woman. Based on this appraisal, the men made an emotional judgment ("I am interested in this woman"). This study supports the idea that people appraise environmental cues to interpret their physiological arousal.

However, some of the specific aspects of the cognitive appraisal theory have been challenged. For example, you learned earlier that arousal states—the activity of the autonomic nervous system—accompanying different emotions are not identical (Friedman, 2010). Therefore, interpretations of at least some emotional experiences may not require appraisal.

What emotions would you be likely to feel if people all around you were wildly cheering your favorite team?

cognitive appraisal theory of emotion A theory stating that the experience of emotion is the joint effect of physiological arousal and cognitive appraisal, which serves to determine how an ambiguous inner state of arousal will be labeled.

Furthermore, experiencing strong arousal without any obvious cause does not lead to a neutral, undifferentiated state, as the theory assumes. Stop for a moment and imagine that, right now, your heart suddenly starts beating quickly, your breathing becomes fast and shallow, your chest muscles tighten, and your palms become drenched with sweat. What interpretation would you put on these symptoms? Are you surprised to learn that people generally interpret *unexplained* physical arousal as *negative,* a sign that something is wrong? In addition, people's search for an explanation tends to be biased toward finding stimuli that will explain or justify this negative interpretation (Marshall & Zimbardo, 1979; Maslach, 1979).

Another critique of the cognitive appraisal theory of emotion comes from researcher **Robert Zajonc** (pronounced *Zy-Onts*). Zajonc demonstrated conditions under which people have preferences—emotional responses to stimuli—without knowing why (Zajonc, 2000, 2001). In an extensive series of experiments on the *mere exposure effect*, participants were presented with a variety of stimuli, such as foreign words, Chinese characters, sets of numbers, and strange faces. These stimuli were flashed so briefly that participants could not consciously recognize the items. Later on, participants were asked how much they liked particular stimuli, some of which were old (that is, those stimuli previously had been flashed below the threshold of consciousness) whereas some were new. The participants tended to give higher ratings to the old items. Because participants experienced these positive emotions without conscious awareness of their origins, the emotional response could not emerge from an appraisal process.

It is probably safest to conclude that cognitive appraisal is an important process of emotional experience but not the only one (Izard, 1993). Under some circumstances, you will, in fact, look to the environment (at least unconsciously) to try to interpret why you feel the way you do. Under other circumstances, however, your emotional experiences may be under the control of the innate links provided by evolution. The physiological response will not require any interpretation. These different routes to emotional experiences suggest that emotions may have a variety of impacts on your day-to-day experiences. We will now consider some of those consequences of moods and emotions.

The Impact of Mood and Emotions

Let's begin with the impact of moods. The moods you experience have a strong effect on how you process information (Clore & Huntsinger, 2007; Forgas, 2008). In particular, people in negative moods tend to process information in a more detailed and effortful fashion than their peers in positive moods. This difference in processing style has a number of consequences. Consider judgment and decision making. You would probably agree that you will often make different judgments and decisions depending on the amount of effort you expend. In that light, think about the consequences of people's moods on the ways they made judgments of guilt or innocence. In one study, participants watched short films that put them in happy, neutral, or sad moods (Forgas & East, 2008). Once the mood was established, participants watched four videotapes of people denying that they had stolen a movie ticket; some of the people were lying. After watching each videotape, the participants judged the person's guilt or innocence. Mood had a major impact on participants' ability to make correct judgments of guilt: Participants in sad moods performed better than chance whereas participants in neutral and happy moods did not. In discussing their results, the researchers suggested that negative moods may make people less gullible. Think about your own life: Are you more skeptical when you are in a sad mood?

Your mood will also have an impact on the way in which information gets committed to memory. Negative moods sharpen the focus of attention whereas positive moods tend to broaden that focus. For that reason, people who are in positive moods may find it harder to ignore irrelevant information. In fact, people have better implicit memory for irrelevant information when they perform tasks in positive (versus neutral) moods (Biss & Hasher, 2011). Can you see how this mood-driven change in focus could have both negative and positive consequences? When you are in a positive mood it's hard for you to concentrate on just critical information. If you need to keep your focus tight, you might want to keep yourself in a slightly negative mood. However, because positive moods produce a broader and more flexible processing style, people in positive moods produce more creative thinking and problem solving than people in neutral moods (Baas et al., 2008). Thus, if you need to be creative, you should try to maintain a positive mood!

Let's turn from long-lasting moods to more acute emotions. Suppose you view a crime in which the perpetrator wields

Why might you worry that a positive mood could make you more gullible?

a gun. You are likely to have negative emotional arousal! That negative emotional arousal will often cause you to fall prey to an effect known as *weapon focus* (Fawcett et al., 2012). Let's see what that means.

Students in a study watched a video of a crime unfolding (Pickel, 2009). In one version of the video, the perpetrator was holding a 9-mm handgun; in the other version, the perpetrator held a music CD in a plastic case. After watching the video, the students completed a questionnaire that tested their ability to recall the perpetrator's appearance. Participants' recall was much lower when the perpetrator was holding the handgun. In different versions of the video, the perpetrator was male or female. Participants performed worst when a female was holding the gun.

Why might the female perpetrator have increased weapon focus? To answer that question, we need to take a step back to consider the more general impact of emotional arousal. Any time you look at the world, some aspects of it are more prominent (because of perceptual properties) or more important to you (because of your goals in the moment). Let's call those types of stimuli *high priority*. Emotional arousal causes people to focus more mental resources on high-priority stimuli (Mather & Sutherland, 2011). That will generally make memory for those stimuli better and memory for other stimuli worse, explaining why the presence of a weapon impairs memory for other details. So, why does a female perpetrator increase weapon focus? A woman holding a gun may be a higher-priority stimulus, a more arousing stimulus, or both. In any case, when you have a strong emotional response to a particular situation, you should expect your perception of and memory for the situation to be quite different than when you have no strong arousal.

Still, it's important to acknowledge that you have some control over the impact your emotions will have on you and on others. You have the capacity for **emotion regulation**, which are processes through which people change the intensity and duration of the emotions they experience (Gyurak et al., 2011). Consider what it's like to be frightened while watching a horror movie. You may remind yourself, "This is only a movie! This is only a movie!" This strategy has two effects. First, you are distracting yourself from the events on screen that are making you anxious. Second, you are engaging in a reappraisal of the source of the arousal. Both distraction and reappraisal are successful strategies for emotion regulation (McCrae et al., 2010). Meanwhile, by making yourself seem less frightened, your successful emotion regulation will change how other people perceive your reaction to the movie.

To complete this exploration of emotions, let's turn to research that addresses individual differences in people's long-term feelings of happiness.

Subjective Well-Being

At the outset of the chapter, you addressed the question, "How are you feeling?" So far, the focus has been on the present moment: What mood or emotion are you experiencing *now*? However, the question can also apply over time, to ask "How are you feeling about your life in general?" This question addresses **subjective well-being**—individuals' overall evaluation of life satisfaction and happiness. In recent years, psychologists have paid considerable research attention to the factors that contribute to people's judgments about their own subjective well-being (Kesebir & Diener, 2008; Tay & Diener, 2011). This research focus reflects, in part, the emergence of **positive psychology** as an important movement within the profession of psychology. The goal of positive psychology is to provide people with the knowledge and skills that allow them to experience fulfilling lives. Positive psychology asks this question: "Can psychologists take what they have learned about the science and practice of treating mental illness and use it to create a practice of making people lastingly happier?" (Seligman et al., 2005, p. 410). Much of the research on subjective well-being focuses on trying to determine why some people are happier than others. As is true in most psychological domains, researchers have tried to assess the impact of genetics and environment.

To understand the impact of genetics, researchers have conducted studies using the classic methodology of behavior genetics: They have examined the extent to which monozygotic (MZ) twins and dizygotic (DZ) twins show similar reports of subjective well-being. For example, in one study, researchers obtained measures of subjective well-being from 4,322 Norwegian twins (Nes et al., 2006). Comparisons between MZ and DZ twins revealed that genetic factors accounted for 51 percent of the variance in subjective well-being for men and 49 percent of the variance for women. The researchers also gathered subjective well-being judgments at two points in time, six years apart. Genetic factors accounted for 85 percent of the correlation across time for men and 78 percent of that correlation for women. Research with a sample of 973 U.S. twin pairs also indicated a large impact of genetics on subjective well-being (Weiss et al., 2008). However, those data also suggested that personality plays an important role in these genetic effects. There is evidence that personality traits are highly heritable. Results from the U.S. twin sample suggest that differences in subjective well-being are consequences of the personality traits people inherit at birth. For example, people who are high in emotional stability and social engagement are also more likely to report high subjective-well being.

We have just seen that genetics has an important impact on individual differences in subjective well-being. Still, life experiences also matter. An important component of people's judgments of subjective well-being is the balance of positive and negative emotions in their lives.

A team of researchers obtained data from 8,557 participants across 46 countries (Kuppens et al., 2008). Participants provided ratings of their life satisfaction by responding to statements such as "In most ways, my life is close to my

emotion regulation The processes through which people change the intensity and duration of the emotions they experience.

subjective well-being Individuals' overall evaluation of life satisfaction and happiness.

positive psychology A movement within psychology that applies research to provide people with the knowledge and skills that allow them to experience fulfilling lives.

ideal" (p. 71) on a 7-point scale that ranged from "strongly disagree" to "strongly agree." They used a 9-point scale—ranging from "not at all" to "all the time"—to indicate how often they had felt positive emotions (such as pride, gratitude, and love) and negative emotions (such as guilt, shame, and jealousy) in the last week. The researchers' analyses disclosed consistent relationships among these measures. In general, participants reported higher levels of life satisfaction when they had more positive emotional experiences and fewer negative emotional experiences. However, positive emotions had about twice as much impact on life satisfaction judgments as did negative emotions. The analyses also revealed somewhat different patterns across cultures. For example, cultures differ with respect to the amount of effort people need to expend to ensure their day-to-day survival. For cultures in which survival is an issue, judgments of life satisfaction depended less on positive emotional experiences.

You can probably relate these results to your own feelings of subjective well-being: As you cast your thoughts over the last week, what types of emotional experiences come readily to mind?

You might also think about the features of your life that gave rise to that particular assortment of emotional experiences. Researchers have tested a variety of hypotheses about life events that may affect subjective well-being. For example, major negative life events, such as the loss of a job or the death of a spouse, often have a damaging impact on subjective well-being (Lucas, 2007). Researchers have also looked at ongoing differences in the circumstances of people's lives. For example, researchers have suggested that "the single most important source of happiness" is good social relationships (Kesebir & Diener, 2008, p. 122). Later in this chapter you'll see that social support is an important resource for coping with stress. Researchers have also tried to understand the relationship between wealth and subjective well-being. When people struggle to meet their basic needs, they often report low levels of life satisfaction and happiness (Diener et al., 2010; Howell & Howell, 2008). However, once people pass the threshold at which those basic needs are secure, the correlation between wealth and subjective well-being is quite modest. If you must make a choice between more money and more friends, the results of positive psychology suggest that you should most often opt for more friends.

We have now explored important short- and long-term consequences of moods and emotions. The next section turns to the topic of stress and how to cope with it. You will learn how to take cognitive control over how you are "feeling."

Stop *and* Review

① What has cross-cultural research revealed about the recognition of facial expressions?

② What role does the autonomous nervous system play in experience of emotions?

③ What is the main claim of the Cannon–Bard theory of emotion?

④ What is the general impact of mood on information processing?

⑤ What might be the single most important source of happiness?

CRITICAL THINKING Recall the study that examined weapon focus. Why might the researcher have chosen to test memory for the perpetrator's appearance?

✔—Study and **Review** on **MyPsychLab**

STRESS OF LIVING

Suppose I asked you to keep track of how you are "feeling" over the course of a day. You might report that for brief periods, you felt happiness, sadness, anger, astonishment, and so on. There is one feeling, however, that people often report as a kind of background noise for much of their day-to-day experience, and that is stress. Modern industrialized society sets a rapid, hectic pace for living. People often have too many demands placed on their time, are worried about uncertain futures, and have little time for family and fun. But would you be better off without stress? A stress-free life would offer no challenge—no difficulties to surmount, no new fields to conquer, and no reasons to sharpen your wits or improve your abilities. Every organism faces challenges from its external environment and from its personal needs. The organism must solve these problems to survive and thrive. 👁

Whether at work or play, individuals in contemporary society are likely to encounter a stressful environment. What situations in your life do you find most stressful?

....

👁 **Watch** the **Video** *The Basics: Stress and Your Health* on **MyPsychLab**

Psychology in Your Life

CAN YOU ACCURATELY PREDICT YOUR FUTURE EMOTIONS?

Suppose you're about to submit an assignment. A researcher stops you and asks you to look into the future. First, he asks you to predict what grade you think you'll get. Next, he asks you to predict how you imagine you will feel—on the dimensions of rejoicing and regret—if your actual grade were higher or lower than that prediction or pretty much accurate. How might you respond?

When researchers conducted this experiment, their goal was to compare students' predictions about their emotional responses to their actual responses (Sevdalis & Harvey, 2007). After the students received their grades, the researchers found them again to ask them how the outcomes made them feel. On average, the students did somewhat better on their assignments than they had predicted. However, those better-than-expected outcomes didn't make them nearly as happy as they thought they would: The students experienced much less rejoicing than they anticipated.

Let's consider a second example of people's predictions about future emotions. Suppose, as a city dweller, you dash down a stairway just in time to watch the doors close on your subway car. How would you feel? Suppose instead you missed the train by a wider margin of time. Now how would you feel?

A team of researchers conducted exactly that study (Gilbert et al., 2004). They approached people on a subway platform and offered them $1 to fill out a brief questionnaire. One group of participants were *Experiencers*. Those people

had actually missed a train by either a narrow margin (one minute) or a wide margin (five minutes). They indicated how regretful they felt by providing a rating on a scale ranging from "not at all" to "extremely." Participants cast in the role of *Forecasters* used the same scale to predict how regretful they imagined they would feel had they missed the train by a narrow or wide margin. (Each Forecaster answered the question for just one margin.)

Forecasters predicted that people would experience more regret for the narrow margin than for the wide margin. However, the Experiencers actually reported nearly the same regret for the narrow margin and the wide margin. Once again, we see that people's predictions about their future feelings aren't very accurate.

Why do people have difficulty predicting how they might respond to particular outcomes? In large part, it seems that people are better than they anticipate at putting outcomes into a broader perspective (Kermer et al., 2006). When people actually miss a subway train, they are able to take that outcome in stride by putting it in the larger context of their unfolding day. They don't dwell on the isolated event in a way that makes them continue to feel negative emotions. By contrast, when people predict how they're going to feel, they aren't able to interpret the outcome in the fuller context. The same is true for positive emotions. You might not rejoice as much as you predict to a better-than-expected grade because that outcome occurs as part of your whole ongoing life.

Stress is the pattern of responses an organism makes to stimulus events that disturb its equilibrium and tax or exceed its ability to cope. The stimulus events include a large variety of external and internal conditions that collectively are called stressors. A **stressor** is a stimulus event that places a demand on an organism for some kind of adaptive response: a bicyclist swerves in front of your car, your professor moves up the due date of your term paper, you're asked to run for class president. An individual's response to the need for change is made up of a diverse combination of reactions taking place on several levels, including physiological, behavioral, emotional, and cognitive. People typically associate stress with *distress*—and assume that all stress is bad. However, you also experience *eustress*. (*Eu* is an ancient Greek suffix meaning "good.") As you'll see by the end of this section, in many circumstances stress can bring about positive changes in your life. ◉▶

Figure 5 diagrams the elements of the stress process. The goal for this section is to give you a clear understanding of all

the features represented in this figure. The section begins by considering general physiological responses to stressors.

Physiological Stress Reactions

How would you respond if you arrived at a class and discovered that you were about to have a pop quiz? You would probably agree that this would cause you some stress, but what does that mean for your body's reactions? Many of the physiological responses that occur for emotional situations are also relevant to

---

◉▶ Simulate the Experiment *How Stressed Are You?* on **MyPsychLab**

stress The pattern of specific and nonspecific responses an organism makes to stimulus events that disturb its equilibrium and tax or exceed its ability to cope.

stressor An internal or external event or stimulus that induces stress.

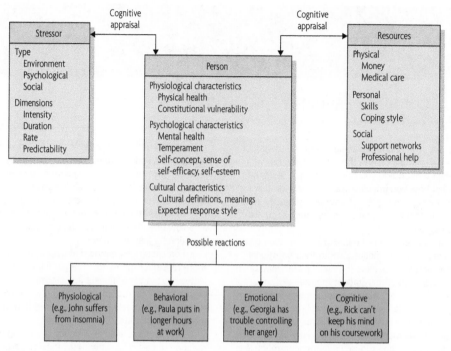

FIGURE 5 A Model of Stress

Cognitive appraisal of the stress situation interacts with the stressor and the physical, social, and personal resources available for dealing with the stressor. Individuals respond to threats on various levels: physiological, behavioral, emotional, and cognitive. Some responses are adaptive, and others are maladaptive or even lethal.

day-to-day instances of stress. Such transient states of arousal, with typically clear onset and offset patterns, are examples of **acute stress**. **Chronic stress,** in contrast, is a state of enduring arousal, continuing over time, in which demands are perceived as greater than the inner and outer resources available for dealing with them. An example of chronic stress might be a continuous frustration with your inability to find time to do all the things you want to do. Let's see how your body responds to these different types of stresses.

Emergency Reactions to Acute Threats In the 1920s, Walter Cannon outlined the first scientific description of the way animals and humans respond to danger. He found that a sequence of activity is triggered in the nerves and glands to prepare the body either to defend itself and struggle or to run

....

Explore the Concept *Virtual Brain: Emotion, Stress, and Health* on MyPsychLab

acute stress A transient state of arousal with typically clear onset and offset patterns.

chronic stress A continuous state of arousal in which an individual perceives demands as greater than the inner and outer resources available for dealing with them.

fight-or-flight response A sequence of internal activities triggered when an organism is faced with a threat; prepares the body for combat and struggle or for running away to safety; recent evidence suggests that the response is characteristic only of males.

away to safety. Cannon called this dual stress response the **fight-or-flight response.** At the center of this stress response is the *hypothalamus*, which is involved in a variety of emotional responses. The hypothalamus has sometimes been referred to as the stress center because of its twin functions in emergencies: (1) It controls the autonomic nervous system (ANS) and (2) it activates the pituitary gland.

The ANS regulates the activities of the body's organs. In stressful conditions, breathing becomes faster and deeper, heart rate increases, blood vessels constrict, and blood pressure rises. In addition to these internal changes, muscles open the passages of the throat and nose to allow more air into the lungs while also producing facial expressions of strong emotion. Messages go to smooth muscles to stop certain bodily functions, such as digestion, that are irrelevant to preparing for the emergency at hand.

Another function of the ANS during stress is to get adrenaline flowing. It signals the inner part of the adrenal glands, the *adrenal medulla,* to release two hormones, *epinephrine* and *norepinephrine,* which, in turn, signal a number of other organs to perform their specialized functions. The spleen releases more red blood corpuscles (to aid in clotting if there is an injury), and the bone marrow is stimulated to make more white corpuscles (to combat possible infection). The liver is stimulated to produce more sugar, building up body energy.

The *pituitary gland* responds to signals from the hypothalamus by secreting two hormones vital to the stress reaction.

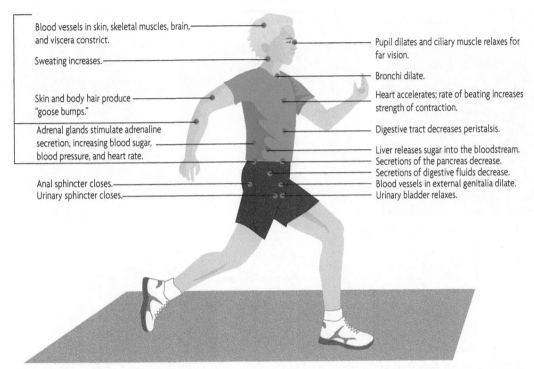

FIGURE 6 The Body's Reaction to Stress

Stress produces a wide range of physiological changes in your body.

The *thyrotropic hormone* (TTH) stimulates the *thyroid gland*, which makes more energy available to the body. The *adreno-corticotropic hormone* (ACTH), known as the "stress hormone," stimulates the outer part of the adrenal glands, the *adrenal cortex*, resulting in the release of hormones that control metabolic processes and the release of sugar from the liver into the blood. ACTH also signals various organs to release about 30 other hormones, each of which plays a role in the body's adjustment to this call to arms. A summary of this physiological stress response is shown in **Figure 6**.

An analysis by health psychologist **Shelley Taylor** and her colleagues (2000; Taylor, 2006) suggests that these physiological responses to stress may have different consequences for females than for males. Taylor and her colleagues suggest that females do not experience *fight-or-flight*. Rather, these researchers argue that stressors lead females to experience a **tend-and-befriend response:** In times of stress, females ensure the safety of their offspring by tending to their needs; females befriend other members of their social group with the same goal of reducing the vulnerability of their offspring. You can see how this analysis of sex differences in stress responses fits with discussions of evolutionary perspectives on human behavior. For example, men and women's *mating strategies* differ, in part, because of the relative roles men and women have played— over the course of evolution—in child rearing. The idea here is very much the same: Because of men and women's different evolutionary niches with respect to nurturing offspring, the same initial physiological responses to stress ultimately produce quite different behaviors.

Unfortunately, neither the fight-or-flight nor the tend-and-befriend response is entirely useful for contemporary lives. Many of the stressors both men and women experience on a day-to-day basis make the physiological stress responses fairly maladaptive. Suppose, for example, you are taking a difficult exam and the clock is swiftly ticking away. Although you might value the heightened attentiveness brought about by your stress response, the rest of the physiological changes do you no good: There's no one to fight or to tend, and so on. The responses that developed in the species as adaptive preparations for dealing with external dangers are counterproductive for dealing with many contemporary types of psychological stressors. This is particularly true because, as you will see next, many people live their lives under circumstances of chronic stress.

The General Adaptation Syndrome (GAS) and Chronic Stress The first modern researcher to investigate the effects of continued severe stress on the body was **Hans Selye** (1907–1982), a Canadian endocrinologist. Beginning in the late 1930s, Selye reported on the complex response of laboratory animals to damaging agents such as bacterial infections, toxins, trauma, forced restraint, heat, cold, and so on. According to Selye's theory of stress, many kinds of stressors can trigger the same reaction or general bodily response. All stressors call for *adaptation:* An organism must maintain or regain its integrity

tend-and-befriend response A response to stressors that is hypothesized to be typical for females; stressors prompt females to protect their offspring and join social groups to reduce vulnerability.

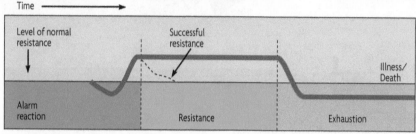

Stage I: Alarm reaction (continuously repeated throughout life)	Stage II: Resistance (continuously repeated throughout life)	Stage III: Exhaustion
• Enlargement of adrenal cortex • Enlargement of lymphatic system • Increase in hormone levels • Response to specific stressor • Epinephrine release associated with high levels of physiological arousal and negative affect • Greater susceptibility to increased intensity of stressor • Heightened susceptibility to illness (If prolonged, the slower components of the GAS are set into motion, beginning with Stage II.)	• Shrinkage of adrenal cortex • Return of lymph nodes to normal size • Sustaining of hormone levels • High physiological arousal • Counteraction of parasympathetic branch of ANS • Enduring of stressor; resistance to further debilitating effects • Heightened sensitivity to stress (If stress continues at intense levels, hormonal reserves are depleted, fatigue sets in, and individual enters Stage III.)	• Enlargement/dysfunction of lymphatic structures • Increase in hormone levels • Depletion of adaptive hormones • Decreased ability to resist either original or extraneous stressors • Affective experience—often depression • Illness • Death

FIGURE 7 The General Adaptation Syndrome (GAS)

Following exposure to a stressor, the body's resistance is diminished until the physiological changes of the corresponding alarm reaction bring it back up to the normal level. If the stressor continues, the bodily signs characteristic of the alarm reaction virtually disappear; resistance to the particular stressor rises above normal but drops for other stressors. This adaptive resistance returns the body to its normal level of functioning. Following prolonged exposure to the stressor, adaptation breaks down; signs of alarm reaction reappear, the stressor effects are irreversible, and the individual becomes ill and may die.

and well-being by restoring equilibrium, or homeostasis. The response to stressors was described by Selye as the **general adaptation syndrome (GAS).** It includes three stages: an alarm reaction, a stage of resistance, and a stage of exhaustion (Selye, 1976a, 1976b). *Alarm reactions* are brief periods of bodily arousal that prepare the body for vigorous activity. If a stressor is prolonged, the body enters a stage of *resistance*—a state of moderate arousal. During the stage of resistance, the organism can endure and *resist* further debilitating effects of prolonged stressors. However, if the stressor is sufficiently long lasting or intense, the body's resources become depleted and the organism enters the stage of *exhaustion.* The three stages are diagrammed and explained in **Figure 7**.

Selye identified some of the dangers associated with the stage of exhaustion. Recall, for example, that ACTH plays a role in the short-term response to stress. In the long term, however, its action reduces the ability of natural killer cells to destroy cancer cells and other life-threatening infections. When the body is stressed chronically, the increased production of "stress hormones" compromises the integrity of the immune system. This application of the general adaptation syndrome has proven valuable to explain **psychosomatic disorders**—illnesses that could not be wholly explained by physical causes—that had baffled physicians who had never considered stress as a cause for illness and disease. What serves the body well in adapting to acute stress impairs the body's response to chronic stress.

Selye's research makes disease seem an inevitable response to stress. We will see, however, that your psychological interpretation of what is stressful and what is not stressful—the way in which you appraise potentially stressful events—has an impact on your body's physiological response. To give a full account of the effect of stress on your body, we will have to combine Selye's foundational physiological theory with later research on psychological factors.

Psychological Stress Reactions

Your physiological stress reactions are automatic, predictable, built-in responses over which you normally have no conscious control. However, many psychological reactions are learned. They depend on perceptions and interpretations of the world. This section will discuss psychological responses to different categories of stressors, such as major life events and traumatic experiences.

general adaptation syndrome (GAS) The pattern of nonspecific adaptational physiological mechanisms that occurs in response to continuing threat by almost any serious stressor.

psychosomatic disorder Physical disorder aggravated by or primarily attributable to prolonged emotional stress or other psychological causes.

What are the physiological consequences of chronic stress?

Major Life Events The influence of life events on subsequent mental and physical health has been a target of considerable research. It started in the 1960s with the development of the Social Readjustment Rating Scale (SRRS), a simple measure for rating the degree of adjustment required by the various life changes, both pleasant and unpleasant, that many people experience. The scale was developed from the responses of adults, from all walks of life, who were asked to identify from a list those life events that applied to them. These adults rated the amount of readjustment required for each change by comparing each to marriage, which was arbitrarily assigned a value of 50 life-change units. Researchers then calculated the total number of **life-change units (LCUs)** an individual had undergone, using the units as a measure of the amount of stress the individual had experienced (Holmes & Rahe, 1967).

The SRRS was updated in the 1990s (see **Figure 8**). The researchers used the same procedure of asking participants

to rate the stress of life events as compared to marriage (Miller & Rahe, 1997). In this update, the LCU estimates went up 45 percent over the original values—that is, participants in the 1990s reported that they were experiencing overall much higher levels of stress than their peers had in the 1960s. Women in the 1990s also reported experiencing more stress in their lives than did men. Researchers continue to relate reports on the SRRS to mental and physical health outcomes. Consider a study in which 268 people completed the scale (Lynch et al., 2005). There was a positive correlation between SRRS scores and participants' total number of medical visits in the following six months: In general, the participants who had the highest SRRS scores also visited their doctors most often.

Researchers have found a variety of ways to examine the relationship between life events and health outcomes. For example, one study followed 16,881 adults for two years (Lietzén et al., 2011). At the beginning of the study, none of the participants had been diagnosed with asthma. Two years later, participants who had experienced high numbers of stressful life events (such as the illness of a family member or marital problems) were considerably more likely to have developed asthma. Consider another study that should have immediate relevance to the choices you make about how to organize your schoolwork.

When a professor gives you an assignment—a stressful life event in every student's life—do you try to take care of it as soon as possible, or do you put it off to the very last minute? Psychologists have developed a measurement

life-change unit (LCU) In stress research, the measure of the stress levels of different types of change experienced during a given period.

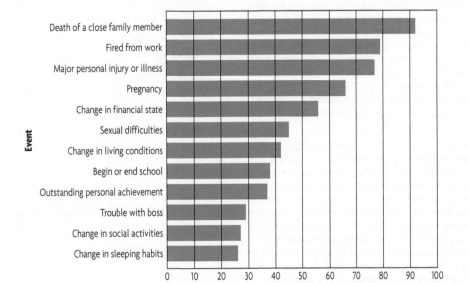

FIGURE 8 Life-Change Units for Some Major Life Events
Students may have to adapt to a number of important changes during their school years. Researchers have calculated the number of life-change units associated with such major life events.

Data from M. A. Miller and R. H. Rahe. Life changes scaling for the 1990s. *Journal of Psychosomatic Research, 43*(3): 279–292, Copyright (1997), with permission from Elsevier.

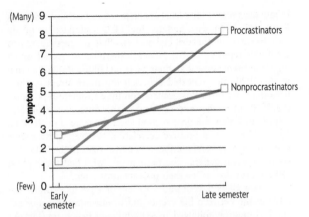

FIGURE 9 The Health Costs of Procrastination
Researchers identified students who were, generally, procrastinators and nonprocrastinators. The students were asked to report, early and late in the semester, how many symptoms of physical illness they had experienced. By late in the semester all students showed increases in symptoms. However—as all their work came due—procrastinators were reporting even more symptoms than their nonprocrastinating peers.

device called the General Procrastination Scale (Lay, 1986) to differentiate those individuals who habitually put things off—procrastinators—from those who don't—nonprocrastinators. A pair of researchers administered this scale to students in a health psychology course who had a paper due late in the semester. The students were also asked to report, early and late in the semester, how many symptoms of physical illness they had experienced. Not surprisingly, procrastinators, on average, turned their papers in later than did nonprocrastinators; procrastinators also, on average, obtained lower grades on those papers. **Figure 9** *displays the effect of procrastination on physical health. As you can see, early in the semester, procrastinators reported fewer symptoms, but by late in the semester, they were reporting more symptoms than their nonprocrastinating peers (Tice & Baumeister, 1997).*

You see in this study why not all life events have the same impact on all people. The nonprocrastinators got to work right away and so experienced stress and symptoms early in the semester. However, the consequence for the procrastinators of avoiding the early semester stress was a great increase in physical illness toward the end of the semester. Therefore, they were likely to be feeling ill just at the point in the semester when they needed to be in good health to complete all the work they had put off! Think about these results as you develop your own plan for navigating each semester. If you believe that you habitually procrastinate, consider consulting with a psychologist or school counselor to modify your behavior. Your grades and health are at stake!

Traumatic Events An event that is negative but also uncontrollable, unpredictable, or ambiguous is particularly stressful.

These conditions hold especially true in the case of *traumatic events.* Some traumatic events, such as rape and automobile crashes, affect individuals. Others, such as earthquakes, tornadoes, and terrorist attacks, have a broader impact. On September 11, 2001, attacks on the World Trade Center and the Pentagon with commercial aircraft led to the deaths of almost 3,000 people. With the goal of providing appropriate mental health care, researchers moved swiftly to assess the psychological aftermath of the attacks.

One particular focus was on the prevalence of **posttraumatic stress disorder (PTSD).** PTSD is a stress reaction in which individuals suffer from persistent reexperiences of the traumatic event in the form, for example, of flashbacks or nightmares (*DSM-IV*, 1994). Sufferers experience an emotional numbing in relation to everyday events and feelings of alienation from other people. Finally, the emotional pain of this reaction can result in an increase in various symptoms, such as sleep problems, guilt about surviving, difficulty in concentrating, and an exaggerated startle response.

A team of researchers wished to assess the long-term impact of the events of 9/11/01 (DiGrande et al., 2011). The study focused on 3,271 civilians who had actually been evacuated from the World Trade Center that morning. The data were collected between September 2003 and November of 2004, two to three years after the attack. As seen in **Table 1**, only 4.4 percent of the participants had no symptoms associated with PTSD. Of the people who had been in the Twin Towers

Table 1 • The Psychological Impact of Exposure to the Events of September 11, 2001

Symptoms of Posttraumatic Stress Disorder	Percent of participants
No symptoms reported	4.4
Reported re-experiences of the events	
Intrusive memories	33.4
Dreams or nightmares	13.5
Reported avoidance of stimuli associated with the event	
Avoidance of thoughts and feelings	31.5
Avoidance of reminders	25.9
Reported increased arousal	
Insomnia	31.6
Irritability or anger	25.4
Probable diagnosis of PTSD	15.0

Data from DiGrande, L., Neria, Y., Brackbill, R. M., Pulliam, P., & Galea, S. (2011). Long-term posttraumatic stress symptoms among 3,271 civilian survivors of the September 11, 2001, terrorist attacks on the World Trade Center. *American Journal of Epidemiology*, 173, 271–281.

posttraumatic stress disorder (PTSD) An anxiety disorder characterized by the persistent re-experience of traumatic events through distressing recollections, dreams, hallucinations, or dissociative flashbacks; develops in response to rapes, life-threatening events, severe injury, and natural disasters.

What factors changed the likelihood that an individual would develop PTSD after the events of September 11, 2001?

the morning of the attack, the vast majority reported some symptoms: re-experiences of the events, avoidance of stimuli associated with the event, and/or increased arousal that stemmed from the event. Despite the passage of two to three years, 15 percent of the sample met the diagnostic criteria for full PTSD. The study revealed several factors that made PTSD more likely. For example, people who were evacuated from higher floors, people who personally witnessed horrors, and people who were themselves injured had higher rates of PTSD.

As noted earlier, people also suffer from individual traumatic events with a negative impact on their psychological health. For example, rape victims often show many of the signs of posttraumatic stress (Ullman et al., 2007). In assessments two weeks after being assaulted, 94 percent of rape victims were diagnosed with PTSD; 12 weeks after the assault, 51 percent of the victims still met diagnostic criteria (Foa & Riggs, 1995). These data illustrate that the emotional responses of posttraumatic stress can occur in an acute form immediately following a trauma and can subside over a period of several months.

Chronic Stressors The discussion of physiological responses to stress made a distinction between stressors that are acute, with clear onsets and offsets, versus those that are chronic—that is, endure over time. With psychological stressors, it's not always easy to draw a sharp distinction. Suppose, for example, your bicycle is stolen. Originally, this is an acute source of stress. However, if you begin to worry constantly that your new bike will also be stolen, the stress associated with this event can become chronic. Researchers have found this pattern in people who suffer from serious illnesses like cancer, HIV

infection, and diabetes (de Ridder et al., 2008; Morris et al., 2011). The chronic stress of coping with the anxiety of a diagnosis and treatment may impair health more rapidly than the disease alone would.

For many people, chronic stress arises from conditions in society and the environment. What cumulative effects do crime, economic conditions, pollution, and the threat of terrorism have on you? How do these and other environmental stressors affect your mental well-being? Some groups of people suffer chronic stress by virtue of their socioeconomic status or racial identity, with stark consequences for overall well-being (Santiago et al., 2011; Sternthal et al., 2011). Consider a longitudinal study of 1,037 New Zealanders that investigated the relationship between socioeconomic disadvantage in childhood and health outcomes when the participants were 32 years old (Danese et al., 2009). Early economic hardship predicted higher levels of adult health risks such as excess weight, high blood pressure, and high cholesterol. Childhood maltreatment by parents and social isolation also had negative consequences for the participants' psychological and physical health as adults. In fact, the more chronic stressors participants had endured as children, the greater the disease risks as adults.

Daily Hassles You may agree that the end of a relationship, an earthquake, or prejudice might cause stress, but what about the smaller stressors you experience on a day-to-day basis? What happened to you yesterday? You probably didn't get a divorce or survive a plane crash. You're more likely to have lost your notes or textbook. Perhaps you were late for an important appointment, or you got a parking ticket, or a noisy neighbor ruined your sleep. These are the types of recurring day-to-day stressors that confront most people, most of the time.

This trader on the floor of the New York Stock Exchange has likely experienced chronic stress as a result of the uncertain economy. What are some possible consequences for his physical and mental health?

In a diary study, a group of White middle-class middle-aged men and women kept track of their daily hassles over a one-year period (along with a record of major life changes and physical symptoms). A clear relationship emerged between hassles and health problems: The more frequent and intense the hassles people reported, the poorer was their health, both physical and mental (Lazarus, 1981, 1984b). Consider a study that demonstrated the impact of daily hassles on adolescents.

A group of 236 adolescents (with an average age of 16.1 years) completed a daily hassles scale. The scale asked the adolescents to indicate how frequently they had experiences such as "Being 'put down' by a family member," "Having to lie to my parents," and "Being bullied or teased" (Wright et al., 2010, p. 222). The adolescents indicated the frequency of such experiences on a 5-point scale that ranged from "never" to "daily." They also completed measures of anxiety, depression, and life satisfaction. In general, the adolescents who reported the highest levels of daily hassles also reported the most negative states of mental health (that is, they reported more anxiety and more depression). In addition, adolescents with more daily hassles reported lower levels of life satisfaction.

This study confirms that daily hassles have a considerable impact on people's sense of well-being.

Although this section has focused on day-to-day hassles, its worth noting that, for many people, daily hassles may be balanced out by daily positive experiences (Lazarus & Lazarus, 1994). For example, one study asked 132 men and women to report the frequency and intensity of the hassles (that is, irritating events) and uplifts (that is, happy events) in their lives (Jain et al., 2007). The researchers also measured the participants' blood levels of substances (such as inflammatory factors) that are indicators of risk for cardiovascular disease. Higher levels of reported hassles were associated with higher levels of these risk indicators; higher levels of reported uplifts were associated with lower levels. Therefore, if we want to predict your life course based on daily hassles, we also need to know something about the daily uplifts your life provides (Lyubomirsky et al., 2005).

You have just learned about many sources of stress in people's lives. Psychologists have recognized for quite a long time that the impact of these different types of stressors depends in large part on how effectively people can cope with them. Let's now consider how people cope successfully and unsuccessfully with stress.

Coping with Stress

If living is inevitably stressful, and if chronic stress can disrupt your life and even kill you, you need to learn how to manage stress. **Coping** refers to the process of dealing with internal or external demands that are perceived as straining or exceeding an individual's resources (Lazarus & Folkman, 1984). Coping

....

 Watch the Video *In the Real World: Reducing Stress, Improving Health* on MyPsychLab

 Explore the Concept *The Effect of Cognitive Appraisal on Responses to Stressors* on MyPsychLab

coping The process of dealing with internal or external demands that are perceived to be threatening or overwhelming.

may consist of behavioral, emotional, or motivational responses and thoughts. This section begins by describing how cognitive appraisal affects what you experience as stressful. We then consider types of coping responses, including both general principles of coping and specific interventions. Finally, we consider some individual differences in individuals' ability to cope with stress.

Appraisal of Stress When you cope with stressful situations, your first step is to define in what ways they are, in fact, stressful. Cognitive appraisal is the cognitive interpretation and evaluation of a stressor. Cognitive appraisal plays a central role in defining the situation—what the demand is, how big a threat it is, and what resources you have for meeting it (Lazarus, 1993; Lazarus & Lazarus, 1994). Some stressors, such as undergoing bodily injury or finding one's house on fire, are experienced as threats by almost everyone. However, many other stressors can be defined in various ways, depending on your personal life situation, the relation of a particular demand to your central goals, your competence in dealing with the demand, and your self-assessment of that competence. The situation that causes acute distress for another person may be all in a day's work for you. Try to notice, and understand, the life events that are different for you and your friends and family: Some situations cause you stress but not your friends and family; other events cause them stress but not you. Why?

Richard Lazarus, whose general theory of appraisal was addressed in the discussion of emotions, distinguished two stages in the cognitive appraisal of demands. *Primary appraisal* describes the initial evaluation of the seriousness of a demand. This evaluation starts with the questions "What's happening?" and "Is this thing good for me, stressful, or irrelevant?" If the answer to the second question is "stressful," you appraise the potential impact of the stressor by determining whether harm has occurred or is likely to and whether action is required (see **Table 2**). Once you decide something must be done, *secondary appraisal* begins. You evaluate the personal and social resources that are available to deal with the stressful circumstance and

Table 2 • Stages in Stable Decision Making/Cognitive Appraisal

Stage	Key Questions
1. Appraising the challenge	Are the risks serious if I don't change?
2. Surveying alternatives	Is this alternative an acceptable means for dealing with the challenge? Have I sufficiently surveyed the available alternatives?
3. Weighing alternatives	Which alternative is best? Could the best alternative meet the essential requirements?
4. Deliberating about commitment	Will I implement the best alternative and allow others to know?
5. Adhering despite negative feedback	Are the risks serious if I *don't* change? Are the risks serious if I *do* change?

consider the action options that are needed. Appraisal continues as coping responses are tried; if the first ones don't work and the stress persists, new responses are initiated, and their effectiveness is evaluated.

Cognitive appraisal is an example of a stress moderator variable. **Stress moderator variables** are those variables that change the impact of a stressor on a given type of stress reaction. Moderator variables filter or modify the usual effects of stressors on the individual's reactions. For example, your level of fatigue and general health status are moderator variables influencing your reaction to a given psychological or physical stressor. When you are in good shape, you can deal with a stressor better than when you aren't. You can see how cognitive appraisal also fits the definition of a moderator variable. The way in which you appraise a stressor will determine the types of coping responses you need to bring to it. Let's now consider general types of coping responses.

Types of Coping Responses Suppose you have a big exam coming up. You've thought about it—you've appraised the situation—and you're quite sure that this is a stressful situation. What can you do? It's important to note that coping can precede a potentially stressful event in the form of **anticipatory coping** (Folkman, 1984). How do you deal with the stress of the upcoming exam? How do you tell your parents that you are dropping out of school or your lover that you are no longer in love? Anticipating a stressful situation leads to many thoughts and feelings that themselves may be stress inducing, as in the cases of interviews, speeches, or blind dates. You need to know how to cope.

The two main ways of coping are defined by whether the goal is to confront the problem directly—*problem-directed coping*—or to lessen the discomfort associated with the stress—*emotion-focused coping* (Billings & Moos, 1982; Lazarus & Folkman, 1984). Several subcategories of these two basic approaches are shown in **Table 3**.

Let's begin with problem-directed coping. "Taking the bull by the horns" is how we usually characterize the strategy of facing up to a problem situation. This approach includes all strategies designed to deal *directly* with the stressor, whether through overt action or through realistic problem-solving activities. You face up to a bully or run away; you try to win him or her over with bribes or other incentives. Your focus is on the problem to be dealt with and on the agent that has induced the stress. You acknowledge the call to action, you appraise the situation and your resources for dealing with it, and

you undertake a response that is appropriate for removing or lessening the threat. Such problem-solving efforts are useful for managing *controllable stressors*—those stressors that you can change or eliminate through your actions, such as overbearing bosses or underwhelming grades.

The emotion-focused approach is useful for managing the impact of more *uncontrollable stressors*. Suppose you are responsible for the care of a parent with Alzheimer's. In that situation, there is no "bully" you can eliminate from the environment; you cannot make the disease go away. Even in this situation, some forms of problem-directed coping would be useful. For example, you could modify your work schedule to make it easier to provide care. However, because you cannot eliminate the source of stress, you also can try to change your feelings and thoughts about the disease. For example, you might take part in a support group for Alzheimer's caregivers or learn relaxation techniques. These approaches still constitute a coping strategy because you are acknowledging that there is a threat to your well-being and you are taking steps to modify that threat.

You will be better off if you have multiple strategies to help you cope in stressful situations (Bonanno et al., 2011). For coping to be successful, your resources need to match the perceived demand. Thus the availability of multiple coping strategies is adaptive because you are more likely to achieve a match and manage the stressful event. Consider a study that examined the ways in which women cope with the stress of undergoing surgery for breast cancer (Roussi et al., 2007). The women reported their distress levels and coping strategies (such as problem-directed and/or emotion-focused strategies) a day before the surgeries, three days after the procedure, and again three months later. The women who reported that they were using multiple coping strategies in the days after their surgeries reported less distress three months later.

Researchers who study coping have discovered that some individuals meet stressors with a particular degree of

....

 Explore the Concept *Coping Strategies and Their Effects* on MyPsychLab

stress moderator variable Variable that changes the impact of a stressor on a given type of stress reaction.

anticipatory coping Efforts made in advance of a potentially stressful event to overcome, reduce, or tolerate the imbalance between perceived demands and available resources.

Table 3 • Taxonomy of Coping Strategies

Type of Coping Strategy	Example
PROBLEM-DIRECTED COPING	
Change stressor or one's relationship to it through direct actions and/or problem-solving strategies	Fight (destroy, remove, or weaken the threat)
	Flight (distance oneself from the threat)
	Seek options to fight-or-flight (negotiating, bargaining, compromising)
	Prevent future stress (act to increase one's resistance or decrease strength of anticipated stress)
EMOTION-FOCUSED COPING	
Change self through activities that make one feel better but do not chnage the stressor	Somatically focused activities (use of antianxiety medication, relaxation, biofeedback)
	Cognitively focused activities (planned distractions, fantasies, thoughts about oneself)
	Therapy to adjust conscious or unconscious processes that lead to additional anxiety

Why are multiple coping strategies beneficial for individuals such as Alzheimer's caregivers?

resilience—they are able to achieve positive outcomes despite serious threats to their well-being (Stewart & Yuen, 2011). Research has focused on the types of coping skills that resilient individuals have acquired and how they have acquired them. An important part of the answer is that children who become resilient have been raised by parents with good parenting skills (Masten, 2011). For example, research with homeless families suggests that higher-quality parenting helps children to acquire the cognitive skills necessary to control their attention and behavior (Herbers et al., 2011). These control skills have positive consequences for the children's performance in school.

Up to now, we have been considering general approaches to coping with stressors. Let's now turn to specific cognitive and social approaches to successful coping.

Modifying Cognitive Strategies   A powerful way to adapt to stress is to change your evaluations of stressors and your self-defeating cognitions about the way you are dealing with them. You need to find a different way to think about a given situation, your role in it, and the causal attributions you make to explain the undesirable outcome. Two ways of mentally coping with stress are *reappraising* the nature of the stressors themselves and *restructuring* your cognitions about your stress reactions.

You have already seen the idea that people control the experience of stress in their lives in part by the way they appraise life events (Lazarus & Lazarus, 1994). Learning to think differently about certain stressors, to relabel them, or to imagine them in a less-threatening (perhaps even funny) context is a form of cognitive reappraisal that can reduce stress. Worried about giving a speech to a large, forbidding audience? One stressor reappraisal technique is to imagine your potential

critics sitting there in the nude—this surely takes away a great deal of their fearsome power. Anxious about being shy at a party you must attend? Think about finding someone who is more shy than you and reducing his or her social anxiety by initiating a conversation.

You can also manage stress by changing what you tell yourself about it and by changing your handling of it. Cognitive-behavior therapist **Donald Meichenbaum** (1977, 1985, 1993) has proposed a three-phase process that allows for such *stress inoculation*. In Phase 1, people work to develop a greater awareness of their actual behavior, what instigates it, and what its results are. One of the best ways of doing this is to keep daily logs. By helping people redefine their problems in terms of their causes and results, these records can increase their feelings of control. You may discover, for example, that your grades are low (a stressor) because you always leave too little time to do a good job on your class assignments. In Phase 2, people begin to identify new behaviors that negate the maladaptive, self-defeating behaviors. Perhaps you might create a fixed "study time" or limit your phone calls to 10 minutes each night. In Phase 3, after adaptive behaviors are being emitted, individuals appraise the consequences of their new behaviors, avoiding the former internal dialogue of put-downs. Instead of telling themselves, "I was lucky the professor called on me when I happened to have read the text," they say, "I'm glad I was prepared for the professor's question. It feels great to be able to respond intelligently in that class."

This three-phase approach means initiating responses and self-statements that are incompatible with previous defeatist cognitions. Once started on this path, people realize that they are changing—and can take full credit for the change, which promotes further successes. **Table 4** gives examples of the new kinds of self-statements that help in dealing with stressful situations. *Stress inoculation training* has been used successfully in a wide variety of domains. Many children live in situations in which, tragically, they are very likely to be exposed to stressful circumstances. Let's consider successful stress inoculation for children.

The teachers of 748 fourth- and fifth-grade students in southern Israel provided a program of stress inoculation in their classrooms (Wolmer et al., 2011). Over the course of 14 weeks, the children received a series of lessons that taught them coping skills and gave them opportunities to rehearse those skills. The lessons also helped students recognize their strong emotions and, again, taught them skills for regulating those emotions. A control group of 740 children did not receive this training. After the training period, a conflict began in the Gaza Strip. All 1,488 of the children experienced three weeks of rocket and mortar attacks. Three months after the conflict ended, the children completed measures to assess the presence of posttraumatic stress disorder. Among the students in the control group, 11.3 percent met criteria for PTSD; among the students who had received the stress inoculation training, 7.2 percent met criteria for PTSD. Thus, stress inoculation training reduced the number of children experiencing PTSD by about one-third.

This study suggests how classroom-based stress inoculation training could help children cope with stressors that,

Table 4 • Examples of Coping Self-Statements

Preparation

I can develop a plan to deal with it.

Just think about what I can do about it. That's better than getting anxious.

No negative self-statements, just think rationally.

Confrontation

One step at a time; I can handle this situation.

This anxiety is what the doctor said I would feel; it's a reminder to use my coping exercises.

Relax; I'm in control. Take a slow, deep breath.

Coping

When fear comes, just pause.

Keep focused on the present; what is it I have to do?

Don't try to eliminate fear totally; just keep it manageable.

It's not the worst thing that can happen.

Just think about something else.

Self-Reinforcement

It worked; I was able to do it.

It wasn't as bad as I expected.

I'm really pleased with the progress I'm making.

quite unfortunately, may be regularly anticipated in some young lives.

Another main component of successful coping is for you to establish **perceived control** over the stressor, a belief that you can make a difference in the course or the consequences of some event or experience (Endler et al., 2000; Roussi, 2002). If you believe that you can affect the course of an illness or the daily symptoms of a disease, you are probably adjusting well to the disorder. However, if you believe that the source of the stress is another person whose behavior you cannot influence or a situation that you cannot change, chances increase for a poor psychological adjustment to your chronic condition. Consider a study of women who had undergone surgery for breast cancer (Bárez et al., 2007). The women who reported higher levels of perceived control experienced the least physical and psychological distress over the whole year following surgery.

While you file away these control strategies for future use, we will turn to a final aspect of coping with stress—the social dimension.

Social Support as a Coping Resource **Social support** refers to the resources others provide, giving the message that one is loved, cared for, esteemed, and connected to other people in a network of communication and mutual obligation. In addition to these forms of *emotional support*, other people may provide *tangible support* (money, transportation, housing) and *informational support* (advice, personal feedback, information). Anyone with whom you have a significant social relationship—such as family members, friends, coworkers, and neighbors—can be part of your social support network in time of need.

Much research points to the power of social support in moderating the vulnerability to stress (Kim et al., 2008). When people have other people to whom they can turn, they are better able to handle job stressors, unemployment, marital disruption, and serious illness, as well as their everyday problems of living. Consider individuals who serve as peacekeepers in the world's many troubled regions. The traumas associated with life in battle zones often leads to posttraumatic stress disorder. However, a study of Dutch peacekeepers who served in Lebanon demonstrated that those individuals who experienced higher levels of positive social interactions had fewer symptoms of PTSD (Dirkzwager et al., 2003).

Researchers are trying to identify which types of social supports provide the most benefit for specific life events. One study examined the impact of informational support and emotional support for men and women who were undergoing facial surgery (Krohne & Slangen, 2005). Overall, people who had more social support anticipated their surgery with less anxiety, required less anesthesia during surgery, and had briefer hospital stays. However, the more specific results differed for men and women. Although patients of both sexes obtained an advantage from greater informational support, only women were much affected by the level of emotional support. More generally, what appears to matter is the match between the type of support an individual needs and what that individual gets. As shown in **Figure 10**, there are four different possibilities for how desires and reality can be related (Reynolds & Perrin, 2004). People are best off when there's a match between what they want and what they get. For a sample of women with breast cancer, they had the worst psychological outcomes when they received support they did not want ("support commission") (Reynolds & Perrin, 2004). This pattern might have emerged because the unwanted assistance made it difficult for women to obtain the emotional support they really needed.

Support is	wanted	not wanted
received	positive congruent support	support commission
not received	support omission	null support

FIGURE 10 Matches and Mismatches for Social Support

When people need to cope with difficult situations, there can be matches or mismatches between the social support they want and the social support they receive.

From Julie S. Reynolds and Nancy Perrin, "Matches and Mismatches for Social Support and Psychosocial Adjustment to Breast Cancer," *Health Psychology, 23*(4), 425–430. Copyright © 2004 by the American Psychological Association. Reprinted with permission.

perceived control The belief that one has the ability to make a difference in the course of the consequences of some event or experience; often helpful in dealing with stressors.

social support Resources, including material aid, socioemotional support, and informational aid, provided by others to help a person cope with stress.

Data from figure "Viral Load" in "Effect of written emotional expression on immune function in patients with human immunodeficiency virus infection: A randomized trial" by Keith J. Petrie, Iris Fontanilla, Mark G. Thomas, Roger J. Booth, and James W. Pennebaker, Psychosomatic Medicine 66(2), March 2004

Why are some forms of social support more welcome than others?

experience stress. One of the most important take-home messages from our study of psychology is that you should always work at being part of a social support network and never let yourself become socially isolated.

Positive Effects of Stress

This section has focused largely on the potential for stress to bring about negative life outcomes. This focus reflects the great effort researchers have expended to help people prevent and overcome those negative outcomes. However, in recent years, psychologists have turned more attention to the potential for stress to have positive effects in people's lives. This new focus is another outcome of the positive psychology movement that you encountered as part of the discussion of subjective well-being. Let's consider stress and coping from a positive psychology perspective.

The initial definition of stress made a distinction between distress and eustress. It's probably easy for you to generate circumstances in which you experienced distress—but what about eustress? Consider the last time you watched any kind of running race. Did you enjoy the experience of seeing who would win? Did you feel your heart race as the runners approached the finish line? Researchers have demonstrated that eustress—the experience of excitement and anxiety—is often an important motivation for people to watch, for example, sporting events (Cohen & Avrahami, 2005; Hu & Tang, 2010). If a team or competitor you favor ultimately- loses, you may experience some distress. However, along the way, you probably have a more positive emotional experience when competitions stimulate eustress. Search your life for other circumstances in which the experience of stressful events gives you pleasure. Here's one more example: Why do you feel happy while you're riding a roller coaster?

For some types of stressful events, it might be hard to anticipate how any positive effects could emerge. However, research has demonstrated that people can experience positive outcomes and personal growth from deeply negative events. One type of research focuses on *benefit finding*—people's ability to identify positive aspects of negative life events (Helgeson et al., 2006; Littlewood et al., 2008). Consider a study of adolescents diagnosed with diabetes.

Researchers are also trying to determine how different coping resources interact to affect responses to stressors. Let's consider a study that examined both perceived control and social support.

The 70 participants in the study all had been diagnosed with colorectal cancer (Dagan et al., 2011). Three months after their diagnosis, the participants completed a scale to indicate their perceptions of personal control over the events in their lives. The participants also completed a scale on which they reported the extent to which their spouses engaged in supportive behaviors (such as providing a context to share feelings) and unsupportive behaviors (such as making disapproving remarks). Six months later, the participants specified the extent of their psychological distress. The researchers looked for relationships between personal control, social support, and participants' distress. Participants who were low on personal control reported less distress if they had good social support and more distress if they had poor social support. However, participants who were relatively high on personal control reported low levels of distress irrespective of the behavior of their spouses.

These results suggest that people who believe they can control their own lives are less likely to look toward others as a coping resource. For that reason, they are less affected by the quality of the available social support.

However, even people with high personal control are likely to discover circumstances in which social support proves valuable. Being part of an effective social support network means that you believe others will be there for you if you need them—even if you don't actually ask for their help when you

A team of researchers recruited 252 adolescents (ages 10 to 14) who had been diagnosed with Type 1 diabetes. The adolescents completed a measure of benefit finding that allowed them to list personally relevant benefits. The adolescents provided a number of benefits: They suggested, for example, that diabetes had made them "feel more independent," had "brought [their] family a lot closer," and had made them "able to accept change easily" (Tran et al., 2011, p. 214). The adolescents also provided information about other aspects of their experience of diabetes, including how effectively they believed they were able to cope with stressful disease-related events and how closely they were able to adhere to their treatment regimens. The researchers found that adolescents who were able to find more benefits were also better able to cope with stressful events and keep up with their treatments.

288

The researchers suggested that benefit finding has the potential to act as a stress buffer: By engaging in benefit finding, people are able to keep negative emotions from overwhelming their coping responses to a disease.

People also may experience *posttraumatic growth*—positive psychological change—in response to serious illnesses, accidents, natural disasters, and other traumatic events. Post-traumatic growth occurs in five domains (Cryder et al., 2006; Tedeschi & Calhoun, 2004):

* New possibilities: "I have new things that I like to do."
* Relating to others: "I feel closer to other people than I did before."
* Personal strength: "I learned I can count on myself."
* Appreciation of life: "I learned that life is important."
* Spiritual change: "I understand religious ideas more."

Not everyone who experiences trauma will experience post-traumatic growth. For example, one study focused on a group of 7- to 10-year-old children affected by Hurricane Katrina in New Orleans (Kilmer & Gil-Rivas, 2010). The children who experienced the most posttraumatic growth were the ones whose thoughts turned frequently back to the original traumatic events. This was true even when the thoughts were distressing. Children focused on the events to try to understand what had happened and make sense of those events.

At many points in this discussion of stress, I have noted the effect of stress on physical or psychological well-being. Let's now turn directly to the ways in which psychologists apply their research knowledge to issues of illness and health.

Stop *and* Review

① What are the three stages of the general adaptation syndrome?
② How did life-change unit estimates change from the 1960s to the 1990s?
③ How do daily hassles and daily pleasures affect well-being?
④ What does it mean to engage in emotion-focused coping?
⑤ Why is perceived control important in the context of coping?
⑥ What is meant by benefit finding?

CRITICAL THINKING Recall the study that demon-strated the value of stress inoculation training. Why might the training have been effective as part of the school curriculum?

✓•⌐**Study** and **Review** on **MyPsychLab**

HEALTH PSYCHOLOGY

How much do your psychological processes contribute to your experiences of illness and wellness? You have already seen ex-amples that suggest that the right answer may be "quite a bit."

This acknowledgment of the importance of psychological and social factors in health has spurred the growth of a new field, health psychology. **Health psychology** is the branch of psy-chology devoted to understanding the way people stay healthy, the reasons they become ill, and the way they respond when they do get ill. **Health** refers to the general condition of the body and mind in terms of soundness and vigor. It is not sim-ply the absence of illness or injury, but is more a matter of how well all the body's component parts are working together. The discussion of health psychology will begin with a discussion of how the field's underlying philosophy departs from a tradi-tional Western medical model of illness. We then consider the contributions of health psychology to the prevention and treat-ment of illness and dysfunction. 👁

The Biopsychosocial Model of Health

Health psychology is guided by a *biopsychosocial model* of health. We can find the roots of this perspective in many non-Western cultures. To arrive at a definition of the biopsycho-social model, this section starts with a description of some of these non-Western traditions.

Traditional Health Practices Psychological principles have been applied in the treatment of illness and the pursuit of health for all of recorded time. Many cultures understand the importance of communal health and relaxation rituals in the enhancement of the quality of life. Among the Navajo, for example, disease, illness, and well-being have been attributed to social harmony and mind–body interactions. The Navajo concept of **hozho** (pronounced *whoa-zo*) means harmony, peace of mind, goodness, ideal family relationships, beauty in arts and crafts, and health of body and spirit. Illness is seen as the outcome of any *disharmony,* caused by evil introduced through violation of taboos, witchcraft, overindulgence, or bad dreams. Traditional healing ceremonies seek to banish illness and restore health, not only through the medicine of the sha-man but also through the combined efforts of all family mem-bers, who work together with the ill person to reachieve a state of hozho. The illness of any member of a tribe is seen not as his or her individual responsibility (and fault) but rather as a sign of broader disharmony that must be repaired by communal healing ceremonies. This cultural orientation guarantees that a powerful social support network will automatically come to the aid of the sufferer.

Toward a Biopsychosocial Model You have just seen that healing practices in non-Western cultures often assumed a link between the body and the mind. By contrast, modern

....

👁 Watch the Video *The Big Picture: Health Psychology* on MyPsychLab

health psychology The field of psychology devoted to understanding the ways people stay healthy, the reasons they become ill, and the ways they respond when they become ill.

health A general condition of soundness and vigor of body and mind; not simply the absence of illness or injury.

hozho A Navajo concept referring to harmony, peace of mind, goodness, ideal family relationships, beauty in arts and crafts, and health of body and spirit.

The Navajo, like people in many other cultures around the world, place a high value on aesthetics, family harmony, and physical health. What do the Navajo people consider to be the origins of illness?

Western scientific thinking has relied almost exclusively on a *biomedical model* that has a dualistic conception of body and mind. According to this model, medicine treats the physical body as separate from the psyche; the mind is important only for emotions and beliefs and has little to do with the reality of the body. Over time, however, researchers have begun to document types of interactions that make the strict biomedical model unworkable. You have already seen some of the evidence: Good and bad life events can affect immune function; people are more or less resilient with respect to the negative consequences of stress; adequate social support can change the length of hospital stays. These realizations yield the three components of the **biopsychosocial model**. The *bio* acknowledges the reality of biological illness. The *psycho* and the *social* acknowledge the psychological and social components of health.

The biopsychosocial model links your physical health to your state of mind and the world around you. Health psychologists view health as a dynamic, multidimensional experience. Optimal health, or **wellness**, incorporates physical, intellectual, emotional, spiritual, social, and environmental aspects of your life. When you undertake an activity for the purpose of preventing disease or detecting it in the asymptomatic stage, you are exhibiting health behavior. The general goal of health psychology is to use psychological knowledge to promote wellness and positive health behaviors. Let's now consider theory and research relevant to this goal.

Health Promotion

Health promotion means developing general strategies and specific tactics to eliminate or reduce the risk that people will get sick. The prevention of illness in the 21st century poses a much different challenge than it did at the beginning of the 20th century. In 1900, the primary cause of death was infectious disease. Health practitioners at that time launched the first revolution in American public health. Over time, through the use of research, public education, the development of vaccines, and changes in public health standards (such as waste control and sewage), they were able to reduce substantially the deaths associated with such diseases as influenza, tuberculosis, polio, measles, and smallpox.

If researchers wish to contribute to the trend toward improved quality of life, they must attempt to decrease those deaths associated with lifestyle factors. Smoking, being overweight, eating foods high in fat and cholesterol, drinking too much alcohol, driving without seat belts, and leading stressful lives all play a role in heart disease, cancer, strokes, accidents, and suicide. Changing behaviors will prevent much illness and premature death. To show you how that works, we now consider a pair of concrete domains: smoking and AIDS. ◉

Smoking It would be impossible to imagine that anyone reading this chapter wouldn't know that smoking is extremely dangerous. In the United States, roughly 443,000 people die each year from smoking-related illnesses and 49,400 people die from exposure to secondhand smoke (Centers for Disease Control and Prevention, 2011). Even so, 58.7 million people in the United States still smoke cigarettes (Substance Abuse and Mental Health Services Administration, 2010). Health psychologists would like to understand both why people begin to smoke—so that the psychologists can help prevent it—and how to assist people in quitting—so they can reap the substantial benefits of becoming ex-smokers.

Analyses of why some people start smoking have focused on interactions of nature and nurture. Studies comparing monozygotic and dizygotic twins for the similarity of their tobacco use consistently find heritability estimates of 0.50 or higher (Munafò & Johnstone, 2008). Consider one study that examined the smoking behavior of 1,198 pairs of adolescent siblings (that is, identical twins, fraternal twins, and nontwin pairs) (Boardman et al., 2008). The researchers reported heritability estimates of 0.51 for whether individuals began to smoke and 0.58 for how much they smoked each day. The study also documented an impact of the environment. For example, when the adolescents attended schools in which

....

◉ **Watch** the **Video** *What's In It For Me?: The Challenge Of Quitting Bad Habits* on **MyPsychLab**

biopsychosocial model A model of health and illness that suggests links among the nervous system, the immune system, behavioral styles, cognitive processing, and environmental domains of health.

wellness Optimal health, incorporating the ability to function fully and actively over the physical, intellectual, emotional, spiritual, social, and environmental domains of health.

health promotion The development and implementation of general strategies and specific tactics to eliminate or reduce the risk that people will become ill.

the popular students were also smokers, genes mattered more: Apparently, in that social context, students could realize their "genetic potential."

To understand the link between genes and smoking, researchers have often focused on personality differences that predict which people will start smoking. One personality type that has been associated with the initiation of smoking is called *sensation seeking* (Zuckerman, 2007). Individuals characterized as sensation seeking are more likely to engage in risky activities. One study measured sensation seeking in several thousand U.S. adolescents, ages 10 to 14 (Sargent et al., 2010). To determine which of the adolescents had become smokers, the researchers contacted them 8, 16, and 24 months after sensation seeking was originally measured. High levels of sensation seeking were a strong predictor of which adolescents would begin smoking in that two-year follow-up period.

The best approach to smoking is never to start at all. But for those of you who have begun to smoke, what has research revealed about quitting? Although many people who try to quit have relapses, an estimated 35 million Americans have quit. Ninety percent have done so on their own, without professional treatment programs. Researchers have identified stages people pass through that represent increasing readiness to quit (Norman et al., 1998, 2000):

* *Precontemplation*. The smoker is not yet thinking about quitting.
* *Contemplation*. The smoker is thinking about quitting but has not yet undertaken any behavioral changes.
* *Preparation*. The smoker is getting ready to quit.
* *Action*. The smoker takes action toward quitting by setting behavioral goals.
* *Maintenance*. The smoker is now a nonsmoker and is trying to stay that way.

This analysis suggests that not all smokers are psychologically equivalent in terms of readiness to quit. Interventions can

Why should interventions recognize that not all smokers are the same with respect to their readiness to quit?

be designed that nudge smokers up the scale of readiness, until, finally, they are psychologically prepared to take healthy action (Velicer et al., 2007).

Successful smoking-cessation treatment requires that both smokers' physiological and psychological needs be met (Fiore et al., 2008). On the physiological side, smokers are best off learning an effective form of *nicotine replacement therapy*, such as nicotine patches or nicotine gum. On the psychological side, smokers must understand that there are huge numbers of ex-smokers and realize that it is possible to quit. Furthermore, smokers must learn strategies to cope with the strong temptations that accompany efforts to quit. Treatments often incorporate the types of cognitive coping techniques described earlier, which allow people to alleviate the effects of a wide range of stressors. For smoking, people are encouraged to find ways to avoid or escape from situations that may bring on a renewed urge to smoke.

AIDS AIDS is an acronym for *acquired immune deficiency syndrome*. Although hundreds of thousands are dying from this virulent disease, many more are now living with HIV infection. **HIV** *(human immunodeficiency virus)* is a virus that attacks the white blood cells (T lymphocytes) in human blood, thus damaging the immune system and weakening the body's ability to fight other diseases. The individual then becomes vulnerable to infection by a host of other viruses and bacteria that can cause such life-threatening illnesses as cancer, meningitis, and pneumonia. The period of time from initial infection with the virus until symptoms occur (incubation period) can be five years or longer. Although most of the estimated millions of those infected with the HIV virus do not have AIDS (a medical diagnosis), they must live with the continual stress that this life-threatening disease might suddenly emerge. At the present time, there are treatments that delay the onset of full-blown AIDS, but there is neither a cure for AIDS nor a vaccine to prevent its spread.

The HIV virus is not airborne; it requires direct access to the bloodstream to produce an infection. The HIV virus is generally passed from one person to another in one of two ways: (1) the exchange of semen or blood during sexual contact and (2) the sharing of intravenous needles and syringes used for injecting drugs. The virus has also been passed through blood transfusions and medical procedures in which infected blood or organs are unwittingly given to healthy people. Many people suffering from hemophilia have gotten AIDS in this way. However, everyone is at risk for AIDS.

The only way to protect oneself from being infected with the AIDS virus is to change those lifestyle habits that put one at risk. This means making permanent changes in patterns of sexual behavior and use of drug paraphernalia. Health psychologist **Thomas Coates** is part of a multidisciplinary research team that is using an array of psychological principles in a concerted effort to prevent the further spread of AIDS (Coates & Szekeres, 2004). The team is involved in many aspects of applied psychology, such as assessing psychosocial

AIDS Acronym for *acquired immune deficiency syndrome*, a syndrome caused by a virus that damages the immune system and weakens the body's ability to fight infection.

HIV Human immunodeficiency virus, a virus that attacks white blood cells (T lymphocytes) in human blood, thereby weakening the functioning of the immune system; HIV causes AIDS.

Critical Thinking in Your Life

CAN HEALTH PSYCHOLOGY HELP YOU GET MORE EXERCISE?

An important goal of health psychology is to increase the likelihood that people will engage in behaviors that are good for their health. High on that list is exercise: People who get enough exercise generally experience better health. The U.S. government makes these recommendations (U.S. Department of Health and Human Services, 2008, p. vii):

- "For substantial health benefits, adults should do at least 150 minutes (2 hours and 30 minutes) a week of moderate-intensity, or 75 minutes (1 hour and 15 minutes) a week of vigorous-intensity aerobic physical activity, or an equivalent combination of moderate- and vigorous-intensity aerobic activity. Aerobic activity should be performed in episodes of at least 10 minutes, and preferably, it should be spread throughout the week."

- "Adults should also do muscle-strengthening activities that are moderate or high intensity and involve all major muscle groups on 2 or more days a week, as these activities provide additional health benefits."

The activities in these recommendations lead to increased fitness of the heart and respiratory systems, improvement of muscle tone and strength, and many other health benefits. So, how can research in health psychology help people reap these benefits?

Researchers have tried to determine what programs or strategies are most effective in getting people to start and continue exercising (Nigg et al., 2008). In fact, much the same model that describes people's readiness to *quit* smoking applies to people's readiness to *begin* exercising (Buckworth et al., 2007). In the *precontemplation* stage, an individual is still more

focused on the barriers to exercise (for example, too little time) rather than the benefits (for example, improves appearance). As the individual moves through the *contemplation* and *preparation* stages, the emphasis shifts from barriers to benefits. People who have been exercising for less than six months are in the *action* stage; those who have exercised regularly for over six months are in the *maintenance* stage.

If you do not exercise regularly now, how can you get beyond precontemplation? Research suggests that individuals can learn strategies that allow them to overcome obstacles to exercise (Scholz et al., 2008). One strategy is to formulate *action plans:* You should create specific plans about when, where, and how you foresee becoming physically active. Another strategy is to formulate *coping plans:* You should anticipate what obstacles might arise to interfere with your action plans and determine how best to cope with those obstacles. In one study, researchers taught patients with coronary heart disease how to formulate these types of plans (Sniehotta et al., 2006). Two months later, patients who combined both types of planning had engaged in considerably more physical activity than patients in the control group (who did not receive the training).

Studies of this sort indicate why you can treat exercise like any other situation in which you can use cognitive appraisal to work toward goals for healthy living.

- Why might the same stages apply to undertaking healthy behaviors and overcoming unhealthy behaviors?

- Why is it stressful to contemplate healthy behaviors such as regular exercise?

risk factors, developing behavioral interventions, training community leaders to be effective in educating people toward healthier patterns of sexual and drug behavior, assisting with the design of media advertisements and community information campaigns, and systematically evaluating changes in relevant attitudes, values, and behaviors (Fernández-Dávila et al., 2008; Hendriksen et al., 2007). Successful AIDS interventions require three components (Starace et al., 2006):

- *Information.* People must be provided with knowledge about how AIDS is transmitted and how its transmission may be prevented; they should be counseled to practice safer sex (for example, use condoms during sexual contact) and use sterile needles.
- *Motivation.* People must be motivated to practice AIDS prevention.
- *Behavioral skills.* People must be taught how to put the knowledge to use.

Why are all three of these components necessary? People might be highly motivated but uninformed, or vice versa. They may have both sufficient knowledge and sufficient motivation but lack requisite skills. In addition, information must be delivered in a fashion that does not undermine people's motivation. For example, people were more likely to participate in HIV-prevention counseling when information was framed so that the participants felt in control of their own behavior (Albarracín et al., 2008).

Treatment

Treatment focuses on helping people adjust to their illnesses and recover from them. This section will look at three aspects of treatment. First, we consider the role of psychologists in encouraging patients to adhere to the regimens prescribed by health-care practitioners. Next, we look at techniques that allow people to explicitly use psychological techniques to take control over the body's responses. Finally, we examine instances in which the mind can contribute to the body's cure.

Patient Adherence   Patients are often given a *treatment regimen*. This might include medications, dietary changes, prescribed periods of bed rest and exercise, and follow-up procedures such as return checkups, rehabilitation training, and chemotherapy. Failing to adhere to treatment regimens is one of the most serious problems in health care (Christensen & Johnson, 2002; Quittner et al., 2008). The rate of patient nonadherence is estimated to be as high as 50 percent for some treatment regimens.

What factors affect the likelihood that patients will adhere to prescribed treatments? One type of research has focused on the relationship between patients' perceptions of the severity of their disease. As you might expect, people who perceive greater threat from a disease also show greater likelihood to adhere to treatments (DiMatteo et al., 2007). However, the relationship becomes more complicated when researchers consider patients' objective health (rather, that is, than patients' subjective perceptions). Patients who face serious diseases that leave them in poor physical health show lower levels of adherence than patients who are less debilitated by the same diseases. This lack of adherence may reflect growing pessimism about the likelihood that the treatment will succeed. A second type of research has demonstrated the importance of social support for patient adherence (DiMatteo, 2004). Patients obtain the greatest benefits when they receive practical support that allows them to accomplish their regimens correctly.

Research has shown that health-care professionals can take steps to improve patient adherence. Consider a study that demonstrated the importance of a match between patients' and physicians' attitudes.

Featured Study

A team of researchers recruited 224 patients and the 18 physicians who had provided them with medical care (Christensen et al., 2010). Both the patients and the physicians completed a questionnaire that assessed their attitudes about the role patients play in their own health outcomes. Patients responded to statements such as "I am in control of my own health" and "When I get sick it is my own behavior which determines how soon I get well again." The physicians responded to a version of the questionnaire that focused on the patients (for example, "Patients are in control of their own health."). To assess the patients' adherence with their treatment regimens, the researchers obtained medication refill information from pharmacy records. The results indicated that patients were more likely to adhere when their attitudes matched their physicians' attitudes.

To understand this result, imagine what might happen when, for example, a patient who believes she is in control of her own health faces a physician who believes otherwise. That mismatch is likely to undermine the patient's trust in her physician. The researchers suggest that physicians should try to understand their patients' attitudes—and modify their behaviors to match those attitudes.

Harnessing the Mind to Heal the Body   More and more often, the treatments to which patients must adhere involve a psychological component. Many investigators now believe that psychological strategies can improve well-being. For example, many people react to stress with tension, resulting in tight muscles and high blood pressure. Fortunately, many tension responses can be controlled by psychological techniques, such as *relaxation* and *biofeedback*.

Relaxation through meditation has ancient roots in many parts of the world. In Eastern cultures, ways to calm the mind and still the body's tensions have been practiced for centuries. Today, Zen discipline and yoga exercises from Japan and India are part of daily life for many people both there and, increasingly, in the West. Growing evidence suggests that complete relaxation is a potent antistress response (Samuelson et al., 2010). The **relaxation response** is a condition in which muscle tension, cortical activity, heart rate, and blood pressure all decrease and breathing slows (Benson, 2000). There is reduced electrical activity in the brain, and input to the central nervous system from the outside environment is lowered. In this low level of arousal, recuperation from stress can take place. Four conditions are regarded as necessary to produce the relaxation response: (1) a quiet environment, (2) closed eyes, (3) a comfortable position, and (4) a repetitive mental device such as the chanting of a brief phrase over and over again. The first three conditions lower input to the nervous system, and the fourth lowers its internal stimulation. ◉▶

Biofeedback is a self-regulatory technique used for a variety of special applications, such as control of blood pressure, relaxation of forehead muscles (involved in tension headaches), and even diminishment of extreme blushing. As pioneered by psychologist **Neal Miller** (1978), biofeedback is a procedure that makes an individual aware of ordinarily weak or internal responses by providing clear external signals. The patient is allowed to "see" his or her own bodily reactions, which are monitored and amplified by equipment that transforms them into lights and sound cues of varying intensity. The patient's task is then to control the level of these external cues.

Let's consider one application of biofeedback. Participants who suffered from either high or low blood pressure were brought into a laboratory (Rau et al., 2003). Feedback from equipment measuring an index of the participants' blood pressure on each heart cycle was delivered to a computer screen so that growing green bars indicated changes in the right direction and growing red bars indicated changes in the wrong direction. In addition, the researchers provided verbal reinforcement: "You did it the right way!" After three training sessions, the participants were able to raise or lower their blood pressure, as

....

◉▶ Simulate the Experiment *Stress and Health* on **MyPsychLab**

relaxation response A condition in which muscle tension, cortical activity, heart rate, and blood pressure decrease and breathing slows.

biofeedback A self-regulatory technique by which an individual acquires voluntary control over nonconscious biological processes.

© Novarc Images/Alamy

Why does relaxation through meditation have health benefits?

flu, you'd like your body to produce abundant antibodies. Those antibodies will lower the probability that you'll get sick. However, people who report more stress in their lives have less antibody response (Pedersen et al., 2009). Thus, for people who experience high levels of stress, vaccinations may be less likely to protect them from illness.

Let's consider another basic function of your immune system, to heal small wounds in your skin. In one study, a research team led by **Janet Kiecolt-Glaser** gave 13 caretakers for relatives with Alzheimer's disease and 13 control participants standardized small wounds to their skin. On average, the Alzheimer's caretakers, who experience chronic stress, took nine days longer for their wounds to heal (Kiecolt-Glaser et al., 1995)! People can also experience chronic stress as a consequence of their own personalities—with similar implications for immune function. For example, individuals who reported having difficulty controlling their anger generally took more days to heal the same type of standardized wounds than individuals with better anger control (Gouin et al., 2008). You can see from these data how small differences in stress level may affect the speed with which a person's body can heal even the smallest scratch or scrape. From that basic insight, you can understand why research suggests that stress responses play an even more profound role with respect to the progression of serious medical conditions such as infectious diseases and cancer. Researchers wish to understand how the mind affects immune function so they can harness that power to slow these serious illnesses.

Psychological Impact on Health Outcomes One last note on treatment. Have you ever had a secret too shameful to tell anyone? If so, talking about the secret could very well improve your health. That is the conclusion from a large body of research by health psychologist **James Pennebaker** (1990, 1997; Petrie et al., 1998), who has shown that suppressing thoughts and feelings associated with personal traumas, failures, and guilty or shameful experiences takes a devastating toll on mental and physical health. Such inhibition is psychologically hard work and, over time, it undermines the body's defenses against illness. The experience of letting go often is followed by improved physical and psychological health weeks and months later. Consider the effects of emotional disclosure on health outcomes for people with HIV infection.

desired. If you ever become concerned about your blood pressure or other physical disorders, results of this sort might encourage you to seek a course of biofeedback to complement a drug regimen.

Psychoneuroimmunology In the early 1980s, researchers made a series of discoveries that confirmed another way in which the mind affects the body: Psychological states can have an impact on immune function. Historically, scientists had assumed that immunological reactions—rapid production of antibodies to counterattack substances that invade and damage the organism—were automatic biological processes that occurred without any involvement of the central nervous system. However, using certain types of conditioning experiments, **Robert Ader** and **Nicholas Cohen** (1981) demonstrated that immune function can be modified by psychological states. Their research gave rise to a new field of study, **psychoneuroimmunology,** which explores interactions of psychological states, the nervous system, and the immune system (Ader & Cohen, 1993; Coe, 1999).

Research over the past 40 years has confirmed that stressors—and how people cope with them—have a consistent impact on the ability of the immune system to function effectively. For example, when you get a vaccination for the

Thirty-seven adults with HIV infection participated in this study. Roughly half of the patients were assigned to an emotional writing group. In four 30-minute sessions on consecutive days, participants wrote about "the most traumatic and emotional experiences of their lives" (Petrie et al., 2004, p. 273). The control group spent the same amount of time on a neutral task, writing accounts, for example, about what they had done in the previous day. To assess the impact of emotional writing, the researchers measured HIV viral load—the number of HIV copies in a milliliter of blood. **Figure 11** *displays the dramatic impact of emotional writing. Those participants who had engaged in emotional writing had consistently lower viral loads two weeks, three months, and six months after the writing sessions.*

psychoneuroimmunology The research area that investigates interactions between psychological processes, such as responses to stress, and the functions of the immune system.

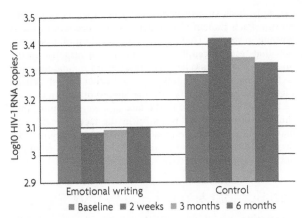

FIGURE 11 The Impact of Emotional Writing on HIV Infection

Participants engaged in four sessions of either emotional or neutral writing. Their HIV viral load was assessed two weeks, three months, and six months after the writing sessions. Participants who had engaged in emotional writing had consistently lower viral loads.

Data from figure "Viral Load" in "Effect of written emotional expression on immune function in patients with human immunodeficiency virus infection: A randomized trial" by Keith J. Petrie, Iris Fontanilla, Mark G. Thomas, Roger J. Booth, and James W. Pennebaker, *Psychosomatic Medicine 66*(2), March 2004.

This result is consistent with other data indicating that an individual's stress level has an impact on the course of HIV infection. Emotional writing helped participants cope with some negative psychological consequences of the infection.

Personality and Health

Do you know a person like this: someone who is driven to succeed, no matter what obstacles; someone whose high school class voted him or her "most likely to have a heart attack before age 20"? Are you that person? As you've observed the way in which some people charge through life while others take a more relaxed pace, you may have wondered whether these different personalities affect health. Research in health psychology strongly suggests that the answer is yes (Deary et al., 2010b). 👁

In the 1950s, Meyer Friedman and Ray Rosenman reported what had been suspected since ancient times: There was a relationship between a constellation of personality traits and the probability of illness, specifically coronary heart disease (Friedman & Rosenman, 1974). These researchers identified two behavior patterns that they labeled Type A and Type B. The **Type A behavior pattern** is a complex pattern of behavior and emotions that includes being excessively competitive, aggressive, impatient, time urgent, and hostile. Type A people are often dissatisfied with some central aspect of their lives and have an intense drive for achievement. The **Type B behavior pattern** is everything Type A is not—individuals are less competitive, less hostile, and so on. Importantly, these behavior patterns have an impact on health. In their original discussion, Friedman and Rosenman reported that people who showed

Type A behavior patterns were stricken with coronary heart disease considerably more often than individuals in the general population.

Because the Type A behavior pattern has many components, researchers have focused their attention on identifying the specific Type A elements that most often put people at risk. A personality trait that has emerged most forcefully as "toxic" is hostility (Chida & Steptoe, 2009).

Featured Study

A longitudinal study began in 1986, with 774 men in the sample who were free of any evidence of cardiovascular disease (Niaura et al., 2002). In 1986, each participant's level of hostility was measured (using a set of questions from the Minnesota Multiphasic Personality Inventory). Hostility is defined as the consistency with which individuals look at the world and other people in a cynical and negative manner. To display the relationship between hostility and coronary heart disease, the researchers divided the hostility scores into percentile groups. As shown in **Figure 12**, *those individuals whose hostility scores were in the upper 20 percent had a dramatically larger number of episodes of incident coronary heart disease in the subsequent years. In this sample of men, hostility was a better predictor of future illness than several behavioral risk factors, such as smoking and drinking.*

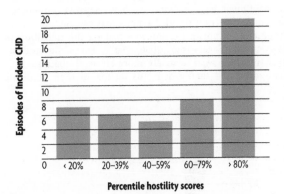

FIGURE 12 Hostility Predicts Coronary Heart Disease

Study participants were divided into percentile groups based on their self-reports of hostility. Men whose scores placed them in the top 20 percent on the measure (that is, the group greater than 80 percent) had the highest levels of coronary heart disease.

Data from Suzanne C. Segerstrom, "Stress, energy and immunity: An Ecological view," *Current directions in Psychological Science*, December 1, 2007, © 2007 by the Association for Psychological Science

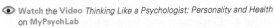 Watch the Video *Thinking Like a Psychologist: Personality and Health* on MyPsychLab

Type A behavior pattern A complex pattern of behaviors and emotions that includes excessive emphasis on competition, aggression, impatience, and hostility; hostility increases the risk of coronary heart disease.

Type B behavior pattern As compared to Type A behavior pattern, a less competitive, less aggressive, less hostile pattern of behavior and emotion.

Hostility may affect health for both physiological reasons—by leading to chronic overarousal of the body's stress responses—and psychological reasons—by leading hostile people to practice poor health habits and avoid social support (Smith & Ruiz, 2002).

The good news is that researchers have begun to implement behavioral treatments to reduce hostility and other aspects of the Type A behavior pattern (Pischke et al., 2008). For example, one intervention focused on African American students in ninth grade (Wright et al., 2011). African Americans are at greater risk than other ethnic groups for heart disease; differences in blood pressure begin to emerge in childhood. These facts provided the motivation for a team of researchers to design an intervention using mindfulness-based stress reduction. The students learned to pay attention to their breathing and to passively observe their thoughts. After three months of training, the students who self-reported lower levels of hostility also had lower blood pressure than at the study's outset. Do you recognize yourself in the definition of hostility? If you do, protect your health by seeking out this type of intervention.

To round out this section on personality and health let's turn to the concept of *optimism*. Optimistic individuals attribute failures to external causes and to events that were unstable or modifiable. This style of coping has a strong impact on the optimist's well-being (Carver et al., 2010). The particular impact depends on the difficulty of the stressor (Segerstrom, 2005). Because optimists believe they can prevail over stressors, they tend to engage them head on. When the stressor is difficult, this strategy of continued engagement may have negative physiological consequences. Consider a study that assessed the health impact of optimism for students making the transition to law school (Segerstrom, 2006, 2007). For some students this transition was relatively more stressful—because they had social and family demands on top of their academic

demands. Each student completed a test that measured optimism. Each student also underwent a procedure to assess immune response. They received an injection of a preparation that tests susceptibility to mumps. In response to the injection, the skin swells. The measure of immune response is the amount of swelling, or *induration*. As shown in **Figure 13**, those students with the highest optimism showed better immune response in the face of lower demands; they showed worse immune response in the face of higher demands. These data suggest that optimists must recognize that there are some stressors for which the best style of coping is not to engage them directly.

Job Burnout and the Health-Care System

One final focus of health psychology is to make recommendations about the design of the health-care system. Researchers, for example, have examined the stress associated with being a health-care provider. Even the most enthusiastic health-care providers run up against the emotional stresses of working intensely with large numbers of people suffering from a variety of personal, physical, and social problems.

The special type of emotional stress experienced by these professional health and welfare practitioners has been termed *burnout* by **Christina Maslach,** a leading researcher on this widespread problem. **Job burnout** is a syndrome of emotional exhaustion, depersonalization, and reduced personal accomplishment that is often experienced by workers in professions that demand high-intensity interpersonal contact with patients, clients, or the public. Health practitioners begin to lose their caring and concern for patients and may come to treat them in detached and even dehumanized ways. They feel bad about themselves and worry that they are failures. Burnout is correlated with greater absenteeism and turnover, impaired job performance, poor relations with coworkers, family problems, and poor personal health (Maslach & Leiter, 2008).

Job burnout in today's workforce is reaching ever higher levels because of the effects of organizational downsizing, job restructuring, and greater concerns for profits than for employee morale and loyalty. Burnout, then, is not merely a concern of workers and health caregivers, but it also reveals organizational dysfunction that needs to be corrected by reexamining goals, values, workloads, and reward structures (Leiter & Maslach, 2005).

What recommendations can be made? Several social and situational factors affect the occurrence and level of burnout and, by implication, suggest ways of preventing or minimizing it (Leiter & Maslach, 2005; Prosser et al., 1997). For example, the quality of the patient–practitioner interaction is greatly influenced by the number of patients for whom a practitioner is providing care—the greater the number, the greater the cognitive, sensory, and emotional overload. Another factor in the quality of that interaction is the amount of direct contact with patients. Longer work hours in continuous direct contact with patients are correlated with greater burnout. This is especially

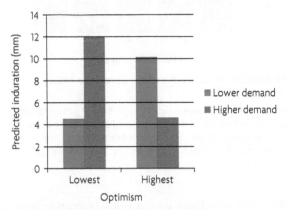

FIGURE 13 Optimism and Immune Function

Students with the highest levels of optimism showed better immune response in the face of lower demands. However, they showed worse immune response in the face of higher demands.

Data from Suzanne C. Segerstrom, "Stress, energy and immunity: An Ecological view," *Current directions in Psychological Science*, December 1, 2007, © 2007 by the Association for Psychological Science.

....

job burnout The syndrome of emotional exhaustion, depersonalization, and reduced personal accomplishment, often experienced by workers in high-stress jobs.

Why are health-care providers particularly prone to job burnout?

true when the nature of the contact is difficult and upsetting, such as contact with patients who are dying (Jackson et al., 2008). The emotional strain of such prolonged contact can be eased by a number of means. For example, practitioners can modify their work schedules to withdraw temporarily from such high-stress situations. They can use teams rather than only individual contact. They can arrange opportunities to get positive feedback for their efforts.

A Toast to Your Health

It's time for some final advice. Instead of waiting for stress or illness to come and then reacting to it, set goals and structure your life in ways that are most likely to forge a healthy foundation. The following nine steps to greater happiness and better mental health are presented as guidelines to encourage you to take a more active role in your own life and to create a more positive psychological environment for yourself and others. Think of the steps as *year-round resolutions.*

1. Never say bad things about yourself. Look for sources of your unhappiness in elements that can be modified by future actions. Give yourself and others only *constructive criticism*—what can be done differently next time to get what you want?
2. Compare your reactions, thoughts, and feelings with those of friends, coworkers, family members, and others so that you can gauge the appropriateness and relevance of your responses against a suitable social norm.
3. Have several close friends with whom you can share feelings, joys, and worries. Work at developing, maintaining, and expanding your social support networks.
4. Develop a sense of *balanced time perspective* in which you can flexibly focus on the demands of the task, the situation, and your needs; be future-oriented when there is work to be done, present-oriented when the goal is achieved and pleasure is at hand, and past-oriented to keep you in touch with your roots.
5. Always take full credit for your successes and happiness (and share your positive feelings with other people). Keep an inventory of all the qualities that make you special and unique—those qualities you can offer others. For example,

a shy person can provide a talkative person with the gift of attentive listening. Know your sources of personal strength and available coping resources.
6. When you feel you are losing control over your emotions, distance yourself from the situation by physically leaving it, role-playing the position of another person in the situation or conflict, projecting your imagination into the future to gain perspective on what seems an overwhelming problem now, or talking to a sympathetic listener. Allow yourself to feel and express your emotions.
7. Remember that failure and disappointment are sometimes blessings in disguise. They may tell you that your goals are not right for you or may save you from bigger letdowns later on. Learn from every failure. Acknowledge setbacks by saying, "I made a mistake," and move on. Every accident, misfortune, or violation of your expectations is potentially a wonderful opportunity in disguise.
8. If you discover you cannot help yourself or another person in distress, seek the counsel of a trained specialist in your student health department or community. In some cases, a problem that appears to be psychological may really be physical, and vice versa. Check out your student mental health services before you need them and use them without concern about being stigmatized.
9. Cultivate healthy pleasures. Take time out to relax, to meditate, to get a massage, to fly a kite, and to enjoy hobbies and activities you can do alone and that help you get in touch with and better appreciate yourself.

So how are you feeling? If the stressors in your life have the potential to put you in a bad mood, try to use cognitive reappraisal to minimize their impact. If you are feeling ill, try to use your mind's healing capacity to speed your way back toward health. Never underestimate the power of these different types of "feelings" to exercise control over your life. Harness that power!

Stop *and* Review

① What has research revealed about the genetics of smoking?
② What are the three components of successful AIDS interventions?
③ What conditions are necessary to produce the relaxation response?
④ What is the central goal for researchers who study psychoneuroimmunology?
⑤ What is the "toxic" aspect of Type A personalities?
⑥ How is job burnout defined?

CRITICAL THINKING Consider the study that examined the health impact of emotional disclosure. Why did the researchers ask participants in the control group to write texts?

✓●─Study and Review on MyPsychLab

Recapping Main Points

Emotions

- Emotions are complex patterns of changes made up of physiological arousal, cognitive appraisal, and behavioral and expressive reactions.
- As a product of evolution, all humans may share a basic set of emotional responses.
- Cultures, however, vary in their rules of appropriateness for displaying emotions.
- Classic theories emphasize different parts of emotional response, such as peripheral bodily reactions or central neural processes.
- More contemporary theories emphasize the appraisal of arousal.
- Moods and emotions affect information processing and memory.
- Subjective well-being is influenced by both genetics and life experiences.

Stress of Living

- Stress can arise from negative or positive events. At the root of most stress are change and the need to adapt to environmental, biological, physical, and social demands.
- Physiological stress reactions are regulated by the hypothalamus and a complex interaction of the hormonal and nervous systems.
- Depending on the type of stressor and its effect over time, stress can be a mild disruption or lead to health-threatening reactions.
- Cognitive appraisal is a primary moderator variable of stress.
- Coping strategies either focus on problems (taking direct actions) or attempt to regulate emotions (indirect or avoidant).

- Cognitive reappraisal and restructuring can be used to cope with stress.
- Social support is also a significant stress moderator, as long as it is appropriate to the circumstances.
- Stress can lead to positive changes such as posttraumatic growth.

Health Psychology

- Health psychology is devoted to treatment and prevention of illness.
- The biopsychosocial model of health and illness looks at the connections among physical, emotional, and environmental factors in illness.
- Illness prevention focuses on lifestyle factors such as smoking and AIDS-risk behaviors.
- Psychological factors influence immune function.
- Psychosocial treatment of illness adds another dimension to patient treatment.
- Individuals who are characterized by Type A (especially hostile), Type B, and optimistic behavior patterns will experience different likelihoods of illness.
- Health-care providers are at risk for burnout, which can be minimized by appropriate situational changes in their helping environment.

Answers for Figure 1

1. happiness
2. surprise
3. anger
4. disgust
5. fear
6. sadness
7. contempt

KEY TERMS

acute stress
AIDS
anticipatory coping
biofeedback
biopsychosocial model
Cannon–Bard theory of emotion
chronic stress
cognitive appraisal theory of emotion
coping
emotion
emotion regulation
fight-or-flight response
general adaptation syndrome (GAS)

health
health promotion
health psychology
HIV
hozho
James–Lange theory of emotion
job burnout
life-change unit (LCU)
perceived control
positive psychology
posttraumatic stress disorder (PTSD)
psychoneuroimmunology
psychosomatic disorder

relaxation response
social support
stress
stress moderator variable
stressor
subjective well-being
tend-and-befriend response
two-factor theory of emotion
Type A behavior pattern
Type B behavior pattern
wellness

• Practice Test

✓•—Study and Review on MyPsychLab

1. Which statement is true of moods, but not emotions?
   a. They may last several days.
   b. They can be either positive or negative.
   c. They may arise from specific events.
   d. They are relatively intense.

2. Which of these facial expressions is *not* among the seven universally recognized expressions of emotion?
   a. concern   c. disgust
   b. contempt   d. happiness

3. The _____ prepares the body for physiological aspects of emotional responses.
   a. hypothalamus
   b. amygdala
   c. autonomous nervous system
   d. hippocampus

4. According to the _____ theory of emotion, you feel after your body reacts.
   a. Cannon–Bard   c. James–Lange
   b. cognitive appraisal d. approach-related

5. Your friend Yasumasa just found out he did better than expected on a calculus exam. An experimenter asks you to predict how happy Yasumasa is feeling. The experimenter also asks Yasumasa the same question. It would probably be the case that your rating would be _____ Yasumas's rating.
   a. equal to   c. higher than
   b. lower than   d. much lower than

6. The brain structure that plays an important role in the fight-or-flight response is the
   a. pituitary gland.   c. hypothalamus.
   b. amygdala.   d. thyroid gland.

7. If you are faced by _____ stressors, the type of coping that is likely to be most useful is _____ coping.
   a. uncontrollable; problem-directed
   b. controllable; emotion-focused
   c. controllable; delay-based
   d. uncontrollable; emotion-focused

8. When May was diagnosed with skin cancer, Al searched the Web to help her learn more about treatment options. This type of social support is _____ support.
   a. tangible   c. emotional
   b. informational   d. inoculation

9. A few months after surviving a tornado, Judy says, "I am grateful for every new day." It sounds like Judy experienced posttraumatic growth in which domain?
   a. spiritual change   c. appreciation of life
   b. relating to others d. personal strength

10. Consider the stages people pass through as they attempt to quit smoking. Which of these pairs is in the wrong order?
   a. preparation; contemplation
   b. contemplation; action
   c. action; maintenance
   d. preparation; maintenance

11. Marsea is participating in a laboratory study. Every time her blood pressure goes up, she sees a "sad face" on a computer display. It seems that Marsea is learning how to use
   a. the relaxation response.   c. anticipatory coping.
   b. biofeedback.   d. stress inoculation.

12. Researchers gave caretakers of Alzheimer's patients and control individuals standardized wounds. What was the result of the study?
   a. The wounds of the Alzheimer's caretakers took longer to heal.
   b. The wounds of the control individuals took longer to heal.
   c. There was no difference in the time it took the wounds to heal.
   d. The wounds of the control individuals were larger.

13. The aspect of the _____ behavior pattern that has the greatest impact on health is _____.
   a. Type B; hostility   c. Type B; pessimism
   b. Type A; optimism   d. Type A; hostility

14. Which of these features is *not* part of the definition of job burnout?
   a. depersonalization
   b. disharmony
   c. emotional exhaustion
   d. reduced personal accomplishment

15. Evanthia is using coping strategies to increase her level of physical activities. Which of these sounds most like a coping plan?
   a. "I will do sit-ups every day before I eat breakfast."
   b. "I will learn how to use an elliptical trainer."
   c. "I will join a gym."
   d. "I will read my textbook while I'm on the treadmill."

ESSAY QUESTIONS

1. What evidence suggests that some emotional responses are innate while others are not?

2. Why does perceived control have an impact on people's ability to cope with stress?

3. What factors affect the likelihood that patients will adhere to treatment regimens?

Stop and Review Answers

Stop and Review (Emotions)

1. Cross-cultural research suggests there are seven facial expressions that people generally recognize around the world.
2. The autonomous nervous system plays an important role to bring about the physiological aspects of emotions—such as a racing heart and sweaty palms.
3. The Cannon–Bard theory suggests that an emotion stimulus produces concurrently arousal and an emotional feeling.
4. People in negative moods tend to process information in a more detailed and effortful fashion than people in positive moods.
5. Research suggests that good social relationships are the single most important source of happiness.

Stop and Review (Stress and Living)

1. The three stages of the GAS are the alarm reaction, resistance, and exhaustion.
2. Participants in the 1990s reported more life-change units, suggesting that they were generally experiencing more stress than people in the 1960s.
3. In general, daily hassles have a negative impact on well-being, and daily pleasures have a positive impact.
4. When people engage in emotion-focused coping, they engage in activities that make them feel better but do not directly change the stressor.

5. When people do not believe they have control over a stressful situation, they are at risk for poor physical and psychological adjustment.
6. People are able to identify positive changes that arise from negative life events.

Stop and Review (Health Psychology)

1. Research comparing MZ and DZ twins for the similarity of their tobacco use indicates that there is a genetic component to people's smoking behaviors.
2. Successful AIDS interventions must provide information, instill motivation, and teach behavioral skills.
3. To produce the relaxation response, people must find a quiet environment in which they can rest in a comfortable position with their eyes closed and use a repetitive mental device.
4. Researchers who study psychoneuroimmunology seek to understand how psychological states have an impact on the immune system.
5. The aspect of Type A personality that puts people at risk for illness is hostility.
6. Job burnout is a state of emotional exhaustion, depersonalization, and reduced sense of personal accomplishment.

Practice Test Answers

1. a	**5.** c	**9.** c	**13.** d
2. a	**6.** c	**10.** a	**14.** b
3. c	**7.** d	**11.** b	**15.** d
4. c	**8.** b	**12.** a	

References

Ader, R., & Cohen, N. (1981). Conditioned immunopharmacological responses. In R. Ader (Ed.), *Psychoneuroimmunology* (pp. 281–319). New York: Academic Press.

Ader, R., & Cohen, N. (1993). Psychoneuroimmunology: Conditioning and stress. *Annual Review of Psychology, 44,* 53–85.

Albarracín, D., Durantini, M. R., Earl, A., Gunnoe, J. B., & Leeper, J. (2008). Beyond the most willing audiences: A meta-intervention to increase exposure to HIV-prevention programs by vulnerable populations. *Health Psychology, 27,* 638–644.

Baas, M., De Creu, C. K. W., & Nijstad, B. A. (2008). A meta-analysis of 25 years of mood-creativity research: Hedonic tone, activation, or regulatory focus? *Psychological Bulletin, 134,* 779–806.

Bárez, M., Blasco, T., Fernández-Castro, J., & Viladrich, C. (2007). A structural model of the relationships between perceived control and the adaptation to illness in women with breast cancer. *Journal of Psychosocial Oncology, 25,* 21–43.

Benson, H. (2000). *The relaxation response* (Updated ed.). New York: HarperCollins.

Biehl, M., Matsumoto, D., Ekman, P., Hearn, V., Heider, K., Kudoh, T., & Ton, V. (1997). Matsumoto and Ekman's Japanese and Caucasian facial expressions of emotion (JACFEE): Reliability data and cross-national differences. *Journal of Nonverbal Behavior, 21,* 3–21.

Billings, A. G., & Moos, R. H. (1982). Family environments and adaptation: A clinically applicable typology. *American Journal of Family Therapy, 20,* 26–38.

Biss, R. K., & Hasher, L. (2011). Delighted and distracted: Positive affect increases priming for irrelevant information. *Emotion, 11,* 1474–1478.

Boardman, J. D., Saint Onge, J. M., Haberstick, B. C., Timberlake, D. S., & Hewitt, J. K. (2008). Do schools moderate the genetic determinants of smoking? *Behavioral Genetics, 38,* 234–246.

Bonanno, G. A., Pat-Horenczyk, R., & Noll, J. (2011). Coping flexibility and trauma: The perceived ability to cope with trauma (PACT) scale. *Psychological Trauma: Theory, Research, Practice, and Policy, 3,* 117–129.

Bornstein, M. H., & Arterberry, M. E. (2003). Recognition, discrimination and categorization of smiling by 5-month-old infants. *Developmental Science, 6,* 585–599.

Buckworth, J., Lee, R. E., Regan, G., Schneider, L. K., & DiClemente, C. C. (2007). Decomposing intrinsic and extrinsic motivation for exercise: Application to stages of motivational readiness. *Psychology of Sport and Exercise, 8,* 441–461.

Camras, L A., & Shutter, J. M. (2010). Emotional facial expressions in infancy. *Emotion Review, 2,* 120–129.

Camras, L. A., Oster, H., Bakeman, R., Meng, Z., Ujiie, T., & Campos, J. L. (2007). Do infants show distinct negative facial expressions for fear and anger? Emotional expression in 11-month-old European American, Chinese, and Japanese infants. *Infancy, 11,* 131–155.

Canli, T., Desmond, J. E., Zhao, Z., Glover, G., & Gabrieli, J. D. E. (1998). Hemispheric asymmetry for emotional stimuli detected with fMRI. *NeuroReport, 9,* 3233–3239.

Cannon, W. B. (1927). The James–Lange theory of emotion: A critical examination and an alternative theory. *American Journal of Psychology, 39,* 106–124.

Cannon, W. B. (1929). *Bodily changes in pain, hunger, fear, and rage* (2nd ed.). New York: Appleton-Century-Crofts.

Carver, C. S., Scheier, M. F., & Segerstrom, S. C. (2010). Optimism. *Clinical Psychology Review, 30,* 879–889.

Centers for Disease Control and Prevention (2011). *Tobacco-related mortality.* Retrieved from www.cdc.gov/tobacco/data_statistics/fact_sheets/health_effects/tobacco_related_mortality.

Chida, Y., & Steptoe, A. (2009). The association of anger and hostility with future coronary heart disease. *Journal of the American College of Cardiology, 53,* 936–946.

Christensen, A. J., Howren, M. B., Hillis, S. L., Kaboli, P., Carter, B. L., Cvengros, J. A., Wallston, K. A., & Rosenthal, G. E. (2010). Patient and physician beliefs about control over health: Association of symmetrical beliefs with medication regimen. *Journal of General Internal Medicine, 25,* 397–402.

Christensen, A. J., & Johnson, J. A. (2002). Patient adherence with medical treatment regimens: An interactive approach. *Current Directions in Psychological Science, 11,* 94–97.

Clore, G. L., & Huntsinger, J. R. (2007). How emotions inform judgment and regulate thought. *Trends in Cognitive Sciences, 11,* 393–399.

Coates, T. J., & Szekeres, G. (2004). A plan for the next generation of HIV prevention research: Seven key policy investigative challenges. *American Psychologist, 59,* 747–757.

Coe, C. L. (1999). Psychosocial factors and psychoneuroimmunology within a lifespan perspective. In D. P. Keating & C. Hertzman (Eds.), *Developmental health and the wealth of nations: Social, biological, and educational dynamics* (pp. 201–219). New York: Guilford Press.

Cohen, A., & Avrahami, A. (2005). Soccer fans' motivation as a predictor of participation in soccer-related activities: An empirical examination in Israel. *Social Behavior and Personality, 33,* 419–434.

Cryder, C. H., Kilmer, R. P., Tedeschi, R. G., & Calhoun, L. G. (2006). An exploratory study of posttraumatic growth in children following a natural disaster. *American Journal of Orthopsychiatry, 76,* 65–69.

Dagan, M., Sanderman, R., Schokker, M. C., Wiggers, T., Baas, P. C., van Haastert, M., & Hagedoorn, M. (2011). Spousal support and changes in distress over time in couples coping with cancer: The role of personal control. *Journal of Family Psychology, 25,* 31–318.

Dailey, M. N., Joyce, C., Lyons, M. J., Kamachi, M., Ishi, H., Gyoba, J., Cottrell, G. W. (2010). Evidence and a computational explanation of cultural differences in facial expression recognition. *Emotion, 10,* 874–893.

Danese, A., Moffitt, T. E., Harrington, H., Milne, B. J., Polanczyk, G., Pariante, C. M., Poulton, R., & Caspi, A. (2009). Adverse childhood experiences and adult risk factors for age-related disease. *Archives of Pediatric & Adolescent Medicine, 163,* 1135–1143.

Darwin, C. (1965). *The expression of emotions in man and animals.* Chicago: University of Chicago Press. (Original work published 1872)

Davidson, R. J., Jackson D.C., & Kalin, N. H. (2000). Emotion, plasticity, context, and regulation: Perspectives for affective neuroscience. *Psychological Bulletin, 126,* 890–909.

de Ridder, D., Geenen, R., Kuijer, R., & van Middendorp, H. (2008). Psychological adjustment to chronic disease. *The Lancet, 372,* 246–255.

Deary, I. J., Weiss, A., & Batty, G. D. (2010b). Intelligence, personality, and health outcomes. *Psychological Science in the Public Interest, 11,* 53–79.

Diener, E., Ng, W., Harter, J., & Arora, R. (2010). Wealth and happiness across the world: Material prosperity predicts life evaluation, whereas psychological prosperity predicts positive feeling. *Journal of Personality and Social Psychology, 99,* 52–61.

DiGrande, L., Neria, Y., Brackbill, R. M., Pulliam, P., & Galea, S. (2011). Long-term posttraumatic stress symptoms among 3,271 civilian survivors of the September 11, 2001, terrorist attacks on the World Trade Center. *American Journal of Epidemiology, 173,* 271–281.

DiMatteo, M. R., Haskard, K. B., & Williams, S. L. (2007). Health beliefs, disease severity, and patient adherence: A meta-analysis. *Medical Care, 45,* 521–528.

Dirkzwager, A. J. E., Bramsen, I., & van der Ploeg, H. M. (2003). Social support, coping, life events, and posttraumatic stress symptoms among former peacekeepers: A prospective study. *Personality and Individual Differences, 34,* 1545–1559.

DSM-IV. (1994). *Diagnostic and statistical manual of mental disorders* (4th ed.). Washington, DC: American Psychiatric Association.

Dutton, D. G., & Aron, A. P. (1974). Some evidence for heightened sexual attraction under conditions of high anxiety. *Journal of Personality and Social Psychology, 30,* 510–517.

Ekman, P. (1984). Expression and the nature of emotion. In K. R. Scherer & P. Ekman (Eds.), *Approaches to emotion.* Hillsdale, NJ: Erlbaum.

Ekman, P. (1994). Strong evidence for universals in facial expressions: A reply to Russell's mistaken critique. *Psychological Bulletin, 115,* 268–287.

Ekman, P., & Friesen, W. V. (1971). Constants across cultures in the face and emotion. *Journal of Personality and Social Psychology, 17,* 124–129.

Ekman, P., & Friesen, W. V. (1986). A new pan-cultural facial expression of emotion. *Motivation and Emotion, 10,* 159–168.

Elfenbein, H. A., Beaupre, M., Levesque, M., & Hess, U. (2007). Toward a dialect theory: Cultural differences in the expression and recognition of posed facial expressions. *Emotion, 7,* 131–146.

Endler, N. S., Macrodimitris, S. D., & Kocovski, N. L. (2000). Controllability in cognitive and interpersonal tasks: Is control good for you? *Personality & Individual Differences, 29,* 951–962.

Fawcett, J. M., Russell, E. M., Peace, K. A., & Christie, J. (2012). Of guns and geese: A meta-analytic review of the "weapon focus" literature. *Psychology, Crime & Law,* in press.

Fernández-Dávila, P., Salazar, X., Cáceres, C. F., Maiorana, A., Kegeles, S., Coates, T. J., & Martinez, J. (2008). Compensated sex and sexual risk: Sexual, social and economic interactions between homosexually- and heterosexually-identified men of low income in two cities of Peru. *Sexualities, 11,* 352–374.

Fiore, M. C., Jaén, C. R., & Baker, T. B. (2008). *Treating tobacco use and dependence: 2008 update.* Rockville, MD: U.S. Department of Health and Human Services. Public Health Service.

Foa, E. B., & Riggs, D. S. (1995). Posttraumatic stress disorder following assault: Theoretical considerations and empirical findings. *Current Directions in Psychological Science, 4,* 61–65.

Folkman, S. (1984). Personal control and stress and coping processes: A theoretical analysis. *Journal of Personality and Social Psychology, 46,* 839–852.

Forgas, J. P. (2008). Affect and cognition. *Perspectives on Psychological Science, 3,* 94–101.

Friedman, B. H. (2010). Feelings and the body: The Jamesian perspective on autonomic specificity of emotion. *Biological Psychology, 84,* 383–393.

Friedman, M., & Rosenman, R. F. (1974). *Type A behavior and your heart*. New York: Knopf.

Gouin, J.-P., Kiecolt-Glaser, J. K., Malarkey, W. B., & Glaser, R. (2008). The influence of anger expression on wound healing. *Brain, Behavior, and Immunity, 22*, 699–708.

Gyurak, A., Gross, J. J., & Etkin, A. (2011). Explicit and implicit emotion regulation: A dual-process framework. *Cognition and Emotion, 25*, 400–412.

Helgeson, V. S., Reynolds, K. A., & Tomich, P. L. (2006). A meta-analytic review of benefit finding and growth. *Journal of Consulting and Clinical Psychology, 74*, 797–816.

Hendriksen, E. S., Pettifor, A., Lee, S.-J., Coates, T. J., & Rees, H. V. (2007). Predictors of condom use among young adults in South Africa: The reproductive health and HIV research unit national youth survey. *American Journal of Public Health, 97*, 1241–1248.

Herbers, J. E., Cutuli, J. J., Lafavor, T. L., Vrieze, D., Leibel, C., Obradović, J., & Masten, A. S. (2011). Direct and indirect effects of parenting on academic functioning of young homeless children. *Early Education and Development, 22*, 77–104.

Hobara, M. (2005). Beliefs about appropriate pain behavior: Cross-cultural and sex differences between Japanese and Euro-Americans. *European Journal of Pain, 9*, 389–393.

Holmes, T. H., & Rahe, R. H. (1967). The social readjustment rating scale. *Journal of Psychosomatic Research, 11*(2), 213–218.

Howell, R. T., & Howell, C. J. (2008). The relation of economic status to subjective well-being in developing countries: A meta-analysis. *Psychological Bulletin, 134*, 536–560.

Hu, A. W.-L., & Tang, L.-R. (2010). Factors motivating sports broadcast viewership with fan identification as a mediator. *Social Behavior and Personality, 38*, 681–690.

Irvine, J. T. (1990). Registering affect: Heteroglossia in the linguistic expression of emotion. In C. A. Lutz & L. Abu-Lughod (Eds.), *Language and the politics of emotions* (pp. 126–161). Cambridge, UK: Cambridge University Press.

Izard, C. E. (1993). Four systems for emotion activation: Cognitive and noncognitive processes. *Psychological Review, 100*, 68–90.

Izard, C. E. (1994). Innate and universal facial expressions: Evidence from developmental and cross-cultural research. *Psychological Bulletin, 115*, 288–299.

Jack, R. E., Blais, C., Scheepers, C., Schyns, P. G., & Caldara, R. (2009). Cultural confusions show that facial expressions are not universal. *Current Biology, 19*, 1543–1548.

Jack, R.E., Caldara, R. & Schyns, P.G. (2012). Internal representations reveal cultural diversity in expectations of facial expressions of emotion. *Journal of Experimental Psychology: General*, in press.

Jackson, V. A., Mack, J., Matsuyama, R., Lakoma, M. D., Sullivan A. M., Arnold, R. M., Weeks, J. C., & Block, S. D. (2008). A qualitative study of oncologists' approaches to end-of-life care. *Journal of Palliative Medicine, 11*, 893–906.

James, W. (1950). *The principles of psychology* (2 vols.). New York: Holt, Rinehart & Wilson. (Original work published 1890)

Kermer, D. A., Driver-Linn, E., Wilson, T. D., & Gilbert, D. T. (2006). Loss aversion is an affective forecasting error. *Psychological Science, 17*, 649–653.

Kesebir, P., & Diener, E. (2008). In pursuit of happiness: Empirical answers to philosophical questions. *Perspectives on Psychological Science, 3*, 117–125.

Kiecolt-Glaser, J. K., Marucha, P. T., Malarkey, P. T., Mercado, A. M., & Glaser, R. (1995). Slowing of wound healing by psychological stress. *Lancet, 346*, 1194–1196.

Kilmer, R. P., & Gil-Rivas, V. (2010). Exploring posttraumatic growth in children impacted by Hurricane Katrina: Correlates of the phenomenon and developmental considerations. *Child Development, 81*, 1211–1227.

Kim, H. S., Sherman, D. K., & Taylor, S. E. (2008). Culture and social support. *American Psychologist, 63*, 518–526.

Kim, M. J., Loucks, R. A., Palmer, A. L., Brown, A. C., Solomon, K. M., Marchante, A. N., & Whalen, P. J. (2011). The structural and functional complexity of the amygdala: From normal emotion to pathological anxiety. *Behavioural Brain Research, 223*, 403–410.

Kobiella, A., Grossmann, T., Reid, V. M., & Striano, T. (2008). The discrimination of angry and fearful facial expressions in 7-month-old infants: An event-related potential study. *Cognition and Emotion, 22*, 133–146.

Krohne, H. W., & Slangen, K. E. (2005). Influence of social support on adaptation to surgery. *Health Psychology, 24*, 101–105.

Kuppens, P., Realo, A., & Diener, E. (2008). The role of positive and negative emotions in life satisfaction judgment across nations. *Journal of Personality and Social Psychology, 95*, 66–75.

Lay, C. H. (1986). At last my research article on procrastination. *Journal of Research in Personality, 20*, 474–495.

Lazarus, R. S. (1981, July). Little hassles can be hazardous to your health. *Psychology Today*, pp. 58–62.

Lazarus, R. S. (1984a). On the primacy of cognition. *American Psychologist, 39*, 124–129.

Lazarus, R. S. (1984b). Puzzles in the study of daily hassles. *Journal of Behavioral Medicine, 7*, 375–389.

Lazarus, R. S. (1991). Cognition and motivation in emotion. *American Psychologist, 46*, 352–367.

Lazarus, R. S. (1993). From psychological stress to the emotions: A history of changing outlooks. *Annual Review of Psychology, 44*, 1–21.

Lazarus, R. S. (1995). Vexing research problems inherent in cognitive-mediational theories of emotion—and some solutions. *Psychological Inquiry, 6*, 183–196.

Lazarus, R. S., & Folkman, S. (1984). *Stress, appraisal, and coping*. New York: Springer.

Lazarus, R. S., & Lazarus, B. N. (1994). *Passion and reason: Making sense of our emotions*. New York: Oxford University Press.

Lea, V. (2004). Mĕbengokre ritual wailing and flagellation: A performative outlet for emotional self-expression. *Indiana, 21*, 113–125.

Leiter, M. P., & Maslach, C. (2005). *Banishing burnout: Six strategies for improving your relationship with work*. San Francisco: Jossey-Bass.

Levenson, R. W., Ekman, P., Heider, K., & Friesen, W. V. (1992). Emotion and autonomic nervous system activity in the Minangkabau of West Sumatra. *Journal of Personality and Social Psychology, 62*, 972–988.

Lietzén, R., Virtanen, P., Kivimäki, M., Sillanmäki, L., Vahtera, J., & Koskenvuo, M. (2011). Stressful life events and the onset of asthma. *European Respiratory Journal, 37*, 1360–1365.

Littlewood, R. A., Venable, P. A., Carey, M. P., & Blair D. C. (2008). The association of benefit finding to psychosocial and health behavior adaptation among HIV1 men and women. *Journal of Behavioral Medicine, 31*, 145–155.

Lucas, R. E. (2007). Adaptation and the set-point model of subjective well-being: Does happiness change after major life events? *Current Directions in Psychological Science, 16*, 75–79.

Lynch, D. J., McGrady, A., Alvarez, E., & Forman, J. (2005). Recent life changes and medical utilization in an academic family practice. *The Journal of Nervous and Mental Disease, 193*, 633–635.

Lyubomirsky, S., King, L., & Diener, E. (2005). The benefits of frequent positive affect: Does happiness lead to success? *Psychological Bulletin, 131*, 803–855.

Marshall, G. D., & Zimbardo, P. G. (1979). Affective consequences of inadequately explained physiological arousal. *Journal of Personality and Social Psychology, 37*, 970–988.

Maslach, C. (1979). Negative emotional biasing of unexplained arousal. *Journal of Personality and Social Psychology, 37*, 953–969.

Maslach, C., & Leiter, M. (2008). Early predictors of job burnout and engagement. *Journal of Applied Psychology, 93*, 498–512.

Masten, A. S. (2011). Resilience in children threatened by extreme adversity: Frameworks for research, practice, and translational synergy. *Development and Psychopathology*, 23, 493–506.

Mather, M., & Sutherland, M. R. (2011). Arousal-based competition in perception and memory. *Perspectives on Psychological Science*, 6, 114–133.

Maxwell, J. S., & Davidson, R. J. (2007). Emotion as motion: Asymmetries in approach and avoidant actions. *Psychological Science*, 18, 1113–1119.

McCrae, R. R., Scally, M., Terracciano, A., Abecasis, G. R., & Costa, P. T., Jr. (2010). An alternative to the search for single polymorphisms: Toward molecular personality scales for the five-factor model. *Journal of Personality and Social Psychology*, 99, 1014–1024.

Meichenbaum, D. (1977). *Cognitive-behavior modification: An integrative approach.* New York: Plenum.

Meichenbaum, D. (1985). *Stress inoculation training.* New York: Pergamon Press.

Meichenbaum, D. (1993). Changing conceptions of cognitive behavior modification: Retrospect and prospect. *Journal of Consulting and Clinical Psychology*, 61, 202–204.

Mesquita, B., & Leu, J. (2007). The cultural psychology of emotion. In S. Kitayama & D. Cohen (Eds.), *Handbook of cultural psychology* (pp. 734–759). New York: Guilford Press.

Miller, N. E. (1978). Biofeedback and visceral learning. *Annual Review of Psychology*, 29, 373–404.

Morris, T., Moore, M., & Morris, F. (2011). Stress and chronic illness: The case of diabetes. *Journal of Adult Development*, 18, 70–80.

Munafò, M. R., & Johnstone, E. C. (2008). Genes and cigarette smoking. *Addiction*, 103, 893–904.

Nes, R. B., Røysamb, E., Tambs, K., Harris, J. R., & Reichborn-Kjennerud, T. (2006). Subjective well-being: Genetic and environmental contributions to stability and change. *Psychological Medicine*, 36, 1033–1042.

Nigg, C. R., Borrelli, B., Maddock, J., & Dishman, R. K. (2008). A theory of physical activity maintenance. *Applied Psychology: An International Review*, 57, 544–560.

Niaura, R., Todaro, J. F., Stroud, L., Spiro, A., III, Ward, K. D., & Weiss, S. (2002). Hostility, the metabolic syndrome, and incident coronary heart disease. *Health Psychology*, 21, 588–593.

Norman, G. J., Velicer, W. F., Fava, J. L., & Prochaska, J. O. (1998). Dynamic topology clustering within the stages of change for smoking cessation. *Addictive Behaviors*, 23, 139–153.

Norman, G. J., Velicer, W. F., Fava, J. L., & Prochaska, J. O. (2000). Cluster subtypes within stage of change in a representative sample of smokers. *Addictive Behaviors*, 25, 183–204.

Pedersen, A. F., Zachariae, R., & Bovbjerg, D. H. (2009). Psychological stress and antibody response to influenza vaccination: A meta-analysis. *Brain, Behavior, and Immunity*, 23, 427–433.

Pennebaker, J. W. (1990). *Opening up: The healing power of confiding in others.* New York: Morrow.

Pennebaker, J. W. (1997). Writing about emotional experiences as a therapeutic process. *Psychological Science*, 8, 162–166.

Petrie, K. J., Booth, R. J., & Pennebaker, J. W. (1998). The immunological effects of thought suppression. *Journal of Personality and Social Psychology*, 75, 1264–1272.

Petrie, K. J., Fontanilla, I., Thomas, M. G., Booth, R. J., & Pennebaker, J. W. (2004). Effect of written emotional expression on immune function in patients with human immunodeficiency virus infection: A randomized trial. *Psychosomatic Medicine*, 66, 272–275.

Pickel, K. L. (2009). The weapon focus effect on memory for female versus male perpetrators. *Memory*, 17, 664–678.

Prosser, D., Johnson, S., Kuipers, E., Szmukler, G., Bebbington, P., & Thornicroft, G. (1997). Perceived sources of work stress and satisfaction among hospital and community mental health staff, and their relation to mental health, burnout, and job satisfaction. *Journal of Psychosomatic Research*, 43, 51–59.

Quittner, A. L., Modi, A., Lemanek, K. L., Ievers-Landis, C. E., & Rapoff, M. A. (2008). Evidence-based assessment of adherence to medical treatments in pediatric psychology. *Journal of Pediatric Psychology*, 33, 916–936.

Rau, H., Bührer, M., & Wietkunat, R. (2003). Biofeedback of R-wave-to-pulse interval normalizes blood pressure. *Applied Psychophysiology and Biofeedback*, 28, 37–46.

Reynolds, J. S., & Perrin, N. A. (2004). Mismatches in social support and psychosocial adjustment. *Health Psychology*, 23, 425–430.

Roussi, P. (2002). Discriminative facility in perceptions of control and its relation to psychological distress. *Anxiety, Stress, & Coping: An International Journal*, 15, 179–191.

Roussi, P., Krikeli, V., Hatzidimitriou, C., & Koutri, I. (2007). Patterns of coping, flexibility in coping and psychological distress in women diagnosed with breast cancer. *Cognitive Therapy and Research*, 31, 97–109.

Samuelson, M., Foret, M., Baim, M., Lerner, J., Fricchione, G., Benson, H., Dusek, J., & Yeung, A. (2010). Exploring the effectiveness of a comprehensive mind–body intervention for medical symptom relief. *The Journal of Alternative and Complementary Medicine*, 16, 187–192.

Santiago, C. D., Wadsworth, M. E., & Stump, J. (2011). Socioeconomic status, neighborhood disadvantage, and poverty-related stress: Prospective effects on psychological syndromes among diverse low-income families. *Journal of Economic Psychology*, 32, 218–230.

Sargent, J. D., Tanski, S., Stoolmiller, M., & Hanewinkel, R. (2010). Using sensation seeking to target adolescents for substance use interventions. *Addiction*, 105, 506–514.

Schachter, S. (1971a). *Emotion, obesity and crime.* New York: Academic Press.

Scholz, U., Schüz, B., Ziegelmann, J., Lippke, S., & Schwarzer, R. (2008). Beyond behavioural intentions: Planning mediates between intentions and physical activity. *British Journal of Health Psychology*, 13, 479–494.

Segerstrom, S. C. (2005). Optimism and immunity: Do positive thoughts always lead to positive effects? *Brain, Behavior, and Immunity*, 19, 195–200.

Segerstrom, S. C. (2006). How does optimism suppress immunity? Evaluation of three affective pathways. *Health Psychology*, 25, 653–657.

Segerstrom, S. C. (2007). Stress, energy, and immunity. *Current Directions in Psychological Science*, 16, 326–330.

Seligman, M. E. P., Steen, T. A., Park, N., & Peterson, C. (2005). Positive psychology progress: Empirical validation of interventions. *American Psychologist*, 60, 410–421.

Selye, H. (1976a). *Stress in health and disease.* Reading, MA: Butterworth.

Selye, H. (1976b). *The stress of life* (2nd ed.). New York: McGraw-Hill.

Sevdalis, N., & Harvey, N. (2007). Biased forecasting of postdecisional affect. *Psychological Science*, 18, 678–681.

Smith, T. W., & Ruiz, J. M. (2002). Psychosocial influences on the development and course of coronary heart disease: Current status and implications for research and practice. *Journal of Consulting and Clinical Psychology*, 70, 548–568.

Sniehotta, F. F., Scholz, U., & Schwarzer, R. (2006). Action plans and coping plans for physical exercise: A longitudinal study in cardiac rehabilitation. *British Journal of Health Psychology*, 11, 23–37.

Starace, F., Massa, A., Amico, K. R., & Fisher, J. D. (2006). Adherence to antiretroviral therapy: An empirical test of the information-motivation-behavioral skills model. *Health Psychology*, 25, 153–162.

Sternthal, M. J., Slopen, N., & Williams, D. R. (2011). Racial disparities in health: How much does stress really matter? *Du Bois Review*, 8, 95–113.

Stewart, D. E., & Yuen, T. (2011). A systematic review of resilience in the physically ill. *Psychosomatics*, 52, 199–209.

Substance Abuse and Mental Health Service Administration (SAMHSA). (2010). *Results from the 2009 national survey on drug use and health: Volume I. Summary of national findings.* Available at www.oas.samhsa.gov/.

Tay, L., & Diener, E. (2011). Needs and subjective well-being around the world. *Journal of Personality and Social Psychology, 101,* 354–365.

Taylor, S. E. (2006). Tend and befriend: Biobehavioral bases of affiliation under stress. *Current Directions in Psychological Science, 15,* 273–277.

Taylor, S. E., Klein, L. C., Lewis, B. P., Gruenewald, T. L., Gurung, R. A. R., & Updegraff, J. A. (2000). Biobehavioral responses to stress in females: Tend-and-befriend, not fight-or-flight. *Psychological Review, 107,* 411–429.

Tedeschi, R. G., & Calhoun, L. G. (2004). Posttraumatic growth: Conceptual foundations and empirical evidence. *Psychological Inquiry, 15,* 1–18.

Tice, D. M., & Baumeister, R. F. (1997). Longitudinal study of procrastination, performance, stress, and health: The costs and benefits of dawdling. *Psychological Science, 8,* 454–458.

Tomkins, S. (1962). *Affect, imagery, consciousness* (Vol. 1). New York: Springer.

Tomkins, S. (1981). The quest for primary motives: Biography and autobiography of an idea. *Journal of Personality and Social Psychology, 41,* 306–329.

Tran, V., Wiebe, D. J., Fortenberry, K. T., Butler, J. M., & Berg, C. A. (2011). Benefit finding, affective reactions to diabetes stress, and diabetes management among early adolescents. *Health Psychology, 30,* 212–219.

Ullman, S. E., Filipas, H. H., Townsend, S. M., & Starzynski, L. L. (2007). Psychosocial correlates of PTSD symptom severity in sexual assault survivors. *Journal of Traumatic Stress, 20,* 821–831.

Velicer, W. F., Redding, C. A., Sun, X., & Prochaska, J. O. (2007). Demographic variables, smoking variables, and outcome across five studies. *Health Psychology, 26,* 278–287.

Weiss, A., Bates, T. C., & Luciano, M. (2008). Happiness is a personal(ity) thing: The genetics of personality and well-being in a representative sample. *Psychological Science, 19,* 205–210.

Wolmer, L., Hamiel, D., & Laor, N. (2011). Preventing children's stress after disaster with teacher-based intervention: A controlled study. *Journal of the Academy of Child & Adolescent Psychiatry, 50,* 340–348.

Wright, A. A., Katz, J. S., Magnotti, J., Elmore, L. C., Babb, S., & Alwin, S. (2010). Testing pigeon memory in a change detection task. *Psychonomic Bulletin & Review, 17,* 243–249.

Wright, L. B., Gregoski, M. J., Tingen, M. S., Barnes, V. A., & Treiber, F. A. (2011). Impact of stress reduction interventions on hostility and ambulatory systolic blood pressure in African American adolescents. *Journal of Black Psychology, 37,* 210–233.

Zajonc, R. B. (2000). Feeling and thinking: Closing the debate over the independence of affect. In J. P. Forgas (Ed.), *Feeling and thinking: The role of affect in social cognition* (pp. 31–58). New York: Cambridge University Press.

Zajonc, R. B. (2001). Mere exposure: A gateway to the subliminal. *Current Directions in Psychological Science, 10,* 224–228.

Zuckerman, M. (2007). *Sensation seeking and risky behavior.* Washington, DC: American Psychological Association.

Therapies for Psychological Disorders

From Chapter 15 of *Psychology and Life*, 20th Edition. Richard J. Gerrig. Copyright © 2013 by Pearson Education, Inc. All rights reserved.

Therapies for Psychological Disorders

Grantpix/Photo Researchers, Inc.

It can be overwhelming to think about all of the ways in which individuals can experience mental illness. Fortunately, psychologists and other providers of mental health care have worked intently to create therapies that address the full range of psychopathology. You will see in this chapter that researchers continue to generate innovations in therapeutic techniques. The more researchers learn about the causes and consequences of psychopathology, the better they are able to fine-tune their repertory of therapies.

This chapter examines the types of therapies that can help restore personal control to individuals with a range of disorders. It surveys the major types of treatments currently used by health-care providers: psychoanalysis, behavior modification, cognitive alteration, humanistic therapies, and drug therapies. We will consider the way these treatments work and assess claims about the likelihood of their success. 👁

As you read this chapter, bear in mind that many people who seek help from therapists haven't been diagnosed with a psychological disorder. There may be times in your life when you can use some help dealing with a variety of psychological stressors. The importance of having a flexible repertory of coping skills cannot be underestimated. Therapists can help you develop strategies for coping with life circumstances that are causing you distress.

THE THERAPEUTIC CONTEXT

There are different types of therapies for mental disorders, and there are many reasons some people seek help (and others who need it do not). The purposes or goals of therapy, the settings in which therapy occurs, and the kinds of therapeutic helpers also vary. Despite any differences between therapies, however, all are *interventions* into a person's life, designed to change the person's functioning in some way.

Goals and Major Therapies

The therapeutic process can involve four primary tasks or goals:

1. Reaching a *diagnosis* about what is wrong, possibly determining an appropriate psychiatric *(DSM-IV-TR)* label for the presenting problem, and classifying the disorder.
2. Proposing a probable *etiology* (cause of the problem)— that is, identifying the probable origins of the disorder and the functions being served by the symptoms.
3. Making a *prognosis*, or estimate, of the course the problem will take with and without any treatment.
4. Prescribing and carrying out some form of *treatment*, a therapy designed to minimize or eliminate the troublesome symptoms and, perhaps, their sources.

Biomedical therapies focus on changing the mechanisms that run the central nervous system. Practiced largely by psychiatrists and physicians, these therapies try to alter brain functioning with chemical or physical interventions, including surgery, electric shock, and drugs that act directly on the brain–body connection.

Psychological therapies, which are collectively called **psychotherapy,** focus on changing the faulty behaviors people have learned: the words, thoughts, interpretations, and feedback that direct daily strategies for living. These therapies are practiced by clinical psychologists as well as by psychiatrists. There are four major types of psychotherapies: psychodynamic, behavioral, cognitive, and existential-humanistic.

The *psychodynamic* approach views suffering as the outer symptom of inner, unresolved traumas and conflicts. Psychodynamic therapists treat mental disorder with a "talking cure," in which a therapist helps a person develop insights about the relation between the overt symptoms and the unresolved hidden conflicts that presumably caused them.

Behavior therapy treats the behaviors themselves as disturbances that must be modified. Disorders are viewed as learned behavior patterns rather than as the symptoms of mental disease. Behaviors are transformed in many ways, including changing reinforcement contingencies for desirable and undesirable responding, extinguishing conditioned responses, and providing models of effective problem solving.

Cognitive therapy tries to restructure the way a person thinks by altering the often distorted self-statements a person makes about the causes of a problem. Restructuring cognitions changes the way a person defines and explains difficulties, often enabling the person to cope with the problems.

Therapies that have emerged from the *humanistic tradition* emphasize the patients' values. They are directed toward self-actualization, psychological growth, the development of more meaningful interpersonal relationships, and the enhancement of freedom of choice. They tend to focus more on improving the functioning of essentially healthy people than on correcting the symptoms of seriously disturbed individuals.

Although I have introduced each type of psychotherapy separately, it is important to note that many psychotherapists take an *integrative* approach to practice: They integrate different theoretical approaches to provide maximum benefit to their patients or clients. In many cases, psychotherapists begin their careers adhering to a particular theoretical orientation. However, as their careers unfold, they begin to mix together the most effective elements of different therapies (Norcross et al., 2005; Thoma & Cecero, 2009). Psychotherapists integrate across virtually every pair of orientations (for example, cognitive and humanistic; behavioral and psychodynamic). However, the most prominent integrative therapies combine aspects of the cognitive and behavioral approaches (Goldfried, 2003; Norcross et al., 2005). Later, the chapter describes integrative cognitive behavioral therapies. 👁

Therapists and Therapeutic Settings

When psychological problems arise, most people initially seek out informal counselors who operate in familiar settings. Many

👁 **Watch the Video** *The Basics, Part 1: Living With Disorder* on MyPsychLab

👁 **Watch the Video** *The Basics, Part 2: Therapies in Action* on MyPsychLab

biomedical therapy Treatment for a psychological disorder that alters brain functioning with chemical or physical interventions such as drug therapy, surgery, or electroconvulsive therapy.

psychotherapy Any of a group of therapies, used to treat psychological disorders, that focus on changing faulty behaviors, thoughts, perceptions, and emotions that may be associated with specific disorders.

Why do many psychotherapists integrate different theoretical approaches in their clinical practices?

people turn to family members, close friends, personal physicians, lawyers, or favorite teachers for support, guidance, and counsel. Those with religious affiliations may seek help from a clergy member. Others get advice and a chance to talk by opening up to bartenders, salesclerks, cabdrivers, or other people willing to listen. In our society, these informal therapists carry the bulk of the daily burden of relieving frustration and conflict. When problems are limited in scope, informal therapists can often help.

Although more people seek out therapy now than in the past, people usually turn to trained mental health professionals only when their psychological problems become severe or persist for extended periods of time. When they do, they can turn to several types of therapists.

A **clinical social worker** is a mental health professional whose specialized training in a school of social work prepares him or her to work in collaboration with psychiatrists and clinical psychologists. Unlike many psychiatrists and psychologists, these counselors are trained to consider the social contexts of people's problems, so these practitioners may also involve other family members in the therapy or at least become acquainted with clients' homes or work settings.

A **pastoral counselor** is a member of a religious group who specializes in the treatment of psychological disorders. Often, these counselors combine spirituality with practical problem solving.

A **clinical psychologist** is required to have concentrated his or her graduate school training in the assessment and treatment of psychological problems, completed a supervised internship in a clinical setting, and earned a PhD or PsyD.

These psychologists tend to have a broader background in psychology, assessment, and research than do psychiatrists.

A **counseling psychologist** also typically has obtained a PhD or PsyD. He or she usually provides guidance in areas such as vocation selection, school problems, drug abuse, and marital conflict. Often, these counselors work in community settings related to the problem areas—within a business, a school, a prison, the military service, or a neighborhood clinic—and use interviews, tests, guidance, and advising to help individuals solve specific problems and make decisions about future options.

A **psychiatrist** must have completed all medical school training for an MD degree and also have undergone some postdoctoral specialty training in mental and emotional disorders. Psychiatrists are largely trained in the biomedical basis of psychological problems.

A **psychoanalyst** is a therapist with either an MD or a PhD degree who has completed specialized postgraduate training in the Freudian approach to understanding and treating mental disorders.

These different types of therapists practice in many settings: hospitals, clinics, schools, and private offices. Some humanistic therapists prefer to conduct group sessions in their homes to work in a more natural environment. Community-based therapies, which take the treatment to the client, may operate out of local storefronts or houses of worship. Finally, some therapists work with clients in the life setting that is associated with their problem. For example, they work in airplanes with clients who suffer from flying phobias or in shopping malls with people who have social phobias. In recent years, psychotherapists have also begun to provide mental health care using the Internet. The *Critical Thinking in Your Life* box explores that topic.

People who enter therapy are usually referred to as either patients or clients. The term **patient** is used by professionals who take a biomedical approach to the treatment of psychological problems. The term **client** is used by professionals who

....

 Watch the Video *Classic Footage of Carl Rogers on Role of a Therapist* on MyPsychLab

clinical social worker A mental health professional whose specialized training prepares him or her to consider the social context of people's problems.

pastoral counselor A member of a religious order who specializes in the treatment of psychological disorders, often combining spirituality with practical problem solving.

clinical psychologist An individual who has earned a doctorate in psychology and whose training is in the assessment and treatment of psychological problems.

counseling psychologist Psychologist who specializes in providing guidance in areas such as vocational selections, school problems, drug abuse, and marital conflict.

psychiatrist An individual who has obtained an MD degree and also has completed postdoctoral specialty training in mental and emotional disorders; a psychiatrist may prescribe medications for the treatment of psychological disorders.

psychoanalyst An individual who has earned either a PhD or an MD degree and has completed postgraduate training in the Freudian approach to understanding and treating mental disorders.

patient The term used by those who take a biomedical approach to the treatment of psychological problems to describe the person being treated.

client The term used by clinicians who think of psychological disorders as problems in living, and not as mental illnesses, to describe those being treated.

think of psychological disorders as "problems in living" and not as mental illnesses. I will use the preferred term for each approach: *patient* for biomedical and psychoanalytic therapies and *client* for other therapies.

Diversity Issues in Psychotherapy

An important goal for clinicians is to provide relief to all people who suffer from psychological disorders. However, that goal is complicated by cultural and gender diversity. To begin, not all cultural groups are equally likely to undergo treatment (Wang et al., 2005; Youman et al., 2010). For example, Caucasians in the United States are more likely to seek treatment than are members of minority groups. An important part of that difference is unequal access to both physical and mental health care. However, cultural norms also affect the extent to which people seek psychological care (Snowden & Yamada, 2005). For example, research suggests that African Americans are more likely to interpret mental illness as physical illness. They are, therefore, less likely to obtain psychotherapy when it would be appropriate (Bolden & Wickes, 2005).

Another diversity issue arises once people actually seek therapy: The important question becomes whether particular therapies are equally effective across all cultural groups. In fact, researchers have begun to demonstrate the importance of *culturally adapted psychotherapy*, which is defined as "the systematic modification of a [treatment] . . . to consider language, culture, and context in such a way that it is compatible with the client's cultural patterns, meanings, and values" (Bernal et al., 2009, p. 362). Cultures differ with respect to their sense of self. One cultural adaptation would be to modify forms of psychotherapy to recognize when people come from individualistic or collectivist cultures (Smith et al., 2011). Recent research suggests that culturally adapted psychotherapy have more therapeutic value than standard therapies for members of racial and ethnic minority groups (Benish et al., 2011; Smith et al., 2011). More research is required to confirm these early results.

Similarly, more research is needed to assess the extent to which men and women benefit from the same therapies (Sigmon et al., 2007). There are gender differences in the prevalence of psychological disorders. For example, women experience more eating disorders than men do. For that reason, most psychotherapies for eating disorders have been developed for girls and young women (Greenberg & Schoen, 2008). Researchers must determine to what extent the same approaches are effective for men. Similarly, researchers must determine whether therapies that clinicians originated to treat men must be modified to bring relief to women.

A final diversity issue arises with respect to the training of psychotherapists: Therapists must be prepared to provide treatments that are sensitive to cultural differences. Researchers have suggested, in particular, that therapists must have *cultural competence* (Imel et al., 2011). Cultural competence has been defined as having three components (Sue, 2006, p. 238):

- "Cultural awareness and beliefs: Provider's sensitivity to her or his personal values and biases and how these may influence perceptions of the client, client's problem, and the counseling relationship."
- "Cultural knowledge: Counselor's knowledge of the client's culture, worldview, and expectations for the counseling relationship."

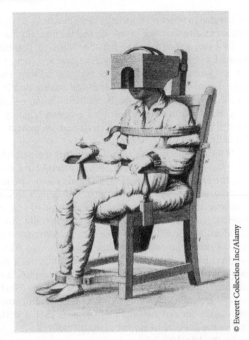

Treatment of mental disorders in the 18th century focused on banishing "ill humors" from the body. Shown here is the "tranquilizing chair" advocated by Philadelphia physician Benjamin Rush. Why did attitudes toward the treatment of people with mental illness change?

- "Cultural skills: Counselor's ability to intervene in a manner that is culturally sensitive and relevant."

Research suggests that therapists with greater cultural competence also have better therapeutic outcomes with patients and clients from diverse groups (Worthington et al., 2008).

Before we turn to contemporary therapies and therapists in more detail, let's first consider the historical contexts in which treatment of the mentally ill was developed.

Historical Perspectives on Institutional Treatment

What kind of treatment might you have received in past centuries if you were suffering from psychological problems? For much of history, chances are the treatment would not have helped and could even have been harmful. This review will trace the institutional treatment of psychological disorders to the 21st century, in which **deinstitutionalization**—the practice of moving people from psychiatric hospitals to other venues for treatment—has become an important issue.

History of Treatment Population increases and migration to big cities in 14th-century Western Europe created unemployment and social alienation. These conditions led to poverty, crime, and psychological problems. Special institutions were

deinstitutionalization The movement to treat people with psychological disorders in the community rather than in psychiatric hospitals.

soon created to warehouse society's three emerging categories of so-called misfits: the poor, criminals, and the mentally disturbed.

In 1403, a London hospital—St. Mary of Bethlehem—admitted its first patient with psychological problems. For the next 300 years, mental patients of the hospital were chained, tortured, and exhibited to an admission-paying public. Over time, a mispronunciation of Bethlehem—*bedlam*—came to mean chaos because of the horrible confusion reigning in the hospital and the dehumanized treatment of patients there (Foucault, 1975).

It wasn't until the late 18th century that the perception of psychological problems as mental illness emerged in Europe. In 1792, the French physician Philippe Pinel received permission from the government installed after the French Revolution to remove the chains from some of the inmates in mental hospitals. In the United States, psychologically disturbed individuals were confined for their own protection and for the safety of the community, but they were given no treatment. However, by the mid-1800s, when psychology as a field of study was gaining some credibility and respectability, "a cult of curability" emerged throughout the country. Spurred on by her firsthand experience working in prison settings, **Dorothea Dix** (1802–1887) labored continuously between 1841 and 1881 to improve the physical treatment of the mentally ill.

In the late 19th and early 20th centuries, many people argued that mental illness arose from the environmental stresses brought on by the turmoil of newly developing cities. To ease those stresses, the disturbed were confined to asylums in rural areas, far from the stress of the city, not only for protection but also for treatment (Rothman, 1971). Unfortunately, many of the asylums that were built became overcrowded. The humane goal of alleviating mental illness was replaced with the pragmatic goal of containing strange people in remote places. These large understaffed state mental hospitals became little more than human warehouses for disturbed individuals (Scull, 1993). Beginning in the 1960s, reformers began to agitate against these warehouses, in favor of the deinstitutionalization of at least those mental patients who could thrive with outpatient treatment and appropriate community supports. Unfortunately, as we'll see next, many deinstitutionalized patients do not obtain adequate assistance in their communities.

Deinstitutionalization and Homelessness In 1986, 41 percent of the money spent for mental health treatment in the United States was spent on inpatient care; in recent years that figure has fallen to 24 percent (Mark et al., 2007). This change reflects the process of deinstitutionalization: Many people with disorders are now treated outside of hospital settings. Deinstitutionalization arose from both social forces (that is, the movement against the warehousing of people with mental illness) and genuine advances in treatment. For example, this chapter later describes drug treatments that allowed people with schizophrenia to live outside of institutions.

Many people have been deinstitutionalized with the assumption that they will receive mental health care in some other setting. Unfortunately, that hasn't always proven to be the case. In fact, many people who leave psychiatric hospitals are not able to cope with their psychological disorders once they are in the community. This reality has led to circumstances that have sometimes been called the "revolving door": People leave institutions for only brief periods of time before needing help once again. For example, one large-scale study looked at 29,373 patients with schizophrenia who had been released from hospitals. The researchers found that 42.5 percent of the patients were readmitted within 30 days of their initial release (Lin et al., 2006). More generally, approximately 40 to 50 percent of psychiatric patients are readmitted within one year after their initial discharge (Bridge & Barbe, 2004). In many of these cases, individuals left institutional care with the symptoms of their psychological disorders at a level that could have allowed them to function in the outside world. Unfortunately, people often do not have appropriate community or personal resources to adhere to treatment outside the structure provided by an institution. In that sense, the problem is not so much with deinstitutionalization as it is with the lack of community resources outside the institutions.

When people cannot get adequate mental health care, they are often unable to maintain jobs or provide for their daily needs. For that reason, a large number of people with mental illnesses like schizophrenia or major depressive disorder become homeless. For example, in one sample of 1,562 chronically homeless people in Philadelphia, 53 percent had been diagnosed with serious mental illnesses (Poulin et al., 2010). The association of homelessness and mental illness also holds outside the United States. In a sample of 32,711 homeless people in Denmark, 62 percent of the men and 58 percent of the women had received diagnoses of psychiatric disorders (Nielsen et al., 2011). Even when people with serious mental illness are not homeless, ongoing mental health issues can cause substantial problems. For example, researchers examined the rate at which people with severe mental illness are the victims of violent crime such as robbery or assault (Teplin et al., 2005). In a sample of 936 men and women, 25.3 percent had experienced a violent crime—a rate 11 times higher than for individuals in the general population. The researchers suggested that the individuals' mental illnesses may prevent them from recognizing risk or appropriately protecting themselves.

As the chapter reviews the range of therapies clinicians have devised to alleviate distress, it's important for you to recognize that many people do not have adequate access to mental health care.

Stop *and* Review

① What are the primary goals of the therapeutic process?
② What special training does a psychoanalyst have?
③ Why is cultural competence important for therapists?
④ With respect to deinstitutionalization, what is meant by the "revolving door"?

✓—[Study and **Review** on **MyPsychLab**

PSYCHODYNAMIC THERAPIES

Psychodynamic therapies assume that a patient's problems have been caused by the psychological tension between unconscious impulses and the constraints of his or her life situation. These therapies locate the core of the disorder inside the disturbed person. This section reviews the origins of this approach in the work of Sigmund Freud and his followers. We will then consider how contemporary clinicians use psychodynamic therapies.

Freudian Psychoanalysis

Psychoanalysis, as developed by Sigmund Freud, is an intensive and prolonged technique for exploring unconscious motivations and conflicts in neurotic, anxiety-ridden individuals. Freudian theory views anxiety disorders as inabilities to resolve adequately the inner conflicts between the unconscious, irrational impulses of the *id* and the internalized social constraints imposed by the *superego*. The goal of psychoanalysis is to establish intrapsychic harmony that expands awareness of the forces of the *id*, reduces overcompliance with the demands of the *superego*, and strengthens the role of the *ego*.

Of central importance to a therapist is to understand the way a patient uses the process of *repression* to handle conflicts. Symptoms are considered to be messages from the unconscious that something is wrong. A psychoanalyst's task is to help a patient bring repressed thoughts to consciousness and to gain *insight* into the relationship between the current symptoms and the repressed conflicts. In this psychodynamic view, therapy succeeds and patients recover when they are "released from repression" established in early childhood. Because a central goal of a therapist is to guide a patient toward discovering insights into the relationships between present symptoms and past origins, psychodynamic therapy is often called **insight therapy.**

Traditional psychoanalysis is an attempt to reconstruct long-standing repressed memories and then work through painful feelings to an effective resolution. The psychodynamic approach includes several techniques to bring repressed conflicts to consciousness and to help a patient resolve them (Luborsky & Barrett, 2006). These techniques include free association, analysis of resistance, dream analysis, and analysis of transference and countertransference.

Free Association and Catharsis The principal procedure used in psychoanalysis to probe the unconscious and release repressed material is called **free association.** A patient, sitting comfortably in a chair or lying in a relaxed position on a couch, lets his or her mind wander freely and gives a running account of thoughts, wishes, physical sensations, and mental images. The patient is encouraged to reveal every thought or feeling, no matter how unimportant it may seem.

Freud maintained that free associations are *predetermined*, not random. The task of an analyst is to track the associations to their source and identify the significant patterns that lie beneath the surface of what are apparently just words. The patient is encouraged to express strong feelings, usually toward authority figures, that have been repressed for fear of punishment or retaliation. Any such emotional release, by this or other processes within the therapeutic context, is called **catharsis.**

Resistance A psychoanalyst attaches particular importance to subjects that a patient does *not* wish to discuss. At some time during the process of free association, a patient will show **resistance**—an inability or unwillingness to discuss certain ideas, desires, or experiences. Such resistances are conceived of as *barriers* between the unconscious and the conscious. This material is often related to an individual's sexual life (which includes all things pleasurable) or to hostile, resentful feelings toward parents.

Why is psychoanalytic therapy, originally practiced in Freud's study, often called the "talking cure"?

When the repressed material is finally brought into the open, a patient generally claims that it is unimportant, absurd, irrelevant, or too unpleasant to discuss. The therapist believes the opposite. Psychoanalysis aims to break down resistances and enable the patient to face these painful ideas, desires, and experiences.

Dream Analysis Psychoanalysts believe that dreams are an important source of information about a patient's unconscious motivations. When a person is asleep, the superego is presumably less on guard against the unacceptable impulses originating in the id, so a motive that cannot be expressed in waking life may find expression in a dream. In analysis, dreams are assumed to have two kinds of content: *manifest* (openly visible) content that people remember upon awakening and *latent* (hidden) content—the actual motives that are seeking expression but are so painful or unacceptable that they are expressed in disguised or symbolic form. Therapists attempt to uncover these hidden motives by using **dream analysis,** a therapeutic technique that examines the content of a person's dreams to discover the underlying or disguised motivations and symbolic meanings of significant life experiences and desires.

Transference and Countertransference During the course of the intensive therapy of psychoanalysis, a patient usually develops an emotional reaction toward the therapist. Often, the therapist is identified with a person who has been at the center of an emotional conflict in the past—most often a parent or a lover.

....

psychoanalysis The form of psychodynamic therapy developed by Freud; an intensive prolonged technique for exploring unconscious motivations and conflicts in neurotic, anxiety-ridden individuals.

insight therapy A technique by which the therapist guides a patient toward discovering insights between present symptoms and past origins.

free association The therapeutic method in which a patient gives a running account of thoughts, wishes, physical sensations, and mental images as they occur.

catharsis The process of expressing strongly felt but usually repressed emotions.

resistance The inability or unwillingness of a patient in psychoanalysis to discuss certain ideas, desires, or experiences.

dream analysis The psychoanalytic interpretation of dreams used to gain insight into a person's unconscious motives or conflicts.

Table 1 • Excerpt from a Session with a Psychodynamic Therapist

Sara [angrily]: I can't connect with you anymore [after two years of twice-a-week treatment]—you don't seem to listen and, anyway, I have nothing to say. I think that after all this time I should have changed, but I'm still distant from my daughter, she still has problems, and she's still in therapy. I want to end this therapy. . . .

Therapist: What's happening now has so much to do with your fantasies about the adoption and your feelings about how your mother could have let you be adopted. Right now, I seem to be standing in for her.

Sara: I do hate you. How can you take a week off? You are leaving me—just like she did. How do I know you'll come back? She never came back—how could she have left me? And here I am, a crying, clinging baby and you'll leave me.

From Hall, J. S. (2004). *Roadblocks on the journey of psychotherapy.* Lanham, MD: Jason Aronson, pp. 73–74. Reprinted by permission.

This emotional reaction is called **transference.** Transference is called *positive transference* when the feelings attached to the therapist are those of love or admiration and *negative transference* when the feelings consist of hostility or envy. Often, a patient's attitude is ambivalent, including a mixture of positive and negative feelings. An analyst's task in handling transference is a difficult one because of the patient's emotional vulnerability; however, it is a crucial part of treatment. A therapist helps a patient to interpret the present transferred feelings by understanding their original source in earlier experiences and attitudes. Please take a moment to read **Table 1**, which provides an excerpt from a therapy session (Hall, 2004, pp. 73–74). The patient was adopted as a child. You can see how Sara's feelings of abandonment have been transferred from her birth mother to her therapist.

Personal feelings are also at work in a therapist's reactions to a patient. **Countertransference** refers to what happens when a therapist comes to like or dislike a patient because the patient is perceived as similar to significant people in the therapist's life. In working through countertransference, a therapist may discover some unconscious dynamics of his or her own. The therapist becomes a "living mirror" for the patient and the patient, in turn, for the therapist. If the therapist fails to recognize the operation of countertransference, the therapy may not be as effective (Hayes et al., 2011). Because of the emotional intensity of this type of therapeutic relationship and the vulnerability of the patient, therapists must be on guard about crossing the boundary between professional caring and personal involvement with their patients. The therapy setting is obviously one with an enormous power imbalance that must be recognized, and honored, by the therapist.

Later Psychodynamic Therapies

Freud's followers retained many of his basic ideas but modified certain of his principles and practices. In general, these therapists

....

transference The process by which a person in psychoanalysis attaches to a therapist feelings formerly held toward some significant person who figured into past emotional conflict.

countertransference Circumstances in which a psychoanalyst develops personal feelings about a client because of perceived similarity of the client to significant people in the therapist's life.

place more emphasis than Freud did on: (1) a patient's *current* social environment (less focus on the past); (2) the continuing influence of life experiences (not just childhood conflicts); (3) the role of social motivation and interpersonal relations of love (rather than of biological instincts and selfish concerns); (4) the significance of ego functioning and development of the self-concept (less on the conflict between id and superego).

Two other prominent theorists are Carl Jung and Alfred Adler. To get a flavor of more contemporary psychodynamic approaches, here we consider the work of Harry Stack Sullivan and of Melanie Klein (see Ruitenbeek, 1973, for a look at other members of the Freudian circle).

Harry Stack Sullivan (1953) felt that Freudian theory and therapy did not recognize the importance of social relationships and a patient's needs for acceptance, respect, and love. Mental disorders, he insisted, involve not only traumatic intrapsychic processes but also troubled interpersonal relationships and even strong societal pressures. Anxiety and other mental ills arise out of insecurities in relations with parents and significant others. Therapy based on this interpersonal view involves observing a *patient's feelings* about the *therapist's attitudes.* The therapeutic interview is seen as a social setting in which each party's feelings and attitudes are influenced by the other's.

Melanie Klein (1975) defected from Freud's emphasis on the Oedipus conflict as the major source of psychopathology. Instead of oedipal sexual conflicts as the most important organizing factors of the psyche, Klein argued that a *death instinct* preceded sexual awareness and led to an innate aggressive impulse that was equally important in organizing the psyche. She contended that the two fundamental organizing forces in the psyche are aggression and love, where love *unites* and aggression *splits* the psyche. On Klein's view, conscious love is connected to remorse over destructive hate and potential violence toward those we love. Thus Klein explained, "one of

Wellcome Library, London

In what ways did the theories of Melanie Klein and Sigmund Freud differ?

Psychology in Your Life

ARE LIVES HAUNTED BY REPRESSED MEMORIES?

In December 1969, a patrolman found the lifeless body of 8-year-old Susan Nason. For 20 years, no one knew who had murdered her. Then, in 1989, Susan's friend Eileen Franklin-Lipsker contacted county investigators. Eileen reported that, with the help of psychotherapy, she had recalled a long-repressed memory of witnessing her father, George Franklin, sexually assault Susan and then bludgeon her to death with a rock (Marcus, 1990; Workman, 1990). This testimony was sufficient to have George Franklin convicted of first-degree murder. Over time, Franklin was released as strong doubts accumulated about the validity of his daughter's memories. Still, a jury had initially found the dramatic recovery of 20-year-old memories quite credible.

How, in theory, had these memories remained hidden for 20 years? The answer to this mystery finds its roots in Sigmund Freud's concept of repressed memories. As you'll recall, Freud (1923) theorized that some people's memories of life experiences become sufficiently threatening to their psychological well-being that the individuals banish the memories from consciousness—they repress them. Clinical psychologists are often able to help clients take control of their lives by interpreting disruptive life patterns as the consequences of repressed memories. But not all experiences of repressed memories remain in the therapist's office. After long intervals of time, individuals will sometimes make accusations about horrifying events, such as murders or childhood sexual abuse. Could these claims be real?

Clinicians worry that therapists who believe in repressed memories may, through the mechanisms of psychotherapy,

implant those beliefs in their patients (Lynn et al., 2003). Therapists who believe in repressed memories may instigate patients' efforts to find these memories—and verbally reward them when the "memories" come to light (de Rivera, 1997). In one study, researchers recruited 128 participants who all claimed that they had experienced childhood sexual abuse (Geraerts et al., 2007). A majority of the participants (71 of the 128) had continuous memories of the abuse. That is, there were no life periods in which they didn't recall the abuse. The other 57 participants had *discontinuous* memories; they believed that they had forgotten the abuse for some period of time. Of that group, 16 had recovered memories of abuse in therapy, whereas the other 41 had recovered the memories without any special prompting. The researchers sent interviewers into the field to try to find evidence to corroborate the participants' memories of abuse. This was possible for 45 percent of the participants with continuous memories and 37 percent of the participants who had recovered memories on their own. However, for participants who recovered memories during therapy the interviewers found 0 percent corroborating evidence.

This study confirms that some reports of recovered memories are based on real occurrences. However, the study also demonstrates the potential for processes of psychotherapy to lead people to create false memories. Belief in the recovery of repressed memories may provide a measurable benefit for patients in psychotherapy. Even so, patients must ensure that they are not passively accepting someone else's version of their life.

the great mysteries that all people face [is] that love and hate—our personal heaven and hell—cannot be separated from one another" (Frager & Fadiman, 1998, p. 135). Klein pioneered the use of forceful therapeutic interpretations of both aggressive and sexual drives in analytic patients.

In contemporary practice, psychodynamic therapists continue to draw upon the foundational concepts of Freud and his followers. Contemporary psychodynamic therapies have several distinctive features (Shedler, 2010). They emphasize patients' emotions and their moments of resistance; they emphasize the importance of past experiences on current reality. They also focus on interpersonal conflict. Against that background, individual therapists may put more or less emphasis on particular processes such as the interpretation of transference (Gibbons et al., 2008). Therapists also differ with respect to how active a role the therapist plays in interpreting the patient's life experiences. Finally, traditional psychoanalysis often takes a long time (several years at least, with as many as five sessions a week). It also requires introspective patients who are verbally fluent,

highly motivated to remain in therapy, and willing and able to undergo considerable expense. Newer forms of psychodynamic therapy are making therapy briefer in total duration.

An important goal of psychodynamic therapy is to provide patients with insights into the interpersonal conflicts that lie at the roots of their psychological disorders. Behavioral therapies, to which we now turn, focus their attention more directly on the maladaptive behaviors that define the disorders.

Stop *and* Review

① Why is psychodynamic therapy also known as insight therapy?

② What is transference?

③ What role did the death instinct play in Melanie Klein's theory?

✓ Study and Review on MyPsychLab

313

BEHAVIOR THERAPIES

Whereas psychodynamic therapies focus on presumed inner causes, behavior therapies focus on observable outer behaviors. Behavior therapists argue that abnormal behaviors are acquired in the same way as normal behaviors—through a learning process that follows the basic principles of conditioning and learning. Behavior therapies apply the principles of conditioning and reinforcement to modify undesirable behavior patterns associated with mental disorders.

The terms **behavior therapy** and **behavior modification** are often used interchangeably. Both refer to the systematic use of principles of learning to increase the frequency of desired behaviors and/or decrease that of problem behaviors. The range of deviant behaviors and personal problems that typically are treated by behavior therapy is extensive and includes fears, compulsions, depression, addictions, aggression, and delinquent behaviors. In general, behavior therapy works best with specific rather than general types of personal problems: It is better for a phobia than for unfocused anxiety. 👁

The therapies that have emerged from the theories of conditioning and learning are grounded in a pragmatic, empirical research tradition. The central task of all living organisms is to learn how to adapt to the demands of the current social and physical environment. When organisms do not learn how to cope effectively, their maladaptive reactions can be overcome by therapy based on principles of learning. The target behavior is not assumed to be a symptom of any underlying process. The symptom itself is the problem. Psychodynamic therapists predicted that treating only the outer behavior without confronting the true, inner problem would result in *symptom substitution,* the appearance of a new physical or psychological problem. However, no evidence has emerged to support the claim that when pathological behaviors are eliminated by behavior therapy, new symptoms are substituted (Tryon, 2008). "On the contrary, patients whose target symptoms improved often reported improvement in other, less important symptoms as well" (Sloane et al., 1975, p. 219).

Let's look at the different forms of behavior therapies that have brought relief to distressed individuals.

Counterconditioning

Why does someone become anxious when faced with a harmless stimulus, such as a spider, a nonpoisonous snake, or social contact? The behavioral explanation is that the anxiety arises due to simple conditioning principles: Strong

Lea Paterson/Science Source

Why are many therapies for anxiety disorders known as exposure therapies?

emotional reactions that disrupt a person's life "for no good reason" are often conditioned responses that the person does not recognize as having been learned previously. In **counterconditioning,** a new response is conditioned to replace, or "counter," a maladaptive response. The earliest recorded use of behavior therapy followed this logic. **Mary Cover Jones** (1924) showed that a fear could be *unlearned* through conditioning.

> Her patient was Peter, a 3-year-old boy who, for some unknown reason, was afraid of rabbits. The therapy involved feeding Peter at one end of a room while the rabbit was brought in at the other end. Over a series of sessions, the rabbit was gradually brought closer until, finally, all fear disappeared and Peter played freely with the rabbit.

Following in Cover Jones's footsteps, behavior therapists now use several counterconditioning techniques, including systematic desensitization, implosion, flooding, and aversion therapy.

Exposure therapies The central component of **exposure therapy** is that individuals are made to confront the object or situation that causes anxiety. The therapeutic principle is that exposure permits counterconditioning—people learn to

---

👁 Watch the Video *Overcoming Fears and Anxieties: Sue Mineka* on MyPsychLab

behavior therapy See behavior modification.

behavior modification The systematic use of principles of learning to increase the frequency of desired behaviors and/or decrease the frequency of problem behaviors.

counterconditioning A technique used in therapy to substitute a new response for a maladaptive one by means of conditioning procedures.

exposure therapy A behavioral technique in which clients are exposed to the objects or situations that cause them anxiety.

Table 2 • Hierarchy of Anxiety-Producing Stimuli for a Test-Anxious College Student (in order of increasing anxiety)

1. A month before an examination.
2. Two weeks before an examination.
3. A week before an examination.
4. Five days before an examination.
5. Four days before an examination.
6. Three days before an examination.
7. Two days before an examination.
8. One day before an examination.
9. The night before an examination.
10. The examination paper face down.
11. Awaiting the distribution of examination papers.
12. Before the unopened doors of the examination room.
13. In the process of answering an examination paper.
14. On the way to the university on the day of an examination.

From Butcher, James N.; Mineka, Susan; Hooley, Jill M., Abnormal Psychology, 13th Ed., © 2007. Reprinted and electronically reproduced by permission of Pearson Education, Inc., Upper Saddle River, New Jersey.

remain relaxed in circumstances that once would have made them highly anxious. Individual exposure therapies differ with respect to the time course and circumstances in which people are exposed to their sources of anxiety.

For example, **Joseph Wolpe** (1958, 1973) observed that the nervous system cannot be relaxed and agitated at the same time because incompatible processes cannot be activated simultaneously. This insight was central to the *theory of reciprocal inhibition* that Wolpe applied to the treatment of fears and phobias. Wolpe taught his patients to *relax* their muscles and then to *imagine* visually their feared situation. They did so in gradual steps that moved from initially remote associations to direct images. Psychologically confronting the feared stimulus while being relaxed and doing so in a *graduated* sequence is the therapeutic technique known as **systematic desensitization.**

Desensitization therapy involves three major steps. First, the client identifies the stimuli that provoke anxiety and arranges them in a hierarchy ranked from weakest to strongest. For example, a student suffering from severe test anxiety constructed the hierarchy in **Table 2**. Note that she rated immediate anticipation of an examination (No. 14) as more stressful than taking the exam itself (No. 13). Second, the client is trained in a system of progressive deep-muscle relaxation. Relaxation training requires several sessions in which the client learns to distinguish between sensations of tension and relaxation and to let go of tension to achieve a state of physical and mental relaxation. Finally, the actual process of desensitization begins: The relaxed client vividly imagines the weakest anxiety stimulus on the list. If it can be visualized without discomfort, the client goes on to the next stronger one. After a number of sessions, the most distressing situations on the list can be imagined without anxiety.

Systematic desensitization represents a gradual course of exposure to stimuli that provoke anxiety. Therapists have explored a variety of other techniques, some of which bring about exposure with less delay. For example, in a technique known as *flooding*, clients agree to be put directly into the phobic situation. A person with claustrophobia is made to sit in a dark closet, and a child with a fear of water is put into a pool. Researchers successfully treated a 21-year-old student's phobia of balloon pops by having him experience three sessions in which he endured hundreds of balloons being popped (Houlihan et al., 1993). In the third session, the student was able to pop the last 115 balloons himself. Another form of flooding therapy begins with the use of imagination. In this procedure, the client may listen to a tape that describes the most terrifying version of the phobic fear in great detail for an hour or two. Once the terror subsides, the client is then taken to the feared situation.

When exposure techniques were first created, therapists brought about exposure through mental imagery or actual contact. In recent years, clinicians have turned to virtual reality to provide exposure therapy (Powers & Emmelkamp, 2008). For example, people have been able to overcome a fear of flying through virtual experiences of flight (for example, sitting in an airplane, taking off, and landing) rather than venturing out to a physical airport (Rothbaum et al., 2006). As a second example, consider a study that used virtual reality therapy to treat a group of women with a phobia of cockroaches.

Featured Study

A team of researchers developed a virtual reality system that provided patients with the illusion that they were seeing cockroaches in their surrounding physical environment (Botella et al., 2010). For example, the system made it possible for patients to see cockroaches crawling on their hands. The system also allowed the therapists to manipulate features such as the number, size, and movement of the insects. Thus, it provided the flexibility the therapists needed to adapt the exposure therapy to suit the needs of each individual patient. The six patients in the study were systematically exposed to the virtual cockroaches in a single session that lasted, on average, just under two hours. After that single session of therapy, the patients showed considerable improvement in their ability, for example, to approach cockroaches. In follow-up assessments 3, 6, and 12 months after the original treatment, the patients continued to show substantial relief from their phobia.

Exposure therapies have proved to be highly effective for treating anxiety disorders. Virtual reality techniques hold the promise of providing powerful exposure experiences without the time and expense of venturing out into the real world.

Exposure therapy has also been used to combat obsessive-compulsive disorders. However, the therapy adds another component: *response prevention*. Not only are clients exposed to what they fear, but they are also prevented from performing the compulsive behaviors that ordinarily reduce their anxiety. Consider a study of 20 children and adolescents with OCD (Bolton & Perrin, 2008). Because each participant had different obsessions and compulsions, the treatment needed to be tailored to each individual. However, the core components remained the same: Each participant was exposed to the objects of his or her obsession while engaging in exercises to prevent the compulsive behaviors. This program of therapy brought about substantial relief.

systematic desensitization A behavioral therapy technique in which a client is taught to prevent the arousal of anxiety by confronting the feared stimulus while relaxed.

 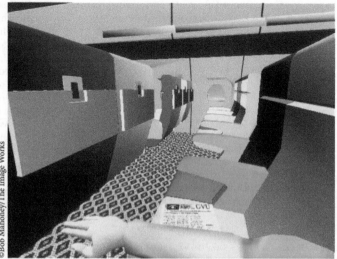

How might a behavior therapist use virtual reality exposure therapy to help a client overcome a fear of flying?

Imitation of models Another form of exposure therapy takes its inspiration from social-learning theory, which predicts that individuals acquire responses through observation. Thus it should be the case that people with phobias should be able to unlearn fear reactions through imitation of models. For example, in treating a phobia of snakes, a therapist will first demonstrate fearless approach behavior at a relatively minor level, perhaps approaching a snake's cage or touching a snake. The client is aided, through demonstration and encouragement, to imitate the modeled behavior. Gradually, the approach behaviors are shaped so that the client can pick up the snake and let it crawl freely over him or her. At no time is the client forced to perform any behavior. Resistance at any level is overcome by having the client return to a previously successful, less threatening level of approach behavior.

The power of this form of **participant modeling** can be seen in research comparing this technique with symbolic modeling, desensitization, and a control condition. In *symbolic modeling therapy*, individuals who had been trained in relaxation techniques watched a film in which several models fearlessly handled snakes; they could stop the film and try to relax whenever a scene made them feel anxious. In the control condition, no therapeutic intervention was used. As you can see in **Figure 1**, participant modeling was clearly the most successful of these techniques. Snake phobia was eliminated in 11 of the 12 individuals in the participant modeling group (Bandura, 1970).

. . . .

participant modeling A therapeutic technique in which a therapist demonstrates the desired behavior and a client is aided, through supportive encouragement, to imitate the modeled behavior.

aversion therapy A type of behavioral therapy used to treat individuals attracted to harmful stimuli; an attractive stimulus is paired with a noxious stimulus in order to elicit a negative reaction to the target stimulus.

contingency management A general treatment strategy involving changing behavior by modifying its consequences.

Aversion therapy The forms of exposure therapy we've considered so far help clients deal directly with stimuli that are not really harmful. What can be done to help those who are *attracted* to stimuli that *are* harmful? Drug addiction, sexual perversions, and uncontrollable violence are human problems in which deviant behavior is elicited by tempting stimuli. **Aversion therapy** uses counterconditioning procedures to pair these stimuli with strong noxious stimuli such as electric shocks or nausea-producing drugs. In time, the same negative reactions are elicited by the tempting stimuli, and the person develops an aversion that replaces his or her former desire.

For example, aversion therapy has been used with individuals who engage in *self-injurious behaviors,* such as hitting their heads or banging their heads against other objects. When an individual performs such a behavior, he or she is given a mild electric shock. This treatment effectively eliminates self-injurious behaviors in some, but not all, patients (van Oorsouw et al., 2008). Because aversion therapies may cause physical harm, ethical considerations require that therapists use them only when other therapies have failed (Prangnell, 2010).

Contingency Management

Counterconditioning procedures are appropriate when one response can be replaced with another. Other behavior modification procedures rely on the principles of operant conditioning that arose in the research tradition pioneered by B. F. Skinner. **Contingency management** refers to the general treatment strategy of changing behavior by modifying its consequences. The two major techniques of contingency management in behavior therapy are *positive reinforcement strategies* and *extinction strategies*.

Positive Reinforcement Strategies When a response is followed immediately by a reward, the response tends to be repeated and to increase in frequency over time. This central principle of operant learning becomes a therapeutic strategy when it is used to modify the frequency of a desirable response

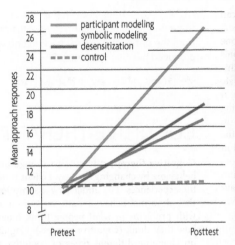

FIGURE 1 Participant Modeling Therapy

The subject shown in the photo first watched a model make a graduated series of snake-approach responses and then repeated them herself. She eventually was able to pick up the snake and let it crawl about on her. The graph compares the number of approach responses subjects made before and after receiving participant modeling therapy (most effective) with the behavior of those exposed to two other therapeutic techniques and a control group.

Albert Bandura, from "Modeling Therapy." Reprinted by permission of Albert Bandura.

as it replaces an undesirable one. Dramatic success has been obtained from the application of positive reinforcement procedures to behavior problems.

In a technique called *shaping*, researchers reinforce successive approximations to a desired behavior. Consider how shaping was used to help smokers reduce the number of cigarettes they smoked (Lamb et al., 2007). The researchers measured the participants' breath carbon monoxide (BCO) to determine initial smoking habits. As the study unfolded, the participants received cash incentives if they were able to get their BCO below particular goal levels (which were set for each smoker). Those goals became more demanding over time—shaping participants toward the desired behavior of abstinence from smoking. Another approach is *token economies*, in which desired behaviors (such as practicing personal care or taking medication) are explicitly defined, and token payoffs are given by institutional staff when the behaviors are performed. These tokens can later be exchanged for an array of rewards and privileges (Dickerson et al., 2005; Matson & Boisjoli, 2009). These systems of reinforcement are especially effective in modifying patients' behaviors regarding self-care, upkeep of their environment, and frequency of their positive social interactions.

In another approach, therapists differentially reinforce behaviors that are incompatible with the maladaptive behavior. This technique has been used successfully with individuals in treatment for drug addiction.

Featured Study

Researchers recruited 87 individuals who were seeking treatment for cocaine dependence into a 12-week study (Petry & Roll, 2011). All the participants received standard treatment of a series of counseling sessions that imparted strategies and skills for overcoming dependence. In addition to this standard treatment, the participants were given the opportunity to win prizes, contingent on negative urine specimens. To win the prizes, participants pulled slips of paper from a bowl. Half of the slips (50 percent) read "good job, try again." However, 44 percent of the slips provided $1 prizes and 6 percent provided $20 prizes. The bowl also had a single slip that resulted in a $100 prize. For the first negative specimen, participants got to pull one slip. For each subsequent negative specimen, they earned an extra one pull. A positive specimen reduced participants back to a single pull. Three months after completing this procedure, 26.9 percent of the participants were still abstinent from cocaine. Note that the actual amount each participant won was determined by the luck they had pulling slips from the bowl. The researchers found that the more prize money a participant had won, the more likely he or she was to be cocaine-free.

This study verifies that contingency management can be used successfully to treat drug dependence. Just for the chance to win prizes, drug users were able to get clean—and stay clean three months later. You might recognize the same philosophy at work here as the one that motivated the counterconditioning procedures described earlier: Basic principles of learning are used to increase the probability of adaptive behaviors.

Extinction Strategies Why do people continue to do something that causes pain and distress when they are capable of doing otherwise? The answer is that many forms of behavior have multiple consequences—some are negative, and some are positive. Often, subtle positive reinforcements keep a behavior going despite its obvious negative consequences. For example, children who are punished for misbehaving may continue to misbehave if punishment is the only form of attention they seem to be able to earn.

Extinction strategies are useful in therapy when dysfunctional behaviors have been maintained by unrecognized reinforcing circumstances. Those reinforcers can be identified through a careful situational analysis, and then a program can be arranged to withhold them in the presence of the undesirable response. When this approach is possible, and everyone in the situation who might inadvertently reinforce the person's behavior cooperates, extinction procedures work to diminish the frequency of the behavior and eventually to eliminate the behavior completely. Consider a classroom example. A boy with attention-deficit/hyperactivity disorder was causing problems for his teachers because he frequently engaged in disruptive off-task behaviors. Researchers discovered that the attention the teachers gave to the student when he engaged in off-task behaviors was positively reinforcing those behaviors (Stahr et al., 2006). When the teachers no longer paid attention to him when he behaved inappropriately, the student's behavior improved.

Generalization Techniques

An ongoing issue of concern for behavior therapists is whether new behavior patterns generated in a therapeutic setting will actually be used in the everyday situations faced by their clients (Kazdin, 1994). This question is important for all therapies, because any measure of treatment effectiveness must include maintenance of long-term changes that go beyond a therapist's couch, clinic, or laboratory.

When essential aspects of a client's real-life setting are absent from the therapy program, behavioral changes accomplished through therapy may be lost over time after therapy terminates. To prevent this gradual loss, it has become common practice to build generalization techniques into the therapeutic procedure itself. These techniques attempt to *increase* the similarity of target behaviors, reinforcers, models, and stimulus demands between therapy and real-life settings. For example, behaviors are taught that are likely to be reinforced naturally in a person's environment, such as showing courtesy or consideration. Rewards are given on a partial reinforcement schedule to ensure that their effect will be maintained in the real world, where rewards are not always forthcoming. Expectation of tangible extrinsic rewards is gradually *faded out* while social approval and more naturally occurring consequences, including reinforcing self-statements, are incorporated.

Behavior therapists, for example, used a fading procedure with a boy (aged 4 years, 10 months) who refused to drink milk (Tiger & Hanley, 2006). To get the boy to drink his milk, the therapists had his teacher mix a small amount of chocolate syrup into a glass of milk. With the chocolate syrup mixed in, the boy drank the milk. Over the next 48 meals, the teacher slowly decreased the amount of chocolate until the boy was offered only plain milk. At the end of this intervention, the boy consistently drank plain milk. This was also true at home, demonstrating generalization from the classroom to an additional setting.

Let's move now to cognitive therapies.

Stop *and* Review

① What is the basic principle of counterconditioning?
② What learning principle is at work when clinicians allow patients to earn prizes?
③ What is the goal of generalization techniques?

CRITICAL THINKING Recall the study that used prizes to treat drug dependence. Why did the number of pulls from the prize bowl get set back to one when participants produced positive specimens?

✔—[Study and Review on MyPsychLab

COGNITIVE THERAPIES

Cognitive therapy attempts to change problem feelings and behaviors by changing the way a client thinks about significant life experiences. The underlying assumption of such therapy is that abnormal behavior patterns and emotional distress start with problems in *what* people think (cognitive content) and *how* they think (cognitive process). Cognitive therapies focus on changing different types of cognitive processes and providing different methods of cognitive restructuring as ways to cope with stress and improve health. This section describes two major forms of cognitive therapy: alteration of false belief systems and cognitive behavioral therapy.

Changing False Beliefs

Some cognitive behavior therapists have, as their primary targets for change, beliefs, attitudes, and habitual thought patterns. These cognitive therapists argue that many psychological problems arise because of the way people think about themselves in relation to other people and the events they face. Faulty thinking can be based on (1) unreasonable attitudes ("Being perfect is the most important trait for a student to have"), (2) false premises ("If I do everything they want me to, then I'll be popular"), and (3) rigid rules that put behavior on automatic pilot so that prior patterns are repeated even when they have not worked ("I must obey authorities"). Emotional distress is caused by cognitive misunderstandings and by failure to distinguish between current reality and one's imagination (or expectations).

Cognitive Therapy for Depression A cognitive therapist helps a client to correct faulty patterns of thinking by substituting more effective problem-solving techniques. Aaron Beck (1976) has successfully pioneered cognitive therapy for the problem of depression. He states the formula for treatment in simple form: "The therapist helps the patient to identify his warped thinking and to learn more realistic ways to formulate his experiences" (p. 20). For example, depressed individuals may be instructed to write down negative thoughts about themselves, figure out why these self-criticisms are unjustified, and come up with more realistic (and less destructive) self-cognitions.

Beck believes that depression is maintained because depressed patients are unaware of the negative automatic thoughts that they habitually formulate, such as "I will never be as good as my brother"; "Nobody would like me if they really knew me"; and "I'm not smart enough to make it in this

cognitive therapy A type of psychotherapeutic treatment that attempts to change feelings and behaviors by changing the way a client thinks about or perceives significant life experiences.

competitive school." A therapist then uses four tactics to change the cognitive foundation that supports the depression (Beck & Rush, 1989; Beck et al., 1979):

- Challenging the client's basic assumptions about his or her functioning.
- Evaluating the evidence the client has for and against the accuracy of automatic thoughts.
- Reattributing blame to situational factors rather than to the patient's incompetence.
- Discussing alternative solutions to complex tasks that could lead to failure experiences.

This therapy is similar to behavior therapies in that it centers on the present state of the client.

One of the worst side effects of being depressed is having to live with all the negative feelings and lethargy associated with depression. Becoming obsessed with thoughts about one's negative mood brings up memories of all the bad times in life, which worsens the depressive feelings. By filtering all input through a darkly colored lens of depression, depressed people see criticism where there is none and hear sarcasm when they listen to praise—further "reasons" for being depressed. Cognitive therapy has proved successful at arresting depression's downward spiral (Hollon et al., 2006).

Rational-Emotive Therapy One of the earliest forms of cognitive therapy was the **rational-emotive therapy (RET)** developed by **Albert Ellis** (1913–2007). RET is a comprehensive system of personality change based on the transformation of irrational beliefs that cause undesirable, highly charged emotional reactions, such as severe anxiety (Ellis, 1962, 1995; Windy & Ellis, 1997). Clients may have core values *demanding* that they succeed and be approved, *insisting* that they be treated fairly, and *dictating* that the universe be more pleasant.

Rational-emotive therapists teach clients how to recognize the "shoulds," "oughts," and "musts" that are controlling their actions and preventing them from choosing the lives they want. They attempt to break through a client's closed-mindedness by showing that an emotional reaction that follows some event is really the effect of unrecognized beliefs about the event. For example, failure to achieve orgasm during intercourse (event) is followed by an emotional reaction of depression and self-derogation. The belief that is causing the emotional reaction is likely to be "I am sexually inadequate and may be impotent because I failed to perform as expected." In therapy, this belief (and others) is openly disputed through rational confrontation and examination of alternative reasons for the event, such as fatigue, alcohol, false notions of sexual performance, or reluctance to engage in intercourse at that time or with that particular partner. This confrontation technique is followed by other interventions that replace dogmatic, irrational thinking with rational, situationally appropriate ideas.

Rational-emotive therapy aims to increase an individual's sense of self-worth and the potential to be self-actualized by getting rid of the system of faulty beliefs that block personal growth. As such, it shares much with humanistic therapies, which we consider later in the chapter.

Cognitive Behavioral Therapy

You are what you tell yourself you can be, and you are guided by what you believe you ought to do. This is a starting assumption

Suppose you were learning to knit. Assuming you wanted to get better at it over time, what would be the best internal message to give yourself about the activity?

of **cognitive behavioral therapy.** This therapeutic approach combines the cognitive emphasis on changing false beliefs with the behavioral focus on reinforcement contingencies in the modification of performance (Goldfried, 2003). Unacceptable behavior patterns are modified by *cognitive restructuring*—changing a person's negative self-statements into constructive coping statements.

A critical part of this therapeutic approach is the discovery by therapist and client of the way the client thinks about and expresses the problem for which therapy is sought. Once both therapist and client understand the kind of thinking that is leading to unproductive or dysfunctional behaviors, they develop new self-statements that are constructive and minimize the use of self-defeating ones that elicit anxiety or reduce self-esteem (Meichenbaum, 1977, 1985, 1993). **Table 3** provides an example of how a session with a cognitive behavioral therapist might unfold. As you can see, the therapist helps the patient to reconsider the evidence that supports her belief that her best friend wants to end their relationship. In addition, as a homework assignment, the patient agrees to gather more evidence to explore other possibilities for her friend's behavior. 👁

Cognitive behavioral therapy has been used as a successful treatment for a variety of disorders. Let's see how it was used to treat clients with *compulsive buying disorder,* which is defined as "excessive and mostly senseless spending or excessive shopping impulses that cause marked distress, interfere with social or occupational functioning, and often result in financial problems" (Mueller et al., 2008, p. 1131).

··

👁 **Watch** the Video *Cognitive Behavioral Therapy for Schizophrenia* on **MyPsychLab**

rational-emotive therapy (RET) A comprehensive system of personality change based on changing irrational beliefs that cause undesirable, highly charged emotional reactions such as severe anxiety.

cognitive behavioral therapy A therapeutic approach that combines the cognitive emphasis on thoughts and attitudes with the behavioral emphasis on changing performance.

Table 3 • A Possible Session with a Cognitive Behavioral Therapist

Patient: I feel like my best friend, Marjorie, is rejecting me.

Therapist: I'm sure that's an unpleasant feeling. What makes you think she's rejecting you?

Patient: When we ran into each other at the mall yesterday, Marjorie barely said hello. She said, "How are you," and then raced off as fast as possible. It really didn't seem like she had any interest in talking to me.

Therapist: Hmm…, you've told me that you've been friends for a long time, right?

Patient: Yeah, but then why was she so rude to me yesterday? She made me feel awful.

Therapist: I can see why you'd feel upset. Can you think of other explanations for her behavior? Let's give that some thought.

Patient: Well, her mother has been sick, and she's moved back home to take care of her. Maybe she was feeling bad about shopping while her mother was home alone. That could be another reason.

Therapist: That could make sense. How could you find out if you're right?

Patient: I suppose I could call her to ask if she's doing okay? I could say that she looked stressed at the mall last night, and see if there's anything I could do to help her out.

Therapist: That sounds like a great way to get some information about your assumptions. Why don't you try that before our next session and then we can talk about what you learned?

Featured Study

Researchers randomly assigned 60 people with compulsive buying disorder to cognitive behavioral therapy or to a control group (Mueller et al., 2008). Participants in the treatment group had one therapy session a week over the course of 12 weeks. The therapy had several components (Burgard & Mitchell, 2000). One component of the therapy was for participants to identify the cues (such as social or psychological situations) in their lives that triggered buying behavior. Once participants identified these cues, the therapists worked with them to develop cognitive strategies to disrupt or avoid the cues' impact. Another component of the therapy was for participants to gain confidence that they could control their behavior. The researchers encouraged participants to undermine negative self-statements (for example, "I cannot control my urge to shop") by gathering evidence against such statements and by generating plans to achieve greater control. This program of therapy led to improvement both at the end of treatment and in follow-up assessment six months after treatment ended.

Note that the researchers needed the control group to demonstrate the effectiveness of the treatment (that is, members of the treatment group showed greater improvement than members of the control group). However, members of the control group were also offered treatment once the study came to an end.

As you can see from this example, cognitive behavioral therapy builds expectations of being effective. Therapists know that building these expectations increases the likelihood that people will behave effectively. Through setting attainable goals, developing realistic strategies for attaining them, and evaluating feedback realistically, you develop a sense of mastery and *self-efficacy* (Bandura, 1992, 1997). Your sense of self-efficacy influences your perceptions, motivation, and performance in many ways. Self-efficacy judgments influence how much effort you expend and how long you persist in the face of difficult life situations (Bandura, 2006). Researchers have demonstrated the importance of self-efficacy in recovery from psychological disorders (Benight et al., 2008; Kadden & Litt, 2011). Consider a study of 108 women with binge eating disorder (Cassin et al., 2008). Women in the control group received a handbook that provided information about the disorder. Women in the treatment group received the handbook but also participated in a therapy session designed to raise self-efficacy. For example, each woman was encouraged to "recall past experiences in which she [had] shown mastery in the face of difficulties and challenges" (p. 421). Sixteen weeks after the treatment, 28 percent of women in the treatment group had refrained from binge eating versus only 11 percent in the control group. Within the treatment group, the women who abstained from binge eating had reported higher levels of self-efficacy. This study provides further evidence that cognitive behavioral approaches to therapy can bring relief.

Stop *and* Review

① What is the underlying assumption of cognitive therapy?
② With respect to rational-emotive therapy, what is the origin of highly charged emotional reactions?
③ Why is increased self-efficacy a goal for cognitive behavioral therapy?

CRITICAL THINKING Recall the study that assessed cognitive behavioral therapy for compulsive buying disorder. Why was it important to identify the cues that triggered buying behavior?

✔●⌐Study and Review on MyPsychLab

HUMANISTIC THERAPIES

Humanistic therapies have at their core the concept of a whole person in the continual process of changing and of becoming. Although environment and heredity place certain restrictions, people always remain free to choose what they will become by creating their own values and committing to them through their own decisions. Along with this *freedom to choose*, however, comes the burden of responsibility. Because you are never fully aware of all the implications of your actions, you experience anxiety and despair. You also suffer from guilt over lost opportunities to achieve your full

How might volunteer work help people to maximize their human potential?

potential. Psychotherapies that apply the principles of this general theory of human nature attempt to help clients define their own freedom, value their experiencing selves and the richness of the present moment, cultivate their individuality, and discover ways of realizing their fullest potential (self-actualization).

In some cases, humanistic therapies also absorbed the lessons of *existentialist* approaches to human experience (May, 1975). This approach emphasizes people's ability to meet or be overwhelmed by the everyday challenges of existence. Existential theorists suggest that individuals suffer from *existential crises:* problems in everyday living, a lack of meaningful human relationships, and an absence of significant goals. A clinical version of existential theory, which integrates its various themes and approaches, assumes that the bewildering realities of modern life give rise to two basic kinds of human maladies. Depressive and obsessive syndromes reflect a retreat from these realities; sociopathic and narcissistic syndromes reflect an exploitation of these realities (Schneider & May, 1995).

The humanistic philosophy also gave rise to the **human-potential movement,** which emerged in the United States in the late 1960s. This movement encompassed methods to enhance the potential of the average human being toward greater levels of performance and greater richness of experience. Through this movement, therapy originally intended for

people with psychological disorders was extended to mentally healthy people who wanted to be more effective, more productive, and happier human beings.

Let's examine two types of therapies in the humanistic tradition: client-centered therapy and Gestalt therapy.

Client-Centered Therapy

As developed by Carl Rogers (1902–1987), *client-centered therapy* has had a significant impact on the way many different kinds of therapists define their relationships to their clients (Rogers, 1951, 1977). The primary goal of **client-centered therapy** is to promote the healthy psychological growth of the individual.

The approach begins with the assumption that all people share the basic tendency to self-actualize—that is, to realize their potential. Rogers believed that "it is the inherent tendency of the organism to develop all its capacities in ways which seem to maintain or enhance the organism" (1959, p. 196). Healthy development is hindered by faulty learning patterns in which a person accepts the evaluation of others in place of those provided by his or her own mind and body. A conflict between the naturally positive self-image and negative external criticisms creates anxiety and unhappiness. This conflict, or *incongruence,* may function outside of awareness, so that a person experiences feelings of unhappiness and low self-worth without knowing why.

The task of Rogerian therapy is to create a therapeutic environment that allows a client to learn how to behave to achieve self-enhancement and self-actualization. Because people are assumed to be basically good, the therapist's task is mainly to help remove barriers that limit the expression of this natural positive tendency. The basic therapeutic strategy is to recognize, accept, and clarify a client's feelings. This is accomplished within an atmosphere of *unconditional positive regard*—nonjudgmental acceptance and respect for the client. The therapist allows his or her own feelings and thoughts to be transparent to the client. In addition to maintaining this genuineness, the therapist tries to experience the client's feelings. Such total empathy requires that the therapist care for the client as a worthy, competent individual—not to be judged or evaluated but to be assisted in discovering his or her individuality (Meador & Rogers, 1979).

The emotional style and attitude of the therapist are instrumental in *empowering* the client to attend once again to the true sources of personal conflict and to remove the distracting influences that suppress self-actualization. Unlike practitioners of other therapies, who interpret, give answers, or instruct, the client-centered therapist is a supportive listener who reflects and, at times, restates the client's evaluative statements and feelings. Client-centered therapy strives to be *nondirective* by having the therapist merely facilitate the client's search for self-awareness and self-acceptance. Table 4 provides an excerpt from a session of client-centered therapy that captures these features (Rogers, 1951, p. 152).

Rogers believed that, once people are freed to relate to others openly and to accept themselves, individuals have the potential to lead themselves back to psychological health. This optimistic view and the humane relationship between

....

human-potential movement The therapy movement that encompasses all those practices and methods that release the potential of the average human being for greater levels of performance and greater richness of experience.

client-centered therapy A humanistic approach to treatment that emphasizes the healthy psychological growth of the individual based on the assumption that all people share the basic tendency of human nature toward self-actualization.

Table 4 • Excerpt from a Session with a Client-Centered Therapist

Alice: It seems—I don't know—It probably goes all the way back into my childhood. I've—for some reason I've—my mother told me that I was the pet of my father. Although I never realized it—I mean they never treated me as a pet at all. And other people always seemed to think I was sort of a privileged one in the family. But I never had any reason to think so. And as far I can see looking back on it now, it's just that the family let the other kids get away with more than they usually did me. And it seems for some reason to have held me to a more rigid standard than they did the other children.

Therapist: You're not so sure you were a pet in any sense, but more that the family situation seemed to hold you to pretty high standards. . . .

Alice: That's really the idea I've had. I think the whole business of my standards, or my values is one that I need to think about rather carefully, since I've been doubting for a long time whether I even have sincere ones.

Therapist: M-hm. Not sure whether you really have any deep values which you are sure of.

Reprinted by permission of Natalie Rogers, executor of the Estate of Carl Rogers.

therapist-as-caring-expert and client-as-person have influenced many practitioners.

Gestalt Therapy

Gestalt therapy focuses on ways to unite mind and body to make a person whole. Its goal of self-awareness is reached by helping clients express pent-up feelings and recognize unfinished business from past conflicts that is carried into new relationships and must be completed for growth to proceed. **Fritz Perls** (1893–1970), the originator of Gestalt therapy, asked clients to act out fantasies concerning conflicts and strong feelings and also to recreate their dreams, which he saw as repressed parts of personality. Perls said, "We have to *re-own* these projected, fragmented parts of our personality, and re-own the hidden potential that appears in the dream" (1969, p. 67).

In Gestalt therapy workshops, therapists encourage participants to regain contact with their "authentic inner voices" (Hatcher & Himelstein, 1996). Among the best known methods of Gestalt therapy is the *empty chair technique.* To carry out this technique, the therapist puts an empty chair near the client. The client is asked to imagine that a feeling, a person, an object, or a situation is occupying the chair. The client then "talks" to the chair's occupant. For example, clients would be encouraged to imagine their mother or father in the chair and reveal feelings they might otherwise be unwilling to reveal. The clients can then imagine those feelings in the chair to "talk" to the feelings about the impact they have on the clients' lives. This technique allows clients to confront and explore strong unexpressed feelings that may interfere with psychological well-being.

....

gestalt therapy Therapy that focuses on ways to unite mind and body to make a person whole.

Stop *and* Review

① What is the goal of the human-potential movement?
② In client-centered therapy, what is meant by unconditional positive regard?
③ In Gestalt therapy, what is the purpose of the empty chair technique?

✓•⌐[Study and **Review** on **MyPsychLab**

GROUP THERAPIES

All the treatment approaches outlined thus far are primarily designed as one-to-one relationships between a patient or client and a therapist. Many people, however, now experience therapy as part of a group. There are several reasons why group therapy has flourished. Some advantages are practical. Group therapy is less expensive to participants and allows small numbers of mental health personnel to help more clients. Other advantages relate to the power of the group setting. The group (1) is a less threatening situation for people who have problems dealing on their own with authority; (2) allows group processes to be used to influence individual maladaptive behavior; (3) provides people with opportunities to observe and practice interpersonal skills within the therapy session; and (4) provides an analogue of the primary family group, which enables corrective emotional experiences to take place.

Group therapy also poses some special problems (Motherwell & Shay, 2005). For example, some groups establish a culture in which little progress can be made—members create a norm of passivity and limited self-disclosure. In addition, the effectiveness of groups can change dramatically when members leave or join the groups. Both arrivals and departures can change the delicate balance that allows groups to function well as a unit. Therapists who specialize in group therapy must take care to address these group dynamics.

Some of the basic premises of group therapies differ from those of individual therapy. The social setting of group therapies provides an opportunity to learn how one comes across to others, how the self-image that is projected differs from the one that is intended or personally experienced. In addition, the

What are some strengths of group therapies?

group provides confirmation that one's symptoms, problems, and "deviant" reactions are not unique but often are quite common. Because people tend to conceal from others negative information about themselves, it is possible for many people with the same problem to believe "It's only me." The shared group experience can help to dispel this pluralistic ignorance in which many share the same false belief about their unique failings. In addition, the group of peers can provide social support outside the therapy setting.

Couple and Family Therapy

Much group therapy consists of strangers coming together periodically to form temporary associations from which they may benefit. Couple and family therapy brings meaningful, existing units into a therapy setting.

Couple therapy for marital problems seeks to clarify the typical communication patterns of the partners and then to improve the quality of their interaction (Snyder & Balderrama-Durbin, 2012). By seeing a couple together, and often by videotaping and replaying their interactions, a therapist can help them appreciate the verbal and nonverbal styles they use to dominate, control, or confuse each other. Each party is taught how to reinforce desirable responding in the other and withdraw reinforcement for undesirable reactions. They are also taught nondirective listening skills to help the other person clarify and express feelings and ideas. Couple therapy has been shown to reduce marital crises and keep marriages intact (Christensen et al., 2006).

In *family therapy*, the client is a whole nuclear family, and each family member is treated as a member of a *system* of relationships (Nutt & Stanton, 2011). A family therapist works with troubled family members to help them perceive what is creating problems for one or more of them. Consider circumstances in which a child has been diagnosed with an anxiety disorder. Research suggests that certain parenting practices may, unfortunately, maintain the child's anxiety (McLeod et al., 2011). For example, if parents do not allow their children sufficient autonomy, the children may never gain enough self-efficacy to cope successfully with novel tasks. Under those circumstances, novel tasks will continue to provoke anxiety. Family therapy can focus on both the child's anxiety and the parent's behaviors that may maintain that anxiety.

Researchers recruited 45 children, ages 9 to 13, to participate in a treatment study (Podell & Kendall, 2011). All the children had been diagnosed with an anxiety disorder (such as generalized anxiety disorder or social phobia). The children received a program of cognitive behavioral therapy that helped them recognize situations that provoked anxiety and develop skills to cope with the anxiety in those situations. The children's mothers and fathers also participated in the therapy sessions. The parents learned coping strategies alongside their children. In addition, the therapy attempted to modify parents' maladaptive behaviors with respect to the children's experience of anxiety and replace those behaviors with constructive responses. The researchers' analyses suggested that children whose parents were more engaged in the therapy sessions showed greater improvement.

This study illustrates the importance of the family therapy approach. By engaging the whole family, the therapeutic intervention changed environmental factors that may have helped maintain the children's levels of anxiety.

Family therapy can reduce tensions within a family and improve the functioning of individual members by helping clients recognize the positive as well as the negative aspects in their relationships. **Virginia Satir** (1916–1988), a developer of family therapy approaches, noted that the family therapist plays many roles, acting as an interpreter and clarifier of the interactions that are taking place in the therapy session and as influence agent, mediator, and referee (Satir, 1967). Most family therapists assume that the problems brought into therapy represent *situational* difficulties between people or problems of social interaction, rather than *dispositional* aspects of individuals. These difficulties may develop over time as members are forced into or accept unsatisfying roles. Nonproductive communication patterns may be set up in response to natural transitions in a family situation—loss of a job, a child going to school, dating, getting married, or having a baby. The job of the family therapist is to understand the structure of the family and the many forces acting on it. Then he or she works with the family members to dissolve "dysfunctional" structural elements while creating and maintaining new, more effective structures (Fishman & Fishman, 2003).

Community Support Groups

A dramatic development in therapy has been the surge of interest and participation in *mutual support groups* and *self-help groups*. There are over 6,000 of these groups in the United States that focus on mental health issues; self-help groups report over 1 million members (Goldstrom et al., 2006). Also, 5 million people over the age of 12 attend self-help groups for alcohol and illicit drugs each year in the United States (Substance Abuse and Mental Health Services Administration, 2008a). These support group sessions are typically free, especially when they are not directed by a health-care professional, and they give people a chance to meet others with the same problems who are surviving and sometimes thriving. The self-help concept applied to community group settings was pioneered by Alcoholics Anonymous (AA), which was founded in 1935. However, it was the women's consciousness-raising movement of the 1960s that helped extend self-help beyond the arena of alcoholism. Now support groups deal with four basic categories of problems: addictive behavior, physical and mental disorders, life transition or other crises, and the traumas experienced by friends or relatives of those with serious problems. In recent years, people have begun to turn to the Internet as another venue for self-help groups (Barak et al., 2008; Finn & Steele, 2010). In general, Internet self-help groups engage the same range of issues as their physical counterparts (Goldstrom et al., 2006). However, the Internet provides a particularly important meeting place for people who suffer from conditions that limit mobility, such as chronic fatigue syndrome and multiple sclerosis: An inability to attend meetings physically no longer denies people the benefits of self-help.

Self-help groups appear to serve a number of functions for their members: For example, they provide people with a sense of hope and control over their problems, they engage social support for people's suffering, and they provide a forum for dispensing and acquiring information about disorders and treatments (Groh et al., 2008). Researchers have begun to demonstrate that self-help groups may help bring relief alongside other forms of therapy. For example, participation in self-help groups has the potential to reduce symptoms of depression (Pfeiffer et al., 2011). 👁

A valuable development in self-help is the application of group therapy techniques to the situations of terminally ill patients. The goals of such therapy are to help patients and their families live lives as fulfilling as possible during their illnesses, to cope realistically with impending death, and to adjust to the terminal illness (Kissane et al., 2004). One general focus of such support groups for the terminally ill is to help patients learn how to live fully until they "say goodbye."

Group therapies are the final examples of types of therapies that are based purely on psychological interventions. Let's now analyze how biomedical therapies work to alter the brain in order to affect the mind.

Stop *and* Review

① How does group therapy help inform participants about the uniqueness of their problems?
② What is a common goal for couple therapy?
③ Under what circumstances are Internet self-help groups particularly valuable?

CRITICAL THINKING   Recall the study that used family therapy to treat children's anxiety disorders. Why was it important to include both parents in the treatment?

✔●[Study and **Review** on **MyPsychLab**

BIOMEDICAL THERAPIES

The ecology of the mind is held in delicate balance. When something goes wrong with the brain, we see the consequences in abnormal patterns of behavior and peculiar cognitive and emotional reactions. Similarly, environmental, social, or behavioral disturbances, such as drugs and violence, can alter brain chemistry and function. Biomedical therapies most often treat mental disorders as problems in the brain. This section describes four biomedical approaches: drug therapies, psychosurgery, electroconvulsive therapy (ECT), and repetitive transcranial magnetic stimulation (rTMS).

Drug Therapy

In the history of the treatment of mental disorders, nothing has rivaled the revolution created by the discovery of drugs that can calm anxious patients, restore contact with reality in withdrawn patients, and suppress hallucinations in psychotic

....

● Watch the Video *In the Real World: Self-Therapy* on MyPsychLab

● Watch the Video *Drugs Commonly Used to Treat Psychiatric Disorders* on MyPsychLab

psychopharmacology The branch of psychology that investigates the effects of drugs on behavior.

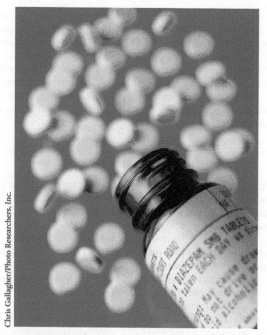

Chris Gallagher/Photo Researchers, Inc.

Why should people be cautious when they undertake drug therapies?

patients. This new therapeutic era began in 1953 with the introduction of tranquilizing drugs, notably *chlorpromazine*, into hospital treatment programs. Emerging drug therapies gained almost instant recognition and status as an effective way to transform patient behavior. **Psychopharmacology** is the branch of psychology that investigates the effects of drugs on behavior. Researchers in psychopharmacology work to understand the effect drugs have on some biological systems and the consequent changes in responding. 👁

The discovery of *drug therapies* had profound effects on the treatment of severely disordered patients. No longer did mental hospital staff have to act as guards, putting patients in seclusion or straitjackets; staff morale improved as rehabilitation replaced mere custodial care of the mentally ill (Swazey, 1974). Moreover, the drug therapy revolution had a great impact on the U.S. mental hospital population. Over half a million people were living in mental institutions in 1955, staying an average of several years. The introduction of chlorpromazine and other drugs reversed the steadily increasing numbers of patients. By the early 1970s, it was estimated that fewer than half the country's mental patients actually resided in mental hospitals; those who did were institutionalized for an average of only a few months.

The drugs that alleviate symptoms of various mental disorders are widely prescribed. As mental health care comes increasingly under the direction of health maintenance organizations (HMOs), cost-cutting practices are limiting the number of patients' visits to therapists for psychological therapies while substituting cheaper drug therapies. Researchers have documented great increases in prescriptions for drug therapies (Stagnitti, 2007). For that reason, it is important to understand the positive and negative features of drug therapies.

Three major categories of drugs are used today in therapy programs: *antipsychotic*, *antidepressant*, and *antianxiety* medications

Table 5 • Drug Therapies for Mental Illness

Disorder	Type of Therapy	Examples
Schizophrenia	Antipsychotic drug	chlorpromazine (Thorazine) haloperidol (Haldol) clozapine (Clozaril)
Depression	Tricyclic antidepressant Selective serotonin reuptake inhibitor Serotonin and norepinephrine reuptake inhibitor MAO inhibitor	imipramine (Tofranil) amitriptyline (Elavil) fluoxetine (Prozac) paroxetine (Paxil) sertraline (Zoloft) milnacipran (Dalcipran) venlafaxine (Effexor) phenelzine (Nardil) isocarboxazid (Marplan)
Bipolar disorder	Mood stabilizer	lithium (Eshalith)
Anxiety disorders	Benzodiazepines Antidepressant drug	diazepam (Valium) alprazolam (Xanax) fluoxetine (Prozac)

(see **Table 5**). As their names suggest, these drugs chemically alter specific brain functions that are responsible for psychotic symptoms, depression, and extreme anxiety.

Antipsychotic Drugs Antipsychotic drugs alter symptoms of schizophrenia such as delusions, hallucinations, social withdrawal, and occasional agitation. Antipsychotic drugs work by reducing the activity of the neurotransmitter dopamine in the brain (Keshavan et al., 2011). The earliest drugs researchers developed, like *chlorpromazine* (marketed under the U.S. brand name *Thorazine*) and *haloperidol* (marketed as *Haldol*) blocked or reduced the sensitivity of dopamine receptors. Although those drugs functioned by decreasing the overall level of brain activity, they were not just tranquilizers. For many patients, they did much more than merely eliminate agitation. They also relieved or reduced the positive symptoms of schizophrenia, including delusions and hallucinations.

There were, unfortunately, negative side effects of these early antipsychotic drugs. Because dopamine plays a role in motor control, muscle disturbances frequently accompany a course of drug treatment. *Tardive dyskinesia* is a particular disturbance of motor control, especially of the facial muscles, caused by antipsychotic drugs. Patients who develop this side effect experience involuntary jaw, lip, and tongue movements.

Over time, researchers created a new category of drugs, which are called *atypical* antipsychotic drugs, that create fewer motor side effects. The first member of this category, *clozapine* (marketed as *Clozaril*), was approved in the United States in 1989. Clozapine both directly decreases dopamine activity and increases the level of serotonin activity, which inhibits the dopamine system. This pattern of activity blocks dopamine receptors more selectively, resulting in a lower probability of motor disturbance. Unfortunately, *agranulocytosis*, a rare disease in which the bone marrow stops making white blood cells, develops in 1 to 2 percent of patients treated with clozapine.

Researchers have created a range of atypical antipsychotic drugs that act in the brain in a fashion similar to clozapine. Large-scale studies suggest that each of these drugs is effective in relieving the symptoms of schizophrenia—but each also has the potential for side effects. For example, people who take these drugs are at risk for weight gain and diabetes (Rummel-Kluge et al., 2010; Smith et al., 2008). Unfortunately, the side effects often prompt patients to discontinue the drug therapy. The rate of relapse when patients go off the drugs is quite high—even by taking lower than recommended doses of the drugs, patients substantially increase the risk of increased symptoms (Subotnik et al., 2011). Patients who remain on the newer drugs such as clozapine still have about a 15 to 20 percent chance of relapse (Leucht et al., 2003). Thus antipsychotic drugs do not cure schizophrenia—they do not eliminate the underlying psychopathology. Fortunately, they are reasonably effective at controlling the disorder's most disruptive symptoms.

Antidepressant Drugs Antidepressant drugs work by increasing the activity of the neurotransmitters norepinephrine and serotonin (Thase & Denko, 2008). Nerve cells communicate by releasing neurotransmitters into synaptic clefts (the small gaps between neurons). *Tricyclics,* such as *Tofranil* and *Elavil,* reduce the reuptake (removal) of the neurotransmitters from the synaptic cleft (see **Figure 2**). Drugs such as *Prozac* are known as *selective serotonin reuptake inhibitors* (SSRIs) because they specifically reduce the reuptake of serotonin. The *monoamine oxidase* (MAO) *inhibitors* limit the action of the enzyme monoamine oxidase, which is responsible for breaking down (metabolizing) norepinephrine. When MAO is inhibited, more of the neurotransmitter is left available. Thus each type of drug leaves more neurotransmitters available to bring about neural signals.

Antidepressant drugs can be successful at relieving the symptoms of depression, although as many as 50 percent of patients will not show improvement (Hollon et al., 2002). In fact, for people with mild or moderate symptoms of depression, antidepressant drugs show little impact beyond placebos (pills containing no active medication); they provide more substantial benefits for people with severe depression (Fournier et al., 2010). Because antidepressant drugs affect important neurotransmitter systems in the brain, they have the potential

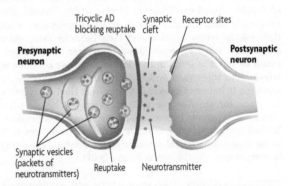

FIGURE 2 **The Brain Mechanisms of Tricyclic Antidepressants**

Tricyclic antidepressants block the reuptake of norepinephrine and serotonin so that the neurotransmitters remain in the synaptic cleft.

From Butcher, James N.; Mineka, Susan; Hooley, Jill M., *Abnormal Psychology*, 13th Ed., © 2007. Reprinted and electronically reproduced by permission of Pearson Education, Inc., Upper Saddle River, New Jersey.

for serious side effects. For example, people taking SSRIs such as Prozac may experience symptoms such as nausea, insomnia, nervousness, and sexual dysfunction. Tricyclics and MAO inhibitors may cause dry mouth, difficulty sleeping, and memory impairment. Research suggests that most of the major antidepressant drugs are roughly equal, across individuals, in their ability to bring relief (Hollon et al., 2002). For that reason, it is important for each individual to find the drug that yields the fewest side effects for him or her personally.

Researchers also continue to search for drugs that will help alleviate the symptoms of depression with fewer side effects. The newest class of drugs is called *serotonin and norepinephrine reuptake inhibitors,* or *SNRIs.* As that name suggests, these drugs, such as *Effexor* and *Dalcipran,* block the reuptake of both serotonin and norepinephrine. Clinical trials using these drugs have not found major differences in effectiveness with respect to SSRIs (Machado & Einarson, 2010). However, researchers still must determine which SNRIs function without serious side effects (Perahia et al., 2008).

In recent years, researchers have examined the important question of whether individuals—and, in particular, children and adolescents—who take antidepressant drugs are at greater risk for suicide. Although conclusions remain controversial, the majority of evidence supports the claim that drug treatment for depression does, in fact, yield a small increase in suicide risk (Möller et al., 2008). The important question is why this is the case. Some researchers believe that the drugs—in particular SSRIs—act in the brain to increase suicidal thoughts. Other researchers suggest that the small increase in suicide risk is an unfortunate consequence of the relief the drugs bring: Because major depressive order impairs motivation, people may be able to carry out suicidal behaviors only once their mental health starts to improve. For that reason, people who start drug treatment for major depressive disorder should receive consistent clinical attention to monitor for possible suicidal thoughts or intentions. Note also that many researchers have argued that, because antidepressant drugs bring relief from depression, they prevent many more suicides than they cause; their benefits outweigh their risks (Bridge et al., 2007).

Lithium salts have proven effective in the treatment of bipolar disorders (Thase & Denko, 2008). People who experience uncontrollable periods of hyperexcitement, when their energy seems limitless and their behavior extravagant and flamboyant, are brought down from their state of manic excess by doses of lithium. In addition, if people continue to take lithium when their symptoms are in remission, they are less likely to have recurrences of the disorder (Biel et al., 2007). However, for those people suffering from bipolar disorders who cycle frequently between manic episodes and depression, lithium appears to be less effective than other treatments such as the drug *valproate,* which was originally developed as a drug to prevent seizures (Cousins & Young, 2007).

Antianxiety Drugs Like antipsychotic and antidepressant drugs, antianxiety drugs generally have their effect by adjusting the levels of neurotransmitter activity in the brain. Different drugs are most effective at relieving different types of anxiety disorders (Hoffman & Mathew, 2008). Generalized anxiety disorder is best treated with a *benzodiazepine,* such as *Valium* or *Xanax,* which increases the activity of the neurotransmitter GABA. Because GABA regulates inhibitory neurons, increases in GABA activity decrease brain activity in areas of the brain relevant to generalized anxiety responses. Panic disorders, as well as agoraphobia and other phobias, can be treated with antidepressant drugs, although researchers do not yet understand the biological mechanism involved. Obsessive-compulsive disorder, which may arise from low levels of serotonin, responds particularly well to drugs, like Prozac, that specifically affect serotonin function.

As with drugs that treat schizophrenia and mood disorders, benzodiazepines affect a major neurotransmitter system and therefore have a range of potential side effects (Macaluso et al., 2010). People who begin a course of therapy may experience daytime drowsiness, slurred speech, and problems with coordination. The drugs may also impair cognitive processes such as attention and memory (Stewart, 2005). Furthermore, people who begin treatment with benzodiazepines often experience drug tolerance—they must increase their dosage to maintain a stable effect. Discontinuation of treatment might also lead to withdrawal symptoms (Tan et al., 2011). Because of the potential for psychological and physical dependence, people should undertake treatment with antianxiety drugs in careful consultation with a health-care provider.

Psychosurgery

When other therapies have failed to bring about relief, doctors have sometimes considered direct interventions in the brain. **Psychosurgery** is the general term for surgical procedures performed on brain tissue to alleviate psychological disorders. Such intervention involves lesioning (severing) connections between parts of the brain or removing small sections of the brain. The best known form of psychosurgery is the **prefrontal lobotomy,** an operation that severs the nerve fibers connecting the frontal lobes of the brain with the diencephalon, especially those fibers of the thalamic and hypothalamic areas. The procedure was developed by neurologist **Egas Moniz** (1874–1955), who, in 1949, won a Nobel Prize for this treatment.

The original candidates for lobotomy were agitated patients with schizophrenia and patients who were compulsive and anxiety ridden. The effects of this psychosurgery were dramatic: A new personality emerged without intense emotional arousal and, thus, without overwhelming anxiety, guilt, or anger. However, the operation permanently destroyed basic aspects of human nature. The lobotomy resulted in inability to plan ahead, indifference to the opinions of others, childlike actions, and the intellectual and emotional flatness of a person without a coherent sense of self. (One of Moniz's own patients was so distressed by these unexpected consequences that she shot Moniz, partially paralyzing him.)

Because the effects of psychosurgery are permanent, its continued use is very limited. Clinicians consider psychosurgery only when other treatments have repeatedly failed. For example, one study evaluated the effectiveness of a procedure called a *cingulotomy,* in which surgeons create lesions in the

....

psychosurgery A surgical procedure performed on brain tissue to alleviate a psychological disorder.

prefrontal lobotomy An operation that severs the nerve fibers connecting the frontal lobes of the brain with the diencephalon, especially those fibers in the thalamic and hypothalamic areas; best known form of psychosurgery.

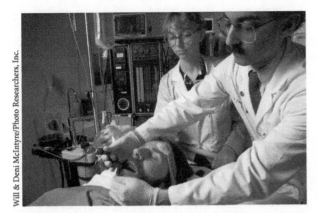
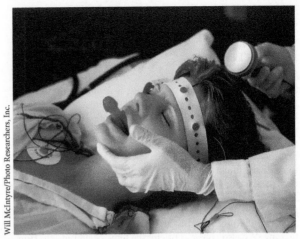

Electroconvulsive therapy has been very effective in cases of severe depression. Why does it remain controversial as a treatment?

limbic system structure called the cingulate gyrus (Shields et al., 2008). The 33 patients in the study had intractable major depression—they had failed to respond to four or more courses of drug treatment as well as other standard treatments. After the surgeries, 75 percent of the patients showed some relief from their symptoms. The cingulotomy procedure has also relieved the symptoms of patients with obsessive-compulsive disorder who were similarly unresponsive to drug treatments (Kim et al., 2003).

ECT and rTMS

Electroconvulsive therapy (ECT) is the use of electric shock applied to the brain to treat psychiatric disorders such as schizophrenia, mania, and, most often, depression. The technique consists of applying weak electric current to a patient's scalp until a seizure occurs. The strength of the current is adjusted to reflect seizure thresholds for particular patients (Kellner et al., 2010). The convulsion usually runs its course in 45 to 60 seconds. Patients are prepared for this traumatic intervention by sedation with a short-acting barbiturate and muscle relaxant, which renders the patient unconscious and minimizes the violent physical reactions.

Electroconvulsive therapy has proven quite successful at alleviating the symptoms of serious depression (Lisanby, 2007). ECT is particularly important because it works quickly. Typically, the symptoms of depression are alleviated in a three- or four-day course of treatment, as compared with the one- to two-week time window for drug therapies. Even so, most therapists hold ECT as a treatment of last resort. ECT is often reserved for emergency treatment for suicidal or severely malnourished, depressed patients and for patients who do not respond to antidepressant drugs or can't tolerate their side effects.

Although ECT is effective, it still remains controversial as a treatment. Scientific unease with ECT centers largely on the lack of understanding of how it works. Researchers have speculated that the treatment might rebalance neurotransmitters or hormones; they have also suggested that the repeated seizures might actually strengthen the brain (Keltner & Boschini, 2009). Much of the uncertainty remains because researchers cannot

ethically conduct experiments on human participants to provide definitive answers.

Critics have also worried about potential side effects of ECT. ECT produces temporary disorientation and a variety of cognitive deficits. For example, patients often suffer amnesia for events in the period of time preceding the treatment as well as difficulty forming new memories (Ingram et al., 2008). However, most patients recover from these deficits in the first few weeks after treatment. As a way of minimizing even short-term deficits, ECT is now often administered to only one side of the brain so as to reduce the possibility of speech impairment. Such unilateral ECT alleviates some of the cognitive consequences of the treatment and also remains an effective antidepressant (Fraser et al., 2008).

In recent years, researchers have explored an alternative to ECT called *repetitive transcranial magnetic stimulation (rTMS)*. People who undergo rTMS receive repeated pulses of magnetic stimulation to the brain. As with ECT, researchers have not yet determined why rTMS can bring relief for major depressive disorder and other forms of psychopathology. However, evidence is mounting that rTMS can be just as effective as some antidepressant drugs (Schutter, 2008). Researchers are working to determine how variables such as the intensity of the magnetic stimulation affect rTMS's ability to bring relief (Daskalakis et al., 2008).

Stop *and* Review

① What advantages do atypical antipsychotic drugs have over early drug therapies for schizophrenia?
② What do SNRIs do in the brain?
③ What are some effects of prefrontal lobotomies?
④ What is the rTMS procedure?

✓• Study and Review on MyPsychLab

....

electroconvulsive therapy (ECT) The use of electroconvulsive shock as an effective treatment for severe depression.

TREATMENT EVALUATION AND PREVENTION STRATEGIES

Suppose you have come to perceive a problem in your life that you believe could be alleviated by interaction with a trained clinician. This chapter has mentioned a great variety of types of therapies. How can you know which one of them will work best to relieve your distress? How can you be sure that *any* of them will work? This section examines the projects researchers undertake to test the effectiveness of particular therapies and make comparisons between different therapies. The general goal is to discover the most efficient way to help people overcome distress. As you will see, this research has also identified some factors that are common to all successful therapy. We also consider briefly the topic of *prevention*: How can psychologists intervene in people's lives to prevent mental illness before it occurs?

Evaluating Therapeutic Effectiveness

British psychologist Hans Eysenck (1952) created a furor some years ago by declaring that psychotherapy does not work at all! He reviewed available publications that reported the effects of various therapies and found that patients who received no therapy had just as high a recovery rate as those who received psychoanalysis or other forms of insight therapy. He claimed that roughly two-thirds of all people with neurotic problems would recover spontaneously within two years of the onset of the problem.

Researchers met Eysenck's challenge by devising more accurate methodologies to evaluate the effectiveness of therapy. What Eysenck's criticism made clear was that researchers needed to have appropriate control groups. For a variety of reasons, *some* percentage of individuals in psychotherapy *does* improve without any professional intervention. This **spontaneous-remission effect** is one *baseline* criterion against which the effectiveness of therapies must be assessed. Simply put, doing something must be shown to lead to a greater percentage of improved cases than doing nothing.

Similarly, researchers generally try to demonstrate that their treatment does more than just take advantage of clients' own expectations of healing. You may be familiar with *placebo* effects: In many cases, people's mental or physical health will improve because they expect that it will improve. The therapeutic situation helps bolster this belief by putting the therapist in the specific social role of *healer* (Frank & Frank, 1991). Although the placebo effects of therapy are an important

···

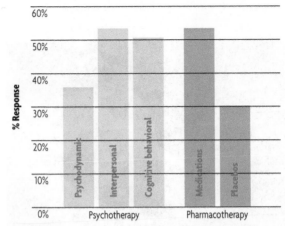

👁 Watch the Video *Thinking Like a Psychologist: Assessing the Effectiveness of Treatments* on MyPsychLab

spontaneous-remission effect The improvement of some mental patients and clients in psychotherapy without any professional intervention; a baseline criterion against which the effectiveness of therapies must be assessed.

placebo therapy A therapy interdependent of any specific clinical procedures that results in client improvement.

meta-analysis A statistical technique for evaluating hypotheses by providing a formal mechanism for detecting the general conclusions found in data from many different experiments.

FIGURE 3 Treatment Evaluation for Depression
The figure displays the results from meta-analyses of treatments for depression. For each treatment, the figure presents the percentage of patients who typically respond to each category of treatment. For example, about 50 percent of patients taking antidepressant medication experience recognizable symptom relief, whereas 50 percent do not.

part of the therapeutic intervention, researchers typically wish to demonstrate that their specific form of therapy is more effective than a **placebo therapy** (a neutral therapy that just creates expectations of healing) (Hyland et al., 2007).

In recent years, researchers have evaluated therapeutic effectiveness using a statistical technique called meta-analysis. **Meta-analysis** provides a formal mechanism for detecting the general conclusions to be found in data from many different experiments. In many psychological experiments, the researcher asks, "Did most of my participants show the effect I predicted?" Meta-analysis treats experiments like participants. With respect to the effectiveness of therapy, the researcher asks, "Did most of the outcome studies show positive changes?" 👁

Consider **Figure 3**, which presents the results of meta-analyses of the research literature on treatments for depression (Hollon et al., 2002). The figure compares results for three types of psychotherapies and medications (averaged across different types of antidepressant drugs) to placebo treatments. The chapter earlier described psychodynamic and cognitive behavioral therapies. Interpersonal therapy focuses on a patient's current life and interpersonal relationships. As you can see, across all the studies reviewed in the meta-analyses that contributed to this figure, interpersonal therapy, cognitive behavioral therapy, and drug therapies had a consistently larger impact than did placebos. At least for treatment of depression, classic psychodynamic therapy did not fare well.

Note that these data reflect the impact of each type of treatment alone. Researchers have assessed the effectiveness of psychotherapy alone versus psychotherapy combined with drug therapy. One study found that combination therapy was most able to bring about full remission from chronic depression (Manber et al., 2008). Of participants who completed a course of treatment, 14 percent of the participants who received only drug therapy met the study's criterion for full remission, as did 14 percent of the participants who received only psychotherapy.

For participants who received both drug therapy and psychotherapy, 29 percent showed the same level of improvement.

Because of such findings, contemporary researchers are less concerned about asking *whether* psychotherapy works and more concerned about asking why it works and whether any one treatment is most effective for any particular problem and for certain types of patients (Goodheart et al., 2006). For example, much treatment evaluation has been carried out in research settings that afford reasonable control over patients (often, the studies exclude individuals who have more than one disorder) and procedures (therapists are rigorously trained to minimize differences in treatment). Researchers need to ensure that therapies that work in research settings also work in community settings in which patients and therapists have more diversity of symptoms and experience (Kazdin, 2008). Another important issue for evaluation research is to assess the likelihood that individuals will complete a course of treatment. In almost all circumstances, some people choose to discontinue treatments (Barrett et al., 2008). Researchers seek to understand who leaves treatment and why—with the ultimate hope of creating treatments to which most everyone can adhere.

Let's turn now from comparisons of individual therapies to an analysis of the common factors that underlie successful therapies.

Common Factors

The last section described how researchers evaluate the effectiveness of specific therapies for particular disorders. However, other researchers have looked across the range of psychotherapies with the goal of identifying **common factors**—shared components that contribute to therapeutic effectiveness (Wampold, 2001). For successful therapies, these factors are most often present:

- The client has positive expectations and hope for improvement.
- The therapist is able to reinforce those expectations and cultivate hope.
- The therapy provides an explanation for how the client will change and allows the client to practice behaviors that will achieve that change.
- The therapy provides a clear plan for treatment.
- The client and therapist form a relationship that is characterized by trust, warmth, and acceptance.

As you consider this list of common factors, take a moment to see how they apply to each of the types of psychotherapy the chapter has reviewed.

Among these common factors, researchers have focused particular attention on the relationship between the therapist and the client. Whatever the form of the treatment, it's important that the individual seeking help enter into an effective therapeutic alliance. A *therapeutic alliance* is a mutual relationship that a client establishes with a therapist: The individual and the therapist collaborate to bring about relief. Research suggests that the quality of the therapeutic alliance has an impact on psychotherapy's ability to bring about improved mental health (Goldfried & Davila, 2005). In general, the more positive the therapeutic alliance, the more relief the client obtains (Horvath et al., 2011). The concept of the therapeutic alliance has several components, each of which also contributes to positive

How can prevention strategies encourage people to build habits to minimize the need for treatment?

outcomes. For example, clients experience more improvement from psychotherapy when they and the therapist share the same perspective on the goals for the therapy and agree on the processes that will achieve those goals (Tryon & Winograd, 2011). If you enter into therapy, you should believe that you can establish a strong therapeutic alliance with the therapist.

The final section of this chapter reflects on an important principle of life: Whatever the effectiveness of treatment, it is often better to prevent a disorder than to heal it once it arises.

Prevention Strategies

The traditional therapies this chapter has examined share the focus of changing a person who is already distressed or disabled. This focus is necessary because, much of the time, people are unaware that they are at risk for psychological disorders. They present themselves for treatment only once they have begun to experience symptoms. However, researchers have identified a number of biological and psychological factors that put people at risk. The goal of *prevention* is to apply knowledge of those risk factors to reduce the likelihood and severity of distress.

Prevention can be realized at several different levels. *Primary* prevention seeks to prevent a condition before it begins. Steps might be taken, for example, to provide individuals with coping skills so they can be more resilient or to change negative aspects of an environment that might lead to anxiety or depression (Boyd et al., 2006; Hudson et al., 2004). *Secondary* prevention attempts to limit the duration and severity of a disorder once it has begun. This goal is realized by means of programs that allow for early identification and prompt treatment. For example, based on assessments of therapeutic effectiveness, a mental health practitioner might recommend a combination of psychotherapy and drug therapy to optimize secondary prevention (Manber et al., 2008). *Tertiary* prevention limits the long-term impact of a

....

▶ **Simulate** the **Experiment** *Ineffective Therapies* on **MyPsychLab**

👁 **Watch** the **Video** *What's In It For Me?: Finding a Therapist if You Need One* on **MyPsychLab**

common factors The components that psychotherapies share that contribute to therapeutic effectiveness.

Critical Thinking in Your Life

CAN INTERNET-BASED THERAPY BE EFFECTIVE?

The therapies described in this chapter all share the common assumption that the therapist and client will meet face-to-face. However, as the Internet has become a standard element of most people's lives, psychotherapists have begun to explore possibilities of providing mental health care without traditional personal contact.

Let's consider an example of a successful program of Internet-based treatment for social phobia. People with social phobia experience anxiety when they anticipate public interactions. For that reason, the Internet holds the promise of providing treatment without requiring people with the disorder to enter the social sphere. In one study, people with social phobia completed a 10-week program of Internet modules that guided them through a course of cognitive behavioral therapy (Berger et al., 2009). Therapists were involved in the process via e-mail. They addressed the patients' questions and delivered motivating messages. At the end of the treatment, the patients' level of distress was compared to that of a control group of individuals who also had been diagnosed with social phobia. The patients who had completed the Internet-based treatment showed considerable improvement with respect to that control group.

Successes of this sort encourage therapists to pioneer innovative therapies delivered via the Internet. However, therapists have also taken a step back to consider some of the particular ethical issues that may arise when therapists and clients remain at a distance (Fitzgerald et al., 2010; Ross, 2011). For example, therapists worry that patients may be misdiagnosed if they present limited or distorted information without the extra scrutiny that is possible face-to-face Furthermore, consumers are rarely able to verify the credentials of online therapists; in cyberspace anyone can claim to be an expert. Finally, therapists who use the Internet are unable to assure their clients of confidentiality. There's a real danger that private information could be "hacked" and dragged into the public domain.

This concern about confidentiality may be particularly urgent because research evidence suggests that online therapy leads to disinhibition: The relative anonymity of this form of therapy allows clients to reveal their most pressing problems and concerns more quickly and with less embarrassment (Richards, 2009). Individuals may be more honest when they don't have to worry about their therapist's overt reactions to their difficult confessions.

But consider that rush of information in the context of the therapeutic alliance. Recall that the quality of the therapeutic alliance has a strong impact on psychotherapy's ability to bring about improved mental health (Goldfried & Davila, 2005; Horvath et al., 2011). Some therapists worry that the therapeutic alliance will necessarily be impaired if they are never face-to-face with their clients (Ross, 2011). Still, other therapists have suggested that Internet-based therapy has the capacity to bring relief because it activates the common factors that underlie the effectiveness of traditional therapies (Peck, 2010).

- In addition to social phobia, for what other psychological disorders might Internet-based therapy be particularly appropriate?
- What might therapists do to cope with confidentiality issues on the Internet?

---

psychological disorder by seeking to prevent a relapse. For example, this chapter noted earlier that individuals with schizophrenia who discontinue drug therapy have a very high rate of relapse (Fournier et al., 2010). To engage in tertiary prevention, mental health practitioners would recommend that their patients with schizophrenia continue their courses of antipsychotic drugs.

Within psychology, the field of *community psychology* plays a particular role in efforts to prevent psychological illness and promote wellness (Schueller, 2009). Community psychologists often design interventions that address the features of communities that put people at risk. For example, researchers have developed community-wide strategies to reduce substance abuse among urban adolescents (Diamond et al., 2009). These programs attempt to change community values with respect to drugs and alcohol and they also provide adolescents with drug-and-alcohol–free social activities.

Preventing mental disorders is a complex and difficult task. It involves not only understanding the relevant causal factors, but overcoming individual, institutional, and governmental resistance to change. A major research effort will be needed to demonstrate the long-range utility of prevention and the public health approach to psychopathology. The ultimate goal of prevention programs is to safeguard the mental health of all members of our society.

Stop and Review

① What conclusions can be drawn from meta-analyses of treatments for depression?
② What has research demonstrated about the importance of the therapeutic alliance?
③ What is the goal of primary prevention?

✓ Study and Review on MyPsychLab

Recapping Main Points

The Therapeutic Context

- Therapy requires that a diagnosis be made and a course of treatment be established.
- Therapy may be medically or psychologically oriented.
- The four major types of psychotherapies are psychodynamic, behavior, cognitive, and humanistic.
- A variety of professionals practice therapy.
- Researchers must assess the effectiveness of psychotherapies across diverse groups.
- Harsh early treatment of those with mental illnesses led to a modern movement for deinstitutionalization.
- Unfortunately, many people do not have adequate resources outside the institution, so they may become homeless or quickly are readmitted to institutions.

Psychodynamic Therapies

- Psychodynamic therapies grew out of Sigmund Freud's psychoanalytic theory.
- Freud emphasized the role of unconscious conflicts in the etiology of psychopathology.
- Psychodynamic therapy seeks to reconcile these conflicts.
- Free association, attention to resistance, dream analysis, transference, and countertransference are all important components of this therapy.
- Other psychodynamic theorists place more emphasis on the patient's current social situation and interpersonal relationships.

Behavior Therapies

- Behavior therapies use the principles of learning and reinforcement to modify or eliminate problem behaviors.
- Counterconditioning techniques replace negative behaviors, like phobic responses, with more adaptive behaviors.
- Exposure is the common element in phobia-modification therapies.
- Contingency management uses operant conditioning to modify behavior, primarily through positive reinforcement and extinction.

Cognitive Therapies

- Cognitive therapy concentrates on changing negative or irrational thought patterns about the self and social relationships.
- Cognitive therapy has been used successfully to treat depression.
- Rational-emotive therapy helps clients recognize that their irrational beliefs about themselves interfere with successful life outcomes.

- Cognitive behavioral therapy calls for the client to learn more constructive thought patterns in reference to a problem and to apply the new technique to other situations.

Humanistic Therapies

- Humanistic therapies work to help individuals become more fully self-actualized.
- Therapists strive to be nondirective in helping their clients establish a positive self-image that can deal with external criticisms.
- Gestalt therapy focuses on the whole person—body, mind, and life setting.

Group Therapies

- Group therapy allows people to observe and engage in social interactions as a means to reduce psychological distress.
- Family and marital therapy concentrates on situational difficulties and interpersonal dynamics of the couple or family group as a system in need of improvement.
- Community and Internet self-help groups allow individuals to obtain information and feelings of control in circumstances of social support.

Biomedical Therapies

- Biomedical therapies concentrate on changing physiological aspects of mental illness.
- Drug therapies include antipsychotic medications for treating schizophrenia as well as antidepressants and antianxiety drugs.
- Psychosurgery is rarely used because of its radical, irreversible effects.
- Electroconvulsive therapy and repetitive transcranial magnetic stimulation (rTMS) can be effective with depressed patients.

Treatment Evaluation and Prevention Strategies

- Research shows that many therapies work better than the mere passage of time or nonspecific placebo treatment.
- Evaluation projects are helping to answer the question of what makes therapy effective.
- Common factors, including the quality of the therapeutic alliance, underlie the effectiveness of therapies.
- Prevention strategies are necessary to stop psychological disorders from occurring and minimize their effects once they have occurred.

KEY TERMS

aversion therapy
behavior modification
behavior therapy
biomedical therapy
catharsis
client
client-centered therapy
clinical psychologist
clinical social worker
cognitive behavioral therapy
cognitive therapy
common factors
contingency management
counseling psychologist

counterconditioning
countertransference
deinstitutionalization
dream analysis
electroconvulsive therapy (ECT)
exposure therapy
free association
Gestalt therapy
human-potential movement
insight therapy
meta-analysis
participant modeling
pastoral counselor
patient

placebo therapy
prefrontal lobotomy
psychiatrist
psychoanalysis
psychoanalyst
psychopharmacology
psychosurgery
psychotherapy
rational-emotive therapy (RET)
resistance
spontaneous-remission effect
systematic desensitization
transference

Practice Test

✔•—Study and Review on MyPsychLab

1. When Sonja begins treatment, her therapist focuses on her inner conflicts, which he believes remain unresolved. It seems that Sonja's therapist takes a _____ approach.
   a. psychodynamic
   b. cognitive
   c. biological
   d. humanist

2. Which of these topics would you be *least* likely to hear about in a lecture on deinstitutionalization?
   a. homelessness
   b. meta-analysis
   c. readmission rates
   d. violent crime

3. In psychodynamic therapy, _____ refers to a patient's inability or unwillingness to discuss certain topics.
   a. catharsis
   b. transference
   c. countertransference
   d. resistance

4. Research on repressed memories suggests that
   a. recovered memories are never accurate.
   b. people's memories are not subject to therapists' influence.
   c. some memories of abuse are implanted by therapists.
   d. most memories are subject to repression.

5. If Roland undergoes _____, he should expect to have a strong noxious stimulus paired with stimuli to which he is attracted.
   a. systematic desensitization
   b. behavioral rehearsal
   c. participant modeling
   d. aversion therapy

6. Every time Janice provides a urine sample that is drug free, she gets vouchers with which she can purchase items she enjoys. This treatment is a form of
   a. systematic desensitization.
   b. contingency management.
   c. participant modeling.
   d. generalization.

7. People can learn the process of _____ to change negative self-statements into positive coping statements.
   a. social learning
   b. self-efficacy
   c. cognitive restructuring
   d. catharsis

8. You hear a therapist talking about how hard he works to communicate unconditional regard. You suspect that he is a _____ therapist.
   a. Gestalt
   b. client-centered
   c. behavioral
   d. psychodynamic

9. In your introductory psychology class, you watch a movie clip of an individual in therapy addressing an empty chair as if it were his abusive boss. This clip demonstrates _____ therapy.
   a. Gestalt
   b. client-centered
   c. aversion
   d. psychodynamic

10. The particular focus of _____ therapy will often be on poor patterns of communication.
    a. Gestalt
    b. client-centered
    c. couple
    d. psychodynamic

11. _____ drugs largely have their impact in the brain by changing the function of the neurotransmitters serotonin and norepinephrine.
    a. Antidepressant
    b. Antianxiety
    c. Antipsychotic
    d. Antimania

12. In clinical research, _____ proven effective at relieving the symptoms of depression.
    a. only ECT has
    b. only rTMS has
    c. neither ECT nor rTMS have
    d. both ECT and rTMS have

13. _____ therapy is the type of treatment *least* likely to provide relief from major depressive disorder.
    a. Placebo
    b. Interpersonal
    c. Cognitive behavioral
    d. Drug

14. When prevention efforts are intended to prevent relapse, it is called _____ prevention.
    a. primary
    b. regulatory
    c. tertiary
    d. secondary

15. Because of the relative anonymity of interactions over the Internet, clients' interactions with therapists may show _____.
    a. countertransference
    b. greater embarrassment
    c. confidentiality
    d. disinhibition

ESSAY QUESTIONS

1. Why do behavior therapies target adaptive and maladaptive behaviors?

2. What features of self-help groups make them beneficial to mental health?

3. Why are therapies compared to placebos to evaluate their effectiveness?

Stop and Review Answers

Stop and Review (The Therapeutic Context)

1. The goals of the process are to reach a diagnosis, propose a probable etiology, make a prognosis, and carry out a treatment.
2. Psychoanalysts have completed postgraduate training in the Freudian approach to therapy.
3. Research suggests that therapists with greater cultural competence achieve better therapeutic outcomes.
4. Substantial numbers of patients who are released from psychiatric institutions are readmitted after a short amount of time.

Stop and Review (Psychodynamic Therapies)

1. Psychodynamic therapy is also known as insight therapy because a central goal is to guide a patient toward insights into the relationships between present symptoms and past conflicts.
2. Transference refers to circumstances in which a patient develops an emotional reaction toward the therapist that often represents an emotional conflict from the patient's life.
3. Klein believed that the death instinct precedes sexual awareness and leads to an innate aggressive impulse.

Stop and Review (Behavior Therapies)

1. Treatments using counterconditioning attempt to replace a maladaptive response (such as fear) with a healthy response (such as relaxation).
2. Typically, clinicians use prizes to provide positive reinforcement for desirable behaviors (such as remaining drug free).
3. Generalization techniques attempt to preserve the positive changes of therapy over time.

Stop and Review (Cognitive Therapies)

1. The underlying assumption of cognitive therapy is that abnormal behavior patterns and emotional distress arise from problems in what and how people think.
2. RET suggests that irrational beliefs lead to maladaptive emotional responses.
3. A goal of cognitive behavioral therapy is to change people's behaviors—it is important that they believe they have the efficacy to perform adaptive behaviors.

Stop and Review (Humanistic Therapies)

1. The goal of the human-potential movement was to enhance individuals' potential toward greater levels of performance and greater richness of experience.

2. A client-centered therapist establishes a setting with unconditional positive regard—nonjudgmental acceptance and respect for the client.
3. In Gestalt therapy, clients imagine that a feeling, person, object, or situation is occupying an empty chair; they talk to the chair's "occupant" to work through issues in their lives.

Stop and Review (Group Therapies)

1. Group therapy gives participants an opportunity to understand that the types of problems they have may actually be quite common.
2. The goal of couple therapy is often to help partners clarify and improve the quality of their interactions.
3. Internet self-help groups are particularly valuable for individuals with mobility issues, who otherwise might not have access to these groups.

Stop and Review (Biomedical Therapies)

1. Atypical antipsychotic drugs help alleviate the symptoms of schizophrenia without causing severe problems in motor control.
2. SNRIs inhibit the reuptake of both serotonin and norepinephrine.
3. The procedure fundamentally alters personalities: People become less emotional, but they also lose their sense of self.
4. When people undergo the rTMS procedure, repeated pulses of magnetic stimulation are focused on their brains.

Stop and Review (Treatment Evaluation and Prevention Strategies)

1. The meta-analyses suggest that many standard treatments for depression (such as cognitive behavioral therapy and drug therapy) provide relief beyond a placebo treatment.
2. Research has demonstrated that, in general, more positive therapeutic alliances bring about more relief from psychological disorders.
3. The goal of primary prevention is to implement programs that lower the probability that individuals will experience mental illnesses.

Practice Test Answers

1. a	**5.** d	**9.** a	**13.** a
2. b	**6.** b	**10.** c	**14.** c
3. d	**7.** c	**11.** a	**15.** d
4. c	**8.** b	**12.** d	

References

Bandura, A. (1970). Modeling therapy. In W. S. Sahakian (Ed.), *Psychopathology today: Experimentation, theory and research.* Itasca, IL: Peacock.

Bandura, A. (1992). Exercise of personal agency through the self-efficacy mechanism. In R. Schwarzer (Ed.), *Self-efficacy: Thought control of action* (pp. 3–38). Washington, DC: Hemisphere.

Bandura, A. (1997). *Self-efficacy: The exercise of control.* New York: Freeman.

Bandura, A. (2006). Toward of psychology of human agency. *Perspectives on Psychological Science, 1,* 164–180.

Barak, A., Boniel-Nissim, M., & Suler, J. (2008). Fostering empowerment in online support groups. *Computers in Human Behavior, 24,* 1867–1883.

Barrett, M. S., Chua, W.-J., Crits-Christoph, P., Gibbons, M. B., & Thompson, D. (2008). Early withdrawal from mental health treatment: Implications for psychotherapy practice. *Psychotherapy Theory, Research, Practice, Training, 45,* 247–267.

Beck, A. T. (1976). *Cognitive therapy and emotional disorders.* New York: International Universities Press.

Beck, A. T., & Rush, A. J. (1989). Cognitive therapy. In H. I. Kaplan & B. Sadock (Eds.), *Comprehensive textbook of psychiatry* (Vol. 5). Baltimore: Williams & Wilkins.

Beck, A. T., Rush, A. J., Shaw, B. F., & Emery, G. (1979). *Cognitive therapy of depression.* New York: Guilford Press.

Benight, C. C., Cieslak, R., Molton, I. R., & Johnson, L. E. (2008). Self-evaluative appraisals of coping capability and posttraumatic distress following motor vehicle accidents. *Journal of Consulting and Clinical Psychology, 76,* 677–685.

Benish, S. G., Quintant, S., & Wampold, B. E. (2011). Culturally adapted psychotherapy and the legitimacy of myth: A direct-comparison meta-analysis. *Journal of Counseling Psychology, 58,* 279–289.

Berger, T., Hold, E., & Caspar, F. (2009). Internet-based treatment for social phobia: A randomized control trial. *Journal of Clinical Psychology, 65,* 1021–1035.

Bernal, G., Jiménez-Chafey, M. I., & Domenech Rodríguez, M. M. (2009). Cultural adaptation of treatments: A resource for considering culture in evidence-based practice. *Professional Psychology: Research and Practice, 40,* 361–368.

Biel, M. B., Preselow, E., Mulcare, L., Case, B. G., & Fieve, R. (2007). Continuation versus discontinuation of lithium in recurrent bipolar illness: A naturalistic study. *Bipolar Disorders, 9,* 435–442.

Bolden, L., & Wicks, M. N. (2005). Length of stay, admission types, psychiatric diagnoses, and the implications of stigma in African Americans in the nationwide inpatient sample. *Issues in Mental Health Nursing, 26,* 1043–1059.

Bolton, D., & Perrin, S. (2008). Evaluation of exposure with response—prevention for obsessive compulsive disorder in childhood and adolescence. *Journal of Behavior Therapy and Experimental Psychiatry, 39,* 11–22.

Botella, C., Bretón-López, J., Quero, S., Baños, R., & García-Palacios, A. (2010). Treating cockroach phobia with augmented reality. *Behavior Therapy, 41,* 401–413.

Boyd, R. C., Diamond, G. S., & Bourolly, J. N. (2006). Developing a family-based depression prevention program in urban community mental health clinics: A qualitative investigation. *Family Process, 45,* 187–203.

Bridge, J. A., & Barbe, R. P. (2004). Reducing hospital readmission in depression and schizophrenia: Current evidence. *Current Opinion in Psychiatry, 17,* 505–511.

Bridge, J. A., Iyengar, S., Salary, C. B., Barbe, R. P., Birmaher, B., Pincus, H. A., Ren, L., & Brent, D. A. (2007). Clinical response and risk for reported suicidal ideation and suicide attempts in pediatric antidepressant treatment: A meta-analysis of randomized controlled trials. *JAMA, 297,* 1683–1696.

Burgard, M., & Mitchell, J. E. (2000). Group cognitive behavioral therapy for buying disorder. In A. L. Benson (Ed.), *I shop therefore I am: Compulsive buying and the search for self* (pp. 367–397). Northvale, NJ: Jason Aronson.

Cassin, S. E., von Ranson, K. M., Heng, K., Brar, J., & Wojtowica, A. E. (2008). Adapted motivational interviewing for women with binge eating disorder: A randomized controlled trial. *Psychology of Addictive Behaviors, 22,* 417–425.

Christensen, A., Atkins, D. C., Yi, J., Baucom, D. H., & George, W. H. (2006). Couple and individual adjustment for 2 years following a randomized clinical trial comparing traditional versus integrative behavioral couple therapy. *Journal of Consulting and Clinical Psychology, 74,* 1180–1191.

Cousins, D. A., & Young, A. H. (2007). The armamentarium of treatments for bipolar disorder: A review of the literature. *International Journal of Neuropsychopharmacology, 10,* 411–431.

Daskalakis, Z. J., Levinson, A. J., & Fitzgerald, P. B. (2008). Repetitive transcranial magnetic stimulation for major depressive disorder: A review. *Canadian Journal of Psychiatry, 53,* 555–566.

de Rivera, J. (1997). The construction of false memory syndrome: The experience of retractors. *Psychological Inquiry, 8,* 271–292.

Diamond, S., Schensul, J. J., Snyder, L. B., Bermudez, A., D'Alessandro, N., & Morgan, D. S. (2009). Building Xperience: A multilevel alcohol and drug prevention intervention. *American Journal of Community Psychology, 43,* 292–312.

Dickerson, F. B., Tenhula, W. N., & Green-Paden, L. D. (2005). The token economy for schizophrenia: Review of the literature and recommendations for future research. *Schizophrenia Research, 75,* 405–416.

Ellis, A. (1962). *Reason and emotion in psychotherapy.* New York: Lyle Stuart.

Ellis, A. (1995). *Better, deeper, and more enduring brief therapy: The rational emotive behavior therapy approach.* New York: Brunner/Mazel.

Eysenck, H. J. (1952). The effects of psychotherapy: An evaluation. *Journal of Consulting Psychology, 16,* 319–324.

Finn, J., & Steele, T. (2010). Online self-help/mutual aid groups in mental health practice. In L. D. Brown & S. Wituk (Eds.), *Mental health self-help* (pp. 87–105). New York: Springer.

Fitzgerald, T. D., Hunter, P. V., Hadjistavropoulos, T., & Koocher, G. P. (2010). Ethical and legal considerations for Internet-based psychotherapy. *Cognitive Behaviour Therapy, 39,* 173–187.

Foucault, M. (1975). *The birth of the clinic.* New York: Vintage Books.

Fournier, J. C., DeRubeis, R. J., Hollon, S. D., Dimidjian, S., Amsterdam, J. D., Shelton, R. C., & Fawcett, J. (2010). Antidepressant drug effects and depression severity: A patient-level meta-analysis. *Journal of the American Medical Association, 303,* 47–53.

Frager, R., & Fadiman, J. (1998). *Personality and personal growth.* New York: Longman.

Frank, J. D., & Frank, J. B. (1991). *Persuasion and healing: A comparative study of psychotherapy* (3rd ed.). Baltimore: Johns Hopkins University Press.

Freud, S. (1923). *Introductory lectures on psychoanalysis* (J. Riviera, Trans.). London: Allen & Unwin.

Geraerts, E., Schooler, J. W., Merckelbach, H., Jelicic, M., Hauer, B. J. A., & Ambadar, Z. (2007). The reality of recovered memories: Corroborating continuous and discontinuous memories of childhood sexual abuse. *Psychological Science, 18,* 564–568.

Gibbons, M. B. C., Crits-Christoph, P., & Hearon, B. (2008). The empirical status of psychodynamic therapies. *Annual Review of Clinical Psychology, 4,* 93–108.

Goldfried, M. R. (2003). Cognitive-behavior therapy: Reflections on the evolution of a therapeutic orientation. *Cognitive Therapy and Research, 27*, 53–69.

Goldfried, M. R. (2003). Cognitive-behavior therapy: Reflections on the evolution of a therapeutic orientation. *Cognitive Therapy and Research, 27*, 53–69.

Goldfried, M. R., & Davila, J. (2005). The role of relationship and technique in therapeutic change. *Psychotherapy: Theory, Research, Practice, Training, 42*, 421–430.

Goldstrom, I. D., Campbell, J., Rogers, J. A., Lambert, D. B., Blacklow, B., Henderson, M. J., & Manderscheid, R. W. (2006). National estimates for mental health support groups, self-help organizations, and consumer-operated services. *Administration and Policy in Mental Health and Mental Health Services Research, 33*, 92–103.

Goodheart, C. D., Kadzin, A. E., & Sternberg, R. J. (2006). *Evidence-based psychotherapy: Where practice and research meet.* Washington, DC: American Psychological Association.

Greenberg, S. T., & Schoen, E. G. (2008). Males and eating disorders: Gender-based therapy for eating disorder recovery. *Professional Psychology: Research and Practice, 39*, 464–471.

Groh, D. R., Jason, L. A., & Keys, C. B. (2008). Social network variables in alcoholics anonymous: A literature review. *Clinical Psychology Review, 28*, 430–450.

Hall, J. S. (2004). *Roadblocks on the journey of psychotherapy.* Lanham, MD: Jason Aronson.

Hatcher, C., & Himelstein, P. (Eds.). (1996). *The handbook of Gestalt therapy.* Northvale, NJ: Jason Aronson.

Hayes, J. A., Gelso, C. J., & Hummel, A. M. (2011). Managing countertransference. *Psychotherapy, 48*, 88–97.

Hoffman, E. J., & Mathew, S. J. (2008). Anxiety disorders: A comprehensive review of pharmacotherapies. *Mount Sanai Journal of Medicine, 75*, 248–262.

Hollon, S. D., Stewart, M. O., & Strunk, D. (2006). Enduring effects for cognitive behavior therapy in the treatment of depression and anxiety. *Annual Review of Psychology, 57*, 285–315.

Hollon, S. D., Thase, M. E., & Markowitz, J. C. (2002). Treatment and prevention of depression. *Psychological Science in the Public Interest, 3*, 39–77.

Horvath, A. O., Del Re, A. C., Flückiger, C., & Symonds, D. (2011). Alliance in individual psychotherapy. *Psychotherapy, 48*, 9–16.

Houlihan, D., Schwartz, C., Miltenberger, R., & Heuton, D. (1993). The rapid treatment of a young man's balloon (noise) phobia using in vivo flooding. *Journal of Behavior Therapy and Experimental Psychiatry, 24*, 233–240.

Hudson, J. L., Flannery-Schroeder, E., & Kendall, P. (2004). Primary prevention of anxiety disorders. In D. J. A. Dozois, & K. S. Dobson (Eds.), *The prevention of anxiety and depression: Theory, research, and practice* (pp. 101–130). Washington, DC: American Psychological Association.

Hyland, M. E., Whalley, B., & Geraghty, A. W. A. (2007). Dispositional predictors of placebo responding: A motivational interpretation of flower essence and gratitude therapy. *Journal of Psychosomatic Research, 62*, 331–340.

Imel, Z. E., Baldwin, S., Atkins, D. C., Owen, J., Baardseth, T., & Wampold, B. E. (2011). Racial/ethnic disparities in therapist effectiveness: A conceptualization and initial study of cultural competence. *Journal of Counseling Psychology, 58*, 290–298.

Ingram, A., Saling, M. M., & Schweitzer, I. (2008). Cognitive side effects of brief pulse electroconvulsive therapy: A review. *The Journal of ECT, 24*, 3–9.

Jones, M. C. (1924). A laboratory study of fear: The case of Peter. *Pedagogical Seminary and Journal of Genetic Psychology, 31*, 308–315.

Kadden, R. M., & Litt, M. D. (2011). The role of self-efficacy in the treatment of substance abuse disorders. *Addictive Behaviors, 36*, 1120–1126.

Kazdin, A. E. (2008). Evidence-based treatment and practice: New opportunities to bridge clinical research and practice, enhance the knowledge base, and improve patient care. *American Psychologist, 63*, 146–159.

Kellner, C. H., Knapp, R., Husain, M. M., Rasmussen, K., Samplson, S., Cullum, M., McClintock, S. M., Tobias, K. G., Martino, C., Mueller, M., Bailine, S. H., Fink, M., & Petrides, G. (2010). Bifrontal, bitemporal and right unilateral placement in ECT: Randomised trial. *The British Journal of Psychiatry, 196*, 226–234.

Keltner, N. L, & Boschini, D. J. (2009). Electroconvulsive therapy. *Perspectives in Psychiatric Care, 45*, 66–70.

Keshavan, M. S., Nasrallah, H. A., & Tandon, R. (2011). Schizophrenia, "Just the facts" 6. Moving ahead with the schizophrenia concept: From the elephant to the mouse. *Schizophrenia Research, 127*, 3–13.

Kim, H. S., Sherman, D. K., & Taylor, S. E. (2008). Culture and social support. *American Psychologist, 63*, 518–526.

Kissane, D. W., Grabsch, B., Clarke, D. M., Christie, G., Clifton, D., Gold, S., Hill, C., Morgan, A., McDermott, F., & Smith, G. C. (2004). Supportive-expressive group therapy: The transformation of existential ambivalence into creative living while enhancing adherence to anticancer therapies. *Psycho-Oncology, 13*, 755–768.

Klein, M. (1975). *The writings of Melanie Klein* (Vols. 1–4). London: Hogarth Press and the Institute of Psychoanalysis.

Lamb, R. J., Morral, A. R., Kirby, K. C., Javors, M. A., Galbicka, G., & Iguchi, M. (2007). Contingencies for change in complacent smokers. *Experimental and Clinical Psychopharmacology, 15*, 245–255.

Leucht, S., Barnes, T. R. E., Kissling, W., Engel, R. R., Correll, C., & Kane, J. M. (2003). Relapse prevention in schizophrenia with new—generation antipsychotics: A systematic review and exploratory meta-analysis of randomized, controlled trials. *American Journal of Psychiatry, 160*, 1209–1222.

Lin, H., Tian, W., Chen, C., Liu, T., Tsai, S., & Lee, H. (2006). The association between readmission rates and length of stay for schizophrenia: A 3-year population based study. *Schizophrenia Research, 83*, 211–214.

Lisanby, S. H. (2007). Electroconvulsive therapy for depression. *New England Journal of Medicine, 357*, 1939–1945.

Luborsky, L., & Barrett, M. S. (2006). The history and empirical status of key psychoanalytic concepts. *Annual Review of Clinical Psychology, 2*, 1–19.

Lynn, S. J., Lock, T., Loftus, E. F., Krackow, E., & Lilienfeld, S. O. (2003). The remembrance of things past: Problematic memory recovery techniques in psychotherapy. In S. O. Lilienfeld, S. J. Lynn, & J. M. Lohr (Eds.), Marcus, A. D. (1990, December 3). Mists of memory cloud some legal proceedings. *Wall Street Journal*, p. B1.

Macaluso, M., Kalia, R., Ali, F., & Khan, A. Y. (2010). The role of benzodiazepines in the treatment of anxiety disorders: A clinical review. *Psychiatric Annals, 40*, 605–610.

Machado, M., & Einarson, T. R. (2010). Comparison of SSRIs and SNRIs in major depressive disorder: A meta-analysis of head-to-head randomized clinical trials. *Journal of Clinical Pharmacy and Therapeutics, 35*, 177–188.

Manber, R., Kraemer, H. C., Arnow, B. A., Trivedi, M. H., Rush, A. J., Thase, M. E., Rothbaum, B. O., Klein, D. N., Kocsis, J. H., Gelenberg, A. J., & Keller, M. E. (2008). Faster remission of chronic depression with combined psychotherapy and medication than with each therapy alone. *Journal of Consulting and Clinical Psychology, 76*, 459–467.

Mark, T. L., Levit, K. R., Buck, J. A., Coffey, R. M., & Vandivort-Warren, R. (2007). Mental health treatment expenditure trends, 1986–2003. *Psychiatric Services, 58*, 1041–1048.

Matson, J. L., & Boisjoli, J. A. (2009). The token economy for children with intellectual disability and/or autism: A review. *Research in Developmental Disabilities, 30*, 240–248.

May, R. (1975). *The courage to create.* New York: Norton.

McLeod, B. D., Wood, J. J., & Avny, S. B. (2011). Parenting and child anxiety disorders. In D. McKay & E. A. Storch (Eds.), *Handbook of child and adolescent anxiety disorders* (pp. 213–228). New York: Springer.

Meador, B. D., & Rogers, C. R. (1979). Person-centered therapy. In R. J. Corsini (Ed.), *Current psychotherapies* (2nd ed., pp. 131–184). Itasca, IL: Peacock.

Meichenbaum, D. (1977). *Cognitive-behavior modification: An integrative approach.* New York: Plenum.

Meichenbaum, D. (1985). *Stress inoculation training.* New York: Pergamon Press.

Meichenbaum, D. (1993). Changing conceptions of cognitive behavior modification: Retrospect and prospect. *Journal of Consulting and Clinical Psychology, 61,* 202–204.

Möller, J.-J., Baldwin, D. S., Goodwin, G., Kasper, S., Okasha, A., Stein, D. J., Tandon, R., Versiani, M., & the WPA section on Pharmacopsychiatry. (2008). Do SSRIs or antidepressants in general increase suicidality? WPA Section on Pharmacopsychiatry: Consensus statement. *European Archives of Psychiatry and Clinical Neuroscience, 258* (Suppl. 3), 3–23.

Motherwell, L., & Shay, J. J. (2005). (Eds.). *Complex dilemmas in group therapy.* New York: Brunner-Routledge.

Mueller, A., Mueller, U., Silbermann, A., Reinecker, H., Bleich, S., Mitchell, J. E., & de Zwaan, M. (2008). A randomized, controlled trial of group cognitive-behavioral therapy for compulsive buying disorder: Posttreatment and 6-month follow-up results. *Journal of Clinical Psychiatry, 69,* 1131–1138.

Nielsen, S. F., Hjorthøj, C. R., Erlangsen, A., & Nordentoft, M. (2011). Psychiatric disorders and mortality among people in homeless shelters in Denmark: A nationwide register-based cohort study. *Lancet, 377,* 2205–2214.

Norcross, J. C., Karpiak, C. P., & Lister, K. M. (2005). What's an integrationist? A study of self-identified and (occasionally) eclectic psychologists. *Journal of Clinical Psychology, 61,* 1587–1594.

Nutt, R. L., & Stanton, M. (2011). Family psychology specialty practice. *Couple and Family Psychology: Research and Practice, 1,* 92–105.

Peck, D. F. (2010). The therapist-client relationship, computerized self-help and active therapy ingredients. *Clinical Psychology and Psychotherapy, 17,* 147–153.

Perahia, D. G. S., Pritchett, Y. L., Kajdasz, D. K., Bauer, M., Jain, R., Russell, J. M., Walker, D. J., Spencer, K. A., Froud, D. M., Raskin, J., & Thase, M. E. (2008). A randomized, double-blind comparison of duloxetine and venlafaxine in the treatment of patients with major depressive disorder. *Journal of Psychiatric Research, 42,* 22–34.

Perls, F. S. (1969). *Gestalt therapy verbatim.* Lafayette, CA: Real People Press.

Petry, N. M., & Roll, J. M. (2011). Amount of earnings during prize contingency management treatment is associated with posttreatment abstinence outcomes. *Experimental and Clinical Psychopharmacology, 19,* 445–450.

Pfeiffer, P. N., Heisler, M., Piette, J. D., Rogers, M. A. M., & Valenstein, M. (2011). Efficacy of peer support interventions for depression: A meta-analysis. *General Hospital Psychiatry, 33,* 29–36.

Podell, J. L., & Kendall, P. C. (2011). Mothers and fathers in family cognitive-behavioral therapy for anxious youth. *Journal of Child and Family Studies, 20,* 182–195.

Poulin, S. R., Maguire, M., Metraux, S., & Culhane, D. P. (2010). Service use and costs for persons experiencing chronic homelessness in Philadelphia: A population-based study. *Psychiatric Services, 61,* 1093–1098.

Powers, M. B., & Emmelkamp, P. M. G. (2008). Virtual reality exposure therapy for anxiety disorders: A meta-analysis. *Journal of Anxiety Disorders, 22,* 561–569.

Prangnell, S. J. (2010). Behavioural interventions for self injurious behaviour: A review of recent evidence (1998–2008). *British Journal of Learning Disabilities, 38,* 259–270.

Richards, D. (2009). Features and benefits of online counselling: Trinity College online mental health community. *British Journal of Guidance and Counselling, 37,* 231–242.

Rogers, C. R. (1951). *Client-centered therapy: Its current practice, implications and theory.* Boston: Houghton Mifflin.

Rogers, C. R. (1959). A theory of therapy, personality, and interpersonal relationships, as developed in the client-centered framework. In S. Koch (Ed.), *Psychology: A study of a science* (Vol. 3). New York: McGraw-Hill.

Rogers, C. R. (1977). *On personal power: Inner strength and its revolutionary impact.* New York: Delacorte.

Ross, W. (2011). Ethical issues involved in online counseling. *Journal of Psychological Issues in Organizational Culture, 2,* 54–66.

Rothbaum, B. O., Anderson, P., Zimand, E., Hodges, L., Lang, D., & Wilson, J. (2006). Virtual reality exposure therapy and standard (in vivo) exposure therapy in the treatment of fear of flying. *Behavior Therapy, 37,* 80–90.

Rothman, D. J. (1971). *The discovery of the asylum: Social order and disorder in the new republic.* Boston: Little, Brown.

Rummel-Kluge, C., Komossa, K., Schwarz, S., Hunger, H., Schmid, F., Lobos, C. A., Kissling, W., Davis, J. M., & Leucht, S. (2010). Head-to-head comparisons of metabolic side effects of second generation antipsychotics in the treatment of schizophrenia: A systematic review. *Schizophrenia Research, 123,* 225–233.

Satir, V. (1967). *Conjoint family therapy* (rev. ed.). Palo Alto, CA: Science and Behavior Books.

Schneider, K., & May, R. (1995). *The psychology of existence: An integrative, clinical perspective.* New York: McGraw-Hill.

Schueller, S. M. (2009). Promoting wellness: Integrating community and positive psychology. *Journal of Community Psychology, 37,* 922–937.

Schutter, D. J. L. G. (2008). Antidepressant efficacy of high-frequency transcranial magnetic stimulation over the left dorsolateral prefrontal cortex in double-blind sham-controlled designs: A meta-analysis. *Psychological Medicine*

Scull, A. (1993). *A most solitary of afflictions: Madness and society in Britain 1700–1900.* London: Yale University Press.

Shedler, J. (2010). The efficacy of psychodynamic therapy. *American Psychologist, 65,* 98–109.

Shields, D. C., Asaad, W., Eskandar, E. N., Jain, F. A., Cosgrove, G. R., Flahtery, A. W., Cassem, E. H., Prince, B. H., Rauch, S. L., & Dougherty, D. D. (2008). Prospective assessment of stereotactic ablative surgery for intractable major depression. *Biological Psychiatry, 64,* 449–454.

Sigmon, S. T., Pells, J. J., Edenfield, T. M., Hermann, B. A., Scharter, J. G., LaMattina, S. M., & Boulard, N. E. (2007). Are we there yet? A review of gender comparisons in three behavioral journals through the 20th century. *Behavior Therapy, 38,* 333–339.

Sloane, R. B., Staples, F. R., Cristol, A. H., Yorkston, N. J., & Whipple, K. (1975). *Psychotherapy versus behavior therapy.* Cambridge, MA: Harvard University Press.

Smith, M., Hopkins, D., Peveler, R. C., Holt, R. I. G., Woodward, M., & Ismail K. (2008). First- v. second-generation antipsychotics and risk for diabetes in schizophrenia: Systematic review and meta-analysis. *The British Journal of Psychiatry, 192,* 406–411.

Smith, T. B., Domenech Rodríguez, M., & Bernal, G. (2011). Culture. *Journal of Clinical Psychology: In Session, 67,* 166–175.

Snowden, L. R., & Yamada, A.-M. (2005). Cultural differences in access to care. *Annual Review of Clinical Psychology, 1,* 143–166.

Snyder, D. K., & Balderrama-Durbin, C. (2012). Integrative approaches to couple therapy: Implications for clinical practice and research. *Behavior Therapy,* in press.

Stagnitti, M. N. (2007). *Trends in the use and expenditures for the therapeutic class prescribed psychotherapeutic agents and a subclasses, 1997 and 2004.* Rockville, MD: Agency for Healthcare Research and Quality. Retrieved from www.meps.ahrq.gov/mepsweb/data_files/publications/st163/stat163.pdf.

Stahr, B., Cushing, D., Lane, K., & Fox, J. (2006). Efficacy of a function-based intervention in decreasing off-task behavior exhibited by a student with ADHD. *Journal of Positive Behavior Interventions, 8,* 201–211.

Stewart, S. A. (2005). The effects of benzodiazepines on cognition. *Journal of Clinical Psychiatry, 66* (Suppl. 2), 9–13.

Subotnik, K. L., Nuechterlein, K. H., Ventura, J., Gitlin, M. J., Marder, S., Mintz, J., Hellemann, G. S., Thornton, L. A., & Singh, I. R. (2011). Risperidone nonadherence and return of positive symptoms in the early course of schizophrenia. *American Journal of Psychiatry, 168,* 286–292.

Sue, S. (2006). Cultural competency: From philosophy to research and practice. *Journal of Community Psychology, 34,* 237–245.

Sullivan, H. S. (1953). *The interpersonal theory of psychiatry.* New York: Norton.

Swazey, J. P. (1974). *Chlorpromazine in psychiatry: A study of therapeutic innovation.* Cambridge, MA: MIT Press.

Tan, K. R., Rudolph, U., & Lüscher, C. (2011). Hooked on benzodiazepines: GABA$_A$ receptor subtypes and addiction. *Trends in Neurosciences, 34,* 188–197.

Teplin, L. A., McClelland, G. M., Abram, K. M., & Weiner, D. A. (2005). Crime victimization in adults with severe mental illness. *Archives of General Psychiatry, 62,* 911–921.

Thase, M. E., & Denko, T. (2008). Pharmacotherapy of mood disorders. *Annual Review of Clinical Psychology, 4,* 53–91.

Thoma, N. C., & Cecero, J. J. (2009). Is integrative use of techniques in psychotherapy the exception or the rule? Results of a national survey of doctoral-level practitioners. *Psychotherapy Theory, Research, Practice, Teaching, 46,* 405–417.

Tiger, J. H., & Hanley, G. P. (2006). Using reinforcer pairing and fading to increase the milk consumption of a preschool child. *Journal of Applied Behavior Analysis, 39,* 399–403.

Tryon, W. W. (2008). Whatever happened to symptom substitution? *Clinical Psychology Review, 28,* 963–968.

Tryon, G. S., & Winograd, G. (2011). Goal consensus and collaboration. *Psychotherapy, 48,* 50–57.

Wampold, B. E. (2001). *The great psychotherapy debate: Models, methods, and findings.* Mahwah, NJ: Erlbaum.

Wang, P. S., Berglund, P., Olfson, M., Pincus, H. A., Wells, K. B., & Kessler, R. C. (2005). Failure and delay in initial treatment contact after first onset of mental disorders in the national comorbidity survey replication. *Archives of General Psychiatry, 62,* 603–613.

Windy, D., & Ellis, A. (1997). *The practice of rational emotive behavior therapy.* New York: Springer.

Wolpe, J. (1958). *Psychotherapy by reciprocal inhibition.* Stanford, CA: Stanford University Press.

Wolpe, J. (1973). *The practice of behavior therapy* (2nd ed.). New York: Pergamon Press.

Workman, B. (1990, December 1). Father guilty of killing daughter's friend, in '69. *San Francisco Examiner-Chronicle,* pp. 1, 4.

Youman, K., Drapalski, A., Stuewig, J., Bagley, K., & Tangney, J. (2010). Race differences in psychopathology and disparities in treatment seeking: Community and jail-based treatment-seeking patterns. *Psychological Services, 7,* 11–26.

Psychological Disorders

© Blend Images/Alamy

Consider these words, written by a 30-year-old woman who was receiving treatment for schizophrenia:

I want to let you know what it is like to be a functional person with schizophrenia in these days and times and what someone with my mental illness faces . . . . I live pretty normal and no one can tell [I'm] mentally ill unless I tell them . . . . The delusions before I got my medicine picked any story line it chose, and changed it at will. As time went by before help, I felt it was taking over my whole brain, and I'd cry wanting my mind and life back.

What are your reactions as you read this young woman's words?

If your reactions are similar to those of other students, you feel a mixture of sadness at her plight, of delight in her willingness to do all she can to cope with the many problems her mental illness creates, of anger toward those who stigmatize her because she may act differently at times, and of hope that, with medication and therapy, her condition may improve. These are but a few of the emotions that clinical and research psychologists and psychiatrists feel as they try to understand and treat mental disorders.

This chapter focuses on the nature and causes of psychological disorders: what they are, why they develop, and how we can explain their causes. Research indicates that 46.4 percent of individuals over age 18 in the United States have suffered from a psychological disorder at some point in their lives (Kessler et al., 2005a). Thus many of you who read this text are likely to benefit directly from knowledge about psychopathology. Facts alone, however, will not convey the serious impact psychological disorders have on the everyday lives of individuals and families. As this chapter discusses categories of psychological disorders, try to envision the real people who live with such a disorder every day. I will share with you their words and lives, as I did at the start of the chapter. Let's begin now with a discussion of the concept of abnormality.

What do you imagine the lives of people with mental illnesses are like?

means that almost everyone has experienced the symptoms of a psychological disorder. This chapter looks at the range of psychological functioning that is considered unhealthy or abnormal, often referred to as *psychopathology* or *psychological disorder*. **Psychopathological functioning** involves disruptions in emotional, behavioral, or thought processes that lead to personal distress or that block one's ability to achieve important goals. The field of **abnormal psychology** is the area of psychological investigation most directly concerned with understanding the nature of individual pathologies of mind, mood, and behavior.

This section begins by exploring a more precise definition of abnormality and then looks at problems of objectivity. We then consider how this definition evolved over hundreds of years of human history.

THE NATURE OF PSYCHOLOGICAL DISORDERS

Have you ever worried excessively? Felt depressed or anxious without really knowing why? Been fearful of something you rationally knew could not harm you? Had thoughts about suicide? Used alcohol or drugs to escape a problem? Almost everyone will answer yes to at least one of these questions, which

Deciding What is Abnormal

What does it mean to say someone is *abnormal* or *suffering from a psychological disorder*? How do psychologists and other clinical practitioners decide what is abnormal? Is it always clear when behavior moves from the normal to the abnormal category? The judgment that someone has a mental disorder is typically based on the evaluation of the individual's *behavioral* functioning by people with some special authority or power. The terms used to describe these phenomena—*mental disorder, mental illness,* or *abnormality*—depend on the particular perspective, training, and cultural background of the evaluator, the situation, and the status of the person being judged. 👁

Let's consider seven criteria you might use to label behavior as "abnormal" (Butcher et al., 2008):

1. *Distress or disability.* An individual experiences personal distress or disabled functioning, which produces a risk of physical or psychological deterioration or loss of freedom of action. For example, a man who cannot leave his home without weeping would be unable to pursue ordinary life goals.
2. *Maladaptiveness.* An individual acts in ways that hinder goals, do not contribute to personal well-being, or interfere strongly with the goals of others and the needs

👁 Watch the Video *The Big Picture: What is Abnormal, Anyway?* on MyPsychLab

psychopathological functioning Disruptions in emotional, behavioral, or thought processes that lead to personal distress or block one's ability to achieve important goals.

abnormal psychology The area of psychological investigation concerned with understanding the nature of individual pathologies of mind, mood, and behavior.

of society. Someone who is drinking so heavily that she cannot hold down a job or who is endangering others through her intoxication is displaying maladaptive behavior.

3. *Irrationality.* An individual acts or talks in ways that are irrational or incomprehensible to others. A man who responds to voices that do not exist in objective reality is behaving irrationally.

4. *Unpredictability.* An individual behaves unpredictably or erratically from situation to situation, as if experiencing a loss of control. A child who smashes his fist through a window for no apparent reason displays unpredictability.

5. *Unconventionality and statistical rarity.* An individual behaves in ways that are statistically rare and that violate social standards of what is acceptable or desirable. Just being statistically unusual, however, does not lead to a psychological judgment of abnormality. For example, possessing genius-level intelligence is extremely rare, but it is also considered desirable. Conversely, having extremely low intelligence is also rare but is considered undesirable; thus it has often been labeled abnormal.

6. *Observer discomfort.* An individual creates discomfort in others by making them feel threatened or distressed in some way. A woman walking down the middle of the sidewalk, having a loud conversation with herself, creates observer discomfort in other pedestrians trying to avoid her.

7. *Violation of moral and ideal standards.* An individual violates expectations for how one ought to behave with respect to societal norms. Thus, if people generally think it is important to provide care to one's offspring, parents who abandoned their children might be considered abnormal.

Can you see why most of these indicators of abnormality may not be immediately apparent to all observers? Consider just the last criterion. Are you mentally ill if you don't wish to work, even if that is abnormal with respect to the norms of society? Or consider a more serious symptom. It is "bad" to have hallucinations in our culture because they are taken as signs of mental disturbance, but it is "good" in cultures in which hallucinations are interpreted as mystical visions from spirit forces. Whose judgment is correct? At the end of this chapter, we will consider some negative consequences and dangers associated with such socially regulated judgments and the decisions based on them.

We are more confident in labeling behavior as "abnormal" when more than just one of the indicators is present and valid. The more extreme and prevalent the indicators are, the more confident we can be that they point to an abnormal condition. None of these criteria is a *necessary* condition shared by all cases of abnormality. For example, during his murder trial, a Stanford University graduate student who had killed his math professor with a hammer, and then taped to his office door a note that read "No office hours today," reported feeling neither guilt nor remorse. Despite the absence of personal suffering, we would not hesitate to label his overall behavior as abnormal. It is also true that no single criterion, by itself, is a *sufficient* condition that distinguishes all cases of abnormal behavior from normal variations in behavior. The distinction between normal and abnormal is not so much a difference between two independent types of behaviors as it is a matter of the degree to which a person's actions resemble a set of agreed-upon criteria of abnormality. Mental disorder is best thought of as a *continuum* that varies between *mental health* and *mental illness*.

How comfortable do you feel with these ideas about abnormality? Although the criteria seem fairly clear-cut, psychologists still worry about the problem of objectivity.

The Problem of Objectivity

The decision to declare someone psychologically disordered or abnormal is always a *judgment* about behavior: The goal for many researchers is to make these judgments *objectively*, without any type of bias. For some psychological disorders, like depression or schizophrenia, diagnosis often easily meets the standards of objectivity. Other cases are more problematic. As you have seen throughout your study of psychology, the meaning of behavior is jointly determined by its *content* and by its *context*. The same act in different settings conveys very different meanings. A man kisses another man; it may signify a gay relationship in the United States, a ritual greeting in France, or a Mafia "kiss of death" in Sicily. The meaning of a behavior always depends on context.

Let's see why objectivity is such an important issue. History is full of examples of situations in which judgments of abnormality were made by individuals to preserve their moral or political power. Consider an 1851 report, entitled "The Diseases and Physical Peculiarities of the Negro Race," published in a medical journal. Its author, Dr. Samuel Cartwright, had been appointed by the Louisiana Medical Association to chair a committee to investigate the "strange" practices of African American slaves. "Incontrovertible scientific evidence" was amassed to justify the practice of slavery. Several "diseases" previously unknown to the White race were discovered. One finding was that Blacks allegedly suffered from a sensory disease that made them insensitive "to pain when being punished" (thus no need to spare the whip). The committee also invented the disease *drapetomania*, a mania to seek freedom—a mental disorder that caused certain slaves to run away from their masters. Runaway slaves needed to be caught so that their illness could be properly treated (Chorover, 1981)!

Once an individual has obtained an "abnormal" label, people are inclined to interpret later behavior to confirm that judgment. **David Rosenhan** (1973, 1975) and his colleagues demonstrated that it may be impossible to be judged "sane" in an "insane place."

Rosenhan and seven other sane people gained admission to different psychiatric hospitals by pretending to have a single symptom: hallucinations. All eight of these pseudopatients were diagnosed on admission as having either paranoid schizophrenia or bipolar disorder. Once admitted, they behaved normally in every way. Rosenhan observed, however, that when a sane person is in an insane place, he or she is likely to be judged insane, and any behavior is likely to be reinterpreted to fit the context. If the pseudopatients discussed their situation in a rational way with the staff, they were reported to be using "intellectualization" defenses, while their taking notes of their observations were evidence of "writing behavior." The pseudopatients remained on the wards for almost three weeks, on average, and not one was identified by

Featured Study

the staff as sane. When they were finally released—only with the help of spouses or colleagues—their discharge diagnosis was still "schizophrenia" but "in remission." That is, their symptoms were no longer active.

Rosenhan's research demonstrates how judgments of abnormality rely on factors beyond behavior itself.

In the view of psychiatrist **Thomas Szasz,** mental illness does not even exist—it is a "myth" (1974, 2004). Szasz argues that the symptoms used as evidence of mental illness are merely medical labels that sanction professional intervention into what are social problems—deviant people violating social norms. Once labeled, these people can be treated either benignly or harshly for their problem "of being different," with no threat of disturbing the existing status quo.

Few clinicians would go this far, in large part because the focus of much research and treatment is on understanding and alleviating personal distress. For most of the disorders this chapter describes, individuals experience their own behavior as abnormal, or poorly adapted to the environment. Even so, this discussion suggests that there can be no altogether objective assessments of abnormality. As you learn about each type of psychological disorder, try to understand why clinicians believe the cluster of symptoms represents behavior patterns that are more serious for the individual than mere violations of social norms.

Classifying Psychological Disorders

Why is it helpful to have a classification system for psychological disorders? What advantages are gained by moving beyond a global assessment that abnormality exists to distinguish among different types of abnormalities? A **psychological diagnosis** is the label given to an abnormality by classifying and categorizing the observed behavior pattern into an approved diagnostic system. Such a diagnosis is in many ways more difficult to make than a medical diagnosis. In the medical context, a doctor can rely on physical evidence, such as X-rays, blood tests, and biopsies, to inform a diagnostic decision. In the case of psychological disorders, the evidence for diagnosis comes from interpretations of a person's actions. To create greater consistency among clinicians and coherence in their diagnostic evaluations, psychologists have helped to develop a system of diagnosis and classification that provides precise descriptions of symptoms, as well as other criteria to help practitioners decide whether a person's behavior is evidence of a particular disorder.

To be most useful, a diagnostic system should provide the following three benefits:

- *Common shorthand language.* To facilitate a quick and clear understanding among clinicians or researchers working in the field of psychopathology, practitioners seek a common set of terms with agreed-upon meanings. A diagnostic category, such as *depression,* summarizes a large and complex collection of information, including characteristic symptoms and the typical course of the

The Salem witchcraft trials were an outgrowth of a desperate attempt to affix blame for frighteningly bizarre behavior among the Puritan colonists. The colonists theorized that the symptoms were the work of the devil, who, through the efforts of earthbound witches, had taken over the minds and bodies of young women.

Photograph courtesy of the Peabody Essex Museum, Salem, Massachusetts

disorder. In clinical settings, such as clinics and hospitals, a diagnostic system allows mental health professionals to communicate more effectively about the people they are helping. Researchers studying different aspects of psychopathology or evaluating treatment programs must agree on the disorder they are observing.

- *Understanding of causality.* Ideally, a diagnosis of a specific disorder should make clear the causes of the symptoms. As is the case for physical illness, the same symptoms may arise for more than one disorder. A goal of a classification system is to indicate why practitioners should interpret particular patterns of symptoms as evidence for specific underlying disorders.
- *Treatment plan.* A diagnosis should also suggest what types of treatments to consider for particular disorders. Researchers and clinicians have found that certain treatments or therapies work most effectively for specific kinds of psychological disorders. For example, drugs that are quite effective in treating schizophrenia do not help and may even hurt people with depression. Further advances in knowledge about the effectiveness and specificity of treatments will make fast and reliable diagnosis even more important.

In 1896, **Emil Kraepelin** (1855–1926), a German psychiatrist, was responsible for creating the first truly comprehensive *classification system* of psychological disorders. Strongly motivated by a belief that there was a physical basis to psychological problems, he gave the process of psychological diagnosis and classification the flavor of medical diagnosis. That flavor remains today in the diagnostic system I now review.

DSM-IV-TR In the United States, the most widely accepted classification scheme is one developed by the American Psychiatric Association. It is called the *Diagnostic and Statistical Manual of Mental Disorders.* The most recent version, published in 2000 as a revision of the fourth edition, is known by

psychological diagnosis The label given to psychological abnormality by classifying and categorizing the observed behavior pattern into an approved diagnostic system.

clinicians and researchers as **DSM-IV-TR.** It classifies, defines, and describes over 200 mental disorders. 👁

To reduce the diagnostic difficulties caused by variability in approaches to psychological disorders, *DSM-IV-TR* emphasizes the *description* of patterns of symptoms and courses of disorders rather than etiological theories or treatment strategies. The purely descriptive terms allow clinicians and researchers to use a common language to describe problems while leaving room for disagreement and continued research about which theoretical models best *explain* the problems.

The first version of *DSM*, which appeared in 1952 *(DSM-I)*, listed several dozen mental illnesses. *DSM-II*, introduced in 1968, revised the diagnostic system to make it more compatible with another popular system, the World Health Organization's *International Classification of Diseases (ICD)*. The fourth edition of the *DSM (DSM-IV*, 1994) emerged after several years of intense work by committees of scholars. To make their changes (from the *DSM-III-Revised*, which appeared in 1987), these committees carefully scrutinized large bodies of research on psychopathology and also tested proposed changes for workability in actual clinical settings. *DSM-IV* is also fully compatible with the 10th edition of the *ICD*. *DSM-IV-TR* (2000) incorporated a review of the research literature that had accumulated since *DSM-IV*. Because the changes largely affected the supporting text, rather than the system of classification, the revision was termed a "text revision," which yielded the name *DSM-IV-TR*. After this brief history of the *DSM*, you probably won't be surprised to learn that committees are meeting to bring the newest research to bear on *DSM-5*, which is scheduled to appear in 2013. In the *Critical Thinking in Your Life* box later in this chapter, you'll get a sense of the process that could lead to the inclusion of new disorders in *DSM-5*.

To encourage clinicians to consider the psychological, social, and physical factors that may be associated with a psychological disorder, *DSM-IV-TR* uses dimensions, or *axes*, that portray information about all these factors (see **Table 1**). Most of the principal clinical disorders are contained on Axis I. Included here are all disorders that emerge in childhood, except for mental retardation. Axis II lists mental retardation as well as personality disorders. These problems may accompany Axis I disorders. Axis III incorporates information about general medical conditions, such as diabetes, that may be relevant to understanding or treating an Axis I or II disorder. Axes IV and

V provide supplemental information that can be useful when planning an individual's treatment or assessing the *prognosis* (predictions of future change). Axis IV assesses psychosocial and environmental problems that may explain patients' stress responses or their resources for coping with stress. On Axis V, a clinician evaluates the global level of an individual's functioning. A full diagnosis in the *DSM-IV-TR* system would involve consideration of each of the axes. ✳

This chapter will provide estimates of the frequency with which individuals experience particular psychological disorders. These estimates arise from research projects in which mental health histories are obtained from large samples of the population. Figures are available for the prevalence of different disorders over one-year and lifetime periods (Kessler et al., 2005a, 2005b). This chapter will generally cite figures from the *National Comorbidity Study (NCS)*, which sampled 9,282 U.S. adults ages 18 and older (Kessler et al., 2005a). It is important to emphasize that often the same individuals have experienced more than one disorder simultaneously at some point in their life span, a phenomenon known as **comorbidity.** (*Morbidity* refers to the occurrence of disease. *Comorbidity* refers to the co-occurrence of diseases.) The NCS found that 45 percent of the people who had experienced one disorder in a 12-month period had actually experienced two or more. Researchers have begun to study intensively the patterns of comorbidity of different psychological disorders (Kessler et al., 2005b).

Evolution of Diagnostic Categories The diagnostic categories and the methods used to organize and present them have shifted with each revision of the *DSM*. These shifts reflect changes in the opinions of a majority of mental health experts about exactly what constitutes a psychological disorder and where the lines between different types of disorders should be

....

👁 Watch the Video *Special Topics: DSM-IV* on **MyPsychLab**

✳ Explore the Concept *The Axes of the DSM* on MyPsychLab

DSM-IV-TR The current diagnostic and statistical manual of the American Psychological Association that classifies, defines, and describes mental disorders.

comorbidity The experience of more than one disorder at the same time.

Table 1 • The Five Axes of *DSM-IV-TR*

Axis	Classes of Information	Description
Axis I	Clinical disorders	These mental disorders present symptoms or patterns of behavioral or psychological problems that typically are painful or impair an area of functioning. Included are disorders that emerge in infancy, childhood, or adolescence.
Axis II	(a) Personality disorders (b) Mental retardation	These are dysfunctional patterns of perceiving and responding to the world.
Axis III	General medical conditions	This axis codes physical problems relevant to understanding or treating an individual's psychological disorders on Axes I and II.
Axis IV	Psychosocial and environmental problems	This axis codes psychosocial and environmental stressors that may affect the diagnosis and treatment of an individual's disorder and the likelihood of recovery.
Axis V	Global assessment of functioning	This axis codes the individual's overall level of current functioning in the psychological, social, and occupational domains.

drawn. They also reflect changing perspectives among the public about what constitutes *abnormality*.

In the revision process of each *DSM*, some diagnostic categories were dropped, and others were added. For example, with the introduction of *DSM-III*, in 1980, the traditional distinction between *neurotic* and *psychotic* disorders was eliminated. **Neurotic disorders,** or *neuroses*, were originally conceived of as relatively common psychological problems in which a person did not have signs of brain abnormalities, did not display grossly irrational thinking, and did not violate basic norms; but he or she did experience subjective distress or a pattern of self-defeating or inadequate coping strategies. **Psychotic disorders,** or *psychoses*, were thought to differ in both quality and severity from neurotic problems. It was believed that psychotic behavior deviated significantly from social norms and was accompanied by a profound disturbance in rational thinking and general emotional and thought processes. The *DSM-III* advisory committees felt that the terms *neurotic disorders* and *psychotic disorders* had become too general in their meaning to have much usefulness as diagnostic categories (however, they continue to be used by many psychiatrists and psychologists to characterize the general level of disturbance in a person).

Let's note one final aspect of classification that has evolved over time. Historically, people with mental illnesses were often labeled with the name of their disorder. For example, clinicians referred to people as "schizophrenics" or "phobics." That didn't happen for physical illnesses—people with cancer were never known as "cancerics." Clinicians and researchers now take care to separate the person from the diagnosis. People have schizophrenic disorders or phobias, just as they have cancer or the flu. The hope is that appropriate treatments can alleviate each condition so they no longer apply to the person.

The Concept of Insanity Before we consider the causes of mental illness, let's turn our attention briefly to the concept of insanity. **Insanity** is not defined in *DSM-IV-TR*; there is no accepted clinical definition of insanity. Rather, insanity is a concept that belongs to popular culture and to the legal system. The treatment of insanity in the law dates back to England in 1843, when Daniel McNaughton was found not guilty of murder by reason of insanity. McNaughton's intended victim was the British prime minister—McNaughton believed that God had instructed him to commit the murder. (He accidentally killed the prime minister's secretary instead.) Because of McNaughton's delusions, he was sent to a mental hospital rather than to prison.

....

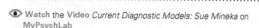

Watch the Video *Current Diagnostic Models: Sue Mineka* on MyPsychLab

neurotic disorder Mental disorder in which a person does not have signs of brain abnormalities and does not display grossly irrational thinking or violate basic norms but does experience subjective distress; a category dropped from *DSM-III*.

psychotic disorder Severe mental disorder in which a person experiences impairments in reality testing manifested through thought, emotional, or perceptual difficulties; no longer used as diagnostic category after *DSM-III*.

insanity The legal (not clinical) designation for the state of an individual judged to be legally irresponsible or incompetent.

etiology The causes of, or factors related to, the development of a disorder.

In an attempt to murder Representative Gabrielle Giffords, Jared Loughner killed six people. Commentators debated whether he qualified as insane. Why has the legal definition of "insanity" changed over time?

The anger surrounding this verdict—even Queen Victoria was infuriated—prompted the House of Lords to articulate a guideline, known as the *McNaughton rule*, to limit claims of insanity. This rule specifies that a criminal must not "know the nature and quality of the act he was doing; or, if he did know it, that he did not know he was doing what was wrong." Does the McNaughton rule seem like a fair test of guilt or innocence? With advances in the understanding of mental illness, researchers became more aware of circumstances in which a criminal might know right from wrong—a criminal might understand that what he or she was doing was illegal or immoral—but still might not be able to suppress the actions.

Despite the great attention that insanity pleas receive in the media—and, thus, the public's great awareness of them—such pleas are quite rare (Kirschner & Galperin, 2001). For example, one study found that in 60,432 indictments in Baltimore, Maryland, only 190 defendants (0.31 percent) entered insanity pleas; of the 190 pleas, only 8 (4.2 percent) were successful (Janofsky et al., 1996). Thus the likelihood that you will ever be asked to sit on a jury and judge another person as sane or insane is quite low.

The Etiology of Psychopathology

Etiology refers to the factors that cause or contribute to the development of psychological and medical problems. Knowing why the disorder occurs, what its origins are, and how it affects thought and emotional and behavioral processes may lead to new ways of treating and, ideally, preventing it. An analysis of causality will be an important part of the discussion of each individual disorder. This section introduces two general categories of causal factors: biological and psychological. 👁

Biological Approaches Building on the heritage of the medical model, modern biological approaches assume that psychological disturbances are directly attributable to underlying biological factors. Biological researchers and clinicians most often investigate structural abnormalities in the brain, biochemical processes, and genetic influences.

The brain is a complex organ whose interrelated elements are held in delicate balance. Subtle alterations in its chemical messengers—the neurotransmitters—or in its tissue can have significant effects. Genetic factors, brain injury, and infection are a few of the causes of these alterations. Technological advances in brain-imaging techniques allow mental health professionals to view the structure of the brain and specific biochemical processes. Using these techniques, biologically oriented researchers are discovering new links between psychological disorders and specific abnormalities in the brain. In addition, continuing advances in the field of behavioral genetics have improved researchers' abilities to identify the links between specific genes and the presence of psychological disorders. We will look to these different types of biological explanations throughout the chapter as we try to understand the nature of various forms of abnormality.

Psychological Approaches Psychological approaches focus on the causal role of psychological or social factors in the development of psychopathology. These approaches perceive personal experiences, traumas, conflicts, and environmental factors as the roots of psychological disorders. There are four dominant psychological models of abnormality: the psychodynamic, the behavioral, the cognitive, and the sociocultural.

Psychodynamic Like the biological approach, the psychodynamic model holds that the causes of psychopathology are located inside the person. However, according to Sigmund Freud, who developed this model, the internal causal factors are psychological rather than biological. Freud believed that many psychological disorders were simply an extension of "normal" processes of psychic conflict and ego defense that all people experience. In the psychodynamic model, early childhood experiences shape both normal and abnormal behavior.

In psychodynamic theory, behavior is motivated by drives and wishes of which people are often unaware. Symptoms of psychopathology have their roots in *unconscious conflict* and thoughts. If the unconscious is conflicted and tension filled, a person will be plagued by anxiety and other disorders. Much of this psychic conflict arises from struggles between the irrational, pleasure-seeking impulses of the *id* and the internalized social constraints imposed by the *superego*. The *ego* is normally the arbiter of this struggle; however, its ability to perform its function can be weakened by abnormal development in childhood. Individuals attempt to avoid the pain caused by conflicting motives and anxiety with *defense mechanisms*, such as repression or denial. Defenses can become overused, distorting reality or leading to self-defeating behaviors. The individual may then expend so much psychic energy in defenses against anxiety and conflict that there is little energy left to provide a productive and satisfying life.

Behavioral Because of their emphasis on observable responses, behavioral theorists have little use for hypothetical psychodynamic processes. These theorists argue that abnormal behaviors are acquired in the same fashion as healthy behaviors—through learning and reinforcement. They do not focus on internal psychological phenomena or early childhood experiences. Instead, they focus on the *current* behavior and the *current* conditions or reinforcements that sustain the behavior. The symptoms of psychological disorders arise because an individual has learned self-defeating or ineffective ways of behaving. By discovering the environmental contingencies that maintain any undesirable, abnormal behavior, an investigator or clinician can then recommend treatment to change those contingencies and extinguish the unwanted behavior. Behaviorists rely on both classical and operant conditioning models to understand the processes that can result in maladaptive behavior.

Cognitive Cognitive perspectives on psychopathology are often used to supplement behavioral views. The cognitive perspective suggests that the origins of psychological disorders cannot always be found in the objective reality of stimulus environments, reinforcers, and overt responses. What matters as well is the way people perceive or think about themselves and about their relations with other people and the environment. Among the cognitive variables that can guide—or misguide—adaptive responses are a person's perceived degree of control over important reinforcers, a person's beliefs in his or her ability to cope with threatening events, and interpretations of events in terms of situational or personal factors. The cognitive approach suggests that psychological problems are the result of distortions in perceptions of the reality of a situation, faulty reasoning, or poor problem solving.

Sociocultural The sociocultural perspective on psychopathology emphasizes the role culture plays in both the diagnosis and etiology of abnormal behavior. You already got a taste of the impact of culture on diagnosis when we considered the problem of objectivity. You saw that behaviors are interpreted in different ways in different cultures: the threshold at which a certain type of behavior will cause an individual problems in adjustment will depend, in part, on how that behavior is viewed in its cultural context. With respect to etiology, the particular cultural circumstances in which people live may define an environment that helps bring about distinctive types or subtypes of psychopathology.

You now have a general sense of the types of explanations researchers give for the emergence of mental illness. It is worth noting that contemporary researchers increasingly take an *interactionist* perspective on psychopathology, seeing it as the product of a complex interaction between a number of biological and psychological factors. For example, genetic predispositions may make a person vulnerable to a psychological disorder by affecting neurotransmitter levels or hormone levels, but psychological or social stresses or certain learned behaviors may be required for the disorder to develop fully.

Now that you have a basic framework for thinking about abnormality, we turn to the core information that you will want to know—the causes and consequences of major psychological disorders, such as anxiety, depression, and schizophrenia. The description of each disorder will begin with an account of what sufferers experience and how they appear to observers. Then we will consider how each of the major biological and psychological approaches to etiology explains the development of these disorders.

There are many other categories of psychopathology that we will not have time to examine. However, what follows is a capsule summary of some of the most important omitted here:

- *Substance-use disorders* include both dependence on and abuse of alcohol and drugs.
- *Sexual disorders* involve problems with sexual inhibition or dysfunction and deviant sexual practices.
- *Eating disorders* include anorexia and bulimia.

As you read about the symptoms and experiences that are typical of the various psychological disturbances, you may begin to feel that some of the characteristics seem to apply to you—at least part of the time—or to someone you know. Beginning students of psychology sometimes fall prey to a version of what has been called *medical students' disease*—the tendency for medical students to diagnose themselves or their acquaintances with each disease about which they are learning. You should try to avoid that tendency with respect to your new knowledge of psychological disorders. Some of the disorders we'll consider are not uncommon, so it would be surprising if they sounded completely alien. Many people have human frailties that appear on the list of criteria for a particular psychological disorder. Recognition of this familiarity can further your understanding of abnormal psychology, but remember that a diagnosis for any disorder depends on a number of criteria and requires the judgment of a trained mental health professional. Please resist the temptation to use this new knowledge to diagnose friends and family members as pathological. However, if the chapter leaves you uneasy about mental health issues, please note that most colleges and universities have counseling centers for students with such concerns.

Stop *and* Review

① Jerry has such an overwhelming fear of spiders that he will not enter a room until someone he trusts assures him the room has no spiders in it. By what criteria might we decide that Jerry's behavior is abnormal?
② What are three important benefits provided by the classification of mental disorders?
③ Why does culture play a role in the diagnosis of psychopathology?

CRITICAL THINKING Consider the study in which David Rosenhan and seven other people were admitted

to psychiatric hospitals. Why might they have chosen "hallucinations" as their pretend symptom?

✓●—Study and Review on MyPsychLab

ANXIETY DISORDERS

Everyone experiences anxiety or fear in certain life situations. For some people, however, anxiety becomes problematic enough to interfere with their ability to function effectively or enjoy everyday life. It has been estimated that 28.8 percent of the adult population has, at some time, experienced symptoms characteristic of the various **anxiety disorders** (Kessler et al., 2005a). Although anxiety plays a key role in each of these disorders, they differ in the extent to which anxiety is experienced, the severity of the anxiety, and the situations that trigger the anxiety. This section reviews five major categories: generalized anxiety disorder, panic disorder, phobic disorder, obsessive-compulsive disorder, and posttraumatic stress disorder. We then consider the causes of these disorders.

Generalized Anxiety Disorder

When a person feels anxious or worried most of the time for at least six months, when not threatened by any specific danger, clinicians diagnose **generalized anxiety disorder.** The anxiety is often focused on specific life circumstances, such as unrealistic concerns about finances or the well-being of a loved one. The way the anxiety is expressed—the specific symptoms—varies from person to person, but for a diagnosis of generalized anxiety disorder to be made, the patient must also suffer from at least three other symptoms, such as muscle tension, fatigue, restlessness, poor concentration, irritability, or sleep difficulties. Among U.S. adults, 5.7 percent have experienced generalized anxiety disorder (Kessler et al., 2005a).

Generalized anxiety disorder leads to impaired functioning because the person's worries cannot be controlled or put aside. With the focus of attention on the sources of anxiety, the individual cannot attend sufficiently to social or job obligations. These difficulties are compounded by the physical symptoms associated with the disorder.

Panic Disorder

In contrast to the chronic presence of anxiety in generalized anxiety disorder, sufferers of **panic disorder** experience unexpected, severe *panic attacks* that may last only minutes. These attacks begin with a feeling of intense apprehension, fear, or terror. Accompanying these feelings are physical symptoms of anxiety, including autonomic hyperactivity (such as rapid heart rate), dizziness, faintness, or sensations of choking or smothering. The attacks are unexpected in the sense that they are not brought about by something concrete in the situation. A panic disorder is diagnosed when an individual has recurrent unexpected panic attacks and also begins to have persistent concerns about the possibility of having more attacks. Research suggests that 4.7 percent of U.S. adults have experienced panic disorder (Kessler et al., 2006b).

anxiety disorder Mental disorder marked by psychological arousal, feeling of tension, and intense apprehension without apparent reason.

generalized anxiety disorder An anxiety disorder in which an individual feels anxious and worried most of the time for at least six months when not threatened by any specific danger or object.

panic disorder An anxiety disorder in which sufferers experience unexpected, severe panic attacks that begin with a feeling of intense apprehension, fear, or terror.

Critical Thinking in Your Life

HOW DO DISORDERS ENTER THE *DSM*?

This chapter will present several descriptions of psychological disorders that are outlined in *DSM-IV-TR* (2000). Before you consider these disorders, it's valuable for you to reflect on the process through which clinicians achieve consensus that a particular disorder belongs in the *DSM*. Although *DSM-IV-TR* is a formidable volume, clinical observation continues to lead to proposals for new disorders: Therapists and researchers pay careful attention to people's symptoms and how those symptoms cluster together. To provide a concrete example of how researchers build the case for a new disorder, we will consider *binge eating disorder*.

Binge eating disorder (BED) is diagnosed when people engage in regular episodes of binge eating without the purges that accompany bulimia nervosa. In addition, people who suffer from BED experience a loss of control during these binges and the binges cause them great distress.

Note two important features of this definition (Striegel-Moore & Franko, 2008). First, the definition suggests how BED is different from other eating disorders, despite the overlap in some symptoms (that is, binge eating). When clinicians propose a new diagnostic category, they must firmly establish that the new disorder is distinct from well-established disorders. Second, the definition mentions a cluster of symptoms. When clinicians propose a new diagnostic category, they are making a strong assertion that a particular set of experiences regularly co-occurs.

The definition of a disorder serves, in a sense, as a hypothesis: The clinicians who propose the disorder are predicting that data will confirm that people experience this distinctive constellation of symptoms. For BED, this has proven to be the case. In one study, researchers engaged in face-to-face interviews with 9,282 adults in the United States (Hudson et al., 2007). To determine whether people suffered from BED, they used criteria from *DSM-IV*. In their sample, 3.5 percent of the women and 2.0 percent of the men met those criteria. These data support the hypothesis that BED exists as a disorder with a unique set of symptoms and consequences.

Still, some data on BED has encouraged researchers to reexamine features of the diagnosis (Striegel-Moore & Franko, 2008). For example, the definitions of other eating disorders include the diagnostic feature "undue influence of body weight or shape on self-evaluation" (*DSM-IV*, 1994, p. 545). Researchers have begun to consider whether this feature should also be included for BED (Grilo et al., 2008). Studies suggest that people who meet the criteria for BED and who also show "undue influence" experience greater distress than people who do not show this influence. However, researchers have yet to reach consensus on how the inclusion of this feature would affect diagnoses of BED.

The goal of research on BED—as well as on other disorders, old and new—is to provide valid diagnoses. Valid diagnoses allow for the provision of appropriate treatments—and, ultimately, for a minimization of people's distress.

- Why do the definitions of disorders include clusters of symptoms?
- Why does improved diagnosis often allow improved treatment?

In *DSM-IV-TR*, panic disorder must be diagnosed as occurring with or without the simultaneous presence of agoraphobia. **Agoraphobia** is an extreme fear of being in public places or open spaces from which escape may be difficult or embarrassing. Individuals with agoraphobia usually fear such places as crowded rooms, malls, and buses. They are often afraid that, if they experience some kind of difficulty outside the home, such as a loss of bladder control or panic attack symptoms, help might not be available or the situation will be embarrassing to them. These fears deprive individuals of their freedom, and, in extreme cases, they become prisoners in their own homes.

Can you see why agoraphobia is related to panic disorder? For some (but not all) people who suffer from panic attacks, the dread of the next attack—the helpless feelings it engenders—can be enough to imprison them. The person suffering from agoraphobia may leave the safety of home but almost always with extreme anxiety.

Phobias

Fear is a rational reaction to an objectively identified external danger (such as a fire in one's home or a mugging attack) that may induce a person to flee or to attack in self-defense. In contrast, a person with a **phobia** suffers from a persistent and irrational fear of a specific object, activity, or situation that is excessive and unreasonable given the reality of the threat.

Watch the Video *Phobias* on MyPsychLab

agoraphobia An extreme fear of being in public places or open spaces from which escape may be difficult or embarrassing.

fear A rational reaction to an objectively identified external danger that may induce a person to flee or attack in self-defense.

phobia A persistent and irrational fear of a specific object, activity, or situation that is excessive and unreasonable, given the reality of the threat.

Table 2 • Common Phobias

Social phobias (fear of being observed doing something humiliating)
Specific phobias
Animal type
Cats (ailurophobia)
Dogs (cynophobia)
Insects (insectophobia)
Spiders (arachnophobia)
Snakes (ophidiophobia)
Rodents (rodentophobia)
Natural environment type
Storms (brontophobia)
Heights (acrophobia)
Blood–injection–injury type
Blood (hemophobia)
Needles (belonephobia)
Situational type
Closed spaces (claustrophobia)
Railways (siderodromophobia)

Many people feel uneasy about spiders or snakes (or even multiple-choice tests). These mild fears do not prevent people from carrying out their everyday activities. Phobias, however, interfere with adjustment, cause significant distress, and inhibit necessary action toward goals. Even a very specific, apparently limited phobia can have a great impact on one's whole life. *DSM-IV-TR* defines two categories of phobias: *social phobias* and *specific phobias* (see **Table 2**).

Social phobia is a persistent, irrational fear that arises in anticipation of a public situation in which an individual can be observed by others. A person with a social phobia fears that he or she will act in ways that could be embarrassing. The person recognizes that the fear is excessive and unreasonable yet feels compelled by the fear to avoid situations in which public scrutiny is possible. Social phobia often involves a self-fulfilling prophecy. A person may be so fearful of the scrutiny and rejection of others that enough anxiety is created to actually impair performance. Even positive social exchanges cause anxiety for people with social phobia: They worry that they have set standards that they will not be able to meet in the future (Weeks et al., 2008). Among U.S. adults, 12.1 percent have experienced a social phobia (Ruscio et al., 2008).

Specific phobias occur in response to several different types of objects or situations. As shown in **Table 2**, specific phobias are further categorized into several subtypes. For example, an individual suffering from an *animal-type specific phobia* might have a phobic response to spiders. In each case,

the phobic response is produced either in the presence of or in anticipation of the feared specific object or situation. Research suggests that 12.5 percent of adults in the United States have experienced a specific phobia (Kessler et al., 2005a).

Obsessive-Compulsive Disorder

Some people with anxiety disorders get locked into specific patterns of thought and behavior. Consider the following case:

> *Only a year or so ago, 17-year-old Jim seemed to be a normal adolescent with many talents and interests. Then, almost overnight, he was transformed into a lonely outsider, excluded from social life by his psychological disabilities. Specifically, he developed an obsession with washing. Haunted by the notion that he was dirty—in spite of what his senses told him—he began to spend more of his time cleansing himself of imaginary dirt. At first, his ritual washings were confined to weekends and evenings, but soon they began to consume all his time, forcing him to drop out of school.* (Rapoport, 1989)

Jim is suffering from a condition known as **obsessive-compulsive disorder (OCD),** which has been estimated to affect 1.6 percent of U.S. adults at some point during their lives (Kessler et al., 2005a). *Obsessions* are thoughts, images, or impulses (such as Jim's belief that he is unclean) that recur or persist despite a person's efforts to suppress them. Obsessions are experienced as an unwanted invasion of consciousness, they seem to be senseless or repugnant, and they are unacceptable to the person experiencing them. You probably have had some sort of mild obsessional experience, such as the intrusion of petty worries—"Did I really lock the door?" or "Did I turn off the oven?" The obsessive thoughts of people

Why might agoraphobia cause people to become "prisoners" in their own homes?

----

social phobia A persistent, irrational fear that arises in anticipation of a public situation in which an individual can be observed by others.

specific phobia Phobia that occurs in response to a specific type of object or situation.

obsessive-compulsive disorder (OCD) A mental disorder characterized by obsessions—recurrent thoughts, images, or impulses that recur or persist despite efforts to suppress them—and compulsions—repetitive, purposeful acts performed according to certain rules or in a ritualized manner.

Why do people with obsessive-compulsive disorder engage in behaviors such as repetitive hand-washing?

with obsessive-compulsive disorder are much more compelling, cause much more distress, and may interfere with their social or occupational functioning. ◉▸

Compulsions are repetitive, purposeful *acts* (such as Jim's washing) performed according to certain rules or in a ritualized manner in response to an obsession. Compulsive behavior is performed to reduce or prevent the discomfort associated with some dreaded situation, but it is either unreasonable or clearly excessive. Typical compulsions include irresistible urges to clean, to check that lights or appliances have been turned off, and to count objects or possessions.

At least initially, people with obsessive-compulsive disorder resist carrying out their compulsions. When they are calm, they view their compulsion as senseless. When anxiety rises, however, the power of the ritual compulsive behavior to relieve tension seems irresistible. Part of the pain experienced by people with this mental problem is created by their frustration at recognizing the irrationality or excessive nature of their obsessions without being able to eliminate them.

Posttraumatic Stress Disorder

There is a noticeable psychological consequence of traumatic events: People experience posttraumatic stress disorder (PTSD), an anxiety disorder that is characterized by the persistent reexperience of those traumatic events through distressing recollections, dreams, hallucinations, or flashbacks. Individuals may develop PTSD in response to rape, life-threatening events or severe injury, and natural disasters. People develop PTSD both when they themselves have been the victim of the trauma and when they have witnessed others being victimized. People who suffer from PTSD are also likely to suffer simultaneously from other psychopathologies, such as major depression, substance-abuse problems, and suicide attempts (Pietrzak et al., 2011).

Research suggests that about 6.4 percent of adults in the United States will experience PTSD at some point during their lifetime (Pietrzak et al., 2011). Studies consistently reveal that most adults have experienced an event that could be defined as traumatic, such as a serious accident, a tragic death, or physical

or sexual abuse (Widom et al., 2005). One study with 1,824 Swedish adults found that 80.8 percent had experienced at least one traumatic event (Frans et al., 2005). In this sample, men had experienced more traumatic events than women, but women were twice as likely to develop PTSD. The researchers suggested that women's greater distress in response to traumatic events helped explain this difference.

Much attention has focused on the prevalence of PTSD in the wake of traumas with widespread impact. For example, one study that found that about 15 percent of individuals who were evacuated from the World Trade Center on September 11, 2001, met diagnostic criteria for PTSD two to three years after the terrorist attack (DiGrande et al., 2011). Similar data emerge from other tragedies. For example, in 2008 the Wenchuan earthquake in China killed almost 70,000 people. In a sample of roughly 2,100 adolescents assessed six months after the earthquake, 15.8 percent met criteria for a diagnosis of PTSD (Fan et al., 2011).

Posttraumatic stress disorder severely disrupts sufferers' lives. How do researchers go about the complex task of exploring the origins of PTSD and other anxiety disorders? Understanding the origins gives hope to eliminating the psychological distress.

Causes of Anxiety Disorders

How do psychologists explain the development of anxiety disorders? Each of the four etiological approaches outlined earlier (biological, psychodynamic, behavioral, and cognitive) emphasizes different factors. Let's analyze how each adds something unique to the understanding of anxiety disorders. ◉

Biological Various investigators have suggested that anxiety disorders have biological origins. One theory attempts to explain why certain phobias, such as those for spiders or heights, are more common than fears of other dangers, such as electricity. Because many fears are shared across cultures, it has been proposed that, at one time in the evolutionary past, certain fears enhanced our ancestors' chances of survival. Perhaps humans are born with a predisposition to fear whatever is related to sources of serious danger in the evolutionary past. This *preparedness hypothesis* suggests that we carry around an evolutionary tendency to respond quickly and "thoughtlessly" to once-feared stimuli (LoBue & DeLoache, 2008; Öhman & Mineka, 2001). However, this hypothesis does not explain types of phobias that develop in response to objects or situations that would not have had survival meaning over evolutionary history, like fear of needles or driving or elevators.

The ability of certain drugs to relieve and of others to produce symptoms of anxiety offers evidence of a biological role in anxiety disorders (Croarkin et al., 2011; Hoffman & Mathew, 2008). For example, when the level of the neurotransmitter GABA in the brain becomes low, people often experience feelings of anxiety. Disorders in the brain's

···

◉▸ Simulate the Experiment *The Obsessive Compulsive Test* on MyPsychLab

◉ Watch the Video *When Does a Fear Become a Phobia: Sue Mineka* on MyPsychLab

use of the neurotransmitter serotonin are also associated with some anxiety disorders. Drugs that affect GABA or serotonin levels are used as successful treatments for some types of anxiety disorders.

Researchers are also using imaging techniques to examine the brain bases of these disorders (Radua et al., 2010; van Tol et al., 2010). For example, PET scans have revealed a difference in the function of serotonin receptors between the brains of individuals who suffer from panic disorder and those of control individuals (Nash et al., 2008). These differences may help explain the onset of panic disorder. As another example, MRI techniques have revealed very widespread abnormalities in OCD patients' brains. For example, patients with OCD have greater cortical thickness in areas of the brain that normally allow people to inhibit behaviors (Narayan et al., 2008). This brain abnormality that potentially hinders communication among neurons may partially explain why people with OCD have difficulty controlling their behavioral compulsions.

Finally, family and twin studies suggest that there is a genetic basis for the predisposition to experience anxiety disorders (Hettema et al., 2005; Li et al., 2011). For example, the probability that a pair of male identical twins both suffered from a social or specific phobia was consistently greater than the probability that both male fraternal twins were sufferers (Kendler et al., 2001). Still, it's important to remember that nature and nurture always interact. For example, many aspects of personality are heritable. Research suggests that part of the influence of genes on PTSD arises because people with different personality traits make life choices that decrease or increase the probability that they will experience traumas (Stein et al., 2002).

Psychodynamic The psychodynamic model begins with the assumption that the symptoms of anxiety disorders come from underlying psychic conflicts or fears. The symptoms are attempts to protect the individual from psychological pain. Thus panic attacks are the result of unconscious conflicts bursting into consciousness. Suppose, for example, a child represses conflicting thoughts about his or her wish to escape a difficult home environment. In later life, a phobia may be activated by an object or situation that symbolizes the conflict. A bridge, for example, might come to symbolize the path that the person must traverse from the world of home and family to the outside world. The sight of a bridge would then force the unconscious conflict into awareness, bringing with it the fear and anxiety common to phobias. Avoiding bridges would be a symbolic attempt to stay clear of anxiety about the childhood experiences at home.

In obsessive-compulsive disorders, the obsessive behavior is seen as an attempt to displace anxiety created by a related but far more feared desire or conflict. By substituting an obsession that symbolically captures the forbidden impulse, a person gains some relief. For example, the obsessive fears of dirt experienced by Jim, the adolescent described earlier, may have their roots in the conflict between his desire to become sexually active and his fear of "dirtying" his reputation. Compulsive preoccupation with carrying out a minor ritualistic task also allows the individual to avoid the original issue that is creating unconscious conflict.

Behavioral Behavioral explanations of anxiety focus on the way symptoms of anxiety disorders are reinforced or conditioned. Investigators do not search for underlying unconscious conflicts or early childhood experiences because these phenomena can't be observed directly. Behavioral theories are often used to explain the development of phobias, which are seen as classically conditioned fears: One famous study involved Little Albert, in whom John Watson and Rosalie Rayner instilled a fear of a white rat. The behavioral account suggests that a previously neutral object or situation becomes a stimulus for a phobia by being paired with a frightening experience. For example, a child whose mother yells a warning when he or she approaches a snake may develop a phobia about snakes. After this experience, even thinking about snakes may produce a wave of fear. Phobias continue to be maintained by the reduction in anxiety that occurs when a person withdraws from the feared situation.

A behavioral analysis of obsessive-compulsive disorders suggests that compulsive behaviors tend to reduce the anxiety associated with obsessive thoughts—thus reinforcing the compulsive behavior. For example, if a woman fears contamination by touching garbage, then washing her hands reduces the anxiety and is therefore reinforcing. In parallel to phobias, obsessive-compulsive disorders continue to be maintained by the reduction in anxiety that follows from the compulsive behaviors.

Cognitive Cognitive perspectives on anxiety concentrate on the perceptual processes or attitudes that may distort a person's estimate of the danger that he or she is facing. A person may either overestimate the nature or reality of a threat or underestimate his or her ability to cope with the threat effectively. For example, before delivering a speech to a large group, a person with a social phobia may feed his or her anxiety:

> *What if I forget what I was going to say? I'll look foolish in front of all these people. Then I'll get even more nervous and start to perspire, and my voice will shake, and I'll look even sillier. Whenever people see me from now on, they'll remember me as the foolish person who tried to give a speech.*

People who suffer from anxiety disorders may often interpret their own distress as a sign of impending disaster. Their reaction may set off a vicious cycle in which the person fears disaster, which leads to an increase in anxiety, which in turn worsens the anxiety sensations and confirms the person's fears (Beck & Emery, 1985).

Psychologists have tested this cognitive account by measuring *anxiety sensitivity*: individuals' beliefs that bodily symptoms—such as shortness of breath or heart palpitations—may have harmful consequences. People high in anxiety sensitivity are likely to agree with statements such as "When I notice that my heart is beating rapidly, I worry that I might have a heart attack." Let's consider a study that demonstrated the role of anxiety sensitivity in phobia for flying.

Participants with flight phobia as well as control participants provided information about their flight anxiety, their bodily symptoms related to flight, and their anxiety sensitivity (Vanden Bogaerde & De Raedt, 2011). The participants provided final data while they were on an actual flight, waiting for the plane to take off. The participants with flight phobia had higher average scores on all measures: They reported

Featured Study

more flight anxiety, more bodily symptoms, and more anxiety sensitivity. However, the relationship among these measures also proved to be important. Consider two participants who experienced the same level of bodily symptoms to the impending flight. In response to those bodily symptoms, a participant with high levels of anxiety sensitivity was likely to experience a great deal of flight anxiety whereas a participant with low levels of anxiety sensitivity was not. The researchers concluded that when participants "experience aversive bodily sensations due to the flying environment," those "with higher levels of [anxiety sensitivity] are prone to interpret these in a threatening way which leads to higher levels of anxiety" (p. 425).

Another study demonstrated the importance of anxiety sensitivity for posttraumatic stress disorder. Researchers assessed the anxiety sensitivity of a group of 68 children, ages 10 to 17, all of whom had been exposed to traumatic events (for example, they had witnessed people being killed) (Leen-Feldner et al., 2008). The researchers found a positive correlation between anxiety sensitivity and the children's symptoms of PTSD: The children who reported the highest levels of anxiety sensitivity were also most likely to report PTSD symptoms. The researchers suggested that high levels of anxiety sensitivity would make reexperiences of traumatic events (such as flashbacks) even more frightening.

Research has also found that anxious patients contribute to the *maintenance* of their anxiety by employing cognitive biases that highlight the threatening stimuli. For example, patients whose symptoms of obsessive-compulsive disorder focused on issues of cleanliness watched a researcher touch a series of objects with a "clean and unused" tissue or a "dirty and already used" tissue. In a later memory test, these OCD patients showed greater ability to recall which objects were "dirty" than which were "clean" (Ceschi et al., 2003). Similarly, people with social anxiety are *more* likely to attend to threatening social information and *less* likely to attend to positive social information. In one study, participants with social anxiety had to give an impromptu five-minute speech—a serious social stressor (Taylor et al., 2010). The participants also completed a task that measured bias against attending to positive social information. The participants who showed the greatest tendency to avoid positive social information also experienced the most distress

giving their five-minute talk. Studies of this type confirm that people suffering from anxiety disorders focus their attention in ways that serve to sustain their anxiety.

Each of the major approaches to anxiety disorders may explain part of the etiological puzzle. Continued research of each approach will clarify causes and, therefore, potential avenues for treatment. Let's turn now to another major category of abnormality—*mood disorders*.

Stop and Review

① What is the relationship between fear and phobias?
② What is the difference between an obsession and a compulsion?
③ With respect to phobias, what is the preparedness hypothesis?
④ What is the impact of anxiety sensitivity?

CRITICAL THINKING Recall the study that focused on the role of anxiety sensitivity for flight phobia. Why was it important for the researchers to collect their data on actual flights?

✓•⬡Study and Review on MyPsychLab

MOOD DISORDERS

There have almost certainly been times in your life when you would have described yourself as terribly depressed or incredibly happy. For some people, however, extremes in mood come to disrupt normal life experiences. A **mood disorder** is an emotional disturbance, such as severe depression or depression alternating with mania. Researchers estimate that 20.8 percent of adults have suffered from mood disorders (Kessler et al., 2005a). We will consider two major categories: major depressive disorder and bipolar disorder.

Major Depressive Disorder

Depression has been characterized as the "common cold of psychopathology," both because it occurs so frequently and because almost everyone has experienced elements of the full-scale disorder at some time in his or her life. Everyone has, at one time or another, experienced grief after the loss of a loved one or felt sad or upset when failing to achieve a desired goal. These sad feelings are only one symptom experienced by people suffering from a **major depressive disorder** (see **Table 3**). Consider one individual's description

How does anxiety sensitivity affect people's fear of flying?

mood disorder A mood disturbance such as severe depression or depression alternating with mania.

major depressive disorder A mood disorder characterized by intense feelings of depression over an extended time, without the manic high phase of bipolar depression.

Table 3 • Characteristics of Major Depressive Disorder

Characteristics	Example
Dysphoric mood	Sad, blue, hopeless; loss of interest or pleasure in almost all usual activities
Appetite	Significant weight loss (while not dieting) or weight gain
Sleep	Insomnia or hypersomnia (sleeping too much)
Motor activity	Markedly slowed down (motor retardation) or agitated
Guilt	Feelings of worthlessness; self-reproach
Concentration	Diminished ability to think or concentrate; forgetfulness
Suicide	Recurrent thoughts of death; suicidal ideas or attempts

of his struggle to carry out normal daily tasks while in the depths of depression:

> *It seemed to take the most colossal effort to do simple things. I remember bursting into tears because I had used up the cake of soap that was in the shower. I cried because one of the keys stuck for a second on my computer. I found everything excruciatingly difficult, and so, for example, the prospect of lifting the telephone receiver seemed to me like bench-pressing four hundred pounds. The reality that I had to put on not just one but two socks and then two shoes so overwhelmed me that I wanted to go back to bed.*
> (Solomon, 2001, pp. 85–86)

This excerpt illustrates some vivid consequences of major depressive disorder.

People diagnosed with depression differ in terms of the severity and duration of their symptoms. Many individuals struggle with clinical depression for only several weeks at one point in their lives, whereas others experience depression episodically or chronically for many years. Estimates of the prevalence of mood disorders reveal that about 16.6 percent of adults suffer from major depression at some time in their lives (Kessler et al., 2005a).

Depression takes an enormous toll on those afflicted, on their families, and on society. A study undertaken on behalf of the World Health Organization estimated the loss of healthy life years that could be attributed to physical and mental illnesses (World Health Organization, 2008). In this analysis, major depressive disorder ranked third (behind lower respiratory infections and diarrheal diseases) in terms of the burden it places on people's lives around the world. For middle- and high-income

countries, major depressive disorder ranked first. In the United States, depression accounts for the majority of all mental hospital admissions, but it is still believed to be underdiagnosed and undertreated. The National Comorbidity Study found that only 37.4 percent of individuals sought treatment in the first year after a major depressive episode (Wang et al., 2005). In fact, the median period people waited between experiencing a major depressive episode and seeking treatment was eight years.

Bipolar Disorder

Bipolar disorder is characterized by periods of severe depression alternating with manic episodes. A person experiencing a **manic episode** generally acts and feels unusually elated and expansive. However, sometimes the individual's predominant mood is irritability rather than elation, especially if the person feels thwarted in some way. During a manic episode, a person often experiences an inflated sense of self-esteem or an unrealistic belief that he or she possesses special abilities or powers. The person may feel a dramatically decreased need to sleep and may engage excessively in work or in social or other pleasurable activities.

Caught up in a manic mood, the person shows unwarranted optimism, takes unnecessary risks, promises anything, and may give everything away.

When the mania begins to diminish, people are left trying to deal with the damage and predicaments they created during their period of frenzy. Manic episodes almost always give way to periods of severe depression.

The duration and frequency of the mood disturbances in bipolar disorder vary from person to person. Some people experience long periods of normal functioning punctuated by occasional short manic or depressive episodes. A small

What are some differences between the occasional feelings of unhappiness that most people feel and the symptoms of major depressive disorder?

---

bipolar disorder A mood disorder characterized by alternating periods of depression and mania.

manic episode A component of bipolar disorder characterized by periods of extreme elation, unbounded euphoria without sufficient reason, and grandiose thoughts or feelings about personal abilities.

percentage of unfortunate individuals go right from manic episodes to clinical depression and back again in continuous, unending cycles that are devastating to them, their families, their friends, and their coworkers. While manic, they may gamble away life savings or give lavish gifts to strangers, acts that later add to guilt feelings when they are in the depressed phase. Bipolar disorder is rarer than major depressive disorder, occurring in about 3.9 percent of adults (Kessler et al., 2005a). ◉

Causes of Mood Disorders

What factors are involved in the development of mood disorders? To address this question, we'll once again visit the biological, psychodynamic, behavioral, and cognitive perspectives. Note that, because of its prevalence, major depressive disorder has been studied more extensively than bipolar disorder. This review will reflect that distribution of research.

Biological Several types of research provide clues to the contribution of biology to mood disorders. For example, the ability of different drugs to relieve manic and depressive symptoms provides evidence that different brain states underlie the two extremes of bipolar disorder (Thase & Denko, 2008). Reduced levels of two chemical messengers in the brain, serotonin and norepinephrine, have been linked to depression; increased levels of these neurotransmitters are associated with mania.

Researchers are using brain-imaging techniques to understand the causes and consequences of mood disorders (Gotlib & Hamilton, 2008). For example, researchers have used fMRI to demonstrate that the brains of people who suffer from bipolar disorder respond differently when they are in depressed versus manic states. One study focused on 36 individuals with bipolar disorder (Blumberg et al., 2003). At the time of the study, 11 were in elevated moods, 10 were in depressed moods, and 15 were in *euthymic* (or balanced) emotional states. All of the individuals performed the same cognitive task—naming the colors in which words were printed—while undergoing fMRI scans. The scans indicated that particular regions of the cortex were more active or less active depending on each individual's particular phase of bipolar disorder.

The contribution of biology to the etiology of mood disorders is also confirmed by evidence that the incidence of mood disorder is influenced by genetic factors (Edvardsen et al., 2008; Kendler et al., 2006). For example, one twin study assessed the likelihood that both twins were diagnosed with bipolar disorder. The correlation was 0.82 for monozygotic (MZ) twins but only 0.07 for dizygotic (DZ) twins. These data led to a heritably estimate of 0.77 (Edvarsen et al., 2008). You will see in the *Psychology in Your Life* discussing nature and nuture that researchers have begun to make progress identifying the way that genes interact with environments to influence individuals' likelihoods of experiencing mood disorders.

Let's see now what the three major psychological approaches can add to your understanding of the onset of mood disorders.

Psychodynamic In the psychodynamic approach, unconscious conflicts and hostile feelings that originate in early childhood are seen to play key roles in the development of depression. Freud was struck by the degree of self-criticism and guilt that depressed people displayed. He believed that the source of this self-reproach was anger, originally directed at someone else, that had been turned inward against the self. The anger was believed to be tied to an especially intense and dependent childhood relationship, such as a parent–child relationship, in which the person's needs or expectations were not met. Losses, real or symbolic, in adulthood reactivate hostile feelings, now directed toward the person's own ego, creating the self-reproach that is characteristic of depression.

Behavioral Rather than searching for the roots of depression in the unconscious, the behavioral approach focuses on the effects of the amount of positive reinforcement and punishments a person receives (Dimidjian et al., 2011). In this view, depressed feelings result when an individual receives insufficient positive reinforcements and experiences many punishments in the environment following a loss or other major life changes. As people begin to experience depression, they will often withdraw from situations they perceive as stressful. This strategy of avoidance often also reduces the opportunities people have to obtain positive reinforcement (Carvalho & Hopko, 2011). Thus, as depression leads to avoidance, the depression will often become more entrenched. In addition, depressed people tend to underestimate positive feedback and overestimate negative feedback (Kennedy & Craighead, 1988).

Cognitive At the center of the cognitive approach to depression are two theories. One theory suggests that negative *cognitive sets*—"set" patterns of perceiving the world—lead people to take a negative view of events in their lives for which they feel responsible. The second theory, the *explanatory style* model, proposes that depression arises from the belief that one has little or no personal control over significant life events. Each of these models explains some aspects of the experience of depression. Let's see how.

Aaron Beck (1967; Disner et al., 2011), a leading researcher on depression, has developed the theory of cognitive sets. Beck has argued that depressed people have three types of negative cognitions, which he calls the *cognitive triad* of depression: negative views of themselves, negative views of ongoing experiences, and negative views of the future. Depressed people tend to view themselves as inadequate or defective in some way, to interpret ongoing experiences in a negative way, and to believe that the future will continue to bring suffering and difficulties. This pattern of negative thinking clouds all experiences and produces the other characteristic signs of depression. An individual who always anticipates a negative outcome is not likely to be motivated to pursue any goal, leading to the *paralysis of will* that is prominent in depression.

In the explanatory style view, pioneered by **Martin Seligman,** individuals believe, correctly or not, that they cannot control future outcomes that are important to them. Seligman's theory evolved from research that demonstrated depressionlike symptoms in dogs (and later in other species). Seligman and Maier (1967) subjected dogs to painful, unavoidable shocks: No matter what the dogs did, there was no way to escape the

◉ Watch the Video *DSM in Context: Speaking Out: Feliziano: Bipolar Disorder* on MyPsychLab

shocks. The dogs developed what Seligman and Maier called **learned helplessness.** Learned helplessness is marked by three types of deficits: *motivational deficits*—the dogs were slow to initiate known actions; *emotional deficits*—they appeared rigid, listless, frightened, and distressed; and *cognitive deficits*—they demonstrated poor learning in new situations. Even when put in a situation in which they could, in fact, avoid shock, they did not learn to do so (Maier & Seligman, 1976).

Seligman believed that depressed people are also in a state of learned helplessness: They have an expectancy that nothing they can do matters (Abramson et al., 1978; Peterson & Seligman, 1984; Seligman, 1975). However, the emergence of this state depends, to a large extent, on how individuals explain their life events. There are three dimensions of explanatory style: *internal–external, global–specific,* and *stable–unstable.* Suppose that you have just received a poor grade on a psychology exam. You attribute the negative outcome on the exam to an internal factor ("I'm stupid"), which makes you feel sad, rather than to an external one ("The exam was really hard"), which would have made you angry. You could have chosen a less stable internal quality than intelligence to explain your performance ("I was tired that day"). Rather than attributing your performance to an internal, stable factor that has global or far-reaching influence (stupidity), you could even have limited your explanation to the psychology exam or course ("I'm not good at psychology courses"). Explanatory style theory suggests that individuals who attribute failure to internal, stable, and global causes are vulnerable to depression. This prediction has been confirmed repeatedly (Lau & Eley, 2008; Peterson & Vaidya, 2001).

Once people begin to experience the negative moods associated with major depressive disorder, ordinary cognitive processes make it more difficult for them to escape those moods. Consider a study that demonstrated that depression changes the way in which people attend to information in the world.

Featured Study

*Researchers recruited a group of 15 depressed participants and 45 control participants (who had never experienced depression) (Kellough et al., 2008). The participants wore a device that allowed the researchers to monitor eye movements while they viewed visual displays. Each display had four photographs that represented the emotion categories sad, threat, positive, and neutral. For example, one display had photographs of a boy crying, a pointing gun, a couple embracing, and a fire hydrant. The participants were told that they were wearing the eye-tracking device so that the researchers could determine the relationship between pupil dilation and emotional images. In fact, the researchers wished to test the hypothesis that depressed individuals would spend more time than control individuals (who had never been depressed) looking at the sad photos and less time looking at the positive photos. The data supported that prediction. As you can see in **Figure 1**, individuals with depression spent more time looking at sad photos whereas individuals who had never experienced depression spent more time looking at positive photos.*

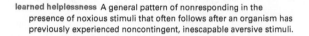

learned helplessness A general pattern of nonresponding in the presence of noxious stimuli that often follows after an organism has previously experienced noncontingent, inescapable aversive stimuli.

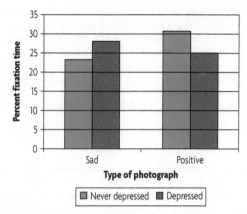

FIGURE 1 Attentional Biases in Major Depressive Disorder

Depressed participants and control participants (who had never been depressed) viewed displays with sad, threat, positive, and neutral photographs. Compared to never-depressed participants, depressed participants spent more time looking at sad photographs and less time looking at positive photographs.

Data from *Behaviour Research and Therapy 46*(11), Kellough, J. L., Beevers, C. G., Ellis, A. J., & Wells, T. T. "Time course of selective attention in clinically depressed young adults," pp 1238–1243, 2008.

This research supports the more general conclusion that people with major depressive disorder find their attention drawn to negative information in the world (Peckham et al., 2010). You can understand how this attentional bias could help make depression feel inescapable.

Insights generated from cognitive theories of depression have given rise to successful forms of therapy. For now, we turn to two other important aspects of the study of depression that we will consider: the large differences between the prevalence of depression in men and women, and the link between depression and suicide.

Gender Differences in Depression

One of the central questions of research on depression is why women are afflicted almost twice as often as men (Hyde et al., 2008). Estimates of the prevalence of mood disorders reveal that about 21 percent of females and 13 percent of males suffer a major depression at some time in their lives (Kessler et al., 1994). This gender difference emerges in adolescence, by about ages 13 to 15. One factor that contributes to this difference is, unfortunately, quite straightforward: On average, women experience more negative events and life stressors than men do (Kendler et al., 2004; Shih et al., 2006). For example, women have a greater likelihood of experiencing physical or sexual abuse, and they are more likely to live in poverty while being the primary caregiver for children and elderly parents. Thus women's lives provide more of the types of experiences that lay the groundwork for serious depression.

Research on gender differences has focused on a number of factors that might make women more vulnerable to depression (Hyde et al., 2008). Some of those factors are biological: There might, for example, be hormonal differences that start

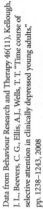

Data from Behaviour Research and Therapy 46(11), Kellough, J. L., Beevers, C. G., Ellis, A.J., Wells, T. T. "Time course of selective attention in clinically depressed young adults," pp. 1238–1243, 2008

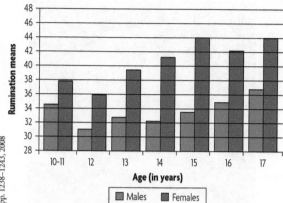

FIGURE 2 Gender Differences in Rumination

Across the adolescent years, the gap grows between girls' and boys' reports of rumination.

Data from Jose, P. E. & Grown, I. "When does the gender difference in rumination begin?" *Journal of Youth and Adolescence 37*(2), 2008, 180–192.

at puberty that put adolescent girls more at risk for depression than their male peers. Researchers have also looked intensively at cognitive factors that set men and women apart. For example, research by **Susan Nolen-Hoeksema** (Nolen-Hoeksema & Hilt, 2009) contrasts the response styles of men and women once they begin to experience negative moods. On this view, when women experience sadness, they tend to think about the possible causes and implications of their feelings. In contrast, men attempt actively to distract themselves from depressed feelings, either by focusing on something else or by engaging in a physical activity that will take their minds off their current mood state.

This model suggests that the more thoughtful, *ruminative* response style of women—the tendency to focus obsessively on their problems—increases women's vulnerability to depression. Consider a study that examined rumination among a large sample of adolescents.

*A group of 1,218 students between the ages of 10 and 17 completed a questionnaire that assessed their responses to life events (Jose & Brown, 2008). The questionnaire included statements like "I sit at home and think about how I feel" and "I think no one will want to be around me if I don't snap out of this mood." The students responded to each statement on a 5-point scale that ranged from "never" to "always." As you can see in **Figure 2**, at the youngest ages there was a modest difference between males and females. However, over the adolescent years the gap grows, with girls engaging in considerably more rumination. The students in the study also completed a measure of depression. For both boys and girls, the students who ruminated the most were also most likely to report the most symptoms of depression. However, the relationship between rumination and depression was even stronger for the girls.*

This study supports the hypothesis that rumination is a risk factor for depression: Paying attention to negative moods can

increase thoughts of negative events, which eventually increases the quantity and/or the intensity of negative feelings. The study also confirms that men who ruminate are also at risk for depression. The gender difference for depression emerges, in part, because more women ruminate.

Suicide

"The will to survive and succeed had been crushed and defeated. . . . There comes a time when all things cease to shine, when the rays of hope are lost" (Shneidman, 1987, p. 57). This sad statement by a suicidal young man reflects the most extreme consequence of any psychological disorder—*suicide*. Although most depressed people do not commit suicide, analyses suggest that many suicides are attempted by those who are suffering from depression (Bolton et al., 2008). In the general U.S. population, the number of deaths officially designated as suicide is around 30,000 each year (Nock et al., 2008). Because many suicides are attributed to accidents or other causes, the actual rate is probably much higher. Because depression occurs more frequently in women, it is not surprising that women *attempt* suicide more often than men do; attempts by men, however, are more often successful (Nock et al., 2008). This difference occurs largely because men use guns more often, and women tend to use less lethal means, such as sleeping pills.

One of the most alarming social problems in recent decades is the rise of *youth suicide*. Although suicide is the eleventh leading cause of death in the United States for all ages, it is third for people ages 15 to 24 (Miniño et al., 2010). For every completed suicide, there may be as many as 8 to

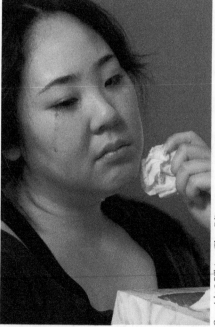

What factors help explain why more women than men experience depression?

20 suicide attempts. To assess the risk of youth suicide, a team of researchers reviewed 128 studies that involved about 500,000 individuals between the ages of 12 and 20 (Evans et al., 2005). Across that broad sample, 29.9 percent of the adolescents had thought about suicide at some point in their lives, and 9.7 percent had actually attempted suicide. Adolescent girls were roughly twice as likely as adolescent boys to have made a suicide attempt.

Youth suicide is not a spur-of-the-moment, impulsive act, but, typically, it occurs as the final stage of a period of inner turmoil and outer distress. The majority of young suicide victims have talked to others about their intentions or have written about them. Thus talk of suicide should always be taken seriously (Rudd et al., 2006). As is the case for adults, adolescents are more likely to attempt suicide when they are experiencing depression (Gutierrez et al., 2004; Nrugham et al., 2008). Feelings of hopelessness and isolation, as well as negative self-concepts, are also associated with suicide risk (Rutter & Behrendt, 2004). Furthermore, gay and lesbian youths are at even higher risk for suicide than are other adolescents. A team of researchers reviewed several studies comparing the suicide rates of heterosexual and "sexual minority youth" (adolescents who reported same-sex attraction and/or behavior). The average rates of suicidal thoughts and behaviors were 28 percent for sexual minority youth and 12 percent for heterosexuals (Marshal et al., 2011). These higher suicide rates undoubtedly reflect the relative lack of social support for homosexual orientation. Suicide is an extreme reaction that occurs especially when adolescents feel unable to cry out to others for help. Being sensitive to signs of suicidal intentions and caring enough to intervene are essential for saving the lives of both youthful and mature people who have come to see no exit for their troubles except total self-destruction.

DFree/Shutterstock.com

Even highly successful individuals, like actor Owen Wilson, are not immune to the feelings of despair that can trigger suicidal thoughts. What has research revealed about the relationship between depression and suicide?

Stop and Review

① What experiences characterize bipolar disorder?
② In Aaron Beck's theory, what types of negative cognitions make up the cognitive triad?
③ How does the ruminative response style help explain gender differences in depression?
④ What are some suicide risk factors for adolescents?

CRITICAL THINKING Recall the study that demonstrated attentional biases in major depressive disorder. Why might participants have been led to believe the study was about pupil dilation?

✓•⌐Study and Review on MyPsychLab

SOMATOFORM AND DISSOCIATIVE DISORDERS

As this chapter has reviewed various types of psychological disorders, you have seen how certain everyday experiences can, pushed to the limit, lead to disability or maladaptive behavior.

For example, everyone experiences anxiety, but for some people those experiences become so severe that they develop an anxiety disorder. Similarly, many people experience symptoms for physical illnesses that don't have any obvious causes; many people have days when they just "don't feel like themselves." However, when those types of experiences impair individuals' day-to-day life, they may indicate *somatoform disorders* or *dissociative disorders*. Let's review the symptoms and etiology of each type of disorder.

Somatoform Disorders

A person suffering from a **somatoform disorder** has physical illnesses or complaints that cannot be fully explained by actual medical conditions. To be diagnosed with one of these disorders, people must experience the illnesses or complaints to an extent that they cause sufficient distress to interfere with their everyday functioning. Let's review *hypochondriasis, somatization disorder,* and *conversion disorder.*

Individuals with **hypochondriasis** believe they have physical illnesses despite assurance from medical practitioners that they do not. Even when they are currently healthy, they may be constantly fearful that they will contact physical illnesses.

....

somatoform disorder A disorder in which people have physical illnesses or complaints that cannot be fully explained by actual medical conditions.

hypochondriasis A disorder in which individuals are preoccupied with having or getting physical ailments despite reassurances that they are healthy.

Psychology in Your Life

HOW CAN WE PINPOINT INTERACTIONS OF NATURE AND NURTURE?

It is evident that people's life outcomes—for example, their attachment to their mothers and their intellectual performance—reflect an interaction of nature and nurture: Environments change the impact of genes. These types of interactions are particularly important in the study of psychopathology. Causal models for many types of mental illness assert that particular genes put people at risk, but features of the environment play an important role to determine whether the risk brings about illness. Let's explore an interaction of nature and nurture for major depressive disorder.

The discussion of mood disorders noted that disruptions in the function of the neurotransmitter serotonin play a role in depression. For that reason, researchers have focused attention on a gene, known as 5-HTTLPR, that has an impact on the serotonin system (Caspi et al., 2010; Karg et al., 2011). The gene comes in short (S) and long (L) forms. In one study with 144 college undergraduates, 19 percent had two short versions of the gene (SS), 53 percent had one short and one long (SL), and 28 percent had two long versions (LL) (Carver et al., 2011). The students themselves provided information about the family circumstances in which they had been raised. They used 5-point scales (1 = not at all; 5 = very often) to provide information about factors such as how often they felt loved and cared for, how often they were insulted, and how often they were abused. Based on those responses, the researchers calculated the extent to which each student had been raised in a "risky family." Each student also underwent a clinical evaluation to determine whether he or she had ever met the diagnostic criteria for major depressive disorder.

In the figure, positive numbers for "Risky families" indicate that the family had more risk factors (so that the student's childhood experience was more stressful). Positive numbers for "Depression diagnosis" indicate a higher probability of a diagnosis. As you can see, the interaction of genes and environments was quite dramatic: For students with two long versions of the gene (LL), a family environment

that was highly risky actually yielded fewer diagnoses of major depressive disorder.

Another study followed people over several decades to evaluate environmental interactions with this same gene (Uher et al., 2011). Participants entered the study when they were small children (some as 3-year-olds and some as 5-year-olds) and maltreatment was assessed during their childhood. They were followed through young adulthood (through ages 32 or 40) to determine which individuals experienced persistent depression. Once again, the impact of childhood maltreatment—with respect to the likelihood of persistent depression—depended on which versions of the 5-HTTLPR gene each participant had inherited.

These studies make plain the importance of both nature and nurture. A known genetic difference in combination with negative life events greatly changes the likelihood that people will experience depression. Breakthroughs in the understanding of the human genome allow researchers to determine exactly how nature and nurture interact.

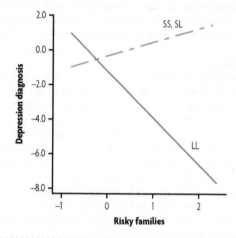

In addition, this preoccupation with being or getting ill causes such sufficient distress that individuals are impaired in their day-to-day lives. To assess the prevalence of hypochondriasis and other somatoform disorders, researchers often focus on people who present themselves for medical treatment. In that context, the question becomes what proportion of people have physical complaints that don't allow medical explanations. Research suggests that 4.7 percent of adults 18 and older who seek medical treatment meet *DSM-IV-TR* criteria for hypochondriasis (Fink et al., 2004).

Individuals with **somatization disorder** present a long history of physical complaints over many years. Those complaints—which remain medically unexplained—must span several medical categories. To meet *DSM-IV-TR* criteria for the diagnosis, individuals must have experienced four pain symptoms (such as headaches or stomachaches), two gastrointestinal

somatization disorder A disorder characterized by unexplained physical complaints in several categories over many years.

What role do attentional biases play in the development of somatoform disorders?

MIXA/Getty Images

The study focused on a 36-year-old woman who had partial paralysis of her upper arm that could not be explained by any physical disorder (Cojan et al., 2009). The patient completed a motor task in which she attempted to use her hands to execute or inhibit responses to visual stimuli on a computer screen. The researchers used fMRI scans to contrast her patterns of brain activity with that of a group of healthy controls who attempted to simulate a left-hand paralysis (in parallel to the patient's symptoms). The patterns of brain activity for the patient and controls showed intriguing differences. For example, the fMRI scans for the simulating controls suggested that they were engaging in conscious effort when they tried not to move their hand. The patient's fMRI scans showed activity in different brain regions—the pattern suggested that her inability to move her hand was not voluntary.

symptoms (such as nausea or diarrhea), one sexual symptom (such as erectile dysfunction or excessive menstrual bleeding), and one neurological symptom (such as paralysis or double vision). Among adults seeking medical treatment, 1.5 percent meet criteria for somatization disorder (Fink et al., 2004).

Both hypochondriasis and somatization disorder are defined by people's complaints about physical symptoms. However, people with hypochondriasis worry about having a specific underlying disease whereas those with somatization disorder focus more on the symptoms themselves. In addition, as you've just seen, to be diagnosed with somatization disorder people must have reported a wide variety of unexplained physical complaints.

Conversion disorder is characterized by a loss of motor or sensory function that cannot be explained by damage to the nervous system or other physical damage. For example, individuals may experience paralysis or blindness without a medical cause. In addition, the onset of the physical symptoms must be preceded by psychological factors such as interpersonal conflict or emotional stressors. Historically, conversion disorder was called *hysteria*—and was believed to represent, in some eras, possession by the devil. Sigmund Freud helped bring about the contemporary understanding of conversion disorder. One of his most enduring insights was that psychological trauma could yield physical symptoms. Conversion disorder is present in 1.5 percent of adults seeking medical treatment (Fink et al., 2004).

Causes of Somatoform Disorders The defining characteristic of somatoform disorders is that individuals experience physical ailments that have no adequate medical explanation. Researchers have attempted to understand how that could be possible: How, for example, could individuals whose motor systems are intact experience paralysis? Studies have used neuroimaging techniques to discover the brain bases of conversion disorder (Mailis-Gagnon & Nicholson, 2011; Ellenstein et al., 2011). Consider a study that demonstrated that an individual with conversion symptoms showed different patterns of brain activity than individuals who were only simulating the same symptoms.

To understand these results, you might take a moment to see what it feels like to simulate paralysis in your left hand. It takes some mental effort not to let the hand move. The study suggests that people with conversion symptoms are not expending any such effort; their symptoms are not just pretense.

Researchers have also examined cognitive processes that contribute to somatoform disorders (Brown, 2004; Rief & Broadbent, 2007). For example, an important aspect of hypochondriasis is an attentional bias in the way that individuals respond to bodily sensations. Suppose you wake up one morning with a scratchy throat. If you have an attentional bias that makes it difficult to divert your thoughts from that scratchy throat, you might come to believe that you are seriously ill. In fact, one study demonstrated that the attention of people who experience a high level of anxiety about their health is drawn to pictures that show health threats (such as a man with a rash on his arms) (Jasper & Witthöft, 2011). The tight focus on symptoms and illness contributes to a vicious cycle: Stress and anxiety have physical consequences (for example, increased sweating and elevated heart rate) that can feel like the symptoms of illness—providing further proof that health-focused anxiety is appropriate. Someone who attributes all physical symptoms to illness may perceive a perilous pattern in the co-occurrence of a scratchy throat, excessive sweating, and a swiftly beating heart. Thus the cognitive biases associated with somatoform disorders serve to exaggerate minor bodily sensations.

Dissociative Disorders

A **dissociative disorder** is a disturbance in the integration of identity, memory, or consciousness. It is important for people to see themselves as being in control of their behavior, including emotions, thoughts, and actions. Essential to this perception of self-control is the sense of selfhood—the consistency of different aspects of the self and the continuity of identity over time and place. Psychologists believe that, in dissociated states, individuals escape from their conflicts by giving up this precious consistency and continuity—in a sense, disowning part of

....

conversion disorder A disorder in which psychological conflict or stress brings about loss of motor or sensory function.

dissociative disorder A personality disorder marked by a disturbance in the integration of identity, memory, or consciousness.

themselves. The forgetting of important personal experiences, a process caused by psychological factors in the absence of any organic dysfunction, called **dissociative amnesia,** is one example of dissociation. For some people, the loss of ability to recall their past is accompanied by an actual flight from their home or place of work. This disorder is called **dissociative fugue.** People may remain in a fugue state for hours, days, or months; they may live with a new identity in a new location.

Dissociative identity disorder (DID), formerly known as *multiple personality disorder,* is a dissociative mental disorder in which two or more distinct personalities exist within the same individual. At any particular time, one of these personalities is dominant in directing the individual's behavior. Dissociative identity disorder is popularly known as *split personality* and sometimes mistakenly called *schizophrenia,* a disorder, as you will see in the next section, in which personality often is impaired but is not split into multiple versions. In DID, each of the emerging personalities contrasts in some significant way with the original self—it might be outgoing if the person is shy, tough if the original personality is weak, and sexually assertive if the other is fearful and sexually naive. Each personality has a unique identity, name, and behavior pattern. In some cases, dozens of different characters emerge to help the person deal with a difficult life situation. Here is an excerpt from a first-person account of a woman who experiences DID (Mason, 1997, p. 44):

> Just as waves turn the ocean inside out and rearrange the water, different ones of us cycle in and out in an ebb and flow that is sometimes gentle, sometimes turbulent. A child colors with Crayola markers. She moves aside to make way for the administrator, who reconciles the bank statement. A moment later, the dead baby takes over and lies paralyzed on the floor. She remains that way for a while, but no one gets upset—it's her turn. The live baby stops in her crawl, engrossed by a speck of dust. The cooker prepares meals for three days and packages each separately—we all have different likes and dislikes. A terrified one screams aloud, a wounded one moans, a grieving one wails.

From Vivian Ann Conan, "Divided She Stands." Originally appeared in New York Magazine August 4, 1997 under the pseudonym Laura Emily Mason. Reprinted by permission of the author.

Can you put yourself in this woman's place, and imagine what it would be like to have this range of "individuals"—the child, the dead baby, the live baby, the cooker, and so on—inside your one head?

Causes of Dissociative Disorders Psychologists who take a psychodynamic perspective have suggested that dissociation serves a vital survival function. They suggest that people who have experienced traumatic stress will sometimes use defense mechanisms to push the traumatic events out of conscious awareness. Consider a study that focused on the life experiences of 891 11- to 17-year-old adolescents in Puerto Rico (Martínez-Taboas et al., 2006). The children completed questionnaires that assessed the presence of victimization experiences and dissociative symptoms in their lives. As you can see in **Figure 3,** relatively few of the children in the sample had experienced high levels of victimization. For example, 74 percent of the adolescents had not experienced any emotional abuse. However, Figure 3 also reveals that increasing levels of emotional, physical, and sexual abuse were accompanied by higher levels of dissociative symptoms.

Although these data—and personal accounts of the type quoted earlier—seem compelling, many psychologists remain skeptical about the link between trauma and dissociation (Giesbrecht et al., 2008). This skepticism has been particularly focused on dissociative identity disorder. No solid data exist about the prevalence of this disorder (*DSM-IV-TR,* 2000). In fact, some critics have suggested that diagnoses of DID have increased because of the media attention paid to individuals who claim to have large numbers of distinct personalities (Lilienfeld & Lynn, 2003). Skeptics have often suggested that therapists who "believe" in DID may create DID—these therapists question their patients, often under hypnosis, in a way that encourages multiple personalities to "emerge." Researchers have tried to find rigorous methods to test the claims people with DID make about the separation between different identities. For example, studies have examined *interidentity amnesia* by assessing the extent to which information acquired by one identity is known to another. Research results fail to support the claim that amnesia occurs between identities (Kong et al., 2008).

Researchers on DID generally acknowledge that not all diagnoses are appropriate. However, many psychologists believe that sufficient evidence has accumulated in favor of the DID diagnosis to indicate that it is not always the product of zealous therapists (Gleaves et al., 2001: Ross, 2009). The safest conclusion may be that, of the group of people diagnosed with DID, some cases are genuine, whereas other cases emerge in response to therapists' demands.

Stop *and* **Review**

① Howard believes that his headaches prove he has a brain tumor, despite his doctor's assurances that he is fine. From which somatoform disorder might Howard suffer?

② How is dissociative amnesia defined?

③ What does research suggest about the life experiences that play a role in the etiology of dissociative identity disorder?

✓—[**Study** and **Review** on **MyPsychLab**

SCHIZOPHRENIC DISORDERS

Everyone knows what it is like to feel depressed or anxious, even though most of us never experience these feelings to the degree of severity that constitutes a disorder. Schizophrenia, however, is a disorder that represents a qualitatively different

....

dissociative amnesia The inability to remember important personal experiences, caused by psychological factors in the absence of any organic dysfunction.

dissociative fugue A disorder characterized by a flight from home or work accompanied by a loss of ability to recall the personal past.

dissociative identity disorder (DID) A dissociative mental disorder in which two or more distinct personalities exist within the same individual; formerly known as multiple personality disorder.

Data from Jose, P. E. & Grown, I. "When does the gender difference in rumination begin?" Journal of Youth and Adolescence 37(2), 2008, 180–192. Excerpt: From Vivian Ann Conan, "Divided She Stands." Originally appeared in New York Magazine August 4, 1997 under the pseudonym Laura Emily Mason. Reprinted by permission of the author

Type of abuse	Percent	Dissociative experiences
Emotional abuse		
No emotional abuse	74%	
Low	15%	
High	11%	

Physical abuse		
No physical abuse	72%	
Low abuse	12%	
Moderate abuse	6%	
High abuse	11%	

Sexual abuse		
No abuse	93%	
Some abuse	7%	

FIGURE 3 Victimization and Dissociative Symptoms

Adolescents provided information about their experiences of victimization and their dissociative symptoms. As indicated by the percent figures, the majority of the children had not experienced any abuse. The children who had been abused reported more dissociative symptoms.

Data from Martínez-Taboas, A. et al. (2006). Prevalence of victimization correlates of pathological dissociation in a community sample of youths, *Journal of Traumatic Stress, 19,* 439–448.

experience from normal functioning. A **schizophrenic disorder** is a severe form of psychopathology in which personality seems to disintegrate, thought and perception are distorted, and emotions are blunted. The person with a schizophrenic disorder is the one you most often conjure up when you think about madness or insanity. Although schizophrenia is relatively rare—approximately 0.7 percent of U.S. adults have suffered from schizophrenia at some point in their lives (Tandon et al., 2008)—this figure translates to around 2 million people affected by this most mysterious and tragic mental disorder.

Mark Vonnegut, son of novelist Kurt Vonnegut, was in his early 20s when he began to experience symptoms of schizophrenia. In *The Eden Express* (1975), he tells the story of his break with reality and his eventual recovery. Once, while pruning some fruit trees, his reality became distorted:

> I began to wonder if I was hurting the trees and found myself apologizing. Each tree began to take on personality. I began to wonder if any of them liked me. I became completely absorbed in looking at each tree and began to notice that they were ever so slightly luminescent, shining with a soft inner light that played around the branches. And from out of nowhere came an incredibly wrinkled, iridescent face. Starting as a small point infinitely distant, it rushed forward, becoming infinitely huge. I could see nothing else. My heart had stopped. The moment stretched forever. I tried to make the face go away but it mocked me.... I tried to look the face in the eyes and realized I had left all familiar ground. (1975, p. 96)

Vonnegut's description gives you a glimpse at the symptoms of schizophrenia.

In the world of schizophrenia, *thinking* becomes illogical; associations among ideas are remote or without apparent pattern. *Hallucinations* often occur, involving imagined sensory perception—sights, smells, or, most commonly, sounds (usually voices)—that patients assume to be real. A person may hear a voice that provides a running commentary on his or her behavior or may hear several voices in conversation. **Delusions** are also common; these are false or irrational beliefs maintained in spite of clear contrary evidence. *Language* may become incoherent—a "word salad" of unrelated or made-up words—or an individual may become mute. *Emotions* may be flat, with no visible expression, or they may be inappropriate to the situation. *Psychomotor behavior* may be disorganized (grimaces, strange mannerisms), or posture may become rigid. Even when only some of these symptoms are present, deteriorated functioning in work and interpersonal relationships is likely as the patient withdraws socially or becomes emotionally detached.

Psychologists divide the symptoms between a positive category and a negative category. During *acute* or *active phases* of schizophrenia, the positive symptoms—hallucinations, delusions, incoherence, and disorganized behavior—are prominent.

....

schizophrenic disorder Severe form of psychopathology characterized by the breakdown of integrated personality functioning, withdrawal from reality, emotional distortions, and disturbed thought processes.

At other times, the negative symptoms—social withdrawal and flattened emotions—become more apparent. Some individuals, such as Mark Vonnegut, experience only one or a couple of acute phases of schizophrenia and recover to live normal lives. Others, often described as chronic sufferers, experience either repeated acute phases with short periods of negative symptoms or occasional acute phases with extended periods of negative symptoms. Even the most seriously disturbed are not acutely delusional all the time.

Major Types of Schizophrenia

Because of the wide variety of symptoms that can characterize schizophrenia, investigators consider it not a single disorder but rather a constellation of separate types. The five most commonly recognized subtypes are outlined in **Table 4**.

Disorganized Type   In this subtype of schizophrenia, a person displays incoherent patterns of thinking and grossly bizarre and disorganized behavior. Emotions are flattened or inappropriate to the situation. Often, a person acts in a silly or childish manner, such as giggling for no apparent reason. Language can become so incoherent, full of unusual words and incomplete sentences, that communication with others breaks down. If delusions or hallucinations occur, they are not organized around a coherent theme.

Catatonic Type   The major feature of the catatonic type of schizophrenia is a disruption in motor activity. Sometimes people with this disorder seem frozen in a stupor. For long periods of time, the individual can remain motionless, often in a bizarre position, showing little or no reaction to anything in the environment. At other times, these patients show excessive motor activity, apparently without purpose and not influenced by external stimuli. The catatonic type is also characterized by extreme *negativism*, an apparently unmotivated resistance to all instructions.

Paranoid Type   Individuals suffering from this form of schizophrenia experience complex and systematized delusions focused around specific themes:

- *Delusions of persecution.* Individuals feel that they are being constantly spied on and plotted against and that they are in mortal danger.

Table 4 • Types of Schizophrenic Disorders

Types of Schizophrenia	Major Symptoms
Disorganized	Inappropriate behavior and emotions; incoherent language
Catatonic	Frozen, rigid, or excitable motor behavior
Paranoid	Delusions of persecution or grandeur
Undifferentiated	Mixed set of symptoms with thought disorders and features from other types
Residual	Free from major symptoms but evidence from minor symptoms of continuation of the disorder

What patterns of thoughts may indicate that a person is experiencing schizophrenia?

- *Delusions of grandeur.* Individuals believe that they are important or exalted beings—millionaires, great inventors, or religious figures such as Jesus Christ. Delusions of persecution may accompany delusions of grandeur—an individual is a great person but is continually opposed by evil forces.
- *Delusional jealousy.* Individuals become convinced—without due cause—that their mates are unfaithful. They contrive data to fit the theory and "prove" the truth of the delusion.

Individuals with paranoid schizophrenia rarely display obviously disorganized behavior. Instead, their behavior is likely to be intense and quite formal.

Undifferentiated Type   This is the grab-bag category of schizophrenia, describing a person who exhibits prominent delusions, hallucinations, incoherent speech, or grossly disorganized behavior that fits the criteria of more than one type or of no clear type. The hodgepodge of symptoms experienced by these individuals does not clearly differentiate among various schizophrenic reactions.

Residual Type   Individuals diagnosed as residual type have usually suffered from a major past episode of schizophrenia but are currently free of major positive symptoms such as hallucinations or delusions. The ongoing presence of the disorder is signaled by minor positive symptoms or negative symptoms like flat emotion. A diagnosis of residual type may indicate that the person's disease is entering *remission*, or becoming dormant.

Causes of Schizophrenia

Different etiological models point to very different initial causes of schizophrenia, different pathways along which it develops,

Explore the Concept *Types and Symptoms of Schizophrenia* on MyPsychLab

delusion False or irrational belief maintained despite clear evidence to the contrary.

Data from Martinez-Taboas, A. et al. (2006). "Prevalence of victimization correlates of pathological dissociation in a community sample of youths." Journal of Traumatic Stress, 19, 439–448

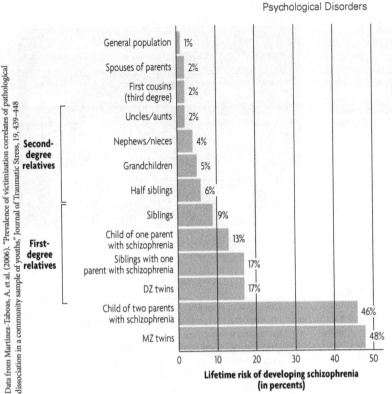

FIGURE 4 Genetic Risk of Developing Schizophrenia

The graph shows average risks for developing schizophrenia. Data were compiled from family and twin studies conducted in European populations between 1920 and 1987; the degree of risk correlates highly with the degree of genetic relatedness. Except when the label indicates otherwise, the data reflect the relationship between an individual and someone who has been diagnosed with schizophrenia. For example, the DZ twin of someone diagnosed with schizophrenia has a 17 percent chance of sharing the diagnosis.

and different avenues for treatment. Let's look at the contributions several of these models can make to an understanding of the way a person may develop a schizophrenic disorder.

Genetic Approaches   It has long been known that schizophrenia tends to run in families (Bleuler, 1978; Kallmann, 1946). Three independent lines of research—family studies, twin studies, and adoption studies—point to a common conclusion: Persons related genetically to someone who has had schizophrenia are more likely to become affected than those who are not (Riley, 2011). A summary of the risks of being affected with schizophrenia through various kinds of relatives is shown in **Figure 4**. Schizophrenia researcher **Irving Gottesman** (1991) pooled these data from about 40 reliable studies conducted in Western Europe between 1920 and 1987; he dropped the poorest data sets. As you can see, the data are arranged according to degree of genetic relatedness, which correlates highly with the degree of risk. For example, when both parents have suffered from schizophrenia, the risk for their offspring is 46 percent, as compared with 1 percent in the general population. When only one parent has had schizophrenia, the risk for the offspring drops sharply, to 13 percent. Note also that the probability that identical twins will both have schizophrenia is roughly three times greater than the probability for fraternal twins.

Because the heritability of schizophrenia is so firmly established, researchers have turned their attention toward discovering the specific genes that may put people at risk for the disorder. As you've seen, there are several major types of schizophrenia with a variety of different symptoms. For that reason, researchers believe that a number of genes will have

an impact on when and how people will be affected: Research evidence has emerged that associates several candidate genes with the disorder (Shi et al., 2008). Different people's experience of schizophrenia—with respect, for example, to the severity of their symptoms—may depend on exactly the combination of genes they inherit. ◉

Brain Function   Another biological approach to the study of schizophrenia is to look for abnormalities in the brains of individuals suffering from the disorder. Much of this research now relies on brain-imaging techniques that allow direct comparisons to be made between the structure and functioning of the brains of individuals with schizophrenia and normal control individuals (Keshavan et al., 2008). For example, as shown in **Figure 5**, magnetic resonance imaging has shown that the *ventricles*—the brain structures through which cerebrospinal fluid flows—are often enlarged in individuals with schizophrenia (Barkataki et al., 2006). MRI studies also demonstrate that individuals with schizophrenia have measurably thinner regions in frontal and temporal lobes of cerebral cortex; the loss of neural tissue presumably relates to the disorder's behavioral abnormalities (Bakken et al., 2011).

Researchers have also begun to document that some brain abnormalities are related to the progress of the disease (Brans et al., 2008). For example, **Figure 6** presents the data from a longitudinal study of 12 individuals who began to experience symptoms of schizophrenia by age 12 (Thompson et al., 2001).

◉ Watch the Video *Genetics Research in Schizophrenia* on MyPsychLab

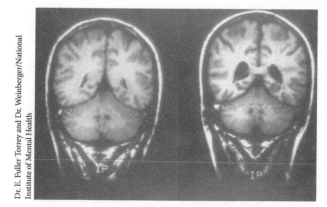

Dr. E. Fuller Torrey and Dr. Weinberger/National Institute of Mental Health

FIGURE 5 Schizophrenia and Ventricle Size

Male identical twins underwent MRI scans. The scan of the twin with schizophrenia (on the right) reveals enlarged ventricles compared to the scan of the twin without the disorder (on the left).

Photo courtesy of Drs. E. Fuller Torrey and Daniel Weinberger.

The study focused on changes in gray matter (largely the cell bodies and dendrites of nerve cells in the cortex) over a five-year period. The 12 patients underwent repeated MRI scans, as did an age-matched group of healthy control participants. Adolescent brains are still undergoing processes of change. That's why even the normal adolescents experience some loss of gray matter. However, as you can see in **Figure 6**, the loss of gray matter for the adolescents with schizophrenia was quite dramatic. By monitoring for such changes in people at genetic risk for schizophrenia, clinicians may be able to offer diagnosis and treatment earlier in the disorder (Wood et al., 2008).

Given the wide range of symptoms of schizophrenia, you are probably not surprised by the comparably wide range of biological abnormalities that may be either causes or consequences of the disorder. What are the ways in which features of the environment may prompt people who are at risk to develop the disease?

Environmental Stressors We have been focusing on genetic and biological aspects of schizophrenia. However, as you can see in **Figure 5**, even in the groups with the greatest genetic similarity, the risk factor is less than 50 percent. This indicates that, although genes play a role, environmental

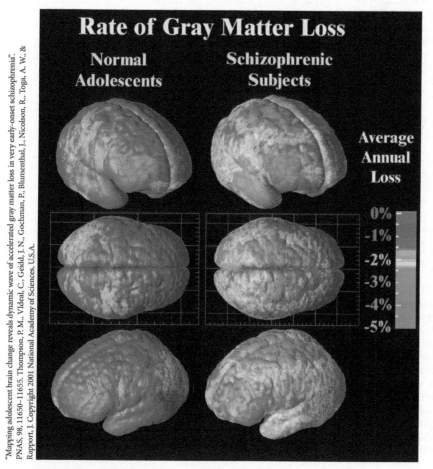

"Mapping adolescent brain change reveals dynamic wave of accelerated gray matter loss in very early-onset schizophrenia". PNAS, 98, 11650–11655. Thompson, P. M., Videal, C., Gedd, J. N., Gochman, P., Blumenthal, J., Nicolson, R., Toga, A. W., & Rapport, J. Copyright 2001 National Academy of Sciences, U.S.A.

FIGURE 6 Gray Matter Loss in Adolescents with Schizophrenia

Researchers carried out MRI scans on 12 adolescents with schizophrenia and 12 age-matched healthy controls. Over a five-year period, the adolescents with schizophrenia showed substantial loss of gray matter in several areas of their brains.

From Thompson, P. M., Vidal, C., Giedd, J. N., Gochman, P., Blumenthal, J., Nicolson, R., Toga, A. W., & Rapoport, J. L. (2001). Mapping adolescent brain change reveals dynamic wave of accelerated gray matter loss in very early-onset schizophrenia. PNAS, 98, 11650–11655.

conditions may also be necessary to give rise to the disorder. A widely accepted hypothesis for the cause of schizophrenia is the *diathesis-stress hypothesis*. According to the **diathesis-stress hypothesis,** genetic factors place the individual at risk, but environmental stress factors must impinge for the potential risk to be manifested as a schizophrenic disorder. Let's consider some of those factors.

For example, research has demonstrated that people who live in urban settings, people who experience greater economic difficulties, and people who have migrated from one country to another all experience higher rates of schizophrenia (Bourque et al., 2011; Tandon et al., 2008). Explanations for these relationships often focus on social stressors and social adversity. Research also suggests that people who experience traumatic life events are at higher risk for schizophrenia. One study examined large samples of individuals in both the United States and Great Britain: The more people had experienced traumas such as physical or sexual abuse, the more likely they were to suffer from a schizophrenic disorder (Shevlin et al., 2008).

Researchers have also examined how life events affect changes in people's symptoms once they have been diagnosed with a schizophrenic disorder. Consider a study that demonstrated a relationship between patients' responses to life events and changes in their symptoms.

*Researchers assessed the symptoms of patients with a schizophrenic disorder at the beginning and end of a nine-month period (Docherty et al., 2009). At the study's outset, the researchers also measured each patient's emotional reactivity—the intensity of an individual's emotional responses to life events. The patients, for example, responded to statements such as "I have big ups and downs in mood" and "I experience very intense emotions" on a scale ranging from "never, or almost never" to "always, or almost always." Nine months later, the patients gave an account of life events from the preceding month. Based on their reports, the researchers sorted them into categories of people who had experienced moderate or severe life events in the past month and those who hadn't. The researchers predicted that negative life events would lead to greater symptoms of schizophrenia—but only for patients who regularly had intense emotional responses to those events. As you can see in **Figure 7**, the data supported the prediction. Only patients who both had negative life events and high emotional reactivity showed increases in symptoms (that is, delusions and hallucinations).*

We saw earlier that differences in people's responses to life events affect the likelihood that they will experience, for example, major depressive disorder. This study demonstrated a similar pattern for symptoms of schizophrenia.

Research has also looked at family stressors that may affect both the likelihood that people develop schizophrenic disorders and the likelihood that they will relapse if the symptoms go into remission (Miklowitz & Tompson, 2003; Schlosser et al., 2010). For example, several studies have focused on the concept of *expressed emotion.* Families are high on expressed emotion if they make a lot of critical comments about the patient, if they are emotionally overinvolved with the patient (that is, if they are

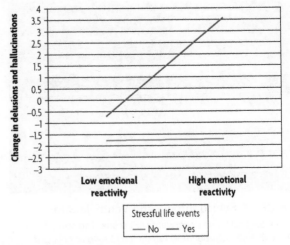

FIGURE 7 Changes in Symptoms of Schizophrenic Disorders

Researchers measured patients' emotional reactivity and symptom change over a nine-month-period. Only patients who both had negative life events and high emotional reactivity showed increases in symptoms (that is, delusions and hallucinations).

Data from Docherty, N. M. et al. (2008). Life events and high-trait reactivity together predict psychotic symptom increases in schizophrenia. *Schizophrenia Bulletin, 35*(3). Reprinted by permission of Oxford University Press.

overprotective and intrusive), and if they have a generally hostile attitude toward the patient. When patients in remission leave hospitals and return to high-expressed-emotion homes, the risk of relapse is more than twice as high as when they return to low-expressed-emotion homes (Hooley, 2007). The implication is that treatment should be for the entire family as a *system*, to change the operating style toward the disturbed child (Kuipers et al., 2010).

The number of explanations of schizophrenia this section has reviewed—and the questions that remain despite significant research—suggests how much there is to learn about this powerful psychological disorder. Complicating understanding is the likelihood that the phenomenon called schizophrenia is probably better thought of as a group of disorders, each with potentially distinct causes. Genetic predispositions, brain processes, and family interactions have all been identified as participants in at least some cases. Researchers must still determine the exact ways in which these elements may combine to bring about schizophrenia.

Stop *and* Review

① Are social withdrawal and flattened emotions positive or negative symptoms of schizophrenia?

diathesis-stress hypothesis A hypothesis about the cause of certain disorders, such as schizophrenia, that suggests that genetic factors predispose an individual to a certain disorder but that environmental stress factors must impinge in order for the potential risk to manifest itself.

② For what type of schizophrenic disorder would delusions of persecution or grandeur be symptoms?

③ What impact does family expressed emotion have on relapse for schizophrenic disorders?

CRITICAL THINKING Recall the study that looked at the impact of life events on symptoms of schizophrenia. Why was emotional reactivity measured at the beginning of the nine-month period?

✓• Study and Review on MyPsychLab

PERSONALITY DISORDERS

A **personality disorder** is a long-standing (chronic), inflexible, maladaptive pattern of perceiving, thinking, or behaving. These patterns can seriously impair an individual's ability to function in social or work settings and can cause significant distress. They are usually recognizable by the time a person reaches adolescence or early adulthood. Personality disorders are coded on Axis II of *DSM-IV-TR*. As shown in **Table 5**, *DSM-IV-TR* organizes 10 types of personality disorders into three clusters.

Diagnoses of personality disorders have sometimes been controversial because of the overlap among the disorders: Some of the same behaviors contribute to diagnoses of different disorders. In addition, researchers have tried to understand the relationship between normal and abnormal personalities. They ask, at what point does an extreme on a particular dimension of personality indicate a disorder (Livesley & Lang, 2005)? For example, most people are somewhat dependent on other people. When does dependence become sufficiently extreme to signal dependent personality disorder? As with other types of psychological disorders, clinicians must understand when and how personality traits become maladaptive—when and how those traits cause either the person or society to suffer. To illustrate that conclusion, this section will focus on *borderline personality disorder* and *antisocial personality disorder*.

Borderline Personality Disorder

Individuals with **borderline personality disorder** experience great instability and intensity in personal relationships. These difficulties arise in part from difficulties controlling anger. The disorder leads people to have frequent fights and temper tantrums. In addition, people with this disorder display great impulsivity in their behaviors—particularly with respect to behaviors that can relate to self-harm, such as substance abuse or suicide attempts. Among adults in the United States, the prevalence of borderline personality disorder is about 1.6 percent (Lenzenweger et al., 2007).

One important component of borderline personality disorder is an intense fear of abandonment (Bornstein et al., 2010). People with this disorder engage in frantic behaviors to prevent abandonment such as frequent phone calls and physical

Table 5 • Personality Disorders

Disorder	Characteristics
Cluster A: People's behavior appears odd or eccentric	
Paranoid	Distrust and suspiciousness about the motives of the individuals with whom they interact
Schizoid	Lack of desire to have social relationships; lack of emotionality in social situations
Schizotypal	Cognitive or perceptual distortions as well as discomfort in social relationships
Cluster B: People's behavior appears dramatic or erratic	
Antisocial	Inability to respect the rights of others; irresponsible or unlawful behavior that violates social norms
Borderline	Instability and intensity in personal relationships; impulsivity, particularly with respect to behaviors that include self-harm
Histrionic	Excessive emotionality and attention seeking; inappropriate sexual or seductive behavior
Narcissistic	Grandiose sense of self-importance and a need for constant admiration; lack of empathy for others
Cluster C: People's behavior appears anxious or fearful	
Avoidant	Avoid interpersonal contact because of risk of rejection; fear criticism and feel inadequate in social situations
Dependent	Need others to take responsibility for major areas of life; feel uncomfortable or helpless without support from other people
Obsessive-Compulsive	Preoccupied with rules and lists; perfectionism interferes with being able to complete tasks

clinging. Let's consider a study that demonstrated a relationship between rejection and rage for individuals with borderline personality disorder.

Featured Study

Researchers recruited 45 individuals who met diagnostic criteria for borderline personality disorder (BPD) and 40 healthy controls (Berenson et al., 2011). The participants carried handheld computers that prompted them for responses at 105 randomly selected times over the course of 21 days. Each time the computer beeped, participants indicated how much rejection they were experiencing at that moment by responding to statements such as "I am abandoned."

....

personality disorder A chronic, inflexible, maladaptive pattern of perceiving, thinking, and behaving that seriously impairs an individual's ability to function in social or other settings.

borderline personality disorder A disorder defined by instability and intensity in personal relationships as well as turbulent emotions and impulsive behaviors.

Participants also reported their feelings of rage at that moment by answering questions such as "Right now to what extent do you feel like lashing out?" Individuals in the BPD group reported both more rejection and more rage over the three-week period. In addition, for the BPD group, small momentary increases in rejection led to relatively large increments in rage. Members of the control group did not react to momentary feelings of rejection with that same pattern of rage.

This study illustrates the difficulties with emotional control that make it quite difficult to maintain relationships with people with borderline personality disorder. One study that followed people with this disorder over the course of 10 years found impaired social functioning across the whole period (Choi-Kain et al., 2010). This research suggests that borderline personality disorder remains stable over time.

Causes of Borderline Personality Disorder As with other disorders, researchers have focused on both the nature and nurture of borderline personality disorder. Twin studies provide strong evidence in favor of a genetic contribution (Distel et al., 2008). For example, one study compared the rate of concordance for monozygotic versus dizygotic twins (Torgersen et al., 2000). When MZ twins had borderline personality disorder, 35.3 percent of their siblings also had the disorder; for DZ twins, only 6.7 percent of their siblings also had the disorder. If Personality traits are strongly heritable, so you might not be surprised that disorders of those traits are also heritable.

Still, research suggests that environmental factors make a strong contribution in the etiology of borderline personality disorder (Cohen et al., 2008; Lieb et al., 2004). One study compared the incidence of early traumatic events for 66 patients with the disorder to 109 healthy controls (Bandelow et al., 2005). The patients had considerably different lives. For example, 73.9 percent of the patients with borderline personality disorder reported childhood sexual abuse; only 5.5 percent of the controls did so. The patients reported, on average, that the abuse started at age 6 and lasted for 3½ years. That early trauma likely contributed to the incidence of the disorder. However, not all people who endure childhood sexual abuse develop borderline personality disorder—witness the 5.5 percent of control participants in this study who survived childhood sexual abuse but did not develop the disorder. It is likely that a combination of genetic risk and traumatic events explains the etiology of the disorder.

Antisocial Personality Disorder

Antisocial personality disorder is marked by a long-standing pattern of irresponsible or unlawful behavior that violates social norms. Lying, stealing, and fighting are common behaviors. People with antisocial personality disorder often do not experience shame or remorse for their hurtful actions. Violations of

....

antisocial personality disorder A disorder characterized by stable patterns of irresponsible or unlawful behavior that violates social norms.

Why do people with antisocial personality disorder often have legal difficulties?

social norms begin early in their lives—disrupting class, getting into fights, and running away from home. Their actions are marked by indifference to the rights of others. Among adults in the United States, the prevalence of antisocial personality disorder is about 1.0 percent (Lenzenweger et al., 2007).

Antisocial personality disorder is often comorbid with other pathologies. For example, in one study of adults with histories of alcohol or drug abuse the prevalence of antisocial personality disorder was 18.3 percent for men and 14.1 percent for women—considerably higher than the 1.0 percent prevalence for the general population (Goldstein et al., 2007). In addition, antisocial personality disorder also puts people at risk for suicide, even in the absence of major depressive disorder (Javdani et al., 2011; Swogger et al., 2009). This suicide risk is likely to be a product of the impulsivity and disregard for safety that characterizes the disorder.

Causes of Antisocial Personality Disorder Researchers have used twin studies to examine genetic components of specific behaviors associated with antisocial personality disorder. For example, one study examined the concordance in behaviors for 3,687 pairs of twins (Viding et al., 2005). Teachers responded to statements about each twin to indicate the presence of callous-unemotional traits (such as "Does not show feelings or emotions") and antisocial behavior (such as "Often fights with other children or bullies them"). The comparisons of MZ and DZ twins suggested that the tendency to display callous-unemotional traits had a strong genetic component. In addition, for twins who displayed high levels of those callous-emotional traits, genetics also made a strong contribution to antisocial behavior.

Research has also focused on the environmental circumstances that give rise to antisocial personality disorder (Paris, 2003). As was the case for borderline personality disorder, people with antisocial personality disorder are more likely than healthy individuals to have experienced childhood abuse. To verify this relationship, one team of researchers searched court records (from around 1970) to compile a sample of 641 individuals whose abuse and neglect as children was officially documented (Horwitz et al., 2001). Those individuals were interviewed 20 years later to assess the prevalence of psychological disorders. Compared to a control group of 510 individuals with no history of abuse, the maltreated individuals were considerably more likely to meet the criteria for antisocial personality disorder. What mattered, in addition, was that the people who had been mistreated as children had often experienced a higher level of stressors throughout their lives. Further research suggests that physical abuse, in particular, puts individuals at risk for antisocial personality disorder (Lobbestael et al., 2010).

Stop *and* Review

① What intense fear do people with borderline personality disorder have with respect to interpersonal relationships?

② How do the early lives of people with borderline personality disorder compare to those of healthy controls?

③ Why are people with antisocial personality disorder at risk for suicide?

CRITICAL THINKING Consider the study that assessed the relationship between rejection and rage for borderline personality disorder. Why was it important that the sampling was done at randomly selected times?

✔—Study and Review on **MyPsychLab**

PSYCHOLOGICAL DISORDERS OF CHILDHOOD

The discussion so far has largely focused on adults who suffer from psychopathology. It is important to note, however, that many individuals begin to experience symptoms of mental illness in childhood and adolescence. Researchers have recently intensified their study of the time course with which psychopathology emerges in young lives (Zahn-Waxler et al., 2008). Researchers often try to identify behavior patterns that allow for early diagnosis and treatment. For example, problems with social functioning may provide clues that children and adolescents are at risk for schizophrenia (Tarbox & Pogue-Geile, 2008).

DSM-IV-TR also identifies a range of disorders that are "usually first diagnosed in infancy, childhood, or adolescence." One of these disorders is *mental retardation*. Here, the focus will be on *attention-deficit hyperactivity disorder* and *autistic disorder*.

Attention-Deficit Hyperactivity Disorder

The definition of **attention-deficit hyperactivity disorder** (ADHD) refers to two clusters of symptoms (*DSM-IV-TR*, 2000). First, children must show a degree of *inattention* that is not consistent with their level of development. They might, for example, have difficulty paying attention in school or often lose items such as toys or school assignments. Second, children must show signs of *hyperactivity-impulsivity* that, once again, is not consistent with their developmental level. Hyperactive behaviors include squirming, fidgeting, and excessive talking; impulsive behaviors include blurting out answers

and interrupting. A diagnosis of ADHD requires that children have shown these patterns of behavior for at least six months before age 7.

Researchers estimate the prevalence of ADHD to be 9 percent among children ages 5 to 17 in the United States (Akinbami et al., 2011). The rate is 12.3 percent for boys and 5.5 percent for girls. Note, however, that research suggests that cultural biases (for example, expectations of gender differences) lead to fewer diagnoses of ADHD among girls than are justified—making it difficult to provide an exact estimate of the gender difference. However, in one large-scale study of adults, 3.2 percent of women and 5.4 percent of men met diagnostic criteria for ADHD (Kessler et al., 2006a). These figures may accurately reflect gender differences across the life span. When they are diagnosed with ADHD, boys and girls show much the same patterns of problematic behavior (Rucklidge, 2010). However, girls may experience more social isolation as a consequence of ADHD than do boys (Elkins et al., 2011).

The diagnosis of ADHD is complicated by the fact that many children are prone to episodes of inattention, hyperactivity, or impulsiveness. For that reason, the diagnosis has sometimes been controversial: People have worried that children's normal disorderliness was being labeled as abnormal. However, there is now a large consensus among clinicians that some children's behavior reaches a level at which it is maladaptive—the children are unable to control their behavior or complete tasks. Although there has often been a popular perception that ADHD is overdiagnosed, research evidence contradicts that perception (Sciutto & Eisenberg, 2007). In fact, as noted earlier, ADHD might actually be underdiagnosed for girls.

As with the other disorders, researchers have considered both the nature and nurture of ADHD. Twin and adoption studies have provided strong evidence for the heritability of the disorder (Greven et al., 2011). Researchers have started to document relationships between specific genes that affect the brain's development and neurotransmitter functions (Poelmans et al., 2011; Smoller et al., 2006). There are also important environmental variables associated with ADHD. For example, children who come from families with economic disadvantages or families with high levels of conflict are more likely to experience the disorder (Akinbami et al., 2011; Biederman et al., 2002). Some environmental variables have greater impact on children in different birth positions. For example, the eldest children in families that lack cohesion—families in which members are not committed to providing support to each other—are more at risk for ADHD than are younger siblings in such families (Pressman et al., 2006). Results of this sort suggest that parenting experience has an impact on the incidence of ADHD.

Autistic Disorder

Children with **autistic disorder** present severe disruption in their ability to form social bonds. They are likely to have greatly delayed and very limited development of spoken language as

....

attention-deficit hyperactivity disorder (ADHD) A disorder of childhood characterized by inattention and hyperactivity-impulsivity.

autistic disorder A developmental disorder characterized by severe disruption of children's ability to form social bonds and use language.

What psychological disorders of childhood might lead to classroom disruptions?

well as very narrow interests in the world. Consider a report on a child who was diagnosed with this disorder:

> [Audrey] seemed frightened by nearly any changes in her customary routine, including the presence of strange people. She either shrank from contact with other children or avoided them altogether, seemingly content to engage in nonfunctional play by herself for hours at a time. When she was with other children, she seldom engaged in reciprocal play or even copied any of their motor movements. (Meyer, 2003, p. 244)

Many children with autistic disorder also engage in repetitive and ritualistic behaviors: They might, for example, place objects in lines or symmetrical patterns (Greaves et al., 2006; Leekam et al., 2011).

Research suggests that the prevalence of autistic disorder (and related disorders) is about one out of 110 children (Centers for Disease Control and Prevention, 2009). Because many of the symptoms of autistic disorder relate to language and social interaction, it has often been difficult to diagnose the disorder until parents notice that their children are failing to use language or interact. However, recent research has begun to document behaviors in the first year of life that predict later diagnoses of autistic disorder (Zwaigenbaum et al., 2005). For example, children at risk for autistic disorder are less likely to smile in response to social smiles and respond to their names than are other children.

Causes of Autistic Disorder   As with ADHD, autistic disorder has a large genetic component. In fact, researchers have begun to identify the variations in the human genome that may predispose individuals to experience the disorder (Vieland et al., 2011). Researchers have also discovered brain markers of the disorder. For example, individuals with autistic disorder experience more rapid brain growth than do their peers (Amaral et al., 2008). The ongoing question is how such brain abnormalities bring about the symptoms of the disorder.

Researchers have suggested that individuals who suffer from autistic disorder have an inability to develop an understanding of other people's mental states (Baron-Cohen, 2008).

Under ordinary circumstances, children develop a theory of mind. At first, they interpret the world only from their own perspective. However, with rapid progress between ages 3 and 4, children develop an understanding that other people have different knowledge, beliefs, and intentions than they do. Research suggests that individuals with autistic disorder lack the ability to develop this understanding. Without a theory of mind, it is quite difficult for people to establish social relationships. Individuals with autistic disorder find it virtually impossible to understand and predict other people's behavior, making everyday life seem mysterious and hostile.

Stop *and* Review

① What types of behaviors characterize ADHD?
② Why has it been difficult to diagnose autistic disorder before age 2 or 3?
③ Why is theory of mind relevant to autistic disorder?

✔•⌐Study and Review on MyPsychLab

THE STIGMA OF MENTAL ILLNESS

One of the most important goals for this chapter has been to demystify mental illness—to help you understand how, in some ways, abnormal behavior is really ordinary. People with psychological disorders are often labeled as *deviant*. However, the deviant label is not true to prevailing realities: When 46.4 percent of adults in the United States report having experienced some psychiatric disorder in their lifetime (Kessler et al., 2005a), psychopathology is, at least statistically, relatively normal.

Even given the frequency with which psychopathology touches "normal lives," people who are psychologically disordered are often stigmatized in ways that most physically ill people are not. A **stigma** is a mark or brand of disgrace; in the psychological context, it is a set of negative attitudes about a person that places him or her apart as unacceptable (Hinshaw & Stier, 2008). The woman with schizophrenia quoted at the beginning of the chapter had this to say: "The patient and public, in my [opinion] needs to be educated about mental illness because people ridicule and mistreat, even misunderstand us at crucial times." Negative attitudes toward the psychologically disturbed come from many sources: The mass media portray psychiatric patients as prone to violent crime; jokes about the mentally ill are acceptable; families deny the mental distress of one of their members; legal terminology stresses mental incompetence. People also stigmatize themselves by hiding current psychological distress or a history of mental health care.

Researchers have documented a number of ways in which the stigma of mental illness has a negative impact on people's

....

stigma The negative reaction of people to an individual or group because of some assumed inferiority or source of difference that is degraded.

lives (Hinshaw & Stier, 2008). In one sample of 84 men who had been hospitalized for mental illness, 6 percent reported having lost a job because of their hospitalization; 10 percent reported having been denied an apartment or room; 37 percent reported being avoided by others; and 45 percent reported that others had used their history of mental illness to hurt their feelings. Only 6 percent of the men reported no incidents of rejection (Link et al., 1997). This group of men went through a yearlong course of treatment that resulted in considerable improvement in their mental health. Even so, at the end of that year, there were no changes in their perception of stigma: Despite their improvements in functioning, the patients did not expect to be treated any more kindly by the world. This type of research shows the great duality of many people's experience with mental disorders: Seeking help—allowing one's problems to be labeled—generally brings both relief *and* stigma.

Unfortunately, many people who suffer from mental illnesses internalize negative stereotypes and stigmatize themselves. In one study, 144 people with serious mental illnesses completed a questionnaire that evaluated internalized stigma (West et al., 2011). The questionnaire assessed, for example, the extent to which participants agreed with negative stereotypes of people with mental illness. In the sample, 41 percent of the women and 35 percent of the men indicated substantial internalized stigma. Such internalized stigma has serious consequences: People with high levels of internalized stigma tend to experience more hopelessness, lower self-esteem, and decreased quality of life (Livingston & Boyd, 2010).

A final note on stigma: Research suggests that people who have had prior contact with individuals with mental illnesses hold attitudes that are less affected by stigma (Couture & Penn, 2003). Let's look at one study that supports this conclusion.

Featured Study

A team of researchers surveyed 911 participants about their personal contact with mental illness (Boyd et al., 2010). Some participants had no contact whereas others had themselves been hospitalized for mental illness or had family members or friends who had been hospitalized. The participants were given vignettes that described an individual who had been diagnosed with either schizophrenia or major depressive disorder. Participants answered a number of questions to indicate how they might respond to the individual. For example, participants indicated how much social distance they would maintain by responding to statements such as, "How willing would you be to make friends with [the patient]?" (p. 1066). Participants with more personal contact indicated that they would establish less personal distance. In addition, people with more personal contact expressed less anger and blame toward the patient.

I hope that one consequence of reading this chapter will be to help modify your beliefs about what it means to be mentally ill—and to increase your tolerance and compassion for mentally ill individuals.

In making sense of psychopathology, you are forced to come to grips with basic conceptions of normality, reality, and social values. In discovering how to understand, treat, and, ideally, prevent psychological disorders, researchers not only help those who are suffering and losing out on the joys of living, they also expand the basic understanding of human nature.

Stop *and* Review

1. In the context of mental illness, how does stigma function?
2. Why does treatment for mental illness often bring about both relief and stigma?
3. What types of experience reduce stigma?

CRITICAL THINKING Consider the study on personal contact and responses to mental illness. Why is social distance an important measure?

✔●–[Study and **Review** on **MyPsychLab**

Recapping Main Points

The Nature of Psychological Disorders

- Abnormality is judged by the degree to which a person's actions resemble a set of indicators that include distress, maladaptiveness, irrationality, unpredictability, unconventionality, observer discomfort, and violation of standards or societal norms.
- Objectivity is an important problem for discussions of mental illness.
- Classification systems for psychological disorders should provide a common shorthand for communicating about general types of psychopathologies and specific cases.
- The most widely accepted diagnostic and classification system is *DSM-IV-TR*.

- The biological approach to the etiology of mental illness concentrates on abnormalities in the brain, biochemical processes, and genetic influences.
- Psychological approaches include psychodynamic, behavioral, cognitive, and sociocultural models.

Anxiety Disorders

- The five major types of anxiety disorders are generalized, panic, phobic, obsessive-compulsive, and posttraumatic stress.
- Research has confirmed genetic and brain bases for anxiety disorders as well as behavioral and cognitive components of causality.

Mood Disorders

- Major depressive disorder is the most common mood disorder; bipolar disorder is much rarer.
- People have genetic predispositions toward mood disorders.
- Mood disorders change the way people respond to life experiences.
- Women's higher levels of major depressive disorder may reflect differences in negative life experiences as well as cognitive responses to those experiences.
- Suicides are most frequent among people suffering from depression.

Somatoform and Dissociative Disorders

- Somatoform disorders such as hypochondriasis, somatization disorder, and conversion disorder are characterized by circumstances in which physical illnesses or complaints cannot be fully explained by actual medical conditions.
- Dissociative disorders involve a disruption of the integrated functioning of memory, consciousness, or personal identity.

Schizophrenic Disorders

- Schizophrenia is a severe form of psychopathology characterized by extreme distortions in perception, thinking, emotion, behavior, and language.

- The five subtypes of schizophrenia are disorganized, catatonic, paranoid, undifferentiated, and residual.
- Evidence for the causes of schizophrenia has been found in a variety of factors, including genetics, brain abnormalities, and environmental stressors.

Personality Disorders

- Personality disorders are patterns of perception, thought, or behavior that are long-standing and inflexible and impair an individual's functioning.
- Both borderline personality disorder and antisocial personality disorder arise because of genetic and environmental factors.

Psychological Disorders of Childhood

- Children with ADHD display inattention and hyperactivity-impulsivity.
- Autistic disorder is characterized by severe disruption of children's ability to form social bonds and use language.

The Stigma of Mental Illness

- Those with psychological disorders are often stigmatized in ways that most physically ill people are not.
- Although treatment for psychological disorders brings about positive changes, the stigma associated with mental illness has a negative impact on quality of life.

KEY TERMS

abnormal psychology
agoraphobia
antisocial personality disorder
anxiety disorder
attention-deficit hyperactivity disorder (ADHD)
autistic disorder
bipolar disorder
borderline personality disorder
comorbidity
conversion disorder
delusion
diathesis-stress hypothesis
dissociative amnesia
dissociative disorder

dissociative fugue
dissociative identity disorder (DID)
DSM-IV-TR
etiology
fear
generalized anxiety disorder
hypochondriasis
insanity
learned helplessness
major depressive disorder
manic episode
mood disorder
neurotic disorder

obsessive-compulsive disorder (OCD)
panic disorder
personality disorder
phobia
psychological diagnosis
psychopathological functioning
psychotic disorder
schizophrenic disorder
social phobia
somatization disorder
somatoform disorder
specific phobia
stigma

Practice Test

1. *Comorbidity* refers to circumstances in which an individual
   a. cannot be accurately diagnosed using *DSM-IV-TR*.
   b. has a neurotic disorder that cannot be easily cured.
   c. has a psychotic disorder that includes a fear of death.
   d. experiences more than one psychological disorder at the same time.

2. Professor Hexter believes that unconscious conflicts often cause psychological disorders. Which approach to psychopathology does Professor Hexter use?
   a. psychodynamic   c. cognitive
   b. sociocultural   d. behavioral

3. Analyses of legal records suggest that the use of the insanity defense is quite _____ and the probability of it succeeding is quite _____.
   a. rare; low   c. common; low
   b. rare; high   d. common; high

4. For binge eating disorder, which criterion is still being researched as a potential part of the diagnosis?
   a. regular episodes of binge eating without purges
   b. a loss of control during binges
   c. binges causing great distress
   d. undue influence of body weight or shape on self-evaluation

5. For over a year, Jane has felt anxious or worried throughout the day. It sounds as though Jane is suffering from
   a. panic disorder.
   b. generalized anxiety disorder.
   c. obsessive-compulsive disorder.
   d. agoraphobia.

6. What attribution style puts people at risk for depression?
   a. internal–specific–stable
   b. external–specific–unstable
   c. internal–global–stable
   d. external–global–unstable

7. When something bad happens, Chris spends a lot of time ruminating about the problem. Based on this behavior, you think it is
   a. more likely that Chris is a man.
   b. equally likely that Chris is a man or a woman.
   c. likely that Chris will develop a specific phobia.
   d. more likely that Chris is a woman.

8. You are trying to assess the probability that Paula will develop major depressive disorder. You would be least concerned if she inherited _____ of the 5-HTTLPR serotonin gene.
   a. two short versions
   b. two long versions
   c. one short and one long version
   d. one or more short versions

9. Nadine alternates between yelling at Tricia and begging her to remain friends. Tricia is convinced that Nadine suffers from _____ personality disorder.
   a. schizotypal   c. borderline
   b. narcissistic   d. obsessive-compulsive

10. To diagnose conversion disorder, you'd try to find _____ that preceded the appearance of symptoms.
   a. a serious physical illness
   b. psychological conflict or stress
   c. a visit to a medical doctor
   d. both pain and gastrointestinal complaints

11. Although Eve doesn't have any organic dysfunction, she often forgets important personal experiences. This could be an instance of
   a. dissociative amnesia.
   b. hypochondriasis.
   c. somatization disorder.
   d. dependent personality disorder.

12. Which of these is a negative symptom of schizophrenia?
   a. hallucinations   c. delusions
   b. incoherent language   d. social withdrawal

13. Which of these behaviors would *not* generally support a diagnosis of attention-deficit hyperactivity disorder?
   a. Manfred blurts out answers during class activities.
   b. Manfred loses his toys and school assignments.
   c. Manfred squirms and fidgets in the classroom.
   d. Manfred cries when other children tease him.

14. Professor Wyatt believes that 1-year-old Brian is at risk for autistic disorder. The professor might observe Brian to determine whether he
   a. fails to respond to his name.
   b. can walk without assistance.
   c. responds appropriately to loud noises.
   d. shows smooth pursuit with his eyes.

15. As part of an introductory psychology class, a professor has her students interview people who have recovered from psychological disorders. This exercise should
   a. prompt the students to be more affected by the stigma of mental illness.
   b. have no impact on the students' experience of stigma.
   c. prompt the students to be less affected by the stigma of mental illness.
   d. decrease the probability that students would seek treatment for mental illness.

ESSAY QUESTIONS

1. Why is it not always possible to be objective about diagnoses of mental illness?

2. What are some benefits of a useful classification system for psychological disorders?

3. What life circumstances lead some people to contemplate suicide?

Stop and Review Answers

Stop and Review (The Nature of Psychological Disorders)

1. The most relevant criteria appear to be "distress or disability" (that is, Jerry's fear causes him personal distress) and "maladaptiveness" (that is, Jerry's fear prevents him from easily pursuing his goals).
2. Classification can provide a common shorthand language, an understanding of causality, and a treatment plan.
3. Behaviors are interpreted in different ways in different cultures—the same behaviors may seem "normal" or "abnormal" in different cultural contexts.

Stop and Review (Anxiety Disorders)

1. People who suffer from phobias experience irrational fears in situations that are not objectively dangerous.
2. Obsessions are thoughts, whereas compulsions are acts.
3. Research suggests that the evolutionary history of the human species leaves people "prepared" to experience phobias with respect to certain stimuli.
4. People who are high on anxiety sensitivity are more likely to believe that bodily symptoms will have harmful consequences.

Stop and Review (Mood Disorders)

1. Bipolar disorder is characterized by periods of severe depression alternating with manic episodes.
2. The cognitive triad refers to negative views of the person him- or herself, negative views of ongoing experiences, and negative views of the future.
3. Research suggests that women are more likely than men to ruminate on their problems, which has the result of increasing negative feelings.
4. Adolescents are at risk for suicide attempts when they feel depressed, hopeless, or isolated and have negative self-concepts.

Stop and Review (Somatoform and Dissociative Disorders)

1. Howard's case fits the definition of hyponchondriasis.
2. Dissociative amnesia is an inability to recall important personal experiences, caused by psychological factors in the absence of any organic dysfunction.

3. Research suggests that nearly all the individuals who develop DID have undergone some form of physical or psychological abuse.

Stop and Review (Schizophrenic Disorders)

1. Social withdrawal and flattened emotions are negative symptoms of schizophrenia.
2. Delusions of persecution or grandeur are symptoms of the paranoid type of schizophrenic disorder.
3. Research suggests that patients who return to families with high expressed emotion are more likely to experience relapses.

Stop and Review (Personality Disorders)

1. People with borderline personality disorder have an intense fear of being abandoned.
2. People with borderline personality disorder have experienced substantially more childhood sexual abuse.
3. Antisocial personality disorder is characterized by both impulsive behaviors and a disregard for safety, which creates a risk for suicide.

Stop and Review (Psychological Disorders of Childhood)

1. ADHD is characterized by degrees of inattention and hyperactivity-impulsivity that are inconsistent with children's levels of development.
2. Many parents start to have concerns only when children fail to meet developmental norms for social interaction or language use starting in the second year.
3. Researchers have suggested that children with autistic disorder fail to develop a standard theory of mind.

Stop and Review (The Stigma of Mental Illness)

1. Negative attitudes about mental illnesses place people apart as unacceptable.
2. When people enter into treatment, they must often publicly acknowledge that they have a mental illness, creating a context for stigma.
3. Research suggests that contact with people who have mental illnesses serves to reduce stigma.

Practice Test Answers

1. d
2. a
3. a
4. d
5. b
6. c
7. d
8. b
9. c
10. b
11. a
12. d
13. d
14. a
15. c

References

Abramson, L. Y., Seligman, M. E. P., & Teasdale, J. D. (1978). Learned helplessness in humans: Critique and reformulation. *Journal of Abnormal Psychology, 87,* 32–48, 49–74.

Akinbami, L. J., Liu, X., Pastor, P. N., & Reuben, C. A. (2011). Attention deficit hyperactivity disorder among children aged 5–17 years in the United States, 1998–2009. *NCHS data brief* (no. 70). Hyattsville, MD: National Center for Health Statistics. Retrieved from www.cdc.gov/nchs/data/databriefs/db70.pdf.

Amaral, D. G., Schumann, C. M., & Nordahl, C. W. (2008). Neuroanatomy of autism. *Trends in Neurosciences, 31,* 137–145.

Bakken, T. E., Bloss, C. S., Roddey, C., Joyner, A. H., Rimol, L. M., Djurovic, S., Melle, I., Sundet, K., Agartz, I., Andreassen, O. A., Dale, A. M., & Schork, N. J. (2011). Association of genetic variants on 15q12 with cortical thickness and cognition in schizophrenia. *Archives of General Psychiatry, 68,* 781–790.

Bandelow, B., Krause, J., Wedekind, D., Broocks, A., Hajak, G., & Rüther, E. (2005). Early traumatic life events, parental attitudes, family history, and birth risk factors in patients with borderline personality disorder and healthy controls. *Psychiatry Research, 134,* 169–179.

Barkataki, I., Kumari, V., Das, M., Taylor, P., & Sharma, T. (2006). Volumetric structural brain abnormalities in men with schizophrenia and antisocial personality disorder. *Behavioural Brain Research, 169,* 239–247.

Baron-Cohen, S. (2008). Theories of the autistic mind. *The Psychologist, 21,* 112–116.

Beck, A. T. (1967). *Depression: Clinical, experimental, and theoretical Aspects.* New York: Harper & Row.

Beck, A. T., & Emery, G. (1985). *Anxiety disorders and phobias: A cognitive perspective.* New York: Basic Books.

Berenson, K. R., Downey, G., Rafaeli, E., Coifman, K. G., & Paquin, N. L. (2011). The rejection-rage contingency in borderline personality disorder. *Journal of Abnormal Psychology, 120,* 681–690.

Biederman, J., Faraone, S. V., & Monteaux, M. C. (2002). Differential effect of environmental adversity by gender: Rutter's index of adversity in a group of boys and girls with and without ADHD. *American Journal of Psychiatry, 159,* 1556–1562.

Bleuler, M. (1978). The long-term course of schizophrenic psychoses. In L. C. Wynne, R. L. Cromwell, & S. Mattysse (Eds.), *The nature of schizophrenia: New approaches to research and treatment* (pp. 631–636). New York: Wiley.

Blumberg, H. P., Leung, H. C., Skudlarski, P., Lacadie, C. M., Fredericks, C. A., Harris, B. C., Charney, D. S., Gore, J. C., Krystal, J. H., & Peterson, B. S. (2003). A functional magnetic resonance imaging study of bipolar disorder. *Archives of General Psychiatry, 60,* 601–609.

Bolton, D., & Perrin, S. (2008). Evaluation of exposure with response-prevention for obsessive compulsive disorder in childhood and adolescence. *Journal of Behavior Therapy and Experimental Psychiatry, 39,* 11–22.

Bornstein, R. F., Becker-Matero, N., Winarick, D. J., & Reichman, A. L. (2010). Interpersonal dependency in borderline personality disorder: Clinical context and empirical evidence. *Journal of Personality Disorders, 24,* 109–127.

Bourque, F., van der Ven, E., & Malla, A. (2011). A meta-analysis of the risk for psychotic disorders among first- and second-generation immigrants. *Psychological Medicine, 41,* 897–910.

Boyd, J. E., Katz, E. P., Link, B. G., & Phelan, J. C. (2010). The relationship of multiple aspects of stigma and personal contact with someone hospitalized for mental illness, in a nationally representative sample. *Social Psychiatry and Psychiatric Epidemiology, 45,* 1063–1070.

Brans, R. G. H., van Haren, N. E. M., van Baal, C. M., Schnack, H. G., Kahn, R. S., & Hulshoff, H. E. (2008). Heritability of changes in brain volume over time in twin pairs discordant for schizophrenia. *Archives of General Psychiatry, 65,* 1259–1268.

Brown, R. J. (2004). Psychological mechanisms in medically unexplained symptoms: An integrative conceptual model. *Psychological Bulletin, 130,* 793–812.

Butcher, J. N., Mineka, S., & Hooley, J. M. (2008). *Abnormal Psychology* (13th ed.). Boston, MA: Allyn & Bacon.

Carvalho, J. P., & Hopko, D. R. (2011). Behavioral theory of depression: Reinforcement as a mediating variable between avoidance and depression. *Journal of Behavior Therapy and Experimental Psychiatry, 42,* 154–162.

Caspi, A., Hariri, A. R., Holmes, A., Uher, R., & Moffitt, T. E. (2010). Genetic sensitivity to the environment: The case of the serotonin transporter gene and its implications for studying complex diseases and traits. *American Journal of Psychiatry, 167,* 509–527.

Centers for Disease Control and Prevention. (2009, December 18). Prevalence of autism spectrum disorders—Autism and Developmental Disabilities Monitoring Network, United States, 2006. *Morbidity and Mortality Weekly Report, 58,* 1–24. Retrieved from ftp://ftp.cdc.gov/pub/publications/mmwr/ss/SS5810.pdf.

Ceschi, G., van der Linden, M., Dunker, D., Perroud, A., & Brédart, S. (2003). Further exploration memory bias in compulsive washers. *Behaviour Research and Therapy, 41,* 737–748.

Choi-Kahn, L. W., Zanarini, M. C., Frankenburg, F. R., Fitzmaurice, G. M., & Reich, D. B. (2010). A longitudinal study of the 10-year course of interpersonal features in borderline personality disorder. *Journal of Personality Disorders, 24,* 365–376.

Chorover, S. (1981, June). *Organizational recruitment in "open" and "closed" social systems: A neuropsychological perspective.* Conference paper presented at the Center for the Study of New Religious Movements, Berkeley, CA.

Cohen, P., Chen, H., Gordon, K., Johnson, J., Brook, J., & Kasen, S. (2008). Socioeconomic background and the developmental course of schizotypal and borderline personality disorder symptoms. *Development and Psychopathology, 20,* 633–650.

Cojan, Y., Waber, L., Carruzzo, A., & Vuilleumier, P. (2009). Motor inhibition in hysterical conversion disorder. *NeuroImage, 47,* 1026–1037.

Couture, S., & Penn, D. (2003). Interpersonal contact and the stigma of mental illness: A review of the literature. *Journal of Mental Health, 12,* 291–306.

Croarkin, P. E., Levinson, A. J., & Daskalakis, Z. J. (2011). Evidence for GABA-ergic inhibitory deficits in major depressive disorder. *Neuroscience and Biobehavioral Reviews, 35,* 818–825.

DiGrande, L., Neria, Y., Brackbill, R. M., Pulliam, P., & Galea, S. (2011). Long-term posttraumatic stress symptoms among 3,271 civilian survivors of the September 11, 2001, terrorist attacks on the World Trade Center. *American Journal of Epidemiology, 173,* 271–281.

Dimidjian, S., Barrera, M., Jr., Martell, C., Muñoz, R. F., & Lewinsohn, P. M. (2011). The origins and current status of behavioral activation treatments for depression. *Annual Review of Clinical Psychology, 7,* 1–38.

Disner, S. G., Beevers, C. G., Haigh, E. A., & Beck, A. T. (2011). Neural mechanisms of the cognitive model of depression. *Nature Reviews Neuro-science, 12,* 467–477.

Distel, M. A., Trull, T. J., Derom, C. A., Thiery, E. W., Grimmer, M. A., Martin, N. G., Willemsen, G., & Boomsma, D. I. (2008). Heritability of borderline personality disorder features is similar across three countries. *Psychological Medicine, 38,* 1219–1229.

Docherty, N. M., St-Hilaire, A., Aakre, J. M., & Seghers, J. P. (2009). Life events and high-trait reactivity together predict psychotic symptom increases in schizophrenia. *Schizophrenia Bulletin 35,* 638–645.

DSM-IV. (1994). *Diagnostic and statistical manual of mental disorders* (4th ed.). Washington, DC: American Psychiatric Association.

DSM-IV-TR. (2000). *Diagnostic and statistical manual of mental disorders* (4th ed., Text revision). Washington, DC: American Psychiatric Association.

Edvardsen, J., Torgersen, S., Røysamb, E., Lygren, S., Skre, I., Onstad, S., & Øien, P. A. (2008). Heritability of bipolar spectrum disorders. Unity or heterogeneity. *Journal of Affective Disorders, 106,* 229–240.

Elkins, I. J., Malone, S., Keyes, M., Iacono, W. G., McGue, M. (2011). The impact of attention-deficit/hyperactivity disorder on preadolescent adjustment may be greater for girls than for boys. *Journal of Clinical Child & Adolescent Psychology, 40,* 532–545.

Ellenstein, A., Kranick, S. M., & Hallet, M. (2011). An update on psychogenic movement disorders. *Current Neurology and Neuroscience Reports, 11,* 396–403.

Evans, E., Hawton, K., Rodham, K., & Deeks, J. (2005). The prevalence of suicidal phenomena in adolescents: A systematic review of population-based studies. *Suicide and Life Threatening Behavior, 35,* 239–250.

Fan, F., Zhang, Y., Yang, Y., Mo, L., & Liu, X. (2011). Symptoms of posttraumatic stress disorder, depression, and anxiety among adolescents following the 2008 Wenchuan earthquake in China. *Journal of Traumatic Stress, 24,* 44–53.

Fink, P., Hansen, M. S., & Oxhøj, M. L. (2004). The prevalence of somatoform disorders among internal medical inpatients. *Journal of Psychosomatic Research, 56,* 413–418.

Frans, Ö., Rimmö, P. A., Åberg, L., & Fredrikson, M. (2005). Trauma exposure and post-traumatic stress disorder in the general population. *Acta Psychiatrica Scandinavica, 111,* 291–299.

Giesbrecht, T., Lynn, S. J., Lilienfeld, S. O., & Merckelbach, H. (2008). Cognitive processes in dissociation: An analysis of core theoretical assumptions. *Psychological Bulletin, 134,* 617–647.

Gleaves, D. H., May, M. C., & Cardeña, E. (2001). An examination of the diagnostic validity of dissociative identity disorder. *Clinical Psychology Review, 21,* 577–608.

Goldstein, R. B., Compton, W. M., Pulay, A. J., Ruan, W. J., Pickering, R. P., Stinson, F. S., & Grant, B. F. (2007). Antisocial behavioral syndromes and DSM-IV drug use disorders in the United States: Results from the National Epidemiologic Survey on Alcohol and Related Conditions. *Drug and Alcohol Dependence, 90,* 145–158.

Gotlib, I. H., & Hamilton, J. P. (2008). Neuroimaging and depression: Current status and unresolved issues. *Current Directions in Psychological Science, 17,* 159–163.

Gottesman, I. I. (1991). *Schizophrenia genesis: The origins of madness.* New York: Freeman.

Greaves, N., Prince, E., Evans, D. W., & Charman, T. (2006). Repetitive and ritualistic behaviour in children with Prader-Willi syndrome and children with autism. *Journal of Intellectual Disability Research, 50,* 92–100.

Greven, C. U., Rijsdijk, F. V., & Plomin, R. (2011). A twin study of ADHD symptoms in early adolescence: Hyperactivity-impulsivity and inattentiveness show substantial genetic overlap but also genetic specificity. *Journal of Abnormal Child Psychology, 39,* 265–275.

Grilo, C. M., Hrabosky, J. I., White, M., Allison, K. C., Stunkard, A. J., & Masheb, R. M. (2008). Overvaluation of shape and weight in binge eating disorder and overweight controls: Refinement of a diagnostic construct. *Journal of Abnormal Psychology, 117,* 414–419.

Gutierrez, P. M., Watkins, R., & Collura, D. (2004). Suicide risk screening in an urban high school. *Suicide and Life-Threatening Behavior, 34,* 421–428.

Hettema, J. M., Prescott, C. A., Myerse, J. M., Neale, M. C., & Kendler, K. S. (2005). The structure of genetic and environmental risk factors for anxiety disorders in men and women. *Archives of General Psychiatry, 62,* 182–189.

Hinshaw, S. P., & Stier, A. (2008). Stigma as related to mental disorders. *Annual Review of Clinical Psychology, 4,* 367–393.

Hoffman, E. J., & Mathew, S. J. (2008). Anxiety disorders: A comprehensive review of pharmacotherapies. *Mount Sanai Journal of Medicine, 75,* 248–262.

Hooley, J. M. (2007). Expressed emotion and relapse of psychopathology. *Annual Review of Clinical Psychology, 3,* 329–352.

Horwitz, A. V., Widom, C. S., McLaughlin, J., & White, H. R. (2001). The impact of abuse and neglect on adult mental health: A prospective study. *Journal of Health and Social Behavior, 42,* 184–201.

Hudson, J. I., Hiripi, E., Pope, H. G. Jr., & Kessler, R. C. (2007). The prevalence and correlates of eating disorders in the national comorbidity survey replication. *Biological Psychiatry, 61,* 348–358.

Hyde, J. S., Mezulis, A. H., & Abramson, L. Y. (2008). The ABCs of depression: Integrating affective, biological, and cognitive models to explain the emergence of the gender difference in depression. *Psychological Review, 115,* 291–313.

Janofsky, J. S., Dunn, M. H., Roskes, E. J., Briskin, J. K., & Rudolph, M. S. L. (1996). Insanity defense pleas in Baltimore city: An analysis of outcome. *American Journal of Psychiatry, 153,* 1464–1468.

Jasper, F., & Witthöft, M. (2011). Health anxiety and attentional bias: The time course of vigilance and avoidance in light of pictorial illness information. *Journal of Anxiety Disorders, 25,* 1131–1138.

Javdani, S., Sadeh, N., & Verona, E. (2011). Suicidality as a function of impulsivity, callous-unemotional traits, and depressive symptoms in youth. *Journal of Abnormal Psychology, 120,* 400–413.

Jose, P. E., & Brown, I. (2008). When does the gender difference in rumination begin? Gender and age differences in the use of rumination by adolescents. *Journal of Youth and Adolescence, 37,* 180–192.

Kallmann, F. J. (1946). The genetic theory of schizophrenia: An analysis of 691 schizophrenic index families. *American Journal of Psychiatry, 103,* 309–322.

Karg, K., Burmeister, M., Shedden, K., & Sen, S. (2011). The serotonin transporter promoter variant (5-HTTLPR), stress, and depression meta-analysis revisited. *Archives of General Psychiatry, 68,* 444–454.

Kellough, J. L., Beevers, C. G., Ellis, A. J., & Wells, T. T. (2008). Time course of selective attention in clinically depressed young adults: An eye tracking study. *Behaviour Research and Therapy, 46,* 1238–1243.

Kendler, K. S., Gatz, M., Gardner, C. O., & Pedersen, N. L. (2006). A Swedish national twin study of lifetime major depression. *American Journal of Psychiatry, 163,* 109–114.

Kendler, K. S., Kuhn, J. W., & Prescott, C. A. (2004). Childhood sexual abuse, stressful life events and risk for major depression in women. *Psychological Medicine, 34,* 1475–1482.

Kennedy, R. E., & Craighead, W. E. (1988). Differential effects of depression and anxiety on recall of feedback in a learning task. *Behavior Therapy, 19,* 437–454.

Keshavan, M. S., Tandon, R., Boutros, N. N., & Nasrallah, H. A. (2008). Schizophrenia, "Just the Facts": What we know in 2008. Part 3: Neurobiology. *Schizophrenia Research, 106,* 89–107.

Kessler, R. C., Adler, L., Barkley, R., Biederman, J., Conners, C. K., Demler, O., Faraone, S. V., Greenhill, L. L., Howes, M. J., Secnik, K., Spencer, T., Ustun, T. B., Walters, E. E., & Zaslavsky, A. M. (2006a). The prevalence and correlates of adult ADHD in the United States: Results form the National Comorbidity Survey Replication. *American Journal of Psychiatry, 163,* 716–723.

Kessler, R. C., Berglund, P., Demler, O., Jin, R., Merikangas, K. R., & Walters, E. E. (2005a). Lifetime prevalence and age-of-onset distributions of *DSM-IV* disorders in the National Comorbidity Survey Replication. *Archives of General Psychiatry, 62,* 593–602.

Kessler, R. C., Chiu, W. T., Demler, O., & Walters, E. E. (2005b). Prevalence, severity, and comorbidity of 12-month *DSM-IV* disorders in the National Comorbidity Survey Replication. *Archives of General Psychiatry, 62,* 617–627.

Kessler, R. C., Chiu, W. T., Jin. R., Ruscio, A. M., Shear, K., & Walters, E. E. (2006b). The epidemiology of panic attacks, panic disorder, and agoraphobia in the National Comorbidity Survey Replication. *Archives of General Psychiatry, 63,* 415–424.

Kessler, R. C., McGonagle, K. A., Zhao, S., Nelson, C. B., Hughes, M., Eshleman, S., Wittchen, H. U., & Kendler, K. S. (1994). Lifetime and 12-month prevalence of *DSM-III-R* psychiatric disorders in the United States. *Archives of General Psychiatry, 51,* 8–19.

Kirschner, S. M., & Galperin, G. J. (2001). Psychiatric defenses in New York County: Pleas and results. *Journal of the American Academy of Psychiatry and the Law, 29,* 194–201.

Kong, L. L., Allen, J. J. B., & Glisky, E. L. (2008). Interidentity memory transfer in dissociative identity disorder. *Journal of Abnormal Psychology, 117,* 686–692.

Kuipers, E., Onwumere, J., & Bebbington, P. (2010). Cognitive model of caregiving in psychosis. *The British Journal of Psychiatry, 196,* 259–265.

Lau, J. Y. F., & Eley, T. C. (2008). Attributional style as a risk marker of genetic effects for adolescent depressive symptoms. *Journal of Abnormal Psychology, 117,* 849–859.

Leekam, S. R., Prior, M. R., & Uljarevic, M. (2011). Restricted and repetitive behaviors in autism spectrum disorders: A review of research in the last decade. *Psychological Bulletin, 137,* 562–593.

Leen-Feldner, E. W., Feldner, M. T., Reardon, L. E., Babson, K. A., & Dixon, L. (2008). Anxiety sensitivity and posttraumatic stress among traumatic event-exposed youth. *Behaviour Research and Therapy, 46,* 548–556.

Lenzenweger, M. F., Lane, M. C., Loranger, A. W., & Kessler, R. C. (2007). *DSM-IV* personality disorders in the National Comorbidity Survey Replication. *Biological Psychiatry, 62,* 553–564.

Li, X., Sundquist, J., & Sundquist, K. (2011). Sibling risk of anxiety disorders based on hospitalizations in Sweden. *Psychiatry and Clinical Neurosciences, 65,* 233–238.

Lilienfeld, S. O., & Lynn, S. J. (2003). Dissociative identity disorder: Multiple personalities, multiple controversies. In S. O. Lilienfeld, S. J. Lynn, & J. M. Lohr (Eds.), *Science and pseudoscience in clinical psychology* (pp. 109–142). New York: Guilford Press.

Link, B. G., Struening, E. L., Rahav, M., Phelan, J. C., & Nuttbrock, L. (1997). On stigma and its consequences: Evidence from a longitudinal study of men with dual diagnoses of mental illness and substance abuse. *Journal of Health and Social Behavior, 38,* 177–190.

Livesley, W. J., & Lang, K. L. (2005). Differentiating normal, abnormal, and disordered personality. *European Journal of Personality, 19,* 257–268.

Livingston, J. D., & Boyd, J. E. (2010). Correlates and consequences of internalized stigma for people living with mental illness: A systematic review and meta-analysis. *Social Science & Medicine, 71,* 2150–2161.

Lobbestael, J., Arntz, A., & Bernstein, D. P. (2010). Disentangling the relationship between different types of childhood maltreatment and personality disorders. *Journal of Personality Disorders, 24,* 285–295.

LoBue, V., & DeLoache, J. (2008). Detecting the snake in the grass: Attention to fear-relevant stimuli by adults and young children. *Psychological Science, 19,* 284–289.

Maier, S. F., & Seligman, M. E. P. (1976). Learned helplessness: Theory and evidence. *Journal of Experimental Psychology, 105,* 3–46.

Mailis-Gagnon, A., & Nicholson, K. (2011). On the nature of nondermatomal somatosensory deficits. *The Clinical Journal of Pain, 27,* 76–84.

Marshal, M. P., Dietz, L. J., Friedman, M. S., Stall, R., Smith, H. A., McGinley, J., Thoma, B., Murray, P. J., D'Augelli, A. R., & Brent, D. A. (2011). Suicidality and depression disparities between sexual minority and heterosexual youth: A meta-analytic review. *Journal of Adolescent Health, 49,* 115–123.

Martínez-Taboas, A., Canino, G., Wang, M. Q., Garcías, P., & Bravo, M. (2006). Prevalence of victimization correlates of pathological dissociation in a community sample of youths. *Journal of Traumatic Stress, 19,* 439–448.

Mason, L. E. (1997, August 4). Divided she stands. *New York,* pp. 42–49.

Meyer, R. G. (2003). *Case studies in abnormal behavior* (6th ed.). Boston: Allyn & Bacon.

Miklowitz, D. J., & Tompson, M. C. (2003). Family variables and interventions in schizophrenia. In G. P. Sholevar & L. D. Schwoeri (Eds.), *Textbook of family and couples therapy: Clinical applications* (pp. 585–617). Washington, DC: American Psychiatric Publishing.

Miniño, A. M., Xu, J., & Kochanek, K. D. (2010). Deaths: Preliminary data for 2008. *National Vital Statistics Reports, 59,* 1–52.

Narayan, V. M., Narr, K. L., Phillips, O. R., Thompson, P. M. Toga, A. W., Szeszko, P. R. (2008). Greater regional cortical gray matter thickness in obsessive-compulsive disorder. *NeuroReport, 19,* 1551–1555.

Nash, J. R., Sargent, P. A., Rabiner, E. A., Hood, S. D., Argyropoulos, S. V., Potokar, J. P., Grasby, P. M., & Nutt, D. J. (2008). Serotonin 5-HT$_{1A}$ receptor binding in people with panic disorder: Positron emission tomography study. *The British Journal of Psychiatry, 193,* 229–234.

Nock, M. K., Borges, G., Bromet, E. J., Cha, C. B., Kessler, R. C., & Lee, S. (2008). Suicide and suicidal behavior. *Epidemiologic Reviews, 30,* 133–154.

Nrugham, L., Larsson, B., & Sund, A. M. (2008). Predictors of suicidal acts across adolescence: Influences of family, peer and individual factors. *Journal of Affective Disorders, 109,* 35–45.

Öhman, A., & Mineka, S. (2001). Fears, phobias, and preparedness: Toward an evolved module of fear and fear learning. *Psychological Review, 108,* 483–522.

Paris, J. (2003). *Personality disorders over time: Precursors, course, and outcome.* Washington, DC: American Psychiatric Publishing.

Peckham, A. D., McHugh, K., & Otto, M. W. (2010). A meta-analysis of the magnitude of biased attention in depression. *Depression and Anxiety, 27,* 1135–1142.

Pedersen, A. F., Zachariae, R., & Bovbjerg, D. H. (2009). Psychological stress and antibody response to influenza vaccination: A meta-analysis. *Brain, Behavior,* Peterson, C., & Seligman, M. E. P. (1984). Causal explanations as a risk factor for depression: Theory and evidence. *Psychological Review, 91,* 347–374.

Peterson, C., & Vaidya, R. S. (2001). Explanatory style, expectations, and depressive symptoms. *Personality and Individual Differences, 31,* 1217–1223.

Pietrzak, R. H., Goldstein, R. B., Southwick, S. M., & Grant, B. F. (2011). Prevalence and Axis I comorbidity of full and partial posttraumatic stress disorder in the United States: Results from wave 2 of the national epidemiological survey on alcohol and related conditions. *Journal of Anxiety Disorders, 25,* 456–465.

Poelmans, G., Pauls, D. L., Buitelaar, J. K., & Franke, B. (2011). *American Journal of Psychiatry, 168,* 365–377.

Pressman, L. J., Loo, S. K., Carpenter, E. M., Asarnow, J. R., Lynn, D., McCracken, J. T., McGough, J. J., Lubke, G. H., Yang, M. H., & Smalley, S. L. (2006). Relationship of family environment and parental psychiatric diagnosis to impairment in ADHD. *Journal of the American Academy of Child and Adolescent Psychiatry, 45,* 346–354.

Radua, J., van den Heuvel, O. A., Surguladze, S., & Mataix-Cols, D. (2010). Meta-analytical comparison of voxel-based morphometry studies in obsessive compulsive disorder vs. other anxiety disorders. *Archives of General Psychiatry, 67,* 701–711.

Rapoport, J. L. (1989, March). The biology of obsessions and compulsions. *Scientific American,* pp. 83–89.

Rief, W., & Broadbent, E. (2007). Explaining medically unexplained symptoms—models and mechanisms. *Clinical Psychology Review, 27,* 821–841.

Riley, B. (2011). Genetic studies of schizophrenia. In J. D. Clelland (Ed.), *Genomics, proteomics, and the nervous system* (pp. 333–380). New York: Springer.

Rosenhan, D. L. (1973). On being sane in insane places. *Science, 179,* 250–258.

Rosenhan, D. L. (1975). The contextual nature of psychiatric diagnoses. *Journal of Abnormal Psychology, 84,* 462–474.

Ross, C. A. (2009). Errors of logic and scholarship concerning dissociative identity disorder. *Journal of Child Sexual Abuse, 18,* 221–231.

Rucklidge, J. J. (2010). Gender differences in attention-deficit/hyperactivity disorder. *Psychiatric Clinics of North America, 33,* 357–373.

Rudd, M. D., Berman, A. L., Joiner, T. E. Jr., Nock, M. K., Silverman, M. M., Mandrusiak, M., Van Orden, K., & Witte, T. (2006). Warning signs for suicide: Theory, research, and clinical applications. *Suicide and Life-Threatening Behavior, 36,* 255–262.

Ruscio, A. M. Brown, T. A., Chiu, W. T., Sareen, J., Stein, M. B., & Kessler, R. C. (2008). Social fears and social phobia in the USA: Results from the National Comorbidity Survey Replication. *Psychological Medicine, 38,* 15–28.

Rutter, P. A., & Behrendt, A. E. (2004). Adolescent suicide risk: Four psychosocial factors. *Adolescence, 39,* 295–302.

Schlosser, D. A., Zinberg, J. L., Loewy, R. L., Casey-Cannon, S., O'Brien, M. P., Bearden, C. E., Vinogradov, S., & Cannon, T. D. (2010). Predicting the longitudinal effects of the family environment on prodromal symptoms and functioning in patients at-risk for psychosis. *Schizophrenia Research, 118,* 69–75.

Sciutto, M. J., & Eisenberg, M. (2007). Evaluating the evidence for and against the overdiagnosis of ADHD. *Journal of Attention Disorders, 11,* 106–113.

Seligman, M. E. P. (1975). *Helplessness: On depression, development, and death.* San Francisco: Freeman.

Seligman, M. E. P., & Maier, S. F. (1967). Failure to escape traumatic shock. *Journal of Experimental Psychology, 74,* 1–9.

Shevlin, M., Houston, J. E., Dorahy, M. J., & Adamson, G. (2008). Cumulative traumas and psychosis: An analysis of the National Comorbidity Study and the British Psychiatric Morbidity Survey. *Schizophrenia Bulletin, 34,* 193–199.

Shi, J., Gershon, E. S., & Liu, C. (2008). Genetic associations with schizophrenia: Meta-analyses of 12 candidate genes. *Schizophrenia Research, 104,* 96–107.

Shih, J. H., Eberhart, N. K., Hammen, C. L., & Brennan, P. A (2006). Differential exposure and reactivity to interpersonal stress predict sex differences in adolescent depression. *Journal of Clinical Child and Adolescent Psychology, 35,* 103–115.

Shneidman, E. S. (1987, March). At the point of no return. *Psychology Today,* pp. 54–59.

Smoller, J. W., Biederman, J., Arbeitman, L., Doyle, A. E., Fagerness, J., Perlis, R. H., Sklar, P., & Faraone, S. V. (2006). Association between the 5HT1B receptor gene (*HTR1B*) and the inattentive subtype of ADHD. *Biological Psychiatry, 59,* 460–467.

Solomon, A. (2001). *The noonday demon.* New York: Scribner.

Stein, M. B., Jang, K. L., Taylor, S., Vernon, P. A., & Livesley, W. J. (2002). Genetic and environmental influences on trauma exposure and posttraumatic stress disorder symptoms: A twin study. *American Journal of Psychiatry, 159,* 1675–1681.

Striegel-Moore, R. H., & Franko, D. L. (2008). Should binge eating disorder be included in *DSM-V*? A critical review of the state of the evidence. *Annual Review of Clinical Psychology, 4,* 305–324.

Swogger, M. T., Conner, K. R., Meldrum, S. C., & Caine, E. D. (2009). Dimensions of psychopathy in relation to suicidal and self-injurious behavior. *Journal of Personality Disorders, 23,* 201–210.

Szasz, T. S. (1974). *The myth of mental illness* (rev. ed.). New York: Harper & Row.

Szasz, T. S. (2004). *Faith in freedom: Libertarian principles and psychiatric practices.* Somerset, NJ: Transaction Publishers.

Tandon, R., Keshavan, M. S., & Nasrallah, H. A. (2008). Schizophrenia, "Just the Facts": What we know in 2008. 2. Epidemiology and etiology. *Schizophrenia Research, 102,* 1–18.

Tarbox, S. I., & Pogue-Geile, M. F. (2008). Development of social functioning in preschizophrenic children and adolescents: A systematic review. *Psychological Bulletin, 34,* 561–583.

Taylor, C. T., Bomyea, J., & Amir, N. (2010). Attentional bias away from positive social information mediates the link between social anxiety and anxiety vulnerability to a social stressor. *Journal of Anxiety Disorders, 24,* 403–408.

Thase, M. E., & Denko, T. (2008). Pharmacotherapy of mood disorders. *Annual Review of Clinical Psychology, 4,* 53–91.

Thompson, P. M., Vidal, C., Giedd, J. N., Gochman, P., Blumenthal, J., Nicolson, R., Toga, A. W., & Rapoport, J. L. (2001). Mapping adolescent brain change reveals dynamic wave of accelerated gray matter loss in very early-onset schizophrenia. *PNAS, 98,* 11650–11655.

Torgersen, S., Lygren, S., Øien, P. A., Skre, I., Onstad, S., Edvardsen, J., Tambs, K., & Kringlen, E. (2000). A twin study of personality disorders. *Comprehensive Psychiatry, 41,* 416–425.

Uher, R., Caspi, A., Houts, R., Sugden, K., Williams, B., Poulton, R., & Moffitt, T. E. (2011). Serotonin transporter gene moderates childhood maltreatment's effects on persistent but not single-episode depression: Replications and implications for resolving inconsistent results. *Journal of Affective Disorders, 135,* 56–65.

van Tol, M.-J., van der Wee, N. J. A., van den Heuvel, O. A., Nielen, M. M. A., Demenescu, L. R., Aleman, A., Renken, R., van Buchem, M. A., Zitman, F. G., & Veltman, D. J. (2010). Regional brain volume in depression and anxiety disorders. *Archives of General Psychiatry, 67,* 1002–1011.

Vanden Bogaerde, A., & De Raedt, R. (2011). The moderational role of anxiety sensitivity in flight phobia. *Journal of Anxiety Disorders, 25,* 422–426.

Viding, E., Blair, J. R., Moffitt, T. E., & Plomin, R. (2005). Evidence for substantial genetic risk for psychopathy in 7-year-olds. *Journal of Child Psychology and Psychiatry, 46,* 592–597.

Vieland, V. J., Hallmayer, J., Huang, Y., Pagnamenta, A. T., Pinto, D. Khan, H., Monaco, A. P., Paterson, A. D., Scherer, S. W., Sutcliffe, J. S., Szatmari, P., & The Autism Genome Project (AGP). (2011). Novel method for combined linkage and genome-wide association analysis finds evidence of distinct genetic architecture for two subtypes of autism. *Journal of Neurodevelopmental Disorders, 3,* 113–123.

Vonnegut, M. (1975). *The Eden express.* New York: Bantam.

Wang, P. S., Berglund, P., Olfson, M., Pincus, H. A., Wells, K. B., & Kessler, R. C. (2005). Failure and delay in initial treatment contact after first onset of mental disorders in the national comorbidity survey replication. *Archives of General Psychiatry, 62,* 603–613.

Weeks, J. W., Heimberg, R. G., Rodebaugh, T. L., & Norton, P. J. (2008). Exploring the relationship between fear of positive evaluation and social anxiety. *Journal of Anxiety Disorders, 22,* 386–400.

West, M. L., Yanos, P. T., Smith, S. M., Roe, D., & Lysaker, P. H. (2011). Prevalence of internalized stigma among persons with severe mental illness. *Stigma Research and Action, 1,* 54–59.

Widom, C. S., Dutton, M. A., Czaja, S. J., & DuMont, K. A. (2005). Development and validation of a new instrument to assess lifetime trauma and victimization history. *Journal of Traumatic Stress, 18,* 519–531.

Wood, S. J., Pantelis, C., Velakoulis, D., Yücel, M., Fornito, A., & McGorry, P. D. (2008). Progressive changes in the development toward schizophrenia: Studies in subjects at increased symptomatic risk. *Schizophrenia Bulletin, 34,* 322–329.

World Health Orgnization. (2008). *The global burden of disease: 2004 update.* Retrieved from www.who.int/healthinfo/global_burden_disease/GBD_report_2004update_full.pdf.

Zahn-Waxler, C., Shirtcliff, E. A., & Marceau, K. (2008). Disorders of childhood and adolescence: Gender and psychopathology. *Annual Review of Clinical Psychology, 4,* 275–303.

Zwaigenbaum, L., Bryson, S., Rogers, T., Roberts, W., Brian, J., & Szatmari, P. (2005). Behavioral manifestations of autism in the first year of life. *International Journal of Developmental Neuroscience, 23,* 143–152.

Index